Cognitive Illusions

"This book is a marvellous achievement. Whereas many edited collections are best dipped into, I recommend reading this one from beginning to end. In doing so one becomes aware of the tantalizing possibility that different psychological phenomena just might share some connection. In addition, the inclusion of classroom demonstrations in each chapter will be an invaluable resource for instructors."

David Hardman, Department of Psychology,
London Metropolitan University

Cognitive Illusions investigates a wide range of fascinating psychological effects in the way we think, judge and remember in our every day lives. At the beginning of each chapter, leading researchers in the field introduce the background to phenomena such as; illusions of control, overconfidence and hindsight bias. This is followed by an explanation of the experimental context in which they can be investigated and a theoretical discussion which draws conclusions about the wider implications of these fallacy and bias effects. Written with researchers and instructors in mind, this tightly edited reader-friendly text provides both an overview of research in the area and many lively pedagogic features such as chapter summaries, further reading lists and experiment suggestions.

Rüdiger F. Pohl is Assistant Professor, Justus Liebig University Giessen, Germany

Cognitive Illusions
A Handbook on Fallacies and Biases in Thinking, Judgement and Memory

Edited by
Rüdiger F. Pohl

Psychology Press
Taylor & Francis Group
HOVE AND NEW YORK

This edition published 2012 by Psychology Press
27 Church Road, Hove, East Sussex, BN32FA
Simultaneously published in the USA and Canada by Psychology Press
711 Third Avenue, New York, NY 10017

First issued in paperback 2012

Psychology Press is an imprint of the Taylor & Francis Group, an informa business

© 2004 Psychology Press

Typeset in Sabon by RefineCatch Ltd, Bungay, Suffolk

All rights reserved. No part of this book may be reprinted or reproduced or utilized in any form or by any electronic, mechanical, or other means, now known or hereafter invented, including photocopying and recording, or in any information storage or retrieval system, without permission in writing from the publishers.

This publication has been produced with paper manufactured to strict environmental standards and with pulp derived from sustainable forests.

British Library Cataloguing in Publication Data
A catalogue record for this book is available from the British Library

Library of Congress Cataloging in Publication Data
Cognitive Illusions : a handbook on fallacies and biases in thinking, judgement and memory / [edited by] Rüdiger Pohl.—1st ed.
    p. cm.
Includes bibliographical references and index.

1. Errors. 2. Prejudices. I. Pohl, Rüdiger, 1954–
BF323.E7C64 2004
153.7′4—dc22   2004009834

ISBN13: 978-0-415-64675-8 (PBK)
ISBN13: 978-1-841-69351-4 (HBK)

Contents

List of tables and figures   vii
List of contributors   xi

Introduction: Cognitive illusions   1
RÜDIGER F. POHL

PART I
Illusions of thinking   21

1   Conjunction fallacy   23
JOHN E. FISK

2   Base rates in Bayesian inference   43
MICHAEL H. BIRNBAUM

3   Statistical formats in Bayesian inference   61
STEPHANIE KURZENHÄUSER AND ANDREA LÜCKING

4   Confirmation bias   79
MARGIT E. OSWALD AND STEFAN GROSJEAN

5   Illusory correlation   97
KLAUS FIEDLER

6   Illusions of control   115
SUZANNE C. THOMPSON

7   Biases in deductive reasoning   127
JONATHAN ST. B. T. EVANS

PART II
Illusions of judgement   145

8   Availability   147
ROLF REBER

9 Judgements by representativeness 165
KARL H. TEIGEN

10 Anchoring effect 183
THOMAS MUSSWEILER, BIRTE ENGLICH, AND FRITZ STRACK

11 Validity effect 201
CATHERINE HACKETT RENNER

12 Mere exposure effect 215
ROBERT F. BORNSTEIN AND CATHERINE CRAVER-LEMLEY

13 Overconfidence 235
ULRICH HOFFRAGE

14 Pollyanna Principle 255
MARGARET W. MATLIN

PART III
Illusions of memory 273

15 Moses illusion 275
HEEKYEONG PARK AND LYNNE M. REDER

16 Orientation illusions in memory 293
GREGORY V. JONES AND MARYANNE MARTIN

17 Associative memory illusions 309
HENRY L. ROEDIGER III AND DAVID A. GALLO

18 Effects of labelling 327
RÜDIGER F. POHL

19 Misinformation effect 345
JACQUELINE E. PICKRELL, DANIEL M. BERNSTEIN, AND ELIZABETH F. LOFTUS

20 Hindsight bias 363
RÜDIGER F. POHL

21 Illusions of change or stability 379
ANNE WILSON AND MICHAEL ROSS

Perspectives 397

22 Suggestion and illusion 399
VLADIMIR A. GHEORGHIU, GÜNTER MOLZ, AND RÜDIGER F. POHL

Author Index 423
Subject Index 433

Tables and Figures

Tables

2.1	Mean judgements of probability that the cab was blue (%)	51
2.2	Bayesian predictions (converted to percentages)	52
3.1	Information of the breast cancer problem represented in four statistical formats	64
5.1	Common notation to describe the correlation between two dichotomous variables	100
6.1	Questions used to demonstrate illusory control over driving	117
7.1	Examples of four kinds of syllogisms presented by Evans et al. (1983) together with the percentage rates of acceptance of each argument as valid over three experiments	139
8.1	Vulnerability to heart disease as a function of type and number of recalled behaviours and family history	159
11.1	Examples of true and false statements	202
14.1	List of skills, mean difficulty rating, mean bias score, number below average, and number above average	257
14.2	Percentage of behaviours recalled from MOPI feedback, as a function of presentation time and the nature of the feedback	262
14.3	Percentage of items recalled, as a function of mood and the nature of the stimulus	263
15.1	The exemplar questions used in the Moses illusion experiment	276
15.2	Mean target reading times and proportion of correct and incorrect responses (in parentheses)	279
18.1	The 12 ambiguous stimuli with two lists of labels (adapted from the original experiment of Carmichael et al., 1932)	331
21.1	Current and retrospective past self-ratings (2 months ago) when the past was described as either recent or distant	383
22.1	Examples for perceiving illusion as reality in different cognitive domains	411

viii *Tables and Figures*

Figures

2.1	Mean inference that the cab was Blue, expressed as a percentage, plotted against the Bayesian solutions, also expressed as percentages (H = high-, M = medium-credibility witness).	52
2.2	Fit of averaging model: Mean judgements of probability that the cab was Blue, plotted as a function of the estimated scale value of the base rate.	53
3.1	Structure of the statistical information in the breast cancer problem in the natural frequency format (left side) and normalized frequency format (right side).	65
5.1	(a) Mean estimated percentage of stereotype-consistent and inconsistent behaviour and (b) mean trait rating on stereotype-consistent and inconsistent scales.	109
10.1	Response latencies for lexical decisions as a function of word type and anchor (Mussweiler & Strack, 2000a).	194
12.1	Effects of stimulus type and exposure frequency on liking ratings of merely exposed stimuli.	224
12.2	Effects of stimulus type and exposure frequency on complexity ratings of merely exposed stimuli.	224
13.1	Left: Calibration curves for representative and selected sets of items. Right: The graphs labelled confidence depict mean confidence judgements minus mean percentage correct, and those labelled frequency depict mean frequency estimates (which have been transformed to percentages to be comparable) minus percentage correct. Data taken from Gigerenzer et al. (1991).	241
15.1	Mean illusion rates from four experiments of Kamas et al. (1996).	288
16.1	Recognition responses (proportional to line lengths) for Comet Hale-Bopp at eight different orientations, for left-handed and for right-handed participants.	299
17.1	The DRM false-recognition effect (Roediger & McDermott, 1995, Exp. 2).	314
17.2	Scatterplot of the relationship between false recall and backward associative strength across 55 DRM lists.	317
17.3	The effects of retention interval on true and false recall (Toglia et al., 1999, Exp. 2).	319
19.1	The effect of the type of information on the proportion of correct answers given on the recognition test 2 days after viewing the slide show and completing the questionnaire.	350

20.1 Mean shift indices for experimental and control items in several studies in the memory design (ordered according to values for experimental items; positive values indicate that the recalled estimates were closer to the solution than the original ones had been). 369

20.2 Scattergram of mean individual shift indices for experimental and control items in one study (Pohl et al., 2003). 370

Contributors

Daniel M. Bernstein
Michael H. Birnbaum
Robert F. Bornstein
Catherine Craver-Lemley
Birte Englich
Jonathan St. B. T. Evans
Klaus Fiedler
John E. Fisk
David A. Gallo
Vladimir A. Gheorghiu
Stefan Grosjean
Catherine Hackett Renner
Ulrich Hoffrage
Gregory V. Jones
Stephanie Kurzenhäuser
Elizabeth F. Loftus
Andrea Lücking
Maryanne Martin
Margaret W. Matlin
Günter Molz
Thomas Mussweiler
Margit E. Oswald

Heekyeong Park

Jacqueline E. Pickrell

Rüdiger F. Pohl, Justus Liebig University Giessen, Germany.

Rolf Reber

Lynne M. Reder

Henry L. Roediger III

Michael Ross

Fritz Strack

Karl H. Teigen

Suzanne C. Thompson

Anne Wilson

Introduction: Cognitive illusions

Rüdiger F. Pohl

Errare humanum est.
(Cicero, 116–43 BC)

That we as humans do make errors in thinking, judgement, and memory is undisputed. Yet the very same fact keeps us puzzled: "Many scholars have found it disturbing that humans might have been rational enough to invent probability theory but not rational enough to use it in their daily thought" (Birnbaum, Anderson, & Hynan, 1990, p. 477). It is exactly this discrepancy that makes cognitive illusions so attractive to experts and laymen alike. In fact, there is a plethora of phenomena showing that we deviate in our thinking, judgement, and memory from some objective and "correct" standard.

This book presents a survey of 21 cognitive illusions that have inspired a wealth of empirical studies and theoretical approaches, in order to better understand the mechanisms (and possible fallacies) of the human information-processing system. In addition to the more "classic" illusions, I have included some more recent (and less well known) ones that promise to provide new and fruitful insights. At the same time, I have deliberately left out a few other illusions, such as misattributions of causality (see, e.g., Kahneman, Slovic, & Tversky, 1982), misconceptions of physics (see, e.g., Krist, Fiedberg, & Wilkening, 1993; Vasta & Liben, 1996), and some other, rather "minor" fallacies.

This introductory chapter gives an overview of cognitive illusions in general, discusses their theoretical status, and describes the intentions of this book.

LOOKING AT COGNITIVE ILLUSIONS

I start this section by asking "What are the defining features of a cognitive illusion?" Then I present the categorization and selection of illusions in this book and briefly review other collections of such illusions. This should give the reader a first feel of the domain in question.

Defining features

The term "cognitive illusion" has evolved in analogy to the better-known domain of "optical illusions" (see Hell, 1993b; Roediger, 1996). The main feature of a phenomenon for it to count as an illusion thus is that it leads to a perception, judgement, or memory that reliably *deviates* from "reality". In cases of optical and memory illusions, it may be immediately evident what constitutes reality (because subjective perception and recall can be compared to external or original stimuli, respectively), but in thinking and judgement, the matter is less clear (Gigerenzer, 1996). The problem concerns how to define an objectively "correct" judgement or decision. Researchers are still disputing in a number of cases which models might be used as norms and which not:

> Note that models, as elements of the theoretical framework of a study, are subject to discussion. They are not necessarily intangible. What is called a bias today may very well lose that status tomorrow if, say, the current framework appears too simplistic, naïve, or based on some superficial apprehension of the situation and the involved processing. In such a situation, the notion of bias loses its relevance.
> (Caverni, Fabre, & Gonzales, 1990b, pp. 8–9)

As a consequence, some cognitive illusions may simply "disappear" (as Gigerenzer, 1991, claimed) if one changes the standard against which to compare human performance (see, e.g., Chapter 2 on the use of base rates).

In addition, the observed phenomenon needs to deviate from the normative standard in a *systematic* fashion (i.e., in a predictable direction) rather than just randomly. Therefore, most designs include a control group, assuming that any deviations in the control group's data result from random error alone, while the experimental group shows in addition a systematic effect. Special care has to be taken if demonstrations of an illusion depend on repeated measures, because this involves the danger of being prone to regression effects, which could possibly lead to false interpretations of the data (as an example, see Chapter 20 on hindsight bias). As a related feature, the mechanisms eventually leading to cognitive illusions are typically rather complex and include a number of probabilistic processes, so that an illusion will not necessarily be observed on each single trial, but may only become evident as a systematic bias if the data are summed across a larger number of trials or participants.

A third aspect of cognitive illusions is that they appear *involuntarily*, that is, without specific instructions or deliberate will. They just happen. This is analogous to what has been found in research on suggestions (see, e.g.,

Gheorghiu, Netter, Eysenck, & Rosenthal, 1989, and Chapter 22): The suggested reaction manifests itself in the given situation without any conscious decision to do so. This does not mean that motivational factors or conscious meta-cognitions may not be influential too, but they are not the ultimate cause of the illusion itself. They only moderate its size (see Pohl, Bender, & Lachmann, 2002, for further discussion). Another aspect is that persons who fell prey to a cognitive illusion usually don't realize what has happened: "Illusions mock our belief that what we perceive, remember, and know is in perfect accord with the state of the external world" (Roediger, 1996, p. 76). That is, illusioned persons are still convinced they have judged, decided, or recalled something to the best of their knowledge.

As a consequence, and this constitutes the fourth cornerstone of the proposed definition, an illusion is *hard if not impossible to avoid*. While this is probably true for all optical illusions, the criterion is much weaker for cognitive ones. For some illusions, a proper instruction, careful selection of the material, or other procedural variations may reduce or even eliminate the illusion (as an example, see Gigerenzer, Hertwig, Hoffrage, & Sedlmeier, in press, and Chapter 3), while for other illusions, most (if not all) attempts to overcome the effect have failed (as an example, see Pohl & Hell, 1996, and Chapter 20).

Finally, to distinguish cognitive illusions from other forms of typical errors, misunderstandings, or faulty memories, illusions often appear as rather *distinct* from the normal course of information processing. An illusion somehow "sticks out" as something special that "piques our curiosity" (as Roediger, 1996, put it) and thus attracts researchers to explain this unexpected but robust finding. In other words, ordinary forms of forgetting (leading to omission errors), drawing schema-based inferences (leading to commission errors), or deviations resulting from simple misunderstandings would not be considered "illusions". Roediger and McDermott (2000) accordingly described these phenomena as "distortions". This is not to say that a cognitive illusion cannot be explained with ordinary and general mechanisms of information processing. In fact, one of the theoretical goals of research on cognitive illusions is to avoid the assumption of any special mechanism that is responsible only for this one phenomenon, but instead to explain the observed effects with what one already knows about cognitive processes in general (see, e.g., Chapter 22).

Categories of cognitive illusions

I ordered the list of cognitive illusions that I came up with when I planned this book into three categories: thinking, judgement, and memory, respectively. While the *memory* category may appear rather clear (something is remembered but deviates in a systematic way from the original), the distinction between *thinking* and *judgement* may be less sharp. This becomes immediately evident if one looks at earlier collections of cognitive illusions (see below): These generally focused either on memory alone or both on thinking and judgement, without clearly differentiating the last two domains. And indeed, categorizing illusions as being related to either thinking or judgement appears rather difficult. But to make things even worse, *all* illusions involve memory processes, like encoding, storage, and retrieval. For some of the judgement illusions, for example, varying the retention interval between experimental phases led to clear effects. On the other hand, memory illusions involve different kinds of thinking and judgement processes. For example, the three classical heuristics proposed by Tversky and Kahneman (1974) are suggested to be responsible not only for biases in judgement but also for several memory illusions. The same is true for some more recently proposed "fast and frugal" heuristics (Gigerenzer, Todd, & the ABC Research Group, 1999b).

As an example of these taxonomic difficulties, the "Moses illusion" (Chapter 15) was initially considered a judgement illusion by me, a thinking illusion by one of the reviewers, and a memory illusion by the authors of that chapter. (I finally endorsed the authors' view.) Other illusions represent similar "borderline" cases. The following distinction should therefore be understood as a pragmatic proposal only.

I have defined illusions of *thinking* (Chapters 1 to 7) as those that involve application of a certain rule (like Bayes' theorem, hypothesis testing, or syllogistic reasoning). These rules are derived from normative models (like probability theory, falsification principle, or logic) and their results usually serve as standards against which human performance is evaluated. The crucial point is that naïve persons usually don't know these rules and therefore behave rather intuitively. Typical tasks are to estimate a probability, to verify a logical conclusion, or to discover a hidden rule. The illusions covered in Chapters 1 to 6 mainly involve inductive inferences, while Chapter 7 focuses on deductive reasoning problems.

In illusions of *judgement* (Chapters 8 to 14), persons are asked to subjectively rate a specific aspect of a given stimulus (e.g., its pleasantness, frequency, or veracity). However, specific features of the situation may bias someone's judgement in a certain direction. These features involve, for example, feelings of familiarity or confidence, the subjective experience of searching one's memory, or the selective activation of one's memory contents. Most importantly, these are all cases of judgements under uncertainty, that is, the person has no knowledge about the correct solution. Instead, he or she is bound to rely on subjective impressions. The classical heuristics described by Tversky and Kahneman (1974) – availability, representativeness, and anchoring (Chapters 8 to 10, respectively) – represent examples of such mechanisms that may in turn lead to judgemental illusions (see the discussion below). In this sense, these heuristics have a different status from the other chapters. They are not cognitive illusions themselves but might be involved as cognitive processes in many different illusions. The last chapter in this category describes the "Pollyanna principle" (Chapter 14), which could as well be categorized as a memory illusion because the appropriate research involves measures of judgement and of memory in about equal shares. I finally decided to put the chapter into the judgement section, because it focuses slightly more on judgement than on memory (including the classroom demonstration of Pollyannaism).

Finally, illusions of *memory* (Chapters 15 to 21) are those in which earlier encoded material has to be remembered later on. The critical test typically involves recall or recognition. I did not restrict this category to those cases where presentation of the original material proceeds under experimental control (Chapters 17 to 21), but also included cases where the original material was encoded pre-experimentally outside the laboratory (Chapters 15 and 16). These latter memory illusions are thus close to the borderline with judgement illusions.

Selection of cognitive illusions

In the paragraphs below, I briefly describe the different cognitive illusions covered in the three main sections of this book and in the final chapter on perspectives.

Thinking

John Fisk (Chapter 1) describes and discusses the "conjunction fallacy". This error occurs whenever the compound of two independent events is considered to be more probable than each of the single events alone. The most prominent task in this domain is the "Linda problem". Problems with "Bayesian inferences" are dealt with in the next two chapters. The central task here is to update a previous probability estimate for a certain hypothesis in the light of new evidence. Michael Birnbaum (Chapter 2) reviews and critically discusses the evidence for the so called "base-rate neglect" in Bayesian inferences – that is, that persons do not attend to the basic frequencies of the included events. In addition, Stephanie Kurzenhäuser and Andrea Lücking (Chapter 3) argue and present evidence that the statistical format in which the data are presented influences people's performance. More precisely, they show that the error rate in Bayesian inferences decreases drastically when the data are given in natural frequencies. Margit Oswald and Stefan Grosjean (Chapter 4) then inspect the "confirmation bias". This bias describes the tendency to selectively look for evidence that confirms one's hypothesis rather than to look for evidence that falsifies it. The following two chapters are devoted to the erroneous detection of a relation where actually none exists. Klaus Fiedler (Chapter 5) investigates cases of "illusory correlation" and Suzanne Thompson (Chapter 6) those of "illusion of control". In the first case, individuals show partly severe failure and inaccuracy in correlation assessment, and in the second, individuals overestimate their personal influence over an outcome. In the final chapter in this section,

Jonathan Evans (Chapter 7) presents an overview about "biases in deductive reasoning". These concern the typical errors associated with veryfying conclusions that logically follow from the given information.

Judgement

The judgement section starts with three chapters that are devoted to the classic heuristics proposed by Tversky and Kahneman (1974). Rolf Reber (Chapter 8) reviews the evidence for the impact of "availability" on people's judgement. Availability is defined as the ease with which relevant instances of a class come to mind, but could also be understood as the number of instances that can be retrieved from memory. Karl Teigen (Chapter 9) then looks critically at judgements that are assumed to be based on "representativeness", that is, on the apparent similarity of the to-be-judged object with its parent population. And Thomas Mussweiler, Birte Englich, and Fritz Strack (Chapter 10) present the latest evidence and explanation for the "anchoring effect", which occurs when people are biased in their numerical judgement by a previously presented value. Following up on these basic heuristics, the next two chapters study the effects of repeated presentations of material. Catherine Hackett Renner (Chapter 11) explores the phenomenon that repeated presentations of unknown assertions may lead to an increased belief in the truth of these assertions ("frequency-validity effect"), and Robert Bornstein and Catherine Craver-Lemley (Chapter 12) review the finding that repeatedly presented material may increase in its positive valence (known as the "mere exposure effect"). "Overconfidence" occurs if one's confidence in the correctness of one's judgements exceeds the corresponding accuracy rate. Ulrich Hoffrage (Chapter 13) discusses this illusion and similar effects in relation to ecological models of human judgement. In the final chapter of this section, Margaret Matlin (Chapter 14) presents an illusion that is probably rather widespread, the "Pollyanna principle". Her collection of cases shows that people tend to maintain inflated judgements about their abilities and characteristics. In addition, similar effects of "positivity" have also been found for memory tasks.

Memory

The first two chapters in the memory section cover memory problems in relation to the retrieval of pre-experimentally encoded semantic and perceptual knowledge. Heekyeong Park and Lynne Reder (Chapter 15) investigate the "Moses illusion", which is the tendency to overlook semantic distortions in statements or questions. Gregory Jones and Maryanne Martin (Chapter 16) discuss evidence showing that we are likely to misremember the spatial orientation of everyday objects. The next illusion, the "associative memory illusion" discussed by Henry Roediger III and David Gallo (Chapter 17), also refers to semantic memory, but here the exposure to the to-be-remembered material is completely under experimental control. In the respective paradigm, persons are likely to falsely recall or recognize a non-represented target word that is highly associated to a list of previously presented words. The following three chapters have in common that they look at the effects of intermediate information for the memory of earlier presented information. The "effects of labelling" (Chapter 18) refer to cases in which verbal labels or descriptions of a previously encountered stimulus deteriorate memory for that stimulus. Similarly, the "misinformation effect" described by Jacquie Pickrell, Daniel Bernstein, and Elizabeth Loftus (Chapter 19) denotes the finding that post-event information may interfere with one's ability to accurately recall the original event. And in hindsight (i.e., after an outcome is known), persons are likely to overestimate what they had (or would have) estimated in foresight, thus leading to "hindsight bias" (Chapter 20). In the last chapter of this section, Anne Wilson and Michael Ross (Chapter 21) present illusions that are connected to erroneous subjective theories of personal development. Generally, persons tend to exaggerate the consistency of their abilities and features across time, but under certain circumstances they prefer to assume change (e.g., improvement).

Perspectives

In the closing chapter (Chapter 22), Vladimir Gheorghiu, Günter Molz, and I attempt to delineate some perspectives for future research and more importantly for a more integrative theoretical framework. In analogy to the domain of suggestionality we introduce a domain of "illusionality", including descriptions of (a) illusive situations and phenomena, (b) illusionability (encompassing general psychological processes as well as individual differences), (c) techniques of producing cognitive illusions, and (d) a theory of illusionality. Under the latter heading we discuss whether cognitive illusions should be considered malfunctions of the human information-processing system ("the pessimistic view") or whether these illusions are adaptive and functional and thus possess advantageous functions ("the optimistic view"; cf. Jungermann, 1983, reprinted 1986; see also the discussion below).

Earlier collections

Of course, the present volume with its selection of cognitive illusions and its attempt to further integrate the field is not the first one to appear. One such collection with examples from thinking, judgement, and memory was published in Germany 10 years ago by Hell, Fiedler, and Gigerenzer (1993). In addition to some of the illusions included in the present volume, Hell et al. also covered problems of attributing causality and developmental misconceptions of physics. Other collections focused on only a few illusions that were related either to thinking and judgement or to memory alone.

Thinking and judgement

Probably one of the most cited papers on biases in judgement was the 1974 *Science* paper of Tversky and Kahneman entitled *Judgment under uncertainty: Heuristics and biases*. The authors presented three general heuristics, namely *availability, representativeness*, and *adjustment and anchoring* (see Chapters 8 to 10, respectively), together with several examples of each. Many of the biases described in that paper also appear in the present volume; for example, biased probability estimates of conjunctive events (Chapter 1), violations of Bayes' rule and the base-rate fallacy (Chapters 2 and 3), illusory correlation (Chapter 5), illusion of validity and subjective probability distributions (Chapter 13), and associative memory illusions (Chapter 17). A collection of some high-impact papers in this domain was later edited by Kahneman, Slovic, and Tversky (1982) under the same title of *Judgment under uncertainty: Heuristics and biases*. The most recent developments of this approach are documented in *Heuristics and biases: The psychology of intuitive judgment* edited by Gilovich, Griffin, and Kahneman (2002). The three major sections of that volume are devoted to (1) theoretical and empirical extensions (including representativeness and availability; anchoring, contamination, and compatibility; forecasting, confidence, and calibration; optimism; and norms and counterfactuals), (2) new theoretical directions (including two systems of reasoning; support theory; and alternative perspectives on heuristics), and (3) real-world applications (including everyday judgement and behaviour; and expert judgement).

Another collection entitled *On cognitive illusions and their implications* was published by Edwards and von Winterfeld (1986). They explored four kinds of intellectual tasks: (1) probability assessments and revision, (2) decision making, (3) intuitive physics, and (4) logic and mental arithmetic. Similarly, Caverni, Fabre, and Gonzales (1990a) looked at *Cognitive biases* related to (1) different cognitive activities (like reasoning and problem solving, categorization, assessment, and judgements of probability and confidence), (2) characteristics of the situation (as given by the context and the external structure of the information), and (3) possible cognitive aids to correct for biases. Still other treatises of biases in human reasoning and thinking were provided by Evans (1989), Gilovich (1991), and Piatelli-Palmarini (1994).

Memory

The earliest book including "memory illusions" that I know of was published by Sully in 1881. He described several illusive phenomena of introspection, perception, memory, and belief under a rather vague definition: "Illusion, as distinguished from correct knowledge, is to put it broadly, deviation of representation from fact" (p. 332).

A few years later, a noteworthy collection of memory errors (also called "illusions" there) was provided by Hodgson and Davey (1886/1887). They rigorously investigated spiritualism in the form of "psychography" (i.e., writing on a hidden slate without any operation of the medium's muscles). That this "clever conjuring trick" was not detected by the devoted followers in such séances was explained mainly through errors of perception and memory. More specifically, the authors described memory errors of omission, substitution, transposition, and interpolation.

Another noteworthy, but more well-known, contribution was provided by Bartlett's (1932) book *Remembering: A study in experimental and social psychology*, which described and experimentally investigated several sources of schematic influences on false recall. Yet the effects of schematic knowledge on encoding and reconstructing memories (see Alba & Hasher, 1983, and Brewer & Nakamura, 1984, for summaries) never came to be considered as "cognitive illusions", perhaps because they represent everyday experiences and thus lack the flavour of a special phenomenon. But the cognitive mechanisms proposed by Bartlett and his successors nevertheless appear in modern explanations of some "true" cognitive illusions.

In more recent times, Schacter, Coyle, Fischbach, Mesulam, and Sullivan (1995) edited a book entitled *Memory distortion: How minds, brains, and societies reconstruct the past*, and Roediger (1996) introduced a special issue of the *Journal of Memory and Language* by focusing on "Memory illusions" (see also Hell, 1993a). The collection of papers in that issue was not intended to systematically and completely cover all known types of illusions, but it gives a fairly good overview of the wide range of memory distortions and illusions. Roediger discussed the included papers under the following topics (which I have rearranged here): fluency illusions (cf. Chapters 8, 11, and 12), relatedness effects (see Chapter 17), verbal overshadowing (see Chapter 18), effects of interference and misleading information (see Chapter 19), and illusions of reality and source monitoring (again, see Chapter 19). In addition, the issue treated a number of phenomena not explicitly covered in the present volume: illusions of perception and memory (which are related to the orientation bias in Chapter 16), illusory conjunctions and memory (which has nothing to do with the "conjunction fallacy" in thinking covered in Chapter 1), and hypnosis and guessing effects (which are related to effects of suggestion and suggestibility; see Chapter 22).

In *The Oxford handbook of memory*, Roediger and McDermott (2000) presented a more systematic coverage of "memory distortions". The two general classes of memory errors – omission and commission – were reviewed according to six factors (p. 160) that seem to be responsible for their occurrence:

> False memories arise from inferences from series of related pieces of information, from interference from events surrounding the event of interest, from imagination of possible events that did not occur, from

retrieval processes, and from social factors. Finally, there are individual differences in susceptibility to these memory illusions.

In closing their overview, Roediger and McDermott expressed their hope that from studying memory illusions "we can elucidate both the nature of these curious and interesting phenomena, but also shed light on processes occurring in 'normal' remembering of events" (p. 160).

UNDERSTANDING COGNITIVE ILLUSIONS

In this section, I summarize the debate on the so-called "heuristics and biases programme" of Tversky and Kahneman (1974). Then I discuss the theoretical status of cognitive illusions in general and what they may tell us about human rationality. I close with some current trends in research.

The debate on heuristics and biases

The underlying idea of Tversky and Kahneman (1974) was that humans employ a small number of simple and quick rules of thumb in many different situations of judgement under uncertainty. With respect to their efficiency, Tversky and Kahneman stated that "in general, these heuristics are quite useful, but sometimes they lead to severe and systematic errors" (p. 1124). Biases caused by these heuristics were thought to represent genuine cognitive strategies of the human information-processing system independent from any motivational influence: "These biases are not attributable to motivational effects such as wishful thinking or the distortion of judgments by payoffs and penalties" (p. 1130). Several of the observed biases and fallacies were thus thought to be explicable with only a few general heuristics. This "heuristics and biases" approach led to an enormous number of studies investigating the intricacies of human judgement (see, e.g., Kahneman et al., 1982, or more recently, Gilovich et al., 2002), which in turn affected scholarship in economics, law, medicine, management, and political science.

However, this approach led to some controversy. In particular, Gigerenzer (1991, 1996; Gigerenzer, Czerlinsky, & Martignon 1999a; Gigerenzer et al., in press) attacked the "heuristics and biases" programme for having "narrow norms and vague heuristics" (Gigenrenzer, 1996: 592) (see also the reply of Kahneman & Tversky, 1996). The criticism centred mainly around three topics, namely one-sided view, artificiality, and lack of explanatory power (see below). As an alternative to the classic heuristics, Gigerenzer et al. (1999b) proposed a set of "fast and frugal" heuristics that were fundamentally different from the classic ones. They were precisely defined, supposed to be ecologically valid, and could be implemented and tested in a computer simulation.

One-sided view

According to Gigerenzer and his co-workers, the collection of biases has focused too much on the few faulty cases of judgement and decision making, thereby ignoring the majority of cases where the same heuristics typically lead to correct or at least useful decisions. This one-sided view may have led some researchers to conclude that "mental illusions should be considered the rule rather than the exception" (Thaler, 1991, p. 4) and that "mistakes of reason rule our minds" (Piatelli-Palmarini, 1994). But this view of human rationality appears overly pessimistic (see the discussion below). Accordingly, Gigerenzer et al. (1999b) summarized their more optimistic view of cognitive illusions in a book entitled *Simple heuristics that make us smart*. As the title implies, the authors' focus was less on errors and fallacies, but rather on how fast and frugal heuristics may lead to optimal decisions under natural time and knowledge constraints. They claimed, moreover, that these heuristics are adaptive and functional.

Artificiality

Gigerenzer (1991) also asserted that not everything that looks like a cognitive illusion really is one. More specifically, he argued that one could "make cognitive illusions disappear" simply by (a) avoiding too narrow norms to evaluate human performance, (b) using an adequate statistical format, and (c) using representative (instead of selected) samples of items. This would lead to a reduction of (at least) three illusions, respectively, namely the conjunction fallacy (see Chapter 1), faulty Bayesian inferences (see Chapters 2 and 3), and overconfidence (see Chapter 13). But Gigerenzer et al. (in press) admitted that the accusation of artificiality applied only to a few illusions, while others are "true illusions" without doubt. In addition, the three proposed methodological remedies generally only *reduced* the respective illusions, but did not make them completely *disappear*. Thus, these illusions still need to be explained apart from any additional (possibly artificial) factor that may have inflated some of the findings of the heuristics and biases programme.

Lack of explanatory power

With respect to their theoretical status, Gigerenzer (1991) claimed that the postulated heuristics are not explanations at all, but rather redescriptions of the observed phenomena: "In the 20 years of 'heuristics and biases' research [. . .], a lack of theoretical progress is possibly the most striking result. The absence of a general theory or even of specific models of underlying cognitive processes has been repeatedly criticized [. . .], but to no avail" (p. 101). Similarly, on the occasion that Daniel Kahneman was awarded the Nobel prize for economics in 2002, one congratulator (MacCoun, 2002, p. 8) noted that "their [Kahneman and Tversky's] core arguments make only sparing use of hypothetical constructs" and that their papers "rely less on elaborate experimentation and psychometrics than on simple but powerful demonstrations of replicable phenomena". This lack of rigorous investigation and detailed modelling is what Gigerenzer so heavily criticized. In his own approach (see Gigerenzer et al., 1999b), he proposed a set of heuristics that are all highly formalized with respect to the underlying cognitive processes.

Unfortunately, there is not enough space here to give a full account of the debate and its current status. A detailed exposition of the "fast and frugal heuristics" approach and its merits has been given by Gigerenzer and Todd (1999) and by Gigerenzer et al. (1999a, reprinted 2002), while the latest state of the discussion on the "heuristics and biases" approach has been summarized by Gilovich and Griffin (2002). According to the last authors, a peaceful coexistence of both approaches or even a theoretical integration may be possible. This view is based on the recent rise of "two systems" models of judgement under uncertainty (as documented in several chapters of the Gilovich et al., 2002, book; see also Sloman, 1996). These models posit "an associationist, parallel processing system ('System 1') that renders quick, holistic judgments [...] and a more deliberate, serial, and rule-based system ('System 2')" (Gilovich & Griffin, 2002, p. 16). Both systems are supposed to operate in parallel, with System 1 always running and System 2 occassionally supplementing or overriding System 1. In this framework, the classical heuristics could be considered to be more connected to System 1 and the fast and frugal heuristics to System 2. More precisely, System 1 is thought to provide "natural assessments" that are based on general-purpose heuristics (like affect, availability, causality, fluency, similarity, and surprise), while System 2 may supply "strategies or rules that are deliberately chosen to ease computational burden" (p. 16f). To me, this new perspective looks promising, but it could be a tedious if not impossible task to satisfactorily disentangle the two systems (see the sceptical comments by Gigerenzer & Regier, 1996).

Status of cognitive illusions

As already mentioned above, several researchers have critically questioned whether the existence of cognitive illusions may serve as proof of the fallibility of the human mind (cf. Jungermann, 1983, 1986, and Chapter 22). For example, "many illusions, in perception and cognition, can be understood as the flipside of otherwise adaptive and prudent algorithms" as Fiedler (Chapter 5) puts it. Similarly, Tversky and Kahneman (1974) acknowledged that heuristics typically lead to useful results, and Gigerenzer et al. (1999b) demonstrated that the fast and frugal heuristics they proposed fared about equally well compared to more complete (but time-consuming) strategies. Our cognitive system is not equipped with a fully-fledged arsenal of highly complex programs (like a computer), but rather consists of a set of fancy "shortcuts" or "rules of thumb" that allow quick and most of the time also very helpful reactions. The question of whether a decision, judgement, or memory is "correct" (in a normative way) is usually secondary to the question of whether that decision, judgement, or memory is helpful in the current situation. Of course, there may be situations in which it appears desirable to have, for example, a perfect memory (as in eyewitness testimony; see Chapter 19). But then, these cases might be relatively rare in our lives, so that in sum we are probably far better off with our heuristics. With respect to memory, Bartlett (1932) accordingly postulated that "in a world of constantly changing environment, literal recall is extraordinarily unimportant" (p. 204). So what we are talking about when we discuss cognitive illusions is the exception and not the rule (which is contrary to what Piatelli-Palmarini, 1994, and Thaler, 1991, had claimed).

Thus, although many illusions provide cogent evidence for erroneous and fallacious cognitive functioning, "one should refrain from premature pessimistic conclusions about human intelligence and rationality" as Fiedler (Chapter 5) claims. Or as Hell (1993b) expressed it: "Systematic deviation [of human performance] is a cue for the necessity to improve one's theory and not a cue for a defective human rationality" (p. 321, my translation). This view of cognitive illusions is explicitly shared by many of the authors of the present volume. "Biases have thus been incorporated into a positive conception of cognitive activity, one that grants them the status of cues, of dependent variables. Biases should indeed be used as indicators likely to clarify our understanding of cognitive functioning, and thus of what is deemed to be normal functioning on the basis of certain criteria" (Caverni et al., 1990b, p. 11). This is probably also what Cicero meant in his famous quote "Errare humanum est" (To err is human).

In analogy to the research on optical illusions, cognitive illusions can therefore tell us much about our "normal" information-processing system (see Roediger & McDermott, 2000). In fact, many of the more detailed explanations of cognitive illusions include only basic processes of encoding, storing, retrieving, and judging that are all well known from cognitive psychology (see, e.g., the SARA model in Chapter 20). That is, these theories refrain from postulating any special (and maybe obscure) mechanism that may have led to the observed illusion. Illusions have thus probably lost some of their previous appeal (just as happened with optical illusions), but at the same time they have been incorporated into what we know about how the human mind works. And that certainly is a true advantage.

Future trends

As the last but not least point in discussing cognitive illusions, I would like to briefly point out three connected areas where research might be beneficial in the future. These are individual differences, applied domains, and neuropsychological foundations.

In a way, individual differences were the very first focus of the study of cognitive illusions (e.g., in research on human suggestibility, intelligence, or repression), but then the scientific community seemed to have somewhat lost interest. The focus shifted to the general architecture of the human information-processing system. In this phase individual differences were often only seen as annoying, but unavoidable sampling error. Only lately, presumably due to the renewed interest in applied perspectives of cognitive functioning, have individual differences gained more attention again (see Chapter 22). For example, Stanovich (1999) asked *Who is rational?*, Dempster and Corkill (1999) looked at individual differences in susceptibility to memory illusions, and Read and Winograd (1998) edited a special issue of *Applied Cognitive Psychology* on "Individual differences and memory distortions". Another area of research, building the bridge to applied perspectives, looked at individual "delusions" as the pathological twin of "illusions". For example, Miller and Karoni (1996) discussed several possible cognitive models of delusions, including "anomalous sensory experiences, distorted attributions, information processing biases, illusory correlations, Bayes' theorem, contingency judgment, and self-monitoring" (p. 487). Another extension of research on individual differences is to look at cultural differences, where different styles of thinking have been postulated and identified for Western as opposed to Eastern cultures (as an example, see Pohl et al., 2002).

With respect to their ecological validity, fallacies and biases have meanwhile been demonstrated in a multitude of applied contexts (as is documented in many papers in, e.g., *Applied Cognitive Psychology*). These include, for example, medical decision making, eyewitness testimony, or memories for childhood sexual abuse (see Roediger & McDermott, 2000). While in the beginning the focus was on possible errors and their costs, other researchers began to ask how illusions could possibly be reduced or even avoided: "Focusing on biases should contribute to the development of cognitive aids or correction procedures that bring together the necessary conditions for reducing if not canceling their effects" (Caverni et al., 1990b, p. 10). However, as research progressed, it became clear that only some of the cognitive illusions could be remedied (see, e.g., Gigerenzer et al., in press), while others proved their robustness (see, e.g., Pohl & Hell, 1996).

With recent substantial improvements in functional imaging techniques, neuropsychological foundations of illusory phenomena moved into the focus of cognitive psychology (see, e.g., Markowitsch, 2000; Schacter, 1998). One ambitious goal, for example, was to disentangle true from false memories (see Johnson, Nolde, Mather, Kounios, Schacter, & Curran, 1997; Schacter et al., 1996; and Chapter 19). But despite some promising first results, there still lies ahead of us much to be discovered.

THE INTENTIONS OF THIS BOOK

Having done research and taught courses on "cognitive illusions" for many years now, I felt it was time to have a representative collection of cognitive illusions in one book instead of dozens of scattered papers. So I took my list of illusions and started to ask colleagues, mostly highly renowned experts in the field, to contribute a chapter to the book. With this enterprise, I had the following intentions in mind.

Hopefully, this dense coverage of cognitive illusions will help to further integrate the field and to foster new *research* and the development of more precise *models* to explain these illusions. This is especially needed, because so far several approaches are still not precise enough to allow rigorous testing. On the other hand, some highly detailed models (even including simulation models) have been developed in the last decade, thus documenting the progress of the field (see, e.g., Pohl, Eisenhauer, & Hard, 2003). A related goal is based on the fact that until recently most of the illusions have been studied in complete isolation from one another without any cross-referencing. As a consequence, a multitude of empirical methods as well as theoretical approaches developed in parallel, thus obscuring the view on any common mechanisms that possibly lie behind larger classes of illusions. Therefore this book is also intended to help in discovering such accordances, in order to untangle the basic cognitive processes responsible for the observed illusions. One such attempt that draws an analogy with the research on suggestion and suggestibility is presented in more detail at the end of this book (Chapter 22).

Besides its hoped-for impact on empirical research and theoretical developments, this book is also intended to serve as a *handbook* to both professionals and informed lay people. It brings together a representative sample of cognitive illusions from various domains, thus allowing a quick overview of this exciting field of cognitive psychology. Each chapter presents the respective state of the art in a comprehensive overview, covering research from the first experiments to the most recent ones. The inclusion of applied perspectives should, moreover, make the chapters informative to experts from applied domains (economics, medicine, law, counselling, forecasting etc.). The discussion of which conditions may increase or reduce (or even eliminate) the respective illusion should also help practitioners to be aware of these distorting influences and of how to possibly reduce their impact by taking appropriate measures. And finally, the references in each chapter were selected to include the most important sources, especially classical demonstrations, high-impact papers, and meta-analytic studies (if available). The mean number of cited references per chapter is around 30 and thus appears to be manageable. If one wants to get further information quickly, a "Further reading" section provides help in each chapter.

As a teacher of cognitive psychology, I always find it beneficial for the students' learning progress if psychological topics are not only talked about, but also personally experienced (which is also more fun). Cognitive illusions offer themselves as such a fruitful possibility, where the single phenomena are generally easy to replicate. Most of the cognitive illusions are robust and will even work under less than optimal conditions, thus rendering them applicable as classroom demonstrations.

So, the last but not least intention of editing this book was to use it as a *textbook* for classes in cognitive psychology. To this end, the chapters are written in such a way as to be informative to the expert but also comprehensible to the beginner. In addition, each chapter (except Chapter 22) follows the same general outline including three main sections (which are further described below), namely (1) a survey of empirical findings, (2) a classroom demonstration, and (3) a discussion of theoretical explanations. Each chapter also contains a concise summary and suggestions for further reading.

The *empirical overview* starts with a definition and an example of the phenomenon in question, and then gives a fair and comprehensive summary of the empirical research so far and how the illusion can possibly be reduced or even eliminated. Not least important, each chapter also includes a discussion of applied aspects.

A separate section provides a detailed description of a prototypical *experiment* that elicits the illusion and that can easily be conducted in the classroom. This can be a classical example already published elsewhere or a new (maybe more simple) variant. The text includes all procedural and statistical details that are necessary to conduct and analyze the described experiment. The materials, instructions, and possibly more detailed information for running the experiment are mostly given in the relevant appendix.

The *theoretical overview* discusses how the illusion can possibly be explained and how any theoretical controversies have extended our understanding. In several chapters, this part also includes critical comments about previous connotations of cognitive illusions as proof of "human irrationality" (see above). Instead, thorough attempts are made to explain cognitive illusions within the framework of "normal" and efficient information processing, drawing on established theoretical concepts, rather than inventing vague and spurious mechanisms. These approaches are, moreover, often embedded in a discussion of the adaptive function of the responsible processes.

EPILOGUE

From research on autobiographical memory it is well known that we might err when we date events from our past. Typically, events of the past do not seem so distant in time as they actually are. This type of error has been called the "forward telescoping" effect (see, e.g., Crawley & Pring, 2000). In preparing this volume, I too experienced several cases of misperceptions of time. In this case, however, they referred to future events (instead of past ones). More precisely, almost all the contributors to this book promised (and even signed a contract) to deliver their chapter no later than the given deadline (which was then about 6 months ahead). However, when the deadline was reached, I had only 6 of the 22 chapters on my desk, which is an annoying but probably typical experience of editors. One of the authors, who was the last one to finally deliver his chapter (exceeding the deadline by 5 months), suggested to me that his apparent "planning fallacy" (Buehler, Griffin, & Ross, 2002) could possibly present a case of "overconfidence" (another well-known cognitive illusion; see Chapter 13): He had simply been too confident that he would make it in time. Presumably, similar misperceptions might have occurred to most of the other authors as well (although to a lesser degree), and I must admit that I am not immune either.

If this were true, the example could again foster a pessimistic view of cognitive illusions – that is, that there exist at least some illusions that are widespread and difficult if not impossible to overcome (which is probably true). But, on the other hand, we may also feel free to think about the positive aspects such an illusion might have for the persons who are afflicted (e.g., making them feel more optimistic, increasing their perseverance, or convincing other people; see also the final remarks in Chapter 13 for such an optimistic and functional view). Or, if we are not afflicted, we could attribute the illusion to some peculiar characteristics of other people and continue to believe that *we* are different and not prone to such biases (which is probably false, but might represent a useful coping strategy, which in turn demonstrates another positive aspect, namely of the erroneous denial of having such illusions).

Finally, several months after my onerous exceeding-the-deadline experiences, I noticed that I began to downplay the negative emotions connected to that event, thus demonstrating my own share of Pollyannaism (see Chapter 14). And in the end, having successfully finished the book and looking back, I feel increasingly certain that things did indeed run quite smoothly and that all the authors were highly cooperative and timely (see Chapter 20 on hindsight bias)!

ACKNOWLEDGEMENTS

This work was supported in part by a grant from the Deutsche Forschungsgemeinschaft (Po 315/6–4). For their helpful comments on an earlier version of this chapter, I thank Martin Heydemann, Michael Bender, Gregor Lachmann, and Ulrich Hoffrage. With respect to the whole book, my sincere thanks go to the 32 international authors who participated in this project. It was a truly inspiring enterprise to work with them. The four reviewers of the book's manuscript – David Hardman, Wolfgang Hell, Tim Rakow, and an anonymous colleague – gave valuable advice on how to further improve the single chapters and the book as a whole. Finally, for always friendly and cooperative guidance in publishing this volume, I would like to express my special thanks to Susan Rudkin and the team from Psychology Press.

REFERENCES

Alba, J. W., & Hasher, L. (1983). Is memory schematic? *Psychological Bulletin, 93*, 203–231.
Bartlett, F. C. (1932). *Remembering: A study in experimental and social psychology.* Cambridge: Cambridge University Press.
Birnbaum, M. H., Anderson, C., & Hynan, L. G. (1990). Theories of bias in probability judgment. In J.-P. Caverni, J. M. Fabre, & M. Gonzalez (Eds.), *Cognitive biases* (pp. 477–498). Amsterdam: North-Holland.
Brewer, W. F., & Nakamura, G. V. (1984). The nature and functions of schemas. In R. S. Wyer, & T. K. Srull (Eds.), *Handbook of social cognition* (Vol. 1; pp. 119–160). Hillsdale, NJ: Lawrence Erlbaum Associates Inc.
Buehler, R., Griffin, D., & Ross, M. (2002). Inside the planning fallacy: The causes and consequences of optimistic time predictions. In T. Gilovich, D. Griffin, & D. Kahneman (Eds.), *Heuristics and biases: The psychology of intuitive judgment* (pp. 250–270). New York: Cambridge University Press.
Caverni, J.-P., Fabre, J. M., & Gonzalez, M. (Eds.). (1990a). *Cognitive biases.* Amsterdam: North-Holland.
Caverni, J.-P., Fabre, J. M., & Gonzalez, M. (1990b). Cognitive biases: Their contribution for understanding human cognitive processes. In J.-P. Caverni, J. M. Fabre, & M. Gonzalez (Eds.), *Cognitive biases* (pp. 7–12), Amsterdam: North-Holland.
Crawley, S. E., & Pring, L. (2000). When did Mrs Thatcher resign? The effects of ageing on the dating of public events. *Memory, 8*, 111–121.
Dempster, F. N., & Corkill, A. J. (1999). Individual differences in susceptibility to interference and general cognitive ability. *Acta Psychologica, 101*, 395–416.
Edwards, W., & von Winterfeldt, D. (1986). On cognitive illusions and their implications. In H. R. Arkes & K. R. Hammond (Eds.), *Judgment and decision making: An interdisciplinary reader* (pp. 642–679). Cambridge: Cambridge University Press.
Evans, J. St. B. T. (1989). *Bias in human reasoning: Causes and consequences.* Hillsdale, NJ: Lawrence Erlbaum Associates Inc.
Gheorghiu, V. A., Netter, P., Eysenck, H. J., & Rosenthal, R. (Eds.). (1989). *Suggestion and suggestibility. Theory and research.* Berlin: Springer.
Gigerenzer, G. (1991). How to make cognitive illusions disappear: Beyond "heuristics and biases". In W. Stroebe & M. Hewstone (Eds.), *European review of social psychology* (Vol. 2; pp. 83–115). Chichester, UK: Wiley.
Gigerenzer, G. (1996). On narrow norms and vague heuristics: A rebuttal to Kahneman and Tversky (1996). *Psychological Review, 103*, 592–596.
Gigerenzer, G., Czerlinski, J., & Martignon, L. (1999a). How good are fast and frugal heuristics? In J. Shanteau, B. Mellers, & D. Schum (Eds.), *Decision research from Bayesian approaches to normative systems: Reflections on the contribution of Ward Edwards* (pp. 81–103). Norwell, MA: Kluwer.
Gigerenzer, G., Czerlinski, J., & Martignon, L. (2002). How good are fast and frugal

heuristics? In T. Gilovich, D. Griffin, & D. Kahneman (Eds.), *Heuristics and biases: The psychology of intuitive judgment* (pp. 559–581). New York: Cambridge University Press. [Reprint of the 1999 paper.]

Gigerenzer, G., Hertwig, R., Hoffrage, U., & Sedlmeier, P. (in press). Cognitive illusions reconsidered. In C. R. Plott, & V. L. Smith (Eds.), *Handbook of experimental economics results*. Amsterdam: Elsevier.

Gigerenzer, G., & Regier, T. (1996). How do we tell an association from a rule? Comment on Sloman (1996). *Psychological Bulletin, 119*, 23–26.

Gigerenzer, G., & Todd, P. M. (1999). Fast and frugal heuristics: The adaptive toolbox. In G. Gigerenzer, P. M. Todd, & the ABC Research Group (Eds.), *Simple heuristics that make us smart* (pp. 3–34). New York: Oxford University Press.

Gigerenzer, G., Todd, P. M., & the ABC Research Group (Eds.). (1999b). *Simple heuristics that make us smart*. New York: Oxford University Press.

Gilovich, T. (1991). *How we know what isn't so: The fallibility of human reason in everyday life*. New York: The Free Press.

Gilovich, T., & Griffin, D. (2002). Introduction – Heuristics and biases: Then and now. In T. Gilovich, D. Griffin, & D. Kahneman (Eds.), *Heuristics and biases: The psychology of intuitive judgment* (pp. 1–18). New York: Cambridge University Press.

Gilovich, T., Griffin, D., & Kahneman, D. (Eds.). (2002). *Heuristics and biases: The psychology of intuitive judgment*. New York: Cambridge University Press.

Hell, W. (1993a). Gedächtnistäuschungen [Memory illusions]. In W. Hell, K. Fiedler, & G. Gigerenzer (Eds.), *Kognitive Täuschungen* [Cognitive illusions] (pp. 13–38). Heidelberg: Spektrum der Wissenschaft.

Hell, W. (1993b). Kognitive und optische Täuschungen [Cognitive and optical illusions]. In W. Hell, K. Fiedler, & G. Gigerenzer (Eds.), *Kognitive Täuschungen* [Cognitive illusions] (pp. 317–324). Heidelberg: Spektrum der Wissenschaft.

Hell, W., Fiedler, K., & Gigerenzer, G. (Eds.). (1993). *Kognitive Täuschungen* [Cognitive illusions]. Heidelberg: Spektrum der Wissenschaft.

Hodgson, R., & Davey, S. J. (1886/1887). The possibilities of mal-observation and lapse of memory from a practical point of view. *Proceedings of the Society for Psychical Research, 4*, 381–495.

Johnson, M. K., Nolde, S. F., Mather, M., Kounios, J., Schacter, D. L., & Curran, T. (1997). The similarity of brain activity associated with true and false recognition memory depends on test format. *Psychological Science, 8*, 250–257.

Jungermann, H. (1983). The two camps on rationality. In R. W. Scholz (Ed.), *Decision making under uncertainty* (pp. 63–86). Amsterdam: North-Holland.

Jungermann, H. (1986). The two camps on rationality. In H. R. Arkes, & K. R. Hammond (Eds.), *Judgment and decision making: An interdisciplinary reader* (pp. 627–641). Cambridge: Cambridge University Press. [Reprint of the 1983 paper.]

Kahneman, D., Slovic, P., & Tversky, A. (Eds.). (1982). *Judgment under uncertainty: Heuristics and biases*. Cambridge: Cambridge University Press.

Kahneman, D., & Tversky, A. (1996). On the reality of cognitive illusions. *Psychological Review, 103*, 582–591.

Krist, H., Fiedberg, E. L., & Wilkening, F. (1993). Intuitive physics in action and judgment: The development of knowledge about projectile motion. *Journal of Experimental Psychology: Learning, Memory, and Cognition, 19*, 952–966.

MacCoun, R. (2002, Dec.). Why a psychologist won the Nobel prize for economics. *APS Observer, 15*, 1 & 8.

Markowitsch, H. J. (2000). Neuroanatomy of memory. In E. Tulving, & F. I. M. Craik (Eds.), *The Oxford handbook of memory* (pp. 465–484). Oxford: Oxford University Press.

Miller, E., & Karoni, P. (1996). The cognitive psychology of delusions: A review. *Applied Cognitive Psychology, 10*, 487–502.

Piatelli-Palmarini, M. (1994). *Inevitable illusions: How mistakes of reason rule our minds*. New York: Wiley.

Pohl, R. F., Bender, M., & Lachmann, G. (2002). Hindsight bias around the world. *Experimental Psychology, 49*, 270–282.

Pohl, R. F., Eisenhauer, M., & Hardt, O. (2003). SARA: A cognitive process model to explain the anchoring effect and hindsight bias. *Memory, 11*, 337–356.

Pohl, R. F., & Hell, W. (1996). No reduction of hindsight bias with complete information and repeated testing. *Organizational Behaviour and Human Decision Processes, 67*, 49–58.

Read, J. D., & Winograd, E. (Eds.). (1998). Individual differences and memory distortions. *Applied Cognitive Psychology, 12*(SI).

Roediger, H. L. III (1996). Memory illusions. *Journal of Memory and Language, 35*, 76–100.

Roediger, H. L. III, & McDermott, K. B. (2000). Distortions of memory. In E. Tulving, & F. I. M. Craik (Eds.), *The Oxford handbook of memory* (pp. 149–162). Oxford: Oxford University Press.

Schacter, D. L. (1998). Illusory memories: A cognitive neuroscience analysis. In G. Mazzoni (Ed.), *Metacognition and cognitive neuropsychology: Monitoring and control processes* (pp. 119–138). Mahwah, NJ: Lawrence Erlbaum Associates Inc.

Schacter, D. L., Coyle, J. T., Fischbach, G. D., Mesulam, M. M., & Sullivan, L. E. (Eds.). (1995). *Memory distortions: How minds, brains, and societies reconstruct the past*. Cambridge, MA: Harvard University Press.

Schacter, D. L., Reiman, E., Curran, T., Yun, L. S., Bandy, D., McDermott, K. B. et al. (1996). Neuroanatomical correlates of veridical and illusory recognition memory: Evidence from positron emission tomography. *Neuron, 17*, 267–274.

Sloman, S. A. (1996). The empirical case for two systems of reasoning. *Psychological Bulletin, 119*, 3–22.

Stanovich, K. E. (1999). *Who is rational? Studies of individual differences in reasoning*. Mahwah, NJ: Lawrence Erlbaum Associates Inc.

Sully, J. (1881). *Illusion: A psychological study*. London: Kegan Paul.

Thaler, R. (1991). *Quasi-rational economics*. New York: Sage.

Tversky, A., & Kahneman, D. (1974). Judgment under uncertainty: Heuristics and biases. *Science, 185*, 1124–1131.

Vasta, R., & Liben, L. S. (1996). The water-level task: An intriguing problem. *Current Directions in Psychological Science, 5*, 171–177.

Part I
Illusions of thinking

1 Conjunction fallacy

John E. Fisk

Violations of the rules of probability theory and associated systematic reasoning biases have been widely demonstrated. When making judgements concerning uncertain events, individuals frequently produce estimates that are consistently too high, or in other situations consistently too low, or they fail to make use of all of the available information in making judgements about probabilistic events. The focus of the present chapter is conjunction-rule violations. Formally, the conjunction rule may be expressed as follows:

$$P(A\&B) = P(A) \times P(B|A) \tag{1}$$

In simple terms, the probability of event A and event B both occurring together is equal to the probability of event A multiplied by the (conditional) probability of event B *given that A has occurred*. For example, the probability that I will *study* (event A) AND *pass* my exams (event B) is equal to the probability that I will study multiplied by the probability that I will pass GIVEN that I have studied:

$$P(\text{Study and Pass}) = P(\text{Study}) \times P(\text{Pass} | \text{Study}) \tag{2}$$

When the two events A and B are independent then Equation 1 simplifies to

$$P(A\&B) = P(A) \times P(B) \tag{3}$$

since for independent events:

$$P(B) = P(B|A) = P(B|\text{not } A) \tag{4}$$

The extent to which individuals make judgements consistent with the conjunction rule has been one of the most investigated areas of probabilistic reasoning with research dating back over 40 years (e.g., Cohen, Dearnaley, & Hansel, 1958). More recently the focus of research has shifted to a particular type of violation of the conjunction rule known as the conjunction fallacy (Agnoli & Krantz, 1989; Donovan & Epstein, 1997; Fiedler, 1988;

Fisk, 1996; Fisk & Pidgeon, 1996, 1997, 1998; Gavanski & Roskos-Ewoldsen, 1991; Tversky & Kahneman, 1983; Wells, 1985; Wolford, Taylor, & Beck, 1990; Yates & Carlson, 1986). The fallacy occurs when the conjunctive probability is assigned a value exceeding that assigned to one or both of the component events, that is,

$$P(A\&B) > P(A) \text{ and/or} \qquad (5)$$

$$P(A\&B) > P(B). \qquad (6)$$

Such judgements, which violate the conjunction rule,[1] are commonplace, with 50–90% of individuals responding in this fashion (Fisk & Pidgeon, 1996; Gavanski & Roskos-Ewoldsen, 1991; Tversky & Kahneman, 1983; Yates & Carlson, 1986).

EXPERIMENT: THE LINDA PROBLEM

Perhaps the best-known example of the conjunction fallacy is the Linda scenario from Tversky and Kahneman's (1983) classic study. Three versions of this problem are presented in Text boxes 1.1, 1.2, and 1.3 respectively, and in the first two versions most individuals rate the conjunction (bank teller and feminist) as more probable than one of the component events (bank teller) thereby committing the fallacy.

Text box 1.1 Version 1 of the Linda scenario

Participants are asked to read the following:

Linda is 31 years old, single, outspoken and very bright. At university she studied philosophy. As a student she was deeply concerned with issues of discrimination and social justice and also participated in anti-nuclear demonstrations.

Now rank each of the following three statements from most to least likely. For the most likely statement enter 1, for the more likely of the remaining two statements enter 2 and for the least likely statement enter 3.

	Linda is a bank teller.
	Linda is active in the feminist movement.
	Linda is active in the feminist movement and is a bank teller.

Text box 1.2 Version 2 of the Linda scenario

Rather than simply rank the alternatives, some researchers (e.g., Fisk & Pidgeon, 1996) have asked participants to provide probability estimates for each of the statements:

In this questionnaire you will be presented with a number of statements about certain events. You will be asked to judge how likely is each event to happen. Please make your judgements by writing down the chances in 100 that you feel that the event will occur. You may choose any number between 0 and 100. Some examples are provided below.

	How many chances in 100? (Enter a number between 0 and 100.)
If you tossed a fair coin how likely would it be to come up "heads"?	50

Since a fair coin is equally likely to come up heads or tails, there is a fifty/fifty or evens chance that it will come up heads and so your answer would be 50.

	How many chances in 100? (Enter a number between 0 and 100.)
Suppose that you had a normal pack of playing cards and that you cut the pack once. How likely would the outcome be a diamond?	25

Since a normal pack of playing cards contains four different suits, hearts, diamonds, clubs, and spades, each suit would be equally likely to be cut from the pack. Therefore you would have a 25% chance of drawing clubs, a 25% chance of spades, a 25% chance of hearts and a 25% chance of diamonds, so the answer is 25 chances in 100 as written above. Please read the following statement:

Linda is 31 years old, single, outspoken and very bright. At university she studied philosophy. As a student she was deeply concerned with issues of discrimination and social justice and also participated in anti-nuclear demonstrations. How likely is it that:

	How many chances in 100? (Enter a number between 0 and 100.)
Linda is a bank teller	
Linda is active in the feminist movement	
Linda is active in the feminist movement and is a bank teller	

> **Text box 1.3** Version 3 of the Linda scenario
>
> The Linda problem has also been posed in terms of frequencies (e.g., Fiedler, 1988):
>
> Linda is 31 years old, single, outspoken and very bright. At university she studied philosophy. As a student she was deeply concerned with issues of discrimination and social justice and also participated in anti-nuclear demonstrations. Imagine that we identified 100 individuals all closely resembling this description of Linda. Please answer the following questions:
>
> Enter a number between 0 and 100
>
> How many of the 100 would be bank tellers?
>
> How many of the 100 would be active in the feminist movement?
>
> How many of the 100 would be active in the feminist movement and bank tellers?

The reader may wish to give each version of the Linda problem to *different* groups of individuals and see what proportion of each group commits the conjunction fallacy. Although sample sizes are typically around 80–90 in our own studies (e.g., Fisk & Pidgeon, 1996), given the large effect size, around 50 participants per group should be sufficient. The reader may score participants' responses according to the following criteria. In Version 1, the participant is defined as having committed the fallacy if the statement "Linda is active in the feminist movement and is a bank teller" is ranked as being more likely than the statement "Linda is a bank teller". In Version 2, the participant is defined as having committed the fallacy if the probability (number of chances in 100) assigned to the former statement exceeds that assigned to the latter. In Version 3, the participant is defined as having committed the fallacy if their estimates are such that there are more feminist bank tellers than there are bank tellers. Having scored each participant on a nominal scale according to whether or not they have committed the fallacy, the reader's own results can be analyzed using χ^2 with the different versions constituting the rows of the design and the numbers committing or not committing the fallacy as the columns. In Tversky and Kaheman's original study (similar to Version 1), 85% committed the fallacy. This compares with 70% for Version 2 (Fisk, 1996) and just 22% with Version 3 (Fiedler, 1988).

EXPLANATIONS

The reason why Version 3 produces the smallest number of fallacies will be discussed below. Focus will now switch to Version 1, in which most participants rank the conjunction (bank teller and feminist) as more probable than its component event (bank teller) thereby committing the conjunction fallacy. Tversky and Kahneman have attempted to explain this outcome in terms of the *representativeness* heuristic (see Chapter 9). Being a feminist is *representative* of or *similar* to the description of Linda and therefore although the conjunction contains the unrepresentative event, bank teller, because it also contains the representative event, feminist, it seems more believable and hence more likely than the unrepresentative event on its own. This same scenario, along with many others with varying contents, has been used in a large number of studies (see above) and the conjunction fallacy has been replicated on numerous occasions. Apart from the potential role of representativeness, many other accounts of the conjunction fallacy have appeared over the past 40 years including:

1   Linguistic misunderstanding
2   Signed summation
3   Frequentist interpretations
4   Applying the wrong probabilistic rule
5   Surprise theory
6   Cognitive experiential self theory (CEST)
7   Mental models
8   Fast and frugal heuristics
9   Averaging

Each of these theoretical perspectives will now be discussed in turn.

Linguistic misunderstanding

It has been suggested that participants misunderstand the single event, assuming that it implicitly includes the negation of the other member of the conjunction. Thus, for example, when asked to evaluate the probability that "Linda is a bank teller", participants actually estimate the probability that "Linda is a bank teller and *not* a feminist". Ranking the latter as less likely than the statement "Linda is a bank teller and a feminist" would not be a violation of the conjunction rule. However, while linguistic misunderstanding might account for a small proportion of conjunction rule violations, the consensus is that it does not offer a comprehensive explanation of the phenomenon (Morrier & Borgida, 1984; Yates & Carlson, 1986).

Signed summation

Signed summation was a heuristic procedure proposed by Yates and Carlson (1986). It has some features in common with the notion of representativeness. The theory proposes that individuals represent degrees of likelihood in terms of a "qualitative likelihood index" (QLI). Unlikely events are represented by negative values on this index, and the more unlikely an event, the more negative the likelihood index becomes. On the other hand, likely events are represented by positive values in the QLI and the more likely an event, the larger will be the value corresponding to it on the index. Unlike standard representations of probability, the QLI is unbounded and can assume negative as well as positive values. According to the theory of signed summation, the likelihood of the conjunction of two events is the signed sum of the QLI values corresponding to the two individual events. Thus the conjunction of a likely event with an unlikely event is the sum of a negative and a positive number. This signed sum will by definition be greater than the QLI for the unlikely event, thus giving rise to the conjunction fallacy. Signed summation also predicts that the conjunction fallacy should not occur for conjunctions of two unlikely events and that for conjunctions of two likely events a double fallacy should occur with both component events being rated more probable than their conjunction. Yates and Carlson's (1986) results are broadly consistent with these expectations. Indeed similar predictions can be derived from the representativeness heuristic (see, e.g., Wells, 1985).

The problem with the signed summation model, and by implication with accounts in terms of representativeness, is that in conjunctions of a likely and an unlikely event, the fallacy is said to arise as a result of the degree of representiveness (or the positive QLI) associated with the likely component. What makes it more likely that Linda is a feminist bank teller is the degree of representativeness of the feminist component. Presumably therefore, the more representative the likely component, the more representative the conjunction will be judged to be. However, in a number of studies utilizing regression analysis, and more recently employing a within-participants design, my co-workers and I found that the probability assigned to the likely component was *not* statistically significant in determining the value of the conjunction. Instead it was the unlikely component that seemed to exert more influence in this regard (Fisk, 2002; Fisk & Pidgeon, 1996, 1997, 1998). Similar results have been obtained by Thüring and Jungermann (1990).

Frequentist interpretations

It has been proposed that when conjunction problems are posed in terms of frequencies, the conjunction fallacy does not occur (Fiedler, 1988). Version 3 of the Linda problem set out in Text box 1.3 is posed in terms of absolute frequencies and is intended to demonstrate this point. For example, in Version 3, participants were not asked to assign numerical single event probabilities. Instead, they were asked to imagine that there were 100 females all of whom fit Linda's description, and to judge how many of these 100 would be feminists, and how many would be bank tellers, and finally how many would be bank tellers and feminists. As noted above, when the problem is posed in this way the incidence of the conjunction fallacy is greatly reduced.

However, this is not to say that frequentist representations of problems are common in everyday life. In fact it seems rather that problems most often manifest themselves in terms of single events. In addition, research has established that individuals do not always understand the relevance or the necessity of obtaining frequency information (Teigen, Brun, & Frydenlund, 1999). Furthermore, Evans and co-workers have shown that frequency versions of probabilistic reasoning problems do not inevitably result in better judgements, indeed sometimes the opposite outcome occurs. Evans has argued that the apparent beneficial effects of frequency formats are not due to the fact that information is expressed in terms of frequencies, but rather that expressing the problem in this manner makes the extensional nature of the relationship between the conjunction and its component more transparent. Indeed Evans has shown that this can be achieved just as easily when problems are posed in probabilistic terms (Evans, Handley, Perham, Over, & Thompson, 2000).

Applying the wrong probabilistic rule

While some researchers have claimed that posing problems in terms of frequencies facilitates adherence to the conjunction rule, others have claimed that the manner in which many of the problems are framed makes it unclear whether the conjunction rule is the appropriate rule to apply. Wolford et al. (1990) argue that in problems like the Linda one, the participant may believe that one of the statements is actually true and that instead of evaluating the probability of the statement, participants are actually evaluating the probability of Linda's description given the statement – that is, instead of evaluating P(feminist and bank teller | Linda) and P(bank teller | Linda) participants are actually evaluating P(Linda | feminist and bank teller) and P(Linda | bank teller) (see Chapter 3). While producing probabilities such as:

P(feminist and bank teller | Linda) > P(bank teller | Linda)

is clearly a violation of the conjunction rule, making judgements such that

P(Linda | feminist and bank teller) > P(Linda | bank teller)

does not necessarily violate any normative rule.

While this suggestion is an appealing one, one of my own studies (Fisk, 1996), in which participants were asked for *both* kinds of probability judgement, showed that participants still violated the conjunction rule in contexts where it clearly should apply. Furthermore, there are some instances where Bayes' theorem does produce a situation in which, depending on the prior probabilities and the information provided:

P(Linda | bank teller) > P(Linda | feminist and bank teller).

However, even in these situations participants still produced estimates such that

P(Linda | feminist and bank teller) > P(Linda | bank teller)

essentially violating Bayes' theorem. Thus while it may be that some participants produce the wrong probability estimates, this does not offer a complete account of the conjunction fallacy, which continues to occur in contexts where the conjunction rule clearly applies.

Surprise theory

In recent years, in our own laboratory, we have attempted to explain conjunction rule violations in terms of Shackle's (1969) theory of "potential surprise". In general terms, the theory states that just as it is possible to assign a probability to an event, so events also possess surprise values. Thus while we might refer to the probability of event B as P(B), equally we can refer to its potential surprise value, that is, y^B (using Shackle's notation). Accordingly, the potential surprise of an event represents the degree of surprise we would experience were that event to occur.

Surprise values can also be defined for conditional events. For example, given two events A and B, y_0^A is defined as the surprise associated with event A, given a situation in which event B is now viewed as perfectly possible. The equivalent concept in probability theory is P(A|B). For *unrelated* or *independent* events, our surprise at the occurrence of A is unaffected by whether or not B occurs and so it follows that $y_0^A = y^A$. On the other hand, for *positively related* events, the occurrence of event B makes event A seem less surprising. For example, the surprise that an individual has had two or more heart attacks (event A) is less given the additional knowledge that he is a heavy smoker (event B), so in this case: $y_0^A < y^A$.

According to Shackle, surprise values can also be defined for conjunctions. The surprise value of the conjunction of events A and B, that is, $y^{A\&B}$, is based on the *greater* of the pair y_0^A and y^B (or for independent events, the greater of the pair y^A and y^B). Thus the relationship is neither additive nor multiplicative. Rather the conjunctive surprise value is dependent on that of its more surprising constituent with the surprise value of the other component exerting no direct influence. For example, imagine that an individual has been selected at random from a sample of persons taking part in a health survey. The surprise value of the conjunction:

> that the individual is a heavy smoker *and* has had two or more heart attacks ($y^{A\&B}$)

is based on the larger of the pair:

> our surprise that the individual is a heavy smoker (y^B)
> our surprise that the individual has had two or more heart attacks given that he is a heavy smoker (y_0^A).

According to Shackle, uncertainty is represented internally in terms of surprise rather than in terms of objective probability. Thus when the individual produces probability estimates these will be based on the subjective surprise values of the events in question. For example, as events become more surprising they will be judged to be progressively less likely. Alternatively, in most cases, likely events would not surprise us at all if they were to occur. Thus, in general, likely events are associated with zero surprise value.

In relation to conjunctive probability judgement, surprise theory predicts that the probability assigned to a conjunction will be determined by the probability of its less likely component. The probability of the more likely component has no direct effect. By way of an analogy, just as a chain can be no stronger than its weakest link, so the conjunction of two or more events is never more surprising than its most surprising constituent (and by implication not less likely than its least likely component). This is contrary to Tversky and Kahneman's emphasis on degree of representativeness of the likely component, from which it would be reasonable to infer that the likely event would play the prominent role in determining the value of the conjunction.

What evidence is there for Shackle's predicted pattern of outcomes? In several studies, my co-workers and I have demonstrated that only the smaller component event probability appears to influence the probability assigned to the conjunction (Fisk, 2002; Fisk & Pidgeon, 1996, 1997, 1998) and similar results have been reported by Christensen (1979), Thüring and Jungermann (1990), and Kariyazono (1991). More recently, Hertwig and Chase (1998) have shown that a substantial number of persons actually set the conjunctive probability *equal* to the probability of the less likely component event.[2] Furthermore, one of my recent studies (Fisk, 2003 submitted) has shown that, just as Shackle predicted, the conjunctive surprise value is indeed determined by the surprise value of the more surprising component with the less surprising component apparently playing no significant role.[3] Furthermore, consistent with Hertwig and Chase's results, in my own lab we found that many individuals set the surprise value of the conjunction exactly *equal* to the surprise value of the more surprising component.

While Shackle's theory is inconsistent with accounts of the conjunction fallacy in terms of representativeness, Tversky and Kahneman (1983) also describe an alternative process that can give rise to the conjunction fallacy. More specifically, they maintain that when a positive conditional relationship exists between two events, the likelihood of the conjunction fallacy is increased. For example, given the following two conjunctions:

Mr X has had two or more heart attacks *and* is a heavy smoker
Mr X has had two or more heart attacks *and* has green eyes

according to Tversky and Kahneman, the former is more likely to give rise to the conjunction fallacy because the two events are conditionally related, that is,

P(two or more heart attacks | heavy smoker) > P(two or more heart attacks).

In this situation, Tversky and Kahneman maintain that the strength of the causal link will unduly inflate the value assigned to the conjunction, potentially giving rise to the conjunction fallacy, even where neither event is particularly representative of the background information. Shackle's theory also predicts that the conjunction fallacy will be most likely where there is a positive conditional relationship between component events (and least likely where the relationship is a negative one). However, contrary to Tversky and Kahneman's account, while the presence of a positive conditional relationship makes the fallacy more likely, according to the surprise theory, the actual *strength* of the relationship exerts no direct influence on the value assigned to the conjunction nor on the extent of the fallacy.[4] All that matters is that a positive relationship exists. Consistent with Shackle's theory, both Fabre, Caverni, and Jungermann (1995) and Fisk and Pidgeon (1998) found that the fallacy was more likely to occur when a positive conditional relationship between the component events existed, *but* that this tendency was unaffected by whether the positive relationship was strong or weak.

If we assume that the surprise values of the component events are used as *cues* to determine the probability of the conjunction, then the emphasis on the more surprising event in Shackle's theory may be compared with the "one-reason" algorithm proposed by Gigerenzer and Goldstein (1996). Rather than combining values on different cues to form a judgement, Gigerenzer argues that judgements may be based on just a single cue. So, by analogy, rather than trying to combine the surprise values of the two component events, individuals may well be following a "one-reason" strategy and basing their conjunctive judgement solely on the more surprising event. From the perspective of ecological validity this makes sense, since in normative judgements an absolute change in the (more surprising) smaller component event probability has a larger impact on the conjunctive probability than the same absolute change applied to the larger component event probability.[5]

Surprise theory can account for a range of results for which other approaches can provide no adequate explanation, however it does possess certain limitations. The theory is essentially axiomatic, and while my co-workers and I (Fisk, 2002, 2003 submitted; Fisk & Pidgeon, 1998) have attempted to provide a justification in psychological terms for some of the underlying assumptions, there is some considerable way to go in this regard.

Cognitive experiential self theory (CEST)

An alternative approach, which has emerged in recent years, is based on Epstein's cognitive-experiential self-theory (CEST). This seeks to explain a range of reasoning errors that occur in judgements of relative frequency as well as conjunction rule violations (e.g., see Donovan & Epstein, 1997). CEST proposes that there are two interactive parallel systems involved in reasoning and decision making, a rational one and an experiential one. "The rational system is a conscious, deliberative, analytical, primarily verbal system with a very brief evolutionary history. The experiential system is a preconscious, automatic, intuitive, primarily imagistic system with a very long evolutionary history" (Donovan & Epstein, 1997, p. 3). The latter system, which is assumed to be the default one, operates using heuristic strategies. It generates judgements that are intrinsically compelling and which can override those generated by the rational system. In relation to the conjunction fallacy, Donovan and Epstein (1997) introduce two distinct dimensions (natural–unnatural and concrete–abstract), which they claim make it possible to identify the conditions under which the fallacy will arise. Concrete representations involve objects or events that can be directly imagined or experienced (e.g., the Linda scenario set out above). Abstract problems cannot be directly experienced or imagined, as for example when the task is to work out the value of the conjunction $P(A\&B)$ given that $P(A) = 0.2$ and $P(B|A) = 0.6$. A natural problem is one that elicits appropriate reasoning strategies, appropriate in the sense that they are capable of producing the correct solution if applied properly. Conversely, unnatural problems are those that elicit inappropriate reasoning strategies. For example, the Linda problem is unnatural since it elicits reasoning based on representativeness, while solution of the problem requires statistical reasoning. Thus in terms of the two dimensions, the Linda scenario is concrete and unnatural. On the other hand, problems such as the one set out in Text box 1.4 (Donovan & Epstein, 1997, p. 19) are concrete and natural since they usually elicit statistical reasoning.

Donovan and Epstein go on to show that the number of conjunction errors in concrete natural problems is significantly less than the number of errors in concrete unnatural problems. The authors claim that the former

> **Text box 1.4** Example of a concrete natural problem (from Donovan & Epstein, 1997)
>
> John goes to the auto races. He bets on two races. In one race he bets on a car driven by an experienced driver with a long history of winning races. In a different race, he bets on a car driven by an inexperienced driver who has won very few races.
>
> Check which of the following you believe is less likely.
>
> _____ The car driven by the inexperienced driver wins.
> _____ The car driven by the inexperienced driver and the car being driven by the experienced driver both win.

elicit the appropriate rational system while the latter elicit the inappropriate experiential system. While representativeness might be appropriate (natural) in judgements of similarity, it is not in judgements of likelihood. Thus Donovan and Epstein argue that the fallacy arises when problems may be categorized as concrete and unnatural. However, there are perhaps some problems with this interpretation. First, the probabilities of the component events in Donovan and Epstein's concrete natural problems are not available (indeed their design involves ranking statements rather than generating actual probability estimates). For example, in relation to the car-racing vignette in Text box 1.4 we generally know from experience that the favourite in a race usually does not win (otherwise bookmakers would go into liquidation). While it may be more likely that the experienced driver will win, nevertheless participants may view both component events as unlikely, and Yates and Carlson (1986) have demonstrated that conjunctions of two unlikely events seldom give rise to the conjunction fallacy. On the other hand the component events in the concrete unnatural Linda problem are viewed by most participants respectively as likely (Linda is a feminist) and unlikely (Linda is a bank teller) (Fisk & Pidgeon, 1997). Again, Yates and Carlson have demonstrated that the fallacy is most common in conjunctions of likely and unlikely events. Thus the difference in the incidence of the fallacy observed by Donovan and Epstein may not in reality be due to the concrete–unnatural, concrete–natural distinction, but may instead be due to the magnitudes of the component event probabilities.

Nonetheless, Epstein and co-workers' notion that there might be two (or more) distinct reasoning systems is an interesting one, and one that has been suggested previously in the literature. For example, Evans and Over (1996) propose that biases in deductive reasoning (see Chapter 7) may be accounted for by the operation of a two-stage heuristic/analytic system. Like Epstein's experiential system, Evans' heuristic mechanism is preconscious and operates in a different manner from the conscious analytical system. Agnoli and Krantz (1989) have also proposed that conjunction errors arise as a consequence of the primacy of representativeness within a competing heuristic framework. This is analogous to the intrinsically compelling nature of judgements generated by the experiential system in Epstein's CEST framework. More recently, the notion of dual reasoning processes has been discussed at length by Stanovich and West (2000) with their contrast between System 1 (heuristic) and System 2 (analytic) processes. The existence of separate reasoning systems might also explain how differently framed problems elicit different answers – for example, frequency-based judgements versus judgements involving single event probabilities.

Mental models

The mental models approach has been influential in accounts of deductive reasoning and more recently it has been applied to probabilistic reasoning and more specifically to conjunctive judgements. For example, Johnson-Laird, Legrenzi, Girotto, Legrenzi, and Caverni (1999) in their second experiment sought judgements of the magnitudes of both P(A&B) and P(A). Three kinds of information were provided in the premises:

1 A or B but not both: There is a box in which there is a yellow card, or a brown card, but not both.
2 A or B or both: There is a box in which there is a yellow card, or a brown card, or both.
3 If A then B   There is a box in which if there is a yellow card then there is a brown card.

For each of these premises, participants generated a range of judgements including the probability that in the box there is at least a yellow card, that is, P(A), and the probability that in the box there is a yellow card and a brown card, that is, P(A&B). The results revealed that the conjunction was assigned a probability of less than its component for the first two sets of premises. However the third premise, if A then B, produced an average percentage probability estimate for the conjunction equal to 68%, while the average for the component event A was 58%, consistent with a number of participants committing the conjunction fallacy. Interestingly, the percentages predicted through the generation of mental models were 50% both for P(A) and for P(A&B), and indeed 9 out of 22 participants did produce these values. In fact none of the predicted outcomes explicitly mentioned in Johnson-Laird et al.'s (1999) second experiment are consistent with the conjunction fallacy, and as such the mental models approach has yet to account for this type of outcome. It seems clear that no unitary theory will adequately account for the range of outcomes associated with conjunctive judgements. Outcomes are likely to be contingent on a range of factors including the way in which the problem is framed.

Fast and frugal heuristics

Hertwig and Chase (1998) have argued that the surface form of the problem will determine what sort of strategy is utilized by the participant. They note that problems requiring numerical probability estimates are generally associated with a lower incidence of the conjunction fallacy relative to problems in which simple rankings are required. Furthermore, this outcome is unrelated to the degree of statistical sophistication of participants. Hertwig and Chase maintain that problems requiring participants to provide numerical estimates are more likely to elicit rule-based strategies, while problems requiring participants to simply rank alternatives produce cue-based strategies. In particular, Hertwig and Chase refer to Gigerenzer's notion of "fast and frugal heuristics" and more specifically of "one-reason decision making", that is, judgements made on the basis of just a single cue.

Consistent with these propositions, in a series of studies Hertwig and Chase found that rule use was more prevalent among those individuals who were asked to provide numerical probability estimates. The particular rules used included the "ceiling rule" (setting the conjunctive probability equal to the smaller component event probability) and a quasi-normative multiplicative rule.[6] Among a group of statistically naïve participants, the majority of those avoiding the conjunction fallacy were found to apply the ceiling rule. On the other hand, among those with statistical training, rather more used the multiplicative rule than the ceiling rule.

Those participants asked to supply ranks appeared to rely on a cue-based strategy. For example, in the Linda scenario, each of the elements in Linda's description may potentially act as a cue. Thus, participating in anti-nuclear demonstrations provides more evidential support for the proposition "feminist bank teller" than it does for the proposition "bank teller", resulting in the former being ranked more highly in probabilistic terms than the latter.

However, it is worthy of note that Hertwig and Chase's proposed mechanism for estimating the cue value essentially corresponds to working out the reverse conditional probabilities. Using the above example, this means that cue values are determined by P(participating in anti-nuclear demonstrations | bank teller) versus P(participating in anti-nuclear demonstrations | feminist bank teller). In this sense Hertwig and Chase's account appears to echo Wolford et al.'s (1990) assertion that conjunction fallacies arise because individuals estimate the wrong probabilities. However, as noted above, my own findings are not wholly supportive of this proposition (Fisk, 1996). While some participants may follow this kind of strategy, my own results clearly demonstrate that it offers only a partial account of the processes underpinning the conjunction fallacy.

Averaging

Turning to the final account of conjunctive probability judgement addressed by the present chapter, this is based on the notion that individuals resort to some form of averaging process in order to derive conjunctive judgements. The idea that individuals utilize some sort of averaging strategy featured in the earliest research into conjunctive judgement, and remains topical today. For example, Wyer (1970) proposed that conjunctive judgements might be (erroneously) derived by simply taking the average of the two component probabilities. Wyer found that participants' conjunctive probability judgements were substantially higher than the normative multiplicative values, and in fact closer in absolute magnitude to the simple average of the component event probabilities. However, the estimates were actually more closely *correlated* with the product of the component event probabilities and with the normative values themselves [i.e., with $P(A) \times P(B)$ and $P(A) \times P(B|A)$]. Following on from Wyer, Goldsmith (1978) found evidence for a number of arithmetic combination rules underpinning conjunctive judgements. Some participants apparently based their judgement on the smaller component event probability (see surprise theory and Hertwig and Chase's "ceiling rule"), others used either the simple average, or the product of the component event probabilities. However, there was less evidence that the more probable event played a significant role (again consistent with surprise theory) and less evidence that the conditional probability was used in forming the conjunctive judgement.

More recently, Birnbaum, Anderson, and Hynan (1990) have proposed a geometric averaging model of conjunctive probability judgement. Birnbaum et al. maintain that in any given context actual probability judgements will be related to the real subjective probabilities plus some error component. Elicited conjunctive judgements will conform to the following equation:

$$q(A\&B) = s(A)^\beta s(B|A)^\alpha + e_{A\&B} \qquad (7)$$

where $s(A)$ and $s(B|A)$ are the subjective component event and conditional probabilities and $e_{A\&B}$ is the random error component. The parameters α and β are estimated, and when they are both equal to one, the above equation is equivalent to the normative model. In an experimental study, Birbaum et al. found that the above equation achieved the best fit to the data when values of the two parameters α and β were substantially less than one. The conjunction fallacy in turn was most likely to occur in situations where participants produced high values for the conditional probability and low values for the component event probability or vice versa. Using regression analysis Fisk (2002) has also applied a logarithmic version of Equation 7 to model conjunctive probability judgements with conditionally independent events. The conjunctions analyzed consisted of a likely and an unlikely event. Perhaps not surprisingly, the values of the two parameters α and β differed between those participants committing the fallacy and those who did not. For the former group, consistent with Birnbaum et al.'s results, values of α and β were substantially less than one, while for the latter group both parameters were close to unity. However, as in my earlier studies, the value of the parameter corresponding to the likely component did not differ significantly from zero. While these functional forms may be successful in modelling some aspects of conjunctive judgements, they do not explain in a systematic manner the psychological processes giving rise to the parameter values evident in the equations. For example, they do not account for why some individuals set the value of the conjunction *exactly equal* to that of the lower component event probability. Equally, they do not explain why some participants apparently produce reverse probability estimates, that is, P(Linda | bank teller & feminist) rather than P(bank teller & feminist | Linda).

CONCLUSIONS

Over the last 40 years or more, many researchers have tried to come up with a parsimonious account of conjunction rule violations and the conjunction fallacy. While we know much about the phenomenon, we are perhaps as far from a complete account of it as we were back in the 1950s. Accounts of the conjunction fallacy in terms of representativeness appear *not* to work (Fisk & Pidgeon, 1997). Furthermore, while some individuals may mistake the single event "B" to mean "B and not A", for example, inferring that "bank teller" means "bank teller and not feminist", such individuals are probably relatively few in number (Morrier & Borgida, 1986). Equally, no doubt some persons when asked to produce probabilities such as P(bank teller and feminist | Linda) may instead produce the reverse probability P(Linda | bank teller and feminist). Again, while this might explain why some individuals appear to commit the conjunction fallacy, it does not offer a complete account (Fisk, 1996). What has become apparent is that conjunction rule violations constitute a highly contingent phenomenon in which the surface form of the problem can affect both the magnitude of the bias and the psychological processes underpinning the judgement.

The two-process theory of reasoning goes some way in providing a conceptual framework that allows for individuals to behave both normatively and non-normatively (Epstein, Lipson, Holstein, & Huh, 1992; Evans & Over, 1996; Stanovich & West, 2000). However, in some respects the distinction between heuristic and analytic processes may not be an entirely useful one. It seems clear that some arithmetic and logical operations are immediate and preconscious in the same way as heuristic processes. For most of us, arithmetic facts and procedures are instantly available. Knowing that $7 \times 6 = 42$ does not require conscious analytical effort for most of us. Equally, if I am buying 3 kg of potatoes at 40 pence per kg, I do not need to consciously retrieve the multiplicative rule, it is available instantly. (Although from an analytical perspective I might plug in the wrong numbers!) It is well known that experts approach problems within their domain in a manner distinct from novices, utilizing well-learned theoretical concepts. Problems are perceived and categorized according to the theoretical rule or construct that must be applied to derive their solution (Larkin, McDermott, Simon, & Simon, 1980). These are *instantly* seen as being appropriate, although again their application may require use of analytic resources. In this sense both logical/mathematical operations and heuristics may be viewed from the perspective of Fodor's (1983) notion of modularity.

The properties of modular functioning according to Fodor may be summarized as perceptual (as opposed to conceptual), domain-specific, mandatory, fast-operating, and localized in neurological terms. They exhibit informational encapsulation and cognitive impenetrability. If we seek to account for probabilistic reasoning in terms of modularity or quasi-modularity (Karmiloff-Smith, 1992), how might the analytical system function? Fodor (1983) has proposed that modules feed a central and non-modular system responsible for rational thought, as well as heuristic processes and the representation of beliefs. This central system is said to be responsible for inferential processes. The central system is fed by different knowledge sources and thus, unlike true modules in Fodor's sense, is not characterized by information encapsulation. The central system also contains a store of lexical information (a mental lexicon) and thus in part supports language-based inferential processes. In addition to the mental lexicon, the central system contains an encyclopaedic knowledge base consisting of factual information, common beliefs, and explicit propositional knowledge. There is assumed to be a free flow of information between these "quasi modules" in the central system including the mental lexicon, and the database of conceptual information (Van der Lely, 1997).

This then might provide an effective model for the analytical system. The challenge posed by this new conceptualization is to account for how the participant's intellectual competence and existing knowledge base interact with particular features of the surface form of the problem to instantly elicit heuristic and/or logical-mathematical operations and, if conflicts between these different representations should emerge, how they are resolved within the analytical system. Thus there remain many questions all in search of adequate answers, both in the context of conjunctive judgement and probabilistic reasoning, and perhaps these will fuel another 40 years research into conjunction errors!

SUMMARY

- The conjunction fallacy arises when individuals assign probabilities to conjunctive events that exceed the probabilities assigned to the component events making up the conjunction.
- In social type judgements where the conjunction combines a likely event with an unlikely event, the proportion of individuals committing the fallacy can be very high, often exceeding 90%.

- Where individuals are asked to provide frequencies instead of probabilities, the incidence of the fallacy is greatly reduced, even in social type judgements.
- Tversky and Kahneman (1983) attempted to account for the occurrence of the fallacy in terms of the representativeness heuristic.
- Other explanations of the fallacy have been offered including linguistic misunderstanding, "signed summation", applying the wrong probabilistic rule, surprise theory, averaging, and the "one-reason" algorithm.
- Subsequent research has cast doubt not only on Tversky and Kahneman's account of the fallacy, but also on alternative explanations of the phenomenon.
- The search for an adequate account of the fallacy remains elusive.

FURTHER READING

Tversky and Kahneman's (1983) classic exposition of the conjunction fallacy is essential reading for anyone interested in the phenomenon. Yates and Carlson's (1986) influential paper served to demonstrate the highly contingent nature of the fallacy, and Wolford, Taylor, and Beck's (1990) critique is relevant not only in terms of its relevance to the present chapter but also to the broader debate on human rationality. In this regard, Stanovich and West's (2000) account of the debate both in terms of the conjunction fallacy and more generally makes fascinating reading.

NOTES

1 The conjunction of two events is defined as: $P(A\&B) = P(A) \times P(B|A)$. Since probabilities cannot exceed 1 then $P(B|A) \leq 1$; therefore $P(A) \times P(B|A) \leq P(A)$ and so $P(A\&B) \leq P(A)$. The same reasoning holds for $P(B)$.
2 Hertwig and Chase describe this outcome in terms of the application of a "ceiling rule" and we shall return to their conceptualization later in the chapter.
3 Until my recent paper (Fisk, 2002), Shackle's theory had not been subjected to direct empirical investigation.
4 Given a positive conditional relationship and given that event A is more surprising than event B, such that $y_0^A < y^B < y^A$, then the conjunctive surprise value will be based on y^B (the larger of y_0^A and y^B). With no conditional relationship then $y^B < y^A = y_0^A$ and the surprise value of the conjunction will be based on y^A (the larger of y^A and y^B). Thus the positive conditional relationship shifts the focus for the conjunctive judgement from the more surprising to the less surprising event, but under most circumstances the actual magnitude of the positive conditional relationship has no direct impact on the conjunctive value.
5 Given the multiplicative nature of the normative relationship, a 0.1 change in the smaller component event probability will produce a larger change in the conjunctive probability than a 0.1 change in the larger component event.
6 In fact, multiplying the component probabilities together to obtain the conjunctive probability is only normative for independent events. Tversky and Kahneman note

that many participants perceive a negative conditional relationship between the two component events in the Linda scenario.

REFERENCES

Agnoli, F., & Krantz, D. H. (1989). Suppressing natural heuristics by formal instruction. The case of the conjunction fallacy. *Cognitive Psychology, 21,* 515–550.

Birnbaum, M. H., Anderson, C., & Hynan, L. G. (1990). Theories of bias in probability judgment. In J.-P. Caverni, J. M. Fabre, & M. Gonzalez (Eds.), *Cognitive biases* (pp. 477–498). Amsterdam: North-Holland.

Christensen, I. P. (1979). Distributional and non-distributional uncertainty. In C. R. Bell (Ed.), *Uncertain outcomes* (pp. 49–59). Lancaster, UK: NTP Press.

Cohen, J., Dearnaley, E. J., & Hansel, C. E. M. (1958). Skill and chance: Variations in estimates of skill with an increasing element of chance. *British Journal of Psychology, 49,* 319–323.

Donovan, S., & Epstein, S. (1997). The difficulty in the Linda conjunction problem can be attributed to its simultaneous concrete and unnatural representation, and not to conversational implicature. *Journal of Experimental Social Psychology, 33,* 1–20.

Epstein, S., Lipson, A., Holstein, C., & Huh, E. (1992). Irrational reactions to negative outcomes: Evidence for two conceptual systems. *Journal of Personality and Social Psychology, 62,* 328–339.

Evans, J. St. B. T., Handley, S. J., Perham, N., Over, D. E., & Thompson, V. A. (2000). Frequency versus probability formats in statistical word problems. *Cognition, 77,* 197–213.

Evans, J. St. B. T., & Over, D. (1996). *Rationality and reasoning.* Hove, UK: Lawrence Erlbaum Associates Ltd.

Fabre, J., Caverni, J. P., & Jungermann, H. (1995). Causality does influence conjunctive probability judgements if context and design allow for it. *Organizational Behaviour and Human Decision Processes, 63,* 1–5.

Fiedler, K. (1988). The dependence of the conjunction fallacy on subtle linguistic factors. *Psychological Research, 50,* 123–129.

Fisk, J. E. (1996). The conjunction effect: Fallacy or Bayesian inference? *Organizational Behaviour and Human Decision Processes, 67,* 76–90.

Fisk, J. E. (2002). Judgements under uncertainty: Representativeness or potential surprise? *British Journal of Psychology, 93,* 431–449.

Fisk, J. E. (2003). *The relationship between surprise and subjective probability: Towards an evaluation of Shackle's theory of potential surprise.* Manuscript submitted for publication.

Fisk, J. E., & Pidgeon, N. (1996). Component probabilities and the conjunction fallacy: Resolving signed summation and the low component model in a contingent approach. *Acta Psychologica, 94,* 1–20.

Fisk, J. E., & Pidgeon, N. (1997). The conjunction fallacy: The case for the existence of competing heuristic strategies. *British Journal of Psychology, 88,* 1–27.

Fisk, J. E., & Pidgeon, N. (1998). Conditional probabilities, potential surprise, and the conjunction fallacy. *Quarterly Journal of Experimental Psychology, 51A,* 655–681.

Fodor, J. (1983). *The modularity of the mind.* Cambridge, MA: MIT Press.

Gavanski, I., & Roskos-Ewoldsen, D. R. (1991). Representativeness and conjoint probability. *Journal of Personality and Social Psychology, 61*, 181–194.

Gigerenzer, G., & Goldstein, D. G. (1996). Reasoning the fast and frugal way: Models of bounded rationality. *Psychological Review, 103*, 650–669.

Goldsmith, R. W. (1978). Assessing probabilities of compound events in a judicial context. *Scandinavian Journal of Psychology, 19*, 103–110.

Hertwig, R., & Chase, V. M. (1998). Many reasons or just one: How response mode affects reasoning in the conjunction problem. *Thinking and Reasoning, 4*, 319–352.

Johnson-Laird, P. N., Legrenzi, P., Girotto, V., Legrenzi, M. S., & Caverni, J. (1999). Naïve probability: A mental model theory of extensional reasoning. *Psychological Review, 106*, 62–88.

Kariyazono, A. (1991). The study of conjunction fallacy in the probability judgment task of compound event. *Japanese Journal of Psychonomic Science, 10*, 57–64. [English abstract.]

Karmiloff-Smith, A. (1992). *Beyond modularity: A developmental perspective on cognitive science*. Cambridge, MA: MIT Press.

Larkin, J. H., McDermott, J., Simon, D. P., & Simon H. A. (1980). Models of competence in solving physics problems. *Cognitive Science, 4*, 317–345.

Morier, D. M., & Borgida, E. (1984). The conjunction fallacy: A task specific phenomenon? *Personality and Social Psychology Bulletin, 10*, 243–252.

Shackle, G. L. S. (1969). *Decision, order and time in human affairs*. Cambridge: Cambridge University Press.

Stanovich, K. E., & West, R. F. (2000). Individual differences in reasoning: Implications for the rationality debate? *Behavioral and Brain Sciences, 23*, 645–726.

Teigen, K. H., Brun, W., & Frydenlund, R. (1999). Judgements of risk and probability: The role of frequentistic information. *Journal of Behavioral Decision Making, 12*, 123–139.

Thüring, M., & Jungermann, H. (1990). The conjunction fallacy: Causality versus event probability. *Journal of Behavioral Decision Making, 3*, 61–74.

Tversky, A., & Kahneman, D. (1983). Extensional versus intuitive reasoning: The conjunction fallacy in probability judgment. *Psychological Review, 90*, 293–315.

Van der Lely, H. K. J. (1997). Language and cognitive development in a grammatical SLI boy: Modularity and innateness. *Journal of Neurolinguistics, 10*, 75–107.

Wells, G. L. (1985). The conjunction error and the representativeness heuristic. *Social Cognition, 3*, 266–279.

Wolford, G., Taylor, H. A., & Beck, J. R. (1990). The conjunction fallacy? *Memory & Cognition, 18*, 47–53.

Wyer, R. S. (1970). Quantitative prediction of belief and opinion change: A further test of a subjective probability model. *Journal of Personality and Social Psychology, 16*, 559–570.

Yates, J. F., & Carlson, B. W. (1986). Conjunction errors: Evidence for multiple judgement procedures including "Signed Summation". *Organizational Behaviour and Human Decision Processes, 37*, 230–253.

2 Base rates in Bayesian inference

Michael H. Birnbaum

What is the probability that a randomly drawn card from a well-shuffled standard deck would be a heart? What is the probability that the German soccer team will win the next world championships?

These two questions are quite different. In the first, we can develop a mathematical theory from the assumption that each card is equally likely. If there are 13 cards each of hearts, diamonds, spades, and clubs, we calculate that the probability of drawing a heart is 13/52, or 1/4. We test this theory by repeating the experiment again and again. After a great deal of evidence (that 25% of the draws are hearts), we have confidence in using this model of past data to predict the future.

The second case (soccer) refers to a unique event that either will or will not occur, and there is no way to calculate a proportion from the past that is clearly relevant. One might examine records of the German team and those of rivals, and ask if the Germans seem healthy – nevertheless players change, conditions change, and it is never really the same experiment. This situation is sometimes referred to as one of *uncertainty*, and the term *subjective probability* is used to refer to psychological strengths of belief.

However, people are willing to use the same term, probability, to express both types of ideas. People gamble on both types of predictions – on repeatable, mechanical games of chance (like dice, cards, and roulette) with known risks, and on unique and uncertain events (like sports, races, and stock markets). In fact, people even use the term "probability" *after* something has happened (a murder, for example), to describe belief that an event occurred (e.g., that this defendant committed the crime). To some philosophers, such usage seemed meaningless. Nevertheless, Reverend Thomas Bayes (1702–1761) derived a theorem for inference from the mathematics of probability. Some philosophers conceeded that this theorem could be interpreted as a calculus for rational formation and revision of beliefs in such cases (see also Chapter 3 in this volume).

BAYES' THEOREM

The following example illustrates Bayes' theorem. Suppose there is a disease that infects one person in 1000, completely at random. Suppose there is a blood test for this disease that yields a "positive" test result in 99.5% of cases of the disease and gives a false "positive" in only 0.5% of those without the disease. If a person tests "positive", what is the probability that he or she has the disease? The solution, according to Bayes' theorem, may seem surprising.

Consider two hypotheses, H and not-H (denoted H'). In this example, they are the hypothesis that the person is sick with the disease (H) and the complementary hypothesis (H') that the person does not have the disease. Let D refer to the datum that is relevant to the hypotheses. In this example, D is a "positive" result and D' is a "negative" result from the blood test.

The problem stated that 1 in 1000 have the disease, so $P(H) = 0.001$; that is, the prior probability (before we test the blood) that a person has the disease is 0.001, so $P(H') = 1 - P(H) = 0.999$.

The conditional probability that a person will test "positive" given that the person has the disease is written as $P(\text{"positive"}|H) = 0.995$, and the conditional probability that a person will test "positive" given he or she is not sick is $P(\text{"positive"}|H') = 0.005$. These conditional probabilities are called the *hit rate* and the *false alarm rate* in signal detection, also known as *power* and *significance* (α). We need to calculate $P(H|D)$, the probability that a person is sick, given the test was "positive". This calculation is known as an *inference*.

The situation in the disease example above is as follows: we know $P(H)$, $P(D|H)$ and $P(D|H')$, and we want to calculate $P(H|D)$. The definition of conditional probability:

$$P(H|D) = \frac{P(H \cap D)}{P(D)} \tag{1}$$

we can also write, $P(H \cap D) = P(D|H) P(H)$. In addition, D can happen in two mutually exclusive ways, either with H or without it, so $P(D) = P(D \cap H) + P(D \cap H')$. Each of these conjunctions can be written in terms of conditionals, therefore:

$$P(H|D) = \frac{P(D|H)P(H)}{P(D|H) P(H) + P(D|H') P(H')} \tag{2}$$

Equation 2 is Bayes' theorem. Substituting the values for the blood test problem yields the following result:

$$P(sick|\text{"positive"}) = \frac{(0.995)(0.001)}{(0.995)(0.001) + (0.005)(0.999)} = 0.166.$$

Does this result seem surprising? Think of it this way: Among 1000 people, only 1 is sick. If all 1000 were tested, the test will likely give a "positive" test to the sick person, but it would also give a "positive" to about 5 others (0.5% of 999 healthy people, about 5, should test positive). Thus, of the six who test "positive," only one is actually sick, so the probability of being sick, given a "positive" test, is only about one in six. Another way to look at the answer is that it is 166 times greater than the probability of being sick given no information (0.001), so there has indeed been considerable revision of opinion given the positive test.

An on-line calculator is available at the following URL:

http://psych.fullerton.edu/mbirnbaum/bayes/bayescalc.htm

The calculator allows one to calculate Bayesian inference in either probability or *odds*, which are a transformation of probability, $\Omega = p/(1 - p)$. For example, if probability = 1/4 (drawing a heart from a deck of cards), then the odds are 1/3 of drawing a heart. Expressed another way, the odds are 3 to 1 against drawing a heart.

In odds form, Bayes' theorem can be written:

$$\Omega_1 = \Omega_0 \left(\frac{P(D|H)}{P(D|H')} \right) \qquad (3)$$

where Ω_1 and Ω_0 are the revised and prior odds, and the ratio of hit rate to false alarm rate, $\frac{P(D|H)}{P(D|H')}$ is also known as the likelihood ratio of the evidence. For example, in the disease problem, the odds of being sick are 999:1 against, or approximately 0.001. The ratio of hit rate to false alarm rate is 0.995/.005 = 199. Multiplying prior odds by this ratio gives revised odds of 0.199, about 5 to 1 against. Converting odds back to probability, $p = \Omega/(1 + \Omega) = 0.166$.

With a logarithmic transformation, Equation 3 becomes additive – prior probabilities and evidence should combine independently; that is, the effect of prior probabilities and evidence should contribute in the same way, at any level of the other factor.

Are humans Bayesian?

Psychologists have wondered if Bayes' theorem describes how people revise their beliefs (Birnbaum, 1983; Birnbaum & Mellers, 1983; Edwards, 1968; Fischhoff, Slovic, & Lichtenstein, 1979; Kahneman & Tversky, 1973; Koehler, 1996; Lyon & Slovic, 1976; Pitz, 1975; Shanteau, 1975; Slovic & Lichtenstein, 1971; Tversky & Kahneman, 1982; Wallsten, 1972). The psychological literature can be divided into three periods. Early work supported Bayes' theorem as a rough descriptive model of how humans combine and update evidence, with the exception that people were described as *conservative*, or less influenced by either base rate or evidence than Bayesian analysis of the objective evidence would warrant (Edwards, 1968; Wallsten, 1972).

The second period was dominated by Kahneman and Tversky's (1973) assertions that people do not use base rates or respond to differences in validity of sources of evidence. It emerged that their conclusions were viable only with certain types of experiments (e.g., Hammerton, 1973), but those experiments were easy to do, so many were done. Perhaps because Kahneman and Tversky (1973) did not cite the body of previous work that contradicted their conclusions, it took some time for those who followed in their footsteps to become aware of the contrary evidence and to rediscover how to replicate it (Novemsky & Kronzon, 1999).

More recent literature supports the early research showing that people do indeed utilize base rates and source credibility (Birnbaum, 2001; Birnbaum & Mellers, 1983; Novemsky & Kronzon, 1999). However, people appear to combine this information by an averaging model (Birnbaum, 1976, 2001; Birnbaum & Mellers, 1983; Birnbaum & Stegner, 1979; Birnbaum, Wong, & Wong, 1976; Troutman & Shanteau, 1977). The Scale-Adjustment Averaging Model of source credibility (Birnbaum & Mellers, 1983; Birnbaum & Stegner, 1979), is not consistent with Bayes' theorem and it also explains "conservatism".

Averaging model of source credibility

The averaging model of source credibility can be written as follows:

$$R = \frac{\sum_{i=0}^{n} w_i s_i}{\sum_{i=0}^{n} w_i} \tag{4}$$

where R is the predicted response, w_i the weights of the sources (which depend on the source's perceived credibility), and s_i is the scale value of the source's testimony (which depends on what the source testified). The initial impression reflects prior opinion (w_0 and s_0). For more on averaging models see Anderson (1981).

In problems such as the disease problem quoted earlier, there are three or more sources of information; first, there is the prior belief, represented by s_0; second, base rate is a source of information; third, the test result is another source of information. For example, suppose that weights of the initial impression and of the base rate are both 1, and the weight of the diagnostic test is 2. Suppose the prior belief is 0.50 (no opinion), scale value of the base rate is 0.001, and the scale value of the "positive" test is 1. This model predicts that the response in the disease problem is as follows:

$$\frac{1 \times 0.5 + 1 \times 0.001 + 2 \times 1}{1 + 1 + 2} = 0.63$$

Thus, this model can predict neglect of the base rate, if people put more weight on witnesses than on base rates.

Birnbaum and Stegner (1979) extended this model to describe how people combine information from sources varying in both validity and bias. Their model also involves configural weighting, in which the weight of a piece of information depends on its relation to other information. For example, when the judge is asked to identify with the buyer of a car, the judge appears to place more weight on lower estimates of the value of a car, whereas people asked to identify with the seller put more weight on higher estimates.

The most important distinction between Bayesian and averaging models is that in the Bayesian model, each piece of independent information has the same effect no matter what the current state of evidence. In the averaging models, however, the effect of any piece of information is inversely related to the number and total weight of other sources of information. In the averaging model, unlike the Bayesian model, the directional impact of information depends on the relation between the new evidence and the current opinion.

Although the full story is beyond the scope of this chapter, three aspects of the literature can be illustrated by data from a single experiment, which can be done two ways – as a within-subjects or a between-subjects study. The next section describes a between-subjects experiment, like the one in Kahneman and Tversky (1973); the section following it will describe how to conduct and analyze a within-subjects design, like that of Birnbaum and Mellers (1983).

EXPERIMENTS: THE CAB PROBLEM

Consider the following question, known as the *cab problem* (Tversky & Kahneman, 1982, pp. 156–157):

> A cab was involved in a hit and run accident at night. There are two cab companies in the city, with 85% of cabs being Green and the other 15% Blue cabs. A witness testified that the cab in the accident was "Blue." The witness was tested for ability to discriminate Green from Blue cabs and was found to be correct 80% of the time. What is the probability that the cab in the accident was Blue as the witness testified?

Between-subjects vs within-subjects designs

If we present a single problem like this to a group of students, the results show a strange distribution of responses. The majority of students (about three out of five) say that the answer is "80%", apparently because the witness was correct 80% of the time. However, there are two other modes: about one in five responds "15%", the base rate; a small group of students give the answer of 12%, apparently the result of multiplying the base rate by the witness's accuracy, and a few people give a scattering of other answers. Supposedly, the "right" answer is 41%, and few people give this answer.

Kahneman and Tversky (1973) argued that people ignore base rate, based on finding that the effect of base rate in such inference problems was not significant. They asked participants to infer whether a person was a lawyer or engineer, based on a description of personality given by a witness. The supposed neglect of base rate found in this *lawyer–engineer* problem and others came to be called the "base-rate fallacy" (see also Hammerton, 1973). However, evidence of a fallacy evaporates when one does the experiment in a slightly different way using a within-subjects design, as we see below (Birnbaum, 2001; Birnbaum & Mellers, 1983; Novemsky & Kronzon, 1999).

There is also another issue with the cab problem and the lawyer–engineer problem as they were formulated. Those problems were not stated clearly enough that one can apply Bayes' theorem without making extra assumptions (Birnbaum, 1983; Schum, 1981). One has to make arbitrary, unrealistic assumptions in order to calculate the supposedly "correct" solution.

Tversky and Kahneman (1982) gave the "correct" answer to this cab problem as 41% and argued that participants who responded "80%" were mistaken. They assumed that the percentage correct of a witness divided by percentage wrong equals the ratio of the hit rate to the false alarm rate. They then took the percentage of cabs in the city as the prior probability for cabs of each colour being in cab accidents at night. It is not clear, however, that both cab companies even operate at night, so it is not clear that percentage of cabs in a city is really an appropriate prior for being in an accident.

Furthermore, we know from signal-detection theory that the percentage correct is not usually equal to hit rate, nor is the ratio of hit rate to false alarm rate for human witnesses invariant when base rate varies. Birnbaum (1983) showed that if one makes reasonable assumptions about the witness in these problems, then the supposedly "wrong" answer of 80% is actually a better solution than the one called "correct" by Tversky and Kahneman.

The problem is to infer how the ratio of hit rate to false alarm rate (in Eq. 3) from the values given for the witness is affected by the base rate. Tversky and Kahneman (1982) implicitly assumed that this ratio is unaffected by base rate. However, experiments in signal detection show that this ratio changes in response to changing base rates. Therefore this complication must be taken into account when computing the solution (Birnbaum, 1983).

Birnbaum's (1983) solution treats the process of signal detection with reference to normal distributions on a subjective continuum, one for the signal and another for the noise. If the observer changes his or her "Green/

Blue" response criterion to maximize percent correct, then the solution of 0.80 is not far from what one would expect if the witness was an ideal observer (for details, see Birnbaum, 1983).

Fragile results in between-subjects research

But perhaps even more troubling to behavioural scientists was the fact that the null results deemed evidence of a "base-rate fallacy" proved very fragile to replication with different procedures (see Gigerenzer & Hoffrage, 1995, and Chapter 3). In a within-subjects design, it is easy to show that people attend to both base rates and source credibility.

Birnbaum and Mellers (1983) reported that within-subjects and between-subjects studies give very different results (see also Fischhoff et al., 1979). Whereas the observed effect of base rate may not be significant in a between-subjects design, the effect is substantial in a within-subjects design. Whereas the distribution of responses in the between-subjects design has three modes (e.g., 80%, 15%, and 12% in the above cab problem), the distribution of responses in within-subjects designs is closer to a bell shape. When the same problem is embedded among others with varied base rates and witness characteristics, Birnbaum and Mellers (1983, Fig. 2) found few responses at the former peaks; the distributions instead appeared bell-shaped.

Birnbaum (1999a) showed that in a between-subjects design, the number 9 is judged to be significantly "bigger" than the number 221. Should we infer from this that there is a "cognitive illusion" a "number fallacy", a "number heuristic", or a "number bias" that makes 9 seem bigger than 221?

Birnbaum (1982, 1999a) argued that many confusing results will be obtained by scientists who try to compare judgements between groups who experience different contexts. When they are asked to judge both numbers, people say 221 is greater than 9. It is only in the between-subjects study that significant and opposite results are obtained. One should not compare judgements between groups without taking the context into account (Birnbaum, 1982).

In the complete between-subjects design, context is completely confounded with the stimulus. Presumably, people asked to judge (only) the number 9 think of a context of small numbers, among which 9 seems "medium", and people judging (only) the number 221 think of a context of larger numbers, among which 221 seems "small".

DEMONSTRATION EXPERIMENT

To illustrate findings within-subjects, a factorial experiment on the cab problem will be presented. This study is similar to one by Birnbaum (2001). It varies the base rate of accidents in which Blue cabs were involved (15%, 30%, 70%, or 85%) and the credibility of a witness (medium or high). The participants' task is to estimate the probability that the car in the accident was a Blue cab. All methodological details are given in Text box 2.1.

Text box 2.1 Method of demonstration experiment

Instructions make base rate relevant and give more precise information on the witnesses. Instructions for this version are as follows:

> A cab was involved in a hit-and-run accident at night. There are two cab companies in the city, the Blue and Green. Your task is to judge (or estimate) the probability that the cab in the accident was a Blue cab.
>
> You will be given information about the percentage of accidents at night that were caused by Blue cabs, and the testimony of a witness who saw the accident. The percentage of night-time cab accidents involving Blue cabs is based on the previous 2 years in the city. In different cities, this percentage was either 15%, 30%, 70%, or 85%. The rest of night-time accidents involved Green cabs. Witnesses were tested for their ability to identify colours at night. They were tested in each city at night, with different numbers of colours matching their proportions in the cities.
>
> The MEDIUM witness correctly identified 60% of the cabs of each colour, calling Green cabs "Blue" 40% of the time and calling Blue cabs "Green" 40% of the time.
>
> The HIGH witness correctly identified 80% of each colour, calling Blue cabs "Green" or Green cabs "Blue" on 20% of the tests.
>
> Both witnesses were found to give the same ratio of correct to false identifications on each colour when tested in each of the cities.

Each participant received 20 situations, in random order, after a warmup of 7 trials. Each situation was composed of a base rate, plus testimony of a high-credibility witness who said the cab was either "Blue" or "Green", testimony of a medium-credibility witness (either "Blue" or "Green"), or there was no witness. A typical trial appeared as follows:

85% of accidents are Blue cabs & medium witness says "Green".

The dependent variable was the judged probability that the cab in the accident was Blue, expressed as a percentage. The 20 experimental trials were composed of the union of a 2 × 2 × 4, Source Credibility (Medium, High) by Source Message ("Green", "Blue") by Base Rate (15%, 30%, 70%, 85%) design, plus a one-way design with four levels of Base Rate and no witness.

Complete materials can be viewed at the following URL:

http://psych.fullerton.edu/mbirnbaum/bayes/CabProblem.htm

The following results are based on data from 103 undergraduates who were recruited from the university "subject pool" and who participated via the worldwide web.

Results and discussion

Mean judgements of probability that the cab in the accident was Blue are presented in Table 2.1. Rows show effects of Base Rate, and columns show combinations of witnesses and their testimony. The first column shows that if Blue cabs were involved in only 15% of cab accidents at night and the high-credibility witness said the cab was "Green", the average response was only 29.1%. When Blue cabs were involved in 85% of accidents, however, the mean judgement was 49.9%. The last column of Table 2.1 shows that when the high-credibility witness said that the cab was "Blue", mean judgements were 55.3% and 80.2% when base rates were 15% and 85%, respectively.

Analysis of variance tests the null hypotheses that people ignored base rate or witness credibility. The ANOVA showed that the main effect of Base Rate was significant, $F(3, 306) = 106.2$, as was Testimony, $F(1, 102) = 158.9$. Credibility of the witness has both significant main effects and interactions with Testimony, $F(1, 102) = 25.5$, and $F(1, 102) = 58.6$, respectively. As shown in Table 2.1, the more diagnostic the witness, the greater the effect of that witness's testimony. These results show that we can reject the hypotheses that people ignored base rates and validity of evidence.

The critical value of $F(1, 60)$ is 4.0, with $a = 0.05$, and the critical value of $F(1, 14)$ is 4.6. Therefore, the observed F-values are more than 10 times their critical values. Because F values are approximately proportional to n for true effects, one should be able to reject the null hypotheses of Kahneman and Tversky (1973) with only 15 participants. However, the purpose of this research is to evaluate models of how people combine evidence, which requires larger samples in order to provide clean results. Experiments conducted via the worldwide web allow one to test large numbers of participants quickly at relatively low cost in time and effort (see Birnbaum, 2001). Therefore, it is best to collect more data than are necessary just to show statistical significance.

Table 2.2 shows Bayesian calculations, simply using Bayes' theorem to calculate with the numbers given. (Probabilities are converted to

Table 2.1 Mean judgements of probability that the cab was Blue (%)

Base rate	Witness credibility and witness testimony				
	High credibility "Green"	Medium credibility "Green"	No witness	Medium credibility "Blue"	High credibility "Blue"
15	29.1	31.3	25.1	41.1	55.3
30	34.1	37.1	36.3	47.4	56.3
70	46.0	50.3	58.5	60.9	73.2
85	49.9	53.8	67.0	71.0	80.2

Each entry is the mean inference judgement, expressed as a percentage.

Table 2.2 Bayesian predictions (converted to percentages)

Base rate	Witness credibility and witness testimony				
	High credibility "Green"	Medium credibility "Green"	No witness	Medium credibility "Blue"	High credibility "Blue"
15	4.2	10.5	15.0	20.9	41.4
30	9.7	22.2	30.0	39.1	63.2
70	36.8	60.9	70.0	77.8	90.3
85	58.6	79.1	85.0	89.5	95.8

percentages.) Figure 2.1 shows a scatterplot of mean judgements against Bayesian calculations. The correlation between Bayes' theorem and the data is 0.948, which might seem "high". It is this way of graphing the data that led to the conclusion of "conservatism", as described in Edwards' (1968) review.

Conservatism described the fact that human judgements are less extreme than Bayes' theorem dictates. For example, when 85% of accidents at night involved Blue cabs and the high-credibility witness said the cab was "Blue", Bayes' theorem gives a probability of 95.8% that the cab was Blue; in contrast, the mean judgement was only 80.2%. Similarly, when base rate was

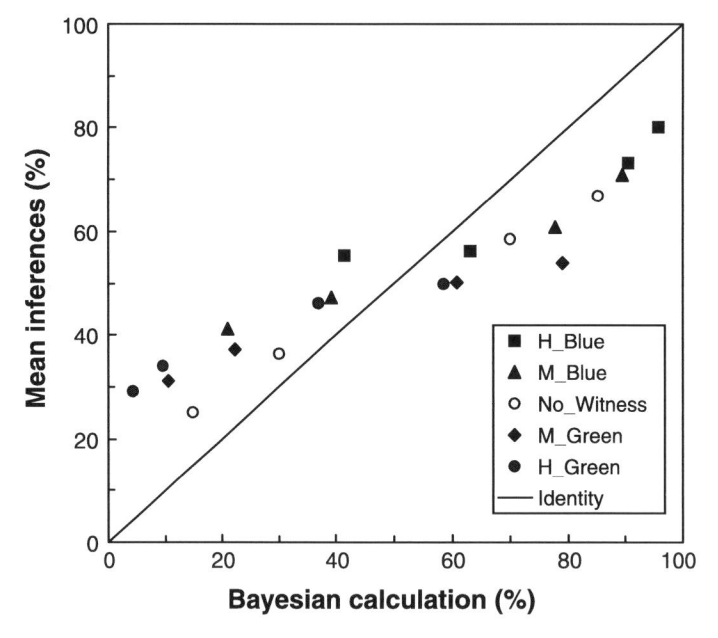

Figure 2.1 Mean inference that the cab was Blue, expressed as a percentage, plotted against the Bayesian solutions, also expressed as percentages (H = high-, M = medium-credibility witness).

15% and the high-credibility witness said the cab was "Green", Bayes' theorem calculates 4.2% and the mean judgement was 29.1%.

A problem with this way of graphing the data is that it does not reveal patterns of systematic deviation, apart from regression. People looking at such scatterplots are often impressed by "high" correlations. Such correlations of fit with such graphs easily lead researchers to wrong conclusions (Birnbaum, 1973). The problem is that "high" correlations can coexist with systematic violations of a theory. Correlations can even be higher for worse models! See Birnbaum (1973) for examples showing how misleading correlations of fit can be.

In order to see the data better, they should graphed as in Figure 2.2, where they are drawn as a function of base rate, with a separate curve for each type of witness and testimony. Notice the unfilled circles, which show judgements for cases with no witness. The cross-over between this curve and others contradicts the additive model, including Wallsten's (1972) subjective Bayesian (additive) model and the additive model rediscovered by Novemsky and Kronzon (1999). The subjective Bayesian model utilizes Bayesian formulas but allows the subjective values of probabilities to differ

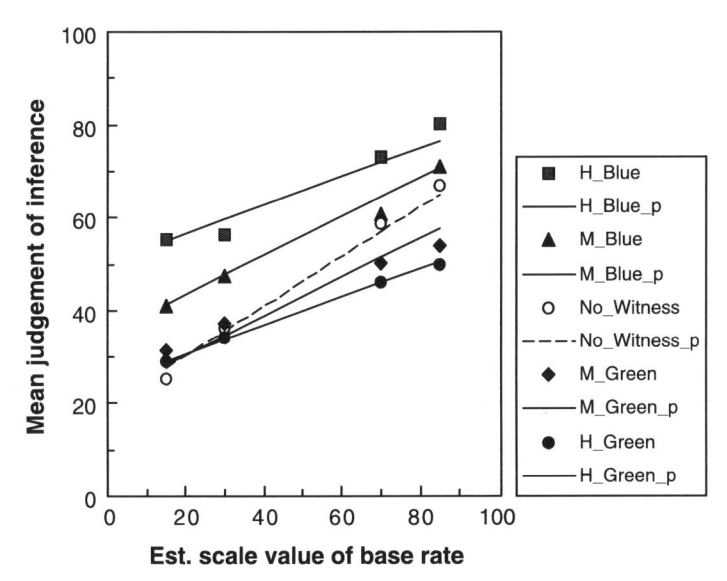

Figure 2.2 Fit of averaging model: Mean judgements of probability that the cab was Blue, plotted as a function of the estimated scale value of the base rate. Filled squares, triangles, diamonds, and circles show results when a high-credibility witness said the cab was "Green", a medium-credibility witness said "Green", a medium-credibility witness said "Blue", or a high-credibility witness said "Blue", respectively. Solid lines show corresponding predictions of the averaging model. Open circles show mean judgements when there was no witness, and the dashed line shows corresponding predictions (H = high-, M = Medium-credibility witness, p = predicted).

from objective values stated in the problem. Instead, the crossover interaction indicates that people are averaging information from base rate with the witness's testimony. When subjects judge the probability that the car was Blue given only a base rate of 15%, the mean judgement was 25.2%. However, when a medium-credibility witness also said that the cab was "Green", which should exonerate the Blue cab and thus *lower* the inference that the cab was Blue, the mean judgement actually *increased* from 25.1% to 31.3%.

Troutman and Shanteau (1977) reported analogous results. They presented non-diagnostic evidence (which should have no effect) that caused people to become less certain. Birnbaum and Mellers (1983) showed that when people have a high opinion of a car, and a low credibility source says the car is "good", it actually makes people think the car is worse. Birnbaum and Mellers (1983) also reported that the effect of base rate is reduced when the source is higher in credibility. These findings are consistent with averaging rather than additive models.

Model fitting

In the old days, one wrote special computer programs to fit models to data (Birnbaum, 1976; Birnbaum & Mellers, 1983; Birnbaum & Stegner, 1979). However, spreadsheet programs such as *Excel* can now be used to fit such models without requiring programming. Methods for fitting models via the Solver in *Excel* are described in detail for this type of study in Birnbaum (2001, Ch. 19).

Each model has been fitted to the data in Table 2.1, by minimizing the sum of squared deviations. Lines in Figure 2.2 show predictions of the averaging model. Estimated parameters are as follows: weight of the initial impression, w_0, was fixed to 1; estimated weights of the base rate, medium-credibility witness, and high-credibility witness were 1.11, 0.58, and 1.56 respectively. The weight of base rate was intermediate between the two witnesses, although it "should" have exceeded the high-credibility witness.

Estimated scale values of base rates of 15%, 30%, 70%, and 85% were 12.1, 28.0, 67.3, and 83.9 respectively, close to the objective values. Estimated scale values for testimony ("Green" or "Blue") were 31.1 and 92.1 respectively. The estimated scale value of the initial impression was 44.5. This 10-parameter model correlated 0.99 with mean judgements. When the scale values of base rate were fixed to their objective values (reducing the model to only six free parameters), the correlation was still 0.99.

The sum of squared deviations (SSD) provides a more useful index of fit in this case. For the null model, which assumes no effect of base rate or source validity, SSD = 3027, which fits better than objective Bayes' theorem (plugging in the given values), with SSD = 5259. However, for the subjective Bayesian (additive) model, SSD = 188, and for the averaging model, SSD = 84. For the simpler averaging model (with subjective base rates set to their objective values), SSD = 85. In summary, the assumption that people attend only to the witness's testimony does fit better than the objective version of Bayes' theorem; however, its fit is much worse than the subjective (additive) version of Bayes' theorem. The averaging model, however, provides the best fit, even when simplified by the assumption that people take the base-rate information at face (objective) value.

OVERVIEW AND CONCLUSIONS

The case of the "base-rate fallacy" illustrates a type of cognitive illusion to which scientists are susceptible when they find non-significant results. The temptation is to say that because I have found no significant effects (of different base rates or source credibilities), there are therefore no effects. However, when results fail to disprove the null hypothesis, they do not prove the null hypothesis. This problem is particularly serious in between-subjects research, where it is easy to get non-significant results, or significant but silly results such as "9 seems bigger than 221".

The conclusions by Kahneman and Tversky (1973) that people neglect base rate and credibility of evidence are quite fragile. One must use a between-subjects design and use only certain wordings. Because I can show that the number 9 seems "bigger" than 221 with this type of design, I put little weight on such fragile between-subjects findings. In within-subjects designs, even the lawyer–engineer task shows effects of base rate (Novemsky & Kronzon, 1999). Although Novemsky and Kronzon argued for an additive model, they did not include the comparisons needed to test the additive model against the averaging model of Birnbaum and Mellers (1983). I believe that had these authors included appropriate designs, they would have been able to reject the additive model. They could have presented additional cases in which there were witness descriptions but no base-rate information, base-rate information but no witnesses (as in the dashed curve of Figure 2.2), different numbers of witnesses, or witnesses with varying amounts of information or different levels of expertise in describing people. Any of these manipulations would have provided of tests between the additive and averaging models.

In any of these manipulations, the implication of the averaging model is that the effect of any source (e.g., the base rate) would be inversely related to the total weight of other sources of information. This type of analysis has consistently favoured averaging over additive models in source credibility studies (e.g., Birnbaum, 1976, Fig. 3; Birnbaum & Mellers, 1983, Fig. 4C; Birnbaum & Stegner, 1979; Birnbaum, Wong, & Wong, 1976, Figs. 2B & 3).

Edwards (1968) noted that human inferences might differ from Bayesian inferences for any of three basic reasons – misperception, misaggregation, or response distortion. People might not absorb or utilize all of the evidence, people might combine the evidence inappropriately, or they might express their subjective probabilities using a response scale that needs transformation. Wallsten's (1972) model was an additive model that allowed misperception and response distortion, but which retained the additive Bayesian aggregation rule (recall that the Bayesian model is additive under monotonic transformation). This additive model is the subjective Bayesian model that appears to give a fairly good fit in Figure 2.1.

When proper analyses are conducted, however, it appears that the aggregation rule violates the additive structure of Bayes' theorem. Instead, the effect of a piece of evidence is not independent of other information available, but instead is diminished by total weight of other information. This is illustrated by the dashed curve in Figure 2.2, which crosses the other curves.

Birnbaum and Stegner (1979) decomposed source credibility into two components, expertise and bias, and distinguished these from the judge's bias, or point of view. Expertise of a source of evidence affects its weight, and is affected by the source's ability to know the truth, reliability of the source, cue correlation, or the source's signal-detection d'. In the case of gambles, weight of a branch is affected by the probability of a consequence. In the experiment described here, witnesses differed in their abilities to distinguish Green from Blue cabs.

In the averaging model, scale values are determined by what the witness says. If the witness said it was a "Green" cab, it tends to exonerate the Blue cab driver, whereas if the witness said the cab was "Blue", it tends to implicate the Blue cab driver. Scale values of base rates were nearly equal to their objective values. In judgements of the value of cars, scale values are determined by estimates provided by sources who drove the car and by the "blue book" values. (The blue book lists the average sale price of a car of a given make, model, and mileage, so it is like a base rate and does not reflect any expert examination or test drive of an individual vehicle.)

Bias reflects a source's tendency to over- as opposed to under-estimate judged value, presumably because sources are differentially rewarded or punished for giving values that are too high or too low. In a court trial, bias would be affected by affiliation with defence or prosecution. In an economic transaction, bias would be affected by association with buyer or seller. Birnbaum and Stegner (1979) showed that source's bias affected the scale value of that source's testimony.

In Birnbaum and Mellers's (1983) study, bias was manipulated by changing the probability that the source would call a car "good" or "bad" independent of the source's diagnostic ability. Whereas expertise was manipulated by varying the difference between hit rate and false alarm rate, bias was manipulated by varying the sum of hit rate plus false alarm rate. Their data were also consistent with the scale-adjustment model that bias affects scale value.

The judge, who combines information, may also have a type of bias, known as the judge's *point of view*. The judge might be combining information to determine buying price, selling price, or "fair price". An example of a "fair" price is when one person damages another's property and a judge is asked to give a judgement of the value of damages so that her judgement is equally fair to both people. Birnbaum and Stegner (1979) showed that the source's viewpoint affects the configural weight of higher- or lower-valued branches. Buyers put more weight on the lower estimates of value and sellers place higher weight on the higher-valued estimates. This model has also proved quite successful in predicting judgements and choices between gambles (Birnbaum, 1999b).

Birnbaum and Mellers (1983, Table 2) drew a table of analogies that can be expanded to show that the same model appears to apply not only to Bayesian inference, but also to numerical prediction, contingent valuation, and a variety of other tasks. To expand the table to include judgements of the values of gambles and decisions between them, let viewpoint depend on the task to judge buying price, selling price, "fair" price, or to choose between gambles. Each discrete probability (event) consequence branch has a weight that depends on probability (or event). The scale value depends on the consequence. Configural weighting of higher- or lower-valued branches depends on identification with the buyer, seller, independent, or decider.

Much research has been developing a catalogue of cognitive illusions, each to be explained by a "heuristic" or "bias" of human thinking. Each time a "bias" is named, one has the cognitive illusion that it has been explained. The notion of a "bias" suggests that if the bias could be avoided, people would suffer no illusions. A better approach to the study of cognitive illusions would be one more directly analogous to the study of visual illusions in perception. Visual illusions can be seen as consequences of a mechanism that allows people to judge actual sizes of objects with different retinal sizes at different distances. A robot that judged size by retinal size only would not be susceptible to the Mueller-Lyer illusion. However, it would also not satisfy size constancy. As an object moved away, it would seem to shrink. So, rather than blame a "bias" of human reasoning, we should seek the algebraic models of judgement that allow one to explain both illusion and constancy with the same model.

SUMMARY

- Early research that compared intuitive judgements of probability and Bayesian calculations concluded that people were "conservative", in that their judgements were closer to uncertainty than dictated by the formula.
- Based on poor studies, it was later argued that people neglect or do not attend to base rates or source validity when making Bayesian inferences.
- Evidence for the so-called "base-rate fallacy" and source neglect is very fragile and does not replicate except in very restricted conditions. When base rates, source, expertise, and testimony are manipulated

- within-subjects, judges do utilize the base rates and attend to source expertise.
- The subjective Bayesian model provides a better fit than the objective model, because it can account for "conservatism" and the nearly additive relationship between base rate and source's opinion.
- However, the data show two phenomena that rule out additive or subjective Bayesian formulations: The effect of the base rate is inversely related to the number and credibility of other sources.
- The data are better described by Birnbaum and Stegner's (1979) scale-adjustment averaging model than by the other models.

FURTHER READING

Reviews of this literature from different viewpoints are presented by Edwards (1968), Tversky and Kahneman (1982), Koehler (1996), and in Chapter 3 of this volume. Birnbaum (1983) showed that the so-called "normative" Bayesian analysis presented by Tversky and Kahneman (1982) made an implausible assumption that made their conclusions unwarranted. Birnbaum and Mellers (1983) showed how to apply the model of Birnbaum and Stegner (1979) to the Bayesian inference task. The model fit here is a special case of that model, which also describes effects of the bias of sources and the viewpoint of the judge.

ACKNOWLEDGEMENT

Support was received from National Science Foundation Grants, SES 99-86436, and BCS-0129453.

REFERENCES

Anderson, N. H. (1981). *Foundations of information integration theory.* New York: Academic Press.

Birnbaum, M. H. (1973). The devil rides again: Correlation as an index of fit. *Psychological Bulletin, 79,* 239–242.

Birnbaum, M. H. (1976). Intuitive numerical prediction. *American Journal of Psychology, 89,* 417–429.

Birnbaum, M. H. (1982). Controversies in psychological measurement. In B. Wegener (Ed.), *Social attitudes and psychophysical measurement* (pp. 401–485). Hillsdale, NJ: Lawrence Erlbaum Associates Inc.

Birnbaum, M. H. (1983). Base rates in Bayesian inference: Signal detection analysis of the cab problem. *American Journal of Psychology, 96,* 85–94.

Birnbaum, M. H. (1999a). How to show that 9 > 221: Collect judgments in a between-subjects design. *Psychological Methods, 4,* 243–249.

Birnbaum, M. H. (1999b). Testing critical properties of decision making on the Internet. *Psychological Science, 10*, 399–407.

Birnbaum, M. H. (2001). *Introduction to behavioral research on the Internet.* Upper Saddle River, NJ: Prentice Hall.

Birnbaum, M. H., & Mellers, B. A. (1983). Bayesian inference: Combining base rates with opinions of sources who vary in credibility. *Journal of Personality and Social Psychology, 45*, 792–804.

Birnbaum, M. H., & Stegner, S. E. (1979). Source credibility in social judgment: Bias, expertise, and the judge's point of view. *Journal of Personality and Social Psychology, 37*, 48–74.

Birnbaum, M. H., Wong, R., & Wong, L. (1976). Combining information from sources that vary in credibility. *Memory & Cognition, 4*, 330–336.

Edwards, W. (1968). Conservatism in human information processing. In B. Kleinmuntz (Eds.), *Formal representation of human judgment* (pp. 17–52). New York: Wiley.

Fischhoff, B., Slovic, P., & Lichtenstein, S. (1979). Subjective sensitivity analysis. *Organizational Behavior and Human Performance, 23*, 339–359.

Gigerenzer, G., & Hoffrage, U. (1995). How to improve Bayesian reasoning without instruction: Frequency format. *Psychological Review, 102*, 684–704.

Hammerton, M. A. (1973). A case of radical probability estimation. *Journal of Experimental Psychology, 101*, 252–254.

Kahneman, D., & Tversky, A. (1973). On the psychology of prediction. *Psychological Review, 80*, 237–251.

Koehler, J. J. (1996). The base-rate fallacy reconsidered: Descriptive, normative, and methodological challenges. *Behavioral and Brain Sciences, 19*, 1–53.

Lyon, D., & Slovic, P. (1976). Dominance of accuracy information and neglect of base rates in probability estimation. *Acta Psychologica, 40*, 287–298.

Novemsky, N., & Kronzon, S. (1999). How are base-rates used, when they are used: A comparison of additive and Bayesian models of base-rate use. *Journal of Behavioral Decision Making, 12*, 55–69.

Pitz, G. (1975). Bayes' theorem: Can a theory of judgment and inference do without it? In F. Restle, R. M. Shiffrin, N. J. Castellan, H. R. Lindman, & D. B. Pisoni (Eds.), *Cognitive theory* (Vol. 1, pp. 131–148). Hillsdale, NJ: Lawrence Erlbaum Associates Inc.

Schum, D. A. (1981). Sorting out the effects of witness sensitivity and response-criterion placement upon the inferential value of testimonial evidence. *Organizational Behavior and Human Performance, 27*, 153–196.

Shanteau, J. (1975). Averaging versus multiplying combination rules of inference judgment. *Acta Psychologica, 39*, 83–89.

Slovic, P., & Lichtenstein, S. (1971). Comparison of Bayesian and regression approaches to the study of information processing in judgment. *Organizational Behavior and Human Performance, 6*, 649–744.

Troutman, C. M., & Shanteau, J. (1977). Inferences based on nondiagnostic information. *Organizational Behavior and Human Performance, 19*, 43–55.

Tversky, A., & Kahneman, D. (1982). Evidential impact of base rates. In D. Kahneman, P. Slovic, & A. Tversky (Eds.), *Judgment under uncertainty: Heuristics and biases* (pp. 153–160). New York: Cambridge University Press.

Wallsten, T. (1972). Conjoint-measurement framework for the study of probabilistic information processing. *Psychological Review, 79*, 245–260.

APPENDIX

The complete materials for this experiment, including HTML that collects the data are available via the WWW from the following URL:

http://psych.fullerton.edu/mbirnbaum/bayes/resources.htm

A sample listing of the trials, including warmup, is given below.

Warmup trials: Judge the probability that the cab was Blue.
  Express your probability judgement as a percentage and type a number from 0 to 100.
  W1 15% of accidents are Blue Cabs & high witness says "Green".
  (There were six additional "warmup" trials that were representative of the experimental trials.)

Please re-read the instructions, check your warmups, and then proceed to the trials below.
  Test trials: What is the probability that the cab was Blue?
  Express your probability judgement as a percentage and type a number from 0 to 100.

1 85% of accidents are Blue Cabs & medium witness says "Green".
2 15% of accidents are Blue Cabs & medium witness says "Blue".
3 15% of accidents are Blue Cabs & medium witness says "Green".
4 15% of accidents are Blue Cabs & there was no witness.
5 30% of accidents are Blue Cabs & high witness says "Blue".
6 15% of accidents are Blue Cabs & high witness says "Green".
7 70% of accidents are Blue Cabs & there was no witness.
8 15% of accidents are Blue Cabs & high witness says "Blue".
9 70% of accidents are Blue Cabs & high witness says "Blue".
10 85% of accidents are Blue Cabs & high witness says "Green".
11 70% of accidents are Blue Cabs & high witness says "Green".
12 85% of accidents are Blue Cabs & medium witness says "Blue".
13 30% of accidents are Blue Cabs & medium witness says "Blue".
14 30% of accidents are Blue Cabs & high witness says "Green".
15 70% of accidents are Blue Cabs & medium witness says "Blue".
16 30% of accidents are Blue Cabs & there was no witness.
17 30% of accidents are Blue Cabs & medium witness says "Green".
18 70% of accidents are Blue Cabs & medium witness says "Green".
19 85% of accidents are Blue Cabs & high witness says "Blue".
20 85% of accidents are Blue Cabs & there was no witness.

3 Statistical formats in Bayesian inference

*Stephanie Kurzenhäuser and
Andrea Lücking*

Although the term "Bayesian inference" may not be common in everyday language, many situations in our daily lives can be described as Bayesian inference problems. Generally speaking, we face such a problem when we want to update our probability estimate for some hypothesis in the light of new evidence, for instance the hypothesis that a soccer team will win the game, given that it is behind at half time, or the hypothesis that a student at a university will pass the next exam, given that she failed before. Or imagine the following situation: You have heard that 40-year-old women have a relatively low probability of developing breast cancer within the next 10 years; about 1%. Therefore, you are not particularly worried when an acquaintance of yours who is in this age group participates in a routine screening for breast cancer. However, the x-ray picture of her breast shows a suspicious lesion that has to be followed up. You are now probably much more worried about your friend *given* this positive test result, because the hypothesis that she has breast cancer seems clearly more likely. In other words, you have updated your *prior probability estimate* for the hypothesis (the base rate for breast cancer in this age group, here 1%) in the light of the new *evidence* (the positive test result) to a somewhat higher *posterior probability estimate* for the hypothesis (the probability of breast cancer in this age group, given a positive test result).

But what exactly does the positive screening result imply – does it indicate the disease with 100% certainty, or 80%, or what? Sometimes, such information about posterior likelihood estimates is directly retrievable, or it may be available after further information search (e.g., you find the information in the Internet; see Krauss & Fiedler, 2003). Whenever this is not the case, the posterior estimate has to be inferred from other information. A normatively correct way to make this inference is to use *Bayes' rule* (named after the English Reverend Thomas Bayes, 1702–1761), which integrates information about the base rate of the hypothesis with information about the quality of the evidence.

Since the 1960s, numerous studies have tested whether human inference follows Bayes' rule. Similar to findings on other base-rate problems (see Chapter 2), the conclusions were mostly negative. People either did not adjust their prior probability estimates sufficiently (a tendency termed "conservatism"; Edwards, 1968), or they seemed to ignore base rates altogether ("base-rate neglect"; see review by Koehler, 1996b). Several factors that influenced the way people dealt with Bayesian inference problems were identified. For instance, base-rate usage in Bayesian inference problems was shown to be affected by the causality of base-rate information (e.g., Tversky & Kahneman, 1980), the credibility of the source (e.g., Birnbaum & Mellers, 1983), experimental design features such as within-subjects variation (e.g., Birnbaum & Mellers, 1983), or direct experience of base rates (e.g., Christensen-Szalanski & Beach, 1982). In the present chapter, we do not attempt to give an overview of all the different factors that influence Bayesian reasoning (for more information, see Chapter 2 and Koehler, 1996b), but focus instead on one that has been at the centre of a lively debate in the Bayesian inference literature of recent years: the *format* in which the statistical information is represented in Bayesian inference problems.

BAYESIAN INFERENCES: BASIC PROBLEM STRUCTURE

Typically, Bayesian inferences have been studied by using text problems. A problem that is very similar to the medical example in the introduction, and which has been widely studied, is the following (Eddy, 1982; Gigerenzer & Hoffrage, 1995):

> *Problem 1:* The probability of breast cancer is 1% for a woman at age forty who participates in routine screening. If a woman has breast cancer, the probability is 80% that she will have a positive mammogram. If a woman does not have breast cancer, the probability is 9.6% that she will also have a positive mammogram. A woman in this age group had a positive mammogram in a routine screening. What is the probability that she actually has breast cancer?____%

This is a basic version of a Bayesian inference problem: The situation consists of a binary hypothesis H or ¬H (here: breast cancer or no breast cancer; the "¬" stands for absence) and one binary cue D or ¬D (D stands for data, here: test positive; ¬D is a negative test result in this example). Three pieces of information are displayed (see Text box 3.1; this is also called a *standard information menu*; for other ways to display the statistical information, see Gigerenzer & Hoffrage, 1995).

The task is to find the posterior probability, or positive predictive value $p(H \mid D)$, namely, the probability of the hypothesis, given the data. Please take a minute to solve this Problem 1 (the normative correct solution will be given in the next paragraph).

Typically, participants who are given this task in Bayesian inference

> **Text box 3.1** The three pieces of information displayed in Problem 1
>
> - The prior probability or *base rate* $p(H)$, here the probability of having breast cancer.
> - The *sensitivity* of the data $p(D \mid H)$, here the proportion of positive mammograms among women with breast cancer.
> - The *false-alarm rate* of the test $p(D \mid \neg H)$, here the proportion of positive mammograms among women without breast cancer.

experiments do not find it easy. Most of them give an incorrect posterior probability estimate, often around 80%, while the correct answer according to Bayes' theorem is 7.8% (computations will be explained below). In fact, numerous experiments have shown that most people fail on Bayesian inference problems, and so it was concluded that the human mind is simply not equipped for Bayesian reasoning problems (e.g., Bar-Hillel, 1980).

REPRESENTATION OF STATISTICAL INFORMATION

In the 1990s, some researchers offered a new interpretation of the results concerning Bayesian reasoning and argued that people are indeed able to solve Bayesian inference problems when given an *external* representation of the data that facilitates rather than complicates human reasoning (Cosmides & Tooby, 1996; Gigerenzer & Hoffrage, 1995). Text box 3.2 gives an illustration of this ecological argument.

> **Text box 3.2** Illustration: Representation of numerical information in the pocket calculator
>
> Think about a pocket calculator: It works perfectly well with Arabic numbers because its algorithms are tuned to this representation format. It would fail badly, however, if the same numerical information were entered in another format, such as binary or Roman numbers.

Natural frequencies

As an alternative way to represent statistical information in Bayesian inference problems, Gigerenzer and Hoffrage (1995) introduced the so-called *natural frequency* format. With natural frequencies, the breast cancer problem has the following wording (adapted from Gigerenzer & Hoffrage, 1995):

Problem 2: Ten out of every 1000 women at age forty who participate in routine screening have breast cancer. Of these 10 women with breast cancer, 8 will have a positive mammogram. Of the remaining 990 women without breast cancer, 95 will still have a positive mammogram. Imagine a sample of women in this age group who had a positive mammogram in a routine screening. How many of these women actually do have breast cancer? ____ out of ____

The only difference between Problem 1 and Problem 2 is the format of the statistical information: Problem 1 contains probabilities for single events; Problem 2 contains natural frequencies. Table 3.1 summarizes the statistical information given in the two problems and also illustrates two other statistical formats, relative frequencies and normalized frequencies, which have been repeatedly used in Bayesian inference research. It is important to note that the statistical information in all four formats is mathematically equivalent.

Gigerenzer and Hoffrage (1995) found that with natural frequencies, considerably more Bayesian inference problems were solved correctly (46%, Study 1) than with single-event probabilities (18%, Study 1). This result was replicated several times and could be shown for lay people as well as for medical and legal experts (Hoffrage & Gigerenzer, 1998, 2004; Hoffrage, Lindsey, Hertwig, & Gigerenzer, 2000). The performance for problems with relative or normalized frequencies was comparable to the low performance

Table 3.1 Information of the breast cancer problem represented in four statistical formats

Information	Example problem wording
	I Natural frequencies
$p(H)$	10 out of every 1000 women have BC
$p(D \mid H)$	8 out of 10 women with BC have a positive M
$p(D \mid \neg H)$	95 out of 990 women without BC have a positive M
	II Normalized frequencies
$p(H)$	10 out of every 1000 women have BC
$p(D \mid H)$	800 out of 1000 women with BC have a positive M
$p(D \mid \neg H)$	96 out of 1000 women without BC have a positive M
	III Single-event probabilities
$p(H)$	The probability is 1% that a woman has BC
$p(D \mid H)$	The probability is 80% that a woman with BC has a positive M
$p(D \mid \neg H)$	The probability is 9.6% that a woman without BC has a positive M
	IV Relative frequencies
$p(H)$	1% of the women have BC
$p(D \mid H)$	80% of the women with BC have a positive M
$p(D \mid \neg H)$	9.6% of the women without BC have a positive M

BC = breast cancer, M = mammogram.

Statistical Formats in Bayesian inference 65

for probability problems (Gigerenzer & Hoffrage, 1995, Study 2; Lewis & Keren, 1999).

Figure 3.1 illustrates the information structure of the breast cancer problem for two statistical formats, natural frequencies and normalized frequencies. First consider the left side of the figure, the natural frequency tree. The tree reveals that natural frequencies are the result of the sequential partitioning of one sample into subsamples. In a first step, the initial sample of 1000 women is partitioned into two subsamples, women with and without breast cancer. In a second step, these samples are again partitioned according to the new evidence; here, it has to be taken into account that each diagnostic test can produce incorrect results. Four possible outcomes result:

- When a woman has breast cancer, she can either get a correct positive (D&H) or a false negative result (¬D&H). The rates of these two outcomes are called sensitivity (or correct positive rate; here, 8 out of 10) and false negative rate (here, 2 out of 10), respectively.
- When a woman does not have breast cancer, she can receive either a correct negative (¬D&¬H) or a false positive (D&¬H) result. The rates of these two outcomes are called the correct negative rate (or specificity; here, 895 out of 990) and false positive rate (here, 95 out of 990), respectively.

Please note that an isolated number, such as 95, is not by itself a natural frequency; it only becomes one because of its relation to other numbers in the tree (Hoffrage, Gigerenzer, Krauss, & Martignon, 2002). Let us return to the actual task: What is the probability that a woman has breast cancer, given the positive mammogram? The correct answer can be directly retrieved from Figure 3.1. There are 103 women with a positive mammogram, and

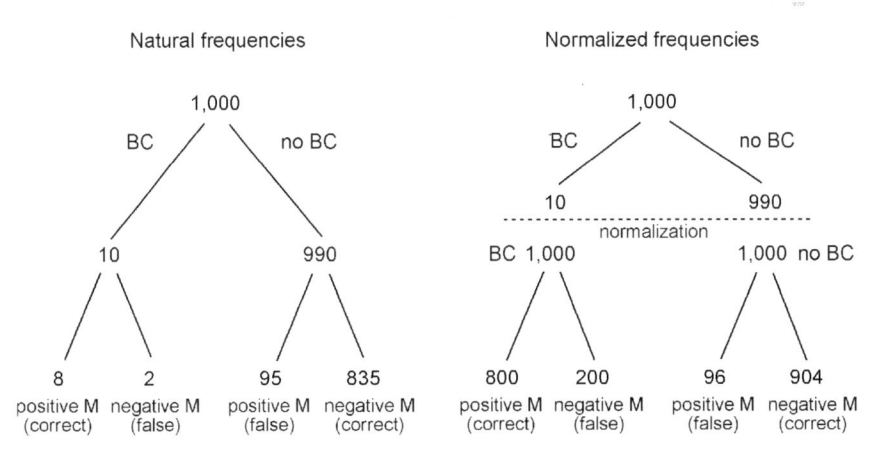

Figure 3.1 Structure of the statistical information in the breast cancer problem in the natural frequency format (left side) and normalized frequency format (right side). BC = breast cancer, M = mammogram.

among them, 8 have breast cancer. In other words, the positive predictive value of the mammogram is 7.8%.

In general, to calculate the probability of a disease given a positive test, the number of correct positive cases D&H has to be divided by the number of all positive cases D, that is, the sum of correct and false positive cases.

$$p(H|D) = \frac{D \& H}{D \& H + D \& \neg H}$$
$$= \frac{8}{8 + 95} = \frac{8}{103} = .078 \quad (1)$$

However, in Problem 1, no natural frequencies are given – only probabilities: the base rate and two *conditional probabilities*, that is, event probabilities that are conditional on the occurrence of some other event (e.g., a positive test *given* breast cancer). Indeed, Bayesian inferences have typically been studied with information given in terms of conditional probabilities. The following equation shows Bayes' rule and how it can be used to solve the Bayesian inference problem with probabilities, percentages, or normalized frequencies:

$$p(H|D) = \frac{p(H)\,p(D|H)}{p(H)\,p(D|H) + p(\neg H)\,p(D|\neg H)}$$
$$= \frac{(.01)(.8)}{(.01)(.8) + (.99)(.096)} = \frac{.008}{.008 + .095} = \frac{.008}{.103} = .078 \quad (2)$$

Both Equations 1 and 2 are versions of Bayes' rule (Gigerenzer & Hoffrage, 1995) and divide the proportion of correct positives by all positives. But in Equation 2, each of the joint frequencies from Equation 1 is replaced by the product of two probabilities. The reason is that the conditional probabilities that enter Equation 2 have been normalized, that is, the values fall within the uniform range of 0 and 1 (or 0% and 100%). In Table 3.1, the statistical formats II, III, and IV are normalized. The benefit of normalization is that the numbers can easily be compared to each other. However, normalization does have a cost. For example, the sensitivity tells us that 80% of women with breast cancer receive a positive test result, but we cannot see from the 80% whether having breast cancer is a frequent or a rare event in the population. To make a Bayesian inference, the base-rate information has to be put back in by multiplying the conditional probabilities by their respective base rates, which makes computation more complex.

The cost of normalization in the context of Bayesian inference problems is illustrated on the right side of Figure 3.1. Because normalized frequencies do not stem from the sequential partitioning of one population, they cannot be displayed in a natural frequency tree (left side of Figure 3.1); rather three different trees describing three different samples have to be drawn. Another important implication of Figure 3.1 is that natural frequencies are not equivalent to any kind of absolute frequencies, because frequency information can also be normalized.

Measures

Performance in Bayesian inference tasks – and thus the difference between statistical formats – is measured by comparing the answers of the participants with the normatively correct answer obtained by Bayes' rule. The posterior probability estimate of the participant is the main dependent variable – in some studies the notes made by the participant while working on the problem to document her strategy are also used. Based on these measures, several ways of scoring performance can be found in the literature:

- *Outcome criterion:* Reports the number of correct inferences. Inferences are scored as correct if the posterior probability estimate of the participant matches the normative solution, either exactly or within a certain range (e.g., Macchi, 2000).
- *Double criterion (outcome and process):* Reports the number of correct inferences. Inferences are scored as correct if the posterior probability estimate matches the normative solution, *and* the participant's notes, calculations, or drawings confirm that not guessing, but a Bayesian computation (Eq. 1 or 2) was used (e.g., Gigerenzer & Hoffrage, 1995).
- *Deviation:* Reports the average deviation of the participant's posterior probability estimate from the normative solution. The smaller the deviation, the higher the performance (e.g., Fiedler, Brinkmann, Betsch, & Wild, 2000).
- *Median and/or modal response:* Reports the median and/or modal posterior probability estimate (e.g., Bar-Hillel, 1980).

If it is not the absolute level of estimates that is the focus of a study, but rather whether participants reasoned in accordance with Bayes' rule, then we would clearly recommend the use of the double criterion. Information about the strategies used by the participant is necessary to differentiate Bayesian inferences from inferences based on incorrect strategies or guessing that, by chance, result in similar estimates (see also Villejoubert and Mandel, 2002).

CLASSROOM EXPERIMENT

The goal of the classroom experiment is to demonstrate how statistical formats influence performance in Bayesian inference tasks. The classroom experiment is an adapted version of the experimental procedures employed by Gigerenzer and Hoffrage (1995, Study 1) and Hoffrage and Gigerenzer (1998, 2004, Study 2). Each participant solves four Bayesian inference problems, two of them with information given in terms of probabilities and two in terms of natural frequencies. The dependent measure is the proportion of correct Bayesian inferences. The procedural details are given in Text box 3.3.

Text box 3.3 Method of the classroom demonstration

Participants

The cited studies had 60 (Gigerenzer & Hoffrage, 1995, Exp. 1), 48 (Hoffrage & Gigerenzer, 1998), and 96 participants (Hoffrage & Gigerenzer, 2004). However, here the number of problems that these participants worked on is more important than the number of participants, because the performance rate is usually expressed as the number of correctly solved problems. In the cited studies, each participant had to solve between 4 and 30 Bayesian inference problems, resulting in the total number of problems in each experimental condition being between 98 (Hoffrage & Gigerenzer, 1998) and 450 (Gigerenzer & Hoffrage, 1995, Exp. 1).

With a within-subjects design and several problems per condition, the format effect can also be reliably shown with fewer participants. For example, in their second experiment Gigerenzer and Hoffrage (1995, Exp. 2) had 15 students who had to solve 72 problems, that is, 36 in each format. However, there are also a number of studies that presented only one problem to each participant with typically between 25 and 40 participants per condition (e.g., Lewis & Keren, 1999; Macchi, 2000; Mellers & McGraw, 1999).

Design

The experiment has a simple design with one factor, namely, statistical format. The factor is tested within-subjects, that is, each participant solves four Bayesian inference problems, two of them with information given in terms of probabilities and two in terms of natural frequencies. The formats and orders of the problems should be systematically varied across the participants to exclude systematic order and material effects. The dependent measure is the proportion of correct Bayesian inferences.

Material

The Appendix provides four medical tasks that were used in two of the cited studies (Hoffrage & Gigerenzer, 1998, 2004). The problems have the basic structure described above.

Procedure

The experiment should be run in one session. Participants should receive a booklet with all four problems, each problem on a single page. They should be instructed to solve the problems in the order presented and not to switch between them. Below each problem, participants should find a sentence that reminds them to write down how they arrived at their solution, including all drawings, calculations, and comments that they thought of while working on the problem. Pocket calculators should not be allowed. Time is not restricted. Participants will need approximately 25 to 40 minutes to solve all four problems. Prior knowledge of Bayesian statistics could distort the results. It is therefore helpful to control for this factor, either by recruiting statistically naïve participants, or by adding a simple questionnaire that asks for familiarity with Bayes' rule.

Analysis

The unit of analysis used here is the task, not the participant. We recommend using the double criterion. In this demonstration, it should be sufficient to score the process notes as being either Bayesian or non-Bayesian (other studies have also analyzed the non-Bayesian strategies in more detail, Gigerenzer & Hoffrage, 1995; Hoffrage & Gigerenzer, 2004). If a participant made an obvious calculation error, but the written notes indicate that the strategy was correct, this case should be treated as if he or she had performed the calculation correctly, because basic arithmetic skills are not addressed in this demonstration.

The cited studies did not use statistical tests to analyze the difference between the performance rates. Some other studies have used chi-square tests (Girotto & Gonzalez, 2001; Macchi, 2000) or Fisher's exact test (Lewis & Keren, 1999) to analyze the proportion of Bayesian answers.

Results

All of the cited studies (Gigerenzer & Hoffrage, 1995; Hoffrage & Gigerenzer, 1998, 2004) found performance rates that were substantially lower for the probability problems than for the natural frequency problems. This result was found to be stable across all task contents used, although the absolute level of performance differed between the contents (see Gigerenzer & Hoffrage, 1999). For the probability format, performance rates ranged from 6 to 18%. For the natural frequency format, the cited studies found performance rates between 46% and 57%.

Discussion

The performance rates for the probability format found in the cited studies were comparable to those found in other studies (Lindsey, Hertwig, & Gigerenzer, 2003; Mellers & McGraw, 1999). Also the performance rates for the natural frequency format were comparable to other studies, but the absolute level of performance seems to be more variable for natural frequencies than for probabilities. Performance rates for natural frequency problems in other studies range from 8% (Mellers & McGraw, 1999, Study 2), to over 53% (Girotto & Gonzalez, 2001, Exp. 5), to 68% (Lindsey, Hertwig, & Gigerenzer, 2003).

The consistently low performance for the probability format could, taken separately, be interpreted as clear evidence for a general inability to solve Bayesian inference problems (especially because not only lay people, but also professionals had these problems). However, as the results for the natural frequency format show, another interpretation seems more appropriate. Just by changing the representation of the statistical information, the performance rate increased by about 30 percentage points. This result indicates that the external representation of information is a rather powerful factor for people's performance in such tasks.

THEORETICAL OVERVIEW AND CONCLUSIONS

Gigerenzer and Hoffrage (1995) offered two related arguments to explain the beneficial effect of natural frequencies. The main argument for the facilitative effect of natural frequencies is computational: Bayesian computations are simpler when the information is represented in natural frequencies rather than in any of the other formats in Table 3.1 (see also Kleiter, 1994). With natural frequencies, the calculations necessary to arrive at the correct solution are equivalent to Equation 1; participants can derive the number of correct positive and false positive cases (8 and 95) directly from the problem text, without having to make any further calculations. With probabilities and relative or normalized frequencies, the calculation is more demanding (Equation 2) because all three formats contain normalized information that has to be multiplied with the respective base rates to arrive at the correct Bayesian solution.

The second explanation brings in an evolutionary perspective. Gigerenzer and Hoffrage (1995; see also Gigerenzer, 1998) argue that the human mind appears to be "tuned" to make inferences from natural frequencies rather than from probabilities and percentages, because for most of their existence, humans have made inferences from information encoded sequentially through direct experience. Natural frequencies are seen as the final tally of such a sequential sampling process (hence the term "natural" frequencies; see Cosmides & Tooby, 1996; Kleiter, 1994). In contrast, mathematical probability did not emerge until the mid-17th century; in other words, probabilities and percentages are much more "recent" in evolutionary terms. Therefore, Gigerenzer and Hoffrage (1995) assume that minds have evolved to deal with natural frequencies rather than with probabilities.

Both explanations have been heavily disputed (see the discussions in Gigerenzer & Hoffrage, 1999; Hoffrage et al., 2002), and the evolutionary argument in particular has been met with scepticism (Fiedler et al., 2000; Girotto & Gonzalez, 2001; Sloman, Over, Slovak, & Stibel, 2003). It should be noted that, strictly speaking, the evolutionary argument has yet to be tested, because it is still not clear how the effects of the two explanations (i.e., computational and evolutionary) can be disentangled (Hoffrage et al.,

2002; for a first step in this direction, see Brase, 2002). Furthermore, many researchers have argued that it is not the use of frequency formats *per se*, but rather some third factor that could be the explanation for the results obtained.

Most alternative accounts refer to the structure of the information entailed by the use of natural frequency formats. For instance, Girotto and Gonzalez (2001) argue that reasoning about conditional probability is mainly affected by two factors, the structure of the problem information and the form of the question asked. They adopt the "mental model theory of probabilistic reasoning" (Johnson-Laird, Legrenzi, Girotto, Sonino-Legrenzi, & Caverni, 1999) and assume that naïve reasoners infer conditional probabilities from so-called subset relations in mental models, rather than from Bayes' rule. People make correct probability evaluations if they are encouraged to apply the *subset principle*, that is, to determine the proportion of the elements of the subset D&H (we have used the term "subsample" so far) in the set of the elements of D. As we saw above, natural frequencies automatically contain these sets, but Girotto and Gonzalez (2001) argue that subset representations can also be elicited without natural frequencies (see also Sloman et al., 2003). They reported that when the form of the question and the structure of the problem were framed so as to encourage the application of the subset principle, naïve individuals solved problems equally well irrespective of whether they were stated in terms of probabilities or frequencies. Other studies showed that subset representations could also be activated by another factor, namely by using so-called *partitive* formulations in the text problems (Macchi, 2000; Macchi & Mosconi, 1998). Partitive formulations clarify the relationship between the subsets to which the probabilities refer. Macchi (2000) reports that not only natural frequencies that are automatically partitive, but also relative frequencies with a partitive formulation, lead to high performance rates.

To date, there is no consensus on the explanation of statistical format effects in Bayesian reasoning (e.g., see Hoffrage et al., 2002; also Girotto & Gonzalez, 2002, for a discussion on whether the subset principle is a mere redescription of a property of natural frequencies). Unfortunately, theoretical advancement in this debate is slowed down by differing empirical methods and recurrent misunderstandings. First, the use of different performance criteria (see above) complicates the direct comparison of performance across studies. Second, the wordings of the text problems often differ considerably between studies. This can be problematic since even small differences can affect performance (Cosmides & Tooby, 1996; Hoffrage et al., 2002). Third, some authors have misinterpreted the results on natural frequencies as a claim that any kind of frequency information would be more helpful than probabilities and percentages (e.g., Lewis & Keren, 1999; Macchi, 2000; for an overview see Hoffrage et al., 2002).

However, although there is an ongoing debate on why the facilitating effect of natural frequencies in Bayesian inferences occurs and what its boundary conditions are (e.g., Mellers & McGraw, 1999), there seems to be a consensus about its existence. As mentioned earlier, the effect has been shown several times for lay people (e.g., Hoffrage & Gigerenzer, 2004; Macchi, 2000) as well as for medical (Hoffrage & Gigerenzer, 1998) and legal experts (Koehler, 1996a; Lindsey et al., 2003). The effect could also be observed in more complex diagnostic problems that invoke data from more than one cue for evaluating the hypothesis, for instance two medical tests in a row (Krauss, Martignon, & Hoffrage, 1999). Moreover, there is evidence that frequency representations can reduce or eliminate other well-known "cognitive illusions" such as the conjunction fallacy (Hertwig & Gigerenzer, 1999; see also Chapter 1) or the overconfidence bias (Gigerenzer, Hoffrage, & Kleinbölting, 1991; see also Chapter 13).

Despite the ongoing theoretical debate, the existing evidence has already inspired researchers to test whether the facilitating effect of natural frequencies could also be used to improve statistical thinking in applied settings. For instance, a 2-hour computerized tutorial was developed with the goal of helping people to deal with the probabilities and percentages that they encounter in textbooks and the media by teaching them how to translate probabilities into natural frequencies (Sedlmeier & Gigerenzer, 2001). This representation-learning approach has led to significantly higher performance, especially in the long run, compared to a traditional approach that teaches how to use Bayes' rule (see also Kurzenhäuser & Hoffrage, 2002, for an adaptation of the tutorial to the traditional classroom setting).

A domain for which the research on statistical formats in Bayesian inference is directly applicable has already been mentioned throughout this chapter: medical risk communication. Given the facilitating effect of natural frequencies in the diagnostic inference problems, it has been proposed that the meaning of medical test results should be communicated to patients in terms of natural frequencies in order to foster understanding (e.g., Gigerenzer, Hoffrage, & Ebert, 1998; Hamm & Smith, 1998).

To give a final example, the representation of risk information is also relevant in the legal domain. In criminal and paternity cases, the general practice in court is to present information in terms of probabilities or ratios of conditional probabilities, with the consequence that jurors, judges, and sometimes the experts themselves are confused and misinterpret the evidence (Koehler, 1996a; Lindsey et al., 2003). It will be most relevant for the development of such legal practices to follow the scientific debate about statistical formats and other representation features in Bayesian inference problems.

SUMMARY

- In Bayesian inferences, a prior probability estimate for a hypothesis is updated in light of new evidence.

- The statistical information that is used in Bayesian inferences can be represented in different statistical formats. The external representation of statistical information is a powerful factor for performance in Bayesian inference tasks.
- The natural frequency format is a statistical format that facilitates Bayesian computations, compared to single-event probabilities or relative frequencies. Natural frequencies are not any kind of frequencies, but a specific type that results from the sequential partitioning of one sample into subsamples.
- While there seems to be a consensus that natural frequencies facilitate Bayesian inferences, there is an ongoing debate on the question of why this effect occurs.
- Nevertheless, natural frequencies can already be used as a tool to facilitate statistical thinking in applied settings such as medical or legal risk communication.

FURTHER READING

Gigerenzer and Hoffrage (1995) wrote the classic paper that introduced natural frequencies as an alternative way of presenting statistical information in Bayesian inference tasks. An overview of the research on natural frequencies since then and a useful clarification of misunderstandings concerning natural frequencies can be found in the paper by Hoffrage et al. (2002). One of the alternative explanations of the effect of natural frequencies in Bayesian inference tasks was proposed by Girotto and Gonzalez (2001). Interesting applications of natural frequencies, for instance in the legal or medical context, can be found in Gigerenzer (2002).

ACKNOWLEDGEMENTS

We are grateful to Barbara Fasolo, Ulrich Hoffrage, Julie Holzhausen, Stefan Krauss, and Gaëlle Villejoubert for helpful comments on an earlier version of this chapter. We also thank Anita Todd and Rona Unrau for editing the manuscript.

REFERENCES

Bar-Hillel, M. (1980). The base-rate fallacy in probability judgments. *Acta Psychologica*, 44, 211–233.

Birnbaum, M. H., & Mellers, B. A. (1983). Bayesian inference: Combining base rates with opinions of sources who vary in credibility. *Journal of Personality and Social Psychology*, 45, 792–804.

Brase, G. (2002). Which statistical formats facilitate what decisions? The perception and influence of different statistical information formats. *Journal of Behavioral Decision Making, 15,* 381–401.

Christensen-Szalanski, J. J., & Beach, L. R. (1982). Experience and the base-rate fallacy. *Organizational Behavior and Human Decision Processes, 29,* 270–278.

Cosmides, L., & Tooby, J. (1996). Are humans good intuitive statisticians after all? Rethinking some conclusions from the literature on judgment under uncertainty. *Cognition, 58,* 1–73.

Eddy, D. M. (1982). Probabilistic reasoning in clinical medicine: Problems and opportunities. In D. Kahneman, P. Slovic, & A. Tversky (Eds.), *Judgment under uncertainty: Heuristics and biases* (pp. 249–267). Cambridge: Cambridge University Press.

Edwards, W. (1968). Conservatism in human information processing. In B. Kleinmuntz (Ed.), *Formal representation of human judgment* (pp. 17–52). New York: Wiley.

Fiedler, K., Brinkmann, B., Betsch, T., & Wild, B. (2000). A sampling approach to biases in conditional probability judgments: Beyond base rate neglect and statistical format. *Journal of Experimental Psychology: General, 129,* 399–418.

Gigerenzer, G. (1998). Ecological intelligence: An adaptation for frequencies. In D. Cummins & C. Allen (Eds.), *The evolution of mind* (pp. 9–29). New York: Oxford University Press.

Gigerenzer, G. (2002). *Reckoning with risk: Learning to live with uncertainty.* London: Penguin Books.

Gigerenzer, G., & Hoffrage, U. (1995). How to improve Bayesian reasoning without instruction: Frequency formats. *Psychological Review, 102,* 684–704.

Gigerenzer, G., & Hoffrage, U. (1999). Overcoming difficulties in Bayesian reasoning: A reply to Lewis and Keren (1999) and Mellers and McGraw (1999). *Psychological Review, 104,* 425–430.

Gigerenzer, G., Hoffrage, U., & Ebert, A. (1998). AIDS counseling for low-risk clients. *AIDS Care, 10,* 197–211.

Gigerenzer, G., Hoffrage, U., & Kleinbölting, H. (1991). Probabilistic mental models: A Brunswikian theory of confidence. *Psychological Review, 98,* 506–528.

Girotto, V., & Gonzalez, M. (2001). Solving probabilistic and statistical problems: A matter of information structure and question form. *Cognition, 78,* 247–276.

Girotto, V., & Gonzalez, M. (2002). Chances and frequencies in probabilistic reasoning: Rejoinder to Hoffrage, Gigerenzer, Krauss, and Martignon. *Cognition, 84,* 353–359.

Hamm, R. M., & Smith, S. L. (1998). The accuracy of patients' judgments of disease probability and test sensitivity and specificity. *The Journal of Family Practice, 47,* 44–52.

Hertwig, R., & Gigerenzer, G. (1999). The "conjunction fallacy" revisited: How intelligent inferences look like reasoning errors. *Journal of Behavioral Decision Making, 12,* 275–305.

Hoffrage, U., & Gigerenzer, G. (1998). Using natural frequencies to improve diagnostic inferences. *Academic Medicine, 73,* 538–540.

Hoffrage, U., & Gigerenzer, G. (2004). How to improve the diagnostic inferences of medical experts. In E. Kurz-Milcke & G. Gigerenzer (Eds.), *Experts in science and society* (pp. 249–268). New York: Kluwer Academic/Plenum Publishers.

Hoffrage, U., Gigerenzer, G., Krauss, S., & Martignon, L. (2002). Representation facilitates reasoning: What natural frequencies are and what they are not. *Cognition, 84*, 343–352.

Hoffrage, U., Lindsey, S., Hertwig, R., & Gigerenzer, G. (2000). Communicating statistical information. *Science, 290*, 2261–2262.

Johnson-Laird, P. N., Legrenzi, P., Girotto, V., Sonino-Legrenzi, M., & Caverni, J.-P. (1999). Naive probability: A mental model theory of extensional reasoning. *Psychological Review, 106*, 62–88.

Kleiter, G. D. (1994). Natural sampling: Rationality without base rates. In G. H. Fischer & D. Laming (Eds.), *Contributions to mathematical psychology, psychometrics, and methodology* (pp. 375–388). New York: Springer.

Koehler, J. J. (1996a). On conveying the probative value of DNA evidence: Frequencies, likelihood ratios, and error rates. *University of Colorado Law Review, 67*, 859–886.

Koehler, J. J. (1996b). The base rate fallacy reconsidered: Descriptive, normative and methodological challenges. *Behavioral and Brain Sciences, 19*, 1–53.

Krauss, S., & Fiedler, K. (2003). *Natural environments and Bayesian reasoning: How natural are "inverse" patterns of information?* Manuscript in preparation.

Krauss, S., Martignon, L., & Hoffrage, U. (1999). Simplifying Bayesian inference: The general case. In L. Magnani, N. Nersessian, & P. Thagard (Eds.), *Model-based reasoning in scientific discovery* (pp. 165–179). New York: Plenum Press.

Kurzenhäuser, S., & Hoffrage, U. (2002). Teaching Bayesian reasoning: An evaluation of a classroom tutorial for medical students. *Medical Teacher, 24*, 531–536.

Lewis, C., & Keren, G. (1999). On the difficulties underlying Bayesian reasoning: A comment on Gigerenzer and Hoffrage. *Psychological Review, 106*, 411–416.

Lindsey, S., Hertwig, R., & Gigerenzer, G. (2003). Communicating statistical DNA evidence. *Jurimetrics, 46*, 147–163.

Macchi, L. (2000). Partitive formulation of information in probabilistic problems: Beyond heuristics and frequency format explanations. *Organizational Behavior and Human Decision Processes, 82*, 217–236.

Macchi, L., & Mosconi, G. (1998). Computational features vs. frequentist phrasing in the base-rate fallacy. *Swiss Journal of Psychology, 57*, 79–85.

Mellers, B., & McGraw, P. (1999). How to improve Bayesian reasoning without instruction: Comment on Gigerenzer and Hoffrage. *Psychological Review, 106*, 417–424.

Sedlmeier, P., & Gigerenzer, G. (2001). Teaching Bayesian reasoning in less than two hours. *Journal of Experimental Psychology: General, 130*, 380–400.

Sloman, S. A., Over, D., Slovak, L., & Stibel, J. M. (2003). Frequency illusions and other fallacies. *Organizational Behavior and Human Decision Processes, 91*, 296–309.

Tversky, A., & Kahneman, D. (1980). Causal schemas in judgments under uncertainty. In M. Fishbein (Ed.), *Progress in social psychology* (pp. 49–72). Hillsdale, NJ: Lawrence Erlbaum Associates Inc.

Villejoubert, G., & Mandel, D. R. (2002). The inverse fallacy: An account of deviations from Bayes's theorem and the additivity principle. *Memory & Cognition, 30*, 171–178.

APPENDIX

The four problems are taken from Hoffrage and Gigerenzer (2004). We present the full text for the two versions of one diagnostic problem. For the other three problems, we present only the natural frequency version, from which the numerical information for the probability versions can easily be derived.

Problem 1: Colorectal cancer

To diagnose colorectal cancer, the haemoccult test – among others – is conducted to detect occult blood in the stool. This test is not only performed from a certain age onward, but also in a routine screening for early detection of colorectal cancer. Imagine conducting a screening using the haemoccult test in a certain region. For symptom-free people over 50 years old who participate in screening using the haemoccult test, the following information is available for this region:

Probabilities

The probability that one of these people has colorectal cancer is 0.3%. If one of these people has colorectal cancer, the probability is 50% that he or she will have a positive haemoccult test. If one of these people does *not* have colorectal cancer, the probability is 3% that he or she will still have a positive haemoccult test. Imagine a person (aged over 50, no symptoms) who has a positive haemoccult test in your screening. What is the probability that this person actually has colorectal cancer? ____%

Natural frequencies

Out of every 10,000 people, 30 have colorectal cancer. Of these 30 people with colorectal cancer, 15 will have a positive haemoccult test. Of the remaining 9970 people *without* colorectal cancer, 300 will still have a positive haemoccult test. Imagine a sample of people (aged over 50, no symptoms) who have positive haemoccult tests in your screening. How many of these people actually do have colorectal cancer? ____ of ____

Problem 2: Breast cancer

To facilitate early detection of breast cancer, from a certain age onward, women are encouraged to participate in routine screening at regular intervals, even if they have no obvious symptoms. Imagine conducting such a breast cancer screening using mammography in a certain geographical region. For symptom-free women aged 40–50 who participate in screening using mammography, the following information is available for this region:

Out of every 1000 women, 10 have breast cancer. Of these 10 women with breast cancer, 8 will have a positive mammogram. Of the remaining 990 women *without* breast cancer, 99 will still have a positive mammogram. Imagine a sample of women (aged 40–50, no symptoms) who have positive mammograms in your breast cancer screening. How many of these women actually do have breast cancer? ___ of ___

Problem 3: Ankylosing spondylitis

To diagnose ankylosing spondylitis (Bekhterev's disease), lymphocyte classification – among other tests – is conducted: For ankylosing spondylitis patients the HL-Antigen-B27 (HLA-B27) is frequently present, whereas healthy people have it comparatively seldom. Of great importance is the presence of HLA-B27 for people with nonspecific rheumatic symptoms, in which case a diagnosis of ankylosing spondylitis will be considered. In this case, lymphocyte classification will be used for differential diagnosis. Imagine conducting an HLA-B27 screening using a lymphatic classification in a certain region. For people with nonspecific rheumatic symptoms who participate in such a screening, the following information is available for this region:

Out of every 1000 people, 50 have ankylosing spondylitis. Of these 50 people with ankylosing spondylitis, 46 will have HLA-B27. Of the remaining 950 people *without* ankylosing spondylitis, 76 will still have HLA-B27. Imagine a sample of people (with nonspecific rheumatic symptoms) who have HLA-B27 in your screening. How many of these people actually do have ankylosing spondylitis? ___ of ___

Problem 4: Phenylketonuria

On the fifth day after birth, blood will be taken from all newborns in a routine screening to test for phenylketonuria (Guthrie test). Imagine working at a women's clinic. The following information is available for newborns in the region in which the clinic is situated:

Out of every 100,000 newborns, 10 have phenylketonuria. Of these 10 newborns with phenylketonuria, all 10 will have a positive Guthrie test. Of the remaining 99,990 newborns *without* phenylketonuria, 50 will still have a positive Guthrie test. Imagine a sample of newborns being delivered at your clinic who have a positive Guthrie test. How many of these newborns do actually have phenylketonuria? ___ of ___

4 Confirmation bias

*Margit E. Oswald and
Stefan Grosjean*

Creating and testing hypotheses represents a crucial feature not only of progress in science, but also in our daily lives in which we set up assumptions about reality and try to test them. However, the lay scientist stands accused of processing his or her hypotheses in such a way that he or she is biased to confirm them. "Confirmation bias" means that information is searched for, interpreted, and remembered in such a way that it systematically impedes the possibility that the hypothesis could be rejected – that is, it fosters the immunity of the hypothesis. Here, the issue is not the use of deceptive strategies to fake data, but forms of information processing that take place more or less unintentionally. In this chapter we are going to study how far the accusation of a confirmation bias in hypothesis testing is justified. But let us first try to solve two problems:

First, assume somebody presents you with the following task:

> I made up a rule for the construction of sequences of numbers. For instance, the three numbers "2–4–6" satisfy this rule. To find out what the rule is, you may construct other sets of three numbers to test your assumption about the rule I have in mind. I gave you one set of three already, and for every three numbers you come up with, I will give you feedback as to whether it satisfies my rule or not. If you are sure you have the solution, you may stop testing, and tell me what you believe the rule to be.

How would you proceed? Which sets of three numbers would you form in order to test your guesses? Please stop your reading at this point to answer this question. Thereafter, continue reading to find out whether you proceeded in manner similar to the participants in a study by Wason (1960).

Wason wanted to demonstrate in his study that most people do not proceed optimally in testing hypotheses. As to what is optimal, Wason followed the lead provided by the philosopher of science Popper (1959). According to Popper, the general mistake consists in trying to *confirm* a hypothesis rather than trying to falsify it. Participants in Wason's experiment typically proceeded in the following manner: Given the sequence of three numbers "2–4–6", they first formed a hypothesis about the rule (e.g., "a sequence of even numbers"). Then they tried to test this rule by proposing more sets of three numbers satisfying this rule (e.g., "4–8–10", "6–8–12", "20–22–24"). The feedback to these examples was always positive ("This set corresponds to my rule"). After several rounds of such testing, many participants felt secure about their hypothesis, and stopped searching since they thought they had found the correct rule. However, when they had stated the rule they assumed to be correct, they were told that they were wrong. Actually, the rule was simply "increasing numbers". Now, since the set of numbers satisfying the rule as hypothesized by the participants represents a subset of all the possible sets of three numbers satisfying the correct rule, the testing strategy of the participants led to a spurious confirmation of their hypothesis. Their testing questions were all answered in the affirmative although the rule assumed was wrong.

What was the participants' mistake? Wason argues that their error consisted in failing to test sets of three numbers that did *not* correspond to what was assumed to be the rule. Thus, a sequence like "4–5–6" would have been an appropriate test. This is because it does *not* correspond to the rule assumed by the participant at this stage, and yet it prompts a positive feedback (since it does correspond to the correct rule). Thus, participants' assumptions about the rule would have been falsified. Therefore it is not surprising that those (very few) participants who generated sequences that did not correspond to their hypothesis (a negative test strategy) needed, on average, fewer rounds of testing than others to find the correct rule.

For the second problem, imagine that you are presenting two scientific studies on the effectiveness of the death penalty to people opposed to it and to people in support of it, as Lord, Ross, and Lepper (1979) did. One of the studies you present supports the conclusion that the death penalty has a deterrent effect, and thus lowers the crime rate. The other study contradicts the effectiveness of the death penalty. Additionally, Lord et al. gave their participants clues hinting at weak points in both studies (e.g., shortcomings of the cross-sectional or longitudinal surveys used). In your opinion, how will research findings that either confirm or deny the death penalty's deterrent effects be judged, and what impact will they have on the supporters and opponents of death penalty? Would you assume that the ambiguity of the findings will lead to greater relativity in both kinds of attitudes?

As the experiment demonstrated, participants gave higher ratings to the study that supported their own opinion, while pointing to shortcomings in the research that questioned their point of view. This pattern was observed even when both studies had supposedly been carried out using the same method. This kind of *confirmation bias* led to the remarkable outcome that participants were even more convinced of their original opinion after reading both studies than before.

From the starting point provided by the studies of Wason (1960) and Lord et al. (1979), we want to discuss in this chapter two questions that represent a kind of thread weaving through the references on hypothesis testing. The first question refers to the procedure people typically use to *search* for information, as in the experiment by Wason (1960). Does this represent a confirmation bias at all, or should we concede, after careful investigation, that this procedure may not be optimal but is still a rather effective testing strategy? The second question refers to the conditions under which a confirmation bias occurs. Is the process of hypothesis confirmation caused by a strong desire for confirmation, or does it also happen in a "cold", that is, non-motivational, fashion? The assumption that individuals more or less constantly seek to confirm their hypotheses is widely shared and not only by lay people (see Bördlein, 2000). This tendency exists not merely because the possibility of rejecting the hypothesis is linked to anxiety or other negative emotions, as in the case of the death penalty (see above), but supposedly also because "cognitive processes are structured in such a way that they inevitably lead to confirmation of hypotheses" (Kunda, 1990, p. 494). However, if this were true, it would entail a serious challenge to the position that attributes to humans the ability to adapt effectively to changing environments by virtue of their evolution (Cosmides, 1989; Gigerenzer & Hug, 1992). We can thus see why different views on the question of hypothesis confirmation entail more profound epistemological problems. Until the 1960s this controversy was mainly the province of philosophers, including philosophers of science. The matter was not studied in psychology until it was introduced by Wason who, while still a student, had become fascinated by the philosophy of science taught by Karl Popper at the London School of Economics from 1946 to 1969.

CONFIRMATION BIAS OR POSITIVE TEST STRATEGY?

To be blunt, Wason (1960) was of the opinion that humans do not try at all to test their hypotheses critically but rather to *confirm* them. This position did not remain unchallenged. Klayman and Ha (1987), for example, presented an approach that disputed the view of humans as "hypotheses confirmers". They showed that the behaviour of the participant in the Wason experiment described above may be interpreted as a "positive test strategy" (see Text box 4.1). The positive test strategy is something different from the attempt to confirm hypotheses, or even to "immunize" them against rejection.

The positive test strategy (PTS) restricts the exploration space: A fundamental problem in testing hypotheses consists in the fact that exploration spaces can become very large if all the cases are considered that might be relevant to the hypothesis. A systematic search through the "whole universe" for events that could falsify the hypothesis can, from a pragmatic point of view, scarcely be accomplished. In this case, the PTS provides a heuristic that aids in restricting the exploration space to those cases that

> **Text box 4.1** A definition of the positive test strategy (PTS)
>
> We propose that many phenomena of human hypothesis testing can be understood in terms of a general *positive test strategy*. According to this strategy, you test a hypothesis by examining instances in which the property or event is expected to occur (to see if it does occur), or by examining instances in which it is known to have occurred (to see if the hypothesized conditions prevail).
>
> (Klayman & Ha, 1987, p. 212)

have some probability of being the relevant ones. Let us take, as an example, the hypothesis "John always becomes aggressive when he is provoked". To test this hypothesis, we could proceed according to the PTS. In this case, we would look for occasions on which John was provoked, in order to see whether he actually reacted aggressively. However, we could also look for occasions on which John did not become aggressive, in order to determine whether he had previously been provoked. Such a search strategy is called a *negative test strategy*, since the *non-occurrence* of the critical event (i.e., John has not been provoked) would confirm the hypothesis.

In this example, the choice of a PTS is very rational. It restricts the exploration space to relevant events without making us the victim of a confirmation strategy: It is always possible to identify occasions on which John was provoked without reacting aggressively. Without any doubt, *falsification* of the hypothesis would be possible. The choice of a *negative test strategy* could become very cumbersome, in this case. The number of cases where John does *not* react aggressively could be very large – moreover, it would not be very conclusive if it only revealed that he was not provoked on these occasions. Only occasions on which John did not react aggressively although he was provoked would count. However, if we hoped to find such events by considering all possible instances in which John did not react aggressively, we would be performing the equivalent of a search for a needle in a haystack. A PTS would enable us to find the "needle" much more easily since we would not have to search the whole "haystack". Here we search explicitly for occasions on which he was provoked – and, as said before, it could result in discovering that he did not become aggressive at all. Following the argument advanced by Klayman and Ha (1987), the PTS as such is not a biasing one. Depending on the structure of the task at hand, the PTS may well result in a falsification of the hypothesis. However, if our task is one in which all events satisfying the current hypothesis (rule) represent a genuine subset of the set of those events that satisfy the correct hypothesis (rule) searched for – as in the 2–4–6 experiment by Wason (1960) – then the PTS does lead to a confirmation bias.

Klayman and Ha (1987) are not the only authors to have critically

Confirmation bias 83

discussed the proposition that people only try to confirm their hypotheses. For example, Trope and Bassok (1982) note that we are justified to call a PTS a confirmation-seeking strategy only if the diagnosticity of the test is deficient. What does that mean? The assumption that a person is, for example, characterized by a certain trait such as honesty or introversion may be tested by asking questions referring to that trait. (For simplicity, we will restrict ourselves in the following to questions that can be answered by "Yes" or "No".) Now, questions that correspond to a PTS are worded in such a way that a "Yes" would confirm the hypothesis. Is it not thinkable that persons select such questions that lead to "Yes" answers independently of whether or not the hypothesis is true? Let us assume a woman who wants to test the hypothesis that her new partner is introverted. To do so, she asks the question "Do you read books occasionally?" and he replies "Yes", confirming her hypothesis. It becomes clear that this is a spurious confirmation when we admit that extraverts do also read books occasionally. Following Trope and Bassok (1982), we could call such a test strategy a "non-diagnostic strategy" since a "Yes" answer is likely both if the hypothesis is true and if its alternative is true. In contrast to this strategy, Trope and Bassok defined a "diagnostic strategy" (see Text box 4.2).

Text box 4.2 A definition of the diagnostic strategy

In this diagnostic strategy, the lay interviewer searches his or her stored representations of personality traits for behavioral features that are distinctively associated *either* with the hypothesized trait category *or* with its alternative(s).
(Trope & Bassok, 1982, p. 561)

Trope and Bassok (1982) ran experiments to solve the problem of whether persons prefer a positive over a negative test strategy even if the questions belonging to the PTS are non-diagnostic. Participants had to select questions in order to test a hypothesis about a person who was previously unknown to them. The result was that diagnostic questions were preferred in all cases, even if they represented instances of a negative test strategy. Devine, Hirt, and Gehrke (1990) replicated these results. Taken together, the studies referred to above suggest that persons prefer diagnostic questions but, whenever possible, they like to phrase their questions in the form of a PTS.

The experiment proposed below illustrates a third condition that may contribute to situations where the application of a PTS leads to a confirmation bias. In these cases, the person searching for information applies predominantly a PTS, and this biased way of interrogation influences the behaviour of the interaction partner. The experiment can be run in a classroom or lecture. It was inspired by the studies of Snyder and Swann (1978) and of Zuckermann, Knee, Hodgins, and Miyake (1995).

84 *Oswald and Grosjean*

However, before we come to the proposal of a classroom experiment, let us summarize those cases in which the application of a PTS may lead to a confirmation bias (see Text box 4.3).

Text box 4.3 Cases in which the positive test strategy (PTS) may lead to a confirmation bias

1. If the correct hypothesis (rule) is *more general* than the one assumed by the person. In this case, necessarily all events corresponding to the hypothesis (rule) of the person also correspond to the correct hypothesis (rule) – as in Wason's (1960) 2–4–6 experiment.
2. If, in addition, the questions asked are *non-diagnostic* and very likely to be answered in the affirmative, independently of the truth of the hypothesis (Devine et al., 1990; Trope & Bassok, 1982).
3. If the interrogation behaviour influences the interaction partner in a way that he or she responds affirmatively (Snyder, Tanke, & Berscheid, 1977; Zuckerman et al., 1995).

AN EXPERIMENT ON THE INFLUENCE OF INTERROGATION BEHAVIOUR

Two groups of participants are supposed to test a social hypothesis (one group tests a target person, the interviewee, as to whether he or she is introverted, and the second group whether he or she is extraverted). Text box 4.4 provides the necessary procedural details to run an appropriate classroom study. The following results are expected:

1. The interviewers test the hypothesis assigned to them by means of a positive test strategy.
2. The interviewee behaves affirmatively (i.e., replies predominantly "Yes").
3. The interviewers in each group give significantly different ratings to the personality of the interviewee with respect to the introversion–extraversion dimension and in the direction of their respective initial hypotheses.

If the results come out as expected, they can be interpreted as follows: The participants applied a PTS in testing the social hypothesis. As we have seen above, this is not yet confirmation bias as such (since the interviewee could very well answer "No", thus rejecting or questioning the hypothesis). However, it is more probable that the interviewee responds affirmatively. According to Zuckerman et al. (1995), this may be due to a selective memory process (see below), or additionally to a social norm according to which "Yes" answers appear more friendly. Now, the confirmation bias occurs

Text box 4.4 Details of the classroom demonstration

Procedure

A person (e.g., an acquaintance of the experimenter) plays the role of the "interviewee". This person should be completely unknown to the participants. It is the task of the interviewee to answer the question put to him or her with a "Yes" or a "No". The interviewee must not hear the instructions given to the other participants.

Before giving the instructions, the class is split into two groups. One stays in the room while the other is sent to another room (not the same room as the interviewee). Both groups are given different instructions: One is asked to test the hypothesis that the interviewee is *extraverted*. To test this, all participants in the group are asked to write a common list of questions they are going to ask the interviewee, and these must be questions that can clearly be answered "Yes" or "No". The other group is asked to test the hypothesis that the interviewee is *introverted*. They, too, are asked to write down the questions to be posed to the interviewee later on, and again these must be clearly answerable with "Yes" or "No".

The participants are allowed about 10 minutes to construct and write down their questions. Thereafter, the interviewee is called into the classroom where only one of the groups is present. The interviewee is ignorant with respect to the instructions given to the two groups. He or she is told to answer questions exclusively with a "Yes" or a "No", and make no further explanations or statements – if necessary, the experimenter has to remind him or her of this instruction. Now the first group is to put questions they have devised and written down in advance. This task is limited to about 10 minutes. During this time, the experimenter records:

1. How many questions are asked, and how many of these are instances of a positive test strategy (all questions that are phrased in such a way that a "Yes" reply would confirm the hypothesis count as instances of a positive test strategy).
2. How often the interviewee replies "Yes".

After the time is up, the experimenter interrupts the interview (whether or not all the questions have been put), and asks the participants to rate the interviewee on a 7-point rating scale from −3 to +3, marked at the ends as "introverted" and "extraverted". The scale may be projected as a transparency by an overhead projector, and the participants are asked to write down the number they would assign.

Following this, the other group is called back to the classroom. Now it is their turn to ask the interviewee the questions they have prepared. The first group may remain present but is urged not to talk during this procedure. The process is exactly the same as before. Finally, the second group is also asked to rate the interviewee on the introversion–extraversion scale.

Thereafter, the following three dependent variables are calculated: (1) the proportion of questions that correspond to a positive test strategy in each group; (2) the proportion of "Yes" replies by the interviewee in each group; (3) the mean ratings of the interviewers on the introversion–extraversion scale in each group. To analyze the data of the classroom experiment proposed above, chi-square tests with $df = 1$ for 2×2 contingency tables could be applied, for Variable 1 with two columns for the groups and two rows for PTS questions and non-PTS questions, and for Variable 2 with two columns for the groups and two rows for "Yes" and for "No" replies. For Variable 3, the difference between the mean ratings of the two groups could be tested by means of a t-test for independent samples, with $df = (n_1 + n_2 - 2)$.

Results

Based on results of similar studies (e.g., Snyder et al., 1977; Zuckerman et al., 1995), the main findings should be as follows:

1. The questions asked correspond predominantly to a positive test strategy (here: Significantly more than half of the questions are phrased in such a way that an affirmative reply would confirm the respective hypotheses).
2. The interviewee responds in the affirmative (here: More than half of the replies are "Yes").
3. The interviewers treat the responses of the interviewee as a confirmation of their hypothesis (here: The group testing the extraversion hypothesis rates the interviewee as significantly more extraverted than the other group testing the introversion hypothesis).

because the interviewer is not aware of this acquiescence tendency – and thus derives unjustified conclusions from the replies of the interviewee. This way a "self-fulfilling prophecy" is generated.

However, we should also consider possible methodological problems: Could it be that questions about extraverted forms of behaviour might differentiate better between introversion and extraversion than do questions about introverted behaviour (see Devine et al., 1990)? Does the result depend on how introverted or extraverted the interviewee is in reality? And does it make sense to test the target person's introversion/extraversion in advance?

EVIDENCE FOR A "TRUE" CONFIRMATION STRATEGY

Since Klayman and Ha (1987), several other authors have postulated that PTS as such is not a confirmation bias. In spite of this, an astonishing confusion is still to be found in the literature. There are two possible reasons for this: (1) Wason (1960, 1968) publicized the concept of "confirmation bias" in his original studies, and therefore this phrase is often employed although what is actually intended is a PTS (see Devine et al., 1990). In those cases, though, some authors additionally note that besides the PTS there also exists a "true confirmation bias" (see Poletiek, 2001). (2) Some authors seem to have real problems differentiating between a confirmation bias and a PTS. According to the PTS, persons have the tendency to ask questions in such a way that their hypothesis *would* be confirmed *if* the answer was affirmative. Those authors seem to miss the conditional clause here and transform it instead into propositions like: "Persons have the tendency to seek only for confirmatory evidence" (Doherty, Mynatt, Tweney, & Schiavo, 1979, p. 113). Although the two statements differ only in a few words, they mean totally different things.

The discussion so far has shown that it is not at all easy to demonstrate a confirmation strategy because we always have to prove that the respective procedure *systematically impedes a possible rejection* of the hypothesis. For this reason, it may be justified to ask if it is possible at all to decide in an unambiguous way whether a certain strategy represents a confirmation strategy. We intend now to elaborate on this question, and will include strategies in addition to those concerned with information search (see Text box 4.5).

Text box 4.5 Three ways of introducing confirmation bias

In addition to strategies applied in the *search* for new information (information-gathering strategies), there are other possibilities not yet discussed here for immunizing hypotheses. In the process of remembering (information-recollection strategies) people may selectively *recall* mainly such information that would confirm their hypotheses. This contributes to a considerable degree to a resistance to change. Also, in the process of interpretation (strategies of information interpretation), persons may systematically *re-interpret* existing information contradicting their hypothesis, or attribute less importance to it than to confirming information, in spite of the objectively equal value of each kind of information.

Based on the discussion presented so far, we may talk of a true confirmation strategy if we can show that, in the search for information, the test (the question asked) will very likely confirm the hypothesis (i.e., be answered affirmatively), and does so independent of the truth of the respective hypotheses. Studies previously undertaken have demonstrated, however, that persons – even children (see Samuels & McDonald, 2002) – are seldom so foolish as to apply such a worthless search strategy.

A true confirmation strategy is also involved if another person's opinion is already known and if it can be assumed that questions will be answered according to one's expectation. Thus, in daily life people often ask like-minded acquaintances for their opinion. Whether, and under what conditions, people systematically search for such sources of information already knowing that a confirmation of their initial assumption is likely, has been little studied to date. The exceptions are those studies inspired by *dissonance theory* in which the phenomenon of "post-decisional regret" has been explored (Frey, 1981; Gagné & Lydon, 2001). According to this theory, people are inclined to avoid sources of information that could question the quality and correctness of a decision that, once made, they are hardly likely to revoke, for example, the purchase of an automobile. However, in such cases it is clear that individuals are no longer neutral with respect to the outcome of their search for information, that is, their starting point is not a "cold" hypothesis. But even in emotionally less involving situations people may search for confirming information, as Betsch, Haberstroh, Glöckner, Haar, and Fiedler (2000) demonstrated in a recent study. If participants have established a *decision routine* in one task, and are expected to test this procedure in another context, they are inclined to maintain this routine. They search mainly for information that can a priori be assumed to favour the routine applied so far.

With respect to *selective remembering*, it has to be said that in recall there seems to be no general advantage for hypothesis-confirming information over hypothesis-contradicting information. Many approaches, inspired by schema theory (Neisser, 1976), assume that schema-consistent information, that is, information consistent with expectations, is not only encoded more easily but also recalled more easily than inconsistent information (Taylor & Crocker, 1981). Other approaches, such as Woll and Graesser's (1982) "schema pointer plus tag model", emphasize that hypothesis-contradicting information will be particularly salient, and thus may be processed more extensively or in a more detailed manner. This kind of processing might make expectancy-disconfirming information particularly likely to be encoded and remembered – perhaps even better than expectancy-congruent material. For both approaches there exists extensive empirical evidence, as is clearly demonstrated in the meta-analysis published by Stangor and McMillan (1992).

Whether the results point to a general advantage in recalling consistent information (congruency effect) or inconsistent information (incongruency effect) seems to depend essentially on the method applied to measure recall. Moreover, an advantage for the recall of consistent information seems to depend on certain additional conditions: (a) Individuals have already established hypotheses, (b) these hypotheses refer to social groups (stereotypes) and not to individuals, and (c) there exists a temporal delay between the processing of stimulus information and the recall or judgement. How far the advantage in recall of congruent data is related to the fact that the hypotheses are motivationally supported was not revealed by this particular meta-analysis.

However, several studies demonstrate that selective, directed recall occurs when people consider a particular personality trait as especially desirable. Sanitioso, Kunda, and Fong (1990) convinced their students in one of the conditions in their experiment that extraverted persons are particularly successful in their academic and professional careers, and in the other condition that this was instead true for introverted persons. In addition, participants were asked to think of possible reasons for this relation between personality and success. Later on, in a seemingly unrelated study, they were asked to list autobiographical memories reflecting their own standing on the introversion–extraversion dimension. The introvert-success induced participants (a) were more likely to list introverted memories first, (b) generated introverted memories faster, and (c) tended to list overall more introverted memories than did the extravert-success induced participants. The "search tends to be biased, so that memories consistent with the desired trait are more likely to be accessed than memories that are inconsistent with it" (Sanitioso et al., 1990, p. 239). The authors could not find any comparable effect when the two personality traits were instead activated by semantic priming. The enhanced accessibility seems to be due to motivational factors rather than to priming of memory.

The other possible means to confirm hypotheses identified above refers to the case where a hypothesis tester gathers information (strategy of information interpretation) and biases the interpretation of that information so that the hypothesis appears to be true. Systematic preservation of the original hypothesis could occur by assessing the expectancy-congruent information systematically to be *more important* than the incongruent information, or by *increasing confidence* in the hypothesis on the basis of congruent information more than such confidence is decreased by incongruent information (cf. Bacon, 1620/1990, p. 109). Of course, here we must assume that the two kinds of information do not differ in their diagnostic relevance.

A difference in the weighting of congruent and incongruent information was clearly demonstrated in the already cited study on one's attitude towards the death penalty (Lord et al., 1979). Participants evaluated information incongruent with their attitude much more critically than congruent information even when both kinds were acquired by the same method. Of course, we can assume in this study that attitudes towards the death penalty are not emotionally neutral, so that the confirmation bias may have been caused motivationally. But it can also be shown with fairly "neutral" hypotheses that data consistent with the hypothesis are accorded a higher weight than inconsistent data (Gadenne & Oswald, 1986; Slowiaczek, Klayman, Sherman, & Skov, 1992). In a study by Gadenne and Oswald (1986), for example, participants were told a crime story in which a theft is committed under circumstances to be clarified. Thereafter, the participants were asked to rate the importance of statements (of medium diagnosticity) pointing to or arguing against the possibility that a certain person, A, committed the theft. Information implicating this suspect was significantly more strongly weighted if participants had already adopted the hypothesis that

A was the offender (such adoption being induced in the experiment) than if this was not the case. Given information exonerating the suspect, the induction of a hypothesis about the identity of the offender had no effect on the weighting of the evidence.

It is not yet clear what causes the bias in weighting of data congruent with the hypothesis. Some evidence suggests that participants confronted with an unexpected event may well ask whether this might be "the exception to the rule", while they simply accept expected events without further questioning as to whether the event might also be compatible with the alternative hypothesis (Kruglanski & Mayseless, 1988). However, as long as the alternative hypothesis itself, or the possibility that the event could be explained by an alternative hypothesis, is not considered, an overestimation of the diagnostic relevance of events congruent with the hypothesis occurs very rapidly.

CAN WE ALWAYS ASSUME A CONFIRMATION BIAS IN THE CASE OF MOTIVATIONALLY SUPPORTED HYPOTHESES?

The analyses reported so far made clear that persons do not principally proceed in a confirmatory fashion when testing a hypothesis. Does this also hold for motivationally supported hypotheses, that is, those hypotheses with respect to which there are positive or negative emotions depending on the outcome of the test? Can we assume that confirmatory strategies are in general applied to testing hypotheses, given the assumption that people are generally motivated to seek positive emotions, and avoid negative ones? Although this will often be true – many studies (e.g., Trope & Liberman, 1996, p. 258) and our daily life provide corroboration here – we will see nonetheless that the answer is not so simple. Obviously, it is not always possible to simply believe what we want to believe.

In this context, Scott-Kakures (2001) drew attention to those many situations in daily life where just the opposite phenomenon occurs, namely a tendency to confirm *undesired* or unwelcome assumptions. Thus, people are not infrequently inclined towards intensive testing of assumptions like "I forgot to turn off the tap in the kitchen when I left home", "The strange red spots on my back might be an indication of cancer", or "My daughter Sabine overestimates her capabilities and will endanger herself mountain climbing". In such cases, it may well be that those events are systematically remembered, or that information is searched for which would increase the probability of the undesired hypothesis rather than decrease it. This tendency to seek confirmation of the negative, however, is incompatible with the general statement that hypothesis confirmation occurs because the hypothesis is desired.

If the confirmation of a hypothesis is desired or is associated with positive emotions, persons will be motivated to use a confirmation strategy. However, they will not do so at the risk of a *spurious confirmation* if this error turns out to be a costly one. Thus it is certainly desirable for most people to confirm the hypothesis that they are healthy. However, if this assumption is based on an error, this would result in the consequence that they erroneously feel safe, and fail to have preventive check-ups which could save them from serious illness. Stated differently, we could say that people generally avoid confirming an undesirable hypothesis, but this could lead to still more negative consequences if they fall victim to self-deceit by erroneously rejecting the hypothesis. In such cases it is possible that people do not readily reject an undesirable hypothesis (see above), nor easily accept a desirable hypothesis. These ideas have been elaborated by Trope and Liberman (1996) who base their theory of hypotheses testing on essential assumptions developed by Friedrich (1993) and Tetlock (1992). A central assumption in their model is that people seek to avoid the possible costs of errors (see Text box 4.6). What does that mean?

Text box 4.6 Possible errors in deciding on hypotheses

Independent of whether we accept or reject a hypothesis, it may be true or not. Thus, with respect to a hypothesis, there are in addition to its correct acceptance and its correct rejection, two kinds of erroneous decisions: acceptance of a hypothesis even though it is not true (error of commission), and rejection of a hypothesis even though it is true (error of omission).

Both kinds of erroneous decisions may carry certain costs. For example, if you do not return to your apartment in spite of your assumption that you forgot to turn off the tap, you risk considerable damage. But if you return, you may risk missing an appointment. How long do you deliberate over this problem, searching your memory for further clues that could inform you whether you turned off the tap or not? How do you weight the various clues you come up with? How sure do you have to be with respect to the correctness of your assumption before you decide to proceed to your appointment or alternatively to return home?

Whether you deliberate over the possibilities for a long period at all depends, according to Trope and Liberman (1996), on your estimated costs of the alternative, possibly erroneous decisions. With higher perceived costs of an erroneous decision, people are more motivated to test their hypothesis. The asymmetry of costs with respect to the two kinds of error determines whether data in favour of or against the hypothesis are weighted differently, or are recalled differently, and whether the hypothesis is accepted or rejected more or less rapidly, given the same information. In our example, the cost of an erroneous rejection of the hypothesis (tap was not turned off) is substantially higher than that of an erroneous acceptance; therefore the hypothesis should not easily be rejected. Cues to the possible neglect of the tap may be preferentially remembered and/or weighted more strongly than contrary cues. In addition, you may need many more hints as to the incorrectness of the assumption before you are ready to reject it (high rejection threshold). This means, in other words, that given an equal number of cues of equal quality for and against the hypothesis, you are more rapidly convinced of the correctness of the assumption already favoured than of its opposite.

Finally, let us consider why it is, as Trope and Liberman (1996) suggested, that the testing of a desired hypothesis is relatively often accompanied by a confirmation bias. In their view, desired hypotheses may be particularly prone to a confirmation strategy because the error of a faulty acceptance (e.g., a person is actually not as intelligent, beautiful, or moral as they think themself to be) is generally associated with small costs: To retain a more positive self-image than is realistic, or to believe that friends are more altruistic and honest than they actually are, involves a lower cost than to become dismayed because of an unrealistic negative self-image, or to lose friends because of chronic distrust (see Text box 4.7). In addition, Trope and Liberman (1996, p. 258) assumed that we probably regard desired hypotheses as more likely than undesired ones because we think of events that confirm the desired hypothesis more easily and rapidly than negative events. In this respect this approach is consistent with the findings of Sanitioso et al.'s (1990) study reviewed above.

Text box 4.7 Confirmation bias with motivationally supported hypotheses

People seem generally to be inclined to proceed in a confirmatory fashion with respect to motivationally supported hypotheses. However, according to Trope and Liberman (1996), if an erroneous *acceptance* of a desired hypothesis were to be associated with high costs, no confirmation bias should occur. And if the costs of an erroneous *rejection* are high, persons might even be inclined to confirm undesired hypothesis (as in the example with the tap left on).

FINAL REMARKS

In daily life, people not only test their hypotheses by *searching for new information* that could support or invalidate their hypothesis. They also try to *evaluate* existing evidence, and to *remember* information from past events that is congruent or incongruent with the hypothesis (see also Chapter 10 on anchoring effects for a similar approach). Of all these phases of information processing – searching, interpretation, and remembering – the confirmation strategy has been studied mainly in the context of information search. Surprisingly, just there it has hardly been proven.

People do indeed search for results that *would* confirm their hypothesis *if* the corresponding results could be found. Klayman and Ha (1987) distinguished this heuristic from a confirmation bias and called it a "positive test strategy (PTS)". A PTS as such does not necessarily lead to preservation of the hypothesis, since the person doing the testing exerts only a restricted influence on the outcome of the search for new information, and is moreover inclined predominantly to ask diagnostically relevant questions. In effect, we have here an effective search strategy which should not be changed. People would, generally speaking, be completely lost if their preference was to search for results that they do *not* expect according to their hypothesis (negative test strategy). The real problem is not that people apply a PTS but that they often entertain only their starting hypothesis. In order to avoid spurious confirmation, people would be better off considering alternative explanations even in the case of events that obviously seem to confirm the hypothesis they have in mind at the outset. This would lead them more or less automatically to apply a PTS original hypothesis, and also to the alternative (cf. Oswald, in press).

A true confirmation bias seems to occur primarily when the hypotheses tested are *already established*, or are *motivationally supported*. In general, we may say that the confirmation bias consists in favouring expectancy-congruent information over incongruent information. This may happen in different ways: (a) memories congruent with the hypothesis are more likely to be accessed than memories that are incongruent with it; (b) undue weight is given to the importance of congruent information, possibly because of the concentration on the hypothesis, and the neglect of alternative explanations; (c) those sources with information that could reject the hypothesis are avoided, provided that the person knows a priori the opinion of the source.

According to the model offered by Trope and Liberman (1996), however, a confirmation bias will not occur even with established and motivationally supported hypotheses if the perceived costs of believing in a hypothesis erroneously are relatively high. People in general are inclined to entertain desired hypotheses, such as having an unrealistic positive self-image (see Chapter 14 on the Pollyanna principle). But they will not be trapped into confirming strategies if they become aware that an overestimation of their self-image will cause more serious problems than its possible underestimation.

SUMMARY

- Whenever people search for, interpret or remember information in such a way that the corroboration of a hypothesis becomes likely, independent of its truth, they show a confirmation bias.
- A confirmation bias happens, for example, if – in a systematic fashion –

hypothesis-confirming information receives more weight, is evaluated less critically, or is better remembered than disconfirming data.
- A positive test strategy (PTS) should not be confused with a confirmation bias, because in many cases this heuristic allows the falsification of the hypothesis.
- Asking mainly questions that *would* confirm rather than disconfirm one's hypothesis, *if* answered in the affirmative (= PTS), seems to be almost unavoidable. However, one could try to ask not only in the light of one's hypothesis but also of at least one alternative explanation.
- Testing desired hypotheses, for example, that my friend is trustworthy, may be particularly prone to a confirmation bias. One reason might be that their erroneous acceptance is generally associated with smaller costs than their erroneous rejection: To believe that friends are more trustworthy than they are involves a lower cost than to lose friends because of chronic distrust.

FURTHER READING

An excellent overview about research on confirmation bias, but also an interesting theoretical approach, is given by Trope and Liberman (1996). The question of whether it is irrational of anxious people to stick to undesired hypotheses, is addressed by Scott-Kakures (2001). A brilliant critique of whether the results of Wason (1960, 1968) can be considered as a proof that people are generally prone to confirm their beliefs is given by Klayman and Ha (1987). See also Poletiek (2001). A nice experiment which shows that even young children have an astonishing capability to ask diagnostically relevant questions is presented by Samuels and McDonald (2002).

REFERENCES

Bacon, F. (1620/1990). *Neues Organon: lateinisch-deutsch* [Novum organum]. Hamburg: Meiner.

Betsch, T., Haberstroh, S., Glöckner, A., Haar, T., & Fiedler, K. (2000). The effects of routine strength on adaption and information search in recurrent decision making. *Organizational Behavior and Human Decision Processes, 84*, 23–53.

Bördlein, C. (2000). Die Bestätigungstendenz. Warum wir (subjektiv) immer Recht behalten [The confirmation bias. Why we are always right (subjectively)]. *Skeptiker, 3*, 132–138.

Cosmides, L. (1989). The logic of social exchange: Has natural selection shaped how humans reason? Studies with the Wason selection task. *Cognition, 31*, 187–276.

Devine, P. G., Hirt, E. R., & Gehrke, E. M. (1990). Diagnostic and confirmation strategies in trait hypothesis testing. *Journal of Personality and Social Psychology, 58*, 952–963.

Doherty, M. E., Mynatt, C. R., Tweney, R. D., & Schiavo, M. D. (1979). Pseudodiagnosticity. *Acta Psychologica*, *43*, 111–121.

Frey, D. (1981). *Informationssuche und Informationsbewertung bei Entscheidungen* [Information seeking and information evaluation in decision making]. Bern: Huber.

Friedrich, J. (1993). Primary error detection and minimization (PEDMIN) strategies in social cognition: A reinterpretation of confirmation bias phenomena. *Psychological Review*, *100*, 298–319.

Gadenne, V., & Oswald, M. (1986). Entstehung und Veränderung von Bestätigungstendenzen beim Testen von Hypothesen [Formation and alteration of confirmatory tendencies during the testing of hypotheses]. *Zeitschrift für Experimentelle und Angewandte Psychologie*, *33*, 360–374.

Gagné, F. M., & Lydon, J. E. (2001). Mind-set and close relationships: When bias leads to (in)accurate predictions. *Journal of Personality and Social Psychology*, *81*, 85–96.

Gigerenzer, G., & Hug, K. (1992). Domain-specific reasoning: Social contracts, cheating, and perspective change. *Cognition*, *43*, 127–171.

Klayman, J., & Ha, Y. (1987). Confirmation, disconfirmation, and information in hypothesis testing. *Psychological Review*, *94*, 211–228.

Kruglanski, A. W., & Mayseless, O. (1988). Contextual effects in hypothesis testing: The role of competing alternatives and epistemic motivations. *Social Cognition*, *6*, 1–20.

Kunda, Z. (1990). The case for motivated reasoning. *Psychological Bulletin*, *108*, 480–498.

Lord, C. G., Ross, L., & Lepper, M. R. (1979). Biased assimilation and attitude polarization: The effects of prior theories on subsequently considered evidence. *Journal of Personality and Social Psychology*, *37*, 2098–2109.

Neisser, U. (1976). *Cognition and reality*. San Francisco, CA: W. H. Freeman.

Oswald, M. E. (in press). When hypotheses override therapists' information about the client. In F. Caspar (Ed.), *The inner processes of psychotherapists. Innovations in clinical training*. Oxford: Oxford University Press.

Poletiek, F. H. (2001). *Hypothesis-testing behaviour*. Philadelphia, PA: Psychology Press.

Popper, K. R. (1959/1974). *The logic of scientific discovery* (3rd Ed.). London: Hutchinson.

Samuels, M. C., & McDonald, J. (2002). Elementary school-age children's capacity to choose positive diagnostic and negative diagnostic tests. *Child Development*, *73*, 857–866.

Sanitioso, R., Kunda, Z., & Fong, G. T. (1990). Motivated recruitment of autobiographical memories. *Journal of Personality and Social Psychology*, *59*, 229–241.

Scott-Kakures, D. (2001). High anxiety: Barnes on what moves the unwelcome believer. *Philosophical Psychology*, *14*, 313–326.

Slowiaczek, L. M., Klayman, J., Sherman, S. J., & Skov, R. B. (1992). Information selection and use in hypothesis testing: What is a good question, and what is a good answer? *Memory & Cognition*, *20*, 392–405.

Snyder, M., & Swann, W. B., Jr. (1978). Hypothesis-testing in social interaction. *Journal of Personality and Social Psychology*, *36*, 1202–1212.

Snyder, M., Tanke, E., & Berscheid, E. (1977). Social perception and interpersonal behavior: On the self-fulfilling nature of social stereotypes. *Journal of Personality and Social Psychology*, *35*, 656–666.

Stangor, C., & McMillan D. (1992). Memory for expectancy-congruent and expectancy-inconcruent information: A review of the social and social developmental literatures. *Psychological Bulletin, 111*, 42–61.

Taylor, S. E., & Crocker, J. (1981). Schematic bases of social information processing. In E. T. Higgins, C. P. Herman, & M. P. Zanna (Eds.), *Social cognition: The Ontario symposium* (Vol. 1, pp. 89–134). Hillsdale, NJ: Lawrence Erlbaum Associates Inc.

Tetlock, P. E. (1992). The impact of accountability on judgment and choice: Toward a social contingency model. In M. P. Zanna (Ed.), *Advances in experimental social psychology* (Vol. 25, pp. 331–376). New York: Academic Press.

Trope, Y., & Bassok, M. (1982). Information-gathering strategies in hypothesis-testing. *Journal of Experimental Social Psychology, 19*, 560–576.

Trope, Y., & Liberman, A. (1996). Social hypothesis testing: Cognitive and motivational mechanisms. In E. T. Higgins & A. W. Kruglanski (Eds.), *Social psychology. Handbook of basic principles* (pp. 239–270). New York: Guilford Press.

Wason, P. C. (1960). On the failure to eliminate hypothesis in a conceptual task. *Quarterly Journal of Experimental Psychology, 14*, 129–140.

Wason, P. C. (1968). Reasoning about a rule. *Quarterly Journal of Experimental Psychology, 20*, 273–281.

Woll, S. B., & Graesser A. C. (1982). Memory discrimination for information typical or atypical of person schemata. *Social Cognition, 1*, 287–310.

Zuckermann, M., Knee, C. R., Hodgins, H. S., & Miyake, K. (1995). Hypothesis confirmation: The joint effect of positive test strategy and aquiescence response set. *Journal of Personality and Social Psychology, 68*, 52–60.

5 Illusory correlation

Klaus Fiedler

As organisms learn to predict and control their environment through serial observation, they have to assess the correlations that exist between important stimulus events. What signals accompany danger and safety? What behaviours are forbidden or allowed? Which traits characterize which social group? Or more generally, which causes precede which effects or consequences? The ability to figure out the correlations that hold between signals and their meanings, behaviours and reinforcements, groups and social attributes, or causes and effects, is a basic module of adaptive intelligence.

THE PHENOMENON OF ILLUSORY CORRELATION

If this central ability is impaired or distorted, organisms can be misled into erroneous predictions and decisions with detrimental consequences. For instance, the failure to learn which stimuli feel pleasant versus painful can cause much discomfort in a young child; erroneously inferred correlations between symptoms and diseases can lead to false medical diagnosis. However, although the accurate detection of environmental correlations appears to be crucial for survival and everyday problem solving, the experimental evidence is split. While many experiments testify to humans' and animals' high sensitivity to differential event frequencies (Alloy & Abramson, 1979; Malmi, 1986), an even larger body of evidence is concerned with subjective correlation assessments that deviate more or less markedly from the correlation actually encountered (Crocker, 1981; Fiedler, 2000). Such an illusion – seeing a correlation that was not really there – is termed an "illusory correlation". More generally, the term applies not only to overestimations of zero correlations but to all kinds of systematic deviations or biases in subjective assessment.

Some prominent examples help to circumscribe the phenomenon. In a classical study on illusory correlations in diagnostic reasoning, Chapman and Chapman (1967) showed their participants a series of draw-a-person test pictures, each with an indication of the problem that characterized the person who had allegedly drawn the picture. Participants persistently believed they had seen correlations that conformed to common diagnostic stereotypes. For instance, they reported that patients with worries about manliness had often produced drawings with pronounced shoulders, whereas patients characterized as suspicious would often highlight the eyes in the drawings, although in fact all combinations appeared equally often. In a similar vein, Hamilton and Rose (1980) used a list of persons described by their vocational categories and their personality traits. Even though all vocational groups appeared equally often with all traits, participants believed they had seen predominantly expected pairings, such as accountant/perfectionist or doctor/helpful.

While the illusions obtained in these two studies obviously originate in the participants' pre-experimental expectancies, or stereotypical knowledge, other variants of illusory correlations can be found when prior beliefs are ruled out by the use of neutral or meaningless stimulus materials. Such a task was used by Kao and Wasserman (1993), as described in Text box 5.1.

Text box 5.1 Experiment conducted by Kao and Wasserman (1993)

The experimental task referred to an unknown exotic plant, the Lanyu. Participants were asked to rate the "value of a fertilizer in promoting the Lanyu to bloom". They were fed with information about the frequencies with which the effect (blooming) occurred or did not occur when the cause (fertilizer) was given or not. When the rate or relative frequency of blooming was the same in the presence and in the absence of fertilizing, the causal influence was judged to be positive when the absolute frequency of blooming in the presence of the fertilizer was high and negative when the absolute frequency of this combination was low. Thus, if the frequencies of blooming and not-blooming were 19 and 7, both with and without the fertilizer, the perceived influence was positive, but if the frequencies were 7 and 19, the perceived influence was negative. Likewise, the perceived influence was positive (negative) if an equal relative rate of blooming and not blooming was absolutely higher (lower) in the presence than in the absence of the cause. The common denominator of these findings is that one event combination, the co-occurrence of a present cause with a present effect, receives the highest weight in correlation assessment.

Finally, consider the famous set finding by Hamilton and Gifford (1976) described in Text box 5.2. Suffice it to mention briefly that Hamilton and Gifford's (1976) finding, which was replicated in countless other experiments, has obvious implications for the creation of minority derogation and discrimination.

The classical examples provided thus far represent three major classes of illusory correlation phenomena: expectancy-based illusory correlations, illusions arising from unequal weighting of information, and illusory correlations reflecting selective attention and encoding.

Text box 5.2 Experiment conducted by Hamilton and Gifford (1976)

Participants were presented with a series of 39 behaviour descriptions, ascribed to members of one of two groups. To rule out prior knowledge, the groups were simply denoted A and B. As 26 behaviours were associated with Group A but only 13 with Group B, A constitutes the majority and B the minority, as it were. Within both groups, there were clearly more positive than negative behaviours, in accordance with the fact that in reality positive behaviour is normal and negative behaviour is norm-deviant and therefore by definition rare. The resulting stimulus distribution comprised 18 positive A behaviours, 8 negative A behaviours, 9 positive B behaviours, and 4 negative B behaviours. Note that the positivity rate was the same for Group A (18/26) as for Group B (9/13), yielding a perfect zero correlation. Nevertheless, participants arrived at systematically less positive judgements of the minority than the majority. This was evident in various dependent measures, such as frequency estimates, evaluative group impression ratings, and selective recall of what positive or negative behaviours had been associated with Groups A and B.

Definitions

To delineate more precisely these different origins or cognitive processes leading to illusory correlations, we introduce the following notation to define the information given in the simplest case of a correlation between two dichotomous variables x and y (see Figure 5.1 later). For convenience, let x denote a cause and y an effect. For a concrete example, think of the causal influence of weather (x) on mood (y). However, note that illusory correlations are not confined to causal relations between dichotomous variables but extend to all kinds of correlations. Keeping within the example, the two levels on the first variable, $x+$ and $x-$, may represent good and bad weather, respectively, and $y+$ and $y-$ indicate good and bad mood, respectively. An elementary stimulus event, $s(x,y)$, in a pertinent stimulus series specifies the joint occurrence of one x-level with one y-level in a person or observation unit. For example, a series of stimuli might consist of pictures showing good or bad weather in the background and a human face expressing good or bad mood in the foreground. The frequency distribution of all four combinations yields a 2 × 2 table as in Table 5.1. Cell entries a, b, c, d indicate the frequencies with which good and bad weather co-occurs with good and bad mood across the stimulus series. Various correlation or contingency coefficients can be defined as a function of a, b, c, d to measure the objectively existing correlation in the series. The degree of a causal relation can be quantified as

$$\Delta = \frac{a}{a+b} - \frac{c}{c+d},$$

which is the difference in the proportion of good mood observations given good weather minus given bad weather. Another convenient measure is the phi coefficient,

$$\Phi = \frac{ad - bc}{\sqrt{ab + cd + ac + bd}}.$$

Although the choice of an arbitrary normative model for correlation assessment presents a problem in its own right, many illusory-correlation findings are robust enough to generalize across most reasonable measures.

Experimental task and dependent measures

In the correlation assessment paradigm, participants are exposed to stimulus materials in which combinations of two attributes, x and y, occur with joint frequencies a, b, c, d. In some studies, frequencies are presented as statistical summary tables, as in Figure 5.1, but richer insights into the entire cognitive process of correlation assessment come from experiments in which participants have to actively extract the event frequencies from a more or less extended series of raw observations (e.g., from photos depicting weather and mood). The assessment task can be explicit in that the relevant stimulus attributes x and y are clearly identified from the beginning and participants are instructed to figure out the correlation. Or the task may be implicit or incidental such that stimuli are observed with another orienting task in mind (e.g., rating photos for pleasantness) and the call for retrospective correlation assessment may come later as a surprise. The amount and complexity of the task can further vary as a function of the total number of observations, their distribution across the four event categories, the visibility of the variables x and y against the background of irrelevant context variables, and the pre-experimental knowledge about the relation of x and y and their meaning.

The cognitive process of correlation assessment encompasses several stages. Stimulus observations must be *classified* as either (a) $x+y+$, (b) $x+y-$,

Table 5.1 Common notation to describe the correlation between two dichotomous variables

	Attribute $y+$ Effect present	Attribute $y-$ Effect absent
Attribute $x+$ Cause present	Cell A Frequency a	Cell B Frequency b
Attribute $x-$ Cause absent	Cell C Frequency c	Cell D Frequency d

(c) x–y+, or (d) x–y–; observations have to be *perceived* and *encoded* attentively, and the distribution of the four event classes has to be somehow extracted and *integrated* in memory. Finally, the resulting memory *representation* has to be transformed to some *judgement* or reaction, which depends on the sign and degree of the observed correlation.

Explicit and implicit dependent measures are used in illusory-correlation experiments. The most common explicit measures include direct ratings of the size of the observed correlation on numerical or graphical scales, or estimates of the event frequencies a, b, c, d, from which the perceived correlation can then be computed (according to the chosen model, Δ, Φ, etc.). Implicit measures of subjective correlations rely on choices or decisions that presuppose correlation knowledge, without asking participants to express this knowledge directly on some quantitative scale. In a prediction or betting task, participants may be asked to predict, across various test stimuli, the value of one attribute given the value of the other. For example, having observed a series of weather–mood combinations, participants may be presented with a series of cards, drawn from the same pool as the stimulus series, that show a smiling or frowning face (symbolizing good or bad mood) on one side, and their task is to predict the weather situation shown on the other side of the card. Note that such an implicit measure leaves it up to participants to utilize correlation knowledge (e.g., how the good-mood rate differs between weather states) or other sources of information (e.g., the base rate of the predicted event).

THEORETICAL ACCOUNTS OF ILLUSORY CORRELATIONS

Different theoretical explanations have been advanced to account for the three classes of illusory correlations depicted at the outset.

Expectancy-based illusory correlations

To begin with, the notion of prior expectancies suggests that observers tend to see the very regularities they expect to find. A major domain of expectancy-driven illusory correlations is the study of social and diagnostic stereotypes. The basic theoretical intention is to demonstrate the top-down impact of prior knowledge that can override the bottom-up processing of the stimulus data proper. For instance, participants may know or believe that mood generally improves when the weather is fine. This prior belief may then be used for guessing when they have to judge under uncertainty the number of smiling and frowning faces associated with good versus bad weather. In such an account, the illusion is attributed to guessing in the final judgement stage. The initial perception and encoding stages may be unbiased, provided the stimulus encoding process is imperfect enough to create uncertainty, as a precondition for guessing. It may be postulated, in addition, that expectancies also influence stimulus learning, giving an advantage to learning expected stimuli (smiling faces & sunny weather; frowning faces & rainy weather) as opposed to unexpected stimuli (smiling & rainy; frowning & sunny). However, this additional assumption is not necessary and, by the way, not supported empirically; there is indeed ample evidence for more effective encoding of unexpected rather than expected events (Stangor & McMillan, 1992).

Expectancy-based illusory correlations are often confused, and essentially equated, with *similarity*-based illusory correlations, which is not justified conceptually. Similarity is a stimulus property whereas expectancies reside within the individual. One can increase the similarity of the stimulus display for good mood and sunny weather by adding several common features (e.g., same colour, common symbols, smile on both the face and the sun, etc.) while holding expectancies constant. Such overlap in common features may enhance the experienced correlation (Fiedler, 2000; Plessner, Freytag, & Fiedler, 2000), but unlike expectancy effects this reflects a stimulus-driven encoding influence.

Unequal weighting of information

Even when all differences in prior knowledge are ruled out, correlation assessment may be biased because the cognitive integration function does not give equal *weight* to all information belonging to the different cells in Table 5.1. In particular, present events and committed behaviours are deemed more important than absent events and omitted behaviours. Thus, when the task focuses on whether the presence of the sun causes good mood (i.e., a slightly revised example), then the critical features are present when there is sunny weather and good mood but absent when there is rainy weather and bad mood. Due to the asymmetry of present and absent features, known as the feature-positive effect (Newman, Wolff, & Hearst, 1980), a typical finding is that cell frequency a (i.e., the number of present effects & present cause) receives the highest weight in correlation assessment (Wasserman, Dorner, & Kao, 1990), followed by b (missing effect & present cause), and c (present effect & absent cause), while the least weight is given to d (missing effect & absent cause). As a consequence, two formally identical correlations can give rise to rather different subjective assessments. Thus, observing $a = 20$ instances of good mood in sunny weather along with a constantly lower frequency in the other cells, $b = c = d = 10$, will be experienced as a stronger correlation than observing $a = b = c = 10$ and $d = 20$ (i.e., an enhanced frequency for the complementary event, bad mood & rainy days). Such unequal weigthing of different attribute levels is typically attributed to the early phase of perception and encoding, as present features are perceptually more salient. However, theoretically, it could also pertain to a subsequent integration stage when observations from all four cells are combined to yield an overall judgement or representation.

Selective attention and encoding

Furthermore, illusory correlations may arise when some observations catch more attention or are more likely to be encoded in memory and remembered than others. One possible source of enhanced salience is the distinctiveness of rare events, in accordance with the famous von-Restorff (1933) effect. Illusory correlations of this type mainly stem from social psychological research on minorities. As mentioned at the outset, the same high proportion of, say, 75% desirable behaviour in a minority (defined by a small absolute number of observations) leads to a less positive impression than the same proportion observed in a majority (large number of observations), although the constant proportion warrants a perfect zero correlation. The *distinctiveness* account (Hamilton & Sherman, 1989) of this frequently replicated finding states that the combination of the two infrequent attribute levels, that is, undesirable behaviour by the minority, has a distinctiveness advantage, rendering these exceptional behaviours particularly salient and therefore likely to be encoded in memory.

However, direct evidence for enhanced encoding and memory of information belonging to the rarest cell is rather weak (Fiedler, Russer, & Gramm, 1993; Klauer & Meiser, 2000) and the phenomenon can be explained alternatively as a *sample-size effect*. Every reasonable learning theory predicts that learning increases with the number of trials. Applying this simple principle, there is more opportunity to learn that most behaviours tend to be desirable in the majority than in the minority, just as a matter of different sample size (Fiedler, 1996).

The sample-size account can be set apart from the distinctiveness account when illusory correlations are studied in a hypothesis-testing paradigm. Translating pertinent findings (cf. Fiedler, Walther, & Nickel, 1999) to the present example, we might ask participants to engage in active information search in order to test the hypothesis that sunny weather produces good mood. This might be accomplished by letting participants search, within a restricted time period, for relevant entries in somebody's diary. The diary can be constructed such that the base rate of good-mood entries is 70%, and this rate is the same for days described as sunny and rainy, yielding an objective zero correlation. A common information search strategy in such a situation is *positive testing* (Klayman & Ha, 1987; see also Chapters 4 and 10); given the hypothesis focus on sunny weather, most participants will attend more to sunny than to rainy days, thus producing a distribution like the following:

    Good mood & sunny: 14
    Bad mood & sunny: 6
    Good mood & rainy: 7
    Bad mood & rainy: 3

Thus, although the good-mood proportion is the same across weather conditions (i.e., 70%), sample size is higher for sunny weather, due to positive testing. As a consequence, the predominant good-mood reaction should be associated more strongly with sunny than rainy days, even though the attention focus, or salience advantage, is not on rare events (bad mood on rainy days) but on the complementary events (good mood on sunny days) focused in the hypothesis to be tested.

This hypothesis-testing approach can be easily extended to investigate the joint influence of different sources of illusory correlations within the same experiment – an issue largely neglected in previously quite isolated approaches. For instance, the hypothesis to be tested might focus on an unexpected event (good mood on rainy days) in order to pit sample-size effects against expectancy effects. Or the hypothesis might focus on an absent rather than present feature, such as when the task is formulated to find out whether good mood appears whenever the sun is missing. Because integrating different sources of illusory correlations within a single comprehensive approach is a major task for future research, this is also the goal of the following demonstration experiment.

ILLUSORY-CORRELATION EXPERIMENT

To illustrate the interplay of top-down expectancy effects and bottom-up stimulus effects in correlation assessment, I now outline an experiment that was never conducted exactly as described here, but which is modelled after a series of experiments published in Fiedler et al. (1999). The procedural details are given in Text box 5.3.

Text box 5.3 Procedural details for a sample experiment

Participants and design

To keep the demonstration simple, the experiment should include only one between-participants factor, *numerosity* (of stereotype-consistent vs inconsistent observations). Including about 20 participants in each of the resulting two experimental groups should be sufficient, as suggested by previous experience with the effect size of the illusion. *Aggression type* (stereotype-consistent vs stereotype-inconsistent aggression) yields an additional repeated-measures factor, based on the comparison of the judged degree of overt and covert aggression in males and females.

If the number of available participants permits, one might in addition manipulate the *focus of hypothesis*, asking different subsets of participants (from each numerosity condition) to find out either whether male overt aggression and female covert aggression is elevated, or whether female overt and male covert aggression is elevated. This additional manipulation could serve to disentangle two aspects of the expectancy effect, the pre-experimental belief and the attention focus imposed by the experimental task instruction. An interesting empirical question is whether simply focusing on unexpected, counter-stereotypical pairings causes a corresponding shift in the reported correlation, even though beliefs point in the opposite direction (i.e., male–overt aggression link) and even though the actual proportion of male and female overt aggression is constant. Orthogonally to the potential impact of beliefs and hypothesis focus, the working hypothesis says that the relative size of the stimulus samples pertaining to stereotypical and counter-stereotypical aggression should have a significant impact on correlation assessment, and should even override the impact of prior beliefs. Given a constantly high aggression rate in all conditions, higher judgements are predicted for the one type of aggressive behaviour (either stereotypical or counter-stereotypical) for which the sample of observations is larger – regardless of whether sample size coincides with hypothesis focus and prior expectancies.

Materials

As already mentioned, each elementary stimulus event consists of a male or female face along with a behaviour description that either confirms or disconfirms an instance of overt or covert aggression. Depending on whether the experiment is run on a computer or not, stimuli could be presented either on screen or mounted on cards or paper sheets. The verbal behaviour description can appear on the same page or screen as the photograph showing the face, or on the reverse side of a card or the next screen appearing shortly after the face. The various stimuli could either all refer to a constant male and female target person – shifting the hypothesis to the overt aggression rate in two individual persons – or each stimulus could exhibit a different exemplar from two groups of male and female persons. All behaviour descriptions should be pilot-tested for reference to overt and covert aggressiveness. For convenience, one might use the same item set as Fiedler et al. (1999) as listed in the Appendix. The constant reference to the aggression theme should help to minimize uncontrolled influences of stimulus contents. Photographs of faces should be easily available; they can be downloaded from many Internet sites.

Altogether, the stimulus set should include 40 to 50 pairings of faces and behaviours. To keep within the parameter range used in previous experiments, the materials in the "numerous stereotypical observations" condition might consist of

- 24 confirmed instances of stereotypical behaviours (12 male overt + 12 female covert)
- 8 disconfirmed instances of stereotypical behaviours (4 male overt + 4 female covert)
- 12 confirmed instances of counter-stereotypical behaviours (6 male covert + 6 female overt)
- 4 disconfirmed instances of counter-stereotypical behaviours (2 male covert + 2 female overt)

The other stimulus set for the "numerous counter-stereotypical observations" condition can be constructed simply by reversing the assignment of male and female pictures to behaviours. This leaves the relative confirmation rate (constantly 75%) unchanged, but the absolute majority of observations then refer to stereotype-inconsistent behaviours. If all participants appear together, as in a lecture-hall demonstration, the association of faces to specific behaviours must inevitably be held constant. If they participate in separate sessions and the experiment is controlled by computer, the procedure can be improved by using new randomized pairings of faces and behaviours for each participant, such that all faces have the same chance of being associated with each stimulus behaviour across participants.

Procedure

For the experimental instruction, a cover story should be constructed to render the task meaningful. In the original study, for example, the hypothesis to be tested was embedded in a diagnostic task setting. Participants were told that partner therapy was contingent on the assumption that the male partner shows enhanced overt aggression whereas the female partner shows enhanced covert aggression. Stimulus behaviours were said to represent the result of extended in vivo behaviour observations. In this context, a constant male and female face is required. Alternatively, the cover story might ask participants to imagine that they begin a new job and that their task is to find out whether overt/covert aggression occurs more frequently among male or female co-workers. In this case, variable faces representing different individuals would be needed.

Further instructions should be as explicit as possible regarding the hypothesis to be tested. Participants might be instructed, for example:

> It is important that you focus on the crucial question of whether it is true that, across the series of all observations, overt aggression is more likely to be paired with male than female persons, whereas covert aggression is more likely to be paired with female than male persons.

Instructions should also clarify that the hypothesis to be tested refers to the relationship between gender and aggression *in the stimulus list*, as distinct from the participants' general beliefs about the correlation in the real world. As soon as all participants have read and understood the instructions, the stimulus series can be presented at a rate of about 12 seconds per item and with an inter-trial interval of 1 or 2 seconds to have a clear delimiter between items. The presentation order should be randomized under the constraint that the distribution of the four stimulus types is roughly the same in all successive parts (e.g., fourths) of the list.

Three dependent measures are suggested for capturing illusory differences between male and female aggression: (a) frequency estimates of the number of observations confirming and disconfirming overt and covert aggression in male versus female context; (b) separate impression ratings of the male and female target on five to ten adjective scales that speak to overt and covert aggression; and (c) a cued-recall test whereby all observed stimulus behaviours

> are presented once more and participants have to recall whether the behaviour has been associated with a male or a female person. The order of the three dependent measures might be varied, but frequency estimates should not follow the cued-recall test, because the repeated presentation of items for cued recall is likely to distort frequency estimates. At the end of the experiment, participants should be asked to rate their actual belief in the stereotype that males are higher in overt aggression whereas females are higher in covert aggression, and they should indicate their confidence in the preceding judgements and also their own gender. Finally, they should be carefully debriefed concerning the study purpose.

Correlation assessment is framed as a hypothesis-testing task. Participants are instructed to test the hypothesis that "Overt aggression is more likely among males than females whereas covert aggression is more likely among females than males". Accordingly, they are presented with a series of photographs showing either a male or female person, coupled with the verbal description of that person's behaviour, which either entails (overt or covert) aggression or absence of aggression. The stimulus series in all experimental conditions is constrained such that the actual correlation is zero; that is, the proportions of observations that exhibit overt and covert aggression are the same for female as for male target persons. This constant proportion is chosen to be quite high (75%); that is, aggression is more likely to be present than absent across all stimulus behaviours, whether associated with males or females and whether aggression is overt or covert.

According to a common gender stereotype, an *expectancy-based illusory correlation* can be predicted such that participants should report to have seen more stereotype-consistent behaviours (overt aggression in males, covert aggression in females) than stereotype-inconsistent behaviours (overt aggression in females, covert aggression in males). However, the actual outcome should depend on another source of bias, which is stimulus-driven rather than expectancy-driven. In two different experimental groups, the number of observations is manipulated such that the stimulus series includes more observations concerning either stereotype-consistent or inconsistent behaviours. The additional manipulation of *sample size* should moderate or even override the expectancy bias, which constantly associates males with overt aggression and females with covert aggression. If the majority of stimuli refer to stereotype-consistent pairings, the stimulus-driven influence should reinforce the expectancy-driven influence, as the predominant behavioural tendency (i.e., the presence of aggression) is most frequently paired with the expected gender category. In contrast, when most stimuli refer to stereotype-inconsistent cases, the overall high rate of overt (covert) aggression can be most often observed in females (males). The associative stimulus influence should thus counteract the impact of stereotypical expectations.

Results

For convenience, the following results are derived by analogy from the actual results obtained in the conceptually similar approach of Fiedler et al. (1999). First, a check on whether most participants really shared the pre-experimental expectancy associating overt aggression to males and covert aggression to females provides support for this premise. The average rating on a graphical scale from −21 to +21 (with positive values indicating an increasing degree of belief that aggression is overt in males and covert in females) was +5.54 and clearly above 0, $t(73) = 4.18$, $p = .00006$.

An expectancy-driven illusory correlation should thus be reflected in higher judgements for stereotype-consistent behaviours. For convenience, the pertinent results for the two numerosity conditions are reported separately, because this manipulation is only optional. In the one numerosity condition, in which sample size is larger for stereotype-consistent observations, the mean estimated percentage of confirmed stereotype-consistent behaviours (pooling over male–overt and female–covert) was 66.7% as compared with 43.5% stereotype-inconsistent confirmations (see Figure 5.1), $F(1, 31) = 16.98$, $p = .0003$. The effect size here amounted to approximately two thirds of a standard deviation. Likewise, the mean rating for stereotypical traits (e.g., male–brutal, female–shining) was higher (+4.58) than for counter-stereotypical traits (−1.27), $F(1, 31) = 8.13$, $p = .008$. The effect size here was about one standard deviation. As evident from Figure 5.1, both the estimated percentage of confirmed aggression and the average impression rating on relevant adjective scales were higher for stereotypical than for counter-stereotypical combinations.

On the cued-recall test, which is not reported in detail, the proportion of aggressive behaviours recalled as belonging to stereotypical pairings (i.e., overt aggression assigned to male persons and covert aggression assigned to females) was higher than items recalled as belonging to counter-stereotypical pairings.

However, Figure 5.1 also shows that in spite of the gender-stereotypic expectancy and in spite of the instruction focus on gender-typical aggression, a strong reversal was obtained when sample size was larger for counter-stereotypical information. Thus, when there was more opportunity to learn the constantly high confirmation rate of 75% aggression in the female–overt and the male–covert domain than in the expected domains, the mean estimated percentage of confirmed aggression was higher for counter-stereotypical (52.4%) than for stereotypical behaviour (43.6%), $F(1, 41) = 4.18$, $p = .045$. Similarly, mean impression ratings were larger for counter-stereotypical traits (+4.29) than for stereotypical traits (+1.14), $F(1, 41) = 8.83$, $p = .005$. Thus, frequency estimates as well as impression ratings reflected the dominant stimulus association between gender and aggression in the stimulus input – in spite of the opposite observer expectancy and hypothesis focus.

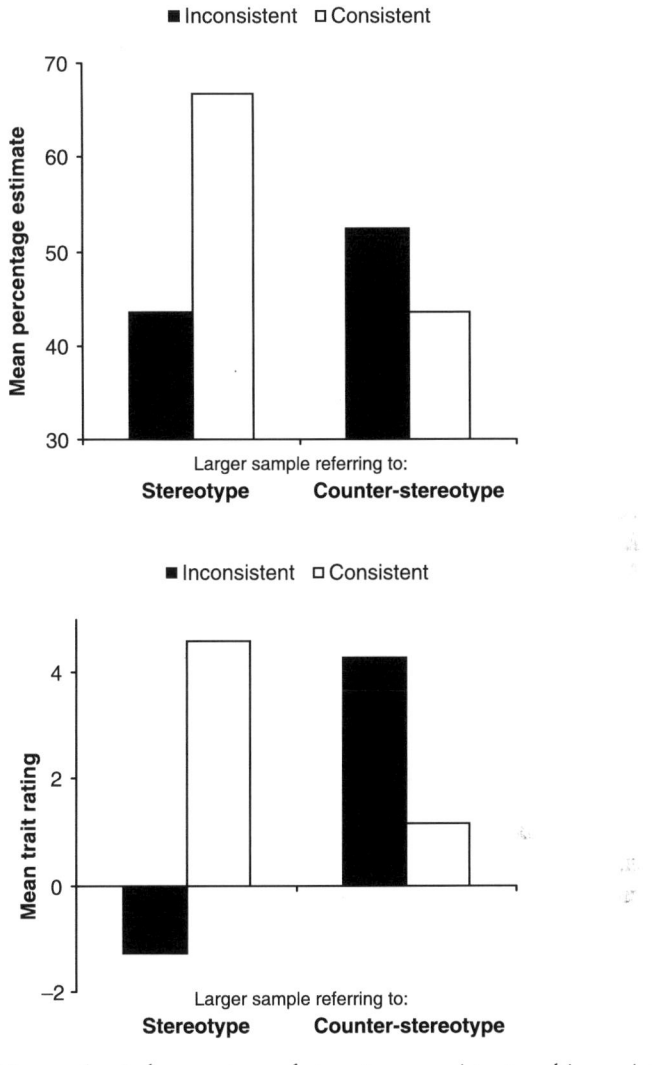

Figure 5.1 (a) Mean estimated percentage of stereotype-consistent and inconsistent behaviour and (b) mean trait rating on stereotype-consistent and inconsistent scales.

Pooling over both numerosity conditions, there presumably will not be an aggression type main effect, or tendency to report more overt or covert aggression in males than females, indicating that prior expectancies were completely overridden by the sample-size manipulation. Suffice it to mention briefly that in the original investigation of Fiedler et al. (1999) the sample-size effect dominated the final judgements regardless of whether the focus of hypothesis was consistent or inconsistent with gender expectancies. However, note also that the present demonstration experiment differs from the original design in some procedural features, thus rendering the outcome less than perfectly certain.

Discussion

The illusory-correlation experiment I have depicted in this section was selected to demonstrate the interplay of different sources of illusory correlations, stemming from separate research traditions. Logically, prior expectancies, attention focus, and sample size do not represent mutually exclusive alternative accounts of illusory correlations, but can exert their influence additively and simultaneously within the same task situation. For a comprehensive approach to correlation assessment, it is thus important to include top-down factors (prior expectancies, focus of attention) and bottom-up factors (sample size) within the same experimental paradigm. Although the different influencing factors may combine additively, it is of theoretical and practical interest to find out, for instance, what size of illusory correlation effects are possible when several factors act in the same direction or, when they operate in opposite directions, which factor dominates and overrides the others. In the context of gender stereotypes, it was suggested here that sample size (a largely neglected factor) may override the stereotypical expectancies concerning gender and aggression (a prominent factor in social psychology). This is not to say, however, that such a finding from a single experiment can be uncritically generalized to expectancy-based and sample-size-based illusory correlations in general. The ultimate purpose of an integrative, multi-factor approach is to study systematically how the relative impact of different sources of bias depends on such boundary conditions as the degree of uncertainty and noise in the stimulus materials, the motivational pay-off structure of the task, the stimulus presentation mode and precise encoding condition, the degree of memory load and decay, and the presence of metacognitive monitoring and correction processes.

CONCLUSIONS

Detecting and estimating correlations between attributes of significant environmental objects is an important module of adaptive intelligence and behaviour. Although humans as well as animals seem to have the competence to assess environmental correlations quite accurately, their performance is often impaired under less than optimal task conditions. Hundreds of experiments conducted during several decades of research on illusory correlations converge in demonstrating that subjective correlation estimates are often distorted as a function of prior knowledge, attention, asymmetric representation of variable levels, sample size, similarity, and motivational factors. Moreover, the degree of distortion can be quite severe and some types of illusory correlations can be reproduced easily and can hardly be eliminated through training. In some theoretical and applied domains, the existence and size of these illusions is interesting in its own right. For instance, economists and consumer researchers are interested in the perceived correlation between price and quality of consumer products. And in social psychology, the perceived correlation between trait attributes and group membership provides a basic building block for theories of stereotyping.

However, although evidence for illusory correlations is strong and uncontested, one should be cautious in drawing ideological conclusions about human irrationality. From a broader theoretical perspective, illusory correlations can also be considered as indicators of adaptive intelligence. Many illusions, in perception and cognition, can be understood as the flipside of otherwise adaptive and prudent algorithms. For instance, the higher weight given to present than to absent attributes might be indispensable for survival. Clearly, the absence of traffic signs would be a less useful guide for driving behaviour than the presence of signs. Similarly, the effect of sample size makes sense if information is unreliable and organisms have to conduct significance tests in addition to correlation assessment. In this regard, an observed proportion of 8 out of 12 is indeed stronger information than an observed proportion of 2 out of 3. The formal model of a correlation – based on probability estimates that are independent of sample size – is but one of several normative models that might be applied rationally. Last but not least, an effectively adapted organism not only has to be accurate but also quick, and must not waste too many resources on each and any task. Using simplified algorithms that produce errors some of the time may thus be preferable to more demanding algorithms in the long run.

In this regard, McKenzie (1994) has shown through Monte Carlo simulations across most reasonable distributions that primitive algorithms of correlation assessment are strongly correlated with more refined correlation measures. For instance, the sum of diagonal cell frequencies ($a + d$ in Figure 5.1) is highly correlated with the fully-fledged Φ coefficient, especially when the marginal frequencies of the two levels on x and y are approximately equal. Thus, if the cutoff points that distinguish between "good versus bad weather" and between "good versus bad mood" are chosen such that each variable level occurs at roughly 50%, then merely counting the diagonal sum (i.e., the relative frequency of good weather & good mood or bad weather & bad mood) provides a perfect estimate of the correlation. The diagonal sum will only be misleading when marginal frequencies are unequal. For instance, if people are in good mood on 900 out of 1000 days and the weather (say, in Spain) is fine on 800 out of 1000 days, then the joint frequency of good weather and good mood (i.e., frequency a), just as the diagonal $a + b$, can be expected to be very high even when there is no correlation. However, from an adaptive-behaviour perspective, highly skewed distributions can render correlation assessment obsolete. Given 90% good mood, the best strategy to predict mood might be to always predict the high base-rate event (i.e., good mood), rather than trying to infer mood from the weather (cf. Kareev, 2000).

Thus, although many illusory correlation experiments provide cogent evidence for erroneous and fallacious reasoning on the specific task, one should refrain from premature pessimistic conclusions about human intelligence and rationality.

SUMMARY

- The detection and assessment of environmental correlations is an important module of adaptive intelligence.
- The phenomenon of illusory correlations refers to partly severe failure and inaccuracy in correlation assessment.
- Different types of illusory correlations can be distinguished in terms of underlying cognitive processes: illusions can be based on expectancies; unequal weighting of present and absent events; differences in attention and encoding elaboration; or sample size.
- The most prominent applied settings for illusory-correlations research include diagnostics, economical decisions, evaluation, hypothesis testing, and the social psychological domain of group stereotypes.

FURTHER READING

More comprehensive reviews of research on illusory correlations in particular and correlation assessment in general can be found in several journal articles. Allan (1993) conceptualizes correlation assessment in an associative-learning framework. An older article by Alloy and Tabachnik (1984) affords an intriguing view on human and animal performance on correlation assessment tasks. Fiedler (2000) provides a review of different variants of illusory correlations that can all be explained within the same connectionist framework.

ACKNOWLEDGEMENTS

The author's own research on illusory correlations has been supported by various grants from the Deutsche Forschungsgemeinschaft. Thanks for helpful comments on a draft of the chapter are due to Myriam Bayer. Readers of this chapter are invited to send feedback and suggestions for improvement in future editions of this volume to kf@psychologie.uni-heidelberg.de

REFERENCES

Allan, L. G. (1993). Human contingency judgments: Rule based or associative? *Psychological Bulletin, 114*, 435–448.

Alloy, L. B., & Abramson, L. Y. (1979). Judgment of contingency in depressed and nondepressed students: Sadder but wiser? *Journal of Experimental Psychology: General, 108*, 441–485.

Alloy, L. B., & Tabachnik, N. (1984). Assessment of covariation by humans and animals: The joint influence of prior expectations and current situational information. *Psychological Review, 91*, 112–149.

Chapman, L. J., & Chapman, J. P. (1967). Genesis of popular but erroneous psychodiagnostic observations. *Journal of Abnormal Psychology, 72*, 193–204.

Crocker, J. (1981). Judgment of covariation by social perceivers. *Psychological Bulletin, 90*, 272–292.

Fiedler, K. (1996). Explaining and simulating judgment biases as an aggregation phenomenon in probabilistic, multiple-cue environments. *Psychological Review, 103*, 193–214.

Fiedler, K. (2000). Illusory correlations: A simple associative algorithm provides a convergent account of seemingly divergent paradigms. *Review of General Psychology, 4*, 25–58.

Fiedler, K., Russer, S., & Gramm, K. (1993). Illusory correlations and memory performance. *Journal of Experimental Social Psychology, 29*, 111–136.

Fiedler, K., Walther, E., & Nickel S. (1999). The autoverification of social hypothesis: Stereotyping and the power of sample size. *Journal of Personality and Social Psychology, 77*, 5–18.

Hamilton, D. L., & Gifford, R. K. (1976). Illusory correlation in interpersonal perception: A cognitive basis of stereotypic judgments. *Journal of Experimental Social Psychology, 12*, 392–407.

Hamilton, D. L., & Rose, R. L. (1980). Illusory correlation and the maintenance of stereotypic beliefs. *Journal of Personality and Social Psychology, 39*, 832–845.

Hamilton, D. L., & Sherman, S. J. (1989). Illusory correlations: Implications for stereotype theory and research. In D. Bar-Tal, C. F. Graumann, A. W. Kruglanski, & W. Stroebe (Eds.), *Stereotype and prejudice: Changing conceptions* (pp. 59–82). New York: Springer.

Kao, S.-F., & Wasserman, E. A. (1993). Assessment of an information integration account of contingency judgment with examination of subjective cell importance and method of information presentation. *Journal of Experimental Psychology: Learning, Memory, and Cognition, 19*, 1363–1386.

Kareev, Y. (2000). Seven (indeed, plus minus two) and the detection of correlations. *Psychological Review, 107*, 397–402.

Klauer, K. C., & Meiser, T. (2000). A source-monitoring analyses of illusory correlations. *Personality and Social Psychology Bulletin, 26*, 1074–1093.

Klayman, J., & Ha, Y. (1987). Confirmation, disconfirmation, and information in hypothesis testing. *Psychological Review, 94*, 211–228.

Malmi, R. A. (1986). Intuitive covariation estimation. *Memory & Cognition, 14*, 501–508.

McKenzie, C. R. M. (1994). The accuracy of intuitive judgment strategies: Covariation assessment and Bayesian inference. *Cognitive Psychology, 26*, 209–239.

Newman, J., Wolff, W. T., & Hearst, E. (1980). The feature-positive effect in adult human subjects. *Journal of Experimental Psychology: Human Learning and Memory, 6*, 630–650.

Plessner, H., Freytag, P., & Fiedler, K. (2000). Expectancy-effects without expectancies: Illusory correlations based on cue-overlap. *European Journal of Social Psychology, 30*, 837–851.

Stangor, C., & McMillan, D. (1992). Memory for expectancy-congruent and expectancy-incongruent information: A review of the social and social developmental literatures. *Psychological Bulletin, 111*, 42–61.

von Restorff, H. (1933). Über die Wirkung von Bereichsbildungen im Spurenfeld [On the influence of area formation in the field of traces]. *Psychologische Forschung, 18*, 299–342.

Wasserman, E. A., Dorner, W. W., & Kao, S.-F. (1990). Contribution of specific cell information to judgments of interevent contingency. *Journal of Experimental Psychology: Learning, Memory, and Cognition, 16*, 509–521.

APPENDIX

Stimulus items representing overt and covert aggression

Overt aggression	*Covert aggression*
1. Tends to use violence	1. Becomes unfair in arguments
2. Quickly goes too far with language	2. Acts as though others were not there
3. Shouts in arguments	3. Enjoys disparaging others
4. Threatens with violence	4. Lies to get an advantage
5. Screams when s/he doesn't like something	5. Makes a pretence of being friendly with everyone
6. Shakes people when angry	6. Makes others feel sorry for him/her
7. Quickly gets into a temper	7. Hangs up when fed up
8. Shouts others down	8. Simply walks out of an argument
9. Doesn't stop short of hitting people	9. Plays with others' feelings
10. Kicks things	10. Gossips about people s/he doesn't like
11. Was involved in a fistfight	11. Cuts others after an argument
12. Throws things around the room	12. Pretends to be unforgiving
13. Gets out of control quickly	13. Schemes
14. Sometimes smashes dishes	14. Sets traps for others
15. Defends his/her rights with violence	15. Sets people against each other
16. Easily gets into a rage	16. Manipulates others to fight each other
17. Likes to argue with people	17. Denigrates others
18. May slap someone's face when in rage	18. Puts up a show
19. Sometimes wants to smash something	19. Pointedly ignores others
20. Quickly has a fit after insults	20. Flatters others

Note. English translations of original German items.

6 Illusions of control

Suzanne C. Thompson

One of the enduring themes of psychological theory and research is that human beings are motivated to have control over the events of their lives (Rodin, 1986; White, 1959). Extensive research has demonstrated that perceived control is associated with many positive outcomes, including successful coping with stressful events, making health-improving lifestyle changes, and better performance on tasks (Thompson & Spacapan, 1991).

The central role of perceived control in many areas of functioning has led to a focus on the accuracy of personal control judgements. Illusions of control occur when individuals overestimate their personal influence over an outcome. For example, Peter takes a herbal supplement, echinacea, with the goal of avoiding colds and the flu. He is likely to attribute a period of good health to the supplement even if, in fact, it has only a minimal effect or perhaps no effect at all. At times individuals may judge that they have control even over an obviously chance process: People who play slot machines have been known to act as if their choice of machine or style of pulling the handle can affect their chances of winning.

Studies of illusions of control have taken three different approaches to demonstrating the existence of control illusions. Ellen Langer conducted the first programmatic study of illusory control. Her approach was to examine people's perceptions of the likelihood of getting a desired outcome when the task involves chance situations with skill elements. In a series of studies, she showed that in chance situations with elements such as familiarity or choice, participants have higher estimates of getting the outcomes they desire (Langer, 1975). For example, in one study, lottery tickets were decorated with familiar or novel symbols. The participants who received the familiar symbols were less likely to exchange their tickets for new ones even though the probability of winning was higher with a new ticket. It was assumed that the unwillingness to exchange the ticket indicated that participants believed they had control, that is, they chose a ticket that was more likely to win. This approach to studying illusory control does not measure control perceptions directly, but relies on preferences for options to infer that participants believe they have control.

A second approach to research on illusions of control has participants work on laboratory tasks where the researcher can set the level of actual control that can be exercised on the task. Typically, participants are given no control over the occurrence of a particular outcome. Then, after working on the task, participants rate the amount of control they believe they had. For example, Alloy and Abramson (1979) used a light-onset task to explore illusions of control. Participants tried to get a light to come on by pressing a button. In actuality there was no relationship between their actions and onset of the light: The light was programmed to come on on either 25% or 75% of the trials. However, when the light came on more frequently (75% of the time), estimates of personal control over onset of the light were high. This work clearly demonstrates that even when people have no control, control judgements can be high.

A third way of researching illusory control asks participants to report on their behaviour under various circumstances. For example, McKenna (1993) used the issue of driving safety and asked participants to rate the likelihoods that, compared to other drivers, they would be involved in a road accident when they are driving and when they are passengers. Participants rated the likelihood of an accident to be lower when they were the driver. In a second study, high and low driver-control scenarios for an accident were used. Participants were particularly likely to judge that they could avoid an accident that involved high driver control (e.g., driving your vehicle into the rear of another car) as opposed to low driver control (e.g., being hit from behind). Thus people show illusory control over avoiding an accident by assuming that they will be able to exert control that others cannot.

These three approaches to researching illusory control have strengths and weaknesses as research strategies. The Langer approach has the advantage of using realistic situations that people are likely to face in everyday life (lotteries and competitive games). In addition, the strategy of using an indirect measure of control allows people to express their feeling of control when they may be reluctant to admit that they believe they can control a chance process. At the same time, it has the disadvantage of not demonstrating whether control *per se* is the critical factor. The laboratory manipulations of control such as Alloy and Abramson (1979) used employ a dependent variable measure that is clearly tapping control judgements, but typically the studies do not use tasks with good external validity. The self-report measures used by McKenna (1993) have good external validity but suffer the disadvantages of self-report methodology. One of the strengths of the illusions of control research as a whole is that studies using these diverse methodologies with their attendant advantages and disadvantages have reached similar conclusions. Text box 6.1 gives examples of the use of these methodologies as classroom demonstrations.

Illusions of control 117

Text box 6.1 Classroom demonstrations

Each of the three ways of researching illusions of control can be used to demonstrate illusions of control in a classroom context. They are discussed below in ascending order of difficulty of preparation and time needed to complete the demonstration.

Demonstration 1: Illusions of control over driving

The questions used by McKenna (1993) can easily be adapted for classroom use. One set of questions focuses on the likelihood of an automobile accident when the participant is the driver vs the passenger of the car (see Q1 and Q2 in Table 6.1). The other four questions focus on the circumstances of an accident with the participant as driver: For two questions (Q3 and Q4), the circumstances are low control; for the other two (Q5 and Q6), the circumstances are high control. These questions are rated on a –5 to +5 scale with 0 = average as the midpoint.

Table 6.1 Questions used to demonstrate illusory control over driving

Q1.	Compared to other drivers, how likely do you think you are to be involved in an automobile accident when you are driving?
Q2.	Compared to other drivers, how likely do you think you are to be involved in an automobile accident when you are a passenger?
Q3.	Compared to the average driver, how likely do you feel you are to be involved in an accident which is caused by another vehicle hitting you from behind?
Q4.	Compared to the average driver, how likely do you feel you are to be involved in an accident which is caused by an unexpected tyre blow-out?
Q5.	Compared to the average driver, how likely do you feel you are to be involved in an accident in which the vehicle you are in is driven into the rear of another vehicle?
Q6.	Compared to the average driver, how likely do you feel you are to be involved in an accident in which the vehicle you are in is changing traffic lanes?

Adapted from McKenna, 1993.

Response scale from –5 (much less likely) through 0 (average) to +5 (much more likely).

In the classroom experiment, students receive a handout with these six questions, which they answer anonymously and hand in. The design is a paired *t*-test, comparing answers to Q1 and Q2, with the independent variable of self as driver or passenger. Additional analyses include averaging the two low-control questions and the two high-control questions and comparing mean differences in those. The results are graphed on overheads or in a Powerpoint file for the next class session. The class is asked to guess the results of the comparison between Q1 and Q2, and they will accurately predict that ratings of the likelihood of an accident will be higher when the participant is listed as the passenger. The discussion of why this would be brings out the idea of illusory control.

The issue of accuracy is often raised, with some students protesting that they (or some of the respondents) are better drivers than someone they might ride with as a passenger. This is a good time to cover the difference between individual and group prediction and the meaning of mean ratings of likelihood of an accident as a driver that are significantly below the midpoint of 0 (average). Another issue this raises is that of being able to accurately assess one's own capabilities. In addition, some especially perceptive students will comment on alternative explanations for the results, in particular that lower ratings of accidents when one is a driver could be a "better than average" effect, but not necessarily one that is due to overestimating one's control. At that point, the second set of graphs that show the comparison between the low-control and high-control accident circumstances can be examined. Typically, the high-control accident circumstances are rated as significantly less likely to lead to an accident than the low-control circumstances. The comparison suggests that perceptions of control make a contribution to the effect.

There are a number of ways that this demonstration can be expanded. For example, number of traffic tickets received, gender, or self-esteem can be added to the questionnaire and analyzed to see if experience or personality measures predict the amount of illusory control.

Overall, this demonstration is easy to prepare and administer, and very likely to yield results that demonstrate illusions of control. Using similar materials, McKenna (1993) found a mean of −1.41 for the driver condition as opposed to 0.01 for the passenger condition. Thus, participants judged that they had less likelihood of being in an accident when driving than the average person, but not less likelihood when they were passengers.

Demonstration 2: Illusions of control in a gambling game

Demonstration 2 is based on Langer's (1975) research on illusory control, using a simple gambling game. The class is divided into pairs and one student in each pair is randomly assigned to be the participant or the observer. Each pair is given a pair of dice and a sheet for recording the outcomes of dice throws. The dice will be rolled 20 times by the participant, and the results of each roll recorded and then summed across all 20 throws. There is a prize for the pair that gets the highest total. Before the dice throwing begins, each participant and observer gets a piece of paper asking them to separately and anonymously rate the chances of getting the prize on a 0–10 scale from "no chance at all" to "an excellent chance". These measures are collected, the dice rolling is done, and the prize distributed. Before the next class, the analysis is done using paired t-tests with role as the independent variable and ratings of chance as the dependent variable.

Even though both the participants and the observers have no control over their dice-throwing score, there will be a slight tendency for the participants to rate the chances of getting the prize higher than the observers will. The results may not be significant with a smaller class, but the data can be saved and aggregated over several classes for stronger effects.

This demonstration uses a fairly realistic context (at least for those who play games of chance). If the demonstration works as proposed, it is an excellent experience for students to analyze the causes and effects of control illusions. If the results are not consistent with Langer's work, then the discussion can focus on the differences in the research set-up used by Langer and that of the demonstration. For instance, students may have felt pressure to make their ratings of their chances of getting the prize in a "rational" way, given the class context. Previous research has found that circumstances that highlight the right or "rational" way to estimate likelihoods reduce or eliminate illusions of control (Thompson, Armstrong, & Thomas, 1998).

Demonstration 3: Illusions of control on the computer

This demonstration requires a more elaborate set-up of equipment and most likely would need to be done outside class time for later discussion. Thompson, Kyle, Osgood, Quist, Phillips, and McClure (2002) adapted for computer use the Alloy and Abramson (1979) light-onset task. In the original task, participants pushed a button to see if they could control the onset of a light. In our adaptation, experiment-presentation software (SuperLab) was used to set up a similar task. The software was used to present either red "0"s or green "X"s on the computer screen. Participants were told that for each of 40 trials, they could choose to press or not press the space bar to get the green "X" screen to appear. Their job was to judge how much control they had over the appearance of the green "X" on the screen. The level of reinforcement was manipulated by the number of times the desired green "X" appeared (25% or 75% of the time). At the end of 40 trials, participants judged their control on a 100-point scale, labelled "0 = no control", "50 = intermediate control", and "100 = complete control". Although participants had no control over the onset of the screens, estimates of control were high, especially in the high reinforcement ($M = 43$) compared to the low reinforcement ($M = 11$) condition.

For use as a demonstration, participants could be randomly assigned to the high or low reinforcement conditions and complete the task of judging their control outside class time. When the results are presented in class, they can provoke discussion of several issues: Why do illusions of control occur? What are their "real world" implications? Why are the overestimations of control so much lower in the low reinforcement condition?

WHEN DO ILLUSIONS OF CONTROL OCCUR?

In a recent review paper, Thompson et al. (1998) reviewed five conditions that have been found to influence control judgements: (1) skill-related factors, (2) success or failure emphasis, (3) need or desire for outcome, (4) mood, and (5) the intrusion of reality.

Skill-related factors

Skill-related factors are attributes associated with situations where skill is an issue, including familiarity, making choices, active engagement with the material, competition, and foreknowledge. According to Langer (1975), when a chance situation contains these elements, people mistakenly think that skill is involved. Hence, they judge that they have some control over the outcomes. For example, the act of choosing options is associated with skilled tasks. Therefore when lottery participants are allowed to choose their own numbers, the game has the feel of a task involving skill and one that is controllable.

Numerous studies have shown that situations with skill-associated features such as familiarity with the materials, personal involvement, competition, and foreknowledge of the possible outcomes lead to overestimations of personal control (see Ayeroff & Abelson, 1976; Dunn & Wilson, 1990; Langer, 1975, for representative studies). For example, in one study, Ayeroff and Abelson (1976) used an extrasensory perception task to examine illusions of control. Two factors were manipulated – choice of symbols used on the task (participants chose vs were assigned symbols) and personal involvement (participants shuffled the symbol deck us someone else did). Both choice and involvement led to higher estimates of success on the extrasensory perception task, presumably because choice and involvement enhanced illusions of control.

Success or failure emphasis

Success or failure emphasis refers to the extent to which the task or the context highlights expectations or perceptions of success vs failure. An emphasis on success enhances illusions of control whereas failure emphasis undermines control illusions. For example, Langer and Roth (1975) showed that a pattern of early successes on a coin-toss task led to higher illusions of control than a pattern of early failures, despite the fact that the overall number of wins was constant. The early successes focused participants' attention and expectations on successes, thereby raising control illusions.

Success emphasis is the likely reason why the frequency of reinforcement has a strong effect on illusory control in the Alloy and Abramson (1979) light-onset task. When the light comes on frequently (regardless of what participants do), participants' actions are frequently followed by the desired outcome and they receive a strong message of "success". With infrequent onset of the light, it appears that their actions result in "failure". In their analysis of the mediators of illusory control effects, Thompson et al. (2002) found that a high level of reinforcement was associated with higher estimates that one's attempts to exert control were successful, and higher control judgements.

Need or desire for the outcome

Need or desire for the outcome refers to situations where people are motivated to believe that they have personal control. Biner, Angle, Park, Mellinger, and Barber (1995) conducted an interesting test of the idea that a motive for control increases illusions of control. In their Study 1, half the participants were motivated to have control over obtaining a hamburger meal because they fasted from solid food on the day they reported for the study; the other half did not fast. Those who had fasted were significantly more confident that they would win the hamburger meal through participation in a draw than were those who were not hungry.

Sometimes the motive for control may be due to the stress-reducing properties of control beliefs. To test this, Friedland, Keinan, and Regev (1992) asked Israeli Air Force cadets to complete an illusions of control measure at a low-stress time or half an hour before they were tested during a critical training flight (high-stress condition). Illusions of control were higher immediately prior to the stressful flight test.

In a further examination of the role of motivation in illusions of control, Thompson et al. (2002) manipulated the motivation to have control by paying participants for each success at a computer screen onset task or having no payments for success. Illusions of control were considerably higher when participants were paid for successes and, presumably, motivated to have control over the onset of the screen.

Mood

A number of studies find that illusions of control are higher when people are in a positive mood. For instance, Alloy, Abramson, and Viscusi (1981) manipulated mood states (positive, negative, or neutral) in depressed and nondepressed individuals. Those participants whose mood was temporarily induced to be positive showed higher illusions of control; those with a temporary more negative mood showed lower illusions of control.

Intrusion of reality

Finally, research has found that situations that focus people on a realistic or rational assessment of control reduce or entirely eliminate illusory control thinking. In one study to test this idea, Bouts and Van Avermaet (1992) had some individuals focus on the objective probabilities of winning a gambling game either before or after placing a bet on a card-drawing gamble. Those who considered the probabilities before placing the bet showed considerably lower illusions of control (i.e., made a lower bet).

THEORIES OF ILLUSORY CONTROL: WHY DOES IT OCCUR?

Langer (1975) offered the earliest theory to explain why people often overestimate their influence even in situations where there is no actual control.

According to Langer, illusions of control occur because people confuse skill and chance situations, especially when chance situations contain elements that are usually associated with skill-based tasks. This theory can be used to explain why the presence of skill-based elements such as familiarity, involvement, and competition lead people to overestimate their control on chance-based tasks. However, in their critique of this theory, Thompson et al. (1998) point out several flaws with this explanation, including (1) all situations contain both skill and chance elements, so it seems likely that people are used to sorting out these influences, and (2) this theory cannot explain why non-skill-based elements such as success-focus or need for the outcome also influence illusions of control.

Thompson et al. (1998) offered an explanation of illusions of control based on a "control heuristic", a shortcut that people use to judge the extent of their personal influence. The control heuristic involves two elements: one's intention to achieve the outcome, and the perceived connection between one's action and the desired outcome. When one acts with the intention of obtaining a particular outcome and there is a relationship (temporal, common meaning, or predictive) between one's action and the outcome, people judge that they had control over the outcome.

Like most heuristics, this shortcut to estimating control often leads to accurate judgements. For example, when we have the ability to influence whether or not we obtain an outcome, we often act with the intention of getting that outcome and there is a connection between our action and the receipt of the desired event. However, we can also act with the intention of getting a desired outcome and see a connection between our action and the outcome in situations where we do not have control. For example, gamblers at slot machines can pull the handle with the intention of getting a winning combination. If the winning items appear, there is a temporal connection between the gambler's action and the appearance of the winning items. Thus using the control heuristic to judge their personal influence can lead gamblers to judge that they have control over getting a winning combination.

In a test of this theory, Thompson et al. (2002) manipulated reinforcement and motive for control in a computer screen onset task. They found that judgements of intentionality mediated the relationship between motives and judgements of control. That is, as would be predicted by the control heuristic theory, the motive to have personal control resulted in higher illusory judgements of control because it affected an element of the control heuristic – intentions to get the outcome. Although judgements of connection were correlated with control judgements, they did not mediate the relationship between motives and illusory control, perhaps because the perceptions of connection were fairly accurate (i.e., people did not overestimate the number of hits they received).

IMPLICATIONS OF ILLUSIONS OF CONTROL

Most of the research focuses on situations that lead to control overestimation rather than the frequency of occurrence of illusory control, so there is little information about how common illusions of control are. However, they do appear to be fairly easy to elicit in psychological studies (e.g., Alloy & Abramson, 1979; Langer, 1975) which may say something about how often they naturally occur. In addition, the strong effects obtained in McKenna's (1993) research on people's perceptions that they can avoid motor vehicle accidents in "controllable" situations suggests that illusory control is a common phenomenon.

Not everyone overestimates their personal control. Moderately depressed individuals tend to have a realistic sense of how much they are contributing to an outcome. Does that mean that we are better off if we overestimate our personal control? Overestimating one's control might have a number of consequences including positive ones (enhanced self-esteem, better motivation for attempting difficult tasks) and negative ones (failure to protect oneself against harm, disappointment when control is disconfirmed, pursuing unrealistic goals, and blaming others for their misfortune). Far less research has focused on this question and the few studies that have been done indicate that both positive and negative consequences can follow from control overestimation.

At least one study has found positive effects of illusory control. Alloy and Clements (1992) used the light-onset task to assess the extent to which college students used illusory control. Students who displayed greater illusions of control had less negative mood after a failure on a lab task, were less likely to become discouraged when they subsequently experienced negative life stressors, and were less likely to get depressed a month later, given the occurrence of a high number of negative life stressors. Thus, individuals who are more susceptible to an illusion of control may be at a decreased risk for depression and discouragement in comparison to those individuals who are not. The idea that "positive illusions" (in this case, illusory control) are associated with adaptive outcomes is consistent with Taylor and Brown's (1988) thesis that positive illusions provide motivation and the confidence to engage in positive action (cf. Chapter 14).

In contrast to this positive finding, there is evidence that overestimating one's control has a number of costs and disadvantages. As an example, Donovan, Leavitt, and Walsh (1990) investigated the influence of illusory control on performance demands associated with child care. The degree of illusory control was measured by having mothers try to terminate the noncontingent crying of an audio-taped baby. A subsequent simulation assessed the mothers' ability to learn effective responses in ceasing an infant's cry. Mothers with a high illusion of control on the first task showed a depressive attribution style, aversive physiological responses to impending infant cries, and less proactive coping. Illusory control thinking is associated with more involvement in gambling (Toneatto, Blitz-Miller, Calderwood, Dragonetti, & Tsanos, 1997) and belief in extrasensory perception (Blackmore & Troscianko, 1985). Reduced self-protection against risk of disease has also been linked to illusory control thinking. College students and gay men who had higher scores on general illusory control thinking felt less vulnerable to HIV and used less effective protection against HIV (Thompson, Kent, Thomas, & Vrungos, 1999). Finally, in some recent unpublished research, my students and I examined the relationship between women's perceptions that they can avoid being the victim of a sexual assault and their propensity to blame women who were assault victims. Perceptions of having control over avoiding an assault were high and were only weakly correlated with having concrete strategies to protect oneself. Thus it seems likely that the women's perceptions of control over avoiding sexual assault were illusory to some extent. Women with higher beliefs that they had control over avoiding assault were more likely to hold other women responsible for being a victim of assault. So it appears that illusory control could have disadvantages both for the people who hold these beliefs and for other people in their social environment.

Which is the correct view: that illusory thinking is generally useful because it leads to positive emotions and motivates people to try challenging tasks, or that people are better off if they have an accurate assessment of themselves and their situation? Another possibility is that sometimes illusory control is adaptive and at other times it is not. For example, illusions of control may be reassuring in stressful situations, but lead people to take unnecessary risks when they occur in a gambling context, or may be a source of blaming others for their misfortunes. The challenge for researchers is to examine the consequences of illusory control in a variety of situations to answer these important questions.

SUMMARY

- Illusions of control occur when individuals overestimate their personal influence over an outcome.
- Three approaches to researching illusions of control are Langer's preference analysis, experimental laboratory studies that directly measure control perceptions, and self-reports of control-related behaviours.
- Illusions of control are affected by skill-related factors, success or failure emphasis, need or desire for the outcome, mood, and intrusion of reality.
- Langer (1975) originally proposed that illusions of control occur because people confuse skill and chance situations. The Thompson et al. (1998) control heuristic explanation can account for more of the findings.
- According to the control heuristic explanation, people use both connection and intention to judge their control. Because both can be present even when control is not, personal control is often overestimated.

- Depending on the circumstances, illusions of control can be adaptive or maladaptive in everyday life.

FURTHER READING

Langer's (1975) classic studies of illusory control in the selection of lottery tickets and games of chance are a good place to start. For a different and equally influential approach to control overestimation, the original Alloy and Abramson (1979) set of studies provides a systematic exploration of this topic and the beginnings of the depressive realism concept. For a comprehensive review of illusions of control research and the control heuristic explanation, see Thompson, Armstrong, and Thomas (1998). A condensed review is also available (Thompson, 1999).

REFERENCES

Alloy, L. B., & Abramson, L. Y. (1979). Judgment of contingency in depressed and nondepressed students: Sadder but wiser? *Journal of Experimental Psychology: General, 108*, 441–485.

Alloy, L. B., Abramson, L. Y., & Viscusi, D. (1981). Induced mood and the illusions of control. *Journal of Personality and Social Psychology, 41*, 1129–1140.

Alloy, L. B., & Clements, C. M. (1992). Illusion of control: Invulnerability to negative affect and depressive symptoms after laboratory and natural stressors. *Journal of Abnormal Psychology, 101*, 234–245.

Ayeroff, F., & Abelson, R. P. (1976). ESP and ESB: Belief in personal success at mental telepathy. *Journal of Personality and Social Psychology, 34*, 240–247.

Biner, P. M., Angle, S. T., Park, J. H., Mellinger, A. E., & Barber, B. C. (1995). Need and the illusion of control. *Personality and Social Psychology Bulletin, 21*, 899–907.

Blackmore, S., & Troscianko, T. (1985). Belief in the paranormal: Probability judgements, illusory control, and the "chance baseline shift". *British Journal of Psychology, 76*, 459–468.

Bouts, P., & Van Avermaet, E. (1992). Drawing familiar or unfamiliar cards: Stimulus familiarity, chance orientation, and the illusions of control. *Personality and Social Psychology Bulletin, 18*, 331–335.

Donovan, W. L., Leavitt, L. A., & Walsh, R. O. (1990). Maternal self-efficacy: Illusory control and its effect on susceptibility to learned helplessness. *Child Development, 61*, 1638–1647.

Dunn, D. S., & Wilson, T. D. (1990). When the stakes are high: A limit to the illusion-of-control effect. *Social Cognition, 8*, 305–323.

Friedland, N., Keinan, G., & Regev, Y. (1992). Controlling the uncontrollable: Effects of stress on perceptions of controllability. *Journal of Personality and Social Psychology, 63*, 923–931.

Langer, E. J. (1975). The illusion of control. *Journal of Personality and Social Psychology, 32*, 311–328.

Langer, E. J., & Roth, J. (1975). Heads I win, tails it's chance: The illusion of control as a function of the sequence of outcomes in a purely chance task. *Journal of Personality and Social Psychology, 32*, 951–955.

McKenna, F. P. (1993). It won't happen to me: Unrealistic optimism or illusion of control? *British Journal of Psychology, 84*, 39–50.

Rodin, J. (1986). Aging and health: Effects of the sense of control. *Science, 233*, 1271–1276.

Taylor, S. E., & Brown, J. D. (1988). Illusion and well-being: A social psychological perspective on mental health. *Psychological Bulletin, 103*, 193–210.

Thompson, S. C. (1999). Illusions of control: How we overestimate our personal influence. *Current Directions in Psychological Science, 8*, 187–190.

Thompson, S. C., Armstrong, W., & Thomas, C. (1998). Illusions of control, underestimations, and accuracy: A control heuristic explanation. *Psychological Bulletin, 123*, 143–161.

Thompson, S. C., Kent, D. R., Thomas, C., & Vrungos, S. (1999). Real and illusory control over exposure to HIV in college students and gay men. *Journal of Applied Social Psychology, 29*, 1128–1150.

Thompson, S. C., Kyle, D., Osgood, A., Quist, R. M., Phillips, D. J., & McClure, M. (2002). *The effects of motives on illusions of control*. Manuscript submitted for publication.

Thompson, S. C., & Spacapan, S. (1991). Perceptions of control in vulnerable populations. *Journal of Social Issues, 47*, 1–21.

Toneatto, T., Blitz-Miller, T., Calderwood, K., Dragonetti, R., & Tsanos, A. (1997). Cognitive distortions in heavy gambling. *Journal of Gambling Studies, 13*, 253–265.

White, R. W. (1959). Motivation reconsidered: The concept of competence. *Psychological Review, 66*, 297–333.

7 Biases in deductive reasoning

Jonathan St. B. T. Evans

Deductive reasoning involves drawing conclusions that necessarily follow from some given information. For example, if I told you that Sally is shorter than Mary and that Mary is taller than Joan, you could safely conclude that Mary is the tallest of the three. However, if I asked you who was taller, Joan or Sally, you could not infer the answer from the information given. This is because the information given is consistent with three possible situations that you might represent in mental models (Johnson-Laird & Byrne, 1991) as follows:

Mary > Sally > Joan (A)
Mary > Joan > Sally (B)
Mary > Sally = Joan (C)

These models allow us to deduce who is tallest, but not, for example, who is shortest. Most people can solve this kind of problem, although they might need to think about it for a few seconds before answering. Consider a more complex reasoning problem, like the following from the study of Handley and Evans (2000):

You urgently need to get hold of your friend Jane. Jane is on holiday somewhere in Britain. You know she is staying in a youth hostel, but you do not know in which city. Jane, being somewhat mysterious, gives you the following information about her whereabouts:

If Jane is in Hastings, then Sam is in Brighton
Either Jane is in Hastings or Sam is in Brighton, but not both

Based on this information, does it follow that:
(a) Jane is in Hastings
(b) Jane is not in Hastings
(c) It is impossible to tell whether or not Jane is in Hastings

The reader may care to give this problem some thought before reading on.

It is possible to draw a definite conclusion that follows logically from the stated information, although it is hard to see. It involves what is called suppositional reasoning, where you need to suppose a possibility for the sake of argument. In this case, let us suppose that Jane is in Hastings and see what follows. Clearly, we can conclude from the first piece of information that Sam is in Brighton. However, the second statement tells us that either Jane is in Hastings or Sam is in Brighton *but not both*. So if Jane is in Hastings, by the second statement it follows that Sam is not in Brighton. So we have a contradiction. Our supposition that Jane is in Hastings has led us to conclude both that Sam is in Brighton and that he is not in Brighton. Since this is an impossible state of affairs, it follows logically that our supposition is false. Hence, we can conclude that Jane is not in Hastings.

This kind of indirect reasoning is very hard for people who are not trained in logic, so don't worry if you didn't get the right answer. Handley and Evans gave this problem, among other similar ones, to undergraduate students as a pencil and paper task in a class setting. Only 9.5% offered the correct answer (b). Of the remainder, 48% said (c), impossible to tell, and an astonishing 42.5% gave answer (a) that is the *opposite* of the correct answer. The authors offered an explanation in terms of mental model theory. According to this theory, people try to imagine states of affairs, or mental models, that are suggested by the information given. We know that the first statement will suggest the model:

Jane is in Hastings; Sam is in Brighton

even though they may realize that there are other possibilities. When they try to integrate the information in the second statement, they ought to reject this model as it is inconsistent. Those concluding that Jane is in Hastings must have overlooked the significance of the phrase "but not both" in the second statement. However, it is likely that those who did notice the inconsistency mostly moved to the other incorrect answer that it is impossible to tell. Although people may acknowledge that the statement "If p then q" allows possibilities other than p and q to be the case, no other state of affairs comes easily to mind for most people, so it seems to them that no conclusion is possible.

Why is it important to study deductive reasoning in psychology? The answer to this question has changed quite radically over the past 40 years or so. The paradigm was developed at a time when Piaget's views were very influential and when most psychologists and philosophers saw logic as the basis for rational thinking (Evans, 2002). Hence it seemed a good idea to give people logical problems and see whether they could solve them, in order to determine how rationally people can reason. This meant giving people problems where they must assume the premises are true, introduce none of their real-world knowledge, and draw only conclusions that strictly and necessarily follow. A large number of experiments of this kind have been conducted from the 1960s onwards, with two general findings (Evans, Newstead, & Byrne, 1993). First of all, people make many errors when their answers are compared with a logical analysis of what is right and wrong. Second, they are highly influenced by the content and context in which the problem is framed, even though that is irrelevant to the logical task they are set.

These findings at first led psychologists to worry that people were highly irrational, but later to question whether logic was a good standard against which to measure real-world reasoning (Evans, 2002). As a consequence, there is now a big debate about logic and rationality. This debate complicates the story of biases in deductive reasoning somewhat. The reason is that "biases" in this field of research are measured relative to logic. A bias is defined as a systematic not random error. It involves people either neglecting some logically relevant information, or being influenced by factors that have nothing to do with the logic of the task. Hence, a bias is only evidence of irrationality if you think that logic is the right way to measure rationality.

The study of reasoning biases is, however, of considerable psychological interest in its own right. The approach I will take in this chapter is to discuss some of the major biases that have been explored in deductive reasoning research and the psychological implications that these have, without making assumptions about whether bias implies irrationality. I will then briefly consider the issue of rationality in reasoning research at the end of the chapter.

THE WASON SELECTION TASK

One of the best-known tasks in the study of deductive reasoning is the Wason selection task or four card problem. Invented by Peter Wason in the 1960s the task became well known after a series of studies was described in the early textbook on reasoning published by Wason and Johnson-Laird (1972). Studies of this task are generally divided between those using abstract problem materials and those using concrete or thematic material. A typical abstract version of the task is the following.

> There are four cards lying on a table. Each has a capital letter on one side and a single figure number on the other side. The visible sides of the cards are as follows:
>
> A   D   3   7
>
> The following statement applies to these four cards and may be true or false:
>
> If there is an A on one side of the card, then there is a 3 on the other side of the card.

Your task is to decide which cards, and only which cards, would need to be turned over in order to check whether the rule is true or false.

Most people give the answer A alone, or A and 3. Neither is logically correct according to the analysis given by Peter Wason and accepted by most later authors in the field. Logically, the statement can only be false if there is a card with an A on one side and without a 3 on the other. For example, if the A is turned over and a 5 is on the back, we know the statement is false. Because turning the A card *could* discover such a case, it is logically necessary to turn it. But by the same argument the 7 card must be turned as well: 7 is a number that it is not a 3, and discovering an A on the back would similarly disprove the statement. Very few people select this card, however. What they often do instead is to choose the 3 card, which is *not* logically necessary. The statement says that As must have 3s on the back, but it does not say that 3s must have As on the back. So if you turn over the 3 and find an A or find a B it would be consistent with the statement either way. In fact, you cannot prove the statement true except by eliminating any possibility that would make it false.

The matching bias effect

Why do people make these logical errors on the Wason selection task? Wason and Johnson-Laird (1972) suggested that people have a *confirmation bias*. There is a wide range of studies on cognitive and social psychology that suggest people may be biased to confirm their hypotheses (Klayman, 1995). The idea is that people tend to look for information that will confirm their hypotheses rather than information that could refute or falsify them. Such a bias could be important in science, since scientists generally agree that they should try to disprove theories in order to test them thoroughly. So how might confirmation bias explain the selection task findings? Wason suggested that people think that the statement would be true if a card were found with an A and a 3 on it. Because they have a confirmation bias, they turn over the A and the 3 cards trying to find this confirming case. They overlook the 7 card because they are not focused on trying to find the disconfirming card that has an A and *not* a 3.

While plausible, this account was abandoned by Wason and others shortly after the publication of his 1972 book with Johnson-Laird. The reason was an experiment reported by Evans and Lynch (1973) that provided strong evidence for an alternative account, known as *matching bias*. Note that the cards people tend to choose, A and 3, are those that are explicitly named in the conditional statement (If there is an A then there is a 3). What if people are simply matching their card choices to these named values? How could we tell if they were doing this, rather than looking for confirmation as Wason suggested? The answer requires a change to the presentation of the task. Suppose we introduce a negative into the conditional statement as follows:

If there is an A on one side of the card, then there is not a 3 on the other side of the card.

The instructions are the same as before. Now what will people choose? If they have a confirmation bias, they should choose the A and the 7 cards, in order to discover a card that has an A on one side and does not have a 3 on the other. If they have a matching bias, on the other hand, they choose A and 3 in order to match the cards to the named items. Note that this is now the logically correct answer, as an A3 card would disprove the statement. The results of the Evans and Lynch study were decisively in favour of the matching bias. In fact once the effects of matching were controlled, there was no evidence of confirmation bias at all in their study. The effect has been replicated many times in subsequent studies using a variety of tasks and linguistic formats (Evans, 1998).

Many researchers in the field were quite disconcerted by this finding when it appeared. Matching bias seemed to make participants in these experiments look rather foolish. How could they ignore the logical reasoning instructions and make such a superficial response? After many years of research, summarized by Evans (1998), the nature of matching bias became a lot clearer, although there is still some dispute as to its exact cause. There is strong evidence to suggest that people only think about the matching cards. If people are asked, in a computer presentation of the task, to point with a mouse at cards they are thinking of choosing, for example, most point little if at all at the 7 card. It is as though the matching bias acts as a kind of preconscious filter, drawing people's attention to the A and 3 cards. (Of course, the actual letters and numbers given vary for different participants.)

When people are asked to "think aloud" on the selection task, it becomes apparent that they are engaged in reasoning and that they do think about the hidden sides of the cards. But once again they focus their attention on the *matching values* that might be on these hidden sides. With the affirmative conditional – If A then 3 – for example, they might well say that they are turning over the A card, because a 3 on the back would prove the statement true. With the negative statement – If A then not 3 – they say they need to turn the A card because a 3 on the back would prove the statement *false*. In either case they think only about the matching cards and end up finding a justification for choosing them.

In the past few years we have learned that matching bias is strongly linked to problems in understanding implicit negation. It seems that the difficulty in choosing the 7 card is due to the fact that people have to interpret the 7 as "not a 3". In experiments where the mismatching cards are described explicitly, for example as "not A" or "not 3", the matching bias effect has been shown to disappear completely (Evans, 1998). In spite of this strong evidence, there is a rival account of matching bias in terms of expected information gain (Oaksford & Chater, 1998). The argument here is that people are prone to choose information that is generally informative in

132 *Evans*

everyday life, and negative information is generally less informative than positive. Evidence for a general positivity bias in thinking and hypothesis testing is quite widespread (Evans, 1989) and other theorists have also argued such a bias reflects a process that would normally be adaptive in everyday life (Klayman & Ha, 1987).

Do realistic materials "debias" reasoning?

Psychologists use the rather ugly word "debias" to refer to factors that remove cognitive biases. Experiments described by Wason and Johnson-Laird (1972) led to a popular hypothesis (now seen as greatly oversimplified) that realistic problem materials facilitate reasoning performance. Of course, we could argue as to whether realistic content debiases performance or whether abstract material biases it! Let us start by examining a version of the Wason selection task that is known to be very easy: the "drinking-age problem" first reported by Griggs and Cox (1982).

> Imagine you are a police officer observing people drinking in a bar. You need to check that they are obeying the following rule:
>
> If a person is drinking beer, then that person must be over 18 years of age.
>
> There are four cards, each representing an individual drinking in the bar. One side shows what beverage they are drinking and the other side shows their age. The four exposed sides of the cards are as follows:
>
> | Drinking Beer | Drinking Coke | 22 years of age | 16 years of age |
> |---|---|---|---|
>
> Which cards would you need to turn over in order to find out whether or not the rule is being obeyed?

These cards are laid out in the same logical order as for the abstract selection task discussed earlier. Hence, the first and last cards are again the correct choices. You should check the person drinking beer and the person who is 16 years of age. The great majority of participants do precisely that. They get this problem right and they show no evidence of matching bias.

What is the difference between this problem and the original selection task? Actually, there are several. The problem is "realistic". It also has a context – the police officer scenario. Brief though it is, this context is critical to the facilitation. If the task is presented without an introductory context, performance is little better than on the abstract version. The logic of the problem is also subtly changed. The standard task asks you to decide whether the rule is true or false. In the drinking-age problem you have to

Biases in deductive reasoning 133

decide whether or not the rule is obeyed. This turns out to be necessary but not sufficient for the full facilitation effect. An abstract task that asks about rules being obeyed does not facilitate, but the benefits of realism are reduced if the task asks for a true/false decision.

You might think that the problem facilitates because people have direct real-world knowledge of drinking-age laws and simply know from experience that underage drinkers are the ones to worry about. However, this is not the correct explanation. The conditional statement in the drinking-age problem is a permission rule. You need to fulfil a condition (over 18) in order to have permission to do something (drink beer). Other problems with permission rules work equally well, even where people have no direct experience of these rules. Consider the following problem – adapted from Manktelow and Over (1991):

> You are a company manager. Your firm is trying to increase business by offering free gifts to people who spend money in its shops. The firm's offer is
>
> If you spend more than £100, then you may take a free gift.
>
> You have been brought in because you have been told that in one of the firm's shops the offer has run into a problem: *you suspect that the store has not given some customers what they were entitled to*. You have four receipts in front of you showing on one side how much a customer spent and on the other whether they took a gift. The exposed sides show:
>
> Spent £120   Spent £85   Took a gift   Did not take a gift

The italicized words were shown in standard type to the participants. I have identified them as they were altered in some versions given to other participants (see below). The above problem has the same structure as the previous selection tasks and again shows the "cards" in the same order. Participants are most unlikely to have direct experience of this permission rule and yet they overwhelmingly chose cards 1 and 4, as on the drinking-age problem. This could lead them to discover someone who had fulfilled the condition (spent over £100) but not received the gift, thus being possibly cheated by the shop.

What exactly is happening here? Are people reasoning logically, or are they acting on their general knowledge of how permission rules work? Suppose the wording of the italicized section is changed to the following: *you suspect that some customers in the store might have been taking more than they were entitled to*. Now Manktelow and Over found a marked shift in card choices. Most people chose cards 2 and 3. This would enable them to tell whether the customers had been cheating the shop: the opposite problem. They could now possibly find cases where people spent less than £100 and still took the gift. Note that the rule is exactly the same in both cases. What differs is the motive that they are given for investigating the rule. This study was followed by others (e.g., Gigerenzer & Hug, 1992) which showed that selections could be changed by altering the perspective of the decision maker and nothing else in the wording.

These findings suggest that facilitation in realistic versions of the selection task is not due to somehow improving people's understanding of conditional logic. Much more likely, the content is eliciting domain-sensitive reasoning procedures of some kind. There is an unresolved debate as to what the nature of these might be, with rival accounts based on pragmatic reasoning schemas, innate cognitive modules, and pragmatic relevance theory (Evans, 2002; Manktelow, 1999).

BIASES IN SYLLOGISTIC REASONING

A popular form of reasoning task that is used in the study of deductive reasoning is the syllogism, originally invented by Aristotle. A syllogism consists of two premises and a conclusion, which are always in one of the following four forms:

All A are B
No A are B
Some A are B
Some A are not B

The syllogism always links three terms together. I will use the convention of assuming that the conclusion links two terms A and C and that each premise therefore connects with a middle term, B. A complete syllogism might be of the form:

All A are B
All C are B
Therefore, all A are C

This argument is a fallacy, that is, its conclusion does not necessarily follow. This can be seen easily if I substitute some realistic terms for A, B, and C as follows:

All dogs are animals
All cats are animals
Therefore, all dogs are cats

The fallacy would be much harder to see if I substituted some different terms as follows:

All tigers are animals
All cats are animals
Therefore, all tigers are cats

People are strongly influenced by whether they agree with conclusions (the belief bias effect, discussed later). However, the task they are set is to say whether or not the conclusion follows in light of the logical structure of the argument. When syllogisms are presented in abstract form – say using letters as in the earlier examples above – error rates are very high indeed. Hundreds of different syllogisms can be formed by varying the terms (technically the mood) used in each premise and conclusion (all, no, some, some not) and by varying the order reference to the terms A, B, and C. With the conclusion in the form A–C the premises can take four different arrangements (or figures as they are technically known): A–B, B–C; A–B, C–B; B–A, B–C; B–A, C–B. With three statements (two premises and a conclusion) in each of four moods and four different figures, you can make 256 logically distinct syllogisms.

Psychological experiments on abstract syllogistic reasoning are reviewed in detail by Evans et al. (1993, Ch. 5). A recent study in which people evaluated every possible logical form was reported by Evans, Handley, Harper, and Johnson-Laird (1999). When syllogisms are given to people to evaluate, they frequently say that the conclusion follows, even though the great majority are actually invalid, or fallacious. The endorsement of fallacies is a strong bias in deductive reasoning research as a whole. With syllogisms people are also biased by both the mood and the figure. For example, they are more likely to say that the conclusion follows if it is of a similar mood to the premises. The first syllogism described above, although invalid, has two "all" premises and an "all" conclusion. This type of fallacy is much more often endorsed than one where the conclusion is incongruent, such as:

All A are B
All C are B
Therefore, no A are C

Note that the conclusion here is possible given the premises, just as it was in the "all" form. People are also biased by the figure of the syllogism. They would, for example, be much more likely to agree with the following argument:

Some A are B
Some B are C
Therefore, some A are C

than this one

> Some A are B
> Some B are C
> Therefore, some C are A

even though both are actually fallacies. In the first case, the terms seem to follow in a natural order. These fallacies and biases of abstract syllogistic reasoning bear a similarity to the matching bias effect discussed above in conditional reasoning. They suggest very superficial processing by most of the participants. They also suggest that the typical populations of undergraduate students find abstract logical reasoning very difficult. However, what if problems are made more realistic and easier to relate to everyday knowledge and thinking? How will that affect people's ability to reason deductively?

BELIEF BIAS: A SAMPLE EXPERIMENT

One of the major phenomena studied in deductive reasoning research is that of *belief bias*. Belief bias is typically described as a tendency to endorse arguments whose conclusions you believe, regardless of whether they are valid or not. This is not very accurate because, as we have already seen, people tend to endorse fallacies when syllogisms have abstract or neutral content. The belief bias effect is really a suppression of fallacies when conclusions are unbelievable, and so might be better called a *debiasing* effect!

The usual method by which belief bias is studied involves giving people syllogisms and asking them whether the conclusion necessarily follows (full details of the experimental method can be found in Text box 7.1). Some of

---

Text box 7.1 Method of a sample experiment on the belief bias

Participants

The effects are typically quite large and have demonstrated with small samples. I recommend a minimum of 32 participants drawn from a population of average or above average intelligence.

Materials

The material consists of syllogisms like those in Table 7.1. Note that there are two logical forms used. The valid form is

> No C are B
> Some A are B
> Therefore, some A are not C

and the invalid form is

> No A are B
> Some C are B
> Therefore, some A are not C

It is necessary to keep these same forms, which were carefully chosen, but the design calls for two syllogisms of each type to be presented. The four shown in Table 7.1 can be used but at least one other set is needed. In order to get a powerful effect, the experimenter needs to make sure that the conclusions follow (believable) or violate (unbelievable) a *class-inclusive* relationship, as do those in the table. For example, all cigarettes are addictive but not all addictive things are cigarettes. So while it is believable, as in the example shown, to say that "some addictive things are not cigarettes" it is unbelievable if it is turned around as "some cigarettes are not addictive". Ideally, the experimenter also checks the believability of the conclusions by asking a separate group of participants to rate them on a 5-point scale from "Highly Unbelievable" to "Highly Believable" and working out the average ratings. About 16 participants is sufficient for the rating study.

Design

The design is within-participants. Each participant will be asked to solve all eight problems, presented in an independently randomized order.

Procedure

A booklet with eight pages is given each participant. Each page contains one of the problems, with a layout like this

> GIVEN
> > No millionaires are hard workers
> > Some rich people are hard workers
> DOES IT FOLLOW THAT
> > Some millionaires are not rich people
> > YES   NO

The experimenter assigns each problem a number from 1 to 8, and uses a random number table or spreadsheet program to work out a separate random sequence for each participant. The problem sheets are numbered in the corner before they are copied and then put together in the right order for each participant. The front cover of the booklet can have the written instructions. The participants are instructed to reason deductively, as otherwise the influence of belief could not be considered a bias. Typical instructions (adapted from Evans et al., 1983) would be:

> This is a test of reasoning ability. You will be given eight problems. In each case you are given two statements that you should assume to be true. You will also be asked if a further statement – that is, a conclusion –

> follows from these two statements. If you think the conclusion *necessarily* follows then mark the word "YES", otherwise mark "NO". Take your time and make sure you have the right answer. Do not go back to a previous problem once you have left it.
>
> *Analysis and results*
>
> There are three effects of interest: an effect of logic, an effect of belief, and an *interaction* between the two. There are too few measures for parametric analysis, but there is a way around this. First, a table can be made up with a row for each participant and a column for each condition, VB, VU, IB, and IU. For each participant the number of Yes answers he or she gave for each type is recorded – these must be between 0 and 2. The next step is to compute for each participant the value of three indices in a further three columns. These indices are computed by adding two different pairs of columns and then subtracting the totals as follows:
>
> Logic Index: (VB + VU) – (IB + IU)
> Belief Index: (VB + IB) – (VU + IU)
> Interaction Index: (VU + IB) – (VB + IU)
>
> The first two are fairly obvious. The Logic Index is the number of valid conclusions accepted minus the number of invalid conclusions accepted with belief balanced. Conversely, the Belief Index measures the difference between the acceptance of believable and unbelievable conclusions with logic controlled. The Interaction Index is designed to measure whether (as is usually found) the belief-bias effect is larger for invalid than for valid syllogisms. One might want to think of this as (IB – IU) – (VB – VU) although it is algebraically equivalent to the above. Tests for statistical significance are simple. For each index it can be determined whether it is significantly above zero by using the sign test. For each index the number of participants with a score above zero are counted and compared with the number at or below zero using the binomial test. Since these effects are well known, one-tailed tests can be used in each case.

the arguments are logically valid and some are not, and some have believable conclusions and some do not. A well-known study by Evans, Barston, and Pollard (1983) is often cited as showing the basic phenomenon. They presented four categories of syllogisms classified as Valid-Believable (VB), Valid-Unbelievable (VU), Invalid-Believable (IB), and Invalid-Unbelievable (IU). Examples of these are shown in Table 7.1 together with the rates at which people accepted them as valid arguments over three experiments.

The higher acceptance rate for believable syllogisms compared to the unbelievable ones, both for valid and invalid cases, indicates the presence of a strong belief bias. The Belief Index (as defined in Text box 7.1) yielded a high score of 0.95, which was moreover higher than the Logic Index (see also Text box 7.1) that yielded a score of only 0.64. But note that both were significantly above zero.

Table 7.1 Examples of four kinds of syllogisms presented by Evans et al. (1983) together with the percentage rates of acceptance of each argument as valid over three experiments

Type	Example	Rate
Valid-Believable	No police dogs are vicious Some highly trained dogs are vicious Therefore, some highly trained dogs are not police dogs	89%
Valid-Unbelievable	No nutritional things are expensive Some vitamin tablets are expensive Therefore, some vitamin tablets are not nutritional	56%
Invalid-Believable	No addictive things are inexpensive Some cigarettes are inexpensive Therefore, some addictive things are not cigarettes	71%
Invalid-Unbelievable	No millionaires are hard workers Some rich people are hard workers Therefore, some millionaires are not rich people	10%

Discussion

Research on the belief-bias effect is reviewed and discussed by Evans et al. (1993) and by Manktelow (1999). Although the effects are large and very reliable, there is considerable theoretical debate about the causes of the bias and its implications. Evans et al. (1983) argued that there were conflicting logical and belief-based processes within individuals competing for control of the task, an idea that accords with currently fashionable "dual processing" accounts of reasoning discussed later (see Evans & Over, 1996; Stanovich, 1999). There has been a debate on the cause of the interaction between belief and logic on this task. One idea is that people accept arguments uncritically if they agree with their conclusions, so they do not notice when believable conclusions are supported by invalid arguments and only check the logic when the conclusion is disagreeable. A different idea is that people are unsure what it means to have a conclusion that "necessarily" follows. If they cannot prove the conclusion valid, they then tend to fall back on belief. The belief bias effect has also figured in debates about whether reasoning research shows people to be irrational (see below).

THEORETICAL ISSUES

Dual process theories of reasoning

In discussing the belief bias effect earlier, I mentioned that there was evidence of a conflict between two types of thought processes, one reasoning logically according to the instructions and the other prompting people to respond on the basis of their prior beliefs. Of particular interest are the problems that bring logic and belief into conflict: Valid-Unbelievable and Invalid-Believable. There is evidence that logical performance on these conflict problems declines sharply with age, while performance on problems where belief and logic agree is unaffected (Gilinsky & Judd, 1994). This can be linked theoretically with findings reported in a large programme of study of individual differences in reasoning ability (Stanovich, 1999). Stanovich found that people with high general intelligence scores were much better able to deal with belief–logic conflict problems, effectively suppressing belief influences in order to find the logical solutions. The link is that the cognitive basis of general intelligence scores, in particular working memory capacity, declines with age.

Stanovich's results generally support a dual processing account of thinking and reasoning (see also Evans & Over, 1996). It seems that we think using two different cognitive systems. The first system introduces prior knowledge based on associative learning and causes us almost compulsively to contextualize any problem we may be given to consider. By this I mean that we relate every problem to prior knowledge that we have which appears relevant to it. Although helpful in many real life situations, this contextualization may result in belief biases when we are supposed to be reasoning abstractly or logically, only considering the information in front of us. The second system does allow abstract reasoning, but only seems to be well developed in people of very high general intelligence. Stanovich has also shown that performance on the abstract form of the Wason selection task is related to general intelligence, whereas performance on realistic versions is not. This makes sense because the first system can provide solutions to typical realistic versions by generalizing past experience, whereas the second system is needed for the abstract task where there is no helpful prior knowledge to be added to the context.

The rationality debate

Research on deductive reasoning was developed during a period in which psychologists were content to follow many philosophers in regarding logic as a model for rational thinking (Evans, 2002). If we hold fast to this view, after the past 40 years or so of intensive investigation of deductive reasoning, then we should feel very concerned indeed about human rationality. As this brief survey has indicated, people – typically university students – given reasoning problems in the laboratory, make many errors. They frequently give logically incorrect answers to abstract reasoning problems and show biases indicative of shallow processing, such as matching bias in conditional reasoning and mood and figural biases in syllogistic reasoning. Introducing realistic content does not induce better logical reasoning, as was once thought. People's reasoning is highly influenced by content and context that are logically irrelevant to the task set, and the knowledge and belief introduced is just as likely to bias as to debias responses from a logical point of view.

Faced with these findings, psychologists (and to a lesser extent philosophers) have felt it necessary to resolve what Evans and Over (1996) term the "paradox of rationality". The human species is highly successful and has succeeded in adapting the environment to its own needs, inventing science, technology, and so on. We seem to be a very intelligent species. So why are representatives of the human race generally so poor at solving reasoning tasks set in the psychological laboratory? Discussions of rationality in reasoning experiments have turned on three major issues. The first of these is the *normative system* problem. Perhaps people seem illogical because formal logic provides a poor framework for assessing the rationality of everyday reasoning. Psychologists have in fact been somewhat naïve in adopting standard textbook logic as a normative reference, and have lacked awareness that such systems have been rejected by contemporary philosophical logicians precisely because they cannot be mapped onto natural language and everyday reasoning (Evans, 2002).

As an example, many psychologists have treated the conditional statement "If p then q" as though it represented a relationship of material implication between p and q. Such a representation means that the conditional is true unless we have a case of p and not-q and logically equivalent to the statement "Either not p or q". Suppose I make this statement:

If I am in London, then I am in France.

If I am in Plymouth when I make this statement and if the conditional is material, then you would have to say the statement is true. A material conditional is equivalent to:

Either I am not in London or I am in France.

Since I am in Plymouth, and therefore not in London, the first part of the disjunction is confirmed so the statement is true. However, it is self-evident that the conditional statement is false. Many philosophers consequently reject the material conditional. What we actually do is to imagine the world in which I am in London and ask whether I would be in France. Evidently we would be in England, so the statement is false.

A second issue is known as the *interpretation problem*. Perhaps participants construe the task differently than the experimenter intended. Then their conclusions may follow logically from their personalized interpretation of the problem. Consider the following inference:

If there is an A on the card, then there is a 3 on the card.
There is a 3 on the card.
Therefore, there is an A on the card.

Many psychologists would regard this as a fallacy and mark anyone endorsing it as committing an error. When presented with abstract materials like these, the evidence is that intelligent adults frequently do agree that this conclusion follows (Evans et al., 1993). The problem is that the inference *does* follow logically if people interpret the statement as meaning "If and only if there is an A on the card, then there is a 3 on the card". Moreover, it is not unreasonable for them to make such an interpretation, as this biconditional reading is often intended when we use conditionals in everyday discourse. When people are given realistic conditionals, then they will make the above "fallacy" when only p seems to lead to q as in:

If he is over 18 years of age, then he is entitled to vote.

but they will not make it when the statement is clearly one way, as in:

If he is 18 years of age, then he is an adult.

In fact, no-one would infer that an adult must be 18 years of age. So the "error" would not occur in everyday reasoning and the abstract problem can be regarded as ambiguous in interpretation.

The third issue is the *external validity* problem. This is the argument that many of the reasoning problems used in the laboratory are artificial and unrepresentative of real-world reasoning. Hence, people may be more rational than the experiments suggest. On this view, problems such as the Wason selection task provide cognitive illusions that tell us interesting things about how people think, but are not to be taken as measures of rationality in reasoning. This is analogous to saying that the visual illusions studied by psychologists are informative about the visual system, even though that system provides highly accurate representations of the world most of the time.

The force of these three arguments, taken together, makes it difficult to argue that the biases observed in deductive reasoning experiments are necessarily indicative of irrationality in human beings. However, this was not the objective for most of the psychologists working in this field anyway. As with topics discussed in many other chapters of this book, the study of biases and cognitive illusions in deductive reasoning has proved very helpful in the development of our theoretical understanding of human thought processes.

SUMMARY

- The deductive reasoning paradigm investigates the ability of ordinary people to solve logical reasoning problems. Hence, systematic departures from logical solutions are normally regarded as biases.
- One such well-established effect is the *matching bias*, which is a tendency

to focus on the explicit content of sentences, such as conditionals, regardless of whether propositions contain a negation that reverses their logical significance.
- While logically irrelevant, the content and context used to frame deductive reasoning problems have marked influence on the responses that participants give. Sometimes realistic material affects people's ability to perceive the logical validity of arguments.
- Dual process theory accounts for some reasoning biases by positing competing systems of reasoning. Pragmatic processes associated with implicit systems of cognition may interfere with people's ability to apply abstract general reasoning in compliance with the instructions.
- Logic is nowadays disputed as the appropriate normative system for evaluating reasoning, so there is a major debate about the implications that reasoning biases have for human rationality.

FURTHER READING

For a broad discussion of the deductive reasoning paradigm and the major psychological phenomena associated with it, the reader is referred to Evans (2002). More detailed discussion of some of the biases in this literature is provided by Manktelow (1999). Those readers who are particularly interested in the implications of this work for the debate about human rationality should consult Evans and Over (1996) and Stanovich (1999).

REFERENCES

Evans, J. St. B. T. (1989). *Bias in human reasoning: Causes and consequences*. Hove, UK: Lawrence Erlbaum Associates Ltd.

Evans, J. St. B. T. (1998). Matching bias in conditional reasoning: Do we understand it after 25 years? *Thinking and Reasoning, 4*, 45–82.

Evans, J. St. B. T. (2002). Logic and human reasoning: An assessment of the deduction paradigm. *Psychological Bulletin, 128*, 978–996.

Evans, J. St. B. T., Barston, J. L., & Pollard, P. (1983). On the conflict between logic and belief in syllogistic reasoning. *Memory & Cognition, 11*, 295–306.

Evans, J. St. B. T., Handley, S. J., Harper, C., & Johnson-Laird, P. N. (1999). Reasoning about necessity and possibility: A test of the mental model theory of deduction. *Journal of Experimental Psychology: Learning, Memory, and Cognition, 25*, 1495–1513.

Evans, J. St. B. T., & Lynch, J. S. (1973). Matching bias in the selection task. *British Journal of Psychology, 64*, 391–397.

Evans, J. St. B. T., Newstead, S. E., & Byrne, R. M. J. (1993). *Human reasoning: The psychology of deduction*. Hove, UK: Lawrence Erlbaum Associates Ltd.

Evans, J. St. B. T., & Over, D. E. (1996). *Rationality and reasoning*. Hove, UK: Psychology Press.

Gigerenzer, G., & Hug, K. (1992). Domain-specific reasoning: Social contracts, cheating and perspective change. *Cognition*, *43*, 127–171.

Gilinsky, A. S., & Judd, B. B. (1994). Working memory and bias in reasoning across the life-span. *Psychology and Aging*, *9*, 356–371.

Griggs, R. A., & Cox, J. R. (1982). The elusive thematic materials effect in the Wason selection task. *British Journal of Psychology*, *73*, 407–420.

Handley, S. J., & Evans, J. St. B. T. (2000). Supposition and representation in human reasoning. *Thinking and Reasoning*, *6*, 273–312.

Johnson-Laird, P. N., & Byrne, R. (1991). *Deduction*. Hove, UK: Lawrence Erlbaum Associates Ltd.

Klayman, J. (1995). Varieties of confirmation bias. *The Psychology of Learning and Motivation*, *32*, 385–417.

Klayman, J., & Ha, Y. W. (1987). Confirmation, disconfirmation and information in hypothesis testing. *Psychological Review*, *94*, 211–228.

Manktelow, K. I. (1999). *Reasoning and thinking*. Hove, UK: Psychology Press.

Manktelow, K. I., & Over, D. E. (1991). Social roles and utilities in reasoning with deontic conditionals. *Cognition*, *39*, 85–105.

Oaksford, M., & Chater, N. (1998). *Rationality in an uncertain world*. Hove, UK: Psychology Press.

Stanovich, K. E. (1999). *Who is rational? Studies of individual differences in reasoning*. Mahway, NJ: Lawrence Erlbaum Associates Inc.

Wason, P. C., & Johnson-Laird, P. N. (1972). *Psychology of reasoning: Structure and content*. London: Batsford.

Part II
Illusions of judgement

8 Availability

Rolf Reber

When you ask each spouse of a married couple to estimate the percentage of their own contribution to the housework, the chances are high that each spouse will overestimate their own contribution, so that the sum exceeds one hundred percent. People normally overestimate their own contribution to the joint product of a group (Ross & Sicoly, 1979). These authors found this effect in naturally occurring discussion groups, basketball players, groups assembled in the laboratory, and married couples. Why do people behave in this way? One explanation would be that people are motivated to see themselves in a positive light and therefore overestimate their contribution to a joint product. It is, however, possible that cognitive processes alone, without any involvement of motivational processes, account for the observed overestimation.

Let us have a closer look at the married couple. If the husband is asked about his contribution to the housework, he retrieves information that is relevant to the question. He recalls instances of preparing meals and cleaning the house. Moreover, he recalls instances of his wife doing the same work. However, this retrieval is biased: He is better at retrieving instances of his own housework than instances of his wife's work. He remembers in some detail how he prepared a tiramisu. He may have forgotten, however, that his wife prepared paella, work that needed about the same time and effort. Even if he remembers the paella, his memories of his own efforts expended for the tiramisu are probably more vivid than the memories of his wife's work. Other instances are remembered in an analogous way, so that in general, he remembers more easily instances of his own contribution to the housework than of his wife's contribution. If he now has to estimate his own contribution, he compares the ease with which he can retrieve instances of his own work with the ease with which he can retrieve instances of his wife's work. As he can more easily remember his own contributions, he overestimates his share of the housework. Of course, his wife does exactly the same, with the consequence that she can retrieve instances of her housework with greater ease, resulting in an overestimation of her contribution.

The mechanism leading to these overestimations might be "availability". This is one of the famous heuristics proposed by Tversky and Kahneman

(1973), along with the representativeness heuristic (see Chapter 9 on representativeness) and anchoring and adjustment (see Chapter 10 on the anchoring effect). Text box 8.1 provides a definition of availability.

Text box 8.1 Definition of availability

The ease with which relevant instances of a class (in our example housework) come to mind has been called "availability" (Tversky & Kahneman, 1973).

Alternative terms to "availability" have been proposed. Higgins (1996), for example, distinguished between availability and accessibility in accordance with Tulving, who used "the term 'availability' to refer to the hypothetical presence of information in the memory store [. . .]. That part of the available information that could be recalled was said to be accessible" (Tulving, 1983, p. 203). Note that the term "availability" is used differently from the way Tversky and Kahneman (1973) used it. Higgins (1996) used "accessibility experiences" to refer to the ease with which instances come to mind. In this chapter, I use the term "availability" as a general heuristic relying on ease or amount of recall, and the term "accessibility experiences" or "ease of recall" when discussing the specific mechanisms behind the availability heuristic.

Let us apply the term "availability" to our example: Both the husband and his wife overestimate their own contribution to the housework because information about their own contribution is more available than information about their spouse's contribution. As they are unable to come to an objective assessment of the proportion of housework that each of them has contributed, they use the availability of information as a heuristic for their estimate. Overestimation of one's contribution to the joint products of a group has been only one of many applications of the availability heuristic. Although availability is often a valid cue to frequencies in the environment, it sometimes causes biased estimates. In this chapter, I shall first describe two of the experiments from the classic paper of Tversky and Kahneman (1973). I then turn to some early applications of the availability heuristic, such as stereotype formation and the effects of vividness of information, before I discuss some studies that tell us what mental mechanisms lie behind availability.

TWO BASIC EXPERIMENTS

I now report two classical studies, Experiments 8 and 3, from Tversky and Kahneman's (1973) seminal paper. For each experiment, I first report methods and results of the original study and then turn to adaptations of the studies for classroom demonstrations.

Experiment 1: The famous-names experiment

The basic idea of Tversky and Kahneman's (1973) Experiment 8 was to show that estimates of frequency of occurrence depend on availability (see Text box 8.2 for a classroom demonstration).

Method

Participants were presented with a tape-recorded list of 39 names, at a rate of 2 seconds per name. The independent variable, manipulated within participants, was fame of the names. Some names were famous (e.g., Richard Nixon, Elizabeth Taylor), others less famous (e.g., William Fulbright, Lana Turner). Some participants heard names of public figures (e.g., Richard Nixon, William Fulbright), others of entertainers (e.g., Elizabeth Taylor, Lana Turner). In one group, 19 of these names were of famous women and the remaining 20 of less famous men. In the other group, 19 names were of famous men and the remaining 20 of less famous women. Note that there were always fewer famous than non-famous names. There were two dependent variables: (a) after listening to the recordings, about half of the participants had to recall as many names as possible; this measure indicated the availability with which an instance can be recalled. Participants were assumed to represent famous names more vividly than non-famous names, and therefore to recall the former more readily than the latter. (b) The other participants had to judge whether the list contained more names of men or of women. If people use the availability heuristic, they are expected to judge that there are more instances with famous names, despite the fact that there were only 19 famous names and 20 less famous names. If 19 famous women and 20 less famous men had been shown, participants were expected to judge that there were more women in the list. In contrast, if 19 famous men and 20 less famous women had been presented, participants were expected to judge that more men were presented.

Results

The results were clear-cut: Those participants who had to recall as many names as possible recalled 12.3 of the 19 famous names and 8.4 of the 20 less famous names. Of 86 participants in the recall condition, 57 recalled more famous than less famous names, and only 13 recalled fewer famous names than less famous names. A sign test revealed that this difference was highly significant. Among the 99 participants who compared the frequency of men and women in the lists, 80 erroneously believed that the class consisting of the more famous names was more frequent. Again, a sign test revealed that this difference was highly significant. The authors concluded that the participants used the availability heuristic because they recalled more famous names and they judged famous names as being more frequent on the list.

> **Text box 8.2** Classroom demonstration of Experiment 1
>
> This is an easy experiment that always worked when I used it as a classroom demonstration. The design of the experiment can be simplified. The experimenter compiles a list of 9 famous women and 10 less famous men, or vice versa. From time to time, he or she has to update the list because some less famous people have risen to stardom and some famous ones have sunk into oblivion. The important part of the experiment is the participants' judgement of the relative frequency of men compared to women, after they have listened to the list read by the experimenter. The idea behind the recall of names is to check whether famous names are indeed recalled more readily than less famous names. As we will see later, however, amount of recalled names is not necessarily a good measure of ease of recall.

Experiment 2: The letter-frequency experiment

Another classic experiment instructs participants to judge word frequency (Tversky & Kahneman, 1973, Exp. 3; see Sedlmeier, Hertwig, & Gigerenzer, 1998, for a critical examination). A classroom adaptation of this experiment can be found in Text box 8.3.

Method

Participants of this study were given the following instructions:

> The frequency of appearance of letters in the English language was studied. A typical text was selected, and the relative frequency with which various letters of the alphabet appeared in the first and third positions in words was recorded. Words of less than three letters were excluded from the count.
>
> You will be given several letters of the alphabet, and you will be asked to judge whether these letters appear more often in the first or in the third position, and to estimate the ratio of the frequency with which they appear in these positions.
>
> (Tversky & Kahneman, 1973, p. 211f)

The authors assessed two dependent variables: First, participants were asked whether a certain letter, for example, R, is more likely to appear in the first or in the third position. The participants had to mark the correct answer. Second, they were asked to estimate the ratio of these two values, that is, Rs in the first position divided by Rs in the third position. In their original study, the authors used five letter, K, L, N, R, and V, all of them occurring more frequently in the third than in the first letter position in English words. There was no manipulation of an independent variable; the authors were interested in the question of whether participants judged these letters to appear more frequently in the first position, despite the fact that all of them were more frequent in the third position in English language.

Results

As it is easier to retrieve letters in the first position than letters in the third position, a majority of participants judged the first position to be more likely for the majority of letters: From 152 participants, 105 judged the first position to be more likely for a majority of the presented letters, and 47 judged the third position to be more likely for a majority of the letters. The authors employed a sign test and found a highly significant preference for the first letter position, $p < .001$. Moreover, each of the five letters was judged to be more frequent in the first rather than in the third position, with a median ratio of about 2:1, despite the fact that each letter was more frequent in the third position.

Text box 8.3 Classroom demonstration of Experiment 2

For a classroom demonstration, the experimenter may choose an uneven number of letters that in his or her language is more frequent in the third than in the first position.[1] The respondents are then asked to indicate whether each of these letters is more frequent in the first position or in the third position. The experimenter then simply counts how many respondents chose the first and how many chose the third position for the majority of letters. As letter position can be ranked, the data can be analyzed with a sign test.

I now turn to an overview of research on the availability heuristic that is partitioned into two sections: First, I review early research that applied the concept of availability, before turning to more recent discussions of mental mechanisms underlying the availability heuristic.

APPLICATIONS OF THE AVAILABILITY HEURISTIC

The concept of availability has become very popular and has gone far beyond estimates of frequencies. Availability had a huge impact, especially on social psychology. In this section, I first discuss how biased encoding and retrieval influence availability of information. I then turn to vividness as a basis of availability of information. Finally, I highlight the role of perspective taking for availability. Perspective taking is an instructive example of how both retrieval processes and vividness jointly contribute to availability.

Biased encoding and retrieval of information

Information A may be more available than information B because information A is presented more frequently than information B (see Chapter 12 on the mere exposure effect). If, for example, an employer sees 50 Dallonians who are lazy, but only 20 industrious Dallonians, information about lazy Dallonians may become more available than information about industrious Dallonians. This information, in turn, may drive the employer's impression about Dallonians as employees and his or her decision whether or not to hire a Dallonian. I discuss two examples of biased encoding and retrieval: Formation of stereotypes and overestimation of frequencies of lethal events.

The formation of stereotypes

How do people form stereotypes of a group? Early theorists emphasized the crucial role of motivational factors in stereotype formation. After Tversky and Kahneman (1973) demonstrated the use of the availability heuristic, however, researchers examined the role of cognitive biases in stereotype formation (see Rothbart, Fulero, Jensen, Howard, & Birrell, 1978, for a discussion); people may arrive at biased stereotypes without any motivation to see others in a biased manner. Let us assume that Joe, Bill, Frank, and Eric belong to the Dallonians. Joe and Bill are lazy, whereas Frank and Eric are industrious. If Jane – who has never seen Dallonians before – meets these four Dallonians twice each, she will conclude that Dallonians are neither especially lazy nor especially industrious people because she has seen two group members who were industrious and two who were not. What happens if Jane meets Joe and Bill four times each and Frank and Eric only twice? If Jane organizes her experiences around persons, she will again believe that Dallonians are neither lazy nor industrious because she has seen two group members who were industrious and two who were not. If, however, she organizes her representations around the group as a whole, she will believe that Dallonians are lazy because she experienced eight instances when they were lazy and only four instances when they were industrious. In this latter case, instances of lazy behaviour come more easily to mind, resulting in the stereotype that Dallonians are lazy.

Rothbart et al. (1978) tested this assumption experimentally. The authors manipulated the proportion of desirable and undesirable traits, the pairing of names and traits, and memory load. Participants in three groups got either (1) more desirable than undesirable traits about Dallonians, (2) as many desirable as undesirable traits, or (3) more undesirable than desirable traits. In the single exposure condition, each name was paired with one instance of the same trait (e.g., Joe–lazy). In the multiple exposure condition, each person was paired with multiple instances of the same trait (e.g., Joe paired four times with lazy; Frank paired twice with industrious); in this condition, the same number of persons had desirable and undesirable traits, although the number of traits was manipulated. Participants in the low memory load condition saw 16 name–trait pairs; those in the high memory load condition saw 64 name–trait pairs. After each person–trait pair was presented, the participants had to estimate the frequency of desirable and undesirable traits, and the attractiveness of Dallonians as a group.

The authors found that people always organized traits around persons when memory load was low. That is, even when Joe was paired four times with lazy and Frank only twice with industrious (and analogically for other undesirable and desirable traits), they found that Dallonians had as many desirable as undesirable traits. If memory load was high, the frequency estimates depended on the exposure condition: In the single exposure condition, frequency estimates were by and large accurate because one name was paired with one trait. In the multiple exposure condition, however, people estimated that Dallonians had more undesirable traits when Joe was paired four times with lazy and Frank only twice with industrious, although there were as many Dallonians with desirable as with undesirable traits. In addition, judgements of group attractiveness paralleled the frequency estimates, and thus biased frequency estimates resulted in a change in judged attractiveness. In sum, this finding suggests that cognitive factors contribute to stereotype formation even if there is no motivation to see others in a biased way.

Overestimation of lethal events

Many people are afraid of becoming a victim of a crime, maybe more than is justified by official crime statistics. One possibility is that more crimes are committed than is revealed in official statistics. An alternative possibility is that people overestimate the prevalence of violent crime because these are exhaustively covered and sensationalized by the media. Due to high media coverage, violent crimes become more available in memory, and their frequency is thus overestimated. Lichtenstein, Slovic, Fischhoff, Layman, and Combs (1978) examined this assumption in a study about judging the frequency of lethal events.

They chose 41 causes of death that varied widely in frequency. It is very uncommon to die from botulism, whereas stroke is one of the more frequent causes of death. Some causes were natural, for example, stomach cancer, whereas others were unnatural, such as homicide. The authors predicted that unnatural causes with high media coverage would be judged to be more frequent than quiet killers like stomach cancer. Their findings matched their predictions: Although stomach cancer is more than five times more frequent than homicide, participants estimated that homicide is about 1.6 times more frequent than stomach cancer. Moreover, media coverage was high for homicides, but zero for stomach cancer, and media coverage predicted the frequency estimates of causes of death. The authors concluded that estimates of frequency of lethal events are based on high availability of vivid or sensational events. Indeed, among the most overestimated causes were sensational events like tornado, flood, homicide, and motor vehicle accidents. Most causes of death that were underestimated were those not much covered by the media, like asthma, tuberculosis, diabetes, stomach cancer, and heart disease.

Vividness of information

Estimations of frequency of lethal events are biased because of the disproportionate media coverage of some sensational, but relatively infrequent, events. Thus, two independent features of the information may cause the increase in availability of homicide compared to stomach cancer: (1) Homicides may be more available because instances of death from homicide are covered more frequently in the media than instances of death from stomach cancer, as discussed above. Or (2) homicides can be more available even if they are not seen more frequently than stomach cancer, because people can imagine violent crimes more vividly than quiet killers. Therefore, frequency of public coverage of an event and its vividness need to be manipulated independently.

Reyes, Thompson, and Bower (1980) were able to show that vividness of presented evidence from a trial affected both its retention and judgements of guilt after a 48-hour delay. The authors presented nine pieces of evidence from the prosecution and nine pieces of evidence from the defence, but for some participants, only the prosecution evidence was vivid, while for the other participants, only the defence evidence was vivid. The participants remembered more evidence of the prosecution and gave higher judgements of the defendant's apparent guilt when the prosecution presented the vivid evidence. In contrast, the participants remembered more evidence of the defence and gave lower judgements of the defendant's apparent guilt when the defence presented vivid evidence. This finding suggests that vividness and imaginability of an instance increase availability of the respective category, which in turn increases judged frequency of occurrence of instances of the category.

There are many examples where vivid cases weigh more than pallid data summaries (see Nisbett & Ross, 1980). For example, in the 20 years after the US Surgeon General published a report that linked cigarette smoking to lung cancer, no decline in average cigarette consumption was observed. There was one exception: physicians, especially radiologists. The probability that a physician smokes is directly related to the distance of the physician's specialty from lung disease. It seems that those who diagnose and treat lung cancer daily have vivid illustrations of the dangers of cigarette smoking, while other people just see statistics that do not activate their imagination.

Adopting the perspective of others

If a husband thinks about how much housework his wife does, he has to adopt her perspective. As he does not see all the housework she does, he can try to think as if he were his wife and then estimate her contribution to joint outcomes. As we have already seen, adopting the other's perspective seems to be difficult, as suggested by the fact that spouses overestimate their own contribution to the housework. Both retrieval biases and vividness may contribute to the resulting bias: When estimating the share of the housework, people can retrieve more instances of their own housework and they probably have more vivid memories of their own housework than of the spouse's housework.

Another well-known phenomenon that can at least partly be explained by the availability heuristic is *unrealistic optimism* about future life events (Weinstein, 1980). When people judge the chances that positive or negative life events happen to them, they believe that, compared with the chances of their classmates, their chances are higher of experiencing positive events and lower of experiencing negative events (cf. Chapter 6 on the illusion of control). Of course, the average of one's chances of experiencing positive or negative events should equal the chances of the whole group. Therefore, the optimism revealed in Weinstein's study is unrealistic. Among several mechanisms that contribute to this illusion, one is availability, which may come into play in two ways: One factor that influences risk assessments is one's own experience. If one has experienced heart disease in one's family, the risk of heart disease is more available than for someone who has no family history of heart disease. A second factor may be people's difficulties in adopting the perspective of others, comparable to the married partners who overestimated their share of the housework (Ross & Sicoly, 1979). People see what they themselves do to increase their probabilities for positive events and lower their probabilities for negative events, but not what others do. If people assess their chances, they may see reasons why they have better chances, but they may not understand that others also think about such reasons and may arrive at similar conclusions. Therefore, people perceive a difference in chances between themselves and others.

A similar lack of adopting the perspective of others may account for the *fundamental attribution error*, a bias in attributing behaviours of others to dispositional factors (see Nisbett & Ross, 1980). Research has shown that actors are more prone to attribute their behaviours to situational factors than observers of the same actions. For example, if a father yells at his child on the bus, he himself probably thinks that this is because he is tired and his child misbehaved for the third time, whereas observers of his behaviour may conclude that he is a loony father. The actor – here the father – explains his behaviour with situational factors that caused him to act as he did, whereas observers explain the father's behaviour with his character or disposition. Actors see the situations and act in them, but they do not so much see themselves acting. For observers, however, the actor is the focus of the observed action. Observers may see that the child behaves awkwardly, but they do not know that the child has misbehaved repeatedly and do not feel how tired the father is.

Summary

So far, we have discussed how biased encoding and retrieval or vividness of information has an impact on the availability of information that, in turn, may influence stereotype formation or judgements of apparent guilt. The lack of ability to adopt another's perspective normally results in both more frequent encoding and more vivid memories of one's own actions, leading to overestimation of one's contribution to joint products, or to attribution of one's own behaviour to situational factors and of another's behaviour to dispositional factors.

Availability has been a very popular theoretical framework to explain different phenomena. Part of this appeal, some critics have stated, has come from the vagueness of the term "availability" (e.g., Betsch & Pohl, 2002): It has been used in a very broad sense, and no process was specified that is unique to availability. It was unclear, for example, whether availability was tied to ease of recall or to amount of recall. Recent research by Norbert Schwarz and his colleagues addressed this issue (see Schwarz, 1998, for a detailed discussion).

AVAILABILITY: EASE OR AMOUNT OF RECALL?

Let us take a closer look at the first of the two basic experiments described above. Tversky and Kahneman (1973) found that people recalled more famous names and judged famous names to be presented more frequently. For example, if 19 famous women and 20 non-famous men were presented, participants responded that more names of women were presented. The authors concluded that people used availability – the ease with which they were able to bring instances to mind – as information to judge whether names of men or women were presented more frequently. But note that there is an ambiguity inherent in this finding: When famous names are more available, people can both retrieve them more easily and retrieve more of them. Ease of recall and amount of recall were confounded in this experiment. Thus, there are two alternative possibilities for how people can arrive at the conclusion that names of (famous) women were more frequent than (non-famous) men: First, they may have recalled the famous women more easily than the non-famous men, concluding that if it is so easy to recall names of women, there must have been more of them in the list. Alternatively, they might have tried to recall names, and recalled more names of women than of men. From the fact that they have recalled more women, they may conclude that there must have been more names of women in the list. There is no way to resolve this ambiguity in the experiments as done by Tversky and Kahneman.

How can this ambiguity be resolved? Schwarz, Bless, Strack, Klumpp, Rittenauer-Schatka, and Simons (1991) used an experimental paradigm that separated ease of recall from amount of recall. They asked people to list 6 or 12 instances where they behaved self-assertively. In pilot studies, these authors had found that it is relatively easy to recall 6 instances of self-assertive behaviours, but it is quite difficult to recall 12 such instances. After the participants recalled these behaviours, they were asked how assertive they are. If people base their judgement of self-assertiveness on the experienced ease of recall, rated assertiveness is expected to be higher after recalling 6 behaviours than after recalling 12 behaviours. In contrast, if people base their judgement on amount of recall, those who recalled 12 assertive behaviours should judge themselves as being more assertive than those who recalled 6 behaviours.

The results supported the ease of recall view: Participants who listed 6 behaviours judged themselves as being more assertive than those who listed 12 behaviours. In other experimental conditions, the authors assessed the judgement of assertiveness after participants listed 6 or 12 instances of unassertive behaviours. The participants again based their judgements on ease of recall and judged themselves to be less assertive after recalling 6 rather than 12 behaviours. If it was easy to recall 6 unassertive behaviours, one cannot be assertive after all. The difficulty of recalling 12 unassertive behaviours, in contrast, seems to indicate that one is rather assertive.

In this study, availability is related to ease of recall, not to amount of recall. However, do people always base their judgements on ease of recall, or are there instances where availability is better captured in terms of amount of recall? Schwarz and his colleagues found several conditions that limited the role of ease of recall, as I will discuss in the next sections.

Effects of misattribution of the recall experience

Imagine that a participant has recalled 6 examples of behaviour where she behaved assertively. She now concludes from the ease with which she was able to recall these behaviours that she must be self-assertive. In a slightly different experiment, a participant under the same experimental condition listens to music, a new-age piece at half speed. He is told that this music *facilitates* the recall of the behaviours. After recalling six instances, he has to judge how assertive he is. What is the difference from the condition without music? The difference lies in the diagnosticity of the recall experience: The participant in the condition without music normally bases her judgement on ease of recall because she believes that ease of recall tells her something about her assertiveness. The participant who hears music experiences the same amount of ease of recall when he recalls instances of self-assertive behaviour, but he believes that the experience of ease is caused by the music played to him. Therefore, he has no reason to base his judgement of assertiveness on the experienced ease of recall. Ease of recall is considered as being undiagnostic as information for the judgement of self-assertiveness.

Another participant has to recall six behaviours and hears music, but she is told that music *inhibits* the recall of examples. It is easy to recall 6 instances of self-assertive behaviour, but the music is supposed to make recall difficult. This participant has reason to argue that if it is easy to recall instances of self-assertive behaviour despite the inhibiting influence of music, she must be highly assertive. In this case, ease of recall is considered as being diagnostic information for self-assertiveness. Schwarz et al. (1991) tested this assumption experimentally and indeed found that people used their recall experience only if it was diagnostic. If the informational value of the recall experience was undermined because participants could attribute these feelings to the music played to them, they no longer relied on their recall experiences.

Direct access to information

When people can access a judgement directly, they do not need to rely on accessibility experiences. For example, people who have thought much about doctor-assisted suicide and are extremely in favour or against it do not need to inspect their feelings to determine how strong their attitude is; they retrieve this information directly. In line with this reasoning, Haddock, Rothman, Reber, and Schwarz (1999) found that experiences of ease of recall influenced judgements of the strength of one's attitude towards doctor-assisted suicide only when the pre-experimentally assessed attitude was not extreme. Those respondents who were strongly in favour or against doctor-assisted suicide did not rely on recall experiences when they judged attitude strength. Processing experiences influenced the participants' judgements about attitude strength only when attitudes were moderate and direct retrieval of information about attitude strength was not possible.

Effects of processing motivation

If you have to list behaviours that increase your risk for heart disease and are then asked to estimate your vulnerability for this disease, you can take it easy if there is no history of heart disease in your family, and you probably base your judgement of vulnerability on ease of recall. However, if heart disease has occurred in your family, you probably do not take it easy. You are much more motivated to process this information systematically, paying attention to the number of risk-increasing behaviours you are able to list. Rothman and Schwarz (1998) explored the consequences of processing motivation in an experiment. Participants had to list either three or eight behaviours that increased or decreased the risk of heart disease. About half of the participants had a family history of heart disease, the others had not. The results are shown in Table 8.1: Participants without a family history of

Table 8.1 Vulnerability to heart disease as a function of type and number of recalled behaviours and family history

	Family history of heart disease	
	Without family history	With family history
Vulnerability judgements		
Risk-increasing behaviour		
3 examples	3.87	4.63
8 examples	3.18	5.37
Risk-decreasing behaviour		
3 examples	3.09	5.75
8 examples	4.25	3.75
Need for behaviour change		
Risk-increasing behaviour		
3 examples	3.37	3.63
8 examples	2.87	6.25
Risk-decreasing behaviour		
3 examples	3.00	5.20
8 examples	5.62	4.70

Adapted from Rothman & Schwarz, 1998.
Judgements of vulnerability and the need to change current behaviour were made on 9-point scales, with higher values indicating greater vulnerability and need to change, respectively.

heart disease based their judgements on ease of recall. They judged themselves to be more vulnerable and thought that they needed more urgently to change their behaviour if they had to recall either *three* rather than *eight* examples of risk-*in*creasing behaviours or *eight* rather than *three* examples of risk-*de*creasing behaviours. This pattern reversed if there existed a family history of heart disease: These participants relied on the amount of information they listed, and therefore judged themselves to be more vulnerable and thought that there was a higher need to change their behaviour if they had to recall either *eight* rather than *three* examples of risk-*in*creasing behaviours or *three* rather than *eight* examples of risk-*de*creasing behaviours. This study demonstrated the effect of processing motivation on the informational implications of processing experience: Participants without a family history of heart disease had a low motivation to examine the processed information and therefore based their judgements on ease of recall. Participants with a history of heart disease, on the other hand, were highly motivated to monitor how many risk-increasing or risk-decreasing behaviours they could list and based their judgements on amount of recall.

The role of naïve theories

Recent work has emphasized the importance of naïve beliefs in linking the experience of ease or difficulty of recall to subjective judgements. For example, Winkielman and Schwarz (2001) showed that the same experience of ease or difficulty in recalling childhood events can lead to opposite judgements, depending on the participant's "theory" about the meaning of the subjective experience. Specifically, these researchers first manipulated recall experience by asking participants to recall few or many childhood events. Then, they manipulated participants' naïve theories about the reason for their specific recall experiences. They told one group of participants that recall can be difficult because pleasant childhood events fade from memory; another group was told that recall can be difficult because unpleasant childhood events fade from memory. As expected, participants reached opposite conclusions about their childhood happiness when the same recall experience was suggested to have different causes: Those participants who experienced easy recall and believed that recall difficulty indicated an unpleasant childhood judged their childhood as more pleasant than those with easy recall and the belief that recall difficulty indicated a pleasant childhood. When recall was difficult, participants who believed that recall difficulty indicated a pleasant childhood judged their childhood to be more pleasant than those who believed that recall difficulty is caused by an unpleasant childhood. These findings show that people use their naïve beliefs to interpret their processing experiences.

CONCLUSIONS

I have discussed in some detail whether availability as a judgemental basis is better described in terms of ease of recall or of amount of recall. In sum, participants relied on ease of recall when they thought that experienced ease was diagnostic for their judgemental task, when they did not have direct access to relevant information, or when they were not very motivated to elaborate on a topic. When people had direct access to relevant information or when they were motivated to process information systematically, participants relied on amount of recall. Moreover, effects of ease of recall may depend on naïve theories people have about the meaning of experienced ease.

How do these findings relate to the frequency judgements assessed in the studies of Tversky and Kahneman (1973) discussed above? Can we conclude that their participants estimated the relative frequency of men and women or of word frequencies on the basis of recall experiences? The use of the availability heuristic is not the only way people can assess frequency. When people are confronted with low frequencies, they simply try to count (Brown, 1995). If, for example, respondents in a survey are asked how many times they have eaten caviar in the last 2 years, most of them are probably able to count the frequency of this event. This means that availability – or ease of recall – may be used only when frequencies are sufficiently high.

Wänke, Schwarz, and Bless (1995) extended Experiment 3 of Tversky and Kahneman (1973) that we discussed above by using a misattribution manipulation similar to that of Schwarz et al. (1991). This misattribution manipulation influenced participants' frequency estimates; therefore, the authors concluded that estimates of letter frequencies were based on ease of recall. However, Sedlmeier et al. (1998), in another extension of the classical letter-frequency study by Tversky and Kahneman, found no evidence for effects of availability on judgements of letter frequencies in the German language; they measured availability in terms of both ease of recall, assessed as speed of recall of a single word, and of amount of recall, assessed as the number of words recalled within a certain time. In line with Hasher and Zacks (1984), these authors concluded that people encode frequency automatically along with information about events. In another study, Reber and Zupanek (2002) manipulated ease of processing at encoding of frequently presented stimulus events, and demonstrated an influence of this manipulation on frequency judgements. In sum, the evidence for or against the use of the availability heuristic in estimating high frequencies is mixed.

The seminal paper by Tversky and Kahneman (1973) opened a new way of thinking about how frequency judgements are performed, and subsequent research has shown the importance of the availability heuristic in different domains. As an important consequence, phenomena that had formerly been discussed in terms of motivational processes were now explained in terms of cognitive mechanisms. Recent research has disentangled some ambiguities about the mechanisms underlying the availability heuristic, and it is easy to think about new research directions that continue this work.

SUMMARY

- Availability is the ease with which relevant instances of a class come to mind.
- Sources of biased availability are biased frequencies, different vividness of information, and the inability to adopt the perspective of another person.
- Availability affects frequency estimates, stereotype formation, and different kinds of judgements.
- Recent work has disentangled the contributions of ease and amount of recall of instances to judgement formation.
- Whether people use ease or amount of recall as information depends on (a) the perceived diagnosticity of experienced ease; (b) direct access to relevant information; and (c) motivation to elaborate on a topic. Moreover, judgements depend on naïve theories about the meaning of experienced ease.

FURTHER READING

The classic piece on this topic is the article by Tversky and Kahnemann (1973) that has been cited over 1400 times to date. I recommend reading some elegant studies into availability, for example by Lichtenstein et al. (1978), Ross and Sicoly (1979), and Schwarz et al. (1991). For early applications of the availability heuristic, see Nisbett and Ross (1980); for recent theoretical developments, see Higgins (1996) and Schwarz (1998).

NOTE

1 In English, the consonants D, K, L, N, R, V, X, and Z appear more frequently in the third than in the first position; the other 12 consonants appear more frequently in the first position (Tversky & Kahneman, 1973; see also Sedlmeier et al., 1998). In German, the letters A, C, E, I, L, N, O, R, U appear more frequently in the second than in the first position, whereas the letters B, F, G, and S are more frequently in the first than in the second position (Sedlmeier et al., 1998).

ACKNOWLEDGEMENTS

Completion of this chapter was supported by the Swiss National Foundation (Grant no. 61–57881.99) and the Meltzer Foundation of the University of Bergen.

REFERENCES

Betsch, T., & Pohl, D. (2002). Tversky and Kahneman's availability approach to frequency judgement: A critical analysis. In P. Sedlmeier & T. Betsch (Eds.), *Etc. Frequency processing and cognition* (pp. 109–119). Oxford: Oxford University Press.

Brown, N. R. (1995). Estimation strategies and the judgment of event frequency. *Journal of Experimental Psychology: Learning, Memory, and Cognition, 21*, 1539–1553.

Haddock, G., Rothman, A. J., Reber, R., & Schwarz, N. (1999). Forming judgments of attitude certainty, intensity, and importance: The role of subjective experiences. *Personality and Social Psychology Bulletin, 25*, 771–782.

Hasher, L., & Zacks, R. T. (1984). Automatic processing of fundamental information: The case of frequency of occurrence. *American Psychologist, 39*, 1372–1388.

Higgins, E. T. (1996). Knowledge activation: Accessibility, applicability, and salience. In E. T. Higgins & A. W. Kruglanski (Eds.), *Social psychology: Handbook of basic principles* (pp. 133–168). New York: Guilford Press.

Lichtenstein, S., Slovic, P., Fischhoff, B., Layman, M., & Combs, B. (1978). Judged frequency of lethal events. *Journal of Experimental Psychology: Human Learning and Memory, 4*, 551–578.

Nisbett, R. E., & Ross, L. (1980). *Human inference: Strategies and shortcomings of social judgment*. Englewood Cliffs, NJ: Prentice Hall.

Reber, R., & Zupanek, N. (2002). Effects of processing fluency on estimates of probability and frequency. In P. Sedlmeier & T. Betsch (Eds.), *Etc. Frequency processing and cognition* (pp. 175–188). Oxford: Oxford University Press.

Reyes, R. M., Thompson, W. C., & Bower, G. H. (1980). Judgmental biases resulting from differing availabilities of arguments. *Journal of Personality and Social Psychology, 39*, 2–12.

Ross, M., & Sicoly, F. (1979). Egocentric biases in availability and attribution. *Journal of Personality and Social Psychology, 37*, 322–336.

Rothbart, M., Fulero, S., Jensen, C., Howard, J., & Birrell, P. (1978). From individual to group impressions: Availability heuristics in stereotype formation. *Journal of Experimental Social Psychology, 14*, 237–255.

Rothman, A. J., & Schwarz, N. (1998). Constructing perceptions of vulnerability: Personal relevance and the use of experiential information in health judgments. *Personality and Social Psychology Bulletin, 24*, 1053–1064.

Schwarz, N. (1998). Accessible content and accessibility experiences: The interplay of declarative and experiential information in judgment. *Personality and Social Psychology Review, 2*, 87–99.

Schwarz, N., Bless, H., Strack, F., Klumpp, G., Rittenauer-Schatka, H., & Simons, A. (1991). Ease of retrieval as information: Another look at the availability heuristic. *Journal of Personality and Social Psychology, 61*, 195–202.

Sedlmeier, P., Hertwig, R., & Gigerenzer, G. (1998). Are judgments of the positional frequencies of letters systematically biased due to availability? *Journal of Experimental Psychology: Learning, Memory, and Cognition, 24*, 754–770.

Tulving, E. (1983). *Elements in episodic memory*. Oxford: Oxford University Press.

Tversky, A., & Kahneman, D. (1973). Availability: A heuristic for judging frequency and probability. *Cognitive Psychology, 5*, 207–232.

Wänke, M., Schwarz, N., & Bless, H. (1995). The availability heuristic revisited: Experienced ease of retrieval in mundane frequency estimates. *Acta Psychologica, 89*, 83–90.

Weinstein, N. D. (1980). Unrealistic optimism about future life events. *Journal of Personality and Social Psychology, 39*, 806–820.

Winkielman, P., & Schwarz, N. (2001). How pleasant was your childhood? Beliefs about memory shape inferences from experienced difficulty of recall. *Psychological Science, 12*, 176–179.

9 Judgements by representativeness

Karl Halvor Teigen

Imagine the following two situations:

- Example 1. You observe a person on the pavement who appears to be talking to himself. He is alone, but smiling and gesturing. You decide that he is probably crazy.
- Example 2. You take part in a raffle where tickets are numbered from 1 to 100. Someone offers you ticket No. 1. You refuse. What about No. 50? You are still not satisfied. You are offered No. 63. You feel much better, and decide to keep the ticket.

These situations are, superficially, quite different from each other. In the first case, you try to explain a person's strange behaviour, by identifying a category where such behaviours appear to belong. You make a tentative diagnosis. In the second case, you want to pick a lottery ticket that maximizes your (subjective) chances of winning. You make a tentative prediction.

But the situations also have something in common. They are uncertain, and require you to make a guess. In both cases, you are searching for a probable solution. How do we make such guesses? You have no available statistics about the proportion of people talking to themselves who are actually crazy, so how can you conclude "he is probably crazy"? You may have some knowledge about the probabilities involved in a raffle, and even be able to calculate that all probabilities are equal, that is, p (ticket No. 1) = p (ticket No. 50) = p (ticket No. 63) = .01. And yet you do not find this knowledge very helpful because it does not tell you which ticket to accept, and worse still, it does not explain your uneasiness about the first two tickets.

In two famous articles Kahneman and Tversky (1972, 1973) suggested that people in such cases make use of a simple and reasonable mental shortcut to arrive at probability judgements. They simply ask themselves: How much does the target *look like* a typical instance of the class, category, or parent population under consideration? How *similar* is this individual's behaviour to that of a typical crazy person? How *representative* are tickets numbered 1, 50, or 63, as random instances of the ticket population?

Judgement by representativeness, commonly referred to as *the representativeness heuristic*, constitutes a most useful way of making probability estimates:

- It is easy, requiring a minimum of cognitive resources.
- It can be used in a number of situations where objective probabilities cannot be calculated (e.g., in singular situations).
- It is often correct. In a unimodal, symmetrical distribution, the central outcome will also be the most frequent one. In many other distributions, including non-ordinal, categorical classifications, the modal outcome is both most probable and most typical. For instance, if I am going to meet a high-ranking military officer, I expect to see a man above 40, rather than a young woman. My stereotype of a "representative" officer corresponds in this case to the actual sex and age distribution of military commanders.

Philosophers from Aristotle to Hume have regarded representativeness, or similarity, as a perfectly legitimate way of estimating probabilities. In the *Rhetoric*, Aristotle lists similarity along with frequency as the basis of sound probability judgements. "If the thing in question *both* happens *oftener* as we represent it and more *as* we represent it, the probability is particularly great" (1941, p. 1433). Even Laplace, one of the founders of modern probability calculus, regarded judgement by analogy to be one of the "diverse means to approach certainty", claiming "the more perfect the similarity, the greater the probability" (1816, p. 263). But Laplace also wrote a chapter on "Illusions in probability estimation", being well aware that our intuitions about probabilities sometimes lead us astray.

In line with this, the representativeness heuristic is not infallible. The "crazy" person in Example 1 may not be crazy, even if he behaves like a typical madman. He could simply be talking in his handsfree mobile phone. The representativeness heuristic may in this case have enticed us to disregard alternative possibilities, and to forget the relative number of madmen compared to mobile phone users. Similarly, the winning number in Example 2 could equally well be 1 or 50 as 63.

To show that people rely on the representativeness heuristic, rather than on more rational calculations of frequencies, we need to construct situations in which probability judgements based on representativeness *differ* from judgements based on more normative considerations. In other words, the emphasis will be on errors of judgements, rather than successful judgements. These errors, or biases, often imply that some other, normative factors are neglected or given insufficient weight. The biases can accordingly be described as "base-rate neglect", "insensitivity to sample size", and similar labels, indicating the principles that are violated. However, it is important to bear in mind that ignoring such principles is a phenomenon that is conceptually distinct from the representativeness heuristic (Bar-Hillel, 1984).

Judgements by representativeness

In addition, we need to show that subjective probability judgements and representativeness judgements are highly correlated. For instance, to check whether 63 is a more representative number than 1 or 50, we could ask people how typical these numbers are, as outcomes of a random draw.

TWO DEMONSTRATIONS

The two most famous, and most intensely debated, demonstrations of representativeness in the research literature are the engineers-and-lawyers problem and the Linda problem. These are discussed in Chapters 1 and 2 of this volume and will not be repeated here. Instead we will focus on two more simple problems, involving people's intuitions about randomness and their sensitivity (or insensitivity) to sample size.

Study 1: Intuitions about random sequences

Consider the problem described in Text box 9.1 When Tversky and Kahneman (1974) asked people to compare alternative (a) and (b) in the

---

Text box 9.1 Intuitions about randomness: Predicting chance

Imagine a person tossing a fair coin six times in a row. In every toss, the outcome can be head (H) or tail (T). Which of the following series is most likely?

(a) H T T H T H
(b) H H H T T T
(c) H H H H H H
(d) H H H H T H

Text-box example, the majority chose (a), because (b) did not "look" random. Sequence (a) was also preferred to (d), which appears biased and thus not representative of a "fair" coin. The truth is, however, that all series, including (c), are equally likely, with a probability of $0.5^6 = 0.016$. This can be shown by writing all possible sequences of heads and tails; there are altogether 64 such series, each of them occurring once.

In a replication, Smith (1998) gave sets (a)–(c) to a sample of college students, and included a fourth option, namely: All rows are equally likely. This (correct) answer was chosen by 40% of the students. However, a majority of 55% still opted for (a). Sequence (b) was chosen by 5%, and nobody chose (c). Smith found a preference for (a) among school children as young as 10 years. The popularity of options (b) and (c) decreased with age, whereas that of the correct answer, that all rows are equally likely, increased.

Significant differences between (a) and (b), or (a) and (c) can be checked using a sign test. For 20 participants, such differences will be significant ($p < .05$) if 15 (75%) or more choose (a). From Smith's results we may expect at least 90% preference for (a) over (b), which will yield a significant result with 95% probability. If we include "equally likely" as an option, participants choosing this alternative can be excluded from the analysis. To test the difference between participants choosing (a) and "equally likely" makes no sense, as no meaningful null hypothesis can be formed. (We don't need a significant majority of errors to identify a bias.)

Explanation

If we think of a fair coin as a device that can produce two equally likely outcomes, a representative series of outcomes should contain an approximate equal number of heads and tails. Three heads and three tails are viewed as more representative than a series containing more heads than tails. This makes (c) and (d) more unlikely than (a) or (b). But why should (a) be preferred to (b)? Two explanations, both invoking the concept of representativeness, are possible.

(1) With a sequence of random tosses, the outcomes should not only be representative for the coin, but also for the process by which the outcomes are produced. Random outcomes should be *typically* random. They should *look* random. The sequence HHHTTT looks too structured, whereas HTTHTH has the proper random look. This explanation presupposes a lay theory about randomness. For most of us, this theory has two parts. First, random outcomes should balance each other out (there should be approximately an equal number of each). This requirement is violated by sequence (c) and (d). Second, random outcomes should not look orderly. This is the criterion that sequence (b) fails to meet.

(2) A slightly different interpretation invokes the concept of *local* representativeness. A random sequence should not only be globally representative (i.e., taken as a whole), we also expect each *part* of the series to reflect the balance between heads and tails, leading to frequent alternations and few runs. HHHTTT consists of two biased parts, whereas HTTHTH can be divided into three balanced pairs.

We can extend the coin experiment by asking participants to predict the result of a *seventh* throw. Suppose that series (c) has actually occurred by chance. What will happen next? According to the so-called *gambler's fallacy*, people will be more ready for a tail than for a seventh head. In series (b), we may feel (although less strongly) that head is due. These predictions are also in line with the notion of representativeness: A seventh head will make the sequence still less representative, whereas a tail will contribute to a more balanced, and hence more probable pattern.

In a study by Holzworth and Doherty (1974) participants were shown random series of nine cards, coloured black or white, and asked to predict the colour of the next card. When the cards were drawn from a 90/10 distribution of black and white cards, the participants predicted (correctly) black cards. But when they believed that the cards came from a 70/30 population, they predicted *white* cards on almost 30% of the trials. This is normatively nonsensical, because black cards have a better chance than white to be drawn in all trials, as long as there are more black than white cards. It makes more sense from a representativeness point of view. After, say, four black cards in a row, one might think that a white card would make the sample more representative of a 70/30 distribution.

Study 2: Intuitions about sample sizes

Consider the problem described in Text box 9.2 (from Tversky & Kahneman, 1972, 1974). In a group of undergraduate college students, 56% answered

---

Text box 9.2 Intuitions about sample size: From population to samples

A certain town is served by two hospitals. In the larger hospital about 45 babies are born each day, and in the smaller hospital about 15 babies are born each day. As you know, about 50% of all babies are boys. However, the exact percentage varies from day to day. Sometimes it may be higher than 50%, sometimes lower. For a period of one year, each hospital recorded the days on which more than 60% of the babies born were boys. Which hospital do you think recorded more such days?

(a) The larger hospital
(b) The smaller hospital
(c) About the same (that is, within 5% of each other)

---

alternative (c), the rest were equally divided between (a) and (b). Thus there was no general preference for either hospital, despite the fact that a large sample is much less likely to be biased than a small sample. That is precisely why investigators prefer large samples! In fact, the "true" probability for random samples of size 15 to have 9 (60%) or more male babies is about 0.30, whereas the probability for samples of size 45 to have 27 (60%) or more male babies is about 0.12 (according to the normal curve approximation of a binomial test). That is, normatively, (b) is the correct answer one.

This demonstration is in no need of a statistical test, because no null hypothesis can be meaningfully formed. The question is rather whether errors, that is, answers of type (a) and (c) are common, rare, or nonexistent. With more answers of type (b) than (c), all we can say is that *some* participants are not insensitive to sample size.

Explanation

Instead of obeying the "law of large numbers" of probability theory, a majority of students seem to think that equally biased samples are equally probable, regardless of n. The more biased, the less probable. This follows from a unique reliance on the representativeness heuristic.

PREDICTION VERSUS DIAGNOSIS

In both demonstrations, people were asked to predict the occurrences of specific outcomes, which they seemed to do by asking themselves: How well do these outcomes match salient features of the populations from which they are drawn? The better the match, the higher the outcome probability.

However, a match can go both ways. In prediction tasks, we know the population, and ask for a matching sample. In other cases, we go from a given sample in search of a matching population. Do people use the representativeness heuristic in both cases? And should they?

Normatively, the probability for a sample, given the population, and the probability for a population, given a sample, are not the same. After a course in inferential statistics, most students know how to calculate $p(\text{Data}|H_o)$, that is, they can predict the probability of a particular outcome occurring by chance. They may also have learned that this probability is not identical to $p(H_o|\text{Data})$, or the probability that the null hypothesis is correct, given the results. Yet these probabilities are often confused; even scientists who should know better sometimes refer to the probabilities involved in significance testing as probabilities for the null hypothesis, rather than probabilities for data, given H_0. A legitimate transition from $p(D|H_0)$ to $p(H_0|D)$ requires additional knowledge of the prior probability of H_0 and H_1, and of the compatibility of data to H_1, as dictated by Bayes' theorem. The tendency to confuse $p(D|H)$ and the inverse probability $p(H|D)$ is a very common error of probabilistic reasoning, which has been labelled the *inverse fallacy* (Villejoubert & Mandel, 2002).

Representativeness was originally described as a prediction rule, leading from a population (a distribution, or a category) to a sample (an instance, or an event). According to Kahneman and Tversky, the representativeness heuristic is used when "the probability of an uncertain event, or a sample, is evaluated by the degree to which it is: (i) similar in essential properties to its parent population; and (ii) reflects the salient features of the process by which it is generated" (1972, p. 431).

In practice, however, representativeness was soon applied to the inverse relationship (cf. Chapter 3 on Bayesian inferences). In the engineer-and-lawyer problem, the cab problem, and several other problems introduced by Kahneman and Tversky (1973), participants were asked to estimate the probability that a particular individual, or event, belonged to a certain

Judgements by representativeness 171

category; in other words, they were invited to make an inference from event to category, or from sample to population, rather than the other way around. Such inferences should perhaps more accurately be termed problems of diagnosis than problems of prediction.

Are such inferences in everyday life also accomplished by a simple matching process, making representativeness a general heuristic for both kinds of probability judgements? To examine this question let us revisit our two demonstration cases, this time from the point of view of diagnosis rather than prediction.

Diagnosing randomness

A diagnosis version of the random sequence problem can be arranged by asking participants to estimate the probability that a particular sequence was actually produced by chance. Consider the example in Text box 9.3

Text box 9.3 Intuitions about randomness: Diagnosing chance

Alice and Susan are asked by their teacher to produce a sequence of heads and tails by tossing a coin six times. One of the girls does as she is told, whereas the other skips the coin and simply invents a sequence. Here are the results:

Alice: H T T H T H
Susan: H H H T T T

What is, in your opinion, more likely:

Alice used a coin / Susan used a coin

(adapted from a study by Ayton & Wright, 1987). Following an "inverted" variant of the representativeness heuristic, we would believe that Alice in Text box 9.3 used a coin, because her sequence looks like a typical random sequence, whereas Susan probably cheated, because her sequence looks arranged.

However, this problem has no single normative answer. We cannot even say that both answers are equally likely, because the true probabilities depend not only on what kind of sequences can occur by chance, but also on what kind of sequences will occur by cheating, which in turn depends on how sophisticated a cheater you are! Susan's sequence looks arranged, but a cheater who tries to mimic chance would hardly produce such a sequence. So perhaps she is not the cheater after all.

172 *Teigen*

Diagnoses based on sample size

A diagnosis version of the birth-clinic problem is more difficult to arrange, because most people will have strong a priori reasons to believe that there are around 50% male newborn babies (or slightly more). We could, however, make a slight change in content, as illustrated by the example in Text box 9.4. In the case described, answer (b) will be more popular than (a), demonstrating that people have more confidence in a greater than a smaller sample (as indeed they should). This should lead us to modify the previous conclusion that representativeness makes people "insensitive" to sample size. Prediction probabilities and diagnostic probabilities need not be the same.

Text box 9.4 Intuitions about sample size: From samples to population

Two teachers want to find out whether there are more male or female students at the university. One of them checks a small class of 15 students, finding 9 (60%) male and 6 female students. The other one studies a larger class of 45, finding 18 (40%) male and 27 female students. What is more probable: (a) There are altogether more male students; (b) there are more female students; (c) there is an equal number of male and female students.

REPRESENTATIVENESS AS A GENERAL-PURPOSE HEURISTIC

The representativeness heuristic has been used to explain a number of judgemental biases. We have discussed the gambler's fallacy and insensitivity to sample size as examples of errors of prediction. In diagnosis problems the representativeness heuristic has been held responsible for *base-rate neglect* (or rather insufficient weight of base rates). This theme has been explored in detail in Chapter 2 of the present volume.

Tversky and Kahneman (1983) further argued that representativeness can lead to the fallacious belief that a combination of one likely and one unlikely event is more likely than the unlikely event taken by itself. This so-called *conjunction fallacy* has been treated in this book in Chapter 1. For instance, people thought it was likely that Bjorn Borg would win the Wimbledon tennis final, because it looked like a typical thing for a champion like Borg to do. They thought it would be rather unlikely for him to lose the first set of the match. This would be less typical of Borg. The conjunction – losing the first set but winning the match – contains a combination of typical and less typical elements. This conjunction was believed by many participants to have an *intermediate* probability, rather than the even lower probability that follows logically from the combination of high and low p events.

Kahneman and Tversky (1973) also showed that use of the representativeness heuristic could lead to *nonregressive predictions*. It has been known since the time of Francis Galton that use of imperfect predictors should lead to less extreme predictions. Extremely tall parents will have tall offspring, but since the heights of parents and offspring are not perfectly correlated, we should expect these children to be, on the average, somewhat shorter than their parents; conversely, children of exceptionally short parents should be in general taller than their parents. Filial regression had, in fact, already been observed by Homer, in a passage of the *Odyssey*: "Few are the sons that are like their father in breed; The most part are worse, scarce any their fathers excel" (Book 2, Verse 277–78, S. O. Andrew's translation). Being exclusively concerned with the superior part of the distribution, Homer failed to comment on the complementary fact that inferior fathers often have sons of a more hopeful breed. Evidently, Homer felt sons to be less representative of their illustrious origins than they ought to have been, documenting a very early instance of the representativeness heuristic failing to square with the facts.

It further follows from the concept of statistical regression that, when a measure is not perfectly reliable, we must expect the top scorers on one occasion to be distributed somewhat closer to the mean on the second occasion (and vice versa). From the point of view of representativeness, however, a typical top scorer should continue to excel, and an individual scoring in the 75th percentile should remain around the 75th percentile on the second occasion also. A drop in performance would accordingly be attributed to change or some other systematic process, rather than to chance. Tversky and Kahneman (1974) tell the story about a flight instructor who used to praise students who had performed exceptionally well, only to find that, as a rule, they performed worse on the next occasion. Instead of realizing that performances are not completely reliable indicators of skill, and thus bound to regress for purely statistical reasons, he felt forced to conclude that praise has a negative rather than the intended positive effect.

A corollary of the problem of non-regressive predictions is that people tend to make the same predictions based on invalid measures as they would do on more reliable and valid ones. So for instance when two groups of participants were asked to predict the grades of hypothetical students based on their relative standing (percentile scores) on (a) a grade point average scale, or (b) a mental concentration test, they produced in both cases almost identical, non-regressive predictions (Kahneman & Tversky, 1973). In other words, they appeared to use the less valid and reliable mental concentration test with the same confidence as a perfectly valid predictor. Extreme predictions based on invalid predictors have been described as manifestations of an *illusion of validity*.

The representativeness heuristic has over the years been applied to an increasing range of phenomena in the field of judgement and decision making. It has been proclaimed to be "perhaps, our most basic cognitive heuristic" (Fiske & Taylor, 1991, p. 384). One of its attractions has been that it seems also to be applicable to expert judgements in a variety of fields. Another is its link to the area of causality judgements.

Expert judgements

In their very first paper on judgemental biases, Tversky and Kahneman (1971) showed that even scientists with a solid background in statistics place too much confidence in the results of small samples. They presented a questionnaire to a group of mathematical psychologists, asking what kind of advice they would give a PhD student who has just performed two small-scale, inconclusive experiments (one barely significant and the other not). Many respondents thought it would be a good idea to speculate about the *difference* between the results (which could have been a statistical artifact). The majority thought that the experiment should be repeated a third time, again with a small sample (which could not be expected to reach significance). Despite their theoretical knowledge of sampling distributions and statistical hypothesis testing, these experts seemed to suppose that small samples are highly representative of their populations, apparently believing in a "law of small numbers" (as a proxy for the well-known "law of large numbers" in statistical theory).

However, domain expertise can sometimes counteract some of the more extreme biases due to representativeness thinking. For instance, experience with the ups and downs of the stock market could make the predictions of a professional investor more regressive than those of a novice. Yet even a real-world economic market may be biased by the power of representative predictions, manifested as overconfidence in stocks, firms, or football teams that have a recent history of good performance (Tassoni, 1996). Moreover, risky stocks tend to be undervalued, and safe stocks overvalued, by representativeness reasoning: Safe stocks come from good companies, and investment in good companies should give good returns, that is, investors assume a match between the company and stock quality, making safe stocks attractive even when they are costly (Shefrin, 2001).

Clinical judgements offer rich possibilities for studying diagnoses as well as predictions. Garb (1996) gave clinical psychologists a case description satisfying the DSM-IIIR criteria for antisocial personality disorder. They were then asked to rate (a) the likelihood for five possible diagnoses, as well as (b) the degree to which the case was similar to the "typical" person with these disorders. Only 27% of the clinicians made the "correct" diagnosis (according to the manual). The correlation between probability judgements and representativeness judgements was extremely high, $r = .97$, indicating that the clinicians used similarity to a prototype rather than a list of criteria to arrive at a diagnosis.

Causality judgements

John Stuart Mill (1856) observed that people, including philosophers, tend to assume a correspondence between cause and effects. Like begets like. Large effects prompt us to look for large causes. Good effects are attributed to good causes, whereas disasters and human suffering must be due to evil forces. While this is in general a sound heuristic – large objects make in general louder noises than smaller objects, and nice people often make us feel good – exceptions are not difficult to find (small whistles can be deafening, and nice people can be boring). The similarity between Mill's correspondence principle and the representativeness heuristic has made many investigators think that judgements by representativeness also apply to judgements of causation.

Again, these inferences may go both ways: from known causes to hypothetical effects, and from known effects to hypothetical causes. We may for instance expect an acknowledged expert to be a source of valid and reliable information. Informed people (causes) should produce informative statements (effects) matching their level of expertise. Unfortunately, experts can be wrong, particularly outside their field of expertise. Even more risky, we may infer the expertise of the speaker from the confidence and specificity of his or her assertions. It is more impressive for a political commentator to announce that Iraq will be attacked on January 27, than simply that war will break out sooner or later. Unfortunately, the specific prediction will be more easily disconfirmed than the vague one, leading to a "preciseness paradox" (Teigen, 1990), where the speaker has to choose between being believed (by sounding like an expert) and being correct (by using more general and approximate terms).

If causes correspond to effects, we should expect people to prefer causes whose salient features match the salient features of the events to be explained. Lupfer and Layman (1996) found that people favour religious explanations of uncontrollable events with life-altering outcomes, whereas they prefer naturalistic explanations for controllable events, and events with more mundane consequences. In each case the religious attributions were made in agreement with characteristics believed to be "representative" for supernatural versus natural sources of causality.

Gavanski and Wells (1989) suggested that representative causes also apply to hypothetical, counterfactual outcomes. For instance, when we think how an *exceptional* outcome could have been prevented, we focus on *exceptional* antecedents, whereas we change *normal* outcomes by changing a *normal* antecedent. Causes, or antecedents, are supposed to match outcomes also in magnitude (Sim & Morris, 1998). If an athlete makes a poor overall performance in a triathlon contest, we will blame the failure on her worst rather than on her average or best exercise, even if they all could, in principle, have been improved.

Representativeness, or similarity reasoning, may play a part in scientific theories as well:

- A stutterer behaves in some respects in a similar way to a nervous person, and may indeed be anxious about not being able to communicate. This has suggested anxiety as an aetiologic factor in some theories about stuttering (Attanasio, Onslow, & Packman, 1998).
- When children show few signs of empathy and social interest, a corresponding lack of empathy and interest on the part of their caregivers looks like a plausible cause. Thus childhood autism, with its remarkable impairment of reciprocal social interaction, was for many years believed to be due to inadequate mothering.

In these cases, representativeness reasoning suggested a false lead. But there are probably many more cases where the same line of reasoning provides valuable hints. For instance, violent and abusive adults have themselves often been abused by their parents. Violence breeds violence. This looks like a similarity inference, but it is also a truth.

Representativeness broadly defined

If representativeness applies to all the cases we have listed in this chapter, the original definition (Kahneman & Tversky, 1972, see above) appears too narrow. A more general formulation was suggested by Tversky and Kahneman (1982, p. 85): "Representativeness is a relation between a process or a model, M, and some instance or event, X, associated with that model," as in the following four basic cases:

- M is a class and X is a value of a variable defined in this class (X could be the typical income of college professors).
- M is a class and X is an instance of that class (X is regarded to be a "representative" American writer).
- M is a class and X is a subset of M (X is a "representative" sample of the US population).
- M is a causal system and X is a possible consequence.

"In summary, a relation of representativeness can be defined for (1) a value and a distribution, (2) an instance and a category, (3) a sample and a population, (4) an effect and a cause. In all four cases, representativeness expresses the degree of correspondence between X and M" (Tversky & Kahneman, 1982, p. 87). This correspondence can be based on statistical beliefs (as in 1), causal beliefs (as in 4), and perceived similarity (as in 2 and 3). When this correspondence has been empirically established, for example by asking people to judge which of two events, X_1 or X_2, is more representative of M, we would expect probability judgements to be influenced by the representativeness relation. If X_1 is regarded as more representative than X_2, it will appear to be more likely.

CRITICISMS

The concept of a representativeness heuristic, as well as the biases it was supposed to explain, have often been challenged. Some of the main criticisms are summarized below.

Conceptual vagueness

Representativeness is a very broad concept, applicable to a number of situations. This generality makes it both imprecise and difficult to falsify. Gigerenzer, the strongest critic of the heuristics-and-biases programme, is not impressed by terms like representativeness, availability, and anchoring: "These one-word labels at once explain too little and too much: too little, because the underlying processes are left unspecified, and too much, because, with sufficient imagination, one of them can be fit to almost any empirical result post hoc" (Gigerenzer. Todd, & the ABC Research Group, 1999, p. 28). This is a serious criticism if we expect a full-fledged theory capable of modelling and predicting human judgements with a high degree of accuracy. However, representativeness was originally proposed as a more descriptive term, capable of elucidating some general characteristics of human reasoning under uncertainty. The concluding section of the present chapter presents some recent speculations about the nature of the "underlying processes".

Biases can disappear

Not all studies show equally strong effects of representativeness. Moreover, in all studies there will be a substantial number of individual participants who appear less susceptible to representativeness reasoning. For instance in the random sequence experiment, many participants will say (correctly) that all sequences have the same probability of occurrence.

Such differences can be attributed to a variety of sources. One is situational transparency. A concrete situation, in which procedures and mechanisms are clearly visible, will increase the chances of a normative response. Within-subjects studies, in which participants are asked directly to compare the alternatives, will typically yield more normative answers than between-subjects designs, in which the focal variables are more disguised. A group in a between-subjects design who are only shown the sequence HTTHTH will probably characterize it as a more likely than participants in another group who are asked to characterize the sequence HHHTTT, whereas individual participants who are asked to compare both sequences may "know" that they are equally likely.

People's use of heuristics is also influenced by their degree of statistical sophistication, ability differences (Stanovich & West, 2000), and more generally whether the task is conceived as a problem that should be solved by mathematical reasoning or simply by "gut feelings".

Probabilities versus frequencies

Problems can sometimes be made more concrete and transparent by translating probabilities into frequencies. Some evidence suggests, indeed, that people reason more normatively with natural frequency formats (Gigerenzer, 1991; see Chapter 3). But despite claims to the contrary, the judgement "illusions" do not disappear. In several of the original demonstrations (including those presented in the first section of the present chapter) participants were in fact asked about frequencies.

Even so, it has been suggested that the representativeness heuristic is especially well suited for unique events, whereas the availability heuristic (see Chapter 8) is more applicable to frequentistic probabilities (Jones, Jones, & Frisch, 1995). Frequency theorists, who believe that probabilities can only be meaningfully assigned to repeated events, have argued that probability judgements by representativeness cannot be given a mathematical interpretation, but invoke instead a credibility or plausibility concept (Hertwig & Gigerenzer, 1999).

Biases are not errors

Some critics have argued that when people appear biased, it is not because they commit errors of judgement, but because the norms do not apply. People may have been asked ambiguous questions, where a particular answer will appear incorrect given a literal interpretation of the task, but justified given a more pragmatic interpretation. For instance, a question about the likelihood of the HTTHTH sequence may be interpreted as a question about a sequence of "this type" (with alternating Hs and Ts) rather than about exactly this sequence. Conjunction tasks and base-rate tasks have similarly been given pragmatic interpretations that make "conjunction errors" and "base-rate neglect" less fallacious than they originally appeared.

A problem with this criticism is that it is typically raised post hoc (when the results are known) and often assumes that the participants are able to draw very fine distinctions in their interpretation of questions. Indeed, the participants are sometimes attributed a more sophisticated grasp of probability theory than the experimenters.

Alternative explanations

Not all the judgement "illusions" that have been attributed to the representativeness heuristic may, in fact, be due to it. The conjunction fallacy may in some cases be due to a misplaced averaging rule, or judgements of surprise, as discussed in Chapter 1. Base-rate neglect, as discussed in Chapter 2, could sometimes be due to inversion errors (Villejoubert & Mandel, 2002). Similarly, the gambler's fallacy may be due to more magical "balancing beliefs", in addition to similarity judgements (Joram & Read, 1996). Finally, when middle numbers in a lottery are preferred to extreme numbers (Teigen, 1983), it could be due to representativeness, but it could also signify a preference for small errors over large ones (with ticket No. 1, one could be very wide of the mark).

REPRESENTATIVENESS REVISITED

In a recent article, Kahneman and Frederick (2002) have offered a wider framework for heuristic judgements. In their view, representativeness illustrates a general feature of intuitive reasoning, where people solve a difficult task (estimation of probabilities) by transforming it into a simpler task (here: judgements of similarity). This can be described as a process of *attribute substitution*. A jury member who is asked to evaluate the probability that the defendant is telling the truth (the target attribute) may instead be performing the much easier evaluation: "How well did he answer the prosecutor's questions" (the heuristic attribute). There often is a valid link between these two attributes; convincing answers may be correlated with actual truth telling. But if the heuristic attribute is given too much credit, biased judgements ensue. A jury member who relies exclusively on his or her gut feelings may decide issues of guilt on the basis of credibility judgements rather than on evidence.

Representativeness reasoning refers, by this account, to two processes:

- A judgement of what is the prototypical, or "representative" exemplar of a category, a population, or a distribution (judgement *of* representativeness).
- A probability judgement based on how similar a target outcome is to this prototype (judgements *by* representativeness).

In some problems, the first assessment is already implied by the instructions; for instance in the birth-clinic problem, participants were told that typically around 50% of babies are boys. In other problems, participants have to make their own typicality judgements, based on previous beliefs. For instance, a player with some coin-tossing experience may be less convinced that HTTHTH is a prototypical random sequence, perhaps it contains too many alternations to be truly "representative". Thus different individuals might arrive at different probability judgements simply by having different opinions about the prototypical chance outcome (or the prototypical engineer, or the prototypical bank teller, as the case may be). Experts could make better probability estimates than novices, not by relying less on representativeness, but by having developed a more differentiated and accurate lexicon of prototypes.

Heuristic judgements are often described as quick, intuitive, effortless, and automatic. This means that they are hard to avoid, yet they do not have to be accepted. If I observe a fellow bus passenger in Oslo (Norway) with a striking similarity to Saddam Hussein, the thought of Saddam himself is unavoidable, but I will quickly convince myself that despite the similarity, the probability of Saddam (or one of his stand-ins) riding the local bus is essentially zero. Similarly, statistical knowledge and logical arguments may convince me that large biased samples occur less frequently than small biased samples, that HHHHHH is a perfectly acceptable random sequence, and that people apparently talking to themselves are not necessarily crazy, especially in places with few crazy people around. These "corrections" are usually due to more deliberate, reflective, and analytic afterthoughts that follow, and sometimes supersede, our initial, spontaneous intuitions.

Leaning on currently popular dual-process models, Kahneman and Frederick (2002) distinguish between the operations of two cognitive systems, System 1 and System 2. System 1 is exemplified by intuitive and spontaneous heuristic processing, whereas System 2 refers to our capacity for reflective, controlled, critical, and effortful thinking, where judgements are evaluated according to rational rules. System 2 will monitor and control the output of System 1, with the implication that judgements by representativeness (as well as other heuristic judgements) are only expressed overtly if endorsed by System 2. We may accordingly think of probability judgements as a compromise between simple and effortless spontaneous processes, on the one hand, and more slow and careful review-and-revise procedures, on the other. Whether, in the end, the judgements will be biased or not, depends on the appropriateness of intuitive thinking, as well as the weight allotted to it by System 2.

SUMMARY

- Representativeness is not in itself a bias (or an illusion), but a procedure for estimating probabilities by means of similarity or typicality judgements. Such judgements are often accurate, but will occasionally lead to biased estimates.
- Representativeness can be used to assess the probability of a particular outcome, based on its similarity with its source or its "parent population" (prediction tasks).
- It can also be used to assess the probability of a hypothesis, or a causal model, based on its match with a set of observations (diagnosis tasks).
- Representativeness was originally described as one of three basic heuristics by Kahneman and Tversky. An over-reliance on representativeness has been used to explain a number of biases, including the conjunction fallacy, base-rate neglect, the gambler's fallacy, belief in "the law of small numbers", nonregressive predictions, and the illusion of validity.
- Representativeness has been studied both in lay and expert judgements

and is related to beliefs in the similarity between causes and consequences.
- Many biases originally described as "due" to representativeness can also be given alternative explanations.

FURTHER READING

Tversky and Kahneman's (1974) classic paper is still the best introduction to their early work on representativeness and other judgemental heuristics. A more thorough conceptual analysis of representativeness is provided by Tversky and Kahneman (1982), and a revised and updated version by Kahneman and Frederick (2002).

REFERENCES

Aristotle (1941). Rhetoric. In R. McKeon (Ed.), *The basic work of Aristotle*. New York: Random House.
Attanasio, J. S., Onslow, M., & Packman, A. (1998). Representativeness reasoning and the search for the origins of stuttering: A return to basic observations. *Journal of Fluency Disorders*, 23, 265–277.
Ayton, P., & Wright, G. (1987). Tests for randomness? *Teaching Mathematics and its Applications*, 6, 83–87.
Bar-Hillel, M. (1984). Representativeness and fallacies of probability judgment. *Acta Psychologica*, 55, 91–107.
Fiske, S. T., & Taylor, S. E. (1991). *Social cognition* (2nd Ed.). New York: McGraw-Hill.
Garb, H. N. (1996). The representativeness and past-behavior heuristics in clinical judgment. *Professional Psychology: Research and Practice*, 27, 272–277.
Gavanski, I., & Wells, G. L. (1989). Counterfactual processing of normal and exceptional events. *Journal of Experimental Social Psychology*, 25, 314–325.
Gigerenzer, G. (1991). How to make cognitive illusions disappear: Beyond "heuristics and biases". *European Review of Social Psychology*, 2, 83–115.
Gigerenzer, G., Todd, P. M., & the ABC Research Group (1999). *Simple heuristics that make us smart*. Oxford: Oxford University Press.
Hertwig, R., & Gigerenzer, G. (1999). The "conjunction fallacy" revisited: How intelligent inferences look like reasoning errors. *Journal of Behavioral Decision Making*, 12, 275–305.
Holzworth, R. J., & Doherty, M. E. (1974). Inferences and predictions: Normative vs. representative responding. *Bulletin of the Psychonomic Society*, 3, 300–302.
Homer's Odyssey (1953), London: Dent.
Jones, S. K., Jones, K. T., & Frisch, D. (1995). Biases of probability assessment: A comparison of frequency and single-case judgments. *Organizational Behavior and Human Decision Processes*, 61, 109–122.
Joram, E., & Read, D. (1996). Two faces of representativeness: The effects of response format on beliefs about random sampling. *Journal of Behavioral Decision Making*, 9, 249–264.

Kahneman, D., & Frederick, S. (2002). Representativeness revisited: Attribution substitution in intuitive judgment. In T. Gilovich, D. Griffin, & D. Kahneman (Eds.), *Heuristics and biases: The psychology of intuitive judgment* (pp. 49–81). Cambridge: Cambridge University Press.

Kahneman, D., & Tversky, A. (1972). Subjective probability: A judgment of representativeness. *Cognitive Psychology, 3*, 430–454.

Kahneman, D., & Tversky, A. (1973). On the psychology of prediction. *Psychological Review, 80*, 237–251.

Laplace, P. S. (1816). *Essai philosophique sur les probabilités*. Paris: Courcier.

Lupfer, M. B., & Layman, E. (1996). Invoking naturalistic and religious attributions: A case of applying the availability heuristic? The representativeness heuristic? *Social Cognition, 14*, 55–76.

Mill, J. S. (1856). *A system of logic*. London: Parker.

Shefrin, H. (2001). Do investors expect higher returns from safer stocks than from riskier stocks? *The Journal of Psychology and Financial Markets, 2*, 176–181.

Sim, D. L. H., & Morris, M. W. (1998). Representativeness and counterfactual thinking: The principle that antecedent and outcome correspond in magnitude. *Personality and Social Psychology Bulletin, 24*, 595–609.

Smith, H. D. (1998). Misconceptions of chance: Developmental differences and similarities in use of the representativeness heuristic. *Psychological Reports, 83*, 703–707.

Stanovich, K. E., & West, R. F. (2000). Individual differences in reasoning: Implications for the rationality debate. *Behavioral and Brain Sciences, 23*, 645–665.

Tassoni, C. J. (1996). Representativeness in the market for bets on national football league games. *Journal of Behavioral Decision Making, 9*, 115–124.

Teigen, K. H. (1983). Studies in subjective probability I: Predictions of random events. *Scandinavian Journal of Psychology, 24*, 13–25.

Teigen, K. H. (1990). To be convincing or to be right: A question of preciseness. In K. Gilhooly, M. Keane, R. Logan, & G. Erdos (Eds.), *Lines of thinking: Reflections on the psychology of thought* (pp. 299–313). Chichester, UK: Wiley.

Tversky, A., & Kahneman, D. (1971). Belief in the law of small numbers. *Psychological Bulletin, 76*, 105–110.

Tversky, A., & Kahneman, D. (1974). Judgments under uncertainty: Heuristics and biases. *Science, 185*, 1124–1131.

Tversky, A., & Kahneman, D. (1982). Judgments of and by representativeness. In D. Kahneman, P. Slovic, & A. Tversky (Eds.), *Judgment under uncertainty: Heuristics and biases* (pp. 84–98). Cambridge: Cambridge University Press.

Tversky, A., & Kahneman, D. (1983). Extensional versus intuitive reasoning: The conjunction fallacy in probability judgment. *Psychological Review, 90*, 293–315.

Villejoubert, G., & Mandel, D. R. (2002). The inverse fallacy: An account of deviations from Bayes's theorem and the additivity principle. *Memory & Cognition, 30*, 171–178.

10 Anchoring effect

Thomas Mussweiler, Birte Englich, and Fritz Strack

Suppose you are the judge in a legal case of rape. The prosecutor and the defender have given their final speeches and you have just closed the court for a lunch break. The next session will start right after lunch, so that you have roughly an hour to make up your mind about the sentence. All the information that is necessary to make this important decision is right in front of you. The protocols of witnesses' statements, the opinions of a series of experts, and the relevant passages from the penal code are spread over your desk. You go through the most important facts once again: The victim's account of what happened that night, the expert's assessment of how likely it is that the defendant will commit rape again, the prosecutor's and the defender's plea. Upon close inspection, the evidence seems mixed and you are uncertain about what to do, what sentence to give. In thinking about the core facts, the final words of the prosecutor echo in your mind "... therefore, your honour, I demand a sentence of 34 months". You wonder, "34 months of prison confinement, is this an appropriate sentence?" Will the prosecutor's demand influence your sentencing decision?

If so, your decision may be biased by one of the most remarkable influences on human judgement, namely the anchoring effect (Tversky & Kahneman, 1974). Because the prosecutor's goal is to obtain a high sentence, being directly influenced by his demand may be against your intentions. At the same time, it would put you in good company. The results of a recent study of ours (Englich & Mussweiler, 2001) indicate that accomplished trial judges with an average of more than 15 years of experience were influenced by sentencing demands, even if the demands were made by non-experts. In fact, the magnitude of this influence proved to be dramatic. Judges who considered a high demand of 34 months gave final sentences that were almost 8 months longer than judges who considered a low demand of 12 months. A difference of 8 months in prison for the identical crime. Notably, this influence occurred although both demands were explicitly made by a non-expert: In our study they were given by a computer science student in the role of the prosecutor.

THE ANCHORING PHENOMENON

As is true in this legal setting, human judgement is often influenced by salient anchors (for a classroom demonstration, see Text box 10.1.). Judgemental

---

Text box 10.1 Anchoring experiment

Anchoring effects are among the most robust and easily replicated findings in psychology. The experimental design we outline as a basis for classroom demonstrations follows the classic anchoring paradigm (Tversky & Kahneman, 1974).

Method

Participants

Anchoring effects are exceptionally strong. Furthermore, simple studies can typically be run in a within-subjects design. For such designs a total of 20 participants is sufficient to produce reliable effects.

Materials

Four pairs of difficult general-knowledge questions pertaining to different content domains are used as materials (see Appendix). The anchors are typically set at one standard above and below the mean estimates of a calibration group that answered absolute questions (Mussweiler & Strack, 1999a).

Each question pair consists of a comparative and an absolute anchoring judgement. In the *comparative* judgements, participants indicate whether the target quantity is higher or lower than the anchor value (e.g., "Is the mean temperature in Antarctica in winter higher or lower than −17°C?"). In the subsequent *absolute* judgements, participants provide their best estimate of the target quantity (e.g., "How high is the mean temperature in Antarctica in winter?"). Two of the comparative judgements include a high anchor, the other two include a low anchor. Two different versions of the questionnaire are constructed to control for content and order effects. In both versions, questions are presented in the same order. In each version, however, the high and low anchor conditions are assigned to different questions, so that across both versions each of the two conditions is realized with each of four critical question pairs.

Procedure

Participants may complete the questionnaires in groups of up to 20. Upon arrival in the lab, they are given the questionnaire and are told to read the instructions carefully. They are informed that they are taking part in a pretest for the construction of a general-knowledge questionnaire. The purpose of the pretest is ostensibly to find the best wording for general-knowledge questions. Importantly, to reduce the perceived informativeness of the anchors and thus to discourage conversational inferences (Grice, 1975) the instructions emphasize that the anchor values were randomly selected. This is typically done by explaining that the anchors were determined by a randomization device that works in a similar way to a wheel of fortune. It is further pointed out that this random selection is necessary to minimize the impact the anchors have on the answers and to thus identify the impact of different question formats. Finally, participants are instructed to answer all of the questions in the given order and to do so as accurately as possible.

Analysis

To pool answers across different content domains, absolute estimates are transformed into z-scores, separately for each question. These scores reflect participants' average deviation from the question mean in units of the pertinent standard deviation. For each participant, the mean z-score for the two questions in the high anchor condition and for the two questions in the low anchor conditions are calculated. These mean scores build the basis for the analysis which in this simple design consists of a t-test for repeated samples.

Results and discussion

Absolute estimates should be reliably assimilated towards the provided anchor values, so that higher mean estimates result for those targets that were compared to high anchors than for those that were compared to low anchors. As we have indicated before, this effect is extremely robust. Even if participants are deliberately trying to work against the anchoring influence, their estimates are typically assimilated towards the anchor values.

anchoring – the assimilation of a numeric judgement to a previously considered standard – may be one of the most remarkable influences on human judgement for at least two reasons. First, anchoring effects are strikingly pervasive and robust. Second, the mechanisms that produce anchoring have long remained an enigma.

Pervasiveness and robustness

Anchoring effects pervade a variety of judgements, from the trivial (i.e., estimates of the mean temperature in Antarctica; Mussweiler & Strack, 1999a) to the apocalyptic (i.e., estimates of the likelihood of nuclear war; Plous, 1989). In particular, they have been observed in a broad array of different judgemental domains, such as general-knowledge questions (Strack & Mussweiler, 1997), price estimates (Mussweiler, Strack, & Pfeiffer, 2000; Northcraft & Neale, 1987), estimates of self-efficacy (Cervone & Peake, 1986), probability assessments (Plous, 1989), evaluations of lotteries and gambles (Chapman & Johnson, 1994), legal judgement (Chapman & Bornstein, 1996; Englich & Mussweiler, 2001), and negotiation (Galinsky & Mussweiler, 2001).

Not only is the anchoring effect influential in a plethora of laboratory and real-world settings, this influence is also remarkably robust. In particular, anchoring is independent of many potentially moderating variables. For one thing, anchoring occurs even if the anchor values are clearly uninformative for the critical estimate, for example because they were randomly selected (e.g., Mussweiler & Strack, 2000b; Tversky & Kahneman, 1974). Moreover, anchoring remains uninfluenced by the extremity of the anchor (e.g., Chapman & Johnson, 1994; Strack & Mussweiler, 1997) so that even implausibly extreme values yield an effect. For example, in one of our own studies (Strack & Mussweiler, 1997) estimates for Mahatma Gandhi's age were assimilated to an unreasonably high anchor value of 140 years. Furthermore, anchoring effects appear to be independent of participants' motivation (e.g., Wilson, Houston, Etling, & Brekke, 1996). Specifically, the attempt to improve accuracy by awarding a prize for the best estimate proved unsuccessful. In addition, it has been demonstrated that anchoring occurs independently of participants' expertise (Englich & Mussweiler, 2001; Northcraft & Neale, 1987). In the above-mentioned study in the legal domain (Englich & Mussweiler, 2001), for example, experienced judges and inexperienced law students were influenced by the anchor sentencing demand given by a computer science student to similar degrees.

Furthermore, anchoring effects are characterized by an exceptional temporal robustness and persist over fairly long periods of time. In one study, for example, anchoring effects were still apparent 1 week after the anchor value had been considered (Mussweiler, 2001). Probably the most striking demonstration of the robustness of the phenomenon, however, stems from research demonstrating that explicit instructions to correct for a potential influence of an anchor do not mitigate the effect (Wilson et al., 1996). Even explicitly forewarning judges about the potential distortion and informing them about its direction does not diminish the effect. This suggests that anchoring is an exceptionally robust phenomenon that is difficult to avoid.

Relevance

Judgemental anchoring is not only a particularly robust judgemental effect that has been demonstrated in a variety of domains, it also constitutes a basic explanatory concept that has been used to explain a wide array of judgemental phenomena. Anchoring has, for example, been used to explain attitudinal phenomena (Quattrone, 1982). More recently, the egocentricity of social judgement has also been attributed to an anchoring mechanism (Gilovich, Medvec, & Savitsky, 2000). Specifically, people may overestimate the extent to which their appearances are noted by others, because they anchor on their own rich experiences. Furthermore, anchoring has been used to explain another eminent cognitive illusion, namely hindsight bias (Fischhoff, 1975; see also Chapter 20), the assimilation of a recollected estimate towards a provided solution.

In the psychology of judgement and decision making, anchoring has been primarily applied to probabilistic inferences. Thus, preference-reversal effects (Lichtenstein & Slovic, 1971), the distortion of estimates for the probability of disjunctive and conjunctive events (Tversky & Kahneman, 1974), and the assessment of subjective probability distributions (Tversky & Kahneman, 1974) have been attributed to judgemental anchoring.

Finally, applications of the anchoring concept are also found in applied contexts, such as negotiations in organizational psychology (Neale & Bazerman, 1991). First offers, for example, may influence the final negotiation outcome, because they serve as judgemental anchors to which the final outcome is assimilated (Galinsky & Mussweiler, 2001). In consumer behaviour, it has been suggested that price claims in advertisements influence consumer behaviour because they function as anchors in product evaluation (Biswas & Burton, 1993).

These accounts bear witness to the great diversity of phenomena that have been explained by the notion of judgemental anchoring. It is important to note, however, that these phenomena are not sufficiently explained by evoking an unspecific notion of anchoring. As such, the anchoring notion does not illuminate the underlying mechanisms, but only describes the direction of the observed influence (assimilation). In this respect, the term "anchoring" constitutes a descriptive rather than an explanatory concept which does not go beyond the terms assimilation and contrast (Strack, 1992). In order to be used as an explanatory concept, however, the psychological mechanisms that underlie anchoring first have to be sufficiently understood.

Paradigms

Anchoring effects are most typically examined in a classic paradigm introduced by Tversky and Kahneman (1974). In this paradigm, anchors are explicitly provided by inducing judges to compare the target to the anchor value. Typically, this is achieved by posing a *comparative* anchoring question and asking participants to indicate whether the target's extension on the judgemental dimension is larger or smaller than the anchor value. In order to reduce the perceived informativeness of the anchor values, they are ostensibly selected at random. This may be obtained by spinning a wheel of fortune (Tversky & Kahneman, 1974), emphasizing the random selection in the instructions (Strack & Mussweiler, 1997), or throwing dice (Mussweiler & Strack, 2000b). In what is probably the best-known demonstration of anchoring in this paradigm, Tversky and Kahneman (1974) asked their research participants two consecutive questions about the percentage of African nations in the UN. In a first comparative anchoring question, participants indicated whether the percentage of African nations in the UN is higher or lower than an arbitrary number (the anchor) that had ostensibly been determined by spinning a wheel of fortune (e.g., 65% or 10%). In the subsequent *absolute* anchoring question, participants then gave their best estimate of this percentage. Absolute judgements were assimilated to the provided anchor value, so that the mean estimate of participants who received the high anchor was 45%, compared to 25% for participants who received the low anchor.

Alternatively, the anchor may be implicitly provided to the participants in cases in which it is clearly informative for the judgement at hand. For example, Northcraft and Neale (1987) demonstrated that real-estate pricing decisions depended on the listing price for the property. They had real-estate agents estimate the value of a property. Participants were given a 10-page booklet including all the information that is important for real-estate pricing. This booklet also contained the listing price of the house, which constituted the central independent variable. The price provided was either above or below the actual appraisal value of the property (e.g., $83,900 vs $65,900). Replicating the typical anchoring finding, participants' estimates for the value of the property were assimilated towards the provided anchors.

In a third paradigm, anchors are self-generated rather than explicitly or implicitly provided by the experimenter (Tversky & Kahneman, 1974). In one such study, participants were given 5 seconds to estimate the result of a product that was either presented in ascending sequence ($1 \times 2 \times \ldots \times 8$) or in descending sequence ($8 \times 7 \times \ldots \times 1$). Participants' estimates for the ascending sequence proved to be lower than for the descending sequence, presumably because participants use the result of calculating the product for the first few numbers (which is lower for the ascending than for the descending sequence) as a self-generated anchor, to which their final estimate was then assimilated. Similarly, judges may assimilate their estimates to self-generated anchors that are closely associated with the target quantity. Participants who are asked to give their best estimate for the freezing point of vodka, for example, may generate 0°C as the freezing point of water as an anchor, and then adjust downwards, because they know that the freezing point of alcohol is lower (Epley & Gilovich, 2001).

Finally, anchoring effects may be obtained by increasing the accessibility of the anchor value in a preceding unrelated task (Wilson et al., 1996). In one experiment (Wilson et al., 1996) demonstrating such *basic* anchoring effects, participants were first induced to copy either five pages of numbers ranging from 4421 to 4579 or five pages of words, and subsequently estimated the number of students at the University of Virginia who will contract cancer within the next 40 years. Those participants who had copied five pages of high numbers estimated this number to be higher than those who had copied five pages of words. Thus, the arbitrary high anchor presented in the preceding task influenced the judgement.

In sum, anchoring effects have been demonstrated using four different experimental paradigms, in which the anchor values are either explicitly or implicitly provided by the experimenter, self-generated, or provided in an unrelated task. Most of the anchoring research, however, uses the standard paradigm that was introduced by Tversky and Kahneman (1974) by first asking participants a comparative and then an absolute anchoring question.

THEORETICAL ACCOUNTS

To date, four theoretical accounts of anchoring effects have been proposed. In particular, it has been suggested that anchoring effects result from (1) insufficient adjustment from a starting point, (2) conversational inferences, (3) numerical priming, and (4) mechanisms of selective accessibility.

Insufficient adjustment

In their initial description of the phenomenon, Tversky and Kahneman (1974) describe anchoring in terms of insufficient adjustment from a starting point. They argue that "[...] people make estimates by starting from an initial value that is adjusted to yield the final answer [...]. Adjustments are typically insufficient. That is, different starting points yield different estimates, which are biased toward the initial value" (p. 1129). Adjustment may be insufficient because it terminates at the boundary of a region of acceptable values for the estimate (Quattrone et al., 1984). For example, participants who are asked whether the percentage of African nations in the UN is higher or lower than 65% may use this anchor value as a starting point, determine whether it is too high or too low, and then adjust in the appropriate direction until the first acceptable value is found. However, such insufficient adjustment to the boundary of a distribution of acceptable values is only possible if the anchor value falls outside this distribution, in that it constitutes an unacceptable value itself. This may be the case because the anchor value is absurdly extreme, or because it is known to be wrong. Participants who, in order to estimate the freezing point of vodka, self-generate the freezing point of water as an anchor, for example, are likely to know that 0°C constitutes an unacceptable value because the freezing point of alcohol is below that of water (Epley & Gilovich, 2001). As a consequence, they may adjust from this unacceptable value until the first acceptable value is reached.

Anchoring effects, however, are not only obtained for clearly implausible and unacceptable anchor values (e.g., Strack & Mussweiler, 1997). It seems difficult to explain effects of plausible and acceptable anchors by an "insufficient adjustment" because for such anchors, there is no reason to adjust in the first place. The scope of the insufficient adjustment account thus appears to be limited to implausible anchors that are clearly unacceptable (for a more extensive discussion, see Mussweiler & Strack, 2001). Consistent with this assumption, it has been demonstrated that insufficient adjustment only appears to contribute to anchoring effects if the critical anchors are unacceptably self-generated, rather than acceptable provided, values (Epley & Gilovich, 2001).

Conversational inferences

A second account attributes anchoring to conversational inferences. According to this reasoning, applying implicit rules of natural conversations (Grice, 1975) to standardized situations (e.g., Schwarz, 1994) allows participants to use the anchor value to infer the actual range of possible answers. Participants who expect the experimenter to be maximally informative (Grice, 1975) in asking his or her questions, may assume that the provided anchor value is close to the actual value and consequently position their estimate in its vicinity. Such conversational inferences may well underlie the effects of considering anchor values that are of clear relevance for the estimate to be made (e.g., Northcraft & Neale, 1987). It is important to note that this account presupposes that the anchor value is indeed seen as informative for the judgement. Anchoring effects, however, also occur if the anchor values are clearly uninformative because they were randomly selected (Tversky & Kahneman, 1974), are implausibly extreme (Strack & Mussweiler, 1997), or are not related to the question at all (Wilson et al., 1996). Thus, although conversational inferences are potential determinants of anchoring in natural situations, they are not a necessary precondition.

Numeric priming

A third theoretical account assumes that anchoring effects are rather superficial and purely numeric in nature (Jacowitz & Kahneman, 1995; Wilson et al., 1996; Wong & Kwong, 2000). In particular, solving a comparative anchoring task may simply render the anchor value itself more accessible, so that this value is likely to influence the subsequent absolute judgement. From this numeric-priming perspective, the sole determinant of anchoring effects is the anchor value itself, regardless of its context, the target with which it is compared, and the judgemental operations in which it is involved. One recent account even goes so far as to claim that anchoring effects may be so superficial that not the anchor itself, but only its absolute value (e.g., "50" for an anchor of "−50°C") is represented in memory and exerts the primary anchoring influence (Wong & Kwong, 2000).

However compelling such a simple numeric account may appear, a careful analysis of anchoring research reveals that focusing exclusively on the numeric anchoring value is insufficient to allow for a complete understanding of judgemental anchoring. In particular, abundant evidence demonstrates that the semantic content that is associated with the anchor necessarily has to be taken into account to understand the complete pattern of findings in the standard paradigm. A purely numeric account cannot, for example, explain that anchoring effects depend on changes in the judgemental dimension (Strack & Mussweiler, 1997). Were anchoring effects indeed evoked by the anchor value itself, then identical effects should result irrespective of the semantic content with which the anchor is associated. For example, comparing the *height* of the Brandenburg Gate to a given anchor value should have identical effects on subsequent judgements of the *height* and the *width* of the Gate, because the numeric properties of the anchor value are left unchanged by changing the judgemental dimension. This, however, is not the case. Rather, the magnitude of the anchoring effect is reduced if the comparative anchoring question pertains to another dimension than the absolute anchoring question (Strack & Mussweiler, 1997).

The temporal robustness of anchoring effects is also at odds with a purely numeric account which implies that anchoring effects are fairly transient and short-lived. Because we are constantly exposed to arbitrary numbers, our daily routines (e.g., calling a friend, paying a bill) should immediately wipe out the effects of solving a comparative anchoring task. The fact that anchoring effects can prevail for a week (Mussweiler, 2001) is clearly in conflict with this implication and further renders a purely numeric conceptualization of the standard anchoring paradigm unconvincing.

Selective accessibility

As a fourth theoretical account, we have proposed a selective accessibility (SA) model of anchoring (Mussweiler, 1997; Mussweiler & Strack, 1999a, 1999b; Strack & Mussweiler, 1997; for a related account, see Chapman & Johnson, 1994, 1999). The starting point of this model is the observation that anchoring occurs in situations in which the consequences of comparing a given target to a numeric standard are assessed with a subsequent absolute judgement of this target (for a more complete discussion of the informational underpinnings of comparison processes, see Mussweiler, 2003). Because – as in any judgement – absolute target judgements reflect the implications of accessible target knowledge, one has to examine the informational consequences of the comparison to understand the mechanisms that lead to the assimilation of absolute estimates towards the anchor. Absolute judgements are likely to be based on the knowledge that is accessible at the time the judgement is made, so that analyzing the accessibility of target knowledge promises to provide a more complete understanding of the anchoring enigma.

The basic assumption of the SA model is that anchoring is in essence a knowledge accessibility effect, and is thus semantic in nature (for more detailed accounts, see Mussweiler & Strack, 1999a, 1999b). The model attempts to explain anchoring by linking it to two principles that are fundamental to social cognition research: (1) *hypothesis-consistent testing* and (2) *semantic priming*. More specifically, the model postulates that comparing the judgemental target to the anchor value changes the accessibility of knowledge about the target. In particular, the accessibility of an anchor-consistent subset of target knowledge is selectively increased. We assume that judges compare the target with the anchor by testing the possibility that the target's value is equal to the anchor value. For example, judges who are asked whether the percentage of African nations in the UN is higher or lower than a high anchor of 65% are assumed to test the possibility that this value actually is 65%. To do so, they selectively retrieve knowledge from memory that is consistent with this assumption (e.g., "Africa is a huge continent", "There are more African nations than I can keep in mind", etc.).

This kind of hypothesis-consistent testing is a general tendency that contributes to a variety of judgemental processes (Klayman & Ha, 1987). As a consequence, the accessibility of anchor-consistent knowledge is increased. In order to generate the final numeric estimate, judges then rely primarily on easily accessible knowledge (Higgins, 1996), so that their estimate is heavily influenced by the anchor-consistent knowledge generated before. In our example, absolute estimates about the percentage of African nations in the UN would thus be based on the specific subset of target knowledge that was deliberately retrieved to be consistent with the assumption that this percentage is fairly high. Conceivably, using this knowledge leads to high estimates, so that the final estimate is assimilated to the anchor value.

Similarities between anchoring and knowledge accessibility effects

This conceptualization of anchoring as a knowledge accessibility effect is consistent with a large body of evidence, which demonstrates that anchoring effects share many of the qualities that are characteristic of knowledge accessibility effects in general (for a review, see Higgins, 1996). For one, anchoring effects critically depend on the applicability of the knowledge that was rendered accessible during the comparative task. It has been demonstrated that the extent to which increasing the accessibility of a concept in a priming task influences a subsequent judgement, is determined by how applicable the activated concept is to this judgement (Higgins, Rholes, & Jones, 1977). In much the same way, the magnitude of anchoring depends on how applicable the knowledge that was rendered accessible during the comparative task is to the critical absolute judgement. As described before, comparing the height of the Brandenburg Gate to a given anchor yields stronger effects on absolute estimates of the height of the Gate than on estimates of its width (Strack & Mussweiler, 1997; see also Chapman & Johnson, 1994). This may be the case because the knowledge generated during the comparative task has more direct implications for estimates of height than for estimates of width (i.e., it is more applicable to judgements of height) so that estimates of height are influenced more strongly. Thus, anchoring effects appear to depend on the applicability criterion (Higgins et al., 1977) in much the same way as is characteristic of knowledge accessibility effects in general.

An additional characteristic that is shared by anchoring and knowledge accessibility effects is that the time that is needed to make a given judgement depends on the degree of accessibility of judgement-relevant knowledge. In a classic priming study, for example, Neely (1977) demonstrated that participants were faster in judging whether a given letter string constitutes a word, if a semantically related word had been presented beforehand. For example, participants were faster in judging the word "robin" if "bird" had been presented before. Paralleling this dependency, response latencies for the absolute anchoring task have been demonstrated to depend on the extent to which the accessibility of judgement-relevant knowledge had been increased during the comparative task (Mussweiler & Strack, 1999a, 2000a, 2000b; Strack & Mussweiler, 1997). For example, judges were faster in giving absolute judgements if they had ample time to generate knowledge during the preceding comparison than when they had made the comparison under time pressure – a condition that is likely to limit the accessibility increase (Mussweiler & Strack, 1999a).

However, different levels of accessibility influence not only response latencies for absolute judgements, but also the content of these judgements. In particular, larger anchoring effects occur under conditions that promote the extensive generation of anchor-consistent target knowledge and thus lead to a more substantial accessibility increase. For example, judges who have more target information available during the comparative task show more anchoring than those who have little information available (Chapman & Johnson, 1999). Furthermore, judges who generate more anchor-consistent knowledge during the comparative task, because they are in a sad mood – a condition that is typically associated with more elaborate processing – show larger anchoring effects than judges in a neutral mood (Bodenhausen, Gabriel, & Lineberger, 2000).

Temporal robustness constitutes yet another characteristic of knowledge accessibility effects that is shared by anchoring. Knowledge accessibility effects often have long lasting effects on judgement. For example, it has been demonstrated that increasing the accessibility of a specific trait concept influences person judgements that are made 1 week after the priming episode (Srull & Wyer, 1980). The same temporal robustness also characterizes judgemental anchoring. In particular, it has been demonstrated that anchoring effects still occur, if the comparative and the absolute question are separated by a 1-week delay (Mussweiler, 2001).

These parallels between anchoring and knowledge accessibility effects in general provide converging evidence in support of the assumption that anchoring effects are indeed knowledge accessibility effects in essence.

Direct support for selective accessibility

The most direct support for this notion, however, stems from a series of studies that directly assessed the accessibility of target knowledge subsequent to the critical comparative judgement (Mussweiler & Strack, 2000a, 2000b). In one of these studies (Mussweiler & Strack, 2000a), participants were asked to compare the average price for a German car to either a high or a low anchor value (40,000 vs 20,000 German Marks). Subsequent to this comparative judgement, we assessed the accessibility of target knowledge with a lexical decision task. In particular, participants made a series of lexical decisions including target words that are closely associated with expensive cars (e.g., Mercedes, BMW) and words associated with inexpensive cars (e.g., VW).

Response latencies for these two types of target words clearly depended on the anchoring condition, as is apparent from Figure 10.1. In particular, judges were faster in recognizing words associated with expensive cars after a comparison with the high anchor than after a comparison with the low anchor. In contrast, words associated with inexpensive cars were recognized faster after a comparison with the low anchor. These findings demonstrate that the accessibility of anchor-consistent semantic knowledge about the target (e.g., knowledge indicating high prices after a comparison with a high anchor) is increased as a consequence of the comparative judgement.

Additional evidence further suggests that this accessibility increase is specific to the judgemental target itself. That is, the knowledge that is rendered accessible specifically pertains to the judgemental target. In one study demonstrating this specificity, for example, comparing the self as a judgemental target to a high anchor of general knowledge only increased the accessibility of knowledge indicating that the self is knowledgeable, whereas the accessibility of knowledge about a close other remained unchanged (Mussweiler & Strack, 2000a). These findings provide direct support for the core assumption of the SA model. Comparing the target to the anchor value does indeed appear to increase the accessibility of anchor-consistent semantic knowledge about the target. Using this knowledge as a basis for the absolute estimate produces the assimilation effect that is known as the typical consequence of anchoring.

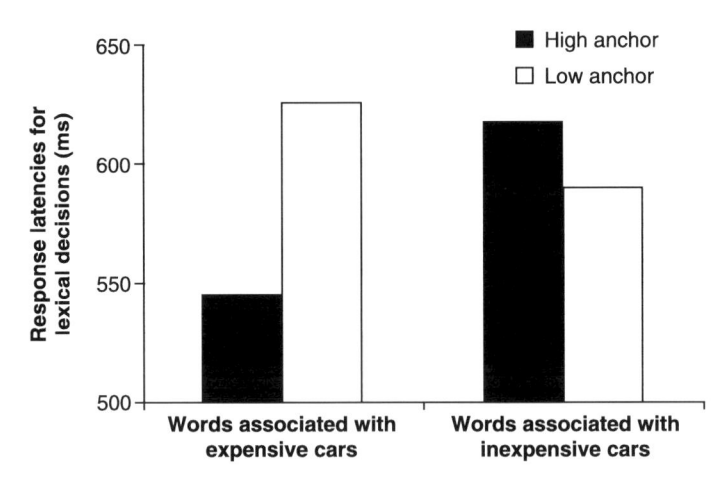

Figure 10.1 Response latencies for lexical decisions as a function of word type and anchor (Mussweiler & Strack, 2000a).

Integration: Anchoring as a two-stage process

The preceding discussion suggests that anchoring effects are in essence knowledge accessibility effects. The critical comparison of the judgemental target with the anchor value appears to involve a selective search for anchor-consistent target knowledge. Although this target–anchor comparison appears to be a core stage in all of the described anchoring paradigms, at least some of these paradigms involve a preceding stage. In those paradigms in which the anchor value is not explicitly provided, the judges first have to select a potential anchor, which can then be compared to the target. That is, at least in some of the anchoring paradigms, judges first have to engage in selection processes before they can carry out the comparison process that is likely to involve mechanisms of selective accessibility. This suggests that to obtain a complete understanding of the anchoring phenomenon, one has to differentiate between two stages which appear to be clearly distinguishable with respect to the processes they involve: the *selection* of a judgemental anchor, and its subsequent *comparison* with the target (for a related view, see Wilson et al., 1996).

Although selection processes do not play much of a role in the standard anchoring paradigm (Tversky & Kahneman, 1974) because here the standard is explicitly provided to the judges, they may constitute an important aspect of many judgements in everyday life. Theorizing in different areas of psychology has pointed out that human judgement is essentially relative or comparative in nature, even if a comparison is not explicitly asked for (e.g., Festinger, 1954; Helson, 1964; Kahneman & Miller, 1986; Mussweiler, 2003). Such a tendency towards comparative evaluation is likely to be especially pronounced in situations in which judges have little target knowledge available, as is typically the case in anchoring studies. Judges who desperately search for information that may help them to estimate a quantity they have never thought about, are likely to consider the target quantity in comparison to a standard it appears to be bringing to mind. Participants who estimate the number of African nations in the UN (Tversky & Kahneman, 1974), for example, may compare this target quantity to a number that comes to their mind because they have previously compared it to the unrelated quantity of the number of physicians listed in the local phone book (Wilson et al., 1996). Thus, an unrelated anchor value may be selected as a comparison standard for the generation of the target estimate, so that this stage of standard selection is open to numeric influences.

At least three mechanisms may influence the initial stage of standard selection. First, a particular value may be selected as an anchor because conversational inferences suggest it as relevant. If a particular anchor is explicitly mentioned by the experimenter, then judges may well use it to subsequently compare it to the target. Second, a value may be selected as an anchor because it is easily accessible and comes to mind during the evaluation of the target. Finally, an anchor may be self-generated via an insufficient adjustment process. Judges who are provided with an implausible anchor, for example, may use this value as a starting point to generate a more plausible value, which is then compared to the target. This suggests that the alternative mechanisms of conversational inference, numeric priming, and insufficient adjustment may contribute to the selection of an anchor value.

The outcome of this process of standard selection is likely to influence the subsequent process of target evaluation. At the same time, selecting a standard by itself is not sufficient to influence how the target is judged. Rather, these effects result from the process of comparing the selected standard to the judgemental target. In order for a selected standard to be helpful for target evaluation, it has to be related to the characteristics of the judgemental target. This process requires the activation of semantic target knowledge and is – in light of the accumulated evidence (see Mussweiler & Strack, 1999b) – likely to involve the process of selective accessibility.

From this perspective, there appear to exist at least two distinguishable types of anchoring effects: a relatively shallow anchoring influence that operates at the stage of standard selection and a deeper anchoring effect that has its roots in the comparison stage. Notably, it is the latter effect that is typically seen as the classic case of anchoring. The actual comparison appears to involve a relatively elaborate process of testing the hypothesis that the target quantity may be similar to the comparison standard by selectively generating target knowledge that supports this assumption. This hypothesis-testing process increases the accessibility of standard-consistent knowledge about the target, which influences subsequent target judgements.

CONCLUSION

Anchoring effects are among the most robust and ubiquitous psychological phenomena in judgement and decision making. Given the diversity of paradigms that have been used to produce "anchoring effects", it seems unsurprising that a careful differentiation of different processes that operate in paradigms which involve clearly different judgemental tasks is called for. Despite this variety of judgemental paradigms and contributing mechanisms, however, the accumulated evidence suggests that the selective accessibility mechanism of generating anchor-consistent target knowledge lies at the core of the anchoring phenomenon. The various paradigms that have been used to examine anchoring effects, however, appear to differ with respect to the additional mechanisms they may involve. With a perspective on psychological processes rather than judgemental effects, we may well find that what has previously been considered as instantiations of one judgemental heuristic called "anchoring" is actually a conglomeration of fairly diverse phenomena whose similarity rests solely on the net outcome they produce.

SUMMARY

- An assimilation of a numeric estimate towards a previously considered standard is defined as judgemental anchoring.
- The core mechanism underlying anchoring appears to be a selective increase in the accessibility of knowledge indicating that the target's extension is similar to the anchor value.
- Anchoring constitutes a ubiquitous phenomenon that occurs in a variety of laboratory and real-world settings.
- Anchoring effects are remarkably robust. They occur even if the anchor values are clearly uninformative or implausibly extreme, are independent of participants' motivation and expertise, persist over long periods of time, and are not reduced by explicit instructions to correct.

FURTHER READING

Recent reviews of anchoring research are given by Chapman and Johnson (2002) as well as Mussweiler and Strack (1999b). Bazerman (2002) provides an interesting discussion of how anchoring effects may influence managerial decision making.

ACKNOWLEDGEMENTS

Our research on anchoring was supported by grants from the German Science Foundation (DFG). We would like to thank the members of the Würzburg Social Cognition Group for numerous discussions of this work.

REFERENCES

Bazerman, M. H. (2002). *Judgment in managerial decision making.* Chichester, UK: Wiley.

Biswas, A., & Burton, S. (1993). Consumer perceptions of tensile price claims in advertisements: An assessment of claim types across different discount levels. *Journal of the Academy of Marketing Science, 21,* 217–229.

Bodenhausen, G. V., Gabriel, S., & Lineberger, M. (2000). Sadness and the susceptibility to judgmental bias: The case of anchoring. *Psychological Science, 11,* 320–323.

Cervone, D., & Peake, P. K. (1986). Anchoring, efficacy, and action: The influence of judgmental heuristics on self-efficacy judgment and behavior. *Journal of Personality and Social Psychology, 50,* 492–501.

Chapman, G. B., & Bornstein, B. H. (1996). The more you ask for, the more you get: Anchoring in personal injury verdicts. *Applied Cognitive Psychology, 10,* 519–540.

Chapman, G. B., & Johnson, E. J. (1994). The limits of anchoring. *Journal of Behavioral Decision Making, 7,* 223–242.

Chapman, G. B., & Johnson, E. J. (1999). Anchoring, activation, and the construction of values. *Organizational Behavior and Human Decision Processes, 79,* 1–39.

Chapman, G. B., & Johnson, E. J. (2002). Incorporating the irrelevant: Anchors in judgments of belief and value. In T. Gilovich, D. Griffin, & D. Kahneman (Eds.), *Heuristics and biases: The psychology of intuitive judgment* (pp. 120–138). Cambridge: Cambridge University Press.

Englich, B., & Mussweiler, T. (2001). Sentencing under uncertainty: Anchoring effects in the courtroom. *Journal of Applied Social Psychology, 31,* 1535–1551.

Epley, N., & Gilovich, T. (2001). Putting adjustment back in the anchoring and adjustment heuristic: Differential processing of self-generated and experimenter-provided anchors. *Psychological Science, 12,* 391–396.

Festinger, L. (1954). A theory of social comparison processes. *Human Relations, 7,* 117–140.

Fischhoff, B. (1975). Hindsight ≠ foresight: The effect of outcome knowledge on judgment under uncertainty. *Journal of Experimental Psychology, 89,* 288–299.

Galinsky, A. D., & Mussweiler, T. (2001). First offers as anchors: The role of perspective-taking and negotiator focus. *Journal of Personality and Social Psychology, 81,* 657–669.

Gilovich, T., Medvec, V. H., & Savitsky, K. (2000). The spotlight effect in social judgment: An egocentric bias in estimates of the salience of one's own actions and appearance. *Journal of Personality and Social Psychology, 78,* 211–222.

Grice, H. P. (1975). Logic and conversation. In P. Cole & J. L. Morgan (Eds.), *Syntax and semantics. Vol. 3: Speech acts* (pp. 41–58). New York: Academic Press.

Helson, H. (1964). *Adaptation level theory: An experimental and systematic approach to behavior.* New York: Harper.

Higgins, E. T. (1996). Knowledge activation: Accessibility, applicability, and salience. In E. T. Higgins, & A. W. Kruglanski (Eds.), *Social psychology: Handbook of basic principles* (pp. 133–168). New York: The Guilford Press.

Higgins, E. T., Rholes, W. S., & Jones, C. R. (1977). Category accessibility and impression formation. *Journal of Experimental Social Psychology, 13,* 141–154.

Jacowitz, K. E., & Kahneman, D. (1995). Measures of anchoring in estimation tasks. *Personality and Social Psychology Bulletin, 21,* 1161–1166.

Kahneman, D., & Miller, D. T. (1986). Norm theory: Comparing reality to its alternatives. *Psychological Review, 93,* 136–153.

Klayman, J., & Ha, Y. W. (1987). Confirmation, disconfirmation, and information in hypothesis testing. *Psychological Review, 94,* 211–228.

Lichtenstein, S., & Slovic, P. (1971). Reversal of preference between bids and choices in gambling decisions. *Journal of Experimental Psychology, 89,* 46–55.

Mussweiler, T. (1997). *A selective accessibility model of anchoring: Linking the anchoring heuristic to hypothesis-consistent testing and semantic priming. Psychologia Universalis (Vol. 11).* Lengerich, Germany: Pabst.

Mussweiler, T. (2001). The durability of anchoring effects. *European Journal of Social Psychology, 31,* 431–442.

Mussweiler, T. (2003). Comparison processes in social judgment: Mechanisms and consequences. *Psychological Review, 110,* 472–489.

Mussweiler, T., & Strack, F. (1999a). Hypothesis-consistent testing and semantic priming in the anchoring paradigm: A selective accessibility model. *Journal of Experimental Social Psychology, 35*, 136–164.

Mussweiler, T., & Strack, F. (1999b). Comparing is believing: A selective accessibility model of judgmental anchoring. In W. Stroebe & M. Hewstone (Eds.), *European review of social psychology* (Vol. 10, pp. 135–167). Chichester, UK: Wiley.

Mussweiler, T., & Strack, F. (2000a). The use of category and exemplar knowledge in the solution of anchoring tasks. *Journal of Personality and Social Psychology, 78*, 1038–1052.

Mussweiler, T., & Strack, F. (2000b). Numeric judgment under uncertainty: The role of knowledge in anchoring. *Journal of Experimental Social Psychology, 36*, 495–518.

Mussweiler, T., & Strack, F. (2001). The semantics of anchoring. *Organizational Behavior and Human Decision Processes, 86*, 234–255.

Mussweiler, T., Strack, F., & Pfeiffer, T. (2000). Overcoming the inevitable anchoring effect: Considering the opposite compensates for selective accessibility. *Personality and Social Psychology Bulletin, 26*, 1142–1150.

Neale, M. A., & Bazerman, M. H. (1991). *Cognition and rationality in negotiation.* New York: The Free Press.

Neely, J. H. (1977). Semantic priming and retrieval from lexical memory: Roles of inhibitionless spreading of activation and limited-capacity attention. *Journal of Experimental Psychology: General, 3*, 226–254.

Northcraft, G. B., & Neale, M. A. (1987). Experts, amateurs, and real estate: An anchoring-and-adjustment perspective on property pricing decisions. *Organizational Behavior and Human Decision Processes, 39*, 84–97.

Plous, S. (1989). Thinking the unthinkable: The effects of anchoring on likelihood estimates of nuclear war. *Journal of Applied Social Psychology, 19*, 67–91.

Quattrone, G. A. (1982). Overattribution and unit formation: When behavior engulfs the person. *Journal of Personality and Social Psychology, 42*, 593–607.

Quattrone, G. A., Lawrence, C. P., Warren, D. L., Souza-Silva, K., Finkel, S. E., & Andrus, D. E. (1984). *Explorations in anchoring: The effects of prior range, anchor extremity, and suggestive hints.* Unpublished manuscript. Palo Alto, CA: Stanford University

Schwarz, N. (1994). Judgment in a social context: Biases, shortcomings, and the logic of conversation. In M. P. Zanna (Ed.), *Advances in experimental social psychology* (pp. 123–162). San Diego, CA: Academic Press.

Srull, T. K., & Wyer, R. S. (1980). Category accessibility and social perception: Some implications for the study of person memory and interpersonal judgments. *Journal of Personality and Social Psychology, 38*, 841–856.

Strack, F. (1992). The different routes to social judgments: Experiential versus informational strategies. In L. L. Martin & A. Tesser (Eds.), *The construction of social judgment* (pp. 249–275). Hillsdale, NJ: Lawrence Erlbaum Associates Inc.

Strack, F., & Mussweiler, T. (1997). Explaining the enigmatic anchoring effect: Mechanisms of selective accessibility. *Journal of Personality and Social Psychology, 73*, 437–446.

Tversky, A., & Kahneman, D. (1974). Judgment under uncertainty: Heuristics and biases. *Science, 185*, 1124–1130.

Wilson, T. D., Houston, C., Etling, K. M., & Brekke, N. (1996). A new look at anchoring effects: Basic anchoring and its antecedents. *Journal of Experimental Psychology: General, 4*, 387–402.

Wong, K. F. E., & Kwong, J. Y. Y. (2000). Is 7300 m equal to 7.3 km? Same semantics but different anchoring effects. *Organizational Behavior and Human Decision Processes, 82*, 314–333.

APPENDIX

Comparative anchoring questions and anchor values:

1. Is the mean temperature in Antarctica higher or lower than −17 (−43) °C?
2. Was Leonardo da Vinci born before or after 1698 (1391) AD?
3. Was Albert Einstein's first visit to the US before or after 1939 (1905)?
4. Was Mahatma Gandhi older or younger than 79 (64) years when he died?

11 Validity effect

Catherine Hackett Renner

The effect of repetition on enhancing the perceived validity of information has long been independently established by several researchers (e.g., Arkes, Hackett, & Boehm, 1989; Bacon, 1979; Begg, Armour, & Kerr, 1979; Gigerenzer, 1984; Gude & Zechmeister, 1975; Hasher, Goldstein, & Toppino, 1977; Schwartz, 1982). Taken together, these studies have all found that if information has been heard previously, people are likely to ascribe more truth or validity to it than if they are hearing it for the first time. This phenomenon, referred to as the "validity effect", occurs regardless of the type of information (factual, nonfactual, or political), regardless of whether the information was originally believed to be true or false, and regardless of whether the exact wording was repeated.

OVERVIEW: DEMONSTRATING AND EXPLAINING THE OCCURRENCE OF THE VALIDITY EFFECT

Establishing the phenomenon of the validity effect

Text box 11.1 includes a detailed description of a typical validity effect experiment that can be used as a classroom demonstration. In 1977, Hasher,

---

Text box 11.1 The typical validity effect experiment

Generating statements

The typical validity effect experiment requires that numerous "trivia" statements be generated and pilot-tested first in order to ascertain how true or false participants perceive them to be. The most recent almanac is an excellent source of information for creating statements of fact. During the pilot test the participants should rate the statements on the same rating scale that will be used in the experiment. The majority of the experiments have used a Likert scale ranging from 1 (definitely false) to 7 (definitely true). Once the statements have been generated and pilot-tested, the process of choosing the statements that will be used in the research or classroom demonstration begins. In most experiments statements that have a neutral mean rating (near 4.0) are chosen. To replicate the Arkes et al. (1989) study, statements that have a mean rating near 2.0 as well as statements that have a mean rating near 6.0 should be chosen. One note of caution: The participants used for the pilot test should not also participate in the research or classroom demonstration.

Implementing the experiment

Participants

Since any experiment in this area will necessarily be a repeated-measures study, having at least 20 participants is important (in order to have enough power to detect differences between the sessions), and the participants must be able to attend two sessions. This type of research lends itself nicely to a classroom setting as most of the participants will return for the necessary subsequent sessions. If the participants are not an already-formed group, it would be wise to anticipate that some will not return for the second session and recruit more participants to the first session than are needed. A drop-out rate of approximately 30% from the first to the second session is fairly typical.

Materials

After the list of factual statements has been pilot-tested, the statements that will be repeated in the second session need to be randomly selected. If it has been decided to use statements that had a pre-tested mean rating near 4.0 and only factually true and factually false statements, then the list will contain 30 true and 30 false statements in the first session with one-third of each type of statement repeated in the second session. In the second session, 20 new true and 20 new false statements will be needed to mix with the 10 true and 10 false statements that will be repeated from the first session. Therefore, each session will have 60 statements, 20 of which will appear in both sessions (see Table 11.1 for examples of statements used in the Arkes et al., 1989, study). The

Table 11.1 Examples of true and false statements*

True statements	False statements
More presidents of the United States were born in Virginia than any other state.	New Delhi, India, is the world's most populous city.
The thigh bone is the largest bone in the human body.	Willie Mays had the most home runs in one season of any National League player.
Canada is the world's largest producer of silver.	New Jersey was the first state to ratify the eighteenth amendment.
Bolivia borders the Pacific Ocean.	The Indian Ocean is the smallest ocean on earth.
The largest dam in the world is in Pakistan.	The planet Venus is larger than the earth.

* At the time of the Arkes et al. (1989) experiment, these statements were factually true and factually false. Since then, the status of some of these statements may have changed. These statements were used in a sample of participants from the United States and therefore reflect some information that is specific to the United States.

statements should be in random order. It is advised that two forms of the lists of statements be used to counterbalance for any potential order or fatigue effects. It would also be a good idea to be sure that the first five to eight statements are always nonrepeated statements, in order to serve as primacy and recency buffers.

Procedure

For ease of explanation, this procedure assumes that the statements will be given in a written list to the participants. In the first session, the participants are instructed to read each statement and to indicate on a 1 (definitely false) to 7 (definitely true) scale how true or false they believe the statement to be. After an interval of time has passed (across studies this interval has varied from 3 days to 1 month), the participants are asked to return for a second session and to engage in the same task of rating statements. In this second session, the participants are told that some of the statements may be repeated from the first session. The second list will comprise the 20 statements repeated from the first session and the 40 new statements.

Statistical analysis

To analyze the data, the mean of the ratings given to the true and false repeated and nonrepeated statements across the two sessions will need to be computed for each participant. Therefore, each participant will have eight mean ratings as follows:

> The mean of statements in Session 1 that were true and will be repeated
> The mean of statements in Session 1 that were true and will not be repeated
> The mean of statements in Session 1 that were false and will be repeated
> The mean of statements in Session 1 that were false and will not be repeated
> The mean of statements in Session 2 that were true and were repeated
> The mean of statements in Session 2 that were true and were not repeated
> The mean of statements in Session 2 that were false and were repeated
> The mean of statements in Session 2 that were false and were not repeated

From here a 2 (Session 1 vs Session 2) × 2 (True vs False Statement) × 2 (Repeated vs Nonrepeated Statements) repeated-measures analysis of variance can be performed. The hallmark of the validity effect is a statistically significant session × repetition interaction. Veracity ratings should increase from Session 1 to Session 2 for repeated statements, but not for the nonrepeated statements.

Goldstein, and Toppino demonstrated that merely repeating a statement to research participants prompted the participants to rate the statement as more true or valid. On three successive occasions, separated by 2-week intervals, Hasher et al. presented participants with 60 factual statements that were either true or false and had been pre-tested in order to ensure that on a 1–7 scale of truth assessment (higher values indicating higher levels of truth) all statements averaged a rating of close to 4.0. The statements were trivia of the type "the population in Greenland is about 50,000". Of the statements from the first session, 20 were repeated in Sessions 2 and 3, the remaining 40 items in each session were new. The results revealed that the rated validity of the repeated statements increased across the sessions regardless of whether the statements were originally true or false. Nonrepeated statements (those presented only once during one of the three sessions) were given approximately the same validity rating during each session. From these results Hasher et al. concluded that the frequency of occurrence is a criterion we use to judge the referential validity of information.

The validity effect as an automatic process

Prior to the work of Hasher and her colleagues, Gude and Zechmeister (1975) had demonstrated the occurrence of the validity effect regardless of whether the exact wording of the sentences was used. In their research, the effect of repetition was found similarly in sentences that were both exact in wording as the original sentences as well as sentences that were not exact in wording but had the same underlying meaning or gist. To further explain this phenomenon, Hasher and Chromiak (1977) performed two studies to ascertain whether detecting frequency may be an automatic process. In this research participants from Grades 2, 4, and 6, and college students, were asked to judge how frequently a word had been presented to them during a testing session. In some of the conditions the participants were explicitly told that some items would be repeated, while in others they were not. The results of this research revealed that the ability to count frequency did not show a developmental trend, nor was it affected by instructions indicating that repetition would occur. This type of finding implies that the validity effect is a cognitive skill that is based on recognition memory, which has historically shown limited development with age (Brown, 1975). However, as we age, this cognitive skill may become practised enough that it becomes an automatic process (i.e., one that is not under the conscious control of the individual). If the ability to detect frequency is an automatic process, it would then make sense that it would be insensitive to explicit instructions regarding whether the information has been repeated, as these instructions now become redundant to the individual.

In sum, the collective works by Hasher suggest that detecting the frequency with which information is heard is an automatic process that, at minimum, is used to determine whether information is new or old, and may be even used to ascertain how likely it is that the information is true. The next question to answer pertains to whether the validity effect occurs for information believed to be repeated regardless of its actual repetition status. Here we turn to Bacon (1979) who demonstrated that the conferral of validity occurred for statements of trivia judged to be repeated whether or not the statements were actually repeated (*note*: "Frederick T. Bacon" is a pseudonym for a research group that included Ian Begg, Grant Harris, John Mitterer, and Douglas Upfold). In this research, statements judged by the participants to be repeated were rated as more true regardless of whether the statement was actually repeated or not. Bacon concluded that it is the judgement that the information was repeated that leads one to believe that the information has been repeated, rather than the actual repetition status. In addition, his research also supports the contention that the repetition sparks recognition memory. Bacon further believes that the validity effect is a recognition effect rather than a repetition effect.

Exploring the types of information that produce the validity effect

In all of the studies mentioned thus far, the statements used in the experiments were trivia statements that had an overall rating of 4.0 on a 1 (definitely false) to 7 (definitely true) scale. In essence, these statements were of neutral truth value to the participants. The statements were also all statements of fact. In the first of two experiments, Arkes et al. (1989) were interested in whether the validity effect would occur for statements that were opinion statements (e.g., "Competition in schools is not good for young children") as well as statements of fact (e.g., "The thigh bone is the largest bone in the human body"). In addition we were also interested in whether the validity effect would occur similarly for statements that were not rated as neutral but were rated on the higher end of the 1–7 truth rating scale as well as the lower end, thus testing the generality of this effect on statements that were obviously true or obviously false.

In a separate sample, Arkes et al. pilot-tested numerous statements to ascertain their perceived truth status. Statements that obtained a mean rating of 1.8–2.8 were used as the "perceived false" statements; statements that obtained a mean rating of 3.95–4.95 were used as the "perceived neutral" statements; and statements that obtained a mean rating of 5.3–6.5 were used as the "perceived true" statements. We labelled these statements as "perceived", as half of the statements in each category chosen were factually false while others were factually true. Therefore we were also able to look at the occurrence of the validity effect within those statements that were erroneously believed to be true and false, as well as those that were correctly believed to be true and false. In two sessions, participants were asked to rate the validity of these statements, with some of the statements in Session 2 being statements repeated from Session 1.

The results of this study revealed that the validity effect occurred similarly for statements of fact as well as statements of opinion, in that repeated statements were given higher ratings at Session 2 than Session 1. In addition, the validity effect occurred similarly for all statements regardless of their perceived truth rating. This means that those statements initially perceived to be false rose in rated validity at Session 2, as did statements initially perceived to be true and those initially perceived to be neutral. This finding separates the validity effect from an attitude-polarization effect. If the effect of repetition was simply an extension of attitude polarization, then the effect of repetition on the statements believed to be true should be that these statements are rated as more true, and by extension, the effect of repetition of the false statements should be that these statements are rated as more false. As stated, this was not the case, repeated statements that were initially perceived to be false were rated as more true (i.e., less false) in the second session.

In conclusion, the validity effect seems to occur for statements of fact as well as statements of opinion. It also occurs similarly for factual and opinion statements that are originally believed to be true as well as those that are originally believed to be false.

The role of the source of information in the validity effect

It is possible that the source of the information could be contributing to the occurrence of the validity effect. In an experimental setting in which participants are hearing statements that they believe they have heard before, it may be the case that they also think they heard the statement elsewhere first (Source 1) and again in the experiment (Source 2). In Experiment 1 of Arkes et al. (1989) participants were asked to indicate whether they had heard the statement before, and if so where (only within the experiment or from a source outside the experiment). The results indicated that information attributed to sources outside the experimental setting was given the highest validity ratings.

This prompted further study by Arkes, Boehm, and Xu (1991). In a series of three studies these researchers sought to further explain the impact of source dissociation, need for cognition, and the outside boundaries of the validity effect (i.e., how many repetitions continue to produce the effect and could the effect be found in statements that are related to assertions but not exact replications). A structural equation model of the relationship between source dissociation, validity, and familiarity found that source dissociation does not affect validity, but it does affect familiarity (which then affects validity). Statements that were attributed to a source outside the experiment were rated as more familiar. In this analysis, need for cognition was not found to be associated with any of the factors studied. With respect to the boundaries of the validity effect, Arkes et al. (1991) replicated and extended the earlier work of Begg et al. (1979). In a second experiment, participants read a passage concerning information about China, and in subsequent weeks rated the validity of sentences that were (a) related to the passage, (b) not related to the passage but related to China, and (c) not related to the passage or China. Those statements that were related to the passage were given higher validity ratings than statements that were related to China but not in the passage or statements that were not related to either the passage or China. This result demonstrates that the validity effect extends beyond the exact presentation of the information and includes information that is similar to what was first heard. Finally, in a third experiment, Arkes et al. (1991) found that across six sessions, the bulk of the validity effect occurred in the second session (i.e., as a result of the first repetition). While rated validity further increased in Sessions 3–6, the increase was not statistically significant. In conclusion, the results of this research demonstrated that it only takes one repetition that is similar (rather than identical) to the first presentation of the information, to increase the rated and perceived validity of information.

The role of expertise in the validity effect

In a second study, Arkes et al. (1989) attempted to explore the impact of levels of knowledge or expertise with the topic on the validity effect. Past research in the area of experts and novices (e.g., Chiesi, Spilich, & Voss, 1979) had consistently found that within their area of expertise, experts have better memory for information than novices. Given this, Arkes et al. questioned whether or not the validity effect would occur for information in the area of one's expertise compared to information not in one's area of expertise. In an attempt to determine if expertise would have an impact, statements that came from seven different categories of information (food, literature, science, art, history, entertainment, and sport) were generated. In the first session, participants were asked to rank-order their knowledge of information in these seven categories before they rated how true the statements were. Participants returned for a second session and rated another list of statements in which some of the statements had been repeated from the first session and some were new. The participants were not asked to rank their knowledge of the seven categories at this session. Analysis of the data from this study revealed that the validity effect occurred only in those topics for which the participants rated themselves as being knowledgeable. Given this, familiarity with information mediates the impact of repetition such that information from topic areas in which one has little knowledge will be rated less valid than information from topic areas in which one has more knowledge.

The validity effect outside the laboratory: Is there ecological validity?

Up to this point the information presented to participants has been trivia statements presented in a university laboratory. The participants are students enrolled in the university and the climate is such that they are encouraged and expected to believe what they are told by professors. It is possible that the validity effect is an epiphenomenon of the setting, and has little ecological validity. It now becomes important to generalize the validity effect to field settings.

That the validity effect occurs in "real life" is not in question here. There are numerous accounts that confirm that the validity effect does in fact occur outside the laboratory. For example, it is well known in the world of advertising that repetition works (Krugman, 1977). Krugman clearly supports that a "frequency of three" is critical for advertising effectiveness. Krugman links each of the three repetitions to awareness in the population, with the first exposure interpreted by the consumer as "What is it?", the second exposure interpreted as "What is the personal relevance of it?", and the third exposure taking the role of a reminder. Krugman goes on to state that with enough mere repetition of product brand names we have a higher tendency to buy the product solely because we recognize it. While researchers in advertising have disagreed with Krugman's "frequency of three", it has only been to provide evidence that increased repetition brings more success. For example, Meyers (1993) demonstrated the need to increase the minimum number of repetitions for effective advertising. Meyers argues that due to media fragmentation, repetition needs to become the most important tool of the advertiser.

But where else might there be a demonstration of the validity effect? One suggestion is in a college classroom. Many introductory psychology instructors can attest to the fact that students often come to them and say they have heard all of this information before and believe they know it already. The source of the information may have been their high-school psychology class, the media in general, or other classes within the college setting that have some degree of overlap with the introductory psychology course (e.g., the information on the brain may well be covered in an introductory biology class). According to the validity effect, each time students hear the information they are then more likely to believe it is true. I was interested in how this truth assessment manifested itself in a learning environment. Given the past research, the repetition is based on recognition, therefore the students would recognize the information as having been heard before. How would this familiarity be interpreted in a learning environment?

In a series of experiments looking at the impact of repetition and familiarity on learning, my colleagues and I explored a number of potential ways in which course content information may have been recognized as a repetition by the students (Renner, Renner, & Shaffer, 2004). In our first experiment, we defined familiarity with course material in two ways. In the first, we assumed that if students had taken the course previously they would be familiar with the material in the course due to the previous exposure. In the second, we compared terms that are more common in the psychological literature to those that are not under the assumption that common terms would have been heard or learned before in other courses. The participants were college students enrolled in a general psychology class, 46% (66/142) of whom had taken high-school psychology.

We needed to develop a measure of knowledge of psychology that was separate from course exams and that would equally represent the various areas in an introductory psychology course. To accomplish this, a 54-item Psychology Information Test (PIT) was constructed. The PIT contained three items from each of the 18 chapters represented in the textbook used by the instructor, which was organized similarly to most contemporary texts. The questions were selected based on the commonness of the term being queried in an introductory psychology text. The determination of commonness came from research by Boneau (1990) who created a list of terms used in general psychology from surveying glossaries and indexes of general psychology textbooks. He then asked textbook authors to rate the list of terms from most to least common. From these data, Boneau created a list of the 100 most common terms in each of the general areas of psychology. For each chapter a highly common term, moderately common term, and less common term was chosen from the Boneau list. A question representing each term was then chosen from the test-item file that accompanied the textbook (all questions were of moderate difficulty level as assessed by the authors of the test-item file). This procedure resulted in a 54-item PIT.

On the first day of class, the students were told that in order to have a general idea of how much knowledge students have of psychology before taking a psychology course, they would be asked to answer the PIT. On the second to last day of class, the students were asked to fill out the PIT again so that the instructor could assess how much information they had gained as a result of the course. The results of this study revealed that terms that are high in commonness resulted in worse performance on the PIT than terms that were low in commonness. Students who had taken a high-school psychology course before taking a college-level psychology course performed significantly worse than students who had not taken a high-school psychology course. Having prior exposure to psychology does not enhance performance in the classroom. We suggest that the prior exposure to the material creates the perception that the material is known. We suspect that the increased familiarity with the information creates a false sense of knowing the information. We designed a second study to attempt to ascertain whether this suspicion is true. In our second study we were interested in determining whether increased familiarity would lead to a false assumption that the material was known. If this is true, students should have a high level of confidence in their knowledge of the material that they indicate is familiar. However, if the material is familiar only because of a previous exposure, this confidence would be misleading and result in poorer class performance.

The participants were students enrolled in an undergraduate psychology course. On the first day of class the instructor explained to the students that she was trying to determine ways to enhance learning of course material. One way to do this was to find out what students knew about the course content before the course started. The students were then given a list of 100 terms that would be discussed throughout the course and asked to indicate (Yes or No) if they had ever heard each of the 100 terms before. Approximately 10 terms were randomly chosen from each chapter for inclusion in the list.

Throughout the course, the items in the terms list appeared on tests. For each term, the percentage of students who had heard of the term, and the percent correct on the course examination for that term, was recorded. We then looked at the accuracy of each term according to the number of students who said they had heard the term before. When these data are plotted, it is clear there is not a linear relationship. The highest accuracy was obtained when the term had never been heard before. For other terms, as the number of students who had heard of the term increased, the percent correct on the terms increased, but never reached that of the group who had never heard of the term before.

The conclusion of these two studies is that there is ecological validity to the validity effect in an educational setting. We suspect familiarity is used by most people as an indication of whether information is known, and then an assumption is made that it is known correctly. Hence "I've heard it before, therefore I know it". Unfortunately, based on our research, this assumption is not true. Familiarity is not a valid predictor for one's knowledge, in that simply having heard something before does not mean there is also a depth of accurate knowledge about that item or topic.

Other theories that might explain this phenomenon

It is important to distinguish the validity effect from other phenomena that have similar characteristics. Tesser (1978) performed a study in which he measured the impact of repetition on affect, and found increased affect with increased repetition among positive items but decreased affect with increased repetition among negative items. Tesser's study better represents the impact of repetition on attitude polarization than the validity effect. Remember that in the Arkes et al. (1989) study, false statements (the most comparable to Tesser's negative items) increased in perceived validity with repetition. If the validity effect were nothing more than attitude polarization, the effect of repetition on the false statements should have prompted the participants to rate the statements as more false rather than more true.

Zajonc (1968) and Harrison (1977) have summarized a large number of studies which suggest that repeated exposure increases the liking for a wide variety of stimuli. This effect has been called the "mere exposure" effect (see Chapter 12). Research in this area used research materials that are not factual in nature (e.g., photographs, melodies, and tastes). The difference between the mere exposure effect and the validity effect lies in the distinction between assessments of liking and validity. It is entirely possible that liking and validity are very different concepts that operate separately and distinctly from each other. Given this, we may come to believe a statement is increasingly true, regardless of whether or not we like the statement.

CONCLUSION

For more than 25 years, the phenomenon of the validity effect has been established by several different researchers, from numerous research laboratories, using different methodologies. Within these studies the validity effect has occurred regardless of age (grade school vs college), types of information (factual vs opinion), length of delay between presentations (same day vs several weeks), type of presentation of the statements (written vs auditory), and precision of the repeated information (exact duplication vs gist). The repeated replication of this phenomenon across time and methods demonstrates that the validity effect is a robust phenomenon.

Attention should now turn to enhancing our understanding of the impact of the validity effect in numerous areas of life. For example, the research by Renner et al. (2004) suggests that students equate repetition of information with familiarity of information that further prompts them to think they are knowledgeable about the information. If this is true, would students who retake courses study less for the course the second time around, because they are under the assumption that they "know" the information since they had heard it before? Is it only necessary to continually repeat to constituents the message a particular political candidate wants them to believe, rather than provide evidence? Finally, does the validity effect deter critical thinking about the information presented? These are all important questions, raising important issues. Finding the role of the validity effect in these situations may assist in moving people from blindly accepting pre-thought thoughts (Gatto, 2001) to employing critical evaluation of information. It is time to move beyond demonstrations that the validity effect occurs, to demonstrations of its extended impact.

SUMMARY

- The validity effect occurs when the mere repetition of information affects the perceived truthfulness of that information.
- The validity effect appears to be based on recognition memory and may be an automatic process.
- The validity effect occurs similarly for statements of fact that are true and false in origin, as well as political or opinion statements.

- Factors such as the belief that the information was heard previously or having some expertise in the content of the statement prompts information to be rated as more valid, even if the information has not been repeated.
- The validity effect is not similar to the mere exposure effect, in that liking and validity are separate and distinct phenomena.
- The validity effect is not similar to attitude polarization, as evidenced by the fact that false statements demonstrate an increase in truth rating with repetition (the validity effect) rather than a stronger rating of being false (attitude polarization).

FURTHER READING

A good place to start in developing an understanding of the beginning research on the validity effect is by reading Hasher, Goldstein, and Toppino's (1977) article. The cognitive processes that do and do not mediate the validity effect are examined in Gude and Zechmeister's (1975) article as well as in Hasher and Chromiak's (1977) article. Familiarity with information and the boundaries of the validity effect are explored in a series of studies by Arkes, Hackett, and Boehm (1989) and Arkes, Boehm, and Xu (1991). Finally, the impact of whether or not we believe the information has been repeated and the subsequent effect on the validity effect is nicely demonstrated in studies by Bacon (1979) and Begg, Armour, and Kerr (1979).

REFERENCES

Arkes, H. R., Boehm, L., & Xu, G. (1991). Determinants of judged validity. *Journal of Experimental Social Psychology, 27,* 576–605.

Arkes, H. R., Hackett, C., & Boehm, L. (1989). The generality of the relation between familiarity and judged validity. *Journal of Behavioral Decision Making, 2,* 81–94.

Bacon, F. T. (1979). Credibility of repeated statements: Memory for trivia. *Journal of Experimental Psychology: Human Learning and Memory, 5,* 241–252.

Begg, I., Armour, V., & Kerr, T. (1979). On believing what we remember. *Canadian Journal of Behavioral Science, 17,* 199–202.

Boneau, A. C. (1990). Psychological literacy: A first approximation. *American Psychologist, 45,* 891–900.

Brown, A. L. (1975). The development of memory: Knowing, knowing about knowing, and knowing how to know. In H. W. Reese (Ed.), *Advances in child development and behavior* (Vol. 10, pp. 327–431). New York: Academic Press.

Chiesi, H. L., Spilich, G. J., & Voss, J. F. (1979). Acquisition of domain-related information for individuals with high and low domain knowledge. *Journal of Verbal Learning and Verbal Behavior, 18,* 275–290.

Gatto, J. T. (2001). *A different kind of teacher: Solving the crisis in American schooling*. Berkeley, CA: Berkeley Hills Books.

Gigerenzer, G. (1984). External validity of laboratory experiments: The frequency–validity relationship. *American Journal of Psychology, 97*, 285–295.

Gude, C., & Zechmeister, E. B. (1975). Frequency judgments for the "gist" of sentences. *American Journal of Psychology, 88*, 385–396.

Harrison, A. A. (1977). Mere exposure. In L. Berkowitz (Ed.), *Advances in experimental social psychology* (Vol. 10, pp. 39–83). New York: Academic Press.

Hasher, L., & Chromiak, W. (1977). The processing of frequency information: An automatic mechanism? *Journal of Verbal Learning and Verbal Behavior, 16*, 173–184.

Hasher, L., Goldstein, D., & Toppino, T. (1977). Frequency and the conference of referential validity. *Journal of Verbal Learning and Verbal Behavior, 16*, 107–112.

Krugman, H. E. (1977). Memory without recall, exposure without perception. *Journal of Advertising Research, 17*, 7–12.

Meyers, J. (1993). More is indeed better. *MediaWeek, 3*, 14.

Renner, C. H., Renner, M. J., & Shaffer, V. A. (2004). "I've heard that before, therefore I know it": The validity effect in the classroom. Manuscript in preparation.

Schwartz, M. (1982). Repetition and rated truth value of statements. *American Journal of Psychology, 95*, 393–407.

Tesser, A. (1978). Self-generated attitude change. In L. Berkowitz (Ed.), *Advances in experimental social psychology* (Vol. 10, pp. 289–338). New York: Academic Press.

Zajonc, R. B. (1968). The attitudinal effects of mere exposure. *Journal of Personality and Social Psychology, 9*, 1–27.

12 Mere exposure effect

Robert F. Bornstein and Catherine Craver-Lemley

Folk wisdom tells us that "familiarity breeds contempt", but studies suggest otherwise. Beginning with the work of Titchener (1910), psychologists have been intrigued by the possibility that repeated, unreinforced exposure to a stimulus would result in increased liking for that stimulus. Zajonc (1968) coined the term *mere exposure effect* (MEE) to describe this phenomenon, and since the publication of Zajonc's seminal (1968) paper, there have been nearly 300 published studies of the MEE. The MEE occurs for a broad array of stimuli (e.g., drawings, photographs, musical selections, real words, nonsense words, ideographs) under a variety of laboratory and real-world conditions. Bornstein's (1989) meta-analysis of research on the MEE indicated that the overall magnitude of the effect (expressed in terms of the correlation coefficient *r*) was .26, a moderate effect size. Subsequent investigations have confirmed this result (e.g., Monahan, Murphy, & Zajonc, 2000; Seamon, McKenna, & Binder, 1998).

Without question, repeated exposure to a stimulus biases our attitude regarding that stimulus: Even though the stimulus itself remains the same, the way we think and feel about the stimulus changes as we become familiar with it (see Chapter 11 for a related discussion). In this respect, researchers agree that the MEE represents a form of cognitive *bias*. But is it a genuine cognitive *illusion*? Is our attitude regarding a repeatedly exposed stimulus changed so profoundly that we can no longer perceive and judge the stimulus accurately, no matter how much effort we devote to the task? Several decades of research can help us resolve this question.

EXAMPLES

There are numerous everyday instances of increased liking following repeated exposure to a stimulus. As these examples illustrate, not only does repeated exposure affect our attitude regarding a stimulus, but the process is so subtle that in most cases we are unaware that mere exposure played a role in altering our judgements and feelings.

Repetition and liking for music

Several MEE experiments have shown that repeated exposure to unfamiliar music leads to more positive ratings of this music (Harrison, 1977). Similar patterns emerge in real-world settings. In fact, the impact of radio exposure on record sales is so strong that it is often illegal (and always unethical) for disk jockeys to accept any sort of compensation from record companies, for fear that this will bias song selection and produce an exposure-induced spike in sales.

Exposure and preference for novel types of art

When Impressionist paintings were first displayed publicly, they received scathing reviews. The same thing occurred when Cubist and Expressionist works first appeared. An initial negative reaction occurs almost any time a new art form emerges, but over time – and with repeated viewings – aesthetic judgements shift, and attitudes regarding the now-familiar style become more positive. What was once despised is now embraced.

Unfamiliar people

To a surprising degree, we affiliate with people we encounter most frequently. This is why first-year college students' friendship patterns are determined in part by housing proximity, and why our attitudes regarding other morning commuters become more positive over time (even if we never exchange a word with our fellow traveller). Mere exposure to an unfamiliar person enhances our attitude towards that person.

DESIGNS

MEE studies use two types of designs: naturalistic and experimental. Each has certain advantages, and certain disadvantages as well.

Naturalistic designs

Naturalistic MEE studies examine the relationship between the naturally occurring frequency of a stimulus and people's attitudes regarding that stimulus. Thus, common names receive more positive liking ratings than do uncommon names, and familiar foods are rated more positively than unfamiliar foods (Bornstein, 1989; Harrison, 1977). The primary advantage of a naturalistic design is that it provides a good approximation of naturally occurring MEEs. The primary disadvantage of a naturalistic design is that it does not allow firm conclusions to be drawn regarding causal relationships between exposure and affect: It may be that common names become better liked because people are exposed to them more frequently, but it is also possible that people are inclined to give their children names that are popular to begin with.

Experimental designs

In experimental MEE studies, participants are exposed to varying numbers of exposures of unfamiliar stimuli (e.g., novel photographs, nonsense words), after which they report how much they like each stimulus. Most experimental studies of the MEE use within-participants designs, so each participant is exposed to an array of stimuli at different frequencies. For example, a participant might rate five different stimuli, with each stimulus having been exposed 0, 1, 2, 5, or 10 times during the familiarization phase of the study.

The primary advantage of an experimental design is that it allows strong conclusions to be drawn regarding the causal relationship between stimulus exposures and subsequent affect ratings. The primary disadvantage of an experimental design is its artificiality: Because novel stimuli are presented under highly controlled laboratory conditions, the degree to which these findings generalize to real-world situations is open to question.

MEASURES

A key aspect of MEE research is assessing participants' attitudes regarding stimuli that vary in familiarity. Three types of measures have been used.

Likert ratings

The most common outcome measure in MEE research is a Likert-type rating of each stimulus. Many different rating dimensions have been used (e.g., liking, pleasantness, attractiveness, interestingness), with the specific rating dimension based on the type of stimulus being investigated (see Seamon et al., 1998). Thus, liking ratings are commonly employed when people (or photographs of people) are used as stimuli; pleasantness or interestingness ratings are often employed when paintings or music selections are used.

Likert ratings are not only the most common MEE outcome measure, they are also the most sensitive. Often participants' liking ratings of a merely exposed stimulus shift by 1 or 2 points on a 9-point scale (e.g., Bornstein, Kale, & Cornell, 1990; Seamon et al., 1998). Although this degree of attitude shift may seem trivial, it is not: If unfamiliar stimuli receive neutral (midpoint) ratings, a 1-point positive shift represents a 20% increase in liking for a familiarized stimulus.

Forced-choice preference judgements

Some MEE studies use forced-choice preference judgements in lieu of Likert-type ratings (e.g., Mandler, Nakamura, & Van Zandt, 1987). In these studies, participants are asked to choose which of two stimuli they like better during the rating phase of the study, with one member of each stimulus pair being previously exposed, and the other being novel. Although forced-choice judgements are less sensitive than Likert-type ratings, they are a better approximation of preference judgements in vivo (e.g., wherein a person must choose between two similar products that vary in familiarity).

Behavioural measures

A small number of MEE studies have used behavioural outcome measures in lieu of self-reports (e.g., Bornstein, Leone, & Galley, 1987). Behavioural outcome measures include agreement with familiarized and unfamiliarized confederates in a laboratory negotiation task, voting behaviour in a campus election, electrodermal responses to familiar versus novel stimuli, and willingness to sample different types of food. Most behavioural outcome measures in MEE studies take the form of dichotomous decisions (e.g., choosing between two foods), but on occasion, behavioural outcome measures are analogous to Likert-type ratings (e.g., when percentages of agreement with familiar and unfamiliar people are used; see Bornstein et al., 1987).

RELEVANCE

The most obvious applications of MEE principles are in product sales, and marketing researchers have incorporated findings from mere exposure research into a number of contemporary advertising programmes (Janiszewski, 1993). Along similar lines, studies suggest that frequency of exposure is a significant determinant of the number of votes garnered by a candidate for elected office, even when other factors (e.g., popularity of the candidate's policy positions) are controlled for statistically (Bornstein, 1989). The impact of repeated exposure on election outcome is not just statistically significant, but ecologically significant as well: The 5–10% shift in voting behaviour attributable to candidate familiarity is enough to alter the outcome of many real-world elections.

Another potentially important application of MEE principles and methods concerns intergroup behaviour. Beginning with the work of Amir (1969), psychologists have investigated the degree to which repeated, unreinforced exposure could enhance the attitudes of different groups towards each other. Findings in this area have been mixed: Although mere exposure can enhance the attitudes of unfamiliar groups, it does not produce a parallel effect – and sometimes even leads to increased tension and conflict –

in groups who have initial negative attitudes (Bornstein, 1993). History is replete with examples of neighbouring groups for whom decades of exposure have only heightened hostility (e.g., Israelis and Palestinians).

MODERATING VARIABLES

Researchers have examined the impact of numerous moderating variables on the MEE. These fall into three categories: (1) stimulus variables; (2) exposure variables; and (3) participant variables. Assessment of moderating variables is not only useful in understanding the parameters of the MEE, but also in testing competing theoretical models. Different frameworks make contrasting predictions regarding the impact of various moderating variables, and the most influential models are those that have shown good predictive power in this domain.

Two general procedures have been used to assess the impact of moderating variables on the MEE: individual experiments (e.g., Murphy & Zajonc, 1993), and meta-analytic reviews of the mere exposure literature (Bornstein, 1989, 1992). Individual experiments allow for *direct* assessment of the impact of a particular variable by comparing the magnitude of the exposure effect under different conditions (e.g., for complex versus simple stimuli). Meta-analyses allow for *indirect* assessment of the impact of a moderating variable by comparing the magnitude of the MEE across different studies (e.g., those that used a brief delay between exposures and ratings versus those that used a longer delay). As is true of research in many areas of psychology, some moderating variables have been assessed within MEE studies, others have been assessed by contrasting outcomes across studies, and still others have been evaluated using both procedures.

Stimulus variables

Two stimulus variables have been assessed by MEE researchers: type of stimulus (e.g., photograph versus drawing), and stimulus complexity.

Type of stimulus

Nine different types of stimuli have been used in MEE studies: nonsense words, meaningful words, ideographs, photographs, drawings, auditory stimuli, gustatory (i.e., food) stimuli, actual people, and objects (e.g., toys). Studies contrasting the magnitude of the MEE as a function of stimulus type have generally found no consistent differences across stimulus classes (e.g., Stang, 1974, 1975). Meta-analytic data support this result, confirming that different types of stimuli produce comparable exposure effects (Bornstein, 1989).

Stimulus complexity

The majority of experiments that compare the magnitude of the MEE produced by simple versus complex stimuli find that complex stimuli yield stronger exposure effects (Berlyne, 1970; Bornstein et al., 1990). Two processes are involved. First, complex stimuli typically produce a more rapid increase in liking at lower exposure frequencies (i.e., 1, 2, and 5 exposures). Second, complex stimuli produce a less pronounced downturn in liking at higher exposure frequencies (i.e., 10 or more exposures). It appears that simple stimuli are less interesting to begin with (hence, the less rapid increase in liking at lower frequencies), and become boring more quickly at higher exposure frequencies (leading to an "overexposure effect").

Exposure variables

The most widely studied exposure variables in MEE studies are number of presentations, stimulus exposure sequence, stimulus exposure duration, and delay between exposures and ratings.

Number of presentations

MEE studies typically present stimuli a maximum of 50 times, although there is considerable variability in this area (Bornstein, 1989). In most studies MEE researchers obtain an increase in liking ratings through about 10 stimulus exposures, after which ratings plateau, and gradually decline to baseline (Kail & Freeman, 1973; Stang, 1974). These frequency–liking patterns characteristic of individual MEE experiments were confirmed in Bornstein's (1989) meta-analysis, which found that – across different stimuli and rating dimensions – the strongest MEEs occurred following a maximum of five to nine stimulus exposures.

Exposure sequence

Significantly stronger MEEs are obtained when stimuli are presented in a heterogeneous (i.e., randomized) sequence than a homogeneous (i.e., massed) sequence during the familiarization phase of the study (Bornstein, 1989). Consistent with the results of individual experiments, meta-analytic comparison of studies indicated that while heterogeneous exposures produce a robust MEE ($r = .30$), homogeneous exposures do not ($r = -.02$).

Exposure duration

There is an inverse relationship between stimulus exposure duration and magnitude of the exposure effect (Bornstein, 1989). Studies that use stimulus exposures less than 1 second produce an overall MEE (r) of .41, whereas studies that use stimulus exposures between 1 and 5 seconds produce an MEE of .16, and those that use longer exposures produce an MEE of .09. Individual studies comparing MEEs in identical stimuli presented at different exposure durations support this meta-analytic result (e.g., Hamid, 1973).

Delay between exposure and rating

Seamon, Brody, and Kauff (1983), and Stang (1975) found stronger exposure effects with increasing delay between stimulus exposures and ratings. These results not only indicate that delay enhances the MEE, but confirm that MEEs can persist for up to 1 week (Seamon et al., 1983), or 2 weeks (Stang, 1975) following stimulus exposures.

Meta-analytic data confirm these experimental results (Bornstein, 1989), and further indicate that naturalistic MEE studies (which examine affect ratings of stimuli whose frequency varies naturally in vivo) produce a stronger exposure effect ($r = .57$) than do laboratory studies ($r = .21$). The particularly strong MEEs produced by real-world stimuli (e.g., common names) are in part a consequence of the comparatively long delays between stimulus exposures and affect ratings in naturalistic settings.

Participant variables

Participant variables have been studied less frequently than other moderating variables in MEE investigations, but in certain respects these variables have yielded the most intriguing results. Researchers have examined the effects of stimulus awareness, imagery, and individual difference (i.e., personality) variables on the magnitude of the MEE.

Stimulus awareness

More than a dozen published studies have obtained robust exposure effects for stimuli that are not recognized at better-than-chance levels (e.g., Bornstein et al., 1987; Kunst-Wilson & Zajonc, 1980; Murphy & Zajonc, 1993; Seamon et al., 1983). Not only do subliminal stimuli produce robust MEEs, but meta-analysis of the MEE literature indicates that stimulus awareness actually inhibits the MEE. Experiments using stimuli that were not recognized at better-than-chance accuracy produce an overall MEE of .53, whereas experiments using briefly presented, recognized stimuli produce an overall MEE of .34. The magnitude of the MEE produced by stimuli that were recognized at 100% (or close to 100%) accuracy is .12 (Bornstein, 1989, 1992).

The inverse relationship between stimulus recognition accuracy and magnitude of the MEE has been replicated in individual experiments as well (Bornstein & D'Agostino, 1992, 1994). For example, Bornstein and

D'Agostino (1992) found that photographs and Welsh figures (i.e., simple line drawings) presented for 5 ms during the exposure phase of a typical MEE experiment produced a significantly greater increase in liking than did identical stimuli presented for 500 ms during the exposure phase. (Follow-up data confirmed that 5 ms stimuli were not recognized at better-than-chance level, whereas 500 ms stimuli were recognized at close to 100% accuracy.)

Additional support for the existence of robust MEEs in the absence of stimulus awareness comes from studies of neurologically impaired participants (e.g., Alzheimer's patients, patients with Korsakoff's syndrome). These experiments confirm that even when neurological deficits obviate explicit memory for previously seen stimuli, robust exposure effects are obtained (Halpern & O'Connor, 2000). In fact, these results are so consistent and compelling that researchers now view MEE-type affect ratings as one of the most reliable indicators of implicit memory for previously encountered stimuli (Whittlesea & Price, 2001).

Imagery effects

Given that MEEs persist for up to 2 weeks in laboratory studies, and almost indefinitely in vivo, repeated exposure to a stimulus must lead to the construction of a mental representation of that stimulus – a representation that is encoded deeply enough to be maintained from exposures through affect ratings (Mandler et al., 1987). With this in mind, Craver-Lemley, Bornstein, Forys, Lake, and Thomas (2002) explored the possibility that self-generated mental images would produce exposure effects comparable to those produced by exposure-based mental images. This hypothesis was confirmed: Repeatedly exposed and repeatedly imagined stimuli yielded comparable MEEs. These results dovetail with reports that self-generated images may share properties with images that are actually perceived (Craver-Lemley, Arterberry, & Reeves, 1999).

Consistent with Craver-Lemley et al.'s (2002) results, evidence indicates that self-generated imagery can moderate – or even obviate – the MEE. Thus, Bornstein, Craver-Lemley, Allison, Horchler, and Mitra (1999) found that when participants were instructed to generate positive or negative images during repeated exposures of photographs, subsequent affect ratings of the individuals pictured in the photographs were biased in the direction of these self-generated images (despite the fact that participants were not asked to generate images during the rating phase of the experiment).

Individual differences

Several individual difference variables have been examined in MEE studies, including need for approval, manifest anxiety, tolerance of ambiguity, evaluation apprehension, boredom-proneness, and sensation-seeking. For the most part, these variables had modest moderating effects, with two exceptions. Bornstein et al. (1990) found that boredom-prone participants produced significantly weaker MEEs than did non-boredom-prone participants. Kruglanski, Freund, and Bar-Tal (1996) found that high levels of evaluation apprehension undermined the MEE. A simplified version of the study by Bornstein et al. (1990) is described in Text box 12.1.

Example of a mere exposure experiment

This section describes Bornstein et al.'s (1990) Experiment 2 illustrating two important principles relevant to a broad array of laboratory and real-world exposure effects: (1) the moderating impact of stimulus complexity; and (2) the downturn in the frequency–affect curve that often occurs after many stimulus exposures. A simplified version of this experiment may be used as a classroom demonstration (see Text box 12.1).

Method

The experiment tested 100 participants with two sets of stimuli. *Simple* stimuli consisted of seven line drawings (Figures 8, 10, 20, 33, 42, 55, and 66) from the Barron-Welsh Art Scale (Barron & Welsh, 1949). *Complex* stimuli consisted of seven line-drawn visual illusions taken from Gregory (1968). Within each stimulus category, stimuli were presented at the following frequencies: 0, 1, 2, 5, 10, 25, or 50. Order of stimuli within the stimulus set was random, and counterbalancing was used to ensure that different stimuli are presented at different frequencies in different participants. Across participants, each stimulus appeared in each frequency condition approximately the same number of times.

The stimuli were presented with a slide projector exposing each stimulus for 5 seconds. Subsequent to the presentation phase, participants rated the seven stimuli of each set on two 9-point rating scales: like–dislike, and simple–complex, both from *Not at all* (1) to *Very* (9).

Results

The results are summarized in Figures 12.1 and 12.2. As Figure 12.1 shows, liking ratings of visual illusions increased through five exposures, then gradually declined to baseline (i.e., 0-frequency levels). Liking ratings of Welsh figures increased slightly through five exposures, then declined below baseline levels at higher exposure frequencies. Statistically, a 2 × 7 within-participants ANOVA showed (1) a significant main effect for stimulus type, $F(1, 99) = 98.88$, $p < .0001$ (with visual illusions receiving more positive ratings than Welsh figures); (2) a significant main effect of exposure frequency, $F(6, 594) = 17.79$, $p < .0001$ (with liking ratings of both types of stimuli increasing through five exposures, then declining); and (3) a

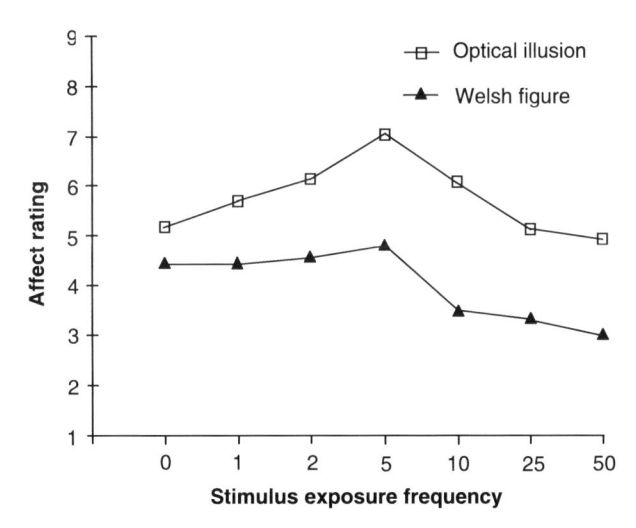

Figure 12.1 Effects of stimulus type and exposure frequency on liking ratings of merely exposed stimuli (from "Boredom as a limiting condition on the mere exposure effect" by Robert F. Bornstein, Amy R. Kale, and Karen R. Cornell, 1990, *Journal of Personality and Social Psychology, 58*, 795. © 1990 American Psychological Association. Adapted with permission of the publisher.)

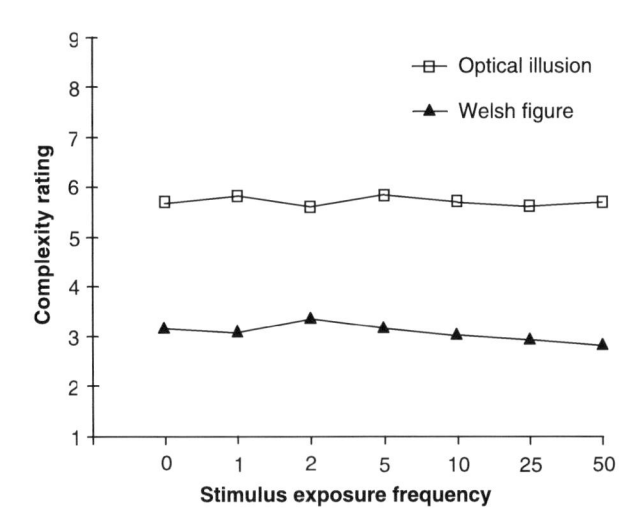

Figure 12.2 Effects of stimulus type and exposure frequency on complexity ratings of merely exposed stimuli (from "Boredom as a limiting condition on the mere exposure effect" by Robert F. Bornstein, Amy R. Kale, and Karen R. Cornell, 1990, *Journal of Personality and Social Psychology, 58*, 796. © 1990 American Psychological Association. Adapted with permission of the publisher.)

significant Stimulus Type x Exposure Frequency interaction, $F(6, 594) = 2.44$, $p < .05$ (with visual illusions showing a more rapid increase in liking than Welsh figures through five stimulus exposures).

Two follow-up ANOVAs assessed the effect of stimulus type and exposure frequency on participants' liking ratings. The first ANOVA assessed the effect of stimulus type and exposure frequency on liking ratings at 0, 1, 2, and 5 exposures; the second assessed the effect of these variables on liking ratings at 5, 10, 25, and 50 exposures. The first ANOVA yielded a significant interaction between stimulus type and exposure frequency, with liking ratings of visual illusions increasing more rapidly than liking ratings of Welsh figures through five exposures. The second ANOVA yielded significant main effects for stimulus type and exposure frequency, but no interaction: Liking ratings of visual illusions and Welsh figures both declined at higher exposure frequencies, with visual illusions continuing to receive more positive ratings than Welsh figures through 50 exposures (see Figure 12.1).

Figure 12.2 summarizes the effects of stimulus type and exposure frequency on simple–complex ratings. As figure 12.2 shows, there was a significant main effect of stimulus type on complexity ratings, with visual illusions receiving higher complexity ratings than Welsh figures at all exposure frequencies, $F(1, 99) = 238.80$, $p<.0001$.

Discussion

The results of this experiment illustrated three aspects of the MEE: (1) Liking increased with increasing stimulus exposures. This is the classic MEE, and it is reflected in the significant increase in liking for both types of stimuli at lower exposure frequencies. (2) Stimulus type moderated the MEE. As noted earlier, complex stimuli tend to yield stronger MEEs than do simple stimuli. This is reflected in the significant Stimulus Type x Exposure Frequency interaction at lower exposure frequencies. (3) The downturn in liking ratings for both types of stimuli illustrates the "overexposure effect": At higher exposure frequencies, stimuli become predictable and boring, and as a result, liking ratings decline.

Text box 12.1 Mere exposure classroom demonstration

This is a simplified version of Bornstein et al.'s (1990) Experiment 2. It focuses on the mere exposure effect for relatively small frequencies and its possible downturn for larger frequencies.

Method

Participants

Because MEE effect sizes are typically moderate, an ideal sample size for this experiment is 80–100 participants when alpha is set at .05. Gender does not

Materials

Deviating from the original experiment, only one set of stimuli is used. These stimuli consist of six line-drawn visual illusions taken from Gregory (1968): the Hering illusion, Wundt's converse of the Hering illusion, the Necker illusion, the Zollner illusion, the Poggendorf illusion, and a reversible figure–ground drawing.

Presentation booklets for the participants contain each of these figures with a frequency of 0, 1, 2, 5, 10, or 25 (the original study also included 50), with one figure per page, resulting in a total of 43 pages. Order of stimuli within the stimulus set is random, and counterbalancing is used to ensure that different stimuli are presented at different frequencies in different participants. Across participants, each stimulus should appear in each frequency condition approximately the same number of times (see the Appendix for instructions regarding construction of stimulus sets).

During the rating phase of the experiment 6-page rating booklets are used. These consist of one copy of each visual illusion (one stimulus per page), along with a 9-point rating scale for each stimulus asking how much the participant likes the stimulus. The rating scale is anchored with the terms *Not at all* (1) and *Very* (9) and appears directly below the relevant stimulus. Within each booklet, stimuli are presented in random order.

Design

This demonstration uses a one-factor within-participants design: Each participant provides ratings of stimuli at all six exposure frequencies. The primary dependent measure is participants' like–dislike ratings.

Procedure

Participants can be tested in class. The experimenter provides standardized instructions:

> This is a study of people's responses to visual stimuli. You will be presented a series of images one at a time, and you should examine each image as it's presented. After all the images have been presented, I'll ask you some questions about your reactions to the stimuli. There are about 40 stimuli in all, and this part of the experiment will take about 4 minutes. I will give you a signal when to turn over to the next page.

After answering any final questions, the experimenter hands out the presentation booklets. Exposure times for each page are manually controlled by the experimenter, who gives a signal every 5 seconds to move on to the next page, until all stimuli have been exposed.

Immediately following stimulus presentations, participants are given the rating booklet, and asked to provide ratings of each stimulus. Participants circle the number on each rating scale corresponding to their rating of the stimulus pictured on that page.

Analysis

The analysis consists of a one-factor within-participants analysis of variance (ANOVA), with stimulus exposure frequency (0, 1, 2, 5, 10, and 25) as independent variable, and participants' like–dislike ratings as the dependent variable.

Results

Results of this experiment should parallel those of Bornstein et al. (1990, Exp. 2) as summarized in Figure 12.1. Liking ratings of visual illusions should increase through five exposures, and then gradually decline to baseline (i.e., 0-frequency level). Statistically, there should be a significant main effect of exposure frequency (with liking ratings increasing through five exposures, then declining).

THEORETICAL ACCOUNTS

Since publication of Zajonc's seminal (1968) paper, more than a dozen theoretical frameworks have been developed to explain the processes that underlie the MEE (see Bornstein, 1989, 1992; Seamon et al., 1998; Whittlesea & Price, 2001; Zajonc, 2001). Five of these models have been particularly influential.

The arousal model

Berlyne's (1970) arousal model contends that unfamiliar stimuli are unpleasant because they produce high levels of physiological arousal. Over time, familiarity-induced habituation leads to less and less arousal following each additional stimulus exposure, while an opponent-process "rebound effect" causes the participant to experience increased liking for the now-familiar stimulus.

Studies support Berlyne's (1970) prediction that unfamiliar stimuli lead to high levels of arousal, in part because of their unpredictability (Kruglanski et al., 1996). Studies also confirm that arousal in response to stimulus presentations diminishes at higher levels of exposure. Despite these supportive findings, Berlyne's (1970) model is incomplete. It cannot account for the moderating effects of stimulus complexity or homogeneous–heterogeneous exposure sequence on the MEE, nor can it explain the downturn in affect ratings that occurs at higher exposure frequencies.

The nonspecific activation model

Mandler et al.'s (1987) nonspecific activation model contends that MEEs result from activation of previously encoded stimulus representations. The basic premise of this perspective is that repeated exposures lead to increasingly elaborated mental images of a stimulus (see also Craver-Lemley et al., 2002). When participants are asked to provide liking ratings during the test phase of the study, the elaborated stimulus representations are easily primed, and participants interpret the resulting ease of processing as evidence that they like the stimulus (cf. Chapter 8 on availability).

A key prediction of the nonspecific activation model is that MEEs should occur for a variety of stimulus judgements, including (but not limited to) affect ratings. In support of this prediction, Mandler et al. (1987) demonstrated that repeated exposure to polygon stimuli led to increases in judgements of stimulus brightness – and stimulus darkness – in addition to the usual increases in liking ratings.

The two-factor model

Stang's (1974) two-factor model contends that MEEs reflect two interacting processes: learning and boredom. Learning leads to increased liking for a stimulus at lower exposure frequencies, as the participant becomes familiar with the properties of the stimulus. Boredom leads to a downturn in the frequency–liking curve at higher exposure frequencies, as the stimulus becomes predictable and uninteresting. The first portion of the two-factor model parallels closely the earlier framework of Berlyne (1970), but emphasizes cognitive processing of the stimulus rather than physiological arousal *per se*. The other important contribution of Stang's (1974) framework is the prediction that boredom will undermine the exposure effect.

Myriad experiments demonstrating that stronger exposure effects are obtained for complex than simple stimuli support this latter prediction of Stang's (1974) two-factor model (Bornstein, 1989). Bornstein et al.'s (1990) results provide further evidence for Stang's (1974) framework: Not only do complex stimuli produce stronger MEEs than simple stimuli, but participants who score high on a measure of boredom-proneness show weaker exposure effects than participants who are not boredom-prone (Bornstein et al., 1990, Experiment 1).

The perceptual fluency/attributional model

Bornstein and D'Agostino's (1992, 1994) perceptual fluency/attributional (PF/A) model interprets the MEE in terms of increased perceptual fluency (i.e., ease of perceptual processing) for repeatedly exposed stimuli (cf. Chapter 8 on availability). Consistent with the perspectives of Seamon et al.

(1983) and Mandler et al. (1987), the PF/A model contends that participants in typical MEE studies misattribute perceptual fluency to increased liking for a stimulus. The PF/A model extends earlier thinking in this area by positing that, to the degree that participants attribute increased fluency to the stimulus familiarization procedure (rather than to properties of the stimulus itself), they will adjust their liking ratings downward, inferring that their reactions to the stimulus are the result of repeated exposure.

The initial portion of the PF/A model is a variation of Mandler et al.'s (1987) hypothesis that repeated exposures lead to the construction of increasingly elaborated mental representations of a stimulus (see also Craver-Lemley et al., 2002). The latter ("attributional") portion of the PF/A model is supported by findings which indicate that: (1) subliminal stimuli produce significantly stronger MEEs than do clearly recognized stimuli; (2) delay between stimulus exposures and ratings enhances the effect; and (3) naturalistic MEE studies yield stronger exposure effects than do laboratory MEE studies (Bornstein, 1989, 1992). All three variables – subliminality, experimentally determined delay, and in vivo delay – interfere with participants' ability to attribute familiarity to stimulus exposures, and prevent them from adjusting downward their liking ratings of the stimuli.

The affective primacy model

Zajonc (1980) argued that MEEs represent a "pure" affective response that occurs with minimal intervening cognitive activity beyond rudimentary encoding of stimulus properties. The existence of MEEs in primates and other mammals supports the affective primacy hypothesis, and in recent years considerable progress has been made in identifying the neurological underpinnings of exposure-based affective responding in humans, even in the absence of higher-level cognitive processing of stimulus elements (Zarate, Sanders, & Garza, 2000).

Zajonc's (1980) affective primacy hypothesis is consistent with findings demonstrating robust MEEs for subliminal stimuli (Murphy & Zajonc, 1993), and with results showing affective "spillover" effects to related – and even unrelated – stimuli following repeated, unreinforced exposures (Monahan et al., 2000). Bornstein et al.'s (1999) finding that repeated association of merely exposed stimuli with positive or negative images altered participants' affective reactions is also consistent with the affective primacy hypothesis.

CONCLUSIONS

Few psychologists question the robustness of the MEE, but researchers continue to debate the processes that underlie the effect. Over time, researchers have divided into two camps with respect to this issue: those who favour an affect-based model of the MEE, and those who focus on the cognitive processes that mediate and moderate the effect. Compelling evidence has been obtained in support of both positions, and in certain respects these two viewpoints are actually quite compatible. It may be that MEEs occur in stages, the first of which is a "pure" affective response that requires minimal cognitive processing beyond rudimentary encoding of stimulus properties. This initial affective response is then moderated by more extensive cognitive processing of the mental representation of the merely exposed stimulus. A key challenge for researchers during the coming years will be to specify the links between affective and cognitive components of the MEE.

Whatever psychological and neurological processes underlie the MEE, there is no doubt that this phenomenon has important implications for a broad array of psychological phenomena. In the cognitive arena, the MEE paradigm has been increasingly applied to the investigation of implicit memory and schema priming effects (e.g., Whittlesea & Price, 2001). Social researchers have used MEE procedures to examine the impact of familiarity on intergroup attitudes and behaviours (Kruglanski et al., 1996). Developmental psychologists have become interested in a very different aspect of the MEE: Because infants show a reverse MEE (i.e., preference for novel over familiar stimuli), while toddlers and older children show typical exposure effects, developmentalists have begun to explore the processes that delay the onset of the MEE beyond the first 2 years of life (Berg & Sternberg, 1985).

One of the most stunning findings in MEE research is the inverse relationship between stimulus awareness and magnitude of the exposure effect. This result – which has now been obtained in more than a dozen independent laboratories – has played a major role in establishing the existence of perception without awareness in mainstream psychology (Bornstein, 1992; Zajonc, 2001). The robustness of subliminal MEEs continues to intrigue researchers interested in the dynamics of unconscious mental processing, and recent research in this area shows great promise in uncovering the neurological pathways that underlie mental processing outside conscious awareness (e.g., Zarate et al., 2000).

The question remains: Given what we know about the MEE, can this phenomenon be described as a genuine cognitive illusion? The answer to this question is a qualified yes. Robust MEEs are produced with a complete absence of stimulus recognition on the part of participants (Zajonc, 2001). Even in situations where participants are aware of having been exposed to stimuli, they rarely attribute their liking for a stimulus to repeated exposure, instead believing that some property of the stimulus itself is particularly attractive or interesting (Bornstein & D'Agostino, 1994). It is here that the crux of the illusion lies: Although repeated exposure does not alter a stimulus at all, it alters attitudes regarding that stimulus. Insofar as people attribute their positive attitude to properties of the stimulus – not familiarity with the stimulus – the true source of this positive attitude remains unknown, and the illusion remains strong.

SUMMARY

- The mere exposure effect (MEE) refers to increased liking for a stimulus that follows repeated, unreinforced exposure to that stimulus.
- MEEs are obtained for a wide variety of stimuli (e.g., visual, auditory), in a broad array of contexts (e.g., laboratory, field).
- MEEs have numerous real-world implications, helping to explain voting behaviour, advertising effects, and attitudes towards people and objects encountered in everyday life.
- Boredom is a limiting condition on the MEE: Simple stimuli and a homogeneous exposure sequence weaken the effect, and liking ratings tend to decrease after a large number of stimulus exposures.
- Stimulus awareness inhibits the MEE: Stronger effects are produced by stimuli perceived without awareness than those that are consciously recognized.
- Myriad theoretical models have attempted to explain the MEE, and it appears that the effect is a product of two processes: a rapid, reflexive affective response followed by more controlled, deliberate cognitive processing of stimulus content.

FURTHER READING

Zajonc's (1968) classic monograph summarizes the history of the mere exposure effect (MEE) and the relationship of the effect to other psychological phenomena. Kunst-Wilson and Zajonc's (1980) experiment has served as a model for most subliminal MEE studies during the past 25 years, while Bornstein's (1989) meta-analysis remains one of the most useful references on the parameters and limiting conditions of the MEE; it not only identifies variables that moderate the effect, but also illustrates how MEEs differ in different situations and settings. Most recently, Whittlesea and Price's (2001) experiments have demonstrated how participants' information-processing strategies can enhance or undermine the effect; Zajonc's (2001) review discusses the implications of the MEE for contemporary models of unconscious mental processing.

REFERENCES

Amir, Y. (1969). Contact hypothesis in ethnic relations. *Psychological Bulletin*, 71, 319–342.

Barron, F., & Welsh, G. S. (1949). *Barron-Welsh art scale*. Palo Alto, CA: Consulting Psychologists Press.

Berg, C. A., & Sternberg, R. J. (1985). Response to novelty: Continuity and discontinuity in the developmental course of intelligence. *Advances in Child Development and Behavior* (Vol. 19, pp. 1–47). New York: Academic Press.

Berlyne, D. E. (1970). Novelty, complexity, and hedonic value. *Perception & Psychophysics, 8,* 279–286.

Bornstein, R. F. (1989). Exposure and affect: Overview and meta-analysis of research, 1968–1987. *Psychological Bulletin, 106,* 265–289.

Bornstein, R. F. (1992). Subliminal mere exposure effects. In R. F. Bornstein & T. S. Pittman (Eds.), *Perception without awareness: Cognitive, clinical, and social perspectives* (pp. 191–210). New York: Guilford Press.

Bornstein, R. F. (1993). Mere exposure effects with outgroup stimuli. In D. M. Mackie & D. L. Hamilton (Eds.), *Affect, cognition, and stereotyping* (pp. 195–211). New York: Academic Press.

Bornstein, R. F., Craver-Lemley, C., Allison, K., Horchler, S., & Mitra, N. (1999). *Visual imagery, verbal association, and the mere exposure effect.* Paper presented at the annual meeting of the Eastern Psychological Association, Providence, RI.

Bornstein, R. F., & D'Agostino, P. R. (1992). Stimulus recognition and the mere exposure effect. *Journal of Personality and Social Psychology, 63,* 545–552.

Bornstein, R. F., & D'Agostino, P. R. (1994). The attribution and discounting of perceptual fluency: Preliminary tests of a perceptual fluency/attributional model of the mere exposure effect. *Social Cognition, 12,* 103–128.

Bornstein, R. F., Kale, A. R., & Cornell, K. R. (1990). Boredom as a limiting condition on the mere exposure effect. *Journal of Personality and Social Psychology, 58,* 791–800.

Bornstein, R. F., Leone, D. R., & Galley, D. J. (1987). The generalizability of subliminal mere exposure effects: Influence of stimuli perceived without awareness on social behavior. *Journal of Personality and Social Psychology, 53,* 1070–1079.

Craver-Lemley, C., Arterberry, M. E., & Reeves, A. (1999). "Illusory" illusory conjunctions: The conjoining of features of visual and imagined stimuli. *Journal of Experimental Psychology: Human Perception and Performance, 25,* 1036–1049.

Craver-Lemley, C., Bornstein, R. F., Forys, K., Lake, C., & Thomas, N. (2002). *Repeatedly exposed and imagined stimuli yield comparable exposure effects.* Paper presented at the annual meeting of the Eastern Psychological Association, Boston, MA.

Gregory, R. L. (1968). Visual illusions. *Scientific American, 219,* 66–76.

Halpern, A. R., & O'Connor, M. G. (2000). Implicit memory for music in Alzheimer's disease. *Neuropsychology, 14,* 391–397.

Hamid, P. N. (1973). Exposure frequency and stimulus preference. *British Journal of Psychology, 64,* 569–577.

Harrison, A. A. (1977). Mere exposure. In L. Berkowitz (Ed.), *Advances in experimental social psychology* (Vol. 10, pp. 39–83). New York: Academic Press.

Janiszewski, C. (1993). Preattentive mere exposure effects. *Journal of Consumer Research, 20,* 376–392.

Kail, R. V., & Freeman, H. R. (1973). Sequence redundancy, rating dimensions, and the exposure effect. *Memory & Cognition, 1,* 454–458.

Kruglanski, A. W., Freund, T., & Bar-Tal, D. (1996). Motivational effects in the mere exposure paradigm. *European Journal of Social Psychology, 26,* 479–499.

Kunst-Wilson, W. R., & Zajonc, R. B. (1980). Affective discrimination of stimuli that cannot be recognized. *Science, 207,* 557–558.

Mandler, G., Nakamura, Y., & Van Zandt, B. J. (1987). Nonspecific effects of exposure to stimuli that cannot be recognized. *Journal of Experimental Psychology: Learning, Memory, and Cognition, 13,* 646–648.

Monahan, J. L., Murphy, S. T., & Zajonc, R. B. (2000). Subliminal mere exposure: Specific, general, and diffuse effects. *Psychological Science, 11*, 462–466.

Murphy, S. T., & Zajonc, R. B. (1993). Affect, cognition, and awareness: Priming with optimal and suboptimal stimulus exposures. *Journal of Personality and Social Psychology, 64*, 723–739.

Seamon, J. G., Brody, N., & Kauff, D. M. (1983). Affective discrimination of stimuli that are not recognized: Effect of delay between study and test. *Bulletin of the Psychonomic Society, 21*, 187–189.

Seamon, J. G., McKenna, P. A., & Binder, N. (1998). The mere exposure effect is differentially sensitive to different judgment tasks. *Consciousness and Cognition, 7*, 85–102.

Stang, D. J. (1974). Methodological factors in mere exposure research. *Psychological Bulletin, 81*, 1014–1025.

Stang, D. J. (1975). Effects of mere exposure on learning and affect. *Journal of Personality and Social Psychology, 31*, 7–12.

Titchener, E. B. (1910). *A textbook of psychology*. New York: Macmillan.

Whittlesea, B. W. A., & Price, J. R. (2001). Implicit/explicit processing versus analytic/nonanalytic processing: Rethinking the mere exposure effect. *Memory & Cognition, 29*, 234–246.

Zajonc, R. B. (1968). Attitudinal effects of mere exposure. *Journal of Personality and Social Psychology Monographs, 9*(2, Part 2), 1–27.

Zajonc, R. B. (1980). Feeling and thinking: Preferences need no inferences. *American Psychologist, 35*, 151–175.

Zajonc, R. B. (2001). Mere exposure: A gateway to the subliminal. *Current Directions in Psychological Science, 10*, 224–228.

Zarate, M. A., Sanders, J. D., & Garza, A. A. (2000). Neurological dissociations of social perception processes. *Social Cognition, 18*, 223–251.

APPENDIX

Construction of stimulus sets

To ensure that each stimulus appears in each exposure-frequency condition approximately the same number of times, the following procedure should be used to construct stimulus sets. As there are six visual-illusions stimuli and six different exposure frequencies, six different presentation booklets need to be constructed. The following table gives these six conditions (A to F) and how many copies of each stimulus should be included in each. Having assembled the 43 pages for each booklet, the pages should be shuffled into random order. Reflecting the six different conditions, it would be preferable to have a sample size of a multiple of six (e.g., 90), and give each sixth one type of booklet. At least, all conditions should be used about equally often.

	Visual illusion					
Condition	V1	V2	V3	V4	V5	V6
A	0	1	2	5	10	25
B	1	2	5	10	25	0
C	2	5	10	25	0	1
D	5	10	25	0	1	2
E	10	25	0	1	2	5
F	25	0	1	2	5	10

V1, ..., V6 = Visual illusion #1 to #6

13 Overconfidence

Ulrich Hoffrage

When the editor of this book asked me whether I would be interested in contributing a chapter on overconfidence, my first question was "What's the deadline?" When Rüdiger said, "In half a year – end of October," I replied, "Impossible. With some luck this is when I could start writing. If the end of November is okay with you, I'm on board, otherwise I have to say no." At the time my confidence in providing the chapter by the end of November was about 80% and my confidence in being done before Christmas was almost 100%.

Christmas came and I had not yet even started. Although this is a quite extreme (and embarrassing) example, milder forms of this "planning fallacy" (Buehler, Griffin, & Ross, 2002) are probably known to many of us. It is ironic that such a thing happened with the chapter on overconfidence, as this is just one illustration of this phenomenon. More generally, overconfidence occurs if our confidence in our judgements, inferences, or predictions is too high when compared to the corresponding accuracy. I will commence with a brief overview of the most frequently used tasks and measures. Text box 13.1 then presents a classroom experiment, the following section summarizes the main findings, and the last section introduces and evaluates the models and theoretical accounts that shed some light on these findings.

OVERCONFIDENCE: TASKS AND MEASURES

The term "overconfidence" has several meanings, reflecting the different methods that have been used to compare subjective beliefs and reality. Specifically, two types of tasks have been used: probability estimates of the correctness of statements or choices, and estimates of confidence intervals. For the first type of task, overconfidence can mean either that participants are miscalibrated, or that average confidence judgements exceed the total percentage of correct statements or choices; for the latter type of task, it means that confidence intervals are too narrow. The present section elaborates on these terms in more detail.

Probability estimates

In an early study, Adams and Adams (1961) asked participants to state their subjective probability (on a full scale of 0 to 100%) for a variety of statements or events. For instance, participants were asked to indicate their confidence in their recalls of nonsense syllables after 1, 2, 4, 8, or 16 trials on a list of 30 syllables. The confidence scale was defined for the participants in terms of expected percentages of correct recalls – that is, of all those recalls made with confidence x, $x\%$ should be correct. Plotting the percentage of correct recalls separately for each confidence category yielded the so-called calibration curve. Data points lined up along the diagonal are said to be well calibrated. Points below indicate overconfidence, that is, unwarrantedly high confidence. For instance, when participants in the 16-trial condition said they were 100% certain that the syllable they recalled was on the list, they were correct in only about 85% of the cases; when their confidence was 80–90%, they were correct in 55%, and so on. Finally, data points above the diagonal indicate underconfidence.[1]

Many if not most of the subsequent studies on calibration have focused on general knowledge questions in which participants – unlike in Adams and Adams' free recall task – have to choose which of two alternatives is correct (two-alternative forced-choice tasks, 2AFC). Examples include "Which city is located farther north: Rome or New York?" and "What is absinthe: a precious stone or a liqueur?" After participants make their choice they are asked to state their confidence in having chosen the correct answer, usually on a scale of 50 to 100%, with 10% increments, and with the instruction to choose confidences such that the percentages of correct choices will match these confidences.

Measures

For both the full and the half scale, the appropriateness of participants' responses can be evaluated with respect to internal and external criteria. Internal criteria include internal consistency (also called normative goodness), and require that subjective probabilities conform to the Kolmogorov axioms of probability and that these subjective probabilities express the assessor's true belief (also called substantive goodness). The external criterion is simply correspondence with reality and reflects how adequate these beliefs are. This can be evaluated with a proper scoring rule, the most popular being the Brier score B (named after Brier, 1950):

$$B = \frac{1}{N} \sum_{i=1}^{N} (r_i - c_i)^2 \qquad (1)$$

where r is the response on the probability scale, c is the correctness of the statement (1 if correct, 0 if wrong) to which this probability has been attached, N is the number of items, and i is the running index for those items. The lower the score, the better: If a full scale is used, optimally all wrong statements are rated with a subjective probability of 0, and all correct statements with 1, resulting in a Brier score of 0. If one is uncertain about the truth of a statement (or the correctness of one's choice in a 2AFC task), the lowest expected Brier score is achieved by stating the true subjective probability. For instance, if a ball is repeatedly and randomly drawn from an urn with 80% red balls and 20% white balls, the best probability one can attach to the statement "a red ball will be drawn" is 80% – all other subjective probabilities will, in the long run, result in a worse (i.e., higher) Brier score.

Several partitionings of the Brier score have been suggested, the most popular by Murphy (1972), which, in the most common case of one response per item, reduces to

$$B = \bar{c}(1-\bar{c}) + \frac{1}{N}\sum_{t=1}^{T} n_t (r_t - \bar{c}_t)^2 - \frac{1}{N}\sum_{t=1}^{T} n_t (\bar{c}_t - \bar{c})^2 \qquad (2)$$

$$= Knowledge + Calibration - Resolution$$

where, in addition to the notation introduced above, $\bar{c}$ is the percentage correct, r_t is the probability assigned to category t (usually these are fixed by the experimenter: 50%, 60%, ..., 100%), and t is the index for these categories – averages with index t are computed within each confidence category; averages without index are computed across all items. These terms can be computed for each participant separately and can be interpreted as follows: *Knowledge* measures the amount of knowledge a participant has about the particular domain, *calibration* measures the (weighted average of the) correspondence between a particular confidence judgement and the proportion of correct statements in this category, and *resolution* reflects the assessor's ability to sort the events into subcategories for which the percentage correct is different from the overall percentage correct (for a discussion of other measures introduced by several colleagues, see Keren, 1991, and Lichtenstein, Fischhoff, & Phillips, 1982).

The measure that is most frequently used in the literature is *over/underconfidence*, which is sometimes also referred to as *calibration-in-the-large* (in contrast to *calibration* as introduced above, which is then referred to as *calibration-in-the-small*). It is simply defined as the agreement between mean confidence (across all items) and percentage correct (across all items), specifically:

$$Over/underconfidence = \bar{r} - \bar{c} \qquad (3)$$

Although this measure is sufficient for many purposes, it is a very coarse one and as such it has drawbacks. For instance, if the experimenter presents 50 correct and 50 wrong statements, the percentage of correct statements is, by experimental design, 50%. If a participant states a subjective probability of 0% for all correct statements (i.e., is absolutely sure that each of them is wrong) and 100% for all wrong statements (i.e., is absolutely sure that each of them is correct), the mean confidence is 50% and thus over/underconfidence is 0 (i.e., as good as could be). At the same time, both the Brier score and calibration are 1 (i.e., as bad as could be). Now imagine another participant who suspects this distribution of correct and wrong statements and always states a probability of 50%. As a result, both over/underconfidence and calibration are 0 (i.e., as good as could be), but resolution would also be 0 (reflecting the inability to discriminate between items), and the Brier score would be 0.25 (a comparatively high, that is, bad value). As these examples show, it is useful to look at the terms into which the Brier score can be partitioned, but looking at any of them alone would be too shortsighted. Before concluding this section on subjective probabilities, it should be noted that a probability of, say, 80% could alternatively be expressed as an odds ratio, namely, that chances are 4 to 1 (for an overview of studies that compared calibration for subjective uncertainties expressed in terms of probabilities, odds ratios, or their transformations to log-odds, see Lichtenstein et al., 1982).

As most studies in calibration research have used subjective probabilities (full and half scale), the present chapter will focus on this type of task. However, for the sake of completeness, the other task that has been employed, namely, estimating confidence intervals, is also briefly introduced in the next section.

Confidence intervals

"What is your best estimate for the length of the Amazon river, that is, the estimate for which you think chances that the true value is above your choice are as high as chances that it is below?" Having received the response the experimenter continues, "Imagine I tell you that your estimate was too high – what is now your best estimate?" and then, "Now imagine that your first estimate was too low – what is now your best estimate?" This is followed by "Now consider again the full range of possible answers. Give me your lowest (highest) estimate – such that your subjective probability for the true value being below (above) this boundary is 1%."

Measures

Let us denote the answers to these questions as x_{50}, x_{25}, x_{75}, x_1, and x_{99}, respectively. We can thus introduce the *interquartile index* as the proportion of true values lying between x_{25} and x_{75} in a series of similar estimation tasks, and the *surprise index* as the proportion of true values lying either below x_1 or above x_{99} in a series of similar estimation tasks (occasionally, similar measures such as the proportion of true values between x_{10} and x_{90} are used). A person is well calibrated if the *interquartile index* is 50% and the *surprise index* is 2%. The typical finding is overconfidence: The *interquartile index* is too low (39% across 27 conditions of several studies reviewed by Lichtenstein et al., 1982) and the *surprise index* is too high (30% across those conditions), indicating that the confidence intervals have been too tight, or, in other words, that people thought their estimates were closer to the true value than they actually were.

Related methods, measures, and findings

For quite another way of structuring the methods and findings the reader is referred to Alba and Hutchinson (2000), who classified the findings into the major sections "remembering the past", "interpreting the present", and "predicting the future", thereby discussing many phenomena such as eye-witness testimony, incidental learning, belief polarization, the reiteration effect, and metamemory (feeling of knowing) in their relation to the overconfidence phenomenon.

TYPICAL FINDINGS

In the present section, I briefly review some findings obtained in calibration research. I commence with a classroom experiment that illustrates the typical procedure and some of the effects listed below.

Text box 13.1 A classroom experiment

Data without theories are like children without parents. The experiment suggested here is adapted from Gigerenzer, Hoffrage, and Kleinbölting (1991) and will produce such children. The parent that can take care of them is the theory of probabilistic mental models (PMMs) and will be introduced later in the chapter.

Method

Design

Calibration is obtained in each of two item sets that Gigerenzer et al. (1991) referred to as the *representative* set and the *selected* set. In the original studies, data were obtained in a within-subjects design, and if time is not a serious constraint, this is also what I would recommend for the classroom demonstration (a within-subjects design allows for a more powerful statistical analysis; moreover, a comparison of their experiences of working in both sets may help students to better understand the theory). Needless to say, order of conditions should be counterbalanced. After completing choices and confidences for an item set, participants should state their frequency estimate, that is, their estimate of the number of correct choices they achieved in a particular set.

Materials

For the *representative* set, Gigerenzer et al. (1991) used a complete paired comparison between 25 (Study 1; 21 for Study 2) German cities that had been randomly drawn from the set of all German cities with more than 100,000 inhabitants. The task was to compare each pair with respect to the cities' population sizes, to choose the larger city, and to provide a confidence rating for this choice (deviating from the original studies, I recommend using the standard scale with 50, 60, . . ., 90, 100 as confidence categories). As an alternative to German cities, one might use countries drawn from the set of all countries of the world (or from subsets, such as from Africa or Europe) and ask participants to compare pairs of countries with respect to any numerical criterion such as area, population, employment rate, or number of medals won at the last Olympic games (other examples are given in Juslin, 1994). It is not necessary to realize a complete paired comparison, but it is important that each object in a given pair has been randomly drawn from a well-specified reference class. It is also not necessary to have as many comparisons as we had in the original studies (300 and 210). Unrepresentative samples, however, must be avoided (samples of 50 comparisons should be sufficient for this purpose; to be on the safe side every participant could get a unique, independent random sample). It can be illustrative to use more than one representative set, which can be realized in either a within-subjects or a between-subjects design.

The *selected* set can be obtained from the author upon request; however, it is recommended to adapt the procedure used by Juslin (1994), who asked people to generate items that they thought would be appropriate to be included in general-knowledge tests. Unlike Juslin, who excluded participants involved in the process of item generation, one could use the same participants for item generation and data collection, although one should make sure that no one works on his or her own items (which could easily be achieved by splitting the classroom in two groups, each providing the items for the other). Having been involved in selecting some "good general-knowledge items" (Juslin, 1994, p. 236) may help the student to understand the results and the theory.

Procedure

Preparation of the materials and data analyses can be done outside the classroom, whereas data can be collected during the course (proceeding through 100 pair comparisons usually does not take longer than 15 minutes).

Participants

The original studies involved 80 and 97 participants from a German university (Study 1 and 2, respectively), but given the large effect size obtained in those studies, a smaller number should be sufficient to demonstrate the effect in the classroom.

Analysis

Data should be analyzed separately for the representative and the selected item set. To obtain the calibration curves (Figure 13.1, left panel) the items of all participants should be pooled.[2] The measures introduced in the last section should be computed for each participant. Given the expected effect sizes, descriptive statistics should be sufficient – if inferential statistics are performed, one should remember that the major independent variables (sampling procedure: representative vs selected set; response format: confidences vs frequency estimates) have been manipulated within subjects, so that the dependent variables for these conditions are treated as repeated measurements.

Results

Figure 13.1 displays the major result of the original studies. The left panel shows that participants were well calibrated in the representative item set, whereas calibration for the selected item set was poor. The right panel shows that there was no overconfidence for the representative item set, yet overconfidence for the selected item set was substantial. In addition, the right panel also displays the differences between mean frequency estimates (which have been transformed to percentages to be comparable) and percentage correct. With this measure, the picture changed: For the selected set, the frequency estimates matched the percentage of correct answers, whereas participants underestimated their performance in the representative set (for the exact numbers, further experimental conditions, and further analyses, see Gigerenzer et al., 1991).

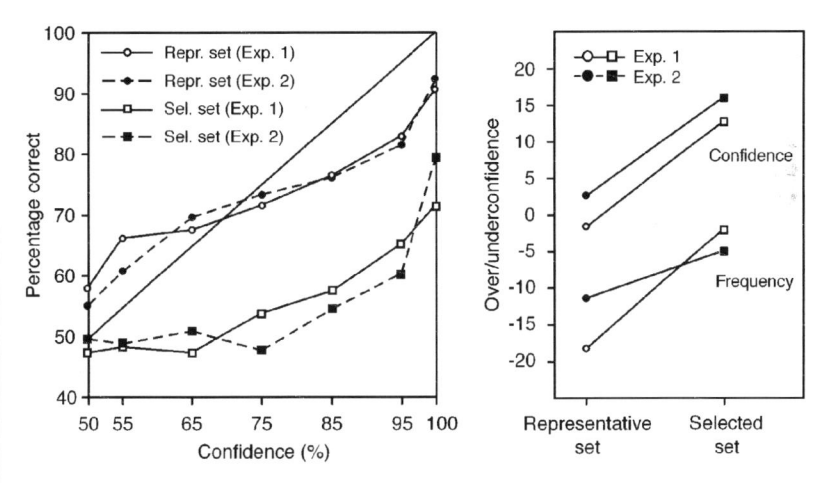

Figure 13.1 Left: Calibration curves for representative and selected sets of items. Right: The graphs labelled *Confidence* depict mean confidence judgements minus mean percentage correct, and those labelled *Frequency* depict mean frequency estimates (which have been transformed to percentages to be comparable) minus percentage correct. Positive differences denote overconfidence, negative differences denote underconfidence. Data taken from Gigerenzer et al. (1991).

Discussion

This experiment has contributed two new insights to the field. First, overconfidence depends on the sampling procedure, and second, it depends on the format that is used to assess performance. Specifically, in the representative set, confidences were well calibrated, but frequency estimates showed underconfidence; in the selected set, confidences showed overconfidence whereas frequency estimates were well calibrated. Given these results it is too shortsighted to discuss whether people are overconfident in general. These results instead call for models of the cognitive processes that are able to capture the quite differentiated picture displayed in Figure 13.1. The theory of these "probabilistic mental models", as Gigerenzer et al. (1991) called them, provides such an approach and will be introduced below.

Most studies on overconfidence used a half-range scale (as in our classroom experiment in Text box 13.1). If not otherwise stated, the findings listed below were obtained in studies that used such a scale. For the sake of brevity, I restrict myself to some well-established results found in many studies, and to some results found in particular studies that have been included because they will be useful when discussing the theoretical approaches in the next section. Comprehensive reviews have been provided by Alba and Hutchinson (2000), Keren (1991), Lichtenstein et al. (1982), O'Connor (1989), and Yates (1990); for two reviews that focus more on models than on findings see McClelland and Bolger (1994) and Juslin and Olsson (1999).

The overconfidence effect

The dominant finding, which also provided the title of this chapter, is overconfidence, that is, mean confidence in the correctness of one's answers tends to exceed percentage correct. Nevertheless, calibration curves usually have a positive slope and, as Alba and Hutchinson (2000) point out, there is still a positive correlation between individuals' reported mean confidences and mean percentages correct (albeit rather low, in one study even as low as .2, but in other studies up to .75). This suggests that using confidence when making decisions is still better than ignoring it.

The hard–easy effect

Overconfidence covaries with item difficulty. Hard item sets (i.e., those with a percentage of correct answers of about 75% or lower), tend to produce overconfidence, whereas easy sets (i.e., those with a percentage correct of about 75% or higher) tend to produce underconfidence.

The importance of sampling

In sets of items that have been representatively drawn from a natural environment of the participants (i.e., an environment for which they have had the chance to acquire some knowledge), confidence judgements tend to be well calibrated. In sets of items that have been selected to be hard – or, which amounts to the same, have been nominated by participants as "good general-knowledge items" – confidence judgements tend to be too high, resulting in poor calibration and in overconfidence. Sampling procedure is confounded with item difficulty: Representative item sets tend to be easier than such selected item sets. Nevertheless, the hard–easy effect and sampling are not only conceptually different, they can also be separated on an empirical basis: In a meta-analysis, Juslin, Winman, and Olsson (2000) conducted a review of 95 independent data sets with selected items and

35 sets in which items had been sampled representatively. Across all selected item sets, overconfidence was 9%, and across all representative sets it was 1% (95% confidence intervals for each of the two sampling procedures were at ±2%). The authors pointed out that this difference could not be explained by differences in percentage correct, as has been claimed by Griffin and Tversky (1992) based on three data points. Moreover, when they controlled for the end effects of the confidence scale and the linear dependence between percentage correct ($\bar{c}$) and the over/underconfidence score (recall that this is $\bar{r} - \bar{c}$), the hard–easy effect almost disappeared for the representative item sets.

The base-rate effect

An effect closely related to sampling (which is obtained for 2AFC and confidence ratings given on a half scale) is the so-called base-rate effect (obtained for statements and a full scale): When the experimenter manipulates the base rate of true statements, participants are unable to adjust their confidence accordingly, showing severe underconfidence (overconfidence) for items set with a high percentage of true (wrong) statements (Ferrell & McGoey, 1980; Lichtenstein et al., 1982).

The confidence–frequency effect

In Figure 13.1 (right panel), we compared confidence with accuracy on the one hand and frequency estimates with accuracy on the other. The direct comparison between the two forms of assessing one's own performance constitutes the confidence–frequency effect: In our studies, confidence exceeded frequency estimates by about 15 percentage points (see also Allwood & Montgomery, 1987; May, 1986; Schneider, 1996).

The expertise effect

Although there are exceptions, many studies with experts have shown that they are well calibrated, at least in their domain of expertise. The most frequently cited example is probably a study by Murphy and Winkler (1977), who found that weather forecasters were almost perfectly calibrated across the whole range of their subjective probabilities from 0 to 100%. Experts' good calibration seems to be domain specific, that is, in domains outside their expertise they are indistinguishable from other people; conversely, other people who had been tested in the experts' field of expertise also fared poorly (for more information on experts' calibration and references to original studies see the reviews mentioned above).

Betting

Quite another way to assess one's own performance is reflected in people's willingness to bet. Fischhoff, Slovic, and Lichtenstein (1977) asked participants whether they were willing to gamble against the experimenter. In the participant's urn were all items for which he estimated the odds of having answered correctly as 50:1 or higher, and in the experimenter's urn were 100 white and 2 red balls. Whenever the participant drew a question from his urn for which he made the wrong choice, he had to pay $1 to the experimenter, and whenever the experimenter drew a red ball from her urn, she had to pay $1 to the participant. Of 42 participants, 27 decided to gamble and almost all lost. In contrast, in their analysis of the bids (which can be translated into subjective probabilities) in a naturalistic setting, namely the horserace betting market, Johnson and Bruce (2001) found an almost perfect calibration.

Simultaneous conservatism (underconfidence) and overconfidence

In research on Bayesian inference, two opposite findings have been reported: (1) People use the representativeness heuristic (which can be defined as putting too much weight on new evidence and not enough weight on base rates; see also Chapters 2 and 9), and (2) people are conservative (indicated by not enough weight given to new evidence and too much weight to the prior probabilities; see also Chapter 2). Conservatism not only poses a problem for the representativeness heuristic, it also seems to challenge the claim that overconfidence is ubiquitous. Why? Imagine two urns: Urn R contains 80% red balls and 20% white balls, and Urn W contains 20% red balls and 80% white balls. One urn is randomly (with $p = .5$) selected and 5 balls are drawn: 4 red, 1 white. Participants typically believe that the sample is drawn from Urn R and estimate the probability of this to be much lower than the objective probability (which for the present case is 93%). Providing estimates that are too low reflects conservatism (by being too close to the prior probability of 50%) and thus underconfidence. Erev, Wallsten, and Budescu (1994) showed that overconfidence and underconfidence can occur simultaneously for the same data set (see next section).

Format dependence

"The population of Bulgaria exceeds 30 million: true or false?" When participants make their own choices for items like this and subsequently state their confidence in the correctness of this choice on a half scale, the calibration curve for this and similar tasks cuts the diagonal at about 75% (with underconfidence in lower and overconfidence in higher confidence categories). However, when the experimenter (randomly) makes the choice and participants state their confidence in their correctness of that choice on a full scale, the calibration curve cuts the diagonal at about 50% (Juslin, Wennerholm, & Olsson, 1999). Finally, participants can be asked to provide the smallest confidence interval within which they are, say, 80% certain that the population of Bulgaria lies – with this method participants tend to be grossly overconfident.

Underconfidence and error independence in sensory-discrimination tasks

Interestingly, calibration of confidence in choices that require sensory discrimination ("Which weight is heavier?" "Which line is longer?") yields quite a different result, namely underconfidence (Juslin, Olsson, & Winman, 1998). Moreover, unlike sets of general-knowledge questions that may contain items that are misleading for a majority of participants (thus leading to less than 50% correct choices), solution probabilities for sensory-discrimination tasks range between 50 and 100%. This suggests that the errors a particular participant makes with general-knowledge items are not independent of the errors other participants make, whereas they seem to be independent for sensory-discrimination tasks.

THEORETICAL ACCOUNTS

"Then are the lifeless fragments in his hand, there only fails, alas! the spirit-band" (from Goethe's *Faust*). How can we understand the findings listed in the last section? For a long time, research in this field could be characterized by a "'dust-bowl empiricism'. Psychological theory is often absent, either as motivation for research or as explanation of the results" (Lichtenstein et al., 1982, p. 333). During the 1990s, however, the picture changed: In fact, most of the studies that led to the findings listed above were theoretically motivated and were conducted after Lichtenstein et al.'s conclusion. As mentioned above, two reviews with a focus on theories and (computational) models have been provided by McClelland and Bolger (1994) and Juslin and Olsson (1999).

Heuristics and biases

During the 1970s and 1980s, when research in judgement and decision making was dominated by the "heuristics and biases programme" associated mainly with Amos Tversky and Daniel Kahneman, the overconfidence phenomenon was considered one of the cornerstones that illustrate shortcomings in human information-processing capacities, thereby marking human irrationality. This is the tone of Lichtenstein et al.'s (1982) review and it thus nicely fits into the context in which it was published. The phenomenon has been taken as a psychological reality and explained in terms of the anchoring and adjustment heuristic (people anchor on 100% confidence and adjust insufficiently downward), or in terms of a confirmation bias (for a critical discussion of this explanation see Gigerenzer et al., 1991; see also Chapter 4). However, this programme cannot account for most of the findings summarized in the last section.

A signal-detection approach

In contrast to the attempts just mentioned, which were not formalized at all, Ferrell and McGoey (1980) proposed a computational approach based on signal-detection theory, which allowed for fitting calibration curves. Beliefs in the truth of true statements and beliefs in the truth of false statements were conceptualized as overlapping probability distributions along a continuous decision variable. By partitioning this continuum into segments, confidences were seen as a function of the area from the distribution of true statements and that of false statements that fell into the particular segment. Although quite specific on the level of the response function, this model is mute about the cognitive processes that are responsible for mapping a particular statement to a particular value on the decision variable. Moreover, given the many free parameters of the model (for n segments one needs $n-1$ cut-off points) it is not very restrictive but quite flexible and thus difficult to falsify (for a critical discussion of this model see the controversy between Suantak, Bolger, & Ferrell, 1996, and Juslin et al., 1998).

Ecological models

Independently, Gigerenzer et al. (1991) with their theory of probabilistic mental models (PMMs) and Juslin (1994) developed what later was termed "ecological models" (McClelland & Bolger, 1994). When solving a task such as "Which city has more inhabitants, A or B?" people construct a PMM (unless they have direct knowledge or can deduce the answer with certainty, which is called a "local mental model"; Gigerenzer et al., 1991). By searching for probabilistic cues that discriminate between the two alternatives, the question is put into a larger context. Imagine that a search hits on the soccer-team cue: City A has a soccer team in the major league and City B does not.[3] Based on literature about automatic frequency processing, PMM theory posits that people are able to estimate the ecological validity of cues (as long as the objects belong to their natural environment, which would also explain the expertise effect mentioned above). This validity is defined by the relative frequency of cases in the environment where the cue indicates the correct answer. For instance, the validity of the soccer-team cue is 90% (in the complete pair comparison of all German cities with more than 100,000 inhabitants). If participants choose the city to which the cue points and report the cue validity as their confidence, they should be well calibrated. This, however, is only true if the cue validities in the item sample reflect the cue validities in the population. If researchers do not sample general-knowledge questions randomly, but over-represent items in which cue-based inferences would lead to wrong choices, overconfidence will occur. Such overconfidence does not reflect fallible reasoning processes but is an artifact of the way the experimenter sampled the stimuli and ultimately misrepresented the cue–criterion relations in the ecology (by applying the same argument to tasks with a full confidence scale one can also account for the base-rate effect mentioned above).

How does PMM theory explain the confidence–frequency effect? While making inferences based on cues and stating cue validities as their confidence values, people are unaware that the cue validities will eventually be lower than in the corresponding reference class, that is, in the population from which the items have been drawn. The question "How many of the last 50 items did you answer correctly?" activates another reference class, namely, one's performance in similar testing situations. And because people know from their experience that general-knowledge items are difficult, they adjust their frequency estimates to that fact and will be well calibrated if items are typical with respect to testing situations, that is, if they are selected to be difficult. In contrast, if items are randomly drawn from a specified reference class and if cue validities in the sample are thus representative of those in the population, those items are, at the same time, untypical for general-knowledge questions. Being easier than expected, these items elicit underconfidence when people are asked to estimate the number of correct inferences.

Error models

While Gigerenzer et al. (1991) focused on the cognitive processes and on the impact of item sampling, they did not make any attempt to elaborate explicitly on the impact of stochastic components of the judgement process. This was achieved in subsequent publications by Erev et al. (1994) and Pfeiffer (1994), who demonstrated that even unbiased response error would deteriorate calibration, simply due to regression effects. To see why, imagine a person who is perfectly calibrated, that is, whenever true confidence is 100%, percentage correct is also 100%, and so on. Further, assume that the overt response is a result of true confidence plus (unbiased) error, which, in the case of a true confidence of, say, 100%, will lead to some responses with a lower confidence than 100%. Conversely, not all overt responses of confidence x% are those with a true confidence of x%. In the case of overt responses of 100%, the error can only pull in one direction, namely, downward. In fact, the representative set in Figure 13.1. shows such regression effects at the ends of the scale.

Yet this is only half the story. If two variables are imperfectly correlated, regression to the mean can be obtained for each of them. Thus, Erev et al.

(1994) could also demonstrate that one simply has to plot mean subjective probabilities for specific events (in their experiments they used, for instance, outcome of basketball games) against their objective probabilities to reverse the typical pattern – that is, to obtain too low confidences at the right end of the scale (events that are correctly predicted by all participants have a subjective probability below 100%) and too high confidences at the left end of the scale. This can also account for conservatism, where a (high) objective probability is taken as the independent and a (lower) subjective probability as the dependent variable (note that in calibration curves objective probability is conditioned on subjective probability).

Combined error models

Whereas Erev et al. (1994) emphasized the role of error without specifying the cognitive processes (as, for instance, PMM theory did), other authors have brought these approaches together (Björkman, 1994; Juslin & Olsson, 1997; Juslin, Olsson, & Björkman, 1997; Juslin et al., 1999; Soll, 1996). Building on PMM theory, Juslin and his colleagues have called the mismatch between cue validities for a sample and for the population the "Brunswikian error" (which is caused either by researcher's violation of a representative design *sensu* Egon Brunswik, or simply by unsystematic sampling error). In contrast, they called the unsystematic response error introduced by Erev et al. the "Thurstonian error". Note that these two errors correspond to two sources of uncertainty. Brunswikian uncertainty is external and reflects less-than-perfect predictability of unknown states of the world (criterion) given known states (cues). Thurstonian uncertainty, in contrast, is internal and reflects less-than-perfect reliability of the information-processing system itself (Juslin & Olsson, 1997). By combining Brunswikian and Thurstonian errors in one single model they could, for instance, explain not only why the calibration curves looked different for different sampling procedures (due to Brunswikian error) but also why they looked different for the half and the full scale (due to Thurstonian error), thus accounting for the format dependence of confidence judgements (Juslin et al., 1999).

Another approach that combined these two kinds of errors is Dougherty's (2001) application of the MINERVA-DM model (MDM, where DM stands for decision making) to the overconfidence phenomenon. Whereas the ecological models and the combined error models assume that confidence emanates from relative frequencies and that this frequency information is stored automatically and separately from memory-trace information, MDM assumes only an instance-based memory representation. By specifying the details of the memory processes involved with confidence judgements, it is able to make predictions that none of the models discussed above could make, such as predictions concerning the effect of depth of encoding of stimuli in a learning phase on accuracy and confidence judgements in a subsequent categorization task. The experiments reported by Dougherty confirm these predictions. A difference between MDM and the other combined error models related to the one just stated is that those other models conceptualize error as response error (mapping covert feelings of confidence to an overt response), whereas MDM sees error as retrieval error without assuming a perturbed response process. For another exemplar model – *PROBEX* – that has been discussed in the context of calibration research see Juslin and Persson (2002); for a comparison between connectionist and exemplar-based memory models see Sieck and Yates (2001), and for an extension of support theory to account for the basic findings presented in this chapter see Brenner (2003).

The sensory sampling model

A special case of Thurstonian uncertainty is neural noise in an organism facing a sensory-discrimination task. If two lines have about the same length, then the impression of which one is longer will most likely vary over time. In their sensory sampling model, Juslin and Olsson (1997) suggested that people (a) decide which line is longer based on the proportion of impressions made within a given short-term memory window that speak for each of the two alternatives, and (b) state this proportion as their confidence. At first glance this reminds one of the rules suggested by PMM theory for stating choice and confidence based on uncertain cues. However, there are two important differences.

First, knowledge about cues is shared by many people and therefore their errors are dependent: If a cue is misleading, it will mislead the majority of people. Stochastic fluctuations in people's sensory systems, in contrast, are independent of each other, as are their errors. Second, if a probabilistic cue makes a correct prediction in 80% of the cases, and confidence is 80%, then a perfect calibration will result in the long run. In a sensory-discrimination task, however, the sensory sampling model predicts underconfidence. Why? Whereas the choice is based on a proportion, that is, on an aggregate, confidence is based on the distribution of single impressions, but not on the distribution of their central tendency. Thus, whereas choice capitalizes on the law of large numbers, confidence does not. For illustration, imagine a large number of balls, say 99, are repeatedly drawn (with replacement) from an urn with 60% red and 40% white balls, and the sample proportion is used to predict whether there are more red or more white balls in the urn. In the long run, the mean percentage of red balls in the samples (and thus the mean confidence) will be 60%, and the proportion of samples with 50 or more red balls (which yields the percentage of correct predictions) will be higher than 60%. As a result, underconfidence occurs.

FINAL REMARKS

The field of overconfidence has seen major changes and developments. The days of "dust-bowl empiricism" are long gone, and some attempts to use the concepts of the heuristics and biases programme did not have the last word. Today we can recognize several precise and highly formalized models of the cognitive processes involved in forming beliefs and generating confidences, indications of the theoretical progress that has been made in the recent past. These models have focused on the psychological mechanisms underlying choices, confidence judgements, and eventually also overconfidence.

Quite another way to look at a particular phenomenon is to ask what function it serves. So put aside, for a moment, the arguments laid out above – namely, that overconfidence may be the result of selected item sampling or statistical regression – and consider the following examples for overconfidence's beneficial effects and, in turn, its potential ultimate causes. A physician may be overconfident that a particular treatment will help her patient, but showing high confidence that it will help may be essential for a placebo effect to occur. If the objective chances that the treatment will help are, a priori, 30%, and if they increase to 60% a posteriori (i.e., after the physician expressed a very high confidence of, say 80%) who wants to blame her for having been overconfident?

As a second example, consider young children's belief that they can master even the most difficult tasks. As long as they grow up in an environment in which they are protected from harming themselves as a result of such overconfidence, this lack of metacognitive abilities is likely to increase the chances that they will attempt such tasks, thereby gaining experience and acquiring skills. Due to this self-fulfilling prophecy (and even if it were only partial) they get an advantage over their peers who have a more realistic – and more pessimistic – view of their own competence (Bjorklund, 1997). Closely related to the adaptive function of children's overconfidence is the planning fallacy that has already been mentioned at the beginning of the present chapter. Had Rüdiger and I been realistic about my time schedule, I would not have committed myself and he would not have accepted me as an author. It was thus the overconfidence phenomenon itself that gave me the opportunity to write about it.

What is the lesson to be learned from our fictitious physician's overconfidence, most children's overconfidence, and some authors' overconfidence? Unwarranted optimism about future developments may function to positively effect those developments.

SUMMARY

- Overconfidence can mean (1) miscalibration, in particular, too low percentages of correctly answered items for a given confidence category, (2) mean confidence ratings exceeding mean percentages of correct answers across all items, and (3) too narrow confidence intervals around a numerical estimate.
- Several effects are well established, including the overconfidence effect, the hard–easy effect, the importance of sampling, the base-rate effect, the confidence–frequency effect, the expertise effect, and the format effect.
- The so-called ecological models have successfully explained overconfidence (and some other effects) as a consequence of item-selection procedures that distort cue validities. In this view, overconfidence is an artifact created by the experimenter.
- The so-called error models have successfully attributed miscalibration to statistical regression of otherwise unbiased information processing.
- Several models are available that combine the strengths of the ecological and the error approaches.
- There are situations in which the benefits of being overconfident clearly outweigh the costs.

FURTHER READING

For review articles about the overconfidence phenomenon see Alba and Hutchinson (2000), Keren (1991), Lichtenstein et al. (1982), O'Connor (1989), and Yates (1990); for two reviews that focus more on models than on findings see McClelland and Bolger (1994) and Juslin and Olsson (1999), and for a meta-analysis on the hard–easy effect see Juslin et al. (2000). Recent computational models that could not have been discussed in the review papers just mentioned have been proposed by Brenner (2003), Dougherty (2001), and Juslin and Persson (2002).

NOTES

1 There is a special case for confidence in the truth of the statement "A is larger than B" that range between 0 and 50%. If the percentage of correct answers here is below the diagonal, this indicates underconfidence rather than overconfidence, because confidence is not as extreme as it should have been.
2 Alternatively, the percentages of correct responses per confidence category can be computed for each participant, and then the average percentages can be plotted. Dawes (1980) obtained virtually no differences between these two procedures.
3 Consistent with Egon Brunswik's notion of vicarious functioning, PMM theory

assumes that search for cues proceeds hierarchically, where cues are ordered according to their validity, and that search is stopped as soon as a cue that discriminates has been found. This process of cue substitution (rather than integration), which bases the decision on one cue only (one-reason decision making) has since been supplemented by the recognition principle and termed Take The Best. The Take The Best heuristic has been shown to perform astonishingly well compared to more complex benchmarks (Gigerenzer & Goldstein, 1996; for further analyses of this and similar heuristics see Martignon & Hoffrage, 2002).

ACKNOWLEDGEMENTS

I would like to thank Gerd Gigerenzer, Wolfgang Hell, Peter Juslin, and Rüdiger Pohl for comments on an earlier draft, and Anita Todd for her careful editing.

REFERENCES

Adams, J. K., & Adams, P. A. (1961). Realism of confidence judgments. *Psychological Review*, 68, 33–45.

Alba, J. W., & Hutchinson, J. W. (2000). Knowledge calibration: What consumers know and what they think they know. *Journal of Consumer Research*, 27, 123–156.

Allwood, C. M., & Montgomery, H. (1987). Response selection strategies and realism of confidence judgments. *Organizational Behavior and Human Decision Processes*, 39, 365–383.

Bjorklund, D. F. (1997). The role of immaturity in human development. *Psychological Bulletin*, 122, 153–169.

Björkman, M. (1994). Internal cue theory: Calibration and resolution of confidence in general knowledge. *Organizational Behavior and Human Decision Processes*, 58, 386–405.

Brenner, L. A. (2003). A random support model of the calibration of subjective probabilities. *Organizational Behavior and Human Decision Processes*, 90, 87–110.

Brier, G. W. (1950). Verification of forecasts expressed in terms of probability. *Monthly Weather Review*, 78, 1–3.

Buehler, R., Griffin, D., & Ross, M. (2002). Inside the planning fallacy: The causes and consequences of optimistic time predictions. In T. Gilovich, D. Griffin, & D. Kahneman (Eds.), *Heuristics and biases: The psychology of intuitive judgment* (pp. 250–270). New York: Cambridge University Press.

Dawes, R. (1980). Confidence in intellectual judgments vs. confidence in perceptual judgments. In E. D. Lantermann & H. Feger (Eds.), *Similarity and choice: Papers in honour of Clyde Coombs* (pp. 327–345). Bern: Huber.

Dougherty, M. R. P. (2001). Integration of the ecological and error models of overconfidence using a multiple-trace memory model. *Journal of Experimental Psychology: General*, 130, 579–599.

Erev, I., Wallsten, T. S., & Budescu, D. V. (1994). Simultaneous over- and underconfidence: The role of error in judgment processes. *Psychological Review*, 101, 519–527.

Ferrell, W. R., & McGoey, P. J. (1980). A model of calibration for subjective probabilities. *Organizational Behavior and Human Performance, 26,* 32–53.

Fischhoff, B., Slovic, P., & Lichtenstein, S. (1977). Knowing with certainty: The appropriateness of extreme confidence. *Journal of Experimental Psychology: Human Perception and Performance, 3,* 552–564.

Gigerenzer, G., & Goldstein, D. (1996). Reasoning the fast and frugal way: Models of bounded rationality. *Psychological Review, 103,* 650–669.

Gigerenzer, G., Hoffrage, U., & Kleinbölting, H. (1991). Probabilistic mental models: A Brunswikian theory of confidence. *Psychological Review, 98,* 506–528.

Griffin, D., & Tversky, A. (1992). The weighing of evidence and the determinants of confidence. *Cognitive Psychology, 24,* 411–435.

Johnson, J. E. V., & Bruce, A. C. (2001). Calibration of subjective probability judgments in a naturalistic setting. *Organizational Behavior and Human Decision Processes, 85,* 265–290.

Juslin, P. (1994). The overconfidence phenomenon as a consequence of informal experimenter-guided selection of almanac items. *Organizational Behavior and Human Decision Processes, 57,* 226–246.

Juslin, P., & Olsson, H. (1997). Thurstonian and Brunswikian origins of uncertainty in judgment: A sampling model of confidence in sensory discrimination. *Psychological Review, 104,* 344–366.

Juslin, P., & Olsson, H. (1999). Computational models of subjective probability calibration. In P. Juslin & H. Montgomery (Eds.), *Judgment and decision making: Neo-Brunswikian and process-tracing approaches* (pp. 67–95). Mahwah, NJ: Lawrence Erlbaum Associates Inc.

Juslin, P., Olsson, H., & Björkman, M. (1997). Brunswikian and Thurstonian origins of bias in probability assessment: On the interpretation of stochastic components of judgment. *Journal of Behavioral Decision Making, 10,* 189–209.

Juslin, P., Olsson, H., & Winman, A. (1998). The calibration issue: Theoretical comments on Suantek, Bolger, and Ferrell (1996). *Organizational Behavior and Human Decision Processes, 73,* 3–26.

Juslin, P., & Persson, M. (2002). PROBabilities from EXemplars (PROBEX): A "lazy" algorithm for probabilistic inference from generic knowledge. *Cognitive Science, 26,* 563–607.

Juslin, P., Wennerholm, P., & Olsson, H. (1999). Format dependence in subjective probability calibration. *Journal of Experimental Psychology: Learning, Memory, and Cognition, 25,* 1038–1052.

Juslin, P., Winman, A., & Olsson, H. (2000). Naive empiricism and dogmatism in confidence research: A critical examination of the hard-easy effect. *Psychological Review, 107,* 384–396.

Keren, G. (1991). Calibration and probability judgments: Conceptual and methodological issues. *Acta Psychologica, 77,* 217–273.

Lichtenstein, S., Fischhoff, B., & Phillips, L. D. (1982). Calibration of probabilities: The state of the art to 1980. In D. Kahneman, P. Slovic, & A. Tversky (Eds.), *Judgment under uncertainty: Heuristics and biases* (pp. 306–334). Cambridge: Cambridge University Press.

Martignon, L., & Hoffrage, U. (2002). Fast, frugal and fit: Simple heuristics for paired comparison. *Theory and Decision, 52,* 29–71.

May, R. S. (1986). Inferences, subjective probability and frequency of correct answers: A cognitive approach to the overconfidence phenomenon. In B. Brehmer,

H. Jungermann, P. Lourens, & G. Sevon (Eds.), *New directions in research on decision making* (pp. 175–189). Amsterdam: North Holland.

McClelland, A. G. R., & Bolger, F. (1994). The calibration of subjective probabilities: Theories and models 1980–94. In G. Wright & P. Ayton (Eds.), *Subjective probability* (pp. 453–482). Chichester, UK: Wiley.

Murphy, A. H. (1972). Scalar and vector partitions of the probability score (Part 1): Two-state situation. *Journal of Applied Meteorology, 12,* 595–600.

Murphy, A. H., & Winkler, R. L. (1977). Can weather forecasters formulate reliable probability forecasts of precipitation and temperature? *National Weather Digest, 2,* 2–9.

O'Connor, M. (1989). Models of human behavior and confidence in judgment: A review. *International Journal of Forecasting, 5,* 159–169.

Pfeiffer, P. E. (1994). Are we overconfident in the belief that probability forecasters are overconfident? *Organizational Behavior and Human Decision Processes, 58,* 203–213.

Schneider, S. (1996). Item difficulty, discrimination, and the confidence–frequency effect in a categorical judgment task. *Organizational Behavior and Human Decision Processes, 61,* 148–167.

Sieck, W. R., & Yates, J. F. (2001). Overconfidence effects in category learning: A comparison of connectionist and exemplar models. *Journal of Experimental Psychology: Learning, Memory, and Cognition, 27,* 1003–1021.

Soll, J. B. (1996). Determinants of overconfidence and miscalibration: The roles of random error and ecological structure. *Organizational Behavior and Human Decision Processes, 65,* 117–137.

Suantak, L., Bolger, F., & Ferrell, W. R. (1996). The hard–easy effect in subjective probability calibration. *Organizational Behavior and Human Decision Processes, 67,* 201–221.

Yates, J. F. (1990). *Judgment and decision making.* Englewood Cliffs, NJ: Prentice-Hall.

14 Pollyanna Principle

Margaret W. Matlin

About 25 years ago, I published a book with David Stang called *The Pollyanna Principle: Selectivity in Language, Memory, and Thought* (Matlin & Stang, 1978). That book was named after Pollyanna Whittier, the child heroine of a book by Eleanor Porter (1913). Soon, "Pollyanna" became a fairly common label for optimists. A Pollyanna is someone who looks on the bright side of every misfortune, who remembers only the happy events, and who believes that the world and its inhabitants are thoroughly delightful.

In 1969, Jerry Boucher and Charles E. Osgood published an article called "The Pollyanna Hypothesis", which described observations about several linguistic phenomena. For example, in a variety of different languages, people use evaluatively positive words more frequently than evaluatively negative words. Stang and I argued, however, that Pollyanna tendencies are pervasive. These tendencies include other positive biases in language, as well as in perception, judgement, and memory. Accordingly, we decided that the Pollyanna hypothesis was so pervasive and strong that it deserved to be upgraded to the "Pollyanna Principle".

In brief, the Pollyanna Principle states that pleasantness predominates: We typically process pleasant items more accurately and efficiently than unpleasant or neutral items, and we tend to make positive judgements about a wide variety of people, events, situations, and objects. (Even distilled water is judged to have a rather pleasant taste.) The present chapter emphasizes the Pollyanna principle in two areas, memory and judgement.

More than two decades have passed since the publication of *The Pollyanna Principle*. Can the world situation in the 21st century support this style of blissful optimism? I wrote this chapter in October 2002, and many examples seemed to deserve the darkest possible pessimism. Consider just two items, the AIDS crisis and the terrorism crisis originating on September 11, 2001. Even in these two crises, people search for optimism.

The AIDS crisis has now killed more than 16 million people throughout the world, and an additional 34 million are currently living with HIV/AIDS. Surely, no one who is actually HIV positive – and anticipating the onset of AIDS – could find an optimistic interpretation of this disease? However, Lather (1999) conducted a remarkable study of HIV-positive women, which shows how some of these women manage to create meaning out of the grimmest circumstances. For example, an interviewer had asked a woman named Rita how being HIV-positive had changed her life. Rita replied:

> This is a gift for me to take a second look at life, at what the value of life really is. I'd probably be dead now if I didn't have HIV. At first, I used it as an excuse; I'm dying anyway. Then my family invited me back home; it was a shock and a relief. I got on methadone and off of the heavy coke and heroin I was on. I sold drugs to support it and the other things you have to do to support your habit. Here was a chance to wipe the slate clean and start over. I just went for it completely. It was just such a relief to go back to being the person I was 15–20 years ago. It was a slice out of my life and then I got to come back and be the person I was when I left here. So I'd probably be dead if it wasn't for HIV, as crazy as that sounds.
>
> (Lather, 1999, p. 141)

The events of September 11, 2001, left many Americans appalled at the horrific deaths of about 3000 people.[1] Even those people who had not lost a relative or a friend were aghast at the enormity of this inhuman attack on the United States. We heard countless interviews with people who had lost a loved one. One year later, many news magazines commemorated the anniversary by revisiting the tragedy and tracking the lives of people who had been forever scarred. The subsequent Letters to the Editor of *Newsweek* magazine revealed many examples of Pollyanna tendencies in the American public. For instance, a woman from Texas wrote,

> I want to ask every American who continues to complain about Mondays, how was your Tuesday, September 11, 2001? I, for one, am grateful for my job. I am more tolerant. . . . I give more compliments. I celebrate diversity, because I still believe we can all work together, no matter what. I recycle much more than I throw away. There is new life in my commitment to my teenage son. And I take a deep breath of fresh air every chance I get.
>
> (Kennedy, 2002, p. 18)

In other words, people often believe that even the greyest clouds can have a silver lining. A deadly disease can lead people to restructure their lives and reunite with their family. A devastating tragedy provides a framework for becoming a more appreciative and caring person.

This chapter will explore many components of the Pollyanna principle. Text box 14.1 describes a research study that illustrates one of these components.

Text box 14.1 Pollyanna research study

One attractive feature of many components of the Pollyanna principle is that they are relatively easy to demonstrate. The research study described in this text box is a variant of a study by Kruger (1999), who examined a phenomenon called "the Lake Wobegon effect". This name requires a brief explanation for those residing outside North America. For many years, public radio stations in the United States and Canada have broadcast a programme called "A Prairie Home Companion". Every week, the programme's host, Garrison Keillor, provides a monologue about a charming but fictional small town in rural Minnesota called Lake Wobegon. Each monologue ends with the sentence, "And that's the news from Lake Wobegon, where all the women are strong, all the men are good looking, and all the children are above average."

To test the generality of the "Lake Wobegon effect", Kruger obtained a list of 14 different skills, which had been rated on a 4-point difficulty scale by students participating in a College Board survey conducted in 1976. He then asked Cornell University undergraduates to rate themselves on each skill, using a scale from 1 (very unskilled) to 10 (very skilled). Kruger discovered that the difficulty rating of each skill was significantly correlated ($r = -.81$) with the percentage of students who rated themselves above average on that skill. For example, 89% of the students rated themselves above average on the ability to get along with others (rated only 3.3 on the difficulty scale), whereas only 38% rated themselves above average on the mechanical scale (rated 6.3 on the difficulty scale).

To provide a wider range of items, I selected 5 skills from Kruger's list and added 16 additional skills, primarily based on skills listed on several graduate-school recommendation forms. Then 25 students in my autumn 2002 course in Cognitive Psychology rated the difficulty of each skill on a 10-point rating scale. The students' mean difficulty ratings for these skills are shown in Table 14.1.

Method

The list of items in the Appendix was photocopied onto a single sheet of paper; also included were the rating scale and instructions that appear at the top of the page. After all students had received a copy, they were reminded, "Please be sure to compare yourself with the average student in this classroom." They were also instructed that they must rate all 21 items on the list. When they appeared to be finished, they were told to fold their sheet in half so that the answers were not visible, then the sheets were collected.

Results and discussion

For each of the 21 skills, the number of students who consider themselves "above average" (ratings of 6, 7, 8, 9, and 10) and the number who consider themselves "below average" (ratings of 1, 2, 3, 4, and 5) was tallied.[2] Then the complete data set could be analyzed. First, (A) the number of skills where the majority of students classified themselves "above average" and (B) the number of skills where the majority of students classified themselves "below average"

Table 14.1 List of skills, mean difficulty rating, mean skill rating, number below average, and number above average

Skill	Mean difficulty rating	Mean skill rating	Number below average	Number above average
1. Ability to understand theoretical issues	5.6	6.6	6	19*
2. Ability to work independently	2.8	7.5	2	23*
3. Ability to work with a research team	4.6	6.1	9	16
4. Compassion for other people	4.6	7.7	2	23*
5. Computer skills	4.5	5.4	13	12
6. Concern about social justice	4.8	7.4	6	19*
7. Creativity	4.6	6.2	9	16
8. Critical thinking	5.2	6.4	7	18*
9. Discussion participant	5.6	5.9	14	11
10. Dependability	4.6	7.4	2	23*
11. Getting along with others	3.4	7.0	1	24*
12. Knowledge about psychology	5.3	6.4	4	21*
13. Leadership	5.9	6.7	6	19*
14. Motivation to achieve in psychology	4.9	6.8	4	21*
15. Oral communication before a group	6.5	6.5	12	13
16. Research design	6.6	5.6	12	13
17. Skill in mathematics	6.1	6.0	9	16
18. Statistics	6.4	6.3	8	17
19. Time management	6.2	6.6	8	17
20. Trustworthiness	4.1	7.8	1	24*
21. Written communication	4.3	6.8	4	21*

Data obtained from my Cognitive Psychology class (autumn 2002)
* The chi-square calculation for each of these items is significant, $p < .05$; on these items, students were significantly more likely to rate themselves "above average" rather than "below average".

were counted. For students in my Cognitive Psychology class, there were 19 skills in Category A – demonstrating the Lake Wobegon effect – and only 2 skills in Category B (see Table 14.1). A chi-square analysis compared the number of skills in Category A with the number in Category B and found this difference to be significant, $\chi^2(1) = 13.762, p < .001$.

The next step was to determine which of those 21 skills were especially likely to generate the Lake Wobegon effect. (The number of people who would need to rate themselves "above average" on a given item, in order to obtain a significant chi-square at the $p < .05$ level of significance, can easily be calculated. For a class of 40 students, 27 students would have to rate themselves "above average" and 13 would have to rate themselves "below average".) Each skill could thus be classified into one of three categories: (a) skills where the Lake Wobegon effect reigns supreme, (b) skills that do not demonstrate a significant difference, and (c) statistically significant "reverse Lake

Wobegon effects". Table 14.1 lists the data for my class; as you can see, 12 of the 21 skills generated a significant Lake Wobegon effect, and none generated a significant "reverse Lake Wobegon effect".

It can be speculated which category of skills is most likely to generate the Lake Wobegon effect. One idea is that the easier tasks are especially likely. To test this idea, a correlation between the skill-difficulty ratings and the mean skill rating (i.e., students' mean ratings per skill) was computed (see Table 14.1). In my class, the correlation was $r = -.53$, $p = .01$, when all 21 of the characteristics were included. In a second analysis, the outlier "Ability to work independently" (which was extremely low on item difficulty) was omitted; a reanalysis of the data for the remaining 20 characteristics produced a correlation of $r = -.46$, $p = .04$.

Depending on the time frame, ratings for the 21 skills on dimensions other than skill difficulty (e.g., social desirability or gender-congruent skills) could be gathered. The overview of the Pollyanna principle in the text may suggest additional factors.

OVERVIEW OF THE POLLYANNA PRINCIPLE

This section will examine in some detail the research about the Pollyanna principle in two important domains, memory and judgement. However, Text box 14.2 illustrates the pervasiveness of this principle in two additional areas, perception and language. The Matlin and Stang (1978) book provides more specific information on each of these points, as well as other phenomena.

It should be noted that some of these phenomena – such as the Lake Wobegon effect (see Text box 14.1) – are clearly cognitive illusions. Other phenomena – such as seeking silver linings – seem to provide adaptive mechanisms for coping with tragedy, enhancing motivation, and facilitating social interactions.

Text box 14.2 Examples of the Pollyanna Principle in perception and language

Perception

1. People seek out pleasant items and avoid unpleasant items. For example, they avoid looking at unpleasant pictures. Like one monkey in the famous trio of Pollyanna-like monkeys, they "see no evil". A consequence is that pleasant stimuli are encountered more often. Notice that this consequence is related in an interesting fashion to the "mere exposure effect" discussed in Chapter 12 of this volume. According to the mere exposure effect, stimuli that are encountered frequently are likely to be rated more positively than low-frequency items.
2. People recognize pleasant or neutral stimuli more quickly than unpleasant or threatening stimuli.

3. Pleasant stimuli are judged larger in size than unpleasant or neutral stimuli.

Language

1. People communicate good news more frequently than bad news; like another monkey in the famous trio, they "speak no evil".
2. Pleasant words usually have higher frequencies in the English language than do less pleasant words, as originally noted by Boucher and Osgood (1969); this tendency also holds true for a variety of other languages. Note once again the relationship between this observation and the mere exposure effect, as discussed in the previous section.
3. In antonym pairs, the more pleasant member typically entered the English language prior to the unpleasant member.
4. The pleasant member of antonym pairs is likely to be linguistically more basic or "unmarked", in the terminology of linguistics. For example, we typically ask "How good is the food in this restaurant?" Someone who asks "How bad is the food in this restaurant?" clearly has reason to anticipate a response in the negative portion of a rating scale.
5. When people construct a list of items, they usually place the pleasant items before the less pleasant items. For example, they list people they like before people they dislike. They also list favourite television programmes, actors, colours, and desserts before nonfavourite ones. Incidentally, a recent study by Silvera, Krull, and Sassler (2002) suggests that this tendency to list pleasant before unpleasant items is limited only to pleasant categories; when listing items for unpleasant categories, people usually list unpleasant items before pleasant ones.

Memory

The research on memory demonstrates selective recall; we tend to remember the delightful and forget the dismal, and we also remember praise better than condemnation. Furthermore, as the saying goes, "Time heals all wounds"; as memory for events fade, the positive events seem slightly less positive, whereas the negative events seem much less negative. Finally, the literature on mood-congruent memory demonstrates that people who are nondepressed or high in self-esteem typically recall pleasant information, whereas people who are unhappy or low in self-esteem are likely to violate the Pollyanna principle.

Accuracy of recall for daily events

During the 1930s and the 1940s, psychologists conducted about a dozen studies that focused on people's recall of their daily experiences. In general, the research in that era supported the Pollyanna principle; people usually recalled pleasant items somewhat more accurately than unpleasant items.

However, the early researchers also identified a second factor – the intensity principle – which operates independently of the Pollyanna principle. According to the intensity principle, intense items often predominate over more neutral items. For example, an intensely positive stimulus will be recalled more accurately than a mildly positive stimulus, and an intensely negative stimulus will be recalled more accurately than a mildly negative stimulus. In order to avoid the confounding variable of intensity, researchers must compare positive and negative stimuli that are matched in their intensity. In other words, it would be unfair to compare (a) recall for learning about the attack on the World Trade Center with (b) recall for receiving a good score on a quiz in a statistics class.

In the more current research on recalling daily experiences, individuals typically record events in a diary. For example, Skowronski, Betz, Thompson, and Shannon (1991) asked undergraduate psychology students to record daily events over a 10-week period. They also rated the pleasantness of these events. At the end of the academic term, a researcher read each entry in random order to the student, who rated how well he or she remembered that event. The students recalled pleasant events more accurately than unpleasant events, supporting the Pollyanna principle. The researchers also found support for the intensity principle; that is, the students recalled extremely pleasant and extremely unpleasant events more accurately than more neutral events.

Accuracy of recall for personal information

If we recall pleasant events about our lives more accurately than unpleasant events, do we also recall pleasant feedback more accurately than unpleasant feedback? Sedikides and Green (2000) conducted a series of studies with a variety of independent variables; we will focus on the research relevant to the Pollyanna principle. In one study, the researchers informed participants that they would take a computerized personality test, which was given the lofty name of the "Michigan Omnibus Personality Inventory" (MOPI). The 45 items on this bogus test included statements such as "I sometimes go to people I consider wise for advice" and "I don't mind visiting places where I have never been before" (Sedikides & Green, 2000, p. 912). During the next phase of the study, the participants were told that they would receive highly accurate feedback about their personality, based on their responses on the MOPI. Half of the feedback statements were positive (e.g., "X would follow through on a promise made to friends") and half were negative (e.g., "X would make fun of others because of their looks"). The results demonstrated that people recalled at a later time significantly more positive descriptions than negative descriptions.

Sedikides and Green speculated that recall may be enhanced for positive descriptions because people spend more time processing them during the feedback phase. In contrast, they spend little time processing negative descriptions in order to protect themselves from self-threat. What would happen if people were allowed only a limited amount of time for both positive and negative descriptions? In another study, these researchers varied both the nature of the feedback (positive versus negative feedback) and the presentation time for each feedback item (an ample time, 8 seconds, versus a limited time, 2 seconds). As you can see in Table 14.2, when people had ample time to inspect the feedback, they recalled a substantially greater percentage of positive items than negative items. In contrast, when time was limited, people actually recalled a substantially greater percentage of negative items.

Memories grow more positive over time

According to another component of the Pollyanna principle, our memory for unpleasant events tends to grow more positive with the passage of time. The dependent variable in these studies is not the number of items recalled, but the qualitative nature of events in our lives. For example, Samuel Clemens (1911) – also known as Mark Twain – described this phenomenon in his book, *Innocents Abroad*. One year after returning from an excursion, he reported that the unpleasant components from his trip had fled from his memory. As a consequence, his overall impressions were glowingly pleasant.

In order to examine whether memories do indeed become more positive, Walker, Vogl, and Thompson (1997) asked undergraduate students to record one personal event each day for about 14 weeks and to rate both the pleasantness and the intensity of the event. After 3 months, the participants returned for a second session. A researcher read each event from the previous list, and the participants were instructed to rate the pleasantness of that event.

According to the analysis of this study's results the rating did not change for those events that were originally considered to be neutral. However, the events originally considered to be pleasant were now considered to be slightly less pleasant. The events originally considered to be unpleasant were now considered to be substantially more pleasant. Consistent with the Pollyanna principle, the change in pleasantness ratings was significantly larger for the unpleasant items than for the pleasant items. Walker and his colleagues found the same pattern of results, for a group of students who had a 1-year retention interval.

Table 14.2 Percentage of behaviours recalled from MOPI feedback, as a function of presentation time and the nature of the feedback

Presentation time	Nature of feedback	
	Positive	Negative
Ample time (8 seconds)	45%	33%
Limited time (2 seconds)	23%	32%

MOPI = Michigan Omnibus Personality Inventory (Sedikides & Green, 2000).

Walker et al. (1997) provide a potential explanation for the results: The strategy of minimizing unpleasant memories serves to maintain a positive self-concept, consistent with Taylor's (1991) mobilization-minimization approach. They argue that social pressure also encourages people to de-emphasize the negative.

Mood-congruent memory

According to the concept of mood-congruent memory, people remember material better if it matches their current mood. In other words, a person who is in a pleasant mood should remember pleasant material better than unpleasant material, whereas a person in an unpleasant mood should remember unpleasant material better. Because most people rate their current mood as positive, the research on mood-congruent memory offers additional support for the Pollyanna principle. However, this research also emphasizes the importance of individual differences: A depressed individual should recall a relatively large number of unpleasant events or personal characteristics. Ruminating about these recollections is likely to increase one's depression still further.

In general, the research on mood-congruent memory is consistent with the predictions (Matlin, in press; Morris, 1999). Consider, for example, a study by Murray, Whitehouse, and Alloy (1999). These researchers located undergraduate students whose scores on two scales of depression allowed them to be consistently categorized as either nondepressed or dysphoric (towards the depressed end of the scales). The participants were instructed to look at a series of 20 positive and 20 negative trait words and to press a key to indicate whether or not each word applied to themselves. After an intervening task, the participants were asked to recall each of the words from the original list. Consistent with previous research, the nondepressed individuals recalled a greater overall percentage of the words than did the dysphoric individuals. More relevant to the Pollyanna principle, the researchers reported a statistically significant interaction between mood and type of stimulus (see Table 14.3). Specifically, the nondepressed students recalled a significantly greater percentage of positive words than negative words. The dysphoric students recalled a slightly greater percentage of

Table 14.3 Percentage of items recalled, as a function of mood and the nature of the stimulus

Mood category	Type of stimulus	
	Positive	Negative
Nondepressed	49%	38%
Dysphoric	35%	39%

(Murray et al., 1999.)

negative words than positive words, but that difference was not statistically significant.

A conceptually similar study by Story (1998) investigated undergraduates who had scored in either the upper third or the lower third on a standard scale of self-esteem. After arriving in the laboratory, the participants completed a set of questionnaires. Next, they were given a bogus feedback sheet providing either positive or negative feedback. Students who were high in self-esteem recalled the positive feedback relatively accurately, and they distorted the negative feedback so that it was more favourable. Students who were low in self-esteem recalled the negative feedback relatively accurately, and they distorted the positive feedback so that it was less favourable. Notice how these tendencies contribute to the stability of our self-concepts (see also Chapter 21). Those who are high in self-esteem will continue to possess a sense of well-being, whereas those who are low in self-esteem will continue to have low opinions about themselves. The remainder of this chapter explores these two topics – well-being and personal attributes – in greater detail.

Judgement

Two components of the Pollyanna principle in judgement are especially active areas of research in the current era. This research demonstrates with considerable consistency that we provide positive judgements about our current happiness and quality of life. Furthermore, we tend to hold inflated opinions about our abilities and other personal attributes.

Rating our happiness and quality of life

In *The Pollyanna Principle*, we reported a number of indications that people believe their lives are generally pleasant (Matlin & Stang, 1978). For instance, people list a larger number of positive life events than negative life events (consistent with the selective recall noted earlier). They are also more likely to report that they are optimists, they proclaim on demographic surveys that they are happy, they rate other people as being happy, and they even carve more smiling pumpkins than frowning pumpkins at Halloween.

This optimism persists in the current era. For example, Quirouette and Pushkar (1999) asked middle-aged university-educated women to contemplate their own expectations about future ageing. The clear majority of the women (84%) had either positive or very positive expectations about their future; 78% also said that it was either easy or very easy to adapt to the ageing process.

Are demographic variables correlated with happiness and well-being? The best answer is one that psychologists supply to virtually every question: "It depends." Let's look at age, income, and culture. With respect to age, for instance, the women in Quirouette and Pushkar's (1999) study speculated that they would be happy when they became old women, but are real elderly women happy? We might expect, for instance, that elderly widows would give themselves relatively low ratings. After all, they are likely to experience poverty, poor health, loneliness, and ageist reactions from younger individuals. However, Neill and Kahn (1999) found that elderly widows gave themselves an average rating of 19 on a life-satisfaction scale where the most negative score was 0 and the highest was 26. Several factors help to explain why these women might be reasonably happy. Specifically, they have learned how to cope effectively with negative emotions, and how to spend time on activities they consider enjoyable. In addition, they have learned to maintain a positive view of themselves, even when faced with disappointments (Whitbourne & Sneed, 2002). Across a variety of studies, age is one demographic variable that is not correlated with well-being.

How about personal income? Most people seem to believe that money can buy happiness, as well as material possessions. However, the correlation between income level and well-being is complex. Yes, in order to be happy, people require a certain minimal income to cover the basic requirements of food, housing, and essential services. But beyond that minimum, the correlation between wealth and well-being is not strong when comparing people who live in the same country (Myers, 2000; Seligman, 2002).

Does culture make a difference? The residents of all but a few countries in a cross-national survey rated themselves on the positive end of the question about life satisfaction (Seligman, 2002). In other research, European American college students were more likely than Japanese college students to provide inflated ratings when rating the pleasantness of the preceding week (Oishi, 2002). In general, however, cultural differences are not large.

Rating our abilities and personal characteristics

We have seen that people typically rate themselves above average on scales of well-being and happiness. What happens when they rate their own abilities and personal characteristics? According to the discussion of this topic in *The Pollyanna Principle*, people are remarkably confident about themselves. In fact, they typically rate themselves above average on a wide variety of attributes (Matlin & Stang, 1978). This tendency is certainly consistent with both the overconfidence effect and the hindsight bias (see Chapters 13 and 20).

In the past 10 years, research on this topic has blossomed, and it is now known by other names, such as the "better-than-average effect", the "optimistic bias", and the "Lake Wobegon effect".

The Pollyanna research study, featured earlier in the chapter (see Text box 14.1), emphasizes that people consider themselves better than average on a variety of academic skills and personal characteristics. Consider some additional research on the Lake Wobegon effect, conducted by Kruger and Dunning (1999). Their first study assessed people's ability to judge which jokes other people would regard as humorous. This ability to identify humour requires subtle knowledge about other people's tastes. Students at Cornell University were asked to rate the humour of 30 jokes from a variety of joke books. The students then evaluated themselves on their own ability to recognize humour, compared to the average student at Cornell. They used a percentile scale ranging from 0 ("I'm at the very bottom") to 50 ("I'm exactly average") to 99 ("I'm at the very top"). Each joke was also assessed by professional comedians, to provide an "expert opinion". Then, for every student, an objective percentile score was calculated in terms of the correspondence between his or her ratings of the jokes and the professional comedians' ratings of the jokes. By definition, the average of these percentile scores was the 50th percentile. However, the average percentile score that the students provided for themselves was the 66th percentile. Even the bottom 25% of the sample provided an average rating at the 58th percentile. Lake Wobegon is apparently also located in Ithaca, New York, where the average student has a sense of humour that is significantly above average!

Other researchers have provided a broad perspective on the Lake Wobegon effect. Text box 14.3 illustrates some representative observations.

Exceptions to the Pollyanna principle in judgement

Despite the prevalence of the Lake Wobegon effect, some factors reduce its power. For example, as emphasized in the research study earlier in the chapter, the better-than-average effect is strong for abilities that are considered relatively easy; in contrast, people may actually rate themselves *below* average on tasks considered to be highly challenging (Kruger, 1999). Furthermore, if people know that they will be required to justify their self-evaluation to someone else – especially someone with expertise in the relevant area – the Lake Wobegon effect is much weaker (Sedikides, Herbst, Hardin, & Dardis, 2002).

Individual differences also play a role in the strength of these positive biases. As you might expect, people who are dysphoric are relatively immune to the Lake Wobegon effect (Helweg-Larsen & Shepperd, 2001). In addition, people raised in a Japanese culture do not inflate their positive attributes; presumably, other Eastern cultures would be similarly reluctant to exaggerate their self-ratings (Heine, Lehman, Markus, & Kitayama, 1999).

Explanations for the Pollyanna principle in judgement

A variety of factors combine to produce a relatively robust tendency for people to rate themselves – and also those in their own group – as better than average. For instance, people pay attention to their own virtues, while ignoring their own vices (Sedikides et al., 2002). In addition, they supply an inflated anchor with respect to assessing their own ability, and they do not make sufficiently large adjustments about the abilities of other people

> **Text box 14.3** Representative examples of the Lake Wobegon effect
>
> 1. People rate themselves more favourably than their friends on a variety of personal characteristics, such as sensitivity, punctuality, insecurity, and sarcasm. They also rate their friends more favourably than their general peer group (Suls, Lemos, & Stwart, 2002).
> 2. People are more positive about themselves now than they are about themselves as they were several years earlier – even when more objective evaluations demonstrate that they have not really improved during this interval (Wilson & Ross, 2001).
> 3. Just as people inflate their own virtues, so they deflate their own risks of encountering a negative outcome. For instance, people believe that they are personally less likely than other people to experience automobile accidents, crimes, unwanted pregnancies, and a variety of psychological and physical health problems (Helweg-Larsen & Shepperd, 2001).
> 4. The Lake Wobegon effect is even more pervasive than many psychologists had imagined. Specifically, people rate other members of their group as being better than the average for that specific group, a phenomenon called "everybody is better than their group's average". For example, suppose that people in a well-established small group (e.g., students in a psychology class) are sitting in a circle, and they are randomly assigned one other member of that group to evaluate, relative to the average group member. The results show that they systematically rate the target person as being better than the group average (Klar, 2002; Klar & Giladi, 1997). In fact, they even demonstrate the Lake Wobegon effect when they are asked to rate an anonymous person in a group, who is identified only by an ID number! In other words, the Lake Wobegon effect does not simply operate in an egocentric fashion. We apparently abandon our logical and mathematical skills (even though our skills are presumably well above average) and proclaim that everyone is better than the average for that group.

(Kruger, 1999; see also Chapter 10). People also tend to recall their virtues more often than their flaws, consistent with the selective recall tendency examined earlier in this chapter (Harrison & Shaffer, 1994).

How can we explain the "everybody in my group is above the group average" phenomenon? One reasonable explanation is that people may focus on the individual group member whom they are evaluating, but not pay sufficient attention to the entire group. For instance, suppose that Susan is asked to make judgements about the friendliness of Rachel, a randomly selected member of her cognitive psychology class. Susan may reason, "Well, Rachel is really friendly," but she may fail to appreciate that most members of this particular class are friendly (Klar, 2002).

The Pollyanna principle and psychology's emphasis on the negative

Anyone who has glanced through psychology journals would certainly contend that the appropriate muse is not young Pollyanna Whittier, but mean-spirited Ebenezer Scrooge from Charles Dickens' *A Christmas Carol*. For example, I was recently exploring the topic of pregnancy for a chapter in a book on women's health. The resource *PsycINFO* was used to identify all English-language references published in the first 5 months of 2002. The four most popular topics related to pregnancy were substance abuse, adolescent pregnancy, sexually transmitted diseases, and psychological disorders. A handful of articles focused on emotionally neutral issues. Not one article looked at women's excitement during a planned pregnancy, their joyous anticipation of holding a newborn baby, or any genuinely positive component of this 9-month period.

Interestingly, a movement called "positive psychology" has been recently initiated in the United States by psychologists such as Seligman and Csikszentmihalyi (2000). According to the positive psychology perspective, psychologists must stop focusing on human pathology and emphasize positive features that make human lives meaningful and hopeful (Seligman, 2002; Snyder & Lopez, 2002). Other researchers, inspired by the extensive work of Isen (1987), have discovered that people perform substantially better on a variety of cognitive tasks when they are in a positive mood. This boost in performance may be traceable to increased brain dopamine levels (Ashby, Isen, & Turken, 1999).

I would like to end this chapter by describing a final application of the Pollyanna principle; this example should be especially useful for professors who assign writing projects in their courses. Most students are overly optimistic about the amount of time they will require to complete a class project. According to research conducted by Taylor, Phan, Rivkin, and Armor (1998), only 14% of students in a control condition completed a particular class project on time. However, students in another condition were told to envision every step in the process of completing this project, such as gathering the resources, organizing the project's basic structure, and so forth. These students were instructed to rehearse these steps for 5 minutes each day. In this condition, 41% completed their projects in time. Clearly, an awareness of the Pollyanna principle can help us devise appropriate precautions so that excessive optimism can be transformed into sadder – but wiser – realism.

SUMMARY

- According to the Pollyanna principle, we typically process pleasant items more accurately than other items, and we typically provide positive judgements about a wide variety of targets.

- The Pollyanna principle is demonstrated in several aspects of perception, such as judging pleasant stimuli to be larger than unpleasant or neutral stimuli.
- This principle is also illustrated in a variety of linguistic phenomena; for example, in a variety of languages, pleasant words have higher frequencies than less pleasant words.
- In memory, people recall pleasant information more accurately than similarly intense unpleasant information, and unpleasant memories typically grow more neutral with the passage of time.
- People typically judge themselves to be happy, and they maintain inflated ideas about their abilities and characteristics.

FURTHER READING

To trace the development of the Pollyanna principle, read Boucher and Osgood's (1969) article about Pollyanna tendencies in language. Matlin and Stang's (1978) book *The Pollyanna Principle* provides an overview of the phenomena in a variety of cognitive and social areas. An article by Walker et al. (1997) is an excellent example of the Pollyanna principle in memory; unpleasant memories become much more neutral with the passage of time. People interested in the implications of the memory research for clinical psychology should also consult the paper by Murray et al. (1999). For illustrations of the Pollyanna principle in judgement, consult the research by Kruger (1999) and by Kruger and Dunning (1999).

NOTES

1. In a Pollyanna-like fashion, most Americans do not choose to learn about the deaths our own country has engineered in dozens of countries throughout the world. For example, I asked my own students how many had known that the United States had been responsible for the deaths of about 30,000 people in Nicaragua, through the US-backed Contras. Not one student raised a hand.
2. Research on the Lake Wobegon effect traditionally employs the number of people who consider themselves above the average, rather than above the median. You might ask your students how this factor might influence the results.

REFERENCES

Ashby, F. G., Isen, A. M., & Turken, A. U. (1999). A neuropsychological theory of positive affect and its influence on cognition. *Psychological Review*, 106, 529–555.

Boucher, J., & Osgood, C. E. (1969). The Pollyanna hypothesis. *Journal of Verbal Learning and Verbal Behavior*, 8, 1–8.

Clemens, S. L. (1911). *The innocents abroad*. New York: Harper.

Harrison, D. A., & Shaffer, M. A. (1994). Comparative examinations of self-reports and perceived absenteeism norms: Wading through Lake Wobegon. *Journal of Applied Psychology, 79*, 240–251.

Heine, S. J., Lehman, D. R., Markus, H. R., & Kitayama, S. (1999). Is there a universal need for positive regard? *Psychological Review, 106*, 766–794.

Helweg-Larsen, M., & Shepperd, J. A. (2001). Do moderators of the optimistic bias affect personal or target risk estimates? A review of the literature. *Personality and Social Psychology Review, 5*, 74–95.

Isen, A. (1987). Positive affect, cognitive processes, and social behavior. *Advances in Experimental Social Psychology, 20*, 203–253.

Kennedy, C. A. (2002, September 23). Letters to the Editor. *Newsweek*, p. 18.

Klar, Y. (2002). Way beyond compare: Nonselective superiority and inferiority biases in judging randomly assigned group members relative to their peers. *Journal of Experimental Social Psychology, 38*, 331–351.

Klar, Y., & Giladi, E. E. (1997). No one in my group can be below the group's average: A robust positivity bias in favor of anonymous peers. *Journal of Personality and Social Psychology, 73*, 885–901.

Kruger, J. (1999). Lake Wobegon be gone! The "below-average effect" and the egocentric nature of comparative ability adjustments. *Journal of Personality and Social Psychology, 77*, 221–232.

Kruger, J., & Dunning, D. (1999). Unskilled and unaware of it: How difficulties in recognizing one's own incompetence lead to inflated self-assessments. *Journal of Personality and Social Psychology, 77*, 1121–1134.

Lather, P. (1999). Naked methodology: Researching the lives of women with HIV/AIDS. In A. E. Clarke & V. L. Olewsen (Eds.), *Revisioning women, health, and healing: Feminist, cultural, and technoscience perspectives* (pp. 136–154). New York: Routledge.

Matlin, M. W. (in press). *Cognition* (6th Ed.). Hoboken, NJ: Wiley.

Matlin, M. W., & Stang, D. J. (1978). *The Pollyanna principle: Selectivity in language, memory, and thought*. Cambridge, MA: Schenkman.

Morris, W. N. (1999). The mood system. In D. Kahneman, E. Diener, & N. Schwartz (Eds.), *Well-being: The foundations of hedonic psychology* (pp. 169–189). New York: Russell Sage.

Murray, L. A., Whitehouse, W. G., & Alloy, L. B. (1999). Mood congruence and depressive deficits in memory: A forced-recall analysis. *Memory, 7*, 175–196.

Myers, D. G. (2000). *The American paradox: Spiritual hunger in an age of plenty*. New Haven: Yale University Press.

Neill, C. M., & Kahn, A. S. (1999). The role of personal spirituality and religious social activity on the life satisfaction of older widowed women. *Sex Roles, 40*, 319–329.

Oishi, S. (2002). The experiencing and remembering of well-being: A cross-cultural analysis. *Personality and Social Psychology Bulletin, 28*, 1398–1406.

Porter, E. H. (1913). *Pollyanna*. Boston: The Page Company.

Quirouette, C. C., & Pushkar, D. (1999). Views of future aging among middle-aged, university educated women. *Canadian Journal on Aging/La Revue canadienne du vieillissement, 18*, 236–258.

Sedikides, C., & Green, J. D. (2000). On the self-protective nature of inconsistency-negativity management: Using the person memory paradigm to examine self-relevant memory. *Journal of Personality and Social Psychology, 79*, 906–922.

Sedikides, C., Herbst, K. C., Hardin, D. P., & Dardis, G. J. (2002). Accountability as a deterrent to self-enhancement: The search for mechanisms. *Journal of Personality and Social Psychology, 83*, 592–605.

Seligman, M. E. P. (2002). *Authentic happiness: Using the new positive psychology to realize your potential for lasting fulfillment.* New York: Free Press.

Seligman, M. E. P., & Csikszentmihalyi, M. (2000). Positive psychology: An introduction. *American Psychologist, 55*, 5–14.

Silvera, D. H., Krull, D. S., & Sassler, M. A. (2002). Typhoid Pollyanna: The effect of category valence on retrieval order of positive and negative category members. *European Journal of Cognitive Psychology, 14*, 227–236.

Skowronski, J. J., Betz, A. L., Thompson, C. P., & Shannon, L. (1991). Social memory in everyday life: Recall of self-events and other-events. *Journal of Personality and Social Psychology, 60*, 831–843.

Snyder, C. R., & Lopez, S. J. (2002). *Handbook of positive psychology.* New York: Oxford University Press.

Story, A. L. (1998). Self-esteem and memory for favorable and unfavorable personality feedback. *Personality and Social Psychology Bulletin, 24*, 51–64.

Suls, J., Lemos, K., & Stewart, H. L. (2002). Self-esteem, construal, and comparisons with the self, friends, and peers. *Journal of Personality and Social Psychology, 82*, 252–261.

Taylor, S. E. (1991). Asymmetrical effects of positive and negative events: The mobilization-minimization hypothesis. *Psychological Bulletin, 110*, 67–85.

Taylor, S. E., Phan, L. B., Rivkin, I. D., & Armor, D. A. (1998). Harnessing the imagination: Mental simulation, self-regulation, and coping. *American Psychologist, 53*, 429–439.

Walker, W. R., Vogl, R. J., & Thompson, C. P. (1997). Autobiographical memory: Unpleasantness fades faster than pleasantness over time. *Applied Cognitive Psychology, 11*, 399–413.

Whitbourne, S. K., & Sneed, J. R. (2002). The paradox of well-being, identity processes, and stereotype threat: Ageism and its potential relationship to the self and later life. In T. D. Nelson (Ed.), *Stereotyping and prejudice against older persons* (pp. 247–273). Cambridge, MA: MIT Press.

Wilson, A. E., & Ross, M. (2001). From chump to champ: People's appraisals of their earlier and present selves. *Journal of Personality and Social Psychology, 80*, 572–584.

APPENDIX

Instructions, rating scale, and list of skills, to be used in the classroom study

Instructions to students: Below is a list of skills that might be relevant for a college student. Using the rating scale below, rate your skill on each item *in comparison to the average student in this classroom*. Place the rating in front of each item. When you are finished, fold each sheet in half and wait until everyone is done. (Do not write your name on this sheet.)

```
     1    2    3    4    5    6    7    8    9    10
Very unskilled              Average                Very skilled
```

Rating Skills

____ 1. Ability to understand theoretical issues
____ 2. Ability to work independently
____ 3. Ability to work with a research team
____ 4. Compassion for other people
____ 5. Computer skills
____ 6. Concern about social justice
____ 7. Creativity
____ 8. Critical thinking
____ 9. Discussion participant
____ 10. Dependability
____ 11. Getting along with others
____ 12. Knowledge about psychology
____ 13. Leadership
____ 14. Motivation to achieve in psychology
____ 15. Oral communication before a group
____ 16. Research design
____ 17. Skill in mathematics
____ 18. Statistics
____ 19. Time management
____ 20. Trustworthiness
____ 21. Written communication

Part III
Illusions of memory

15 Moses illusion

*Heekyeong Park and
Lynne M. Reder*

When asked "How many animals of each kind did Moses take on the Ark?" most people respond "two", even though they know that it was Noah, not Moses, who took the animals on the Ark (Erickson & Mattson, 1981). When a term in a sentence or a question is replaced with a semantically similar but incorrect term, people have difficulty in detecting the distortion. This tendency to overlook distortions in statements is known as the *Moses illusion*.

The Moses illusion was first explored as a scientific issue of inquiry by Erickson and Mattson (1981). They found that people frequently failed to notice the distorted term "Moses" when asked to answer the question, despite reading the question aloud before answering it and despite knowing the name of the correct agent in this role. Even when warned about possible distortions, there was still a great tendency not to note the distortions until they were pointed out. This phenomenon is so robust that it does not require time pressure to elicit the illusion.

Studies of the Moses illusion have focused on when the illusion occurs, what factors influence the illusion, and what mechanisms are responsible for this seeming liability in cognitive performance. That is, what are the mechanisms that underlie the failure to notice mismatches between what is actually presented and what you believe is being asked of you? This chapter will review these issues and present various theoretical accounts that have been proposed to explain these failures, summarizing relevant studies that support or disconfirm each particular account. In the course of this review, the chapter will focus on how people parse questions, query memory, and decide whether the requisite information has been found. We also try to answer the question of why this illusion occurs. Understanding human vulnerability to the Moses illusion can shed light on the memory processes involved in question answering and text comprehension, and will help illuminate the nature of human cognitive architecture.

Text box 15.1 A prototypical Moses illusion experiment

The prototypical Moses illusion experiment described here is based on Experiment 1 of Reder and Kusbit (1991). Participants are asked to answer questions, half distorted and half undistorted. If the question is perceived to be distorted, participants are told to respond "can't say". Otherwise, they are to give the answer to the undistorted question. Accuracy of detecting distorted questions and reaction times to answer them serve as dependent measures.

Method

Participants

A sample size between 20 to 50 participants has provided significant results in the past.

Materials

A list of questions that can be used to produce the illusion is shown in Table 15.1. Each question is listed in two forms, one distorted and one undistorted, along with the answer for the undistorted question. The questions are subject to the following constraints: (1) each substituted term or phrase has to be semantically confusable with the original term; (2) each substituted term has to be syntactically the same part of speech as the original term; (3) the distorted question should not be differently interpretable; (4) the base form of the question should be answerable in the absence of the critical term; and (5) the pair of questions should not differ in length.

Design and procedure

Each participant is presented with only one version of a given question. The questions are randomly assigned for each participant to be presented in either the normal or distorted form, with the constraint that half are seen each way. All participants are told that questions will be presented one at a time on a computer screen and instructed to answer as quickly as possible while remaining accurate. Participants are instructed to treat each question literally and not to give an answer to a question that seems distorted. When a question seems distorted, the participant should respond "can't say". Participants are instructed to respond "don't know" if they do not know the answer to a question.

Analysis

Besides accuracy and response time data, it is necessary to determine whether participants are actually good at detecting distortions. There is a possibility that participants could be biased for calling a question distorted no matter whether the question is distorted or not. Then, the accuracy of distortion detection for a distorted question simply reflects the bias for calling a question

Table 15.1 The exemplar questions used in the Moses illusion experiment

	Questions	Answer
1	How many animals of each kind did Moses take on the Ark? How many animals of each kind did Noah take on the Ark?	two
2	What country was Margaret Thatcher president of? What country was Margaret Thatcher prime minister of?	England
3	What kind of tree did Lincoln chop down? What kind of tree did Washington chop down?	cherry
4	By flying a kite, what did Edison discover? By flying a kite, what did Franklin discover?	electricity
5	What did Goldie-Locks eat at the Three Little Pigs' house? What did Goldie-Locks eat at the Three Bears' house?	porridge
6	Who found the glass slipper left at the ball by Snow White? Who found the glass slipper left at the ball by Cinderella?	prince
7	What is the name of the Mexican dip made with mashed-up artichokes? What is the name of the Mexican dip made with mashed-up avocados?	guacamole
8	What is the name of the shape whose circumference is "pi-r-squared"? What is the name of the shape whose area is "pi-r-squared"?	circle
9	What country is famous for cuckoo clocks, chocolate, stock markets and pocketknives? What country is famous for cuckoo clocks, chocolate, banks and pocketknives?	Switzerland
10	In the biblical story, what was Joshua swallowed by? In the biblical story, what was Jonah swallowed by?	whale

From "Locus of the Moses illusion: Imperfect encoding, retrieval, or match?", L. M. Reder and G. W. Kusbit (1991). *Journal of Memory and Language*, 30, 403–406. © 1991 Elsevier Science. Adapted with permission of Elsevier Science.

distorted rather than sensitivity to distortion detection. In a study by Kamas, Reder, and Ayers (1996), nonparametric measures of sensitivity and bias were calculated. Hit rate (A') is the proportion of "can't say" responses to distorted questions and reflects the proportion of correctly detected distorted questions. False alarm rate ($B'd$) is the proportion of "can't say" responses to undistorted questions and reflects a response bias towards identifying questions as distorted.

Results

An analysis of the accuracy and response time results typically showed that undistorted questions were answered much more accurately and quickly than were distorted questions. Moreover the analysis of hit and false alarm rates tended to show that the manipulation of encoding and retrieval did not affect detection of distortions.

THE LOCUS OF THE MOSES ILLUSION: EXPLANATIONS

In this section we review evidence supporting or disconfirming several proposed explanations for the Moses illusion. These explanations include: (1) the cooperative principle – the listener notices the distortion, but believes that the speaker intended the correct term and so ignores the distortion; (2) imperfect encoding – people simply did not read or hear the distorted term in the sentence; (3) imperfect memory retrieval – the question is correctly heard but the information retrieved from memory is incomplete; and (4) imperfect matching of the question terms to memory.

Cooperation hypothesis/conversational postulate

In everyday situations, people often misspeak and it might be considered rude to jump on one's conversation partner and quickly point out every flaw in his or her utterance. From this observation, it might seem reasonable to view the "failure to detect distortions" in the Moses illusion as merely an extension of the everyday behaviour of cooperating with the speaker. In terms of the "conversational postulate" (Grice, 1975), people notice the distortion but choose not to comment on it because they believe that they know what the speaker intended to say. Being cooperative, they know what was meant by the question and therefore respond in a way that reflects the shared knowledge.

Although this explanation seems plausible, it implies that people are explicitly "overlooking" or ignoring a distortion, which means that the task would be easier if the listener/question-answerer did not feel obliged to inhibit correcting or noting the distortion. If so, people should find it easier to detect distortions than to ignore them, and people should find it easy to report a distortion when requested to do so. However, experimental research suggests otherwise: People still exhibit the Moses illusion when explicitly instructed to watch out for any distortion in a sentence (Reder & Kusbit, 1991, Exp. 1). Contrary to the conversational postulate, participants found it harder to detect distortions (responded more slowly and made more errors) when asked to detect distortions than when told to ignore any distortion and just answer the *gist* of the question (as dictated by the conversational postulate). Response times were significantly faster in the so-called gist condition than in the literal condition, in which the participants were asked to monitor for and report any distortion in a question.

Other studies have also called the cooperative principle into question (e.g., Bredart & Modolo, 1988; van Oostendorp & de Mul, 1990). In those experiments, participants were not asked to answer the questions but rather to verify the validity of statements. Clearly, in that situation, politely ignoring distortions would not be appropriate. Nonetheless, the illusion was still found.

Imperfect encoding hypothesis

When information is not encoded, it is not processed, and it cannot be used to make decisions. The second explanation of the illusion assumes that people might not carefully listen to or read the distorted element in a question. It is possible that people already know what the questioner is going to ask once they hear a part of a question. The question would then be understood without encoding distorted information presented later in the sentence. In that case, the Ark question might be processed as "How many animals of each kind were taken on the Ark?" Otherwise, perhaps, encoding might be so expectation-driven that people expect to read or hear "Noah" when they begin to process a question that begins with "How many animals of each kind . . ." In other words, is the failure to notice the mismatch due to imperfect encoding?

If the Moses illusion were due to encoding failure of a distorted word, then a manipulation to ensure encoding of distorted information should eliminate it. In order to investigate this possibility, Erickson and Mattson (1981) required participants to read the sentence out loud before answering the question. Despite this requirement, the illusion still occurred. Conceivably this requirement invoked an automatic reading to speech response, but participants were apparently not *really* processing what they were reading. Perhaps the weak encoding hypothesis could be salvaged if participants are shown to process the critical, distorted word less well when they failed to notice the distortion. In a study of Reder and Kusbit (1991, Exp. 4), word-by-word reading times were collected while participants read and answered questions. The results are displayed in Table 15.2. Reading times for distorted words were faster when participants noticed the distortion than when the distortion was ignored. This result is consistent with the result of van Oostendorp and de Mul (1990), in which failures to detect distortions were found to be slower than detections. If reading time for a critical word is an indication of the amount of time spent encoding that word, the imperfect encoding hypothesis would suggest that participants should have read a distorted word faster when the distortion was not noticed than when the distortion was noticed. The results demonstrate that the illusion is not based

Table 15.2 Mean target reading times and proportion of correct and incorrect responses (in parentheses)

	Literal task		Gist task	
	Correct	Errors	Correct	Errors
Normal	525ms (0.79)	515ms (0.21)	429ms (0.82)	618ms (0.18)
Distorted	539ms (0.57)	633ms (0.43)	441ms (0.76)	771ms (0.24)

From "Locus of the Moses Illusion: Imperfect encoding, retrieval, or match?" L. M. Reder and G. W. Kusbit (1991). *Journal of Memory and Language*, *30*, 397. © 1991 Elsevier Science. Adapted with permission of Elsevier Science.

on either encoding failure of the critical word or hasty responding to the question.

Inadequate retrieval hypothesis

Although people correctly encode the distorted question, they might not retrieve the required information to detect the distortion. The information retrieved from memory might be incomplete, sometimes omitting the distorted term, thereby explaining the failure to detect the distortion. For example, people might fall for the Moses question because the retrieved proposition about the number of animals on the Ark would not include the critical information about who took the animals on the Ark. If the illusion were due to imperfect memory retrievals, then one would expect that manipulations improving access to memory should improve detection of distortions as well; however, study results did not support such a notion.

Neither studying nor memorizing the correct version of queried facts before attempting to answer the questions facilitated detection of distortions (Reder & Kusbit, 1991, Exp. 2). Participants studied a series of relevant facts before the questioning, such as "Noah took two animals of each kind on the Ark." Later, after studying half of the facts to be queried, the participants were given half of the questions in their distorted form and half in the undistorted form, making four conditions (studied-distorted, studied-undistorted, not-studied-distorted, not-studied-undistorted) that were crossed with answer instruction types (gist vs literal). Strengthening the memory trace of the correct information should have affected the probability of detecting the distorted term if the illusion were simply based on weak knowledge of the critical term. However, such priming to make relevant information more accessible did not make it easier to detect a mismatch between the underlying information and a distorted question. Participants were just as vulnerable to the illusion after studying the correct information, although the number of wrong answers (e.g., "three" for the Moses question) and "don't know" responses was reduced.

If access to the correct information had affected one's ability to detect mismatches, the gist condition would be expected to suffer relative to the literal condition, because the primed knowledge should make distortions easier to notice and harder to ignore; however, after studying the queried facts prior to answering the questions, participants were much faster and more accurate for studied statements in both conditions. The results reflected an increase in accessibility of relevant knowledge, yet the basic pattern of results was still the same as in other studies: Performance in the literal condition was still slower and less accurate than performance in the gist condition.

Memorizing facts reliably facilitated question answering for undistorted questions both in terms of speed and accuracy of responding; however, a concomitant facilitation was not shown for the distorted questions. This means that the manipulation had an effect, but not the hypothesized effect of reducing susceptibility to the illusion. In sum, given that strengthening the memory trace by familiarizing the relevant knowledge did not reduce the tendency to fall for the illusion, we can reject the imperfect memory retrieval hypothesis as a plausible explanation for the underlying mechanism of the illusion.

Partial match hypothesis

The final explanation we consider suggests that the illusion results from an incomplete or partial match between the probe and the memory structures. That is, as cognitive processors, people make incomplete matches of a complete representation of the question (or memory probe) and a complete representation of the stored proposition that contains the answer. As a question is read, the terms are matched to memory so that the answer may be retrieved. Not every word in the question will be matched exactly to a corresponding memory structure. When the input does not exactly match the memory representation, a term will nonetheless be accepted if it passes a criterion of sufficient match, enabling comprehension. If the degree of match does not reach this criterion, the input query will be regarded as incorrect or incomprehensible. What is the basis for this criterion for comprehension? How much is sufficient to pass the criterion?

With a "game show" paradigm, Reder and her colleagues (Reder & Ritter, 1992; Reder & Schunn, 1996; Schunn, Reder, Nhouyvanisvong, Richards, & Stroffolino, 1997) established that people can erroneously believe that they know the answer to a math problem if it shares features with a problem that they already know. In these experiments, participants were given a math problem, similar to one that they had studied and answered many times in the past, but with the replacement of an operator between the two operands. Thus the correct answer to the altered problem was not available, but the partial match of aspects of the problem led participants to think that it was. This partial match process was modelled within a framework called SAC, for Source of Activation Confusion (Reder & Schunn, 1996; Schunn et al., 1997). This activation-based model of partial matching may represent a prototype for the kind of process involved in question-answering situations that produce the Moses illusion.

It is not unreasonable to think that partial matching might be a general aspect of cognition and as such be a viable explanation for the illusion. Consider, for example, face recognition in a real-world setting. Chances are that a face experienced earlier may be viewed in a different location, with a different expression, and with a different clothes or hairstyle. Despite all of these changes, more likely than not the face will still be recognized.

On the other hand, it would be unreasonable to assume that partial matching would always prevent detection of distortions. For example, it seems likely that people would notice the distortion in a question such as

"How many animals of each kind did Nixon take on the Ark?" Although *Nixon* has the same number of syllables and the same initial phoneme as *Noah*, participants readily noticed the misinformation (Erickson & Mattson, 1981; van Oostendorp & Kok, 1990). While "Nixon" was easy for participants to detect as out of place in that question, not all other names would have the same effect. Then what does affect the detectability of a mismatch? We will consider two proposals, one that the partial match is based on semantic features, and the other that it is based on phonological features.

The case for semantic feature overlap

In the study of Erickson and Mattson (1981), the difficulty of noting a distortion was aggravated when the replaced term in the probe was semantically related to the original term. Erickson and Mattson suggested that a crucial component of the illusion might be the semantic similarity between distorted term and the original term. When the semantic similarity between two terms is high, the replaced term does not seem to flag a mismatch. Conversely, when the semantic similarity between distorted and undistorted terms is low, people more often notice that something is wrong and go on to analyze the critical term in more detail. This, of course, begs the question, in the sense that the original term cannot be in conscious awareness as part of this comparison; if it were, the detection would be trivial. Presumably, this semantic similarity cannot be computed at a lexical level for the two terms.

The view that distortion detection involves a two-pass process – the first to flag a potential mismatch and the second to invoke a careful inspection that might confirm an erroneous term in the question – has support from other types of cognitive tasks. For example, Reder (1987) proposed a two-stage model of question answering that involved strategy selection based on semantic similarity. The first stage consisted of an automatic or implicit evaluation stage in which queries are rapidly assessed for answerability. This initial assessment affects the second stage in which people choose either to search memory in order to answer a question or to base their answer on a plausibility strategy. In the first stage, familiarity and relatedness of terms in the question are evaluated. This assessment is based on semantic relatedness and lexical priming. When the terms seem very familiar (as if the words have been heard recently), people tend to answer the question based on a direct search for the answer; if the terms themselves do not seem as if they were just mentioned, then the question is assessed for general semantic relatedness or familiarity, to decide whether to answer the question in some other way or to decide that it is not answerable.

These ideas may be extendable to question answering for a Moses illusion question. If semantic relatedness among terms in the probe is low, this may suggest the need for further processing before attempting to answer the question. That is, when semantic relatedness between the terms is high, as in the case of the Moses illusion, further processing is less likely to be invoked.

We propose that when a substituted term shares low semantic similarity with an original term, the substitution will be easily detected and thereby cause the checking mechanism to confirm the mismatch. Conversely, substituted terms that bear high semantic similarity to the terms they replace would likely go unnoticed, enabling the adoption of a direct retrieval strategy for finding the answer. Given that *Moses* and *Noah* share many semantic features (e.g., both are central figures in a well-known Biblical story, both stories involved water, they were both old for most of the story, etc.), the substitution of one for the other would likely be undetected. Supporting this suggestion, participants in the study of van Oostendorp and de Mul (1990) frequently failed to notice a distortion when the distorted term was highly semantically related to the original term. Moreover, participants took more time to accurately reject a query in the high semantic similarity condition than in the low semantic similarity condition. This result provides further support that people tend to make more errors when semantic overlap is high and that accurate monitoring of highly semantically related lures is a difficult task.

Semantic cohesion of the critical term with the embedding context or proposition also affects the occurrence of the illusion (van Oostendorp & Kok, 1990). When the distorted terms are totally unrelated to the script that is queried, the discrepancy is readily noticed. On the other hand, when the replaced term is related to the remainder of the proposition or the general context of the query, noticing the distortions is quite difficult. In other words, the more consistent the critical terms in the question are with the script or knowledge structure associated with taking animals on the Ark, the harder it is to notice that the wrong term is used. Moses, a biblical figure, is loosely related to the Ark script, whereas Nixon, a modern politician, is not (Erickson & Mattson, 1981). This is another reason why Moses is frequently accepted in the Ark question, whereas Nixon does not produce (illusory) answers to the question.

Hannon and Daneman (2001) also showed that semantic relatedness of both the words and surrounding context were necessary to elicit semantic illusions such as the Moses illusion. As we mentioned earlier, semantic relatedness might be a function of the number of associations that are shared between two terms. It is more difficult to detect distortions when more terms are related to the theme of the question, suggesting that activation relevant to an answer influences processing of distortions (Reder & Kusbit, 1991). We will discuss this issue in detail in the following section.

Is partial matching based on phonological features?

There is an interesting phenomenon called the "Armstrong illusion" (Shafto & MacKay, 2000) which makes a strong case that a partial matching strategy cannot be based solely on semantic similarity. The Armstrong illusion refers to people's inability to detect the distortion in the question "What was the famous line uttered by Louis Armstrong when he first set foot on the moon?" As in the case of the Moses illusion, people tend to take the question as comprehensible and give an answer to the question, despite knowing that Louis Armstrong was a jazz musician, and that the correct name of the astronaut who visited the moon was Neil Armstrong. Shafto and MacKay argued that the underlying mechanism for the illusion is phonetic similarity between Louis Armstrong and Neil Armstrong, and that phonological input of *Armstrong* and semantic input from the remainder of the question lead to people to overlook the distortion. They went on to argue that the Moses illusion could be explained in the same manner. Although *Moses* is presented in the question, the name *Moses* receives only one source of bottom-up priming from the physical presentation of the name; however the correct, but non-presented name, *Noah* is assumed to receive priming from two sources. The term *Noah* is primed by the terms "Ark" and "animals of each kind" in the question because *Noah* is already pre-associated with those concepts in the Ark script. *Noah* is already primed from the name *Moses* because the two names share many semantic similarities and are strongly associated. That is, although the name actually presented was *Moses*, the name *Noah* receives more priming because of pre-associations in semantic memory and semantic linking between two terms. Since the name *Noah* receives more priming by two convergent priming processes, people often fail to notice that an important term has been replaced. In this framework, the Moses illusion is considered to be the result of miscomprehension of *Moses* as *Noah*.

Further, Shafto and MacKay (2000) proposed that phonetic similarity of a substituted term with an original term primes the original term, thereby facilitating the illusion. While the semantic similarity aspect of their explanation is consistent with experimental results, the phonetic similarity aspect is not. As was mentioned earlier, the name *Nixon*, which is closer phonetically to *Noah* than *Moses*, does not elicit the illusion. Given that phonetic similarity does not always produce the illusion, we need to consider other accounts of the Armstrong illusion. The name "Armstrong" is frequently cited when the topic of the first astronaut who landed on the moon is mentioned. Although the last name is not always needed to identify an individual (e.g., "Elvis") and sometimes the last name is not sufficient to identify an individual (e.g., "Taylor"), the last name is frequently used in a non-familiar context for purposes of identification. Perhaps "Armstrong" boosts the activation of *Neil Armstrong* and semantic cohesiveness of the name, and the remainder of the sentence leads to the illusion due to high-relatedness of the name "Armstrong" and the moon-landing script. The Armstrong illusion by itself could be accommodated by either the phonetic or the semantic partial matching story; however, considering the other data on illusions, it seems that semantic overlap is still the most important factor contributing to the occurrence of the illusion.

Partial match and spreading activation

Let us consider in more detail how much semantic similarity or semantic feature overlap is required between the distorted and original term in order to produce the illusion. One possible mechanism would involve bringing the entire memory trace or schema related to the probed information into working memory. In such a situation, not every term of the memory trace would be carefully matched to the test question before "reading off" the answer. It seems reasonable that this partial matching process could be our default process for memory matching. In most situations the form of a question is not likely to match closely with the memory representation it queries. Slight mismatches would be expected even when the input is a statement rather than a question. Indeed, everything we see is varied from different perspectives, so we need to perform partial matches to recognize virtually anything. Consequently, people are accustomed to being tolerant of discrepancies, and highly similar terms are allowed to slip by or are folded into existing representations. In our view, the normal mode of processing strives to be as effortless as possible, and that includes comprehension.

Partial match is sufficient to retrieve information from memory and is itself an important matching process involved in memory retrieval. The amount of overlap between the working memory representation and the long-term memory structure affects the likelihood of accepting the partial match as sufficient. The degree of acceptable overlap is primarily a function of the amount of activation arriving at the higher-level structure that is being matched (see Reder & Schunn, 1996; Schunn et al., 1997, for more details).

Kamas and Reder (1995) suggested that the Moses illusion might be explained by positing the spreading of activation among related concepts in semantic memory. When a person is asked a question, processes operate on this semantic network in search of the queried element. The more activation that accrues at a concept through its connections to the remainder of the concepts in the question, the more likely the person is to accept the retrieved concept as being acceptable and not a distortion. When a term in the question does not match the stored representation, the probability of detecting this mismatch is a function of the number and strength of connections from the distorted word to the schematic node that is queried. The more connections between the schema and the distorted term, and the stronger those connections, the more likely the distorted term will go undetected. Since Noah and Moses share many features, there would be a large number of connections between Noah and Moses leading the substitution of *Moses* for *Noah* to go unnoticed. In contrast, *Nixon* has no obvious semantic connections with the Noah schema, thereby making the mismatch easier to detect. Further, activation is divided among all the concepts in the probe and is assumed to be finite (e.g., Anderson, Reder, & Lebiere, 1996). Thus a mismatching word with no connections to the remaining concepts in the question (e.g., *Nixon*) takes away activation that could be spread to the relevant script, further facilitating distortion detection.

Hannon and Daneman (2001) proposed that knowledge access regulated processing of the related terms while working memory span regulated processing of the context of the terms involved. In their regression analysis, combined factors of knowledge access for critical terms and working memory span accounted for substantial amount of variance for occurrence of semantic illusion. The portion accounted for by knowledge access was greater than that accounted for by working memory span, further supporting the claim that the illusion is due to semantic similarity.

What affects failure to detect a distortion? Whether or not one assumes that partial matching is the mechanism that causes the Moses illusion, one can still ask what factors modulate the likelihood of a distortion being detected.

Limited cognitive capacity?

Conceivably, our cognitive capacity is sufficiently limited that it is difficult to monitor for distortions. Under the assumption that the process searching for the answer competes with the process searching for distortions in the question, there might not be enough cognitive resources to adequately monitor for distortions. If so, reducing cognitive load by removing the requirement of answering the question, and instead only requiring that distortions be found, might be easier. When participants were required only to monitor for distortions and not to answer the questions, more distorted questions were detected, but there was also an increase in false alarms to undistorted questions (Kamas et al., 1996, Exp. 2). This result suggests that reducing the cognitive demands only affected the response bias, but not participants' ability to detect true distortions.

Failure to focus attention on the relevant terms?

Although the inability to detect distortions seems not to be due to insufficient cognitive capacity, perhaps this cognitive error arises from insufficient attention to the critical terms. Bredart and Modolo (1988) examined whether focus of the sentences affected the Moses illusion, using cleft sentences such as "It was Moses who took two animals of each kind on the Ark" and "It was two animals of each kind that Moses took on the Ark". If the focus of the sentences were to have an effect on the illusion, the illusion rate would have been greater for the statements directing focus on to something other than the distorted information. Participants often noticed the discrepancy when the inconsistent part of the statement was in focus, whereas they were not good at detecting a discrepancy when the consistent part was in focus. With this result, Bredart and Modolo argued that only the terms in the focus of attention were compared to the memory structure, and that attention focus was the factor contributing to the illusion. It is important to note, however, that Bredart and Modolo did not include correct sentences such as "It was Noah who took two animals of each kind on the Ark". Conceivably, in their study too, the manipulation may have affected response bias rather than true sensitivity to the distortions.

Kamas et al. (1996, Exp. 1) tested the same idea as Bredart and Modolo but did include non-distorted versions of each question in order to estimate response bias from the false alarms. They manipulated focus by having participants study the relevant fact before answering the questions and varied which part of the statement was emphasized. Three different types of focus were used, manipulated by the terms that were capitalized in the study sentence: (1) The answer was capitalized (e.g., "Noah took TWO animals of each kind on the ark"); (2) the critical term was capitalized (e.g., "NOAH took two animals of each kind on the ark"); or (3) neither term was capitalized. Participants were significantly *less likely* to notice the distortion if the *answer* had been capitalized during study. On the other hand, emphasizing (capitalizing) the critical word in the study sentence made participants more prone to detect the distortion.

Although these results seem to suggest that the ease of detecting the distortion depends not only on the semantic similarity but also on the amount of attention, the same problem noted earlier occurred here as well. The capitalization manipulation not only increased detection of distortions, but it also increased the error rate for undistorted questions, suggesting that the effect of focus only affects response bias, not sensitivity. A signal-detection analysis confirmed that capitalization of the critical term only affected bias. Moreover the failure of detection of distortions was high even when the distorted word was capitalized (Figure 15.1). Thus, it seems that the cause of the illusion cannot be attributed to insufficient allocation of attention.

In sum, people are not good at adopting an explicit word-by-word checking procedure, and they cannot easily become more vigilant at detecting distortions even when they try very hard. We are left with the conclusion that it is not easy to change the basic nature of the partial match process. The next question to ask is, at what level does the partial match occur?

Word vs feature level for partial matching?

To investigate at which level partial matching occurs, Kamas et al. (1996, Exp. 4) made various types of features of the distorted term salient in a question preceding the critical question phase. Participants were presented with questions that (1) emphasized features shared between the original and distorted terms (e.g., "What religions study the story of Moses?"); (2) emphasized features that distinguished the distorted term from the term it replaced (e.g., "What sea did Moses part?"); or (3) contained irrelevant features to the illusion questions (e.g., "What is the name of the once-outlawed Polish labour union?"). After presenting the primed question, participants

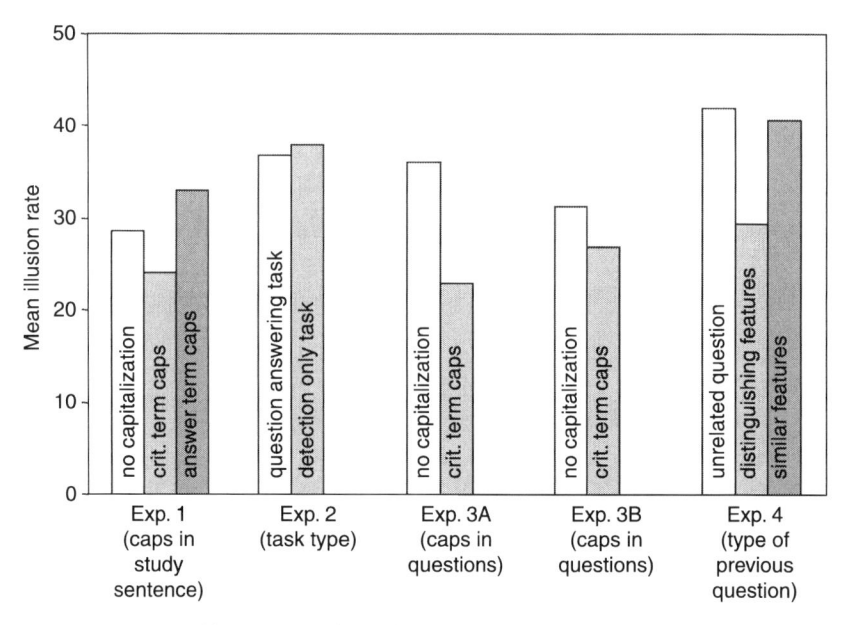

Figure 15.1 Mean illusion rates from four experiments of Kamas et al. (1996) from "Partial matching in the Moses illusion: Response bias not sensitivity" E. N. Kamas, L. M. Reder, and M. S. Ayers (1996) *Memory & Cognition*, 24, 696. © 1996. Psychonomic Society Inc. Reproduced with permission of Psychonomic Society Inc.

were required to answer the critical illusion question. Unlike previously discussed manipulations, detection rates did improve when a preceding question emphasized features that distinguished the original term from its replacement, suggesting that the partial match process operates at the feature level rather than at the word level. It was the focus on the distinguishing features between the original and distorted term that actually improved detection rates as opposed to only affecting response bias.

This result begs the question of why other manipulations at word level did not produce a comparable improvement in detection. It would seem that a manipulation at word level makes more salient both the similar and dissimilar features of the correct and distorted terms, due to their semantic connections in memory. Since the priming at word level does not alter the relative distribution of activation from the word node to its constituent features, the proportion of activation sent from the similar features has not been changed. This explains why the manipulations at the word level did not affect the rate of distortion detection.

In the Moses illusion paradigm, the distorted term shares semantic features with the undistorted term, suggesting that the word is consistent with the basic conceptual representation of the queried information, or at least the features that overlap with it. When the distorted term is activated within the conceptual representation of the question, such as *Moses* in the

Ark question, the distorted term has more chance of being accepted in place of the correct term. Then it can also be predicted that the mere presence of the distorted term will affect the schematic representations for a short period of time. Participants in Kamas et al. (1996) were given a *post-test* to ensure that any failures to detect a distortion were not due to a lack of knowledge of the correct information (e.g., Noah took the animals on the ark). Participants were less likely to give the correct answer on the post-test for those questions that had been distorted during the experiment. Tendency to give the correct answer was not improved by getting the undistorted version as compared with a neutral version (e.g., "How many animals of each kind were taken on the Ark?"). One explanation of this result is that the features of the distorted term were already connected to the schema and that these links were strengthened by the previous experimental presentation (see Reder & Schunn, 1996; Reder, Nhouyvanisvong, Schunn, Ayers, Angstadt, & Hiraki, 2000, for more details). Also it has been shown that participants tend to give a wrong answer to a question that has been primed by a semantically similar one (Kelley & Lindsay, 1993). Potter and Lombardi (1990) also demonstrated that priming of a synonym can cause people to intrude the wrong word in a "verbatim" recall of a recently presented sentence. Of course, we expect all these effects to be short-lived; that is, that the probability of giving the distorted term as a response will decrease with time, as activation decays.

CONCLUSION

Research on the Moses illusion demonstrates that people have difficulty in detecting distortions or inaccuracies when a distorted element is semantically related to the theme of the sentence. Why should our cognitive system be so tolerant of distortions and find it so difficult to do careful matches to memory? It might seem that partial matching is a less-than-ideal way to process information; however, the partial match process is not only common and normal but also a necessary mechanism of our cognitive system. This partial match process enables useful communication and comprehension. Very few things that we see or hear will perfectly match the representation that we already have stored in memory. In order to answer questions, we need to be able to use an acceptable match. In order to understand a new situation and map it onto something we have already seen or done, we must accept slight variations. Every day at many levels, we accept slight distortions without even noticing the process. Occasionally we notice a distortion and choose to ignore it, but more frequently, we do not even realize that distortions have occurred. A rigid comprehension system would have a difficult time indeed. Many of our cognitive operations are driven by familiarity-based heuristics rather than careful matching operations. The Moses illusion is an example of how the adaptive, human cognitive system works. Everyday cognitive processing must be based on simple heuristics such as matching sets of features rather than exact matches, as very few tasks require exact matches. Sentences do not match stored information, faces change, voices may change slightly, even our pets and friends change over time. Therefore it makes sense that people do use partial matches in the normal course of matching to memory. Partial matching is immutable because it is the most efficient way for memory to operate, given the nature of the environment in which we live.

SUMMARY

- When a term in a sentence or a question is replaced with a similar but incorrect term, people have difficulty in detecting the distortion. This is called the Moses illusion.
- The illusion results from a partial match process between the memory probe and the memory representation structures.
- The Moses illusion is an example of how human cognition works in an adaptive and efficient way.

FURTHER READING

Erickson and Mattson (1981) was the first paper to explore the Moses illusion. A comprehensive theoretical account of the illusion and empirical support for the explanation are provided in Reder and Kusbit (1991), and Kamas et al. (1996).

ACKNOWLEDGEMENTS

Preparation of this chapter was supported by Grant 2-R01-MH52808 from the National Institute of Mental Health. We thank Kaia Vilberg for comments on an earlier draft of this chapter.

REFERENCES

Anderson, J. R., & Lebiere, C. (1998). *The atomic components of thoughts.* Mahwah, NJ: Lawrence Erlbaum Associates Inc.

Anderson, J. R., Reder, L. M., & Lebiere, C. (1996). Working memory: Activation limitations on retrieval. *Cognitive Psychology, 30,* 221–256.

Bredart, S., & Modolo, K. (1988). Moses strikes again: Focalization effect on a semantic illusion. *Acta Psychologica, 67,* 135–144.

Erickson, T. A., & Mattson, M. E. (1981). From words to meaning: A semantic illusion. *Journal of Verbal Learning and Verbal Behavior, 20,* 540–552.

Grice, H. P. (1975). Logic and conversation. In P. Cole & J. L. Morgan (Eds.), *Syntax and semantics: Speech acts* (Vol. 3, pp. 41–58). New York: Seminar Press [Originally published from William James Lectures, Harvard University.]

Hannon, B., & Daneman, M. (2001). Susceptibility to semantic illusions: An individual-difference perspective. *Memory & Cognition, 29*, 449–460.

Kamas, E. N., & Reder, L. M. (1995). The role of familiarity in cognitive processing. In R. F. Lorch & E. J. O'Brien (Eds.), *Sources of coherence in reading* (pp. 177–202). Hillsdale, NJ: Lawrence Erlbaum Associates Inc.

Kamas, E. N., Reder, L. M., & Ayers, M. S. (1996). Partial matching in the Moses Illusion: Response bias not sensitivity. *Memory & Cognition, 24*, 687–699.

Kelley, C. M., & Lindsay, D. S. (1993). Remembering mistaken for knowing: Ease of retrieval as a basis for confidence in answers to general knowledge questions. *Journal of Memory and Language, 32*, 1–24.

Potter, M. C., & Lombardi, L. (1990). Regeneration in the short-term recall of sentences. *Journal of Memory and Language, 29*, 633–654.

Reder, L. M. (1987). Strategy selection in question answering. *Cognitive Psychology, 19*, 90–138.

Reder, L. M., & Kusbit, G. W. (1991). Locus of the Moses illusion: Imperfect encoding, retrieval, or match? *Journal of Memory and Language, 30*, 385–406.

Reder, L. M., Nhouyvanisvong, A., Schunn, C. D., Ayers, M. S., Angstadt, P., & Hiraki, K. (2000). A mechanistic account of the mirror effect for word frequency: A computational model of remember–know judgments in a continuous recognition paradigm. *Journal of Experimental Psychology: Learning, Memory, and Cognition, 26*, 294–320.

Reder, L. M., & Ritter, F. (1992). What determines initial feeling of knowing? Familiarity with question terms, not with the answer. *Journal of Experimental Psychology: Learning, Memory, and Cognition, 18*, 435–451.

Reder, L. M., & Schunn, C. D. (1996). Metacognition does not imply awareness: Strategy choice is governed by implicit learning and memory. In L. M. Reder (Ed.), *Implicit memory and metacognition* (pp. 45–77). Hillsdale, NJ: Lawrence Erlbaum Associates Inc.

Schunn, C. D., Reder, L. M., Nhouyvanisvong, A., Richards, D. R., & Stroffolino, P. J. (1997). To calculate or not calculate: A source activation confusion (SAC) model of problem-familarity's role in strategy selection. *Journal of Experimental Psychology: Learning, Memory, and Cognition, 23*, 1–27.

Shafto, M., & MacKay, D. G. (2000). The Moses, Mega-Moses, and Armstrong illusions: Integrating language comprehension and semantic memory. *Psychological Science, 11*, 372–378.

van Oostendorp, H., & de Mul, S. (1990). Moses beats Adam: A semantic relatedness effect on a semantic illusion. *Acta Psychologica, 74*, 35–46.

van Oostendorp, H., & Kok, I. (1990). Failing to notice errors in sentences. *Languages and Cognitive Processes, 5*, 105–113.

16 Orientation illusions in memory

*Gregory V. Jones and
Maryanne Martin*

A few years ago, we observed that many people appear to be subject to a striking mnemonic illusion (Jones & Martin, 1992; Martin & Jones, 1992). They tend systematically to misremember certain spatial orientations. For example, the head depicted on British coins always faces to the viewer's right but, notwithstanding a lifetime's experience of this, the majority of people who were sampled in Britain were found to remember the head as facing to the left (Jones & Martin, 1992). Subsequent research has shown that this illusion is representative of a quite widespread class of distortions in memory for orientation – a set of linked illusions rather than a single illusion – and has begun to shed light on the underlying processes that are responsible.

EXPERIMENT

Unlike some illusions of perception, the distortions of judgement that are manifest in memory for spatial orientation are not usually observed in all individuals. Instead, in common with most other psychological phenomena, they emerge as overall trends within a group. Nevertheless, in some cases – as with the coin-head illusion – the misremembering of spatial orientation may be so firmly established that its unmasking can cause some participants real surprise, scepticism being dispelled only by examining the actual coins in their pockets. It is usually difficult to demonstrate highly unexpected phenomena in the field of autobiographical memory, and thus there is particular interest in investigating illusions of spatial orientation in memory for materials encountered outside the laboratory. Text box 16.1 sketches one possible line of investigation.

If misremembering of spatial orientation is observed, how can it be explained? Recent work shows that there seem to be two principal factors involved. One involves the influence of related but misleading knowledge (cf. Chapter 19), and the other involves the influence of lateralized behaviour in general. These factors are considered here in turn, with misremembering of orientation considered first as an overgeneralization effect and second as a handedness effect.

Text box 16.1 Investigating memory for spatial orientation

Method

Materials

A hazard of studying memory for everyday materials is that their design is often culturally dependent, in which case the stimuli used will also have to differ from place to place. This is certainly true when memory is studied for the appearance of cultural artefacts such as coins. For the present purposes, the simplest option is to select as stimulus a local coin that bears a right-facing head (e.g., any British coin, or the US cent). In some places, however, this option is either not available or at least requires careful specification.

Consider for example the 12 European Community (EC) countries that on 1 January 2002 adopted the euro. These countries issue coins that each have one side that is common to the 12 countries (showing the denomination, a map, and 12 stars – but no head), and another side that is specific to the issuing country. In only a few cases does this country-specific side regularly depict a head – Luxembourg coins always bear the right-facing profile of Grand Duke Henri, and Belgium and the Netherlands always bear the left-facing profiles of King Albert II and Queen Beatrix, respectively. Also relevant are some individual coins of the other nine EC countries – for example, the 1 euro coin of Austria bears the right-facing head of Wolfgang Amadeus Mozart. However, even testing memory for the appearance of, for example, Luxembourg coins is complicated by the fact that the coins from all 12 countries are permitted to circulate freely in each country. Thus instructions for the recall of, say, the Mozart euro in Austria would need to focus specifically on this particular version of the euro coin.

If no suitable coins are available locally, objects bearing right-facing designs may be selected instead from other universally encountered artefacts, such as banknotes, postage stamps, and road signs.

Procedure

For the selected coin or other artefact, the participant is simply asked the direction in which its head faces (i.e., to the viewer's left or the viewer's right). In addition, the handedness of each participant should be elicited, for example by asking which is the hand used for drawing.

Results

Statistical analysis is also straightforward. If responses were the outcome simply of guessing, then the expected numbers of left and right responses would be equal. An excess of right responses is evidence of correct remembering, whereas an excess of left responses is evidence of systematic *mis*remembering – that is, a mnemonic illusion. If l and r are the numbers of participants who are observed to respond that the head faces to the left and to the right, respectively, then statistical analysis focuses on the question of whether these frequencies differ significantly from each other. This may be addressed using a one-sample chi-square analysis in which the observed values, l and r, are compared with the expected value, $(l + r)/2$. This comparison results in the function $(l - r)^2/(l + r)$, whose value may be compared with tabulated values of chi-square with one degree of freedom. If $l > r$, and the significance level indicated by chi-square is less than 0.05, then it may be concluded that systematic misremembering has been observed – that is, performance is at a level below even that to be expected by chance. For example, with a sample of 100 participants, 60 or more left responses would provide significant evidence of misremembering.

If the number of left-handed participants is sufficiently large to make comparisons meaningful, a similar two-sample chi-square analysis can be carried out on the separate results for left-handed and for right-handed participants, to determine whether the two groups differ significantly in susceptibility to the mnemonic illusion.

OVERGENERALIZATION EFFECT

The influence of overgeneralizing on recall of spatial orientation was first noted by Rubin and Kontis (1983). When participants were asked to draw the US cent (together with other US coins), Rubin and Kontis found that the majority of them (62%) portrayed the head of President Lincoln facing to the viewer's left, instead of correctly to the right. Rubin and Kontis pointed out that the different heads on all the other US coins did indeed face to the left. They thus hypothesized that exposure to US coins leads to the formation of a single coin schema whose generic head, dominated by all these other denominations, faces to the left.

The finding of Rubin and Kontis (1983) in the USA was replicated in France by Martin and Jones (1992). As with US coins, the heads on French coins (before their replacement by euro coins in 2002) were generally left-facing, but that of General de Gaulle, on a commemorative 1-franc coin, was right-facing. Of the French participants who said that they did indeed know this coin, a significant majority (68.1%) were nevertheless prey to the mnemonic illusion that de Gaulle faced to the left. In a further experiment, Martin and Jones (1992) provided direct evidence of the role of overgeneralization in this result. Participants unfamiliar with French coins were tested in Britain, with half the participants shown a picture of French coins other than the de Gaulle franc, and half not shown this picture. Participants were asked to hypothesize the direction in which de Gaulle's head would face on a commemorative coin, and it was found that exposure to the picture of other French coins did indeed significantly increase the number of left-facing responses, from 56.5% to 71.3%.

In contrast to the US and French situations, all British coins in circulation bear the head of Queen Elizabeth II facing to the right, and it might be anticipated that in this case the recall of spatial orientation would be veridical.

In fact, however, Jones (1990) found that misremembering was even more severe. In each of three experiments participants drew a British coin, and in each case a significant majority of participants (ranging from 67% to 88%) drew the head facing to the left rather than the right. With the same task, Richardson (1992) found similarly that 70% of profiles were drawn facing incorrectly to the left and in a second experiment, using verbal responses, that 61% were incorrect, again significantly worse than chance (though Kelly, Burton, Kato, & Akamatsu, 2001, failed to observe misremembering in a visual recognition version of the experiment). However, the results with British coins could be explained as the consequence of inappropriate overgeneralization from the orientation of the head not on other coins, but instead on postage stamps. The head on all British stamps faces to the left and stamps, unlike coins, are generally viewed in their canonical orientation (when on envelopes). Jones (1990) therefore proposed that for this population a joint coin–stamp head schema is formed, dominated by input from the viewing of stamps, and leading to the mnemonic illusion that the head faces to the left on British coins.

Thus, by the early 1990s, it appeared that the coin-head illusion was a relatively specific phenomenon that could be attributed solely to inappropriate overgeneralization on the basis of knowledge about related but conflicting spatial materials. If so, the only issues that would remain to be resolved would concern the precise mechanisms by which memory for an object's orientation is influenced by knowledge of other stimuli. For example, work on the way in which people appear to construct situation models has shown that spatial information often fails to be encoded into integrated mental representations unless it is of clear functional significance (Radvansky & Copeland, 2000). It soon transpired, however, that illusions of spatial orientation in memory are more diverse in their origins than had initially been suspected.

Martin and Jones (1995) examined Danish participants' recall of their 20 kroner coin, on which the profile of Queen Margrethe II faced to the viewer's right. If Danish coins carried a head, it always faced to the right, and Danish stamps bore a full-face rather than a profile portrait. In this case, therefore, overgeneralization neither from other coins nor from postage stamps could produce the illusional memory of a left-facing head. Yet Martin and Jones (1995) found that the illusion was still present, with a significant majority (72%) believing incorrectly that the head on the 20 kroner coin faced to the left. Martin and Jones concluded that, in this case at least, the mnemonic illusion must be the product not of overgeneralization but of some other factor, which they identified as handedness.

Portrait asymmetry

Before turning to a consideration of handedness, it should be added that the prior assumptions that lead people to overgeneralize incorrectly when misremembering orientation may derive not from an immediate source such as a set of coins, but instead from a more abstract expectation. There is evidence that portraits in general tend to display more left-facing than right-facing heads, at least in Western European art, and it may be that people's experience of this imbalance influences their remembering of individual portraits on objects such as coins. Examining a large number of portraits by artists, McManus and Humphrey (1973) found that the majority of male subjects, 56%, and an even higher proportion of female subjects, 68%, faced to the viewer's left. What is the origin of this portrait asymmetry? There is some evidence that it derives from the behaviour of the subject rather than that of the artist.

Nicholls, Clode, Wood, and Wood (1999) asked people to adopt a pose that either would portray emotion and would be suitable for giving to members of their family, or would not portray emotion at all and would be suitable for the gallery of the Royal Society. In the emotional condition, they found that the majority of people faced to the viewer's left (59%), whereas in the impassive condition the majority faced to the right (57%). Nicholls et al. thus suggest that the left-facing portrait effect reflects an overall tendency by portrait subjects – stronger among female subjects – to attempt to display emotion rather than to conceal it. However, it has also been argued by David Hockney, the contemporary artist, that for some artists at least (e.g., Caravaggio) the subject's pose is likely to have been reversed by the use of optical aids (Hockney, 2001, pp. 114–119), adding a further twist to the interpretation of whether or not the subject was attempting to display emotion. Nevertheless, the existence of a general tendency for portraits by artists to face to the left, for whatever reason, does provide a further possible basis for incorrect overgeneralization in the recall of orientation.

HANDEDNESS EFFECT: PHENOMENA

Leftward illusion for right-handed people

Attention was first drawn to a hitherto unsuspected factor influencing the orientation illusion in memory by McKelvie and Aikins (1993). They investigated memory for the head of Queen Elizabeth II on the coins of Canada. Canadian postage stamps, unlike British ones, do not generally carry a conflicting head and therefore, as with Denmark, overgeneralization does not provide a reason to expect an orientation illusion to be experienced. Nevertheless, McKelvie and Aikins tested equal numbers of right-handed and left-handed participants in each of two experiments and, combining their results, discovered that the illusion that the head faces to the left was held by significantly more right-handed people (62%) than left-handed people (41%). Subsequent research has confirmed and extended this finding, and started to clarify its origin.

Jones and Martin (1997) similarly examined memory for the head on British coins for equal numbers of right-handed and left-handed participants, and also found that the illusion that the head faces to the left was held by significantly more right-handed (74%) than left-handed (54%) people. The incidences of right-handedness and left-handedness in the general population are typically of the order of 90% and 10%, respectively (see, e.g., McManus, 2002), and thus it may be seen that the figures of 74% and 54% in the preceding sentence imply an overall susceptibility to this illusion in the general population that is of the order of 72% (i.e., 0.9 × 0.74 plus 0.1 × 0.54), consistent with previous findings. In a further experiment, Jones and Martin (1997) examined memory not only for the right-facing head on coins but also for the left-facing head on stamps, with a balanced order of testing. They found for coins that there was a smaller but again significant difference in susceptibility to the orientation illusion, with 66% and 55% of right-handed and left-handed participants, respectively, misremembering the head as facing to the left. For stamps, on the other hand, the head was correctly remembered as facing to the left by the majority of both right-handed participants (71%) and left-handed participants (68%).

Why should right-handed people tend to be more likely than left-handed people to misremember a coin portrait as being left-facing? The responsible effect could be one of two different types. First, an asymmetric, unilateral effect could be influencing the recollections of everyone in a leftward direction, with the influence being merely of greater magnitude for right-handed than for left-handed people. Second, a symmetric, contralateral effect might be influencing the recollections only of right-handed people in a leftward direction, at the same time influencing the recollections of left-handed people in a rightward direction. This latter, contralateral hypothesis implies that it should be possible to detect an illusion which is the converse of that observed by McKelvie and Aikins (1993) and Jones & Martin (1997).

Rightward illusion for left-handed people

The principle of contralaterality suggests that whereas right-handed people were found to be significantly more susceptible to mnemonic illusion than left-handed people when remembering the appearance of a right-facing head on a coin, left-handed people might be more susceptible than right-handed people to misremembering the appearance of a left-facing object. Martin and Jones (1999a) investigated this hypothesis in the context of memory for the appearance of Comet Hale-Bopp, which during 1997 had been clearly visible to the naked eye. Its normal appearance to participants in the sky had been as a head facing to the left and downwards, with a tail trailing behind it (its tail in the evening's northern sky streamed away from the sun towards the east). Participants were asked both to recall and to recognize the appearance of the comet, and it was found as hypothesized that, for both methods, right-handed people remembered the orientation of this stimulus

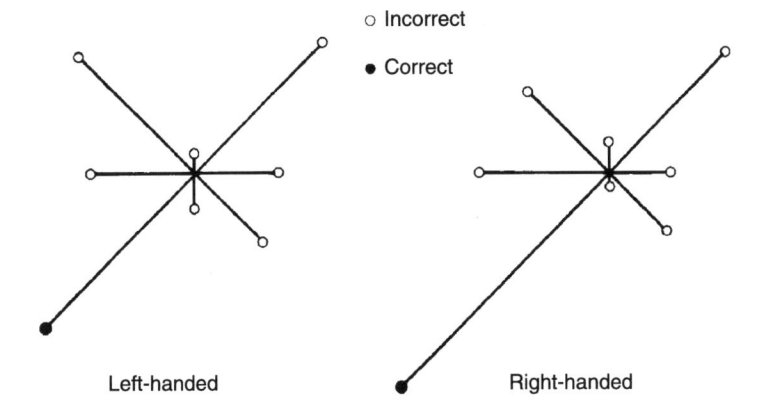

Figure 16.1 Recognition responses (proportional to line lengths) for Comet Hale-Bopp at eight different orientations, for left-handed and for right-handed participants.

significantly more accurately – 40% of right-handed participants, but only 26% of left-handed participants, correctly drew the comet facing down to the left (see Figure 16.1).

As a control, Martin and Jones (1999a) also examined frequency of viewing the comet and semantic memory regarding it (e.g., recall of its name), but found no significant influence of handedness except upon memory for orientation. The study therefore provided evidence that complemented previous findings in supporting a principle of contralaterality in memory for orientation. In addition, the area of application was broadened, because the influence of handedness on memory for orientation was shown to apply not only to the design of a constructed artefact (such as a coin) but also to an entirely natural scene – and, furthermore, a scene that did not involve the human figure.

Contralateral illusions

Is it possible to demonstrate the occurrence of both halves of the contralateral effect within a single experiment? Martin and Jones (1998) examined recall by left-handed people and right-handed people of British road signs showing either a left-facing person (digging, to signal road works) or a right-facing person (walking, to signal a pedestrian crossing). The results provided direct evidence of contralaterality. As with memory for coin-head orientation, the orientation of the right-facing stimulus was significantly more likely to be correctly recalled by the left-handed participants (60%) than by the right-handed participants (48%). In addition, however, the orientation of the left-facing stimulus was significantly more likely to be correctly recalled by the right-handed participants (64%) than by the left-handed participants (44%).

It should be noted that contralaterality is of course not a ubiquitous finding. For example, Nicholls et al. (1999) examined whether the tendency of artists overall (and therefore predominantly right-handed) to depict their subjects as facing to the left was reversed for left-handed artists. They reported evidence that it was not, because the same tendency towards left-facing portraits was observed in the work of two left-handed artists, Raphael (70% leftward) and Hans Holbein the Younger (56% leftward). Instead, as discussed earlier, the portrait effect appears to be driven primarily by the subject of the portrait, rather than by the artist's handedness.

To this point, handedness has been treated implicitly as a binary variable. An alternative approach is to consider handedness as a multivalued variable, and thus Martin and Jones (1998) also assessed participants in terms of a 25-point handedness scale. The results proved to be equivalent to those for the binary variable. Regression analyses showed that people's scores on the handedness scale significantly predicted their accuracy of recall of orientation both for the right-facing stimulus and for the left-facing stimulus, and that these two regression functions possessed gradients of opposite polarity. That is, as handedness moved from left-handed to right-handed, the level of recall of orientation increased for the left-facing stimulus and, contralaterally, decreased for the right-facing stimulus.

The studies considered thus far have focused on the occurrence of spatial illusions within autobiographical memory. They have thus left open the question of whether orientation illusions arise only for material that has been incidentally learned as a result of repeated exposure in the everyday world, or whether they also occur for material presented in a single episode within the laboratory.

Illusion after a single presentation

To explore learning within the laboratory, Martin and Jones (1999b) presented participants with sets of 40 photographs of people's heads in profile, half facing to the left and half to the right. Subsequently participants received a recognition test in which each stimulus was shown alongside its mirror image, and the original item had to be identified. A significant contralateral effect was observed, in that recognition of left-facing heads was 4.1% more accurate for right-handed than for left-handed participants, whereas recognition of right-facing heads was 2.7% more accurate for left-handed than for right-handed participants. The study also provided information on whether the contralateral effect has its origin within memory processing itself, or alternatively as some form of bias within guessing. Participants recorded their confidence in each response on a 5-point scale, and the analysis of the recognition responses was repeated separately for only those responses that had been produced with high or with low confidence. This more detailed analysis showed that the contralateral effect was confined to the high-confidence responses, confirming its mnemonic origin.

HANDEDNESS EFFECT: THEORIES

Hemispheric differences

The finding that a person's handedness has a tendency to influence the accuracy of their recollection of orientation received an explanation first from McKelvie and Aikins (1993). This explanation attributed the finding to differential patterns of processing in the cerebral hemispheres, and takes a form similar to explanations in the field of chimeric perception (e.g., Gilbert & Bakan, 1973; Luh, Redl, & Levy, 1994).

Chimeric perception

Chimeric faces are composed of separate depictions of left and right halves of faces which have been artificially combined. Gilbert and Bakan showed people a series of photographs of faces, in each case asking them to select which of two chimeric faces more closely resembled the original photograph. These two chimeric faces consisted of either the left-hand side of the original photograph and its mirror image, or the right-hand side and its mirror image. With participants who were unselected as to handedness (and hence presumably of the order of 90% right-handed), Gilbert and Bakan found that the chimeric face produced from the left-hand side of the original photograph was selected significantly more frequently than that produced from the right-hand side (e.g., in their Exp. 1, 58% vs 42%, i.e., 16% difference). However, when left-handed and right-handed participants were tested separately (Exp. 4), it was found that although right-handed participants displayed, as expected, a significant tendency to select chimeric images produced from left-hand (rather than right-hand) sides of original photographs (20% difference), left-handed participants displayed a nonsignificant tendency in the opposite direction, towards selecting chimeric images produced from right-hand sides (1% difference).

The explanations that have been offered in terms of hemispheric differences for the handedness effects in chimeric perception (e.g., Gilbert & Bakan, 1973; Luh et al., 1994) and in memory for orientation (e.g., McKelvie & Aikins, 1993) are substantially similar. A crucial but problematic assumption is that visual information arising in the general area to the observer's left (i.e., left *spatial* field) tends to be processed in the right cerebral hemisphere. In addition, it is assumed that the processing of facial information tends also to be localized in the right hemisphere, producing a processing advantage for faces on the viewer's left. Finally, it is assumed that, compared to right-handed people, left-handed people tend to have a lesser degree of cerebral lateralization (or even a reversed lateralization), and thus display a reduced (or even reversed) tendency towards favouring faces that are on the left. It is well established (see McManus, 2002) that left-hemisphere dominance for language is less extensive among left-handed than among right-handed people (approximately 70% and 95%, respectively).

There appears to be little compelling evidence for at least the first assumption of the hemispheric hypothesis – in particular, the existence of an association between left spatial field and right hemisphere does not follow from the well-known linkage between left *visual* field and right hemisphere, because this is normally evinced only under conditions of tachistoscopic presentation and central fixation. For free-vision handedness dependencies, on the other hand, it appears appropriate to consider alternative explanations. We have proposed (e.g., Martin & Jones, 1999b) that these dependencies derive from specific patterns of cerebral motor activation, not from general differences in function between the cerebral hemispheres.

Motor imagery

In recent years, extensive evidence has been amassed that brain processes that are associated with physical movement tend to be activated even when no overt movement is made – the phenomenon of motor imagery (see Jeannerod, 1997). For example, Parsons et al. (1995) demonstrated using positron emission tomography (PET) that areas such as frontal motor cortex, which are activated not only during actual movement but also during imagined movement, are also strongly activated even when participants are merely discriminating between views of left and right hands. Similarly, using functional magnetic resonance imaging (fMRI), Cohen et al. (1996) detected considerable activation of hand somatosensory cortex and premotor cortex when people carried out a mental rotation task, judging whether pairs of angled stimuli were either identical or mirror images.

Clearly, the patterns of motor activation that underlie many typical movements are strongly dependent on handedness, because they are weighted towards controlling the left hand in left-handed people and the right hand in right-handed people. It follows, therefore, that the patterns of motor activation that have been shown to occur even in the absence of physical movement must also differ between left-handed and right-handed people. Our proposal is that it is this difference between characteristic patterns of motor imagery that is responsible for observed effects of handedness in both perception and memory.

It is well established that left-handed and right-handed people tend to depict the same object in different ways. For example, Shanon (1979) asked participants to draw a horizontal line, and found that almost all right-handed people (99%) drew it from left to right, whereas almost all left-handed people (89%) drew it from right to left. For the slightly more complex task of drawing the letter H, again almost all right-handed people (97%) drew its middle bar from left to right, whereas most left-handed people (66%) drew it from right to left. For Shanon's most complex task, of drawing a face in profile, most right-handed people (81%) drew it facing to the left, whereas the majority of left-handed people (56%) drew it facing to the right (as noted earlier, however, Nicholls et al., 1999, did not find a similar tendency in the portraits produced professionally by two left-handed artists). The motor imagery account proposes that these large and stable handedness differences in motor behaviour can influence parallel aspects of perception and memory even in the absence of overt movement. For example, there is an obvious isomorphism between Shanon's results and the finding of Martin and Jones (1999b), described earlier, that recognition of left-facing heads is slightly better for right-handed than for left-handed participants, whereas recognition of right-facing heads is slightly better for left-handed than for right-handed participants.

Martin and Jones (1999b) also compared remembering and drawing within a single experiment, and found the same isomorphism. In addition, the experiment included a mental imagery condition for which, similarly, a majority of right-handed participants (58.9%) reported a left-facing image, whereas a majority of left-handed participants (51.4%) reported a right-facing image. This study had focused on someone whose face would be known to all participants, Diana, Princess of Wales, with testing undertaken several months before her tragic death. Her death in 1997 led to the expression of grief on an unprecedented scale, and over a million bouquets of flowers were placed at her residence, Kensington Palace, and other London locations. There was an accidental, indirect relevance to the laboratory study, because of the production of a large number of pictures of the late Princess. Particularly moving were the hand-drawn pictures, poems, and other mementos often placed with the flowers. When a series of such pictures were viewed, it was found that the proportion facing to the left, as opposed to the right, was 79%. Since the people creating the pictures were presumably of the order of 90% right-handed, it is apparent that the same contralateral relation was manifest in spontaneous, unprompted circumstances as was found in a laboratory study. Furthermore, this relation could not be attributed to mirroring of the very large numbers of photographs of the Princess which appeared at that time in the media, because a sample of these showed that their proportions of left-facing and right-facing photographs did not differ significantly.

The way in which orientation information is processed at the neural level, important for exploring how it may be influenced by patterns of motor activation, is as yet not fully understood. However, work that has been carried out within cognitive neuropsychology suggests that the processing of orientation may be distinct from that of other forms of visual information. Thus Warrington and Davidoff (2000) have described the case of a patient (JBA) with probable Alzheimer's disease, who displayed a paradoxical relation between identification and orientation processes. The patient was shown a picture of an object that was accompanied either by an identical picture or else by its mirror image, and asked both to identify the object and to decide whether or not the second picture was identical. When the object was correctly identified, 64% of orientation decisions were correct, but when identification was incorrect, the accuracy of the orientation decisions improved to 94%. Warrington and Davidoff interpreted this finding in terms of cortically distant systems which are dedicated to identification and positioning processes, and which possess a relationship of reciprocal inhibition.

Object identification

Viggiano and Vannucci (2002) have shown that the motor imagery hypothesis is also helpful in understanding object identification. In their first experiment, they asked participants to draw a wide range of objects whose names were mainly taken from the widely used set of pictures provided by Snodgrass and Vanderwart (1980). They found that mobile objects (namely, animals and vehicles) were mostly drawn facing to the left by right-handed participants (71% and 58%, respectively) but drawn facing to the right by left-handed participants (65% and 66%, respectively), whereas there were no significant differences in directionality for immobile objects (namely, vegetables, tools, and furniture).

In their second experiment, Viggiano and Vannucci compared the visual identification of fragmented versions of Snodgrass pictures of mobile objects (animals and vehicles) and immobile objects (tools and furniture). Each fragmented picture was presented in three ascending levels of completeness, and both threshold level and reaction time for correct identification were recorded (see Viggiano & Kutas, 2000). With mobile objects, it was found that for right-handed participants the mean reaction time was approximately 26 ms less for left-facing than for right-facing objects, whereas for left-handed participants it was approximately 35 ms less for right-facing than for left-facing objects; for immobile objects, there was no significant effect. In addition to the significant contralateral handedness effect on reaction times for the identification of mobile objects, for the sub-category of animals there was also a significant effect on threshold level, with right-handed participants identifying left-facing animals at a lower level than right-facing animals (with no significant difference for left-handed participants). The authors concluded that motor imagery provides the underlying link to explain the isomorphic effects of handedness on object drawing and object identification:

> According to the Motor Image Theory (Jeannerod, 1997; Martin & Jones, 1999b), the same neural system should be activated in different tasks that require the manipulation, identification or memory recognition of the same visual object. Our main result is that mental representations, involved in motor acts such as object drawing and visual processes such as object identification, contain a description of the directionality of object relevant elements.
>
> (Viggiano & Vannucci, 2002, p. 1485)

Writing system

The motor imagery hypothesis suggests the possibility of detecting the influence upon perception and memory of habitual patterns of motor behaviour other than those associated with the factor of handedness. Another such factor is that of writing system. As an example, Gilbert and Bakan (1973) were helped by Daniel Kahneman – later to be 2002 Nobel laureate for Economics – to examine in their Experiment 3 chimeric perception among people (unselected as to handedness) who were native readers of Hebrew (a language that is written from right to left, as opposed to the left to right of English). For the same set of stimuli, the magnitude of the tendency to match an original face with the chimeric image produced from its left-hand side rather than its right-hand side (i.e., left matches minus right matches) was found for users of English to be 21%, but for users of Hebrew to be only 9%.

In another study of the effect on spatial processing of reading and writing behaviour, Chokron and De Agostini (2000) examined choice between mirror-image pairs of pictures in terms of how aesthetically pleasing or interesting they were to look at. The pictures portrayed either moving directional objects (e.g., a vehicle), static directional objects (e.g., a statue), or landscapes; all participants were right-handed. Chokron and De Agostini found that for both types of directional picture, on the majority of occasions adult French participants preferred right-facing objects (62%), whereas adult Israeli participants preferred left-facing objects (60%); for landscapes, both groups displayed some preference for pictures with their most important features on the right side. This pattern of empirical contralaterality accords well with the predictions of the motor imagery hypothesis, but again is difficult to reconcile with an interpretation in terms of hemispheric differences: "There is neither experimental nor clinical argument for a reverse pattern of cerebral lateralization in subjects with opposite reading habits" (Chokron & De Agostini, 2000, p. 48).

An incidental observation is that the rightward direction of aesthetic preference of French participants in the study of Chokron and De Agostini contrasts with the leftward direction of memory misremembering observed in 1992 by Martin and Jones, also for French participants who were presumably predominantly right-handed, since unselected as to handedness. This contrast is a natural consequence of the fact that the way in which motor imagery is utilized is expected to be task-dependent. It may be, for example, that contralateral tendencies tend to be positively weighted when the task is to remember previous stimuli, but negatively weighted when the task is to seek interesting new stimuli. This interpretation will remain speculative, however, until a broader range of tasks has been examined.

SUMMARY

- The evidence reviewed here shows that our processing of information concerning spatial orientation is subject to subtle patterns of modulation which can result in systematic misremembering.
- At least two major kinds of influence on memory for orientation can be distinguished.
- The first type takes the form of overgeneralization, the incorporation of conflicting knowledge about contrasting (or broader) stimulus categories.
- The second type is associated with variation in handedness, where contralateral tendencies in the recall of orientation appear to be underlain by asymmetric patterns of motor imagery.

FURTHER READING

An interesting review of one area of research into memory for spatial orientation was provided by Richardson (1993). McKelvie and Aikins (1993) pioneered investigation of the link with handedness, examined from a range of perspectives by McManus (2002). Recent work has demonstrated unexpected asymmetries with regard to left–right spatial orientation in a number of other areas of human behaviour, ranging from walking (Scharine & McBeath, 2002) to embracing (Güntürkün, 2003).

ACKNOWLEDGEMENT

Research support has been provided by ESRC (UK) Grant R000236216.

REFERENCES

Chokron, S., & De Agostini, M. (2000). Reading habits influence aesthetic preference. *Cognitive Brain Research*, *10*, 45–49.

Cohen, M. S., Kosslyn, S. M., Breiter, H. C., DiGirolamo, G. J., Thompson, W. L., Anderson, A. K. et al. (1996). Changes in cortical activity during mental rotation: A mapping study using functional MRI. *Brain*, *119*, 89–100.

Gilbert, C., & Bakan, P. (1973). Visual asymmetry in the perception of faces. *Neuropsychologia*, *11*, 355–362.

Güntürkün, O. (2003). Adult persistence of head-turning asymmetry. *Nature*, *421*, 711, & *422*, 834.

Hockney, D. (2001). *Secret knowledge: Rediscovering the lost techniques of the Old Masters*. London: Thames & Hudson.

Jeannerod, M. (1997). *The cognitive neuroscience of action*. Oxford: Blackwell.

Jones, G. V. (1990). Misremembering a common object: When left is not right. *Memory & Cognition*, *18*, 174–182.

Jones, G. V., & Martin, M. (1992). Misremembering a familiar object: Mnemonic illusion, not drawing bias. *Memory & Cognition, 20*, 211–213.

Jones, G. V., & Martin, M. (1997). Handedness dependency in recall from everyday memory. *British Journal of Psychology, 88*, 609–619.

Kelly, S. W., Burton, A. M., Kato, T., & Akamatsu, S. (2001). Incidental learning of real-world regularities. *Psychological Science, 12*, 86–89.

Luh, K. E., Redl, J., & Levy, J. (1994). Left- and right-handers see people differently: Free-vision perceptual asymmetries for chimeric stimuli. *Brain and Cognition, 25*, 141–160.

Martin, M., & Jones, G. V. (1992). Exploring a mnemonic illusion: When does General de Gaulle turn to the left? *Cahiers de Psychologie Cognitive, 12*, 103–113.

Martin, M., & Jones, G. V. (1995). Danegeld remembered: Taxing further the coin head illusion. *Memory, 3*, 97–104.

Martin, M., & Jones, G. V. (1998). Generalizing everyday memory: Signs and handedness. *Memory & Cognition, 26*, 193–200.

Martin, M., & Jones, G. V. (1999a). Hale-Bopp and handedness: Individual differences in memory for orientation. *Psychological Science, 10*, 267–270.

Martin, M., & Jones, G. V. (1999b). Motor imagery theory of a contralateral handedness effect in recognition memory: Toward a chiral psychology of cognition. *Journal of Experimental Psychology: General, 128*, 265–282.

McKelvie, S. J., & Aikins, S. (1993). Why is coin head orientation misremembered? Tests of schema interference and handedness hypotheses. *British Journal of Psychology, 84*, 355–363.

McManus, C. (2002). *Right hand, left hand*. London: Weidenfeld & Nicolson.

McManus, I. C., & Humphrey, N. K. (1973). Turning the left cheek. *Nature, 243*, 271–272.

Nicholls, M. E. R., Clode, D., Wood, S. J., & Wood, A. G. (1999). Laterality of expression in portraiture: Putting your best cheek forward. *Proceedings of the Royal Society of London, Series B, 266*, 1517–1522.

Parsons, L. M., Fox, P. T., Downs, J. H., Glass, T., Hirsch, T. B., Martin, C. C. et al. (1995). Use of implicit motor imagery for visual shape-discrimination as revealed by PET. *Nature, 375*, 54–58.

Radvansky, G. A., & Copeland, D. E. (2000). Functionality and spatial relations in memory and language. *Memory & Cognition, 28*, 987–992.

Richardson, J. T. E. (1992). Remembering the appearance of familiar objects: A study of monarchic memory. *Bulletin of the Psychonomic Society, 30*, 389–392.

Richardson, J. T. E. (1993). The curious case of coins: Remembering the appearance of familiar objects. *The Psychologist, 6*, 360–366.

Rubin, D. C., & Kontis, T. C. (1983). A schema for common cents. *Memory & Cognition, 11*, 335–341.

Scharine, A. A., & McBeath, M. K. (2002). Right-handers and Americans favor turning to the right. *Human Factors, 44*, 248–256.

Shanon, B. (1979). Graphological patterns as a function of handedness and culture. *Neuropsychologia, 17*, 457–465.

Snodgrass, J. G., & Vanderwart, M. (1980). A standardized set of 260 pictures: Norms for name agreement, image agreement, familiarity, and visual complexity. *Journal of Experimental Psychology: Human Learning and Memory, 6*, 174–215.

Viggiano, M. P., & Kutas, M. (2000). Overt and covert identification of fragmented objects inferred from performance and electrophysiological measures. *Journal of Experimental Psychology: General, 129,* 107–125.

Viggiano, M. P., & Vannucci, M. (2002). Drawing and identifying objects in relation to semantic category and handedness. *Neuropsychologia, 40,* 1482–1487.

Warrington, E. K., & Davidoff, J. (2000). Failure at object identification improves mirror image matching. *Neuropsychologia, 38,* 1229–1234.

17 Associative memory illusions

Henry L. Roediger III and
David A. Gallo

Distortions of memory arise from many causes. Several types of memory illusions reviewed in this volume are created from external sources. In recollecting some target event from the past, people will often confuse events that happened before or after the target event with the event itself. (These confusions are examples of proactive and retroactive interference, respectively.) On the other hand, the illusion described in this chapter involves the remembering of events that never actually occurred. This erroneous information is internally created by processes that would otherwise lead to good memory for actual events. As such, these errors are part and parcel of the natural memory process, and they are extremely difficult to avoid. Although most of the research reviewed here involves a tightly controlled laboratory paradigm using word lists, we believe (and will cite evidence to support) the claim that similar processes occur whenever people try to comprehend the world around them – reading a newspaper or novel, watching television, or even perceiving scenes with little verbal encoding at all (Roediger & McDermott, 2000b).

THE ASSOCIATIVE TRADITION

Scholars have always assumed that memory is fundamentally associative in nature. The associative doctrine maintains that mental processes and phenomena can be explained by invisible bonds – associations – that link basic mental representations. Some 2300 years ago Aristotle (384–322 BC) theorized in *De Memoria et Reminiscentia* that "acts of recollection, as they occur in experience, are due to the fact that one movement [that is, one thought] has by nature another that succeeds it in regular order." Associationism became a more formal theory in the work of the great British associationists Thomas Hobbes, John Locke, and David Hartley, among others, in the 17th and 18th centuries. Hobbes wrote of the "trayne of thoughts" and Locke proposed "the association of ideas" as a fundamental mental mechanism, whereas Hartley tried to provide a physiological explanation of associations (see Roediger, McDermott, & Robinson, 1998, for a fuller discussion).

Early experimental psychologists drew on associative ideas for experimental inspiration. Hermann Ebbinghaus's pioneering memory studies, published in his monograph *On Memory* (1885/1913), assumed that memories were retained through associative chains. His methodology (serial anticipation learning) helped to uncover the mechanisms of direct and remote associations. Several years later, Mary Calkins developed the paired-associate learning technique to directly measure the formation of associations. Even pioneers of research on animal learning, such as Edward Thorndike and Ivan Pavlov, assumed that the process was fundamentally associative. There was really no competing theory.

Modern work in human memory has continued this associative tradition. John Anderson published several theories (e.g., Free Recall by Associative Nets and Human Associative Memory; FRAN and HAM, respectively) with an unabashedly associative character in the early 1970s. In the 1980s, Jeroen Raiijmakers and Richard Shiffrin proposed the highly influential model SAM – Search of Associative Memory – which also relies heavily on the associative nature of memory (see also SARA in Chapter 20 of this volume), as do all of the connectionist theories (such as those initially proposed by David Rumelhart and James McClelland and colleagues) that are currently in vogue in areas of computational modelling and artificial intelligence.

In all these theories, associations are viewed as a powerful positive force to support remembering – the stronger the associative bond between two elements, the more probable is retrieval of the second element when given the first as a cue. The idea that associative connections might have a dark side – that they may lead to errors of memory – has hardly ever been considered. However, the point of this chapter is that memory distortions can indeed be induced by associative means.

As far as we know, this idea was first suggested, quite offhandedly, in a paper by Kirkpatrick (1894). Kirkpatrick was interested in whether items presented as visual objects were better retained than those presented as words, but his side observations are of interest for present purposes and worth quoting:

> About a week previously in experimenting upon mental imagery I had pronounced to the students ten common words . . . it appears that when such words as "spool," "thimble" and "knife" were pronounced many students at once thought of "thread," "needle," and "fork," which are so frequently associated with them. The result was that many gave those words as belonging to the list. This is an excellent illustration of how things suggested to a person by an experience may be honestly reported by him as part of the experience.
>
> (Kirkpatrick, 1894, p. 608)

Associative memory illusions

The process described by Kirkpatrick is the topic of this chapter, how items associated to presented items are often actually remembered as having been overtly presented (rather than inferred covertly). Underwood (1965) suggested the same idea many years later and showed that if a word such as *table* were presented in a list, participants would be somewhat more likely to falsely recognize an associated word such as *chair* in a later test (than if *table* had not been in the list). Underwood's effect was quite small, however, and the technique presented in the next section produces much more robust effects. Indeed, false recognition can sometimes be more likely than true recognition when elicited by this newer technique. A simplified version of such an experiment that can be used as a classroom demonstration is described in Text box 17.1.

Text box 17.1 Classroom demonstration

This demonstration can be used to create false memories in only a few minutes. For best results, participants should not be told that the demonstration is on false memories until after the experiment.

Material

The material consists of four lists with 15 words each that are all associated to a critical, but not included, target word.

List 1: *bed, rest, awake, tired, dream, wake, snooze, blanket, doze, slumber, snore, nap, peace, yawn, drowsy.*
List 2: *door, glass, pane, shade, ledge, sill, house, open, curtain, frame, view, breeze, sash, screen, shutter.*
List 3: *nurse, sick, lawyer, medicine, health, hospital, dentist, physician, ill, patient, office, stethoscope, surgeon, clinic, cure.*
List 4: *sour, candy, sugar, bitter, good, taste, tooth, nice, honey, soda, chocolate, heart, cake, tart, pie.*

The critical target words are *sleep, window, doctor,* and *sweet*, respectively.

Procedure

The experimenter tells the participants that this will be a memory demonstration, and that they should have a piece of scrap paper and a pen ready for the memory test. The experimenter then tells them that s/he will read lists of words, and that they should try to remember these words. The participants should not be allowed to write the words down as they are being read. The experimenter then reads the first list, at a steady rate of one word every 1 to 2 seconds. After the final word, the participants are asked to write down as many words as they can remember, in any order, without guessing. Participants usually take less than a minute to recall each list. This procedure is then repeated for the next three lists.

Analysis

After the final list is recalled, the experimenter counts separately for each list the number of participants (by having them raise their hands or by tallying the recall sheets) who recalled the critical word. As these critical associates were never presented, their recall represents false memories.

SAMPLE EXPERIMENT: THE DRM PARADIGM

Roediger and McDermott (1995) adapted a paradigm first used by Deese (1959) for a somewhat different purpose. The paradigm produces a very strong associative memory illusion and (owing to a suggestion by Endel Tulving) is now called the DRM paradigm (for Deese-Roediger-McDermott). The paradigm and variants of it are frequently used as a straightforward technique for gaining measures of both veridical and false memories using both recall and recognition techniques. We describe a somewhat simplified version of Experiment 2 in Roediger and McDermott (1995).

Typical method

A set of 24 associative lists were developed, each list being the 15 strongest associates to a nonstudied word, as found in word association norms. These norms are based on a free association task, in which participants were presented a stimulus word (e.g., *rough*) and told to generate the first word that comes to mind. To create each of our lists, we took the 15 words that had been elicited most often by the stimulus word (e.g., the words *smooth, bumpy, road, tough, sandpaper, jagged, ready, coarse, uneven, riders, rugged, sand, boards, ground,* and *gravel*; see Stadler, Roediger, & McDermott, 1999, for a set of 36 lists with normative false recall and recognition data). These study lists were presented to new participants, and their memory was subsequently tested. Critically, the stimulus word (*rough* in this case) was never studied by these participants. Our interest centred on the possible false recall or false recognition of this critical word. If a participant were like a computer or tape recorder, recording and retrieving the words perfectly, one would not expect such systematic memory errors.

A total of 30 undergraduate participants were auditorily presented with 16 of the 24 word lists, one word at a time. Participants recalled half of the lists immediately after their presentation (with 2 minutes provided for recall), and they were instructed not to guess but only to recall the words they were reasonably sure had been in the list. They performed arithmetic problems for 2 minutes after each of the other lists. Shortly after all 16 of the lists had been presented in this way, participants took a yes/no recognition test that covered all 24 lists. Because only 16 lists had been studied, items from the other 8 lists served as lures or distractors to which participants should respond "no" (it was not on the list). The recognition test was composed of 96 words, with 48 having been studied and 48 new words. Importantly, 16 of these new words were the critical missing lures (words like *rough*) that were strongly associated to the studied words.

After each word that they recognized as having been in the list (the ones judged "yes"), participants made a second judgement. They were asked to judge whether they remembered the moment of occurrence of the word in the list – say by being able to remember the word before or after it – what they were thinking when they heard the word, or some other specific detail. This is called a *remember* judgement and is thought to reflect the human ability to mentally travel back in time and re-experience events cognitively. If they were sure the word had been in the list, perhaps because it was highly familiar, but could not remember its specific moment of occurrence, they were told to make a *know* judgement. The remember/know procedure was developed by Endel Tulving in 1985, and has since been used by many researchers in order to measure the phenomenal basis of recognition judgements (see Gardiner & Richardson-Klavehn, 2000, for an overview).

Typical results

Let us consider the immediate free recall results first. Recall of list items followed the typical serial position curve, with marked primacy and recency effects reflecting good recall at the beginning (primacy) and end (recency) of the list. Consider next false recall of the critical nonpresented word such as *rough* (in our sample list used above). Despite the fact that recall occurred immediately after each list and participants were told not to guess, they still recalled the critical nonpresented item 55% of the time. In this experiment, recall of the critical nonpresented item was actually higher than recall of the items that were presented in the middle of the list. In other studies, the probability of recall of critical items often approximates recall of items in the middle of the list, with the particular outcome depending on such factors as presentation rate of the lists (1.5 seconds in this study) and whether the lists are presented auditorily or visually. The important point is that false recall was very high.

The recognition test also revealed a powerful associative memory illusion. The basic data are presented in Figure 17.1. Shown in the two panels are data from the eight lists that were studied and recalled (the right panel) and from the eight lists that were studied but not previously recalled. Within each panel, the left bar shows veridical or true recognition (the hit rate) of items actually studied, whereas the right bar shows false recognition of the critical lures like *rough* (the critical-lure false alarm rate). The false alarm rates to the items from the eight nonstudied lists that appeared on the test are given in the figure caption. Finally, each bar is divided into a dark portion (items called old and judged to be *remembered*) and a white portion (items called old and judged to be *known*).

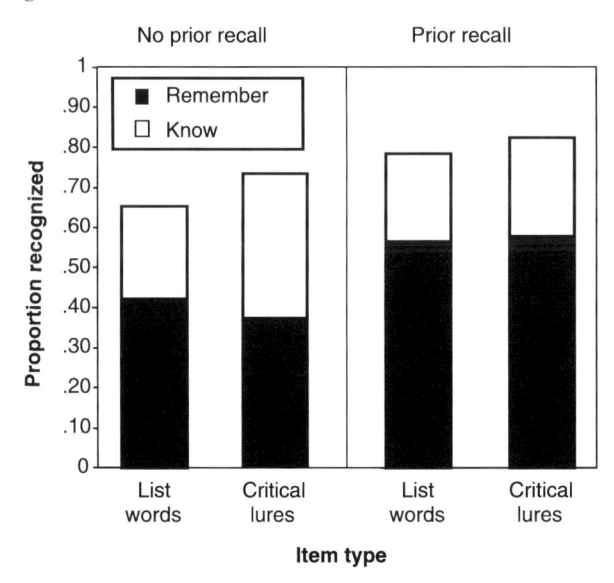

Figure 17.1 The DRM false-recognition effect (Roediger & McDermott, 1995, Exp. 2). False recognition of critical lures approximated the hit rate for list items. False alarms to list words from nonstudied lists were 0.11, and those to critical words from nonstudied lists were 0.16.

Figure 17.1 shows the very large false recognition effect that is typical of the DRM paradigm. For example, for lists that were studied and had been recalled, participants recognized 79% of the list words as old and said they remembered 57% of the words. Nearly three-quarters of the words called old were judged to be remembered (i.e., 57/79 = 72%). Surprisingly, the data for the critical lures (which, again, were not actually presented) were practically the same! Participants recognized 81% as old and even judged 58% *remembered*; and, just as for studied words, 72% of the words judged old were remembered (58/81 = 72%). So, in the DRM paradigm, the level of false recognition and false remembering is about the same as veridical recognition and remembering of list words. The situation is much the same for the lists that were studied but not recalled, with false recognition of critical lures being as high as (or even higher than) veridical recognition of list words. Note, however, that remember judgements were lower on the recognition test (for both kinds of items) when the lists had not been recalled. In some ways, the data in the left panel show effects of recognition that are "purer" in that they were not contaminated by prior false recall. Nonetheless, striking levels of false recognition and "remember" judgements were obtained.

Discussion

Perhaps because the effect is so robust, a sceptical reaction after learning about the effect is common: Participants are obviously not trying to remember at all. Instead, this reasoning continues, participants are faced with too many words to remember, and so make educated guesses as to which words were presented. In particular, they realize that the lists consist of associated items, so they infer that critical items (which are associated to the study lists) were also presented. Miller and Wolford (1999) formalized this sort of decision process in terms of a liberal criterion shift to any test word that is perceived as related to the study list (i.e., the critical items). This model was primarily directed at false recognition, although a generate/recognize component was included to account for false recall. In either case, it is assumed that participants try to capitalize on the related nature of the lists (via some sort of liberal criterion to related items), in the hopes of facilitating their memory for studied words.

Gallo, Roediger, and McDermott (2001) directly tested this account by informing participants about the illusion and telling them to avoid false recognition of nonstudied but related words. The critical condition was when participants were warned between study of the lists and the recognition test, thereby precluding a liberal guessing strategy for related items. The results were straightforward: Warning participants between study and test had negligible effects on false recognition (relative to a no-warning control condition), even though other conditions revealed that warned participants were trying to avoid false recognition. This pattern is also obtained in false recall (e.g., Neuschatz, Payne, Lampinen, & Toglia, 2001). Gallo et al. (2001) reasoned that warned participants did not adopt a liberal strategy to related items because, after all, they were trying to avoid false alarms to these items. Thus, robust false memory effects following warnings were not due to such strategic decision processes alone, but instead were due to processes that are inherent in the memory system. This conclusion is bolstered by the finding that participants will often claim that these false memories are subjectively detailed and compelling (as reviewed below).

In sum, the DRM paradigm produces very high levels of false recall, false recognition, and false remembering, as great as any memory illusion ever studied. As noted above, similar associatively based errors have been obtained using a wide variety of materials, including pictures, sentences, and stories, although these errors are usually not as frequent as those observed in the DRM paradigm (see Roediger & McDermott, 2000a, 2000b, for an overview). In general, any set of materials that strongly implies the presence of some object or event that is not actually presented lends itself to producing false recall and false recognition of the missing but implied event (cf. Chapter 19 on the misinformation effect). Why, then, are the false memories produced by the DRM paradigm so robust?

There are several answers to this question, but we will concentrate on the most critical one: the number of associated events that are studied. The DRM paradigm, in contrast to most other memory illusions, relies on the presentation of multiple associates to the critical nonstudied word, thereby taking full advantage of the power of associations. Robinson and Roediger (1997) directly examined the effect of number of associated words on false recall and false recognition. In one experiment, they presented participants with lists of 15 words prior to recall and recognition tests, but the number of words associated to a critical missing word was varied to be 3, 6, 9, 12, or 15. Increasing numbers of associated words steadily increased false recall of the critical nonpresented word, from 3% (with 3 words) to 30% (with 15 words). (A similar increase was found in false recognition.) Thus, even though the total number of words studied was the same in all conditions, the number of studied associates to the critical word had a considerable influence on the strength of this memory illusion. We discuss the theoretical implications of this finding in the next section.

THEORIES AND DATA

In this section we consider the processes that may be involved and how they might interact to give rise to the associative false-recognition effect. This discussion is divided into two main sections: processes that cause the effect and opposing processes that reduce the effect. Our goal is not to exhaustively review all of the DRM findings – that would be well beyond the scope of this chapter. Rather, we highlight the main theoretical issues and discuss those DRM findings that we feel critically inform these issues. In many instances, more than one group of researchers reported relevant findings, but for brevity we cite only one or two findings to illustrate the point.

Processes that cause the effect

The dominant theories of the DRM effect fall into two classes: *association-based* and *similarity-based*. These classes differ in the types of information or representation that is proposed to cause false remembering (and in terms of the processes that allegedly give rise to these representations). Nevertheless, these theories are not mutually exclusive, and evidence suggests that both types of mechanism make a unique contribution to the effect. We discuss each in turn, followed by a brief consideration of attribution processes that may contribute to the subjectively detailed nature of associative false memories.

Association-based theories

According to the association-based theories, a pre-existing representation of the critical nonpresented word becomes activated when its associates are

Associative memory illusions 317

presented. Thus, presenting *bed, rest, awake* etc. activates the mental representation of the word *sleep*. Under this theory, false remembering occurs when the participant mistakes associative activation with actual presentation, which can be conceptualized as a reality-monitoring error (Johnson, Hashtroudi, & Lindsay, 1993). This theory uses Underwood's (1965) classic idea of the implicit associative response (IAR), and is consistent with Deese's (1959) finding that the degree of association between the list words and the critical nonpresented word (dubbed Backward Associative Strength, or BAS) was highly predictive of false recall. That is, the more items in the list have the critical item as an associate (BAS), the more likely the list is to produce false recollection.

Deese's (1959) finding was recently replicated and extended by Roediger, Watson, McDermott, and Gallo (2001) who reported that BAS predicted most of the variance in false recall (among several candidate variables) using multiple regression analysis. A scatterplot illustrating the relationship between false recall and BAS is presented in Figure 17.2. Roediger et al. (2001) interpreted this relationship as evidence for associative activation. The notion is that associates activate the lexical representation of the critical word, and this activation supports the thought of the item on a recall test. They also found that BAS was related to false recognition, suggesting that activation might be a common cause of false recall and false recognition, although the differences in recognition tend to be somewhat smaller than

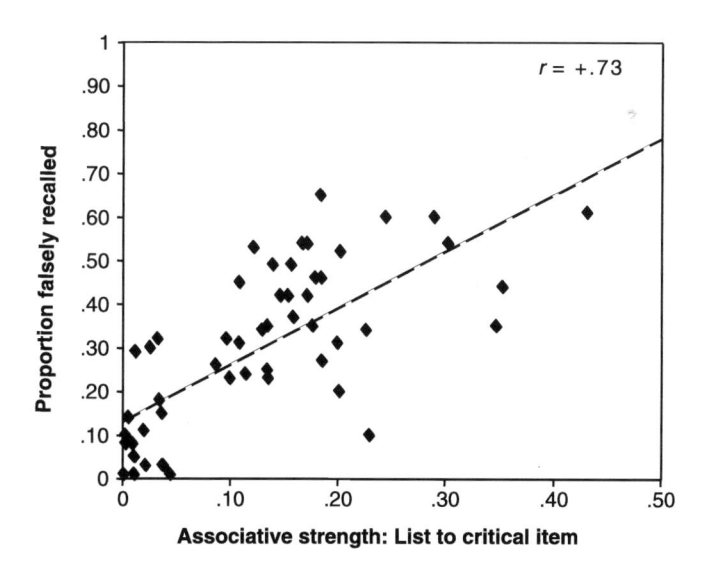

Figure 17.2 Scatterplot of the relationship between false recall and backward associative strength across 55 DRM lists. Backward associative strength refers to the tendency of list items to elicit the critical item in free association norms. The dashed line illustrates the strong positive correlation (see Roediger et al., 2001).

those found in recall (see Gallo & Roediger, 2002). The aforementioned list-length effect (e.g., Robinson & Roediger, 1997) is also consistent with an associative activation mechanism: increasing the number of associates studied increases associative activation, and hence increases false recall and recognition.

Two obvious questions concern the form of this activation (conscious or nonconscious?) and when it occurs (study or test?). The fact that false recall and false recognition occur even with very rapid study presentation rates (under 40 ms per item, or less than a second per list) suggests that conscious thoughts of the critical item during study are not necessary to elicit false memory (see McDermott & Watson, 2001, for recall evidence, and Seamon, Luo, & Gallo, 1998, for recognition evidence). This is consistent with semantic priming models, which suggest that associative activation at study can automatically spread from one word node to another (see Roediger, Balota, & Watson, 2001). However, just because conscious thoughts of the critical item may not be necessary to elicit false remembering does not imply that they do not occur at the relatively slower presentation rates (e.g., 1 s per item) that are typically used in the paradigm. At more standard rates, overt rehearsal protocols indicate that participants often think of the critical item during study, and the frequency of these thoughts predicts subsequent false recall (e.g., Goodwin, Meissner, & Ericsson, 2001).

Additional evidence that associative activation occurs at study has been obtained using implicit tests. After presenting participants with several DRM lists, McDermott (1997) found priming for the critical items on several implicit memory tests, and these effects have since been replicated. McDermott (1997) argued that such priming was due to lexical activation of the critical item at study.

Similarity-based theories

Within the second class of theories, it is proposed that DRM false remembering is caused by similarity between the critical item and the studied items, as opposed to associative activation of the critical item. These theories have primarily been used to explain false recognition. For instance, the fuzzy trace theory of memory representations (e.g., Brainerd, Wright, Reyna, & Mojardin, 2001) postulates that studying a list of associates results in the formation of two types of memory traces. Verbatim traces represent detailed, item-specific information, whereas gist traces represent the more general thematic characteristics of the lists. At test, words that are consistent with the gist of the list (such as the critical item) will be highly familiar, and hence falsely remembered. A different similarity-based account was developed by Arndt and Hirshman (1998), as an extension of exemplar-based models of memory. Under their proposal, a separate "gist" representation need not be encoded. Instead, each studied item is encoded as a set of sensory and semantic features. At retrieval, the similarity between the features of the critical item and the encoded features will make this item familiar, and lead to false remembering.

Despite these differences, both of these similarity-based theories explain DRM false recognition via familiarity caused by semantic similarity, and neither theory appeals to activation of the critical item through associative links. This last point poses important constraints on these theories. Without positing some sort of item-specific activation of the critical item, it is difficult to understand how these theories would explain the generation of this item on a recall test or on perceptually driven implicit memory tests (such as word stem completion).

Perhaps the strongest evidence that similarity-based processes might be involved in addition to associative activation are the effects of retention interval. It has been found that true recall decreases more over a delay than false recall (e.g., Toglia, Neuschatz, & Goodwin, 1999). Illustrative data from Toglia et al. (1999) are presented in Figure 17.3. True recall declined rapidly over a 3-week retention interval, whereas false recall persisted at high levels. Fuzzy trace theory can account for such results because it holds that gist traces are more resistant to forgetting than verbatim traces. As a result, memory for list items (which is supported more by verbatim traces) decreases at a more rapid rate than memory for critical items (which is supported more by gist traces) as retention interval is increased.

Associative-based theories cannot account for such effects without

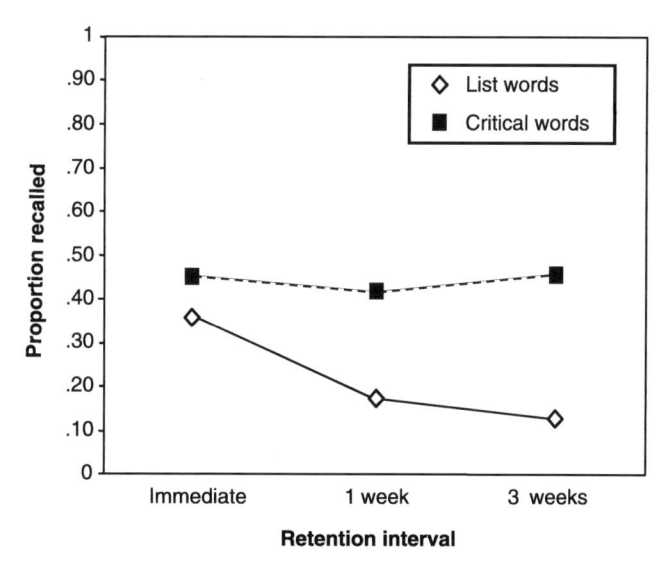

Figure 17.3 The effects of retention interval on true and false recall (Toglia et al., 1999, Exp. 2). Participants studied five DRM lists, and were given a final free recall test at one of three retention intervals (between-subjects). Data are collapsed across blocked and mixed study presentation, although similar patterns were obtained at each level.

additional assumptions. In the strongest form of these theories, the critical item would be activated multiple times at study and rehearsed like a list item. To the extent that the critical item is encoded like a studied item, the two should have similar forgetting functions (especially when initial levels of true and false remembering were matched). In return, it is unclear how a similarity-based mechanism could account for the powerful relationship between associative strength and false remembering. For example, many of the words in the *whisky* list seem to converge on the meaning of that word (e.g., *drink, drunk, beer, liquor*, etc.) just as words in the *window* list converge on its meaning (e.g., *door, glass, pane, shade*, etc.). Nevertheless, these lists differ greatly in associative strength (0.022 vs 0.184), and in turn, they elicit dramatically different levels of false recall (3% vs 65%; for additional discussion see Gallo & Roediger, 2002; Roediger et al., 2001). In sum, it appears that both associative activation and semantic similarity play a role (cf. the partial-match hypothesis in Chapter 15).

Fluency-based attributions

Although they can explain false recall and false recognition, neither the associative-based account or the similarity-based account can explain the perceptually detailed nature of DRM false memories very well. Roediger and McDermott (1995) found that false recognition of critical items was accompanied with high levels of confidence and frequent *remember* judgements. Both of these findings can be explained by thoughts of the critical item at study, but even this account cannot explain more detailed recollections. For instance, when lists are presented by multiple sources (auditory vs visual, or different voices), participants are often willing to assign a source to critical items that are falsely recognized (Gallo, McDermott, Percer, & Roediger, 2001) or recalled (Hicks & Marsh, 1999). Similarly, using the Memory Characteristics Questionnaire (MCQ), participants often claim to recollect specific details about a critical item's presentation at study, such as perceptual features, list position, and personal reactions to the word (e.g., Mather, Henkel, & Johnson, 1997).

One explanation for these subjective phenomena is a *fluency-based attribution* process. Gallo and Roediger (2003) proposed that, at test, participants imagine having been presented with the critical item at study, perhaps in an effort to determine whether it was presented. This imagination is then mistaken for actual presentation because it is processed more fluently, or more easily, than would have otherwise been expected (cf. Chapter 19 on the misinformation effect). If the attribution process occurs automatically, or nonconsciously, then the phenomenological experience would be one of remembering (see Jacoby, Kelley, & Dywan, 1989). Both the associative-based and similarity-based theories predict that processing of the critical word will be enhanced by presentation of the related list, so that a fluency-based attribution process is consistent with either theory.

Recent data provide some clues that associative activation is involved. As previously discussed, Gallo and Roediger (2002) found that lists with greater BAS were more likely to elicit false recall and false recognition than lists with lower BAS. They also found that false recognition from lists with greater BAS was accompanied by greater confidence and more "remember" judgements than was false recognition from lists with lower BAS. Thus, not only do lists with strong BAS elicit false remembering relatively more often, but when they do, it is more compelling than that from lists with weaker BAS. Using the aforementioned MCQ scale, we also found that critical items from longer lists tended to elicit stronger illusory recollection of various aspects of an item's presentation, such as its source, perceptual details, and emotional reactions (Gallo & Roediger, 2003). Under the assumption that presenting more associates increases associative activation, this outcome is again consistent with the notion that associative activation can drive illusory recollections.

Processes that reduce the effect

So far we have discussed processes that drive the DRM effect. No theoretical account would be complete, though, without considering editing processes that oppose these forces and reduce false remembering. Such processes have been conceptualized as *reality monitoring* under association-based theories (e.g., activation/monitoring theory), and item-specific or verbatim-based editing in similarity-based theories (e.g., fuzzy trace theory).

Evidence that such additional processes are involved comes primarily from presentation manipulations that should not affect associative activation or semantic similarity, but nevertheless influence false remembering. These include presentation format (e.g., switching presentation from words to pictures, which has been found to reduce false recognition; Schacter, Israel, & Racine, 1999) and presentation modality (e.g., switching presentation from auditory to visual, which reduces both false recall and false recognition; Gallo, McDermott et al., 2001). Other evidence comes from presentation manipulations that should increase similarity or associative processes, but actually decrease false remembering. These include increasing the number of presentations of the study lists before a recognition test (e.g., Benjamin, 2001), and slowing presentation rate (which has been found to eventually reduce false recall, but not necessarily false recognition; Gallo & Roediger, 2002).

To illustrate, consider a presentation-rate study by McDermott and Watson (2001). In those conditions that are relevant here, participants studied DRM lists at a range of visual presentation durations (20, 250, 1000, 3000, and 5000 ms, between-subjects), and took an immediate free recall test after each list. As expected, true recall increased with more study time (0.17, 0.31, 0.42, 0.50, and 0.51). The pattern for false recall was more striking, with an initial increase and an eventual decrease (0.14, 0.31, 0.22,

0.14, and 0.14). The initial increase suggests that, within this range of extremely rapid presentation rates, slowing the duration afforded more meaningful processing and thus enhanced those activation-based or similarity-based processes that drive false recall. In contrast, the eventual decrease suggests that slowing presentation rates also increases item-specific processing of the list items. Apparently, the accrual of this item-specific information eventually reached a point where it began to facilitate monitoring processes that opposed false recall.

Although these data (and others) suggest that monitoring or editing processes influence DRM false remembering, the exact nature of each of these processes is still unclear. One explanation is that making the studied items more memorable or distinctive allows participants to better discriminate (at study or at test) between thoughts of the critical item and actually presented items. In a sense, participants realize that a generated item was not actually presented. Alternatively, it could be that generation (and subsequent editing) of the critical item plays no role. Instead, making studied items more distinctive might allow participants to use a more conservative response criterion, overall, thereby reducing false remembering. Both explanations are possible.

We have discussed how both activation/similarity and editing processes may play a role in creating DRM false memories. Further support for the distinction between these two opposing processes comes from neuropsychological data. Amnesics with varied aetiologies (e.g., Korsakoff's or anoxia) tend to show decreased DRM false recognition relative to age-matched controls (e.g., Schacter, Verfaellie, Anes, & Racine, 1998). Due to their neurological deficits, it is improbable that the decreased effect in these participants was due to enhanced editing relative to their controls. Instead, this decrease implies that damage to medial temporal regions (which were the primary but not the sole areas that were damaged) reduces the likelihood of remembering the associative relations or gist that can cause false remembering, much as damage to these regions has traditionally been found to reduce true recall and recognition.

In contrast to the reduced effect in amnesics, patients with frontal lobe lesions showed enhanced DRM false recognition relative to age-matched controls (e.g., Budson, Sullivan, Mayer, Daffner, Black, & Schacter, 2002). Again, given their neurological deficit, it is unlikely that these patients showed increased false recognition because they were better able to encode the gist of the list, or its associative relations. It is more likely that, because the frontal lobes have traditionally been implicated in source-monitoring processes, the elevated levels of false recognition in this population were due to a breakdown in false-memory editing. Consistent with this logic, false alarms to unrelated lures were also elevated in frontal patients. Considered as a whole, the data from these two populations nicely illustrate the opposing influences of activation/similarity and editing processes in the DRM paradigm.

CONCLUSION

Associative memory illusions arise when information from the external world activates internal representations that may later be confused with the actual external events that sparked the association. As we have emphasized, we believe that this process is a general one with wide implications, because such associative activation is a pervasive fact of cognition. To use Jerome Bruner's famous phrase, people frequently go "beyond the information given" in drawing inferences, making suppositions, and creating possible future scenarios. Although these mental activities make us clever, they can also lead to errors when we confuse what we thought with what actually happened. The DRM paradigm provides a tractable laboratory task that helps open these processes to careful experimental study, and it also provides a rich arena for testing theories of internally generated false memories.

SUMMARY

- People can falsely remember nonpresented events that are associated to events that occurred.
- Research has identified two sets of factors that are critical for the creation of these types of false memories: activation processes and monitoring processes.
- Activation processes, such as the mental generation of associative information, cause people to believe that the nonpresented event had actually occurred. The similarity between nonstudied events and studied events also plays an important role.
- Monitoring processes refer to the strategic editing of these retrieval products, in an effort to reduce false remembering.
- The frequent occurrence of these systematic errors provides important insights into the cognitive mechanisms of memory.

FURTHER READING

For an early investigation of individual differences in susceptibility to false memories in the DRM task, Winograd, Peluso, and Glover (1998) provide a thoughtful analysis. This article is found in a special issue of *Applied Cognitive Psychology* (Vol. 12), devoted solely to the issue of individual differences in false memories. For an overview of neuropsychological findings in the DRM paradigm, and for additional discussion of underlying neural mechanisms, Schacter, Norman and Koutstaal (1998) is a good place to start. Finally, Bruce and Winograd (1998) provide a historical analysis of the DRM task, and give several reasons for its rise in popularity among memory researchers in the past decade.

REFERENCES

Arndt, J., & Hirshman, E. (1998). True and false recognition in MINERVA2: Explanations from a global matching perspective. *Journal of Memory and Language*, 39, 371–391.

Benjamin, A. S. (2001). On the dual effects of repetition on false recognition. *Journal of Experimental Psychology: Learning, Memory, and Cognition*, 27, 941–947.

Brainerd, C. J., Wright, R., Reyna, V. F., & Mojardin, A. H. (2001). Conjoint recognition and phantom recollection. *Journal of Experimental Psychology: Learning, Memory, and Cognition*, 27, 307–327.

Bruce, D., & Winograd, E. (1998). Remembering Deese's 1959 articles: The Zeitgeist, the sociology of science, and false memories. *Psychonomic Bulletin and Review*, 5, 615–624.

Budson, A. E., Sullivan, A. L., Mayer, E., Daffner, K. R., Black, P. M., & Schacter, D. L. (2002). Suppression of false recognition in Alzheimer's disease and in patients with frontal lobe lesions. *Brain*, 125, 2750–2765.

Deese, J. (1959). On the prediction of occurrence of particular verbal intrusions in immediate recall. *Journal of Experimental Psychology*, 58, 17–22.

Ebbinghaus, H. (1885/1913). *On memory: A contribution to experimental psychology*. New York: Dover.

Gallo, D. A., McDermott, K. B., Percer, J. M., & Roediger, H. L. III (2001). Modality effects in false recall and false recognition. *Journal of Experimental Psychology: Learning, Memory, and Cognition*, 27, 339–353.

Gallo, D. A., & Roediger, H. L. III (2002). Variability among word lists in eliciting memory illusions: Evidence for associative activation and monitoring. *Journal of Memory and Language*, 47, 469–497.

Gallo, D. A., & Roediger, H. L. III (2003). The effects of association and aging on illusory recollection, *Memory & Cognition*, 31, 1036–1044.

Gallo, D. A., Roediger, H. L. III, & McDermott, K. B. (2001). Associative false recognition occurs without strategic criterion shifts. *Psychonomic Bulletin and Review*, 8, 579–586.

Gardiner, J. M., & Richardson-Klavehn, A. (2000). Remembering and knowing. In E. Tulving & F. I. M. Craik (Eds.), *The Oxford handbook of memory* (pp. 229–244). New York: Oxford University Press.

Goodwin, K. A., Meissner, C. A., & Ericsson, K. A. (2001). Toward a model of false recall: Experimental manipulations of encoding context and the collection of verbal reports. *Memory & Cognition*, 29, 806–819.

Hicks, J. L., & Marsh, R. L. (1999). Attempts to reduce the incidence of false recall with source monitoring. *Journal of Experimental Psychology: Learning, Memory, & Cognition*, 25, 1195–1209.

Jacoby, L. L., Kelley, C. M., & Dywan, J. (1989). Memory attributions. In H. L. Roediger & F. I. M. Craik (Eds.), *Varieties of memory and consciousness: Essays in honor of Endel Tulving* (pp. 391–422). Hillsdale, NJ: Lawrence Erlbaum Associates Inc.

Johnson, M. K., Hashtroudi, S., & Lindsay, D. S. (1993). Source monitoring. *Psychological Bulletin*, 114, 3–28.

Kirkpatrick, E. A. (1894). An experimental study of memory. *Psychological Review*, 1, 602–609.

Mather, M., Henkel, L. A., & Johnson, M. K. (1997). Evaluating characteristics of false memories: Remember/know judgements and memory characteristics questionnaire compared. *Memory & Cognition, 25,* 826–837.

McDermott, K. B. (1997). Priming on perceptual implicit memory tests can be achieved through presentation of associates. *Psychonomic Bulletin and Review, 4,* 582–586.

McDermott, K. B., & Watson, J. M. (2001). The rise and fall of false recall: The impact of presentation duration. *Journal of Memory and Language, 45,* 160–176.

Miller, M. B., & Wolford, G. L. (1999). Theoretical commentary: The role of criterion shift in false memory. *Psychological Review, 106,* 398–405.

Neuschatz, J. S., Payne, D. G., Lampinen, J. M., & Toglia, M. P. (2001). Assessing the effectiveness of warnings and the phenomenological characteristics of false memories. *Memory, 9,* 53–71.

Robinson, K. J., & Roediger, H. L. III (1997). Associative processes in false recall and false recognition. *Psychological Science, 8,* 231–237.

Roediger, H. L. III, Balota, D. A., & Watson, J. M. (2001). Spreading activation and the arousal of false memories. In H. L. Roediger, J. S. Nairne, I. Neath, & A. M. Suprenant (Eds.), *The nature of remembering: Essays in honor of Robert G. Crowder* (pp. 95–115). Washington, DC: American Psychological Association Press.

Roediger, H. L. III, & McDermott, K. B. (1995). Creating false memories: Remembering words not presented in lists. *Journal of Experimental Psychology: Learning, Memory, and Cognition, 21,* 803–814.

Roediger, H. L. III, & McDermott, K. B. (2000a). Distortions of memory. In E. Tulving & F. I. M. Craik (Eds.), *The Oxford handbook of memory* (pp. 149–162). New York: Oxford University Press.

Roediger, H. L. III, & McDermott, K. B. (2000b). Tricks of memory. *Current Directions in Psychological Science, 9,* 123–127.

Roediger, H. L. III, McDermott, K. B., & Robinson, K. J. (1998). The role of associative processes in creating false memories. In M. A. Conway, S. E. Gathercole, & C. Cornoldi (Eds.), *Theories of memory II* (pp. 187–245). Hove, UK: Psychology Press.

Roediger, H. L. III, Watson, J. M., McDermott, K. B., & Gallo, D. A. (2001). Factors that determine false recall: A multiple regression analysis. *Psychonomic Bulletin and Review, 8,* 385–407.

Schacter, D. L., Israel, L., & Racine, C. (1999). Suppressing false recognition in younger and older adults: The distinctiveness heuristic. *Journal of Memory and Language, 40,* 1–24.

Schacter, D. L., Norman, K. A., & Koutstaal, W. (1998). The cognitive neuroscience of constructive memory. *Annual Review of Psychology, 49,* 289–318.

Schacter, D. L., Verfaellie, M., Anes, M. D., & Racine, C. (1998). When true recognition suppresses false recognition: Evidence from amnesic patients. *Journal of Cognitive Neuroscience, 10,* 668–679.

Seamon, J. G., Luo, C. R., & Gallo, D. A. (1998). Creating false memories of words with or without recognition of list items: Evidence for nonconscious processes. *Psychological Science, 9,* 20–26.

Stadler, M. A., Roediger, H. L. III, & McDermott, K. B. (1999). Norms for word lists that create false memories. *Memory & Cognition, 27,* 494–500.

Toglia, M. P., Neuschatz, J. S., & Goodwin, K. A. (1999). Recall accuracy and illusory memories: When more is less. *Memory, 7,* 233–256.

Tulving, E. (1985). Memory and consciousness. *Canadian Psychology, 26*, 1–12.
Underwood, B. J. (1965). False recognition produced by implicit verbal responses. *Journal of Experimental Psychology, 70*, 122–129.
Winograd, E., Peluso, J. P., & Glover, T. A. (1998). Individual differences in susceptibility to memory illusions. *Applied Cognitive Psychology, 12*, S5–S27.

18 Effects of labelling

Rüdiger F. Pohl

> A label is something that is affixed.
> (Link & Phelan, 2001, p. 368)

In labelling cases, a specific label is affixed to a stimulus and exerts its distorting influence in subsequent judgement or recall (cf. the anchoring effect in Chapter 10, the misinformation effect in Chapter 19, and the hindsight bias in Chapter 20). Text box 18.1 lists a number of examples demonstrating labelling effects in different domains. This list already suggests that labelling effects may be rather widespread in our lives. More examples, from more applied domains, are given at the end of this chapter in Text box 18.3.

Text box 18.1 Examples of labelling effects from different experimental domains

- If a white wine was labelled as "sweet", students who tasted the wine assigned larger amounts of residual sugar to it than when the same wine was labelled as "dry" (Pohl, Schwarz, Sczesny, & Stahlberg, 2003).
- An odour that was introduced as "pleasant" received higher hedonic ratings than the same odour introduced as "unpleasant" (Herz & von Clef, 2001).
- Ambiguous line drawings that were labelled with a concrete noun were in many cases reproduced more in line with what the given label suggested than what the original figure actually contained (Carmichael, Hogan, & Walters, 1932).
- A blue-green colour that was labelled as "bluish" ("greenish") was later recalled as more blue (green) than it really was (Bornstein, 1976).
- Eyewitnesses who saw a car accident on video, and were then asked to estimate the speed of the cars involved, were influenced by the wording of the question. They estimated a higher speed when the question asked "About how fast were the cars going when they *smashed* into each other?" than when the question was "How fast were the cars going when they *hit* each other?" (Loftus & Palmer, 1974).

Before turning to a detailed discussion of (a) the empirical evidence from labelling research in cognitive psychology and (b) the theoretical accounts of labelling effects, Text box 18.2 describes a classroom demonstration of labelling effects, which has been adapted from the classical experiment by Carmichael et al. (1932). The original study that investigated the effects of labelling on the reproduction of visual forms is described in more detail later

Text box 18.2 A classroom experiment demonstrating the labelling effect

As a classroom demonstration of labelling effects, this is an adapted version of the classical experiment by Carmichael et al. (1932) on the effects of labelling on the reproduction of ambiguous line drawings.

Method

Materials and participants

The complete material is given in Table 18.1. It consists of a series of 12 ambiguous line drawings (as used in the original experiment), together with two lists of labels that serve to influence participant's memory. Although not reported in the original study, the observed effect size was apparently rather large, suggesting that a total sample size of $N = 30$ would suffice (χ^2 tests with $\alpha = 0.05$ and $\beta = 0.20$).

Design and analysis

The participants are divided into three groups. One group receives the labels of List 1, one those of List 2, and the third one no labels at all (control). If the number of available participants is limited, you may drop the control group. If, on the other hand, enough participants are available (i.e., at least 50), you may introduce a further manipulation and split the two experimental groups. You could introduce the label to half of the participants before presenting the stimulus (i.e., in the learning phase) and to the other half after presenting it (i.e., in the recall phase), thus investigating how strongly the label affects the figure's encoding vs reconstruction processes (cf. Hanawalt & Demarest, 1939). The dependent measures are the frequencies of reproduced figures classified into four categories: (1) reproductions that resemble the original drawing, (2) those that resemble Label 1, (3) those that resemble Label 2, and (4) those that cannot be assigned to any of the three preceding categories. Classification should be done by two (or more) independent judges who are blind to the individual experimental condition.

Procedure

The experiment is run in two sessions. In the first session, participants are instructed that they will see 12 line drawings that they should try to memorize in order to later recall them. Then all stimuli together with either Label 1, Label 2, or no label are presented, one at a time, for about 5 seconds each. Each label is given immediately before showing the corresponding figure. After the presentation phase, a retention interval of at least 1 day, or better 1 week, should follow, because the labelling effect generally increases with increasing retention interval. In the second session, participants are asked to reproduce all figures. If the time of presenting the labels is varied, then only half of the participants in the two experimental groups receive the labels at the encoding phase (Session 1). The other half receives the label at the recall phase (Session 2),

> prompting the participant separately for each stimulus to reproduce "The figure that resembled x" (with x being replaced by the appropriate label from List 1 or 2). The latter groups as well as the control group are finally asked to indicate whether they had initially used any self-generated label to better memorize the figure, and if so which one (cf. Hanawalt & Demarest, 1939).
>
> **Results**
>
> In line with the classic results of Carmichael et al. (1932), the number of reproductions resembling the labels of List 1 should be larger in the List-1 group than in the List-2 group, and vice versa for reproductions resembling the labels of List 2 (χ^2 tests with $df = 1$). In addition, the number of correct reproductions (i.e., those that were classified as resembling the original drawing) should be larger in the control group than in both experimental groups (again, χ^2 tests with $df = 1$). The false reproductions in the control group serve to identify which (if any) of the labels were spontaneously used to encode the figures or which other self-generated labels were influential (as Hanawalt & Demarest, 1939, had observed in the majority of cases). If the time of presenting the labels is varied, fewer correct recalls and more reproductions in line with the given labels should be observed when labels were presented at the recall phase than when they were presented at the encoding phase (cf. Daniel, 1972; Hanawalt & Demarest, 1939).

in this chapter. This classroom demonstration is a simplified version and should be fairly easy to set up and to analyze.

LABELLING EFFECTS AND THEIR THEORETICAL ACCOUNTS

This section presents five cognitive domains in which labelling effects have been found. I begin with the classic examples studying the effects of labelling on the memory for ambiguous line drawings. Using the misinformation design (see Chapter 19), other researchers investigated how labelling might affect the memory for colour or speed. Another domain of labelling concerns judgements of taste and odour. And finally, in a more recently studied paradigm, self-generated verbal descriptions of difficult-to-describe visual stimuli (like faces) were found to deteriorate subsequent memory performance ("verbal overshadowing").

Memory for visual forms

In one of the most influential studies on the labelling effect, Carmichael et al. (1932) used 12 relative ambiguous line drawings that were presented one after another to 86 participants split into two groups. Immediately before seeing a figure, each participant received one of two words (Label 1 or 2) describing the figure that was presented next (see Table 18.1 for the complete material). These words had different meanings but could both be applied to name the same ambiguous figure. Participants of Group 1 received Label 1 and those of Group 2 Label 2. After all 12 figures had been presented, participants were asked to draw the figures from memory in any order. If one or more of these reproductions were not recognizable, the whole procedure was repeated right from the beginning, that is, all names and original drawings were presented again. Overall, the number of trials that were required to reach the criterion was between two and eight (with an average of three repetitions).

Two of the authors then rated the quality of all reproductions (from all trials, not only the last one) with respect to the original figure and classified them into five quality categories. Category 5, with drawings that were most deviant from the original ones, received 905 entries (25.9%), which were then further analyzed with respect to whether or not they resembled the objects that were described by the attached labels. The authors found that 74% and 73% of all Category 5 reproductions in Groups 1 and 2, respectively, could be classified as being closer to the named object than to the original figure. This observation, compared to only 45% of such cases in a control group (with nine participants), led Carmichael et al. (1932) to state that "naming a form immediately before it is visually presented may in many cases change the manner in which it will be reproduced" (p. 81).

These results conform to the process of "assimilative perception" as proposed by the first experimental psychologist, Wilhelm Wundt, and later taken up by James Gibson, who coined the term "figure assimilation" to denote the effect of verbal labels on the perception of form. These mental manipulations were supposed to provide a greater stability and precision to the perceived form, rendering it "as good as possible" conforming to the "Law of Prägnanz", as the gestalt psychologists had claimed.

Following up on Carmichael et al. (1932), Hanawalt and Demarest (1939) questioned whether the effect of verbal suggestions on the reproductions of visual forms was grounded in a change of the corresponding memory trace. They assumed that the labels did not change the memory representation of the perceived forms, but rather that the labels were used as an aid in reconstructing forgotten parts of the figure. In the spirit of Frederick Bartlett's theory on remembering, Hanawalt and Demarest emphasized that "reproduction is a construction and hence only partially dependent upon the trace" (p. 160). In their experiment, the authors used the same 12 ambiguous figures together with two lists of labels as in the original work by Carmichael et al. (1932). However, the procedure was quite different. In the learning phase, all figures were shown only once to the participants (148 students), at a pace of 10 seconds per figure with a 10-second interval between presentations. No labelling occurred at this stage. The sample was then divided into three groups, namely Group 1 (receiving List 1 suggestions), Group 2 (receiving List 2 suggestions), and a control group (receiving

Table 18.1 The 12 ambiguous stimuli with two lists of labels (adapted from the original experiment of Carmichael et al. (1932). An experimental study of the effect of language on the reproduction of visually perceived forms. *Journal of Experimental Psychology, 15*, 73–86.

List 1	Figures	List 2
Bottle		Stirrup
Crescent moon		Letter "C"
Bee hive		Hat
Eye glasses		Dumbbells
Seven		Four
Ship's wheel		Sun
Hour glass		Table
Kidney bean		Canoe
Pine tree		Trowel
Gun		Broom
Two		Eight
Curtains in a window		Diamond in a rectangle

no suggestions). As a further between-subjects manipulation, the retention interval was either zero (immediately), 2 days, or 7 days. In the following reproduction phase, participants in the experimental groups were instructed, separately for each of the previously seen figures, to "Draw the figure which resembled x" (with x being replaced by the appropriate label of the suggestion list). Unlike in the study by Carmichael et al., each item was reproduced only once.

In a post-experimental questionnaire, participants indicated in over 90% of all cases that they had spontaneously associated the given figure with an object in the learning phase. With increasing retention interval the reproductions of control-group participants showed an increasing percentage of drawings that contained changes in the direction of the individually associated concepts, from 63% to 93%. These percentages were considerably lower in the experimental groups and showed no increase with the retention interval. Instead, the percentage of drawings that resembled the suggested label increased with the retention interval from 12% to 33% and from 23% to 45%, in Groups 1 and 2 respectively. Thus, the data clearly revealed that while the original figure was more and more forgotten (due to longer retention intervals), the individually associated concepts (in the control group) and the suggested labels (in the experimental groups) played an increasingly important role in helping to reconstruct the figure. As a consequence, the reproductions were biased in the direction of the objects denoted by the labels. In accordance with the authors' hypothesis, the results are best understood in assuming that the labels did not change the memory trace of the original figure, but rather were effective only in the reproduction phase.

Another experiment using the Carmichael et al. (1932) drawings was reported by Prentice (1954). Like Hanawalt and Demarest (1939), Prentice also claimed that labels "operate on S's response in the testing phase (...) rather than on the process of memory that makes such reproductions possible" (p. 315). He based his conclusion on the finding that a recognition test that he applied was unaffected by the given labels. In the learning phase of his experiment, Prentice presented the series of 12 drawings twice at a pace of 4 seconds per item to 60 students. Each drawing was labelled by the experimenter, before it was presented, by announcing that "The next one is something like x" (with x being replaced by the appropriate label). Immediately after the learning phase, a large sheet containing 60 drawings was given to the participant. The 60 randomly ordered drawings were composed of the 12 original figures plus 4 variations of each. Of these, two resembled in varying degree the concept denoted by the corresponding label of List 1 and the other two the concept denoted by the label of List 2. In the recognition test, participants made on average 3.68 errors. Of these, 2.01 deviated in the direction of the label, while 1.68 did not. These frequencies were not significantly different, suggesting that participants were simply guessing. The author therefore concluded, in contrast to what Carmichael et al.

(1932) had claimed, that "the use of labels during learning does not modify the original experience or its memorial process" (p. 320).

Daniel (1972), however, found that labelling did affect recognition. He used different materials, namely four series of 12 different shapes. In a later recognition test (immediately after exposure, or after a delay of 5 minutes, 20 minutes, or 2 days), the "recognized" stimulus shifted away from the original stimulus towards the object denoted by the given label. This effect increased with increasing retention interval. As this occurred in a recognition test (and not only in a reproduction test as before), the author concluded that "the introduction of the label very likely influenced Ss' initial encoding of the form" (p. 156). He also assumed that, even if he had not given the label, participants would have provided their own labels (just as in the study of Hanawalt & Demarest, 1939), which in this case would have been highly similar to the ones used. Daniel explained the difference of his findings from those of Prentice (1954) with differences in the recognition tests applied. While Prentice presented all test stimuli simultaneously on a large sheet, so that participants had ample time to compare all of them, Daniel presented each stimulus alone, requiring a rating within a relatively short response interval (of 5 seconds), so that recognition was more difficult than in the Prentice study.

Memory for colour

Another group of researchers looked at the effects of labelling on the memory for colour. For example, Thomas and DeCapito (1966) found that an ambiguous blue-green colour (with 490 nm) that was called either "blue" or "green" by individual participants led to a differential generalization to bluer or greener colours, respectively.

Following this experimental idea, Bornstein (1976) first determined the point of subjective equality (PSE) for calling a colour "blue" or "green" for each of 13 participants by using a colour-naming task with nine colour stimuli (between 470 and 510 nm). After 1 day, the PSE stimuli were presented again in a recognition test, in randomized order together with eight distractors (with four items having shorter and four having longer wavelengths than the PSE stimulus). The recognition test was then repeated after 1 week. Both tests were highly similar and differed only in the label applied to the target stimulus. The instruction stated that a "bluish" (or "greenish") standard stimulus would be presented for 30 seconds and that this standard had to be recognized in a subsequent test with different stimuli (by responding "same" or "different"). The standard was always the individually devised PSE stimulus.

The results showed a strong labelling effect. The distribution of mean probabilities of saying "same colour" moved towards the blue colours when the label was "bluish", and towards the green colours when the label was "greenish". The mean probabilities of correctly identifying the original PSE stimuli were 0.62 and 0.72 for "bluish" and "greenish" labels, respectively. Comparing the probabilities for the two neighbouring stimuli (with PSE ± 5 nm) showed asymmetric distributions in both label conditions. After the "bluish" label, the bluer (greener) colour received a probability of 0.67 (0.10), while after the "greenish" label, the greener (bluer) colour received a probability of 0.48 (0.18). Thus, the results confirmed that "memory for ambiguous hues can indeed come under the control of linguistic labels" (Bornstein, 1976, p. 275).

Administering a different method, namely a post-event misinformation design (see Chapter 19), Loftus (1977) let 100 students first view a series of 30 colour slides depicting an auto–pedestrian accident. One slide involved a green car that passed by the scene. Immediately after the end of the series, participants were asked to answer 12 questions with respect to the slides they saw. For half of the participants, one question was, "Did the blue car that drove past the accident have a ski rack on the roof?", thus introducing the misinformation "blue". The other half (serving as controls) received the same question without any colour term. After a 20-minute filler task, a colour recognition test was applied to both groups. It consisted of 30 simultaneously presented colour strips (corresponding to colours from 425 to 675 nm, thus covering the whole range of visible colours). Participants were asked to identify the colour for 10 objects that were depicted in the slides seen previously. The critical item was the (originally green) car that passed by the accident. Relative to the controls, the participants with the "blue" misinformation selected significantly more blue and fewer green colours. At the same time, the percentage of correct colour choices dropped from 28% in the control group to 8% in the experimental group. Loftus interpreted these results as showing the blending of the original trace with the subsequently presented false information (see also Belli, 1988, and Pohl & Gawlik, 1995, for more evidence on blends in memory as well as a critical discussion of theoretical conclusions).

In a more recent misinformation experiment on colour memory, Braun and Loftus (1998) investigated the role of wrong advertisement information on a previously experienced product encounter. In the experiment, 96 undergraduates viewed a green wrapper around a chocolate bar in an alleged taste study. After a 15-minute filler task, they either saw a blue wrapper around the chocolate bar (visual misinformation), or were told that it was blue (verbal misinformation), or received no such information (control). After another 15-minute distractor task, the same recognition test as in the Loftus (1977) study was administered. Participants were asked to pick the correct colours from 30 colour strips for 10 previously seen objects, among them the wrapper of the chocolate bar as the critical item. While 73% of control participants chose the correct (green) colour, only 34% and 32% did so in the visually and verbally misled groups, respectively. In addition, misled participants more than controls chose blue or bluish-green hues, thus demonstrating the biasing influence of the misinformation. In accordance with Belli (1988), but unlike in the Loftus (1977) study, replacements (selecting blue instead of green) were observed more often than blends (selecting a mixture of blue and green), thus suggesting that original and misinformation had coexisted in memory.

Memory for speed

Estimating (or memorizing) speed represents another domain with stimuli that are difficult to verbalize and may thus be easily susceptible to labelling effects. In a now famous study, Loftus and Palmer (1974) presented seven short films of traffic accidents to 45 students. Following each film, the spectators were asked to write a short account of the accident and then to fill in a questionnaire. The critical question had five versions (between-subjects): "About how fast were the cars going when they contacted [hit, bumped, collided with, smashed into] each other?" The authors assumed that the specific verb used in the question would act as a label and thus influence the subsequent speed estimate. The data confirmed this expectation. The mean speed estimates significantly increased from 31.8 mph when the verb was "contacted", to 40.8 mph when it was "smashed into". In a second, highly similar experiment with only one film and a sample of 150 students, only the labels "hit" and "smashed" were used and again led to significantly different speed estimates. After a retention interval of 1 week, the verbs also led to different percentages of false memories that there had been broken glass in the film (when in fact there had been none). More precisely, 32% of the participants of the "smashed" group as opposed to only 14% of the "hit" group falsely remembered having seen broken glass.

Loftus and Palmer (1974) assumed that two kinds of information, namely the perception of the original event and external information supplied after the event, may be integrated over time. As a consequence, it would be difficult (if not impossible) to disentangle the different sources of information: "All we have is one memory" (p. 588). In other words, the use of labels apparently changed the memory representation of the original event. That position, however, was a matter of heated debate in the 1980s and 1990s. Opponents argued that labels did not change memory, but rather only biased the retrieval from memory (cf. the arguments of Prentice, 1954, for memory of visual form; presented above). Nowadays, it appears that both sides peacefully coexist and accept each other's position, acknowledging that both processes may add to the observed labelling effects (see the discussion in Chapter 19 and the SARA model in Chapter 20).

However, more critique of the Loftus and Palmer (1974) results accrued when two attempts to replicate them failed (McAllister, Bregman, & Lipscomb, 1988; Read, Barnsley, Ankers, & Whishaw, 1978). Presumably, labelling is not as robust as supposed. Or perhaps its effects depend on the complexity of the material to which the labels are affixed. The other studies (referred to above and below) all used rather simple materials (line drawings, colour, taste, or odour), while the films with accident scenes used here were rather complex and were, moreover, followed by a questionnaire that consisted of a larger series of questions. This complexity may have elicited other cognitive processes that could have obscured or prevented any labelling effect.

Judgements of taste and odour

A few studies investigated the effects of labels on taste judgements. Although these studies did not directly address the question of how labelling influences memory, it appears fairly safe to conclude that the observed judgement distortions also generalize to corresponding memory distortions (cf. Chapter 20). Besides, there is at least one explicit demonstration of labelling effects on taste memory (Melcher & Schooler, 1996; see the next section on "verbal overshadowing").

In a study on food preferences (Woolfolk, Castellan, & Brooks, 1983, Exp. 1), 60 students tasted two allegedly different brands of cola from different cups marked either "L" or "S". Earlier studies had found the letter "L" (for peculiar reasons) to be more disliked than the letter "S". Consequently, most participants judged the cola in cup "S" to taste better than the one in cup "L", although both cups contained the identical beverage. In a further study by the same authors (Exp. 2), 30 students first stated whether they preferred Pepsi or Coke. Then they received both a Coke and a Pepsi bottle and were asked to verify their stated preference by tasting both brands. The trick, however, was that each bottle contained exactly the other brand to the one on the bottle's label. The most interesting question accordingly was whether participants would base their judgement on their taste or on the label. The results revealed the latter to be true. Most participants (i.e., 22 out of 30) continued to prefer their favourite brand as given by the label of the bottle and not as given by its true contents.

In another study demonstrating labelling effects (Wardle & Solomons, 1994), 40 persons from university staff first tasted cheese-spread sandwiches and strawberry yoghurt that were labelled as either "low-fat" or as "full-fat", and then rated the food's tastiness. The results showed that food labelled as "low-fat" was rated lower in liking than food labelled as "full-fat", although both foods had in fact been identical.

In a further attempt to investigate the influence of labelling on taste judgements, Pohl et al. (2003, Exp. 1) asked 81 students to taste a white wine and to estimate its sweetness. In advance, however, half of the participants were informed that the wine was "sweet" (with 15 g of residual sugar per litre) and the other half that it was "dry" (with 5 g/L). Subsequent ratings (on a scale from 0 to 18 g/L) revealed clear effects of the given label: The allegedly "sweet" wine was judged to contain 12.02 g/L of residual sugar, while the allegedly "dry" wine was judged to contain only 9.40 g/L. This finding reminds one of other systematically distorted numerical judgements, as found in anchoring or hindsight bias studies (see Chapters 10 and 20, respectively). For example, in a hindsight bias memory design, participants will first judge the sweetness of the wine, then receive the true value, and are finally (after a retention interval) asked to recall their earlier given judgement. Typically, the recalled values will be closer to the true value than the original estimates had been, thus demonstrating the influence of hindsight bias (see Chapter 20 for more details).

Recently, labelling effects were also reported for odour perception. Herz and von Clef (2001) presented a set of five different odours repeatedly in two sessions (1 week apart) to 80 undergraduates. Each odour was accompanied by one of two labels (in Sessions 1 and 2, respectively) suggesting either a pleasant or an unpleasant hedonic impression. It is noteworthy that, in contrast to other labelling studies, the hedonic-value suggestion was manipulated as a within-subjects factor, thus allowing a strong test of the labelling effect. Would the same participants change their hedonic rating of the same odour, if a different label was given? The five odours (violet leaf, patchouli, pine oil, menthol, and a mixture of isovaleric and butyric acid) were selected as materials because they were perceived as rather ambiguous in their hedonic value in pilot studies. The labels were also collected in a pilot study asking participants to describe the odours. As a result, each odour was combined with a positive and a negative label, e.g., "pine oil" was either labelled as "Christmas tree" (positive), or as "spray disinfectant" (negative). These labels were given in the experiment immediately before each odour was sniffed (e.g., "this is Christmas tree"). After sniffing an odour, participants immediately answered a questionnaire with a 9-point hedonic rating scale among other items. The results of Herz and von Clef (2001) revealed clear effects of the given labels. If an odour was suggested to be pleasant (positive), it received much higher hedonic ratings than when the same odour was suggested to be unpleasant (negative). Recall that these ratings were given by the same participants (and not different ones), thus showing indeed strong labelling effects.

Verbal overshadowing

While, for the examples presented so far, the label was always provided by the experimenter, labelling effects could also occur if the labels were self-generated by the participants. In these cases, however, the label does not consist of a single word, but rather entails a more elaborated verbalization.

Introducing the concept of "verbal overshadowing", Schooler and Engstler-Schooler (1990) studied the negative effects of verbalization on visual memories (faces and colours). In their Experiment 3, for example, one of three different colour swatches (red, blue, or green) was shown to 30 undergraduates. Immediately after that, participants either wrote descriptions of the seen colour (verbal), visualized it (visual), or did an unrelated task (control) for 30 seconds. In a subsequent recognition test, the target colour was shown together with five distractors containing similar colour hues. The whole procedure was then repeated for the other two colour swatches.

The results showed that, compared to the control condition, recognition for the original colour was impaired when it was verbally described prior to the recognition test, while visualizing the colour had no such effect. The percentages of correctly identified colours were 33% in the verbalization, 64% in the visualization, and 73% in the control condition. Interpreting the results of this and a former experiment, the authors assumed that "detrimental memory recoding results from the mismatch between the original visual stimulus and the subsequent verbalization" (p. 52). In this case, verbalization of the given hue could have been rather difficult, so that the resulting labels apparently deviated from the original stimulus.

The authors argued that visual memories can be represented in multiple codes, for example, a visual code for the perceptual information and a verbal code for the labelling information (cf. Allan Paivio's dual code theory). Generally, most studies have found that an additional (verbal) code (as in elaboration) will be helpful in remembering visual information rather than impeding it. So what makes the difference between positive and negative effects of a verbal label on visual memories? Some researchers have suggested that verbal processing diminishes the resources left to visual processing, thus impairing encoding of the latter. Others claimed that the verbal code interferes with the use of the visual code, thus impairing memory performance. Memory errors might then be caused by a "recoding interference" that gives the verbal code more weight than the visual one.

From these considerations, Schooler and Engstler-Schooler (1990) concluded that "verbalization does not eradicate the original representation of the memory [...] but rather produces some form of interference" (p. 61). The authors therefore preferred the term "verbal overshadowing" to denote the effects of verbal labels on the memory for visual information. In an attempt to generalize their findings, the authors further assumed that verbal overshadowing may occur with any stimulus that defies complete linguistic description. This may apply not only to visual stimuli, but equally well to taste, touch, smell, sound, and other stimuli. Two of these, namely taste and odour, were discussed above.

Extending those studies from judgement to memory, Melcher and Schooler (1996) tested the effect of verbalization on taste memory. Their participants tasted two red wines, then verbally described the wines' taste (experimental group) or not (control group), and were then asked to recognise the wines among others. In the recognition test, each wine was accompanied by three distractor wines. A verbal overshadowing effect, that is, a drop in recognition performance after verbalization (compared to the control group), was observed, but only for the first wine tasted and only for participants who were categorized as "intermediates". These persons drank regularly wine, but had little verbal wine expertise. There was neither an effect for the second wine, nor for novices and wine experts. The authors concluded that it was the difference between perceptual and verbal experience that made the "intermediates" vulnerable to the verbal overshadowing effect. At the same time, the results also suggests that the effect is not very robust.

In the last decade, the processes leading to verbal overshadowing have received much attention (see Schooler, Fiore, & Brandimonte, 1997, for a review, and Meissner & Brigham, 2001, for a meta-analysis). Negative effects of verbalization on memory have meanwhile been shown for shapes, colours, faces, voices, music, taste spatial maps, and problem solving. An excellent collection of papers representing the state of the art was recently edited by Memon and Meissner (2002). In one of these papers, Ericsson (2002) claimed that "the reactive effects of 'verbal overshadowing' can be linked to the requirement of producing prescribed types of verbalization and are thus not caused merely by spontaneous verbal expression of one's thoughts" (p. 981). This conclusion reflects that the meta-analysis of Meissner and Brigham (2001) had revealed only a small general effect of verbalization, but a much larger one of the particular type of instruction and procedure used to elicit verbalization. Besides, some studies failed to replicate the overshadowing effect, leading Schooler et al. (1997) to admit that the effect is somewhat fragile. What is nevertheless important (from a theoretical as well as an applied perspective) is how the reactive effect is produced and, accordingly, how it can be avoided. Ericsson (2002) assumed that it is the forced-verbalization condition that most likely causes the overshadowing effect by leading to an increased number of inaccurate descriptions.

This view, however, was challenged by Schooler (2002). He reported that so far no relationship has been observed between description quality and recognition performance. Moreover, verbal overshadowing may well extend beyond the particular stimulus verbalized, but may also be entirely eradicated if participants engaged in a non-verbal task prior to the memory test. These findings led Schooler to drop his earlier "recoding interference" explanation (Schooler & Engstler-Schooler, 1990) and to propose a "transfer inappropriate retrieval" explanation instead. According to this idea, "verbalization produces a 'transfer inappropriate processing shift' whereby the cognitive operations engaged in during verbalization dampen the activation of brain regions associated with critical non-verbal operations" (p. 989). The assumed shift could result from limited-capacity competitions (a) between right and left hemisphere processes and (b) between automatic and controlled processes. The right hemisphere is more associated with non-verbal configural processes, while the left one is more associated with language-based processes. Thus, the act of verbalization could shift the centre of control from right to left hemisphere regions. Similarly, automatic ("reflexive") processes are associated with other brain regions (amygdala, basal ganglia, and lateral temporal cortex) than are controlled ("reflective") processes (anterior cingulate cortex, prefrontal cortex, and medial temporal lobe). Verbalization could then lead to a shift from more reflexive to more reflective processes. However, in order to reach this generalized processing shift, extensive verbal processes appear to be required (Ericsson, 2002; Schooler, 2002).

In this sense then, verbal overshadowing clearly deviates from the other labelling effects as presented above. There, a single word was sufficient to change memory performance. However, and in accordance with verbal overshadowing, all labelling effects have been criticized for their fragility (as indicated by failures to replicate them), suggesting that labelling effects are largely dependent on the specific experimental procedure used, and thus cannot be considered a robust phenomenon.

In addition, one might legitimately ask whether "verbal overshadowing" represents a cognitive illusion at all. One cornerstone of the definition of a cognitive illusion was that the observed behaviour deviates in a systematic fashion from the norm (see Introduction). The other labelling effects discussed above show exactly that: Memory deviates in the direction suggested by the label. But here, in the case of verbal overshadowing, the direction of error is not explicitly considered. Only the overall percentage of correct recall or recognition is reported. It thus remains to be shown whether the direction of error after verbalization is systematically related to the content of one's verbalization.

CONCLUSIONS

Having presented a range of examples, a classroom demonstration, experimental results, and theoretical accounts, this chapter will close with some more theoretical as well as some applied considerations. Text box 18.3 lists

---

Text box 18.3 Applied domains where labelling effects might occur

Apart from the cognitive paradigms reviewed above, labelling occurs in other, more applied contexts as well. For example, developmental psychologists study the effects of labelling on young infants' ability to categorize objects by transitive inference (e.g., Sloutsky, Lo, & Fisher, 2001; Welder & Graham, 2001). Social psychologists are interested on how labelling contributes to impression formation (Higgins, Rholes, & Jones, 1977), and may thus foster stereotyping, prejudice, and stigmatization (e.g., Link & Phelan, 2001). In clinical psychology, the acceptability of psychological treatment methods was found to depend on the specific labels used to describe these methods (Woolfolk, Woolfolk, & Wilson, 1977; but see Katz, Cacciapaglia, & Cabral, 2000). The same reasoning also applies to the large domain of advertisement research studying, for example, how product acceptability (and thus the decision to buy) may be reached through the use of favourable product labels (e.g., Woolfolk et al., 1983). And finally, the question of how eye- or ear-witnesses can be influenced (and even misled) by such simple changes as using different words in a question, is of major importance to forensic psychologists. Thus, labelling appears to play its role on quite a number of stages (many more than are reviewed in this chapter), infiltrating much of our daily lives.

Effects of labelling 341

several applied domains where labelling effects have been observed and are currently being investigated.

Generally, labelling could be considered a type of suggestion. In typical labelling experiments, persons either receive some sort of ambiguous information or information that is difficult (if not impossible) to verbalize, or they are simply left in a state of uncertainty. The label that is provided next contains some specific information that allows a reduction in the subjective ambiguity or uncertainty (cf. also Chapter 10 on the anchoring effect). However, by doing so it acts like a suggestion and drives reinterpretation or reconstruction in a specific direction. As a consequence, subsequent judgements or memories for the original stimulus may be systematically distorted (see Pohl, 2000). Gheorghiu and Walbott (1994, pp. 122, 123) described the characteristics of such a suggestive situation and of suggestive techniques in general (cf. Chapter 22):

> A suggestive situation is primarily characterized by the fact that it contains some directivity in attribution of meaning. A person influenced by a suggestive situation may directly or indirectly, explicitly or implicitly be influenced to follow certain cues (within a certain context). [...]
>
> Suggestive techniques encompass all techniques which attempt to influence a person in his/her appraisals, decisions, and actions in line with the attempted (suggested) direction.

That is exactly what a label does. It gives meaning to an otherwise more or less obscure situation and thus reduces or even eliminates ambiguity or uncertainty. Such effects of labelling have been observed in a variety of domains and contexts, and with a variety of experimental procedures. This would lead one to conclude that labelling is a widespread and robust phenomenon. However, several of the studies reviewed above delineated the possible limits of this effect. In more complex situations, labelling might be overridden by other information that is available and that can be used to reduce uncertainty and thus improve memory. Most of the experiments demonstrating labelling effects, however, used rather simple materials (like line drawings or colours), so that encoding or reconstruction processes relied more heavily on the scanty but relatively "helpful" information provided by the label. The dark side of this is that subsequent judgements or memories may be biased towards the label's content.

Whether the label exerts its influence during encoding, thus possibly altering the memory representation itself, or only serves as a retrieval cue during recall, is still a matter of debate and empirical research. However, as discussed above, both sides have presented evidence in favour of their position, so that it is likely that both are correct in their assumptions (cf. the discussions in Chapters 19 and 20).

SUMMARY

- A label is something that is affixed to a stimulus. A labelling effect occurs if judging or recalling that stimulus is systematically influenced by the label.
- Labelling effects have been found for the recall of visual forms and colour, and for the judgement of speed, taste, and odour.
- Labelling effects may depend on the complexity of the material used. The more complex the material, the more fragile the effect.
- Under the name of "verbal overshadowing", verbal self-descriptions of visual stimuli (faces, colours, and other stimuli) were found to deteriorate memory for these stimuli.
- The label may apparently exert its influence during encoding as well as during recall.
- In general, labelling could be understood as a suggestive process.

FURTHER READING

An enlightening exercise in classical experimenting is to read the original labelling study by Carmichael et al. (1932). As examples of less well researched labelling domains, the studies by Pohl et al. (2003) on taste and by Herz and von Clef (2001) on odour judgement are noteworthy. With respect to "verbal overshadowing", Schooler, Fiore, and Brandimonte (1997) present a review of the field, and Meissner and Brigham (2001) a meta-analysis. Schooler (2002) discusses in detail the latest theories on verbal overshadowing.

REFERENCES

Belli, R. F. (1988). Color blend retrievals: Compromise memories or deliberate compromise responses? *Memory & Cognition, 16*, 314–326.

Bornstein, M. H. (1976). Name codes and color memory. *American Journal of Psychology, 89*, 269–279.

Braun, K. A., & Loftus, E. F. (1998). Advertising's misinformation effect. *Applied Cognitive Psychology, 12*, 569–591.

Bushman, B. J. (1998). Effects of warning and information labels on consumption of full-fat, reduced-fat, and no-fat products. *Journal of Applied Psychology, 83*, 97–101.

Carmichael, L., Hogan, H. P., & Walters, A. A. (1932). An experimental study of the effect of language on the reproduction of visually perceived form. *Journal of Experimental Psychology, 15*, 73–86.

Daniel, T. C. (1972). Nature of the effect of verbal labels on recognition memory for form. *Journal of Experimental Psychology, 96*, 152–157.

Ericsson, K. A. (2002). Towards a procedure for eliciting verbal expression of non-verbal experience without reactivity: Interpreting the verbal overshadowing effect within the theoretical framework for protocol analysis. *Applied Cognitive Psychology, 16*, 981–987.

Gheorghiu, V. A., & Wallbott, H. G. (1994). Suggestion and attribution of meaning: A cognitive and social psychological perspective, *Communicazioni Scientifiche di Psicologia Generale/Scientific Contributions to General Psychology* [Special issue: Ipnosi e suggestione: Aspetti cognitivi e psicofisiologici/Hypnosis and suggestion: Cognitive and psychophysiological aspects], *12*, 117–139.

Hanawalt, N. G., & Demarest, I. H. (1939). The effect of verbal suggestion in the recall period upon the reproduction of visually perceived forms. *Journal of Experimental Psychology, 25*, 159–174.

Herz, R. S., & von Clef, J. (2001). The influence of verbal labeling on the perception of odors: Evidence for olfactory illusions? *Perception, 30*, 381–391.

Higgins, E. T., Rholes, W. S., & Jones, C. R. (1977). Category accessibility and impression formation. *Journal of Experimental Social Psychology, 13*, 141–154.

Katz, R. C., Cacciapaglia, H., & Cabral, K. (2000). Labeling bias and attitudes toward behavior modification revisited. *Journal of Behavior Therapy and Experimental Psychiatry, 31*, 67–72.

Link, B. G., & Phelan, J. C. (2001). Conceptualizing stigma. *Annual Review of Sociology, 27*, 363–385.

Loftus, E. F. (1977). Shifting human color memory. *Memory & Cognition, 5*, 696–699.

Loftus, E. F., & Palmer, J. C. (1974). Reconstruction of automobile destruction: An example of the interaction between language and memory. *Journal of Verbal Learning and Verbal Behavior, 13*, 585–589.

McAllister, H. A., Bregman, N. J., & Lipscomb, T. J. (1988). Speed estimates by eyewitnesses and earwitnesses: How vulnerable to postevent information? *Journal of General Psychology, 73*, 25–36.

Meissner, C. A., & Brigham, J. C. (2001). A meta-analysis of the verbal overshadowing effect in face identification. *Applied Cognitive Psychology, 15*, 603–616.

Melcher, J. M., & Schooler, J. W. (1996). The misremembrance of wines past: Verbal and perceptual expertise differentially mediate verbal overshadowing of taste memory. *Journal of Memory and Language, 35*, 231–245.

Memon, A., & Meissner, C. A. (Eds.). (2002). Investigations of the effects of verbalization on memory [Special Issue]. *Applied Cognitive Psychology, 16*(8).

Pohl, R. F. (2000). Suggestibility and anchoring. In V. De Pascalis, V. A. Gheorghiu, P. W. Sheehan, & I. Kirsch (Eds.), *Suggestion and suggestibility: Advances in theory and research* (pp. 137–151). Munich: M.E.G.-Stiftung.

Pohl, R. F., & Gawlik, B. (1995). Hindsight bias and misinformation effect: Separating blended recollections from other recollection types. *Memory, 3*, 21–55.

Pohl, R. F., Schwarz, S., Sczesny, S., & Stahlberg, D. (2003). Hindsight bias in gustatory judgments. *Experimental Psychology, 50*, 107–115.

Prentice, W. C. H. (1954). Visual recognition of verbally labeled figures. *American Journal of Psychology, 67*, 315–320.

Read, J. D., Barnsley, R. H., Akers, K., & Whishaw, I. Q. (1978). Variations in severity of verbs and eyewitness' testimony: An alternate interpretation. *Perceptual and Motor Skills, 46*, 795–800.

Schooler, J. W. (2002). Verbalization produces a transfer inappropriate processing shift. *Applied Cognitive Psychology, 16*, 989–997.

Schooler, J. W., & Engstler-Schooler, T. Y. (1990). Verbal overshadowing of visual memories: Some things are better left unsaid. *Cognitive Psychology, 22,* 36–71.

Schooler, J. W., Fiore, S. M., & Brandimonte, M. A. (1997). At a loss from words: Verbal overshadowing of perceptual memories. In D. L. Medin (Ed.), *The psychology of learning and motivation* (Vol. 37, pp. 293–334). San Diego, CA: Academic Press.

Sloutsky, V. M., Lo, Y. F., & Fisher, A. V. (2001). How much does a shared name make things similar? Linguistic labels, similarity, and the development of inductive inference. *Child Development, 72,* 1695–1709.

Thomas, D. R., & DeCapito, A. (1966). Role of stimulus labeling in stimulus generalization. *Journal of Experimental Psychology, 71,* 913–915.

Wardle, J., & Solomons, W. (1994). Naughty but nice: A laboratory study of health information and food preferences in a community sample. *Health Psychology, 13,* 180–183.

Welder, A. N., & Graham, S. A. (2001). The influences of shape similarity and shared labels on infants' inductive inferences about nonobvious object properties. *Child Development, 72,* 1653–1673.

Woolfolk, A., Woolfolk, R., & Wilson, T. (1977). A rose by any other name. Labeling bias and attitudes toward behavior modification. *Journal of Consulting and Clinical Psychology, 45,* 184–191.

Woolfolk, M. E., Castellan, W., & Brooks, C. I. (1983). Pepsi versus Coke: Labels, not tastes, prevail. *Psychological Reports, 52,* 185–186.

19 Misinformation effect

Jacqueline E. Pickrell, Daniel M. Bernstein, and Elizabeth F. Loftus

> Memory is a complicated thing, a relative to truth, but not its twin.
> Barbara Kingsolver, *Animal Dreams*

Ah, memories ... they comfort us, inform us, disturb us, and yes, even define us. Memory is often taken for granted and really only reflected upon when it fails us. In general, our memory is an amazing entity with the ability to provide us with the continuous sense of *self* described by William James. Memory operates in an extremely efficient manner, allowing us to recall more pleasant than unpleasant memories and enough detail to reconstruct past experiences with reasonable accuracy. It is, however, subject to distortion, the study of which has historically been rooted in interference theory. Interference theory, a theory of forgetting, states that the reason we forget is that other memories in long-term memory impair our ability to retrieve the target memory. Memory involves a reconstructive process: It is vulnerable to interference from other experiences, especially from experiences that occur after a to-be-remembered event.

In this chapter, we describe contemporary studies of memory distortion, focusing primarily on the "misinformation effect". This effect refers to the tendency for post-event misleading information to reduce one's memory accuracy for the original event. We begin our discussion with a brief overview of forgetting as a function of event encoding and event retrieval errors. We discuss various laboratory techniques that demonstrate the misinformation effect. The existence of the misinformation effect is rarely disputed, as it is a robust phenomenon. However, the parameters and mechanism underlying the effect are less clear. For example, who is particularly susceptible to the influence of misinformation? What kind of post-event information is necessary to distort a memory, and just how much can we distort that memory? What does the misinformation effect say about the permanence of memory? Beginning with the naturally occurring distortions of memory, through use of the suggestion of misleading details, we will discuss evidence in support of the misinformation effect, including the most complex misinformation effect of all: the creation of memories for entirely false events.

We briefly describe some new data from an experiment that examined consequences of creating a false memory of being attacked by a small dog as a young child, and provide a simple methodology for demonstrating the misinformation effect in a classroom. Finally, we explore the difficulty in distinguishing true from false memories.

MEMORY PRIMER: ENCODING, STORAGE, AND RETRIEVAL

Memory consists primarily of information encoded and stored in such a way as to facilitate retrieval of that information The quality of what is encoded along with the way it is encoded directly influences the subsequent retrieval of that information. Numerous factors affect the encoding process, beginning with attention. In order for the encoding process to be successful, the information must be attended to. Additionally, the depth of processing that one does on the encoded details influences the encoding process. Elaborating on information that is observed, particularly by linking the event or detail to previously learned information rather than experiencing the information with no conscious effort to remember it, will lead to better encoding of the information. In addition, unusual or unexpected information will tend to stand out in our mind and may result in being encoded more effectively than ordinary or familiar details. In general it is safe to say that the accessibility of information that is poorly encoded or not encoded in memory at all will not improve with the passage of time.

Information retrieval is a reconstructive process. The memory for an event is not stored in its entirety, as an exact replica of the event. Rather, the event is broken and organized into personally meaningful pieces. These mental representations capture the gist or essential meaning of the event. The retrieval process involves a mental re-enactment of the original experience, reproducing as many details as possible. This reconstructive process will invariably involve distortions, in the form of omissions, elaborations, or misperceptions. Some theorists have argued that the success of retrieving previously encoded details depends, to a large degree, on the extent to which the retrieval context matches the original encoding context (Tulving & Thompson, 1973).

Related to the organization of memory is research done on schematic memory. The definition of schema is an organized pattern of thought about some aspect of the world, such as events, situations, objects, or a class of people (Bartlett, 1932). Our schematic knowledge may dictate what we pay attention to and what we use to guide our understanding. Schematic knowledge can also be very useful in the reconstructive process of memory. Unfortunately, schema can distort memory because as we store schematic knowledge we do not have to attend to everything in our environment. When we rely on our schematic knowledge to report a memory, we usually remember things as being quite typical. Because we use our knowledge to identify an event or situation and to form a representation of that event, the errors committed when we "fill in the gaps" may negatively influence our memory.

MISINFORMATION

By the middle of the 20th century, many scientists were engaged in a vain search for the engram, a hypothetical memory trace that left an identifiable and indelible physical trace in the brain. The engram was believed to be both permanent and localizable, two views that dominated early cognitive neuroscience. The permanence theory gained support in the 1950s when neurosurgeon Wilder Penfield began operating on patients with epilepsy. During surgery, he kept patients awake but anaesthetized them so they could respond when he stimulated certain areas of the brain. He claimed that by using this technique he accessed memories. The media jumped on this concept and the hype was communicated to the public as well as to the scientific community. The permanence theory was given a big boost. In reality, Penfield operated on 1100 patients, and only 40 responded by producing anything like a memorial response when the temporal lobe was stimulated. Only 5 of those 40 reported a complete episodic memory, and some of these could be ruled out as real memories by other evidence.

When Elizabeth Loftus and her colleagues (Loftus, 1975; Loftus, Miller, & Burns, 1978; Loftus & Palmer, 1974) claimed that people's memories are malleable after exposure to misleading post-event information, the social and theoretical implications of this finding caused a flurry of interest in the misinformation effect.

In their original studies, Loftus and colleagues demonstrated how question wording and the introduction of misleading post-event information influence what is remembered (see Chapter 18). In one study, Loftus (1975) showed participants a film of an automobile accident, and then asked half of them, "How fast was the white sports car going when it passed the barn while travelling along the country road?" No barn was shown in the film; however, many of the participants who had been asked about the barn claimed to have seen it in the film. In another study, participants answered one of the following questions about a car accident depicted in a film that they had seen: (1) How fast were the cars going when they *hit* each other? or (2) How fast were the cars going when they *smashed into* each other? (Loftus & Palmer, 1974). The researchers found that the latter question produced higher speed estimates than did the former question. Simply changing the word "hit" to "smashed into" affected the subject-witness's memory for the original event. In another study, participants watched a slide sequence involving a car/pedestrian accident. In the slide sequence, a car arrives at an intersection, turns right and hits a pedestrian. A yield sign was shown to half the participants, while a stop sign was shown to the remaining participants. Later, some participants were asked a question containing a misleading suggestion about either a stop sign or a yield sign (whichever sign they had not seen in the slide sequence). When tested for their memory of the original slides they had seen, many of the misled participants mistakenly claimed that they had seen the sign that had been suggested, rather than the sign that they had actually seen (Loftus et al., 1978). These studies demonstrate that misleading post-event information affects what people erroneously report about the past.

Theoretical accounts of the misinformation effect

About the same time as the first misinformation studies were being published, we saw a rising concern regarding the reliability of eyewitness testimony. This was an important practical implication. Soon thereafter, an important theoretical issue arose. The very nature of memory was now in question. When participants had seen a stop sign, but received a suggestion about a yield sign, and then claimed that they saw a yield sign, what had happened to the stop sign in their memory? Was it still there, but perhaps harder to retrieve? Was it erased or altered in the process of absorbing the suggestive information? McCloskey and Zaragoza (1985) attacked the memory-impairment hypotheses claiming, "misleading post-event information has no effect on memory for the original event" (p. 2). The misinformation results were not in question, but the interpretation and procedure were. McCloskey and Zaragoza's key arguments involved the procedure used in these studies. They argued that the acceptance of misinformation occurred because:

- participants never encoded the original information and remembered the post-event information;
- participants encoded both the original and the post-event information and deliberated about what to report, eventually falling sway to the social desirability bias;
- the original information was just forgotten.

McCloskey and Zaragoza proposed a more appropriate procedure in an attempt to account for participants who may fall into any of the above categories. They conducted six experiments using both this new procedure and the original. The *modified* test procedure was identical to the original procedure except that the test was different. The original procedure has participants choose from either the original event/item or the misleading event/item. In the modified procedure, participants are asked to choose between the original event/item and a *novel* event/item. The misleading information is not an option. McCloskey and Zaragoza hypothesized that if the misleading information alters memory for the original event, when that

Text box 19.1 Misinformation study

As a classroom demonstration of the misinformation effect we suggest using a modified version of Loftus et al.'s (1978) study. In order to demonstrate the effect in the most straightforward manner, we will use one independent variable, the type of information, with three levels (consistent, inconsistent, neutral).

Method

Materials

A series of eight colour slides are shown in a sequential manner to depict an auto–pedestrian accident. This modified set is a subset of the original series of 30 colour slides used by Loftus et. al. (1978). The modified set includes the following:

- a red car leaving a parking lot
- the red car approaching an intersection with a bus on the left
- the bus moving through the intersection in front of the red car
- *the red car stopped at a stop sign*
- a male pedestrian crossing the street in front of the red car
- the pedestrian lying on the road in front of the red car
- the arrival of a police car and a female pedestrian
- the police car pulled over to the side of the road

Eight questions, including one critical question are administered immediately after participants have viewed the slides. These questions serve as a memory test for the information presented in the slide sequence, and are as follows (note that the critical question is in italics):

- Did you see the red car leaving the parking lot?
- Did you see a bicycle?
- Did the bus pass in front of the red car from the right or left?
- *Did another car pass the red car while it was stopped at the intersection with the yield sign?*
- Did you see the taxi cab?
- Was the pedestrian who was hit a man or a woman?
- Was the second pedestrian a man or a woman?
- Did the police officer get out of the car?

After participants have answered each of these questions, they are shown eight pairs of slides. Each pair of test slides contains the original slide and a distractor slide similar to its counterpart except for one key detail. For example, if the original slide depicted the pedestrian lying in front of the red car, the distractor might depict the driver of the red car getting out of the car. For each pair of test slides, participants report which slide they saw before.

Procedure

All participants view the slide sequence showing a stop sign at the intersection. Participants are then randomly assigned to receive consistent, inconsistent, or neutral information with respect to the original traffic sign viewed in the slide sequence. Participants receiving information asking about the stop sign are receiving information consistent with the slide series (Consistent). Another third of the participants receive information where it is suggested that they saw a yield sign (Inconsistent). The final control condition participants receive no information (Neutral).

A yes–no recognition test is administered after a brief (we suggest 15–20 minute) filler task. Eight pair of test slides are shown to participants, who report which slide of each pair they saw before. The critical slide pair, the scene showing either the original stop sign or the misleading yield sign, is randomly placed within the eight pairs of slides.

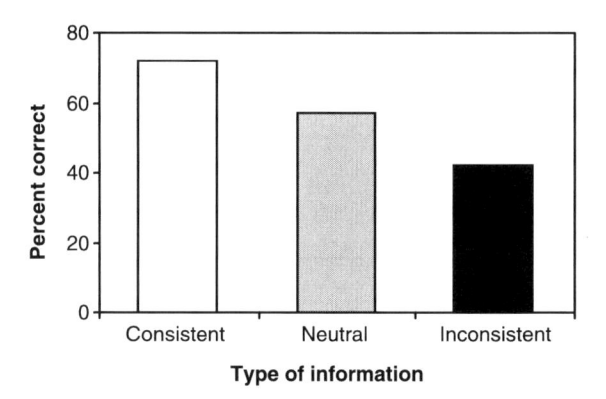

Figure 19.1 The effect of the type of information on the proportion of correct answers given on the recognition test 2 days after viewing the slide show and completing the questionnaire.

Results

What proportion of participants correctly chooses the stop sign from the original slide-show sequence? With the recognition test administered immediately after the exposure to the misinformation, Loftus et al. (1978) found that participants who received the information that was inconsistent with what they had actually seen were much less accurate in their responses compared to the participants in the other two conditions. In addition, when the retention interval is increased to 2 days (see Figure 19.1), and we compare the response of those in the neutral condition with the other two groups, receiving the consistent information improved performance on the recognition task. Along with the fact that the type of information has an effect on memory for the original information, Loftus et al. demonstrated that delay of the questionnaire containing the misleading information also hindered memory performance. Apparently, time allows the original memory trace to weaken, thus making it easier for an erroneous memory report to be given.

information was not an option at test, memory for the original information would be selected less often than selected by those in the control condition.

Collapsing over numerous experiments, McCloskey and Zaragoza successfully replicated the misinformation effect using the original procedure. Participants in the control condition correctly reported the original information 72% of the time whereas the misled participants correctly reported the original information only 37% of the time. However, the results looked quite different in the modified procedure. Here, Controls correctly reported the original information 75% of the time, while Misled participants correctly reported the original information 72% of the time. The researchers' conclusions were direct:

> We conclude from these results that misleading post-event information does not impair participants' ability to remember what they originally saw. In other words, misleading information neither erases the original information nor renders it inaccessible.
> (McCloskey & Zaragoza, 1985, p. 7)

McCloskey and Zaragoza want to explain these results with factors other than memory impairment, specifically, either task demands, or strategic effects. Zaragoza, McCloskey, and Jamis (1987) proceeded to test the modified and original procedures with recall rather than recognition and supported their belief that differences between the misled and control conditions in the original procedure are due to factors other than the impairment of memory. McCloskey and Zaragoza assert that the test should be such that process-of-elimination strategies can be controlled.

More recent experiments designed to reduce or eliminate strategic effects have demonstrated effects of impaired memory (see Ayers & Reder, 1998, for review). In addition, the modified test may be insensitive to memory impairment. When overall memory performance is low, the effect may need the additional strength of the exposure to the misleading information once again at test.

It seems that each of the explanations offered accounts for some of the findings, but as yet we have not developed a theory to explain all of the results. Metcalfe (1990, in Ayers & Reder, 1998, p. 19) proposed her CHARM theory, a memory model that accounts for the misinformation data by means of memory trace alteration. This is a single-trace model that explains the integrated and blended memory data but falls short of explaining the small effects sometimes seen using the modified procedure.

Ayers and Reder (1998) proposed an activation-based model that might explain the various misinformation effect findings in terms of a source of activation confusion (SAC) model of memory. This multi-trace model predicts that in our classic misinformation example, a participant might be aware of the high activation of the concept "yield sign", but be unaware of the reason that it was activated. Yield sign would be more highly activated at test than the original stop sign because it had been activated more recently. This model is consistent with the ideas expressed by Kelley and Jacoby (1996) that, under some conditions, the source of activation is unclear. If the source is either unavailable or unknown, it may be misattributed, resulting in memory errors. This model is, however, at direct odds with an integration/blending theory. If the memory trace is altered or overwritten, there can be no source misattribution because there is only one source. In summary, our colleagues at Western Washington University may have said it best: "Although the misinformation effect is easily replicated, the explanation of such memory errors is hotly contested" (Hyman & Pentland, 1996, p. 101).

Today, there seems to be a consensus among cognitive psychologists that no single process is responsible for all of the misinformation effects. The debate involves several different explanations for the results. While some favour the impairment hypothesis, others favour the co-existence hypothesis. Whichever view is correct, the misinformation effect data support the reconstructive nature of memory and illustrate how this reconstruction leaves memory susceptible to errors.

Manipulations of the misinformation effect

Many factors influence the effectiveness of misinformation. First, the passage of time renders the original memory less accessible, thereby allowing misinformation to "creep in" undetected. Second, the subtler the discrepancies are between the original information and the post-event information, the stronger the misinformation effect. Third, the more ignorant one is of the potentially misleading effects of post-event information, the more susceptible one will be to the misinformation effect.

Who is susceptible to the misinformation effect? Perhaps the largest misinformation study ever conducted provides insight into just *who* is most likely to accept misinformation (Loftus, Levidow, & Duensing, 1992). At a science museum in San Francisco, approximately 2000 visitors participated in a typical misinformation study. Participants viewed a short film and then some of the participants were given misinformation while others were not. All of the participants then answered questions about the film. While the majority of misinformation studies have been conducted in university laboratories with college students, this particular study included people ranging in age from 5 to 75 years, providing a unique opportunity to gather information on the effect of age and misinformation. Consistent with other studies involving children (Ceci, Ross, & Toglia, 1987), the youngest participants showed large misinformation effects. Additionally, the elderly showed a large misinformation effect, too (Loftus et al., 1992).

The preceding discussion has focused primarily on the fact that memory details are sensitive to misinformation. For example, subtle word choice embedded within post-event information can influence memory (for more examples see Chapter 18). Such memory distortion can be seen even in highly salient memories, or memories that some theorists have dubbed "flashbulb memories" for their highly emotional, meaningful, and subjectively permanent nature. One could imagine how the following, subtly worded question could lead people to remember seeing details about the September 11 terrorist attacks that they never saw: "Did you see the explosion after seeing the plane crash into the Pentagon during the September 11 terrorist attacks?" There was no footage of the plane crashing into the Pentagon. However, the question suggests that such footage not only exists, but that the individual might have seen it. This suggestion, coupled with the knowledge that a plane did, in fact, crash into the Pentagon, might lead people to think mistakenly that they saw the plane crash.

In addition to changing memory for details, misinformation can also change entire memories. In one study, 25% of participants either partially or wholly accepted the false suggestion that they had been lost in a shopping mall at the age of 5 (Loftus & Pickrell, 1995). Likewise, Hyman, Husband, and Billings (1995) convinced many of their participants that, as children, they had knocked over a punch bowl at a wedding and spilled punch on the bride's parents. Both studies utilized a procedure in which the researchers acquired three true memories from the participants' parents. The researchers then provided participants with the true memories and the false memory. Participants were asked to try to remember the events and to describe them in detail. Not only did nearly one quarter of the participants come to believe that the false event had occurred, but they also elaborated on the false event (e.g., "I do remember her [an elderly lady] asking me if I was lost, ... and asking my name and then saying something about taking me to security", Loftus & Pickrell, 1995, p. 724).

There are, of course, other ways to increase one's confidence in various childhood events. Mock personality profiles and dream interpretations are procedures that utilize the power of suggestion to increase one's subjective confidence in events that never actually occurred (see Chapter 22). Participants might be told that their personality profiles reveal that, as young children, they had been attacked by a dog. Or a dream "expert" might interpret a dream as meaning that, as a young child, one had to be rescued by a lifeguard. Such misinformation can increase participants' confidence in the critical events (Mazzoni, Loftus, Seitz, & Lynn, 1999).

Another form of suggestion used to inflate confidence in childhood events involves imagining in detail an event that never occurred. For example, Garry, Manning, Loftus, and Sherman (1996) asked participants about a variety of childhood events, including whether they had broken a window with their hand. Next, some participants were asked to imagine in detail running through the house as a child, and tripping, falling, and breaking a window with their hand, cutting themselves and bleeding. This type of imagination exercise significantly increased participants' confidence that the event in question occurred in their childhood. Additional research on "imagination inflation" has established the utility of this procedure.

More recent techniques have also been developed. Drivdahl and Zaragoza (2001) asked participants to view a film depicting a bank robbery. Participants then read a narrative of the event that contained misleading suggestions, in addition to questions designed to produce perceptual elaboration of details for events that were not in the film. For instance, a participant answers specific questions about the physical appearance or location of a suggested but false event ("Was the ring that the thief stole in a box?"). By focusing on perceptual details, the participant creates an image of the scene, imbuing it with life. This perceptual elaboration, in turn, increased participants' confidence in the false event.

Another recent technique used to create false memories involves altered photographs. Wade, Garry, Read, and Lindsay (2002) asked participants about a variety of childhood events, including riding in a hot air balloon. The researchers then obtained childhood photographs of their participants and inserted these pictures into a photograph depicting a hot air balloon ride. After participants saw themselves riding in a hot air balloon, they began to "remember" the ride, even though the experience had been completely fabricated.

Consequences

We know that there are consequences of true experiences that we no longer remember. One of us (JP) knows firsthand of an individual (her daughter) who retained her fear of dogs long after she had forgotten having been attacked by a large dog when she was 2 years old. What if the daughter had had a false belief about being attacked? Would this also lead to a similar kind of lingering fear? More generally, are there long-range consequences associated with the planting of false beliefs or memories? If a person comes to believe they were attacked by a dog while a young child, might they be more inclined as an adult to own a cat instead of a dog? To address this issue a study was designed in our lab, and carried out by Collins (2001) as part of her senior honours thesis. The question addressed in the study is whether there are verifiable consequences to having a false memory. In this case, the false memory was one of being attacked by a small dog.

Introductory psychology students at the University of Washington completed a pre-test where they were asked how confident they were that each of 58 life events had occurred to them in their childhood. Additionally, participants completed a preference questionnaire on which they indicated their preference towards certain things, such as what kind of pet they might like to own and what breed of dog they preferred.

Participants who indicated with a low rating that it was highly unlikely that they "Were unexpectedly attacked by a small dog" were contacted and asked to participate in a future experiment for additional credit. For Session 2, those in the experimental group returned to the laboratory, and were told that their responses on various personality scales during the pre-testing indicated that, as young children, they likely had been attacked by a small dog. Those assigned to the control condition participated in other unrelated experiments during Session 2. During Session 3, all participants returned to the laboratory to complete the post-test questionnaires, identical in content to the pre-test questionnaire, but this time administered on computers.

Participants who originally claimed not to have been attacked by a small dog as children were led to believe that they had, in fact, been attacked. Simply telling participants that their initial responses were indicative of someone who had been attacked by a dog as a child significantly increased their confidence that they had been attacked. What is perhaps more surprising and chilling, though, is that these participants were less likely to claim to want to own a dog as a pet after receiving the false feedback. The results of this experiment demonstrate that not only is it possible to increase people's beliefs in an entire false event, but that this false belief can be accompanied by important, negative consequences. Given these findings, it also should be theoretically possible to alter one's memory and to *positively* influence one's attitudes.

Braun (1999) examined the effects of misinformation, in the form of an advertisement, on one's subsequent memory for the taste of orange juice. Braun asked participants to taste orange juice and to describe its flavour. Some participants then evaluated the effectiveness of a false advertisement that described the orange juice that they had tasted 15 minutes earlier as being "sweet, pulpy and pure" (p. 323). The misinformation in this advertisement significantly altered participants' memories a few minutes later for the original orange juice that they had tasted. Specifically, the false advertisement made participants think that the orange juice that they had tasted earlier was better than it in fact had been (see Chapter 18). The results of Braun's work and of the dog-bite study that we discussed above suggest that it is possible to alter a true memory and to plant a false memory, with either positive or negative consequences.

Possible mechanisms

What is not clear from the work described up to this point are the precise boundary conditions of the misinformation effect and the underlying mechanism responsible for memory distortion. Some have investigated the limits to what types of memories can be created through suggestion or imagination. Pezdek, Finger, and Hodge (1997) could not convince their participants that they had received an enema as a child. Mazzoni, Loftus, and Kirsch (2001) have argued that an event must be seen as plausible in the rememberer's culture and that it must be seen as personally plausible before the person comes to incorporate the experience into his/her own autobiographical memory.

One possible mechanism that might explain memory distortion after different forms of misinformation is that of familiarity (Garry et al., 1996).

Larry Jacoby and colleagues (e.g., Jacoby, Kelly, & Dywan, 1989) have argued that many false memories arise through the misattribution of familiarity. According to this notion, when participants fluently process an event or experience, they experience a feeling of familiarity. They then search for reasons that might explain this processing fluency. If they are unable to detect an obvious source, they may attribute the fluency to past experience.

Familiarity attribution may help explain why people accept misinformation and why they increase their confidence for childhood events after imagining these events or after being told that the events likely occurred. In such cases, people will process the imagined or suggested event more fluently than they would otherwise have processed it. They will, in turn, evaluate their present processing experience. Instead of correctly focusing on the misinformation, the imagination exercise, or the suggestion as the source of familiarity, they mistakenly attribute the familiarity to their childhood.

DISTINGUISHING TRUE FROM FALSE MEMORIES

Unfortunately, it is very difficult to tell whether an individual memory is real or imagined. In fact, research over the past 20 years suggests that it is virtually impossible to determine whether or not a particular memory is real. In one study, Loftus and Pickrell (1995) compared participants' reports for true and false memories. The participants used more words when describing their true memories, and rated the clarity of their true memories higher than they rated the clarity of their false memories. Confidence ratings revealed that people were less confident in their false memories than they were in their true memories.

Hyman and Pentland (1996) used a paradigm similar to that of Loftus and Pickrell to investigate the role that mental imagery plays in the creation of false memories. After successfully planting false memories, additional questions were asked in an attempt to compare recovered true memories with false memories. True memories that were never recovered or those remembered all along were different from those recovered. The emotional strength of the false memories was comparable to the recovered true memories; the clarity ratings for these two groups were also in the same range. Additionally, the confidence ratings were similar between these two groups. Hyman and Pentland (1996, p.111) claim, "The overall pattern of ratings leads us to two conclusions. First, it will be difficult to discern any differences between recovered true memories and created false memories. Second, one reason for this difficulty may be that the recovered true memories are actually creations as well."

Roediger and McDermott (1995) created false memories for words not presented in lists (see Chapter 17). Not only were false memories as common as true memories in the study, but participants expressed as much confidence in their false memories as they did in their true memories. Perhaps even more upsetting to those who hope to be able to accurately distinguish true and false memories, participants claimed to "remember" (or mentally to relive) the experience of having heard words before that they had not heard. Thus, false memories were easily created, and they were virtually indistinguishable from the true memories.

Porter, Yuille, and Lehman (1999) investigated whether phenomenological and content features could discriminate between real and false memories, in an effort to systematically assess the credibility of childhood memories. Porter et al. employed the Memory Assessment Procedure (MAP) criteria. This consists of seven items designed to record phenomenological (subjective) features, and five items designed to record the specific features of memories. Content analysis revealed that participants rated true memories as more vivid/clear and more detailed. Participants also expressed more confidence in true memories when compared to the implanted memories. No difference was measured in stress levels. Additionally, 40% of participants recalled the real memory from a participant perspective. That is to say, they "re-experienced the event from their own eyes" (p. 28). The remaining 60% of participants viewed the real memory from the observer perspective, meaning they could view themselves as if watching a movie. The percentages were exactly reversed when participants recalled the implanted memory: 60% saw it from the participant perspective and 40% from the observer perspective. Although this was not a reliable difference, it does suggest that real and false memories may possibly differ in terms of their phenomenological and content features.

Heaps and Nash (2001) conducted another recent examination of differences between true and false memories. A variation of the Loftus and Pickrell paradigm was employed in order to plant false memories in participants. In other words, they used information from relatives to suggest to people that they had had certain experiences. The researchers replicated the basic finding of greater detail remembered for the true memories when compared to the false memories. On first pass, the true memories appeared different from the false memories, because they were rated as being more important, more emotionally intense, and more typical, and as having clearer imagery. These distinctions were eliminated when rehearsal frequency was used as a covariate in the statistical analyses. This suggests that increased rehearsal shifts the false memory closer to the recollective experience of true memories. A final observation concerned the consequences of the target event. False memories contained less information about any consequences of the event.

The move into the legal arena will clearly lag behind the scientific advances. It will be long after we are able to distinguish false memories from true ones in the lab that we may apply such standards to tests in the courtroom. Heaps and Nash (2001) illustrate the problem, "... the possibility [exists] that repeated remembering of false memories over greater periods of time [longer than 3 weeks] may make recollective experience more complete and more like that found in true autobiographical memories" (p. 17). Few things are more rehearsed than legal testimony, traumatic memories, and events made important by police and legal proceedings. Currently, external corroboration remains the only reliable way to determine the veracity of a memory.

Finally, there have been recent attempts to distinguish true from false memories at the physiological level using highly sophisticated brain-imaging techniques such as event-related potentials (ERPs), positron emission tomography (PET), and functional magnetic resonance imaging (fMRI). If in fact different "sensory signatures" in the brain can be used to differentiate true and false memories, then these physiological differences might hold great promise to memory researchers (Fabiani, Stadler & Wessels, 2000). To date, the results of this line of exploration are mixed. Perhaps most importantly, current brain-imaging techniques are most reliable when reporting group averages. Group averages, while valuable sources of information, tell the memory researcher very little about the real or illusory quality of a *particular* memory. While assessing the reliability of brainwave activity measured with an electroencephalograph (EEG), Hassett (1978) reported that one group of researchers may have put it best when they said, "we are like blind men trying to understand the workings of a factory by listening outside the walls" (as cited in Kassin, 2001, p. 51).

CONCLUSION

What is clear from the myriad studies conducted in the area of memory distortion, and specifically those exploring the parameters of the misinformation effect, is that misinformation can lead to memory changes ranging from minute details of events to memory for entire false events. While the misinformation effect is an extremely robust phenomenon, it can affect people in a number of ways. It can add to memory, it can just change what people report, and it sometimes appears to lead to impairments in previously stored memories.

The current comparison of true and false memories shows us that in general, the phenomenological experiences of both types of memory are indistinguishable (for details see Chapter 17). While some studies point to participants being clearer and more confident in their true memories (Loftus & Pickrell, 1995; Porter et al., 1999), others report less discernible evidence (Heaps & Nash, 2001; Roediger & McDermott, 1995). Along with technological advances in brain-imaging techniques comes the potential to distinguish between true and false memories at a physiological level. The ability to determine the "true" nature of a memory and exactly which areas of the brain are activated during the remembering process holds promise for both the courtroom and the therapist's office.

Heaps and Nash (2001) showed that false memories contained less information about consequences of the false event when compared to the consequences revealed when the memory was true. Future research on the consequences of memory distortion may also open a window on the issue of distinguishing true from false memories. The dog-bite study discussed here illustrates an overlooked power inherent in the acceptance of misinformation, namely the consequences of such behaviour. The applied perspectives are important as we look at not only the legal implications but also potential consequences under less extreme circumstances. The need to understand false memory reports and the impact on everyday actions becomes more important when we realize we are all susceptible to misinformation in myriad ways.

And given that we can manipulate positive events resulting in positive consequences as well as negative, there may be therapeutic implications whereby changes in memory and associations might be beneficial in changing future behaviours.

SUMMARY

- The misinformation effect occurs when a person receives post-event information (e.g., new information after the original event) that interferes with the person's ability to accurately recall the original event.
- The misinformation effect is a very robust phenomenon.
- The underlying cognitive mechanism remains less clear. As explanation, cognitive theories claim that either the original memory trace is altered or the original memory trace remains intact but inaccessible.
- The effect has been found with a variety of materials and experimental procedures, ranging from changing details of an event to planting false memories of an entire event.
- The consequences of memory distortions have important implications for several applied problems.
- As yet, we have no reliable means of distinguishing true from false memories.

FURTHER READING

An excellent overview about research on the misinformation effect was given by Ayers and Reder (1998). In addition, practical legal applications are explored in depth in Elizabeth F. Loftus and Katherine Ketcham (1991) *Witness for the defense: The accused, the eyewitness, and the expert who puts memory on trial*. For recent empirical articles, the *Journal of Applied Cognitive Psychology* (published by John Wiley & Sons) covers theoretical, empirical, as well as applied aspects of the misinformation effect. For information regarding the misinformation effect in children, see Ceci, Ross and Toglia (1987).

REFERENCES

Ayers, M. S., & Reder, L. M. (1998). A theoretical review of the misinformation effect: Predictions from an activation-based memory model. *Psychonomic Bulletin and Review*, 5, 1–21.

Bartlett, F. C. (1932/1995). *Remembering: A study in experimental and social psychology*. Cambridge: Cambridge University Press.

Braun, K. A. (1999). Postexperience advertising effects on consumer memory. *Journal of Marketing Research*, 25, 319–334.

Ceci, S. J., Ross, D. F., & Toglia, M. P. (1987). Suggestibility of children's memory: Psycholegal implications. *Journal of Experimental Psychology: General*, 116, 38–49.

Collins, H. R. (2001). *Another reason to dislike Chihuahuas and other small dogs: Behavioral consequences of false memories*. Unpublished honors thesis, University of Washington, USA.

Drivdahl, S. B., & Zaragoza, M. S. (2001). The role of perceptual elaboration and individual differences in the creation of false memories for suggested events. *Applied Cognitive Psychology*, 15, 265–281.

Fabiani, M., Stadler, M. A., & Wessels, P. M. (2000). True but not false memories produce a sensory signature in human lateralized brain potentials. *Journal of Cognitive Neuroscience*, 12, 941–949.

Garry, M., Manning, C. G., Loftus, E. F., & Sherman, S. J. (1996). Imagination inflation: Imagining a childhood event inflates confidence that it occurred. *Psychonomic Bulletin and Review*, 3, 208–214.

Heaps, C. M., & Nash, M. (2001). Comparing recollective experience in true and false autobiographical memories. *Journal of Experimental Psychology: Learning, Memory, and Cognition*, 27, 920–930.

Hyman, I. E. Jr., Husband, T. H., & Billings, F. J. (1995). False memories of childhood experiences. *Applied Cognitive Psychology*, 9, 181–197.

Hyman, I. E., & Pentland, J. (1996). The role of mental imagery in the creation of false childhood memories. *Journal of Memory and Language*, 35, 101–117.

Jacoby, L. L., Kelley, C. M., & Dywan, J. (1989). Memory attributions. In H. L. Roediger III, & F. I. M. Craik (Eds.), *Varieties of memory and consciousness: Essays in honour of Endel Tulving* (pp. 391–422). Hillsdale, NJ: Lawrence Erlbaum Associates Inc.

Kassin, S. (2001). *Psychology*. Upper Saddle River, NJ: Prentice-Hall.

Kelley, C. M., & Jacoby, L. L. (1996). Memory attributions: Remembering, knowing, and feeling of knowing. In L. M. Reder (Ed.), *Implicit memory and metacognition* (pp. 287–307). Hillsdale, NJ: Lawrence Erlbaum Associates Inc.

Loftus, E. F. (1975). Leading questions and the eyewitness report. *Cognitive Psychology*, 7, 560–572.

Loftus, E. F., & Ketcham, K. (1991). *Witness for the defense: The accused, the eyewitness, and the expert who puts memory on trial*. New York: St. Martin's Press.

Loftus, E. F., Levidow, B., & Duensing, S. (1992). Who remembers best? Individual differences in memory for events that occurred in a science museum. *Applied Cognitive Psychology*, 6, 93–107.

Loftus, E. F., Miller, D. G., & Burns, H. J. (1978). Semantic integration of verbal information into a visual memory. *Journal of Experimental Psychology: Human Learning and Memory*, 4, 19–31.

Loftus, E. F., & Palmer, J. C. (1974). Reconstruction of automobile destruction: An example of the interaction between language and memory. *Journal of Verbal Learning and Verbal Behavior, 13,* 585–589.

Loftus, E. F., & Pickrell, J. E. (1995). The formation of false memories. *Psychiatric Annals, 25,* 720–725.

Mazzoni, G. A. L., Loftus, E. F., & Kirsch, I. (2001). Changing beliefs about implausible autobiographical events: A little plausibility goes a long way. *Journal of Experimental Psychology: Applied, 7,* 51–59.

Mazzoni, G. A. L., Loftus, E. F., Seitz, A., & Lynn, S. (1999). Changing beliefs and memories through dream interpretation. *Applied Cognitive Psychology, 13,* 125–144.

McCloskey, M., & Zaragoza, M. (1985). Misleading postevent information and memory for events: Arguments and evidence against memory impairment hypotheses. *Journal of Experimental Psychology: General, 114,* 1–16.

Pezdek, K., Finger, K., & Hodge, D. (1997). Planting false childhood memories. *Psychological Science, 8,* 437–441.

Porter, S., Yuille, J. C., & Lehman, D. R. (1999). The nature of real, implanted, and fabricated memories for emotional childhood events: Implications for the recovered memory debate. *Law and Human Behavior, 23,* 517–537.

Roediger, H. L., III., & McDermott, K. B. (1995). Creating false memories: Remembering words not presented in lists. *Journal of Experimental Psychology: Learning, Memory, and Cognition, 21,* 803–814.

Tulving, E., & Thompson, D. M. (1973). Encoding specificity and retrieval processes in episodic memory. *Psychological Review, 80,* 352–373.

Wade, K. A., Garry, M., Read, J. D., & Lindsay, D. S. (2002). A picture is worth a thousand lies: Using false photographs to create false childhood memories. *Psychonomic Bulletin and Review, 9,* 597–603.

Zaragoza, M. S., McCloskey, M., & Jamis, M. (1987). Misleading postevent information and recall of the original event: Further evidence against the memory impairment hypothesis. *Journal of Experimental Psychology: Learning, Memory, and Cognition, 13,* 36–44.

20 Hindsight bias

Rüdiger F. Pohl

> Judgments about what is good and what is bad, what is worthwhile and what is a waste of talent, what is useful and what is less so, are judgments that seldom can be made in the present. They can safely be made only by posterity.
>
> (Tulving, 1991, p. 42)

In hindsight, we tend to exaggerate what we had known in foresight. For example, after being told that "absinthe" is not a precious stone but rather a liqueur, we are likely to express inflated confidence that we knew the solution all along (Fischhoff, 1975). This effect has been termed "hindsight bias" or the "knew-it-along effect" (Fischhoff, 1975) and has been observed in numerous studies to date (Christensen-Szalanski & Willham, 1991; Hawkins & Hastie, 1990; Hoffrage & Pohl, 2003). Common to all studies is that participants are in a state of uncertainty (which is necessary in order to observe the effect) usually accomplished by using rather difficult knowledge questions or uncertain events. As a result of these studies, it appears that after knowing the solution or outcome we are simply unable to access our uncontaminated foresight knowledge state (Pohl & Hell, 1996). Moreover, we are generally even unaware of the biasing process itself, that is, of how the solution might have influenced our recollection.

THE PHENOMENON OF HINDSIGHT BIAS

Designs

As the examples in Text box 20.1 demonstrate, the designs, materials, and measures used in hindsight studies are quite diverse. Most importantly, two different general experimental procedures have been employed. In the *memory* design (Examples 1 and 2 in Text box 20.1), people first give an (unbiased) estimate, then receive the solution, and are finally asked to recall their earlier estimate. In the *hypothetical* design (Examples 3 and 4), people receive the solution (or some other value) right away and are then asked to

> **Text box 20.1** Examples of hindsight bias
>
> (1) After a political election, people's recollections of their pre-election estimates were on average closer to the actual outcome than the original estimates had been.
> (2) In an unpublished study from our lab, 46 participants were asked – among other questions – to estimate the number of books Agatha Christie had written. The mean of the estimates was "51". Later the participants received the true solution of "67", and then recalled their original estimates. The mean of the recalled estimates was "63", that is, too close to the solution.
> (3) Being asked after the end of a basketball match and in comparison to other people's pre-game predictions, spectators were convinced that they would have correctly predicted the winning team (Pezzo, 2003).
> (4) In a cross-cultural Internet study on hindsight bias (Pohl, Bender, & Lachman, 2002), 227 participants received 20 numerical almanac questions, with half of them accompanied by the true solution (experimental items) and the other half not (control items). Participants were instructed to ignore the solutions (if given) and to generate their estimates independently. However, the mean distance between estimates and solutions was significantly smaller for experimental than for control items, namely 1.20 vs 1.65 (given in z-score units).

give an estimate as if they did not know the solution (hence the term "hypothetical"): "What would you have estimated?" Typically, hindsight bias is smaller in the memory than in the hypothetical design. However, this may only be due to the fact that correct recollections (with a bias of zero) are only possible in the memory design, thus diminishing the overall effect (see Pohl, Eisenhauer, & Hardt, 2003; Schwarz & Stahlberg, 2003).

The hypothetical design reminds one of the similar *anchoring* design (see Chapter 10). The only difference is that in the former the participants are simply informed about the solution and are then asked what they would have estimated before, while in the latter the solution (or some other value) is most often introduced as an allegedly random value and participants are first asked to indicate whether the true solution lies above or below this value before they then give an exact estimate. Both procedures lead to comparable distortions, suggesting that the same cognitive processes might be involved (Pohl et al., 2003), however, both designs are still treated separately in the literature.

Measures

In order to measure the amount of hindsight bias, different possibilities exist. The most common ones compare pre- and post-outcome estimates with respect to their distance to the solution. One such shift measure is given by the "ΔE" index (Pohl, 1992) that computes the difference between two distances, namely the distance between the original estimate O and the solution S and the distance between the recalled estimate R and the solution S, or more formally,

$$\Delta E = |O - S| - |R - S|.$$

A value of zero would indicate the absence of hindsight bias; any positive value its existence. To allow averaging across differently scaled questions as well as a more meaningful comparison between experiments, the data should be standardized (z-score transformation), so that the amount of hindsight bias will be expressed in standard deviation units. The according index "Δz" (Pohl, 1992) is accordingly defined as

$$\Delta z = |z_O - z_S| - |z_R - z_S|.$$

The standardizing is done separately for each question, but across all original and recalled estimates irrespective of experimental condition. The means and standard deviations per item are then used to also standardize the solutions. In Example 2 in Text box 20.1, the mean shift index (averaged across the individual indices) for the Agatha Christie question was $\Delta z = 0.284$, which was significantly larger than zero, $t(45) = 3.563$, $p < .001$. More examples of z-scored measures of hindsight bias are given below.

Definition

Generally, hindsight bias may be said to exist whenever the posterior estimates lie closer to the solution than the original ones did, that is, whenever the shift index is significantly larger than zero. However, an improvement in the estimates' quality may also simply result from thinking twice about the same question. Another source of "improvement" is given by possible regression effects (Pohl, 1995), because if the first estimates are distributed around the solution, then the chances of recollecting an estimate that deviates in the direction of the solution or even beyond are on the mean larger than of recollecting one that is in the opposite direction. Therefore, one needs to control presentation of the solution, in order to attribute hindsight bias to knowing the solution and not to repeated thinking or regression effects. This can be done by presenting some of the questions together with the solution (experimental items) and others without (control items). The definition of hindsight bias then needs to be extended accordingly to include that the shift index in the experimental condition should be positive and larger than in the control condition. Text box 20.2 provides an application of these considerations.

Text box 20.2 Application of the hindsight-bias index Δz

To continue the Agatha Christie example from Text box 20.1, a group of 45 other participants served as controls in that study, that is, they did not receive the solution. They gave a mean estimate of "51 books" and later recalled their estimates to have been "52" (on the mean). The corresponding mean Δz index (again averaged across the individual indices) was found to be −0.190. Note that while the absolute means indicate a slight shift *towards* the solution (which was "67"), the Δz index yields a *negative* score, which signals that some recalled estimates must have "moved" far beyond the solution and were even farther away from the solution than the original estimates had been.

Comparing the indices for experimental and control participants in our example, namely, $\Delta z = 0.284$ and −0.190, respectively, showed a significant difference, $t(89) = 4.299$, $p < 0.001$, with a large effect size, $d = 0.89$, thus suggesting the existence of hindsight bias.

Relevance

Besides its relevance for theories about storage and retrieval of information (Pohl et al., 2003), hindsight bias also has several practical implications (Christensen-Szalanski & Willham, 1991). For example, consider a researcher who is asked to review a manuscript but knows the results of a previous review from someone else, or a physician who is asked for a second opinion on a serious diagnosis but knows the first one. Many studies have demonstrated that in these cases the new and allegedly independent judgements are most likely biased towards the already available ones (see Hawkins & Hastie, 1990). In other words, second judgements are less independent than we and the judges themselves like to think they are. This could have serious consequences, especially if the first judgement is poor, dubious, arbitrary, or simply wrong.

A general problem with hindsight bias might be that feeling wiser after the outcome is known could also lead us to a too optimistic evaluation of our prior knowledge state. But if we consider ourselves more knowledgeable than we really were, we could easily overestimate our abilities for similar situations in the future. For example, having understood – in hindsight – how an accident came about, or why two nations went to war, could lull us into a false sense of security. The opposite problem occurs if, for example, relatives and friends of suicide victims feel guilty because they overestimate their prior chances of predicting, and possibly preventing, the suicide. Hindsight bias may be at least partially responsible for this inflated feeling of guilt. Similar influences have been discussed in connection with depression or the chronification of pain.

HINDSIGHT-BIAS EXPERIMENT

As a classroom demonstration of hindsight bias, I suggest an adapted version of the experimental procedure employed by several studies (e.g., Hell, Gigerenzer, Gauggel, Mall, & Müller, 1988; Pohl, 1998; Pohl et al., 2003; Pohl & Hell, 1996, Exp. 1). These experiments used numerical almanac questions in the memory design with a 1-week retention interval. Text box 20.3 provides all necessary details to set up a simplified classroom experiment.

Text box 20.3 A classroom demonstration of hindsight bias

Method

Participants

Setting $\alpha = 0.05$ and $\beta = 0.20$, the experiment needs 40 participants to optimally test for a large effect size ($f = 0.40$), or 100 participants to test for a medium effect size ($f = 0.25$). From my experience with hindsight studies, the effect sizes are usually between medium and large, so that any sample size between 40 and 100 should suffice.

Material

A total of 40 difficult numerical almanac questions from different domains are used as materials (see Appendix). Examples are "How old was Mahatma Gandhi when he was shot?" or "How many islands make up Hawaii?" These or similar questions have been used in the cited studies, which used between 40 and 88 such items.

Design

The simplest design is used here, with only one within-subject factor. Participants receive the solution to half the questions (experimental condition), but not to the other half (control condition). Dependent measures are the percentage of correct recollections and the shift index Δz (as given above).

Procedure

The experiment is run in the memory design with a 1-week retention interval between sessions. In Session 1, participants receive a questionnaire with the 40 questions (without the solutions), are asked to estimate the answers to the questions as exactly as possible, and to write these in the open spaces next to each question. In order to avoid frustration on the part of the participants, instructions should stress that the questions were deliberately selected to be very difficult and that it is not expected from the participant that he or she knows the exact solutions. There is no time limit, but participants should be encouraged to work fluently through the questionnaire, not musing too long on single questions. At the end of the session, participants are kindly requested not to look up any of the questions and not to talk to other persons about their estimates. They will get all the solutions in Session 2.

In Session 2, a week later, participants receive the same questionnaire as in the first session, but now accompanied by the solutions to half of the questions. Which half is given with the solution and which one without should be counterbalanced across participants, so that each question serves equally often as experimental and as control item. Participants are instructed to carefully read through the questions and the solutions and to try to recall as exactly as possible their estimates from last week, and to write these in the open spaces next to each question. At the end, participants are debriefed about the purpose of the study and are given the remaining solutions if they wish.

Analysis

In order to take care of extreme estimates, a convenient procedure is to delete all estimates that are outside the median plus or minus three times the interquartile range for each question. The remaining data are then transformed into *z*-scores separately for each question.

Every recalled estimate that exactly matches the original one is counted as a correct recollection. The absolute frequencies of correct recollections in experimental and control conditions can be compared with a paired t-test (with $df = N - 1$). For the remaining pairs of original and incorrectly recalled estimates, the shift indices Δz are computed and then averaged across all items in the same condition for each participant. As a result, two mean shift indices are obtained for each participant, one for the experimental and one for the control items. The overall means of these two conditions can then be compared by running a paired t-test (with $df = N - 1$).

Results

Correct recollections

After 1 week, approximately 20–30% of the original estimates were correctly recalled. Pohl (1998) reported percentages of 19, 22, and 26 for his Experiments 1 to 3, respectively. Similarly, Pohl et al. (2003) observed an overall percentage of 26.5% and Pohl (1992) one of 26%. Using fewer items and thus probably enhancing memory, Pohl and Hell (Exp. 2) found a higher proportion of 36% correctly recalled estimates after 1 week. Similarly, Hell et al. (1988), who requested reasons from their participants for half of their estimates, found a relatively high 35.1%.

With respect to the comparison of experimental and control conditions, only two of the cited studies reported small but statistically significant differences. Pohl (1988, Exp. 3) found 24% and 27% of correctly recalled estimates for experimental and control items, respectively. The corresponding numbers in the Pohl et al. (2003) study were highly similar, namely 24.5% and 28.4%, respectively. In other words, if anything, original estimates tend

Hindsight bias

Comparing the mean shift indices for experimental and control items showed significant differences in all of the cited studies (see Figure 20.1; the results of Hell et al., 1988, were not included, because the authors used a different measure). When the solution was given, the recalled estimates were (on the mean) much closer to the solution than the original estimates, but remained virtually unchanged (on the mean) when the solution was not given. Presenting the solution obviously led to a strong hindsight bias. More precisely, recalled estimates in the experimental condition "moved" about one fifth of a standard deviation towards the solutions. Looking at the individual studies revealed some differences in the amount of hindsight bias that varied from $\Delta z = 0.11$ to 0.27 in the experimental conditions of these studies (see Figure 20.1). This could, of course, be due to random error or to other variables that were manipulated in those studies, but were omitted here for the sake of simplicity. Another way to look at the data is given in Text box 20.4.

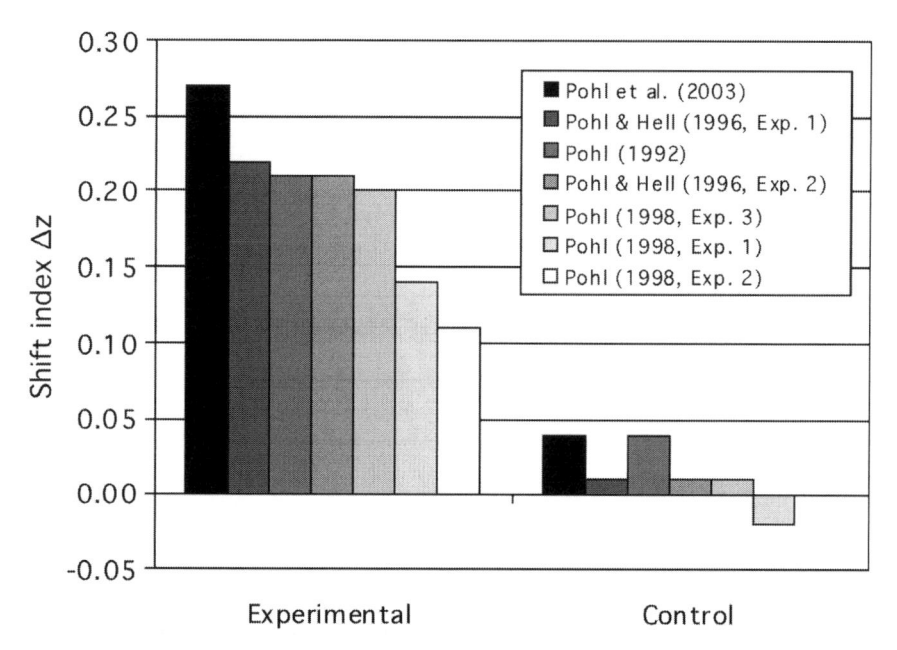

Figure 20.1 Mean shift indices for experimental and control items in several studies in the memory design (ordered according to values for experimental items; positive values indicate that the recalled estimates were closer to the solution than the original ones had been).

Text box 20.4 Distribution of individual hindsight bias indices for experimental and control items

Another and possibly more instructive way of presenting the results of a hindsight bias study is to look at the *distribution* of the individual pairs of hindsight bias indices for experimental and control items. Taking the Pohl et al. (2003) study as an example, Figure 20.2 depicts these data, with each dot respresenting one participant ($N = 99$). For experimental items, many more participants showed a positive shift index than a negative one (i.e., 83 vs 16 persons, respectively), suggesting a systematic distortion, namely hindsight bias. In contrast, the distribution of positive and negative shifts for control items was completely balanced (i.e., 44 vs 45 persons, respectively), suggesting that no systematic influence governed the reconstruction of one's estimates for these questions.

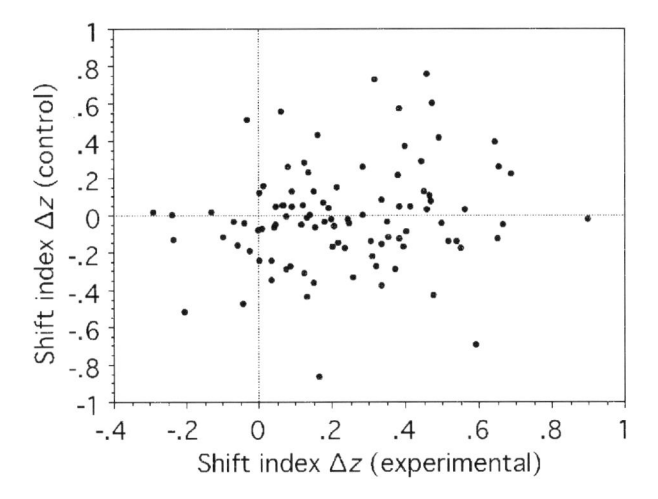

Figure 20.2 Scattergram of mean individual shift indices for experimental and control items in one study (Pohl et al., 2003).

Discussion

In all of the cited studies on which the classroom demonstration was based, participants generated estimates as answers to difficult almanac-type knowledge questions, received the solutions to half of these questions after 1 week, and then tried to recall their original estimates. The results showed two stable findings.

First, about one fourth of all estimates were correctly recalled. This percentage was similar for experimental items (i.e., questions with the solution given) and control items (i.e., questions without the solution), except in a few cases in which the percentage was slightly, but statistically significantly, lower in the experimental condition (Pohl, 1988, Exp. 3; Pohl et al., 2003; see also Schwarz & Stahlberg, 2003, Exp. 2).

As the second stable result, all studies provided clear evidence of hindsight bias. If the solutions were given prior to the recall test, estimates were recalled as being closer to the solutions than they had actually been, as indicated by a positive shift index Δz. In contrast, estimates in the control condition, in which the solution was not given, were not recalled with a systematic bias. The stability of this result conforms to the finding of Christensen-Szalanski and Willham (1991) who conducted a meta-analysis and detected among 122 experiments on hindsight bias only 6 without the typical effect. It appears that participants are simply not able to avoid utilizing the solution in reconstructing their earlier knowledge state (Fischhoff, 1975; Hawkins & Hastie, 1990; Hoffrage, Hertwig, & Gigerenzer, 2000). Which processes might be responsible for this, is discussed in the next section.

THEORETICAL ACCOUNTS

Despite the impressive evidence for the existence of hindsight bias, the underlying mechanisms that are responsible for hindsight bias are still under debate (see Hoffrage et al., 2000; Pohl et al., 2003; Schwarz & Stahlberg, 2003; Stahlberg & Maass, 1998). Besides assuming specific cognitive processes (that have recently even been simulated in computational models), some approaches question the role of metacognitions and individual differences in general.

Cognitive processes

Most prominent among the proposed explanations are *cognitive* accounts which assume that hindsight bias results from an inability to ignore the solution. Among the early approaches are the following three: (1) Fischhoff (1975) assumed an immediate and irreversible assimilation of the solution into one's knowledge base. As a consequence, the reconstructed estimate will be biased towards the solution. (2) Tversky and Kahneman (1974) proposed a cognitive heuristic for the anchoring effect, named anchoring and insufficient adjustment (cf. Chapter 10). The same mechanism may apply here, if the solution is assumed to serve as an "anchor" in the reconstruction process. The reconstruction starts from this anchor and is then adjusted in the direction of one's knowledge base. However, this adjustment process may stop too early, for example at the point where the first plausible value is reached, thus leading to a biased reconstruction. (3) Hell et al. (1988) argued that the relative trace strengths of the original estimate and of the solution might predict the amount of hindsight bias. The stronger the trace strength of the solution relative to that of the original estimate, the larger hindsight bias should be.

The ongoing debate on how to explain hindsight bias through cognitive processes has recently focused on the point in time at which hindsight bias may be caused (Hertwig, Fanselow, & Hoffrage, 2003; Pohl et al., 2003; Schwarz & Stahlberg, 2003). Is the distortion an effect of irreversibly encoding the solution, thus altering one's knowledge base (as Fischhoff, 1975, had suggested), or an effect of the solution biasing one's memory search during reconstruction?

In their "biased-reconstruction theory", Stahlberg and Maas (1998) adopted the latter view. They proposed that biased reconstruction instead of memory impairment is responsible for hindsight bias. They followed the criticism that was levelled against the memory-impairment hypotheses in eyewitness-misinformation studies (cf. Chapter 19). More precisely, the authors assumed that presenting the solution does not alter one's knowledge base, but leads to the solution being used as a retrieval cue in the reconstruction process (see also Schwarz & Stahlberg, 2003). As a consequence, the percentage of perfectly recalled estimates should not be diminished by presenting the solution. Most studies showed indeed no difference between experimental and control condition. However, whenever a significant (albeit small) difference was detected, it was always in favour of the control condition. In other words, the percentage of perfectly recalled estimates was either identical or slightly (but significantly) less in the experimental as compared to the control condition, suggesting that memory could be at least marginally affected by presenting the solution (see Schwarz & Stahlberg, 2003).

Apart from this debate, it seems undisputed that solutions may serve as retrieval cues thereby biasing memory search. Most likely, a solution activates knowledge that is most similar to it (cf. the "confirmation bias" in Chapter 4), thus leading to a search result that may not be representative of the given knowledge base. Alternatively, the solution is used to update uncertain knowledge (see Hoffrage et al., 2000, and Hertwig et al., 2003).

Computational model

Pohl et al. (2003) introduced a cognitive process model, named SARA (*Selective Activation and Reconstructive Anchoring*), which incorporates both of the possible mechanisms discussed above. The model makes detailed assumptions about the memorial representation of the item-specific knowledge base and the cognitive processes operating thereupon. The SARA model assumes that the item-specific knowledge base consists of a number of units (called "images") that are associatively connected according to their degree of similarity. Based on this knowledge (the "image set"), cyclic search and retrieval processes (called "sampling") are used to generate an estimate, to encode the solution, and to later recall or reconstruct the original estimate. Sampling (as well as forgetting) modifies the matrix of association strengths among the images themselves and between images and externally provided retrieval cues (like the question or the solution). The total activation strength of an image determines its likelihood of being found and retrieved in memory search. New images (e.g., estimates and solutions) can be added to one's image set.

Hindsight bias is assumed to be the result of "selective activation", "biased sampling", or both: Encoding the solution may change the association strengths within the image set (selective activation), and at retrieval the solution may bias the memory search towards solution-related images (biased sampling), or both. The first process represents a change within long-term memory (as, e.g., proposed in the assimilation theory; Fischhoff, 1975), while the second one represents an effect of the retrieval process (as, e.g., proposed in the biased-reconstruction theory; Stahlberg & Mass, 1998; Schwarz & Stahlberg, 2003). The result of both processes is that the set of images retrieved during reconstruction most likely differs in a systematic way from the set of images retrieved during the generation of the original estimate. As a consequence, the reconstructed estimate will most likely be biased towards the solution.

The model is devised to capture all changes in each participant's individual knowledge base in each phase of the experimental procedure. The model is thus able to predict the participant's performance at any point in time. The computational precision of the model exceeds previous approaches, so that SARA has been successfully implemented as a computer program that allows simulation of empirical data as well as prediction of new findings (see Hoffrage et al., 2000, and Hertwig et al., 2003, for another computational but more limited model).

Metacognitions

Several studies showed that metacognitions might significantly moderate and even eliminate or reverse hindsight bias (e.g., Pezzo, 2003; Pohl, 1998; Schwarz & Stahlberg, 2003). One area of research looked at the role of *surprise* that someone may perceive when receiving the solution. In these studies, hindsight bias was often reduced or even totally absent (Pezzo, 2003). Instead of "having known it all along", participants might experience in these cases a feeling of "I would never have known that". Accordingly, they managed neither to integrate the solution into their knowledge base nor to use it as a retrieval cue. Schwarz and Stahlberg (2003, Exp. 2) manipulated participants' assumptions of how close their original estimates allegedly were to the solutions. The authors found that hindsight bias was significantly larger when participants believed their estimates had been rather good than when they thought they had been rather poor. In a different approach, Pohl (1998, Exp. 2 and 3) found that only solutions that were considered plausible by the participants led to hindsight bias, while those that were considered implausible did not.

Summarizing these and other studies, it appears that certain metacognitions may prevent (or hamper) the solution from exerting its biasing effects.

However, the processes linked to metacognitions are not intentionally controllable, as one might be tempted to think. Rather, these cognitive processes are still automatic in nature. Otherwise it would be easy to avoid the bias.

Individual differences

Whereas cognitive explanations have been the most often cited and also most successful models in hindsight bias research, several authors have repeatedly addressed the question of *individual differences*. They measured (or manipulated) appropriate variables and found significant correlations with the amount of hindsight bias (see Christensen-Szalanski & Willham, 1991, and Musch, 2003, for summaries).

For example, Musch (2003) found that hindsight bias (in the hypothetical design) was positively related to field dependence, to the tendency for a favourable self-presentation, to the participants' conscientiousness, and to their need for predictability and control (see also Campbell & Tesser, 1983). The motive of *self-presentation* has possibly gained the most attention (Campbell & Tesser, 1983; Fischhoff, 1975; Stahlberg & Maass, 1998). Besides, when informed about the hindsight bias phenomenon, most people suggest that a self-presentation motive could be the cause for the observed "distortion". According to this view, participants of hindsight studies simply try to appear smarter than they really are (see Hawkins & Hastie, 1990, p. 316). The popular connotation of the term "knew-it-all-along" effect (Fischhoff, 1975) denotes the same issue. In addition, Campbell and Tesser (1983) reported a positive correlation between hindsight bias and the amount of ego involvement.

In their meta-analysis of hindsight studies, Christensen-Szalanski and Willham (1991) pointed to another influential individual factor, namely the level of familiarity (or expertise) with the material (see also Hertwig et al., 2003). The more familiar the material (or the more knowledgeable the participant), the smaller the hindsight bias.

Summarizing the findings on individual differences in hindsight bias, one may conclude that some effects have been found, but that these were mostly small and difficult to replicate. Several studies (not cited here) failed to find corresponding effects. The same conclusion was drawn in a recent cross-cultural Internet study on hindsight bias with 225 participants from four continents (Pohl et al., 2002; Example 4 in Text box 20.1). Musch (2003), however, reported some medium-sized correlations between hindsight bias and personal characteristics so that individual differences should not be dismissed as possible source of influence.

CONCLUSIONS

Hindsight bias is an extremely robust phenomenon that can easily be demonstrated (Christensen-Szalanski & Willham, 1991; Hawkins & Hastie, 1990). The first computational models have been advanced recently allowing precise simulation and testing of the processes assumed to be responsible for hindsight bias (Hoffrage et al., 2000; Pohl et al., 2003). These models promise to improve our understanding of the underlying mechanisms. This may also be helpful in trying to overcome the bias or at least to take it appropriately into account in everyday settings.

Finally, some authors argued that hindsight bias is not necessarily a bothersome consequence of a "faulty" information processing system, but that it may rather represent an unavoidable by-product of an evolutionary evolved function, namely adaptive learning (e.g., Campbell & Tesser, 1983; Hertwig et al., 2003; Hoffrage et al., 2000; Pohl et al., 2002). According to this view, hindsight bias is seen as the consequence of our most valuable ability to update previously held knowledge. This may be seen as a necessary process in order to prevent memory overload and thus to maintain normal cognitive functioning. Besides, updating allows us to keep our knowledge more coherent and to draw better inferences. Of course, there are situations in which one may wish to exactly assess one's previous knowledge state. But these cases might be relatively rare in real life, so that the disadvantage of a biased memory reconstruction (as exemplified in hindsight bias) is probably more than outweighed by the benefits of adaptive learning. Going beyond this view, some authors have even suggested that hindsight bias itself represents an adaptive function (see Pohl et al., 2002). Being in hindsight, thus, may also be advantageous for us (see Chapter 22). This is an intriguing, but presently rather speculative, idea that certainly deserves future research.

SUMMARY

- Hindsight bias occurs when persons in hindsight (e.g., after an outcome is known) overestimate what they had (or would have) estimated in foresight.
- As explanation, cognitive theories claim that either the knowledge base is altered or that memory search is biased by the known outcome.
- Hindsight bias is a very robust phenomenon that cannot be reduced intentionally.
- The effect has been found with a variety of materials and experimental procedures.
- Metacognitions (like surprise) may moderate the amount of hindsight bias.
- Motivational factors and individual differences play only minor roles.

- The phenomenon has important implications for several applied problems.

FURTHER READING

An excellent overview about research on hindsight bias was given by Hawkins and Hastie (1990). In addition, Christensen-Szalanski and Willham (1991) published an instructive meta-analysis. The empirical development since then and a detailed cognitive process model are described by Pohl et al. (2003). This paper and a selection of others recently appeared as a special issue of *Memory* (Hoffrage & Pohl, 2003), covering theoretical, empirical, as well as applied aspects of hindsight bias.

ACKNOWLEDGEMENTS

The cited studies of the author have been supported by grants from the Deutsche Forschungsgemeinschaft. Helpful comments on an earlier version of this chapter were provided by Michael Bender, Martin Heydemann, and Gregor Lachmann. The citation at the beginning of the chapter was taken from Tulving, E. (1991). Memory research is not a zero-sum game. *American Scientist*, 46, 41–42.

REFERENCES

Campbell, J. D., & Tesser, A. (1983). Motivational interpretations of hindsight bias: An individual difference analysis. *Journal of Personality*, 51, 605–620.

Christensen-Szalanski, J. J. J., & Willham, C. F. (1991). The hindsight bias: A meta-analysis. *Organizational Behavior and Human Decision Processes*, 48, 147–168.

Fischhoff, B. (1975). Hindsight ≠ foresight: The effect of outcome knowledge on judgment under uncertainty. *Journal of Experimental Psychology: Human Perception and Performance*, 1, 288–299.

Hawkins, S. A., & Hastie, R. (1990). Hindsight: Biased judgments of past events after the outcomes are known. *Psychological Bulletin*, 107, 311–327.

Hell, W., Gigerenzer, G., Gauggel, S., Mall, M., & Müller, M. (1988). Hindsight bias: An interaction of automatic and motivational factors? *Memory & Cognition*, 16, 533–538.

Hertwig, R., Fanselow, C., & Hoffrage, U. (2003). Hindsight bias: How does foresight knowledge and its processing affect our reconstruction of the past? *Memory*, 11, 357–377.

Hoffrage, U., Hertwig, R., & Gigerenzer, G. (2000). Hindsight bias: A by-product of knowledge-updating? *Journal of Experimental Psychology: Learning, Memory, and Cognition*, 26, 566–581.

Hoffrage, U., & Pohl, R. F. (Eds.). (2003). Hindsight bias [Special Issue]. *Memory*, 11(4/5).

Musch, J. (2003). Personality differences in hindsight bias. *Memory, 11*, 473–489.

Pezzo, M. V. (2003). Surprise, defence, or making sense: What removes the hindsight bias? *Memory, 11*, 421–441.

Pohl, R. F. (1992). Der Rückschau-Fehler: systematische Verfälschung der Erinnerung bei Experten und Novizen [Hindsight bias: Systematic distortions of the memory of experts and laymen]. *Kognitionswissenschaft, 3*, 38–44.

Pohl, R. F. (1995). Disenchanting hindsight bias. In J.-P. Caverni, M. Bar-Hillel, F. H. Barron, & H. Jungermann (Eds.), *Contributions to decision making* (pp. 323–334). Amsterdam: Elsevier.

Pohl, R. F. (1998). The effects of feedback source and plausibility on hindsight bias. *European Journal of Cognitive Psychology, 10*, 191–212.

Pohl, R. F., Bender, M., & Lachmann, G. (2002). Hindsight bias around the world. *Experimental Psychology, 49*, 270–282.

Pohl, R. F., Eisenhauer, M., & Hardt, O. (2003). SARA – A cognitive process model to simulate anchoring effect and hindsight bias. *Memory, 11*, 337–356.

Pohl, R. F., & Hell, W. (1996). No reduction of hindsight bias with complete information and repeated testing. *Organizational Behavior and Human Decision Processes, 67*, 49–58.

Schwarz, S., & Stahlberg, D. (2003). Strength of the hindsight bias as a consequence of meta-cognitions. *Memory, 11*, 395–410.

Stahlberg, D., & Maass, A. (1998). Hindsight bias: Impaired memory or biased reconstruction? In W. Stroebe & M. Hewstone (Eds.), *European review of social psychology* (Vol. 8, pp. 105–132), Chichester, UK: Wiley.

Tversky, A., & Kahneman, D. (1974). Judgment under uncertainty: Heuristics and biases. *Science, 185*, 1124–1131.

APPENDIX

Almanac questions and solutions [in brackets]

1. What percentage of the surface of the earth consists of water? [71%]
2. What is the mean life expectancy of a canary in years? [25 years]
3. How often on average does the heart of a mouse beat in one minute? [650 times]
4. How many times larger is the diameter of the planet Jupiter compared to the Earth? [11 times]
5. How many different kind of insects inhabit the Antarctic? [52 kinds]
6. How many keys does a piano have? [88]
7. How long is the life expectancy of a healthy red blood corpuscle (in days)? [120 days]
8. How many teeth has a dog? [42]
9. How many prime numbers does the interval between 1 and 1000 contain? [168]
10. How many days does it take the sun to fully rotate around its axis? [25.4 days]
11. When did the first manned space flight take place? [1961]

12 How many bones does a human have? [214]
13 How old was Mahatma Gandhi when he was shot? [78 years]
14 What is the length of pregnancy of a rat in days? [25 days]
15 How old is the oldest tree on earth (in years)? [4600 years]
16 How many crime novels were written by Agatha Christie? [67]
17 In what year did the first Olympiad of the modern era take place? [1896]
18 What is the maximum length of a total solar eclipse (in minutes)? [7 min]
19 What is the radius of the earth (in kilometres)? [6378 km]
20 In what year did Leonardo Da Vinci paint the "Mona Lisa"? [1503]
21 How high is the Statue of Liberty in New York (in metres)? [93 m]
22 What is the average length of a human adult's kidney (in centimetres)? [12 cm]
23 In what year was a human heart transplanted for the first time? [1967]
24 What is the mean body temperature of a ground hog (in °C)? [31.7 °C]
25 How long is an international sea mile in metres? [1852 m]
26 How old was Martin Luther King when he was shot? [39 years]
27 What is the height of the Mount Everest (in metres)? [8848 m]
28 In what year did the Roman Emperor Nero commit suicide? [68 AD]
29 How high is the Cheops pyramid in Egypt (in metres)? [147 m]
30 What is the airline distance between New York and Berlin, Germany? [6374 km]
31 In what year was the North Atlantic Treaty Organization (NATO) founded? [1949]
32 What is the weight of a regular tennis ball (in grams)? [57 g]
33 How long is the mean pregnancy period of a female elephant in days? [631 days]
34 What is the average winter temperature in the Antarctic (in °C)? [−68 °C]
35 How many star constellations (including the zodiac signs) are officially recognized? [88]
36 When did Albert Einstein first visit the USA? [1921]
37 At what temperature does tin ore begin to melt (in °C)? [232 °C]
38 How long is the Great Wall of China (in kilometres)? [2450 km]
39 How many islands make up Hawaii? [132]
40 How long is the Panama canal (in kilometres)? [81.6 km]

21 Illusions of change or stability

Anne Wilson and Michael Ross

> I do not know myself, and God forbid that I should.
>
> Johann Wolfgang von Goethe (1749–1832)

Despite Goethe's disclaimer and Freud's claims about the unconscious, people probably know themselves better than they know anyone else. We alone have direct access to our private thoughts and feelings. We alone have witnessed and experienced every event in our lives. Even close relatives and lovers know only some of our private thoughts and some of our experiences. For many of us, the self is uniquely fascinating, as well as familiar. Dedicated personal historians, we dwell on our past experiences in thought and conversation.

Occasionally other people share our interest in our personal histories. Friends ask, "What's new?" Our children are curious about what we were like as kids. Were we shy? Were we good students? Our co-workers request a description of a business meeting that they did not attend. Who talked, what did they say, how did people react? Physicians ask us for our medical histories. How often do we have headaches, what medications do we take, when and why did we have any operations? Consumer surveyors ask us to report our purchases and our experiences with anything from motor vehicle accidents to Internet use. Research psychologists, too, rely on respondents' memories. A psychologist studying family conflict might ask spouses to describe their conflicts with each other and their children.

Although we have lived through the experiences and are enthusiastic and dedicated personal historians, we are often handicapped by our memories as we struggle to answer such questions. When we search our recollections, we often find that the best we can do is to retrieve bits and pieces of memories. We are pretty certain that we were shyer and less hardworking as children than now, but we remember only a few relevant childhood incidents. Similarly, we recall some but not all aspects of a business meeting, a few but not all features of a family conflict, and some recent headaches but not their frequency.

With no more than fragments of the past to work with, we reconstruct our memories much as a palaeontologist recreates a dinosaur from only a few bits of bone (e.g., Bartlett, 1932; Neisser, 1967). These fragments of the past are rarely sufficient to yield a full representation of the past. Both the personal historian and the palaeontologist use their current knowledge and beliefs to interpret the fragments and fill in gaps. Palaeontologists' understanding of geology, biology, and prehistory guide their restoration of the fossil. Similarly, personal historians' current knowledge and beliefs about themselves and others help them to recreate the past. Also like palaeontologists, personal historians are guided by theories as they reconstruct the past.

Suppose, for example, a bank manager tries to remember how she felt about a subordinate 5 years ago when she first interviewed him for a job. Her memory for the interview is likely to be hazy – she has interviewed many other job applicants since. As she struggles to remember the interview, she is likely to be very aware of her current knowledge and feelings ("He is lazy"); she has to decide whether she was uncertain or enthusiastic during the interview (Ross, 1989). Her answer will depend both on any evidence she can recall from the interview and on her theories about herself (e.g., my feelings of people tend not to change much; I am a good judge of character; I hired him, so I must have liked him).

One intriguing aspect of knowledge and theories is that they sometimes shift over time. Palaeontologists' beliefs about dinosaur biology have changed dramatically in the last couple of decades. Consequently, many of the older dinosaur reconstructions presently displayed in museums are thought to be misrepresentations, akin to false memories of a distant past. Just as scientific knowledge about dinosaurs shifts over time, so too do personal historians' knowledge and beliefs about themselves and other people. Despite her current opinion, the bank manager could have been very enthusiastic when she hired the subordinate; and the subordinate might have been a good worker back then. Although people and beliefs change, rememberers often seem to exaggerate the similarity between the past and the present. They construct a past that too closely resembles the present.

ILLUSIONS OF STABILITY

We haven't studied bank managers, but we have studied lovers. McFarland and Ross (1987) asked university students to report their feelings about their dating partner at two points in time. Between the two assessment periods, some participants fell more in love. When asked to recall how they felt about their partner at the first assessment period, these participants remembered being more complimentary towards their partner, and more in love, than they reported in their earlier assessments. In contrast, those who fell less in love with their partner recalled being less complimentary and less in love than their earlier assessments had indicated. People appeared to project their current feelings backwards into the past. If their partner is lovable now, they presume he or she must always have been so (How could one not love such a splendid person?). A relationship that turns sour was never so great (How could one ever love such a loser?). Along these same lines, one of the small tragedies of marital break-up is that divorcing couples often seem to have difficulty remembering their earlier affection for each other and their good times together.

Other researchers have obtained evidence of an illusion of stability. As with romantic partners, people fall in and out of love with politicians and in doing so underestimate the degree to which their attitudes have changed (Levine, 1997). Perhaps the most startling demonstration of the illusion of stability was conducted by Goethals and Reckman (1973) who experimentally manipulated participants' attitudes in a two-session study. During the first session, high-school students completed a questionnaire in which they reported their opinions on various social issues. Several days to a couple of weeks later, the students participated in a "rigged" group discussion that massively altered their attitudes on one specific social issue, "bussing" to achieve racial integration in the schools. The bussing issue dealt with whether school children should be sent (by bus) to schools outside their neighbourhoods to achieve racially mixed schools. The issue was very controversial at the time of the study. Following the discussion of bussing which changed their attitudes, students were given a blank version of the questionnaire that they had completed in the first session. They were asked to answer the items on the questionnaire exactly as they had during the first session. In responding to this questionnaire, students showed little awareness of their changed attitudes. Although their opinions on bussing had shifted considerably, they recalled having the same views as they *currently* held.

How could the participants apparently forget their earlier opinions so quickly and on such an important attitude issue? To answer this question, put yourself in the place of these students as they tried to recall their earlier attitudes. Presumably, their current attitude toward bussing is more accessible than any previous attitude. They know how they feel about bussing now and they know the arguments to support their opinion. If their previous attitude is not readily accessible, they might attempt to infer it in order to answer the item on the questionnaire. They have to decide whether a few days or weeks earlier their attitude was different from their current opinion. In general, individuals expect their attitudes to be stable over short periods of time (Ross, 1989). Also, they did not enter the study wanting or expecting a change in attitudes. Nor did they think that the experiment was designed to alter their views. Its true purpose was disguised by the experimenters. When people change their opinions in such circumstances, are they likely to recognize that they have done so? Perhaps not, because cues that might lead people to suppose a change in attitudes are absent (e.g., a long time period, a desire for change, or effort directed towards change).

ILLUSIONS OF CHANGE

The analysis of the Goethals and Reckman (1973) study indicates that people should not always infer that the past mirrors the present. There are circumstances that lead individuals to assume change. When people's beliefs about change are exaggerated, they recall a past as having been more divergent from the present than it actually was. For example, people typically expect self-help programmes (e.g., weight loss, study skills) to be effective. Despite the proliferation of self-help books, tapes, and courses, however, most self-help programmes fail (e.g., Polivy & Herman, 2002). Conway and Ross (1984) studied the effect of a study skills programme on perceptions of change and memory. They found that participants who went through an ineffective study skills programme still reported improvement in study skills, compared to a group randomly assigned to receive no training. Also, programme participants recalled their study skills as being significantly worse before they took the programme than they had reported initially. By revising the past downwards, participants were able to claim improvement in the apparent absence of any actual change. Safer and Keuler (2002) reported similar findings when examining psychotherapy patients' recall of their pre-therapy levels of distress.

We suspect that, at the end of the treatment, participants in many self-improvement programmes essentially say to themselves: "I may not be perfect now, but I was much worse before I took the programme." If participants do say this to themselves, they are often partly right and partly wrong. They are right that they are not perfect now. They are wrong that they were much worse before they took to the programme. Such biased illusions of change might help explain why the self-help industry thrives despite its ineffectiveness.

Although Greenwald (1980) suggested that illusions of change represent a "special case" and should be less common than illusions of stability, there is considerable evidence for these unwarranted perceptions of personal change. In particular, people seem inclined to exaggerate their degree of improvement. For example, Woodruff and Birren (1972) studied individuals who had completed a test of personal and social adjustment 25 years earlier. Woodruff and Birren retested these individuals on the same adjustment measure, and found considerable stability in people's scores over 25 years. Woodruff and Birren also asked participants to complete the adjustment measure as they thought they had 25 years earlier. Participants recalled being much less well-adjusted in the past than they currently were and less well-adjusted than they had reported earlier.

We found that it did not require a span of 25 years for people to claim false improvement on personal characteristics (Wilson & Ross, 2001, Study 3). University students used an 11-point scale to rate themselves on a variety of attributes (e.g., social skills, self-confidence, life satisfaction) in September, near the beginning of the school semester. Two months later, in

November, they rated themselves again on the same attributes. Their self-assessments did not shift dramatically over this time; if anything, they rated themselves a little less favourably later in the term (Ms = 6.35 in September; 6.05 in November). In November, they were also asked to remember what they were like in September. In retrospect, students downgraded their earlier self. They rated their September self (M = 5.74) as inferior to their November self, and worse than they had originally indicated. The students apparently perceived illusory improvement in the face of actual minor decline.

In additional research, we found that people would recall a former self as inferior to their current self only when they *perceived* the time interval between the two to be long enough to justify improvement (Wilson & Ross, 2001, Study 6). Interestingly, the subjective experience of time is malleable and can be quite independent of actual time (Ross & Wilson, 2002). In this study, we kept actual time constant (2 months) but altered the *appearance* of time. Participants were instructed either to "Think of a point in time *in the recent past*, the beginning of this term" or to "*Think all the way back to* the beginning of the term". Participants then evaluated what they were like at the beginning of the term on a variety of attributes. When the beginning of the term was represented as recent, participants evaluated their former self and present self similarly. When the beginning of the term was portrayed as distant, respondents evaluated their earlier self as inferior to their current self (see Table 21.1).

Karney and Frye (2002) found that people also perceive illusory improvement in their marital relationships. People's satisfaction with their marriage tends to decline a little over the early years of a marriage. Yet when people are asked to recall how their marital satisfaction has changed with time, they remember being less satisfied in the recent past than they had reported at the time, as well as being less satisfied than they are now. By revising their satisfaction downwards, individuals can view their marriage as getting better lately. Like the participants in Woodruff and Birren's (1972) study of social adjustment, Conway and Ross's (1984) study of study skills, and our own study of personal attributes (Wilson and Ross, 2001), marriage partners manufacture improvement out of thin air by rewriting history.

Table 21.1 Current and retrospective past self-ratings (2 months ago) when the past was described as either recent or distant

Subjective distance	Self-ratings	
	Retrospective past	Present
Past described as recent	6.10	6.08
Past described as distant	5.58	6.15

Wilson & Ross, 2001, Study 6.
Higher numbers indicate more favourable ratings.

DESIGNS FOR STUDYING ILLUSIONS OF CHANGE OR STABILITY

Two measurement points

One common method to assess illusions of change or stability involves two sessions. In the first session (Time 1), present standing on some dimension is assessed. This will be the point in time that participants are later asked to recall. Next, a period of time passes. To examine the illusion of stability, a period of time is usually chosen during which some change may occur, for example attitudes towards a political figure or romantic partner (e.g., Levine, 1997; McFarland & Ross, 1987). Alternatively, attitudes (e.g., towards a social issue) may actually be experimentally altered at Time 2 (e.g., Goethals & Reckman, 1973).

In the second session, participants are sometimes asked again for their current standing on the attitude, attribute, or feeling. Then (in all cases), they are asked to think back to the earlier point in time (that they had reported on at Time 1) and retrospectively to report their past standing. In some cases, self-presentation and consistency pressures are attenuated by explicitly reminding participants that the experimenters have their earlier ratings and will assess the accuracy of their recall.

The same method is used to examine illusions of change. Often, the time period chosen is one where participants' expectations for change outweigh their actual likelihood of change, such as during a self-help programme or therapy (e.g., Conway & Ross, 1984; Safer & Keuler, 2002). Sometimes, studies are simply conducted over a period of time (Karney & Frye, 2002; Wilson & Ross, 2001, Study 3; Woodruff & Birren, 1972). Self-ratings are obtained at Time 1, and again at Time 2. In addition, at Time 2, participants are asked to recall the attributes they had possessed at Time 1.

Measuring illusion

In studies with two points of measurement, Time 1 concurrent scores are compared to Time 2 concurrent scores to determine actual change over time. Next, the retrospective ratings at Time 2 are compared with Time 1 scores to determine the degree of difference between the actual past and remembered past. Finally, the degree of difference between Time 2 scores and retrospective scores are assessed to examine the degree of perceived change or stability. The extent to which this *perceived* change differs from the measure of *actual* change from Time 1 to Time 2 is the *illusion* of change or stability.

In addition to testing mean differences in standing, these illusions can be examined by computing correlations between (1) actual past standing and recalled past standing, and (2) present standing and recalled past standing. The former correlation assesses accuracy in recall and the latter captures the association between present state and recollection (see the classroom experiment in Text box 21.1 for more details).

Text box 21.1 Experimental demonstration of illusions of stability and change

There are several designs used to examine illusions of stability and change. However, not all are equally feasible as classroom demonstrations. In such a setting it might be inappropriate or inconvenient to conduct a study involving deception (e.g., altering participants' attitudes towards an issue) or to implement a time-consuming manipulation (e.g., random assignment to a study skills class). In addition, if one plans to measure initial status at Time 1 and then return at Time 2, a period of at least several weeks (more often months or longer) is necessary. This may not be feasible in scheduling for some classes.

We have chosen a relatively straightforward demonstration, essentially a replication of Wilson and Ross (2001, Study 6). In this study, participants are asked to rate their present self and are then induced to see the past as relatively recent or distant. Participants should remember the past self to be inferior to the present self in the "distant" condition, but recall the past to be similar to the present in the "recent" condition.

Method

Participants

The current study is a between-subjects design with one experimental factor. In Wilson and Ross (2001, Study 6), 56 students participated. A total of 25–30 participants per condition is recommended.

Materials and procedure

First, select a variety of attributes and ask participants to rate themselves on these dimensions as they are now, in the present, relative to their same-aged peers. A sample questionnaire can be found in the Appendix, but you might alter the dimensions as appropriate.

Participants should be randomly assigned to receive one of two versions of the questionnaire. Both versions begin with identical instructions to rate the current self. Next, participants read one of the following two descriptions, depending on their condition. In the *recent past* condition, participants will read: "Now, take a moment to think of a point in time *in the recent past, the beginning of this term*. What were you like then? Please rate yourself on the following attributes, *as you were at the beginning of this term*." In contrast, those in the *distant past* condition will read: "Now, take a moment to think back to another point in time. *Think all the way back to the beginning of the term*. What were you like way back then? Please rate yourself on the following attributes, *as you were way back then, at the beginning of the term*."

Note that these exact instructions require that students complete this questionnaire about 2 months after the start of a school semester. Change "the beginning of the term" to another time period if necessary. For example, the instruction could read "think all the way back to the beginning of March."

Next, participants in both conditions are asked to rate themselves in the past (at whatever time point they were just asked to think about), relative to their same-aged peers. Respondents rate each of the attributes that they earlier rated for their present self.

Analysis

First, identify any negative attributes (e.g., immature, naïve) and recode them so that 0 = 10; 1 = 9, etc. All attributes should be coded in the same direction, so that higher numbers indicate a more favourable self-appraisal. If you have access to statistical software, compute a Cronbach's alpha internal consistency coefficient for all attributes (separately for present and past). If internal consistency is acceptable, calculate an average score for all attributes (present and past separately) and analyze as an aggregate. If internal consistency is low, or if you want to examine more precisely the pattern of results across each dimension, then you should analyze each attribute separately.

Next, conduct a 2 (Time: Present, Recalled Past) × 2 (Distance: Recent, Distant) Mixed ANOVA. Time is a repeated-measures factor, as all participants generate both a present and past score. Distance is a between-subjects factor, as participants are randomly assigned to one or another condition. Planned comparisons should be conducted to compare the means in the past (Recent vs Distant) and the means in the present. In addition, test the difference between past and present appraisals for the Recent condition, and for the Distant condition.

Results

A significant Time × Distance interaction is predicted (see Table 21.1). Planned comparisons should reveal that present scores do not differ by Distance condition (since present scores were collected prior to the manipulation), but recalled scores should differ. Participants in the Distant condition should recall their past self to be significantly worse than should participants in the Recent condition. In addition, the remembered self should be significantly inferior to the present self in the Distant condition, but evaluations of present and past selves should be similar in the Recent condition.

Additional analyses

Note that participants use scales on which they compare themselves to their peers. You can examine how they think they compare to their peers now and in the past. Do they always view themselves as above average (i.e., significantly above 5), even in the more distant past? We found that participants always viewed themselves as above average (cf. Chapter 14 on the Pollyanna principle), but that they viewed their past selves as closer to average than they viewed their present selves.

People vary in the degree of improvement they see in themselves. Can you account for some of this variance? You could examine the possibility of gender differences, although we did not find evidence of gender differences. You could also include various personality measures in your study to examine their correlation with perceived improvement. In our research, we have found that individuals with high self-esteem tend to perceive more improvement than do individuals with low self-esteem.

Discussion

The study described above was chosen as a demonstration, not because it is most representative of the literature on illusions of change/stability, but because it is straightforward and easy to conduct in a single classroom session. In addition, the single study can demonstrate how memory may be biased both in the direction of stability or of change (most studies can only examine one illusion or the other). Granted, without a Time 1 measurement, one can only speculate about the accuracy of recall because participants' memories cannot be compared with their original self-views. If you have the time and resources, the study could be extended by taking a Time 1 measurement, as described in the following section.

A possible extension

If you are able to schedule a "Time 1" session, then you could compare actual ratings at the earlier time period with remembered self-ratings. For example, a short questionnaire could be administered at the beginning of the term, in which participants are asked to rate themselves in the present. Then, approximately 2 months later, the study as described above could be administered (Time 2). Make sure you have a way to match participants' Time 1 ratings with their Time 2 responses. This would allow you to examine both the alteration in memory as a result of the distance manipulation, and the comparison between actual Time 1 ratings and retrospective ratings.

Analysis

If you are able to take a Time 1 measure 2 months prior to the experimental session, then additional analyses can be conducted. First, create an average score for Time 1 attributes in the same manner as conducted previously. Next, conduct a 3 (Time: Time 1, Time 2, Recall of Time 1) × 2 (Distance: Recent, Distant) Mixed ANOVA. Time is a repeated-measures factor as all participants generate a self-rating for all three times. Distance is a between-subjects factor, as participants are randomly assigned to one or another condition. In addition to analyses conducted previously, planned comparisons should be conducted to test the difference between Time 1 and Time 2 in each condition. These indicate the degree to which participants reported actual change in their contemporaneous ratings. Test the difference between recalled ratings of Time 1 (obtained at Time 2) and actual Time 1 scores to determine the discrepancy between actual and recalled past scores.

Finally, correlations can be conducted for each attribute. Specifically, compute the correlation (a) between Time 1 and recalled Time 1 scores; and (b) between Time 2 and recalled Time 1 scores.

Results

It is expected that relatively little change will be demonstrated between Time 1 and Time 2, and that the degree of change will not be affected by the distance manipulation. In contrast, the difference between actual Time 1 ratings and recalled Time 1 ratings should be greater in the Distant condition than in the Recent condition (such that, in the Distant condition, recalled ratings are significantly lower than actual Time 1 ratings).

Finally, correlations between Time 1 and recalled Time 1 scores should be lower, on average, than correlations between Time 2 and recalled Time 1 scores. This would indicate that recall of Time 1 is more associated with present state (i.e., state at Time 2) than it is guided by actual, accurate recollection of the details of that past time period.

Discussion

Without a Time 1 measurement, the classroom experiment can demonstrate that participants reconstruct the past to be either similar to or different from the present, depending on the subjective distance of the past point in time. If the experiment is extended to include a Time 1 measurement, it can additionally demonstrate that one illusion (probably the illusion of change) has been displayed more readily than the other illusion. This prediction assumes that participants' present self-ratings did not in fact change much over the 2-month period, but that those in the Distant condition still recalled illusory change. However, if participants did report some change in their present ratings over the 2 months, then the illusion of stability would also be demonstrated in the Recent condition, where participants recalled the past to be the same as the present.

One measurement point

In one of the studies reported above (Wilson & Ross, 2001, Study 6), we examined an alternative method of studying illusions of both change and stability. Typically, people expect little change from the recent past and greater change from the more distant past. We hypothesized that, regardless of the *actual* passage of time, if a past point in time *appeared to be recent*, little change would be perceived. If the same former point in time *appeared to be distant*, then more change would be estimated. Because the past point in time remained constant (2 months ago), logically there should be no differences in memory of past self between conditions.

Note that one cannot determine exactly where the illusion lies, without actually measuring the same perceived attribute at a Time 1 session. For example, if people did not actually change over the 2 months, then the "recent" condition might have appeared more accurate. If improvement was reported contemporaneously, then the "distant" condition might appear more correct. However, in either of these instances, the past may still have been reconstructed based on current beliefs, goals, and self-knowledge.

RELEVANCE

These illusions of stability and change can have some important implications. In a general sense, if our memories of the past are constructed from the present, then this calls into question any instance when we are asked to report on our own pasts. For example, our reports to physicians, social and consumer surveyors, and psychologists may be influenced by our current state. Information compiled by these methods could be systematically inaccurate, possibly skewing important decisions such as medical diagnoses or the implementation of social policies.

In addition, illusions of stability might help to account for some commonly observed social phenomena: As people age, they often look upon younger generations as inferior to the standards they set in the "good old days". Parents wonder about their children's manners, teachers about their students' abilities, and concerned citizens worry about the general state of societal decline. Indeed, this view of consecutive generations going "downhill" is pervasive and can be found throughout history (e.g., Bork, 1996). Eibach, Libby, and Gilovich (2003) have suggested that people often don't recognize the degree to which they themselves have changed over time. Rather than recognizing change within themselves, they perceive others and their environment as changing around them. For example, a teacher's writing skills might have improved vastly since her youth, but she may not be aware of the degree of change. Adjusting insufficiently for how inferior her former skills were, she compares her remembered self (a highly skilled writer) with the comparably terrible skills of the students in her class. Not recognizing her own improvement, she concludes that the change must be external: Each generation of students is becoming less and less capable.

Illusions of change may have a different set of consequences. First, they may play an important role in keeping the self-help industry afloat, and might explain why people spend large amounts of money and time on ineffective therapists, fad diets, and "change your life" schemes. In addition, in some cases illusory change could reduce motivation for real change: When individuals perceive illusory improvement, then there may be little impetus for taking actions to improve a situation in fact. On the other hand, it may allow people to maintain satisfaction with circumstances that are unlikely to change or are beyond their control. People can find satisfaction in the belief that, even if circumstances are not ideal, they are much better than they had been in the past.

THEORETICAL ACCOUNTS

Implicit theories

As discussed earlier, illusions of change and stability may often be influenced by implicit theories that guide memory reconstruction (e.g., people expect change over time or as a result of self-improvement programmes; they believe that their attitudes remain stable over relatively short periods of time; Ross, 1989). When people cannot recall former attributes or attitudes, they may rely on the following strategy to reconstruct their memory: First, a person might ask "What is my current status or opinion?" and second, ask "Is there any reason to believe that I have changed over the time in question?" Individuals may believe they have changed or remained stable for many reasons, but these beliefs may often be founded in people's general theories about how they should expect to develop over time or in response to certain circumstances.

However, when people demonstrate illusions of change, we have observed that there is an interesting uniformity to the quality of the supposed change. Almost all of the illusions of change that we have reported seem quite flattering. The implication is that motivation may also play a role in these memory biases. The role of motivation in illusions of stability is perhaps more subtle, but there are reasons why people might be motivated to recall either stability or change.

Motivational bases of stability illusions

People are often motivated to find evidence or support for their opinions and self-views; one way to do so is to recall past behaviours, opinions, and attributes that support their preferred views (e.g., Sanitoso, Kunda, & Fong, 1990). In addition, Albert (1977) suggested that people are motivated to see themselves as coherent and stable over time; recalling exaggerated personal consistency may support this goal. Indeed, some researchers have suggested that perceived stability over time is associated with better psychological well-being (Keyes & Ryff, 2000). Similarly, cognitive dissonance theorists have maintained that perceiving inconsistency within the self leads to tension and discomfort (Festinger, 1957).

Motivational bases of change illusions

Self-consistency is not always a preferred state. People are also motivated to perceive change (usually improvement) in the self. Temporal self-appraisal theory (Ross & Wilson, 2000; Wilson & Ross, 2001) begins with the well-supported premise that, at least in Western culture, people are motivated to think highly of themselves. In this theory we propose that people often tend to recall their past selves in a manner that enhances or flatters the present. In some cases, people benefit from praising past glories. In other instances, people prefer to deprecate past selves, creating an illusion of improvement even when no actual change occurred. We suggest that psychologically recent selves will be praised as highly as the current self, because recent selves reflect directly on the present self. In other words, little change is expected from the recent past to the present, so any strengths or weaknesses attributed to a recent past self are likely also to characterize the present self. When a past self is psychologically distant, it seems more plausible that an individual might have changed on the dimension. People are free, then, to recall their more distant past self unfavourably. These distant shortcomings no longer taint the present self, but instead may provide a gratifying sense of improvement over time.

Why do we suggest that these temporal appraisals are motivated, rather than simply arguing that they reflect implicit theories? We present two types of evidence suggesting that motivation influences recall of past selves, over and above whatever influence might be due to implicit theories. First, culturally shared implicit theories should influence a person's recall of his or her personal past, but should also guide recollections of other people's past attributes and behaviours. For example, suppose that students believe that social adjustment increases over the first year of university, but that this belief is false. If so, then they might exaggerate their own inadequacies as they look back towards the start of university. In addition, this implicit theory should lead them to exaggerate the inadequacies of other university students. We argued that if participants recall more change in themselves than in others, this may reflect a motivation to perceive personal improvement. Participants in our research did see themselves as improving at a greater rate than "same-aged peers", and also reported more improvement for self than for specific other individuals (an acquaintance, a sibling) over the same period of time (Wilson & Ross, 2001). In addition, we reasoned that because personally important attributes should have greater consequences for self-regard than should less valued dimensions, people would be more inclined to be critical of their former self on important than on unimportant attributes. As expected, participants praised recent and deprecated distant past selves on their most valued trait, but did not show the same pattern of recall for the least important attribute (Wilson & Ross, 2001, Study 6). Ironically, people are most critical of a past self on the very dimensions that they care most about.

Several other researchers have also suggested that people are sometimes motivated to perceive an illusion of improvement to enhance their current well-being or self-worth (Karney & Frye, 2002; McFarland & Alvaro, 2000). In addition, perceptions of improvement have been found to predict psychological well-being (Fleeson & Baltes, 1998), as well as optimism in close relationships (Karney & Frye, 2002).

Finally, it should be noted that although we have found that young adults criticize their former selves on a wide variety of attributes, there are likely to be cases where people will *not* be inclined to deprecate even very distant selves. Specifically, when people believe that a particular attribute is stable or fixed, then even very distant failures or bad behaviours might have implications for current character. They might be motivated to forget or downplay these former flaws, regardless of how much time has passed.

Related theoretical accounts

The research presented in Chapter 10 (Anchoring effect) and Chapter 20 (Hindsight bias) offers other theoretical accounts that are potentially relevant to the memory effects described in this chapter. There are notable parallels between the anchoring effect, hindsight bias, and illusions of stability and change. Anchoring occurs when people adjust their judgements about a particular estimate to be more in accordance with a previously established standard or level. One could argue that the present acts as an "anchor" (or standard) for memories of the past, contributing to exaggerated stability. Similarly, the hindsight bias demonstrates that people's knowledge of an event's outcome can lead them to revise their memories of how they expected the episode to happen (i.e., "I knew it all along"). Conceivably, the hindsight phenomenon could partly account for people's downward revisions of former selves. For example, a student might, in September, have considered himself to be above average in intelligence. Several months later, that student might have knowledge (test outcomes, etc.) calling into question that conclusion. The student's knowledge of outcomes might result in a downward revision of the intelligence of past self (e.g., "I wasn't as smart as I thought I was"). In the case of each of these phenomena, present knowledge exerts a powerful impact on the judgement in question.

CONCLUSIONS

One might be tempted to conclude that memory is not to be trusted: We may *believe* we are recalling our past attitudes and attributes, but in fact our present state, beliefs, and goals determine how our past is reconstructed (Bartlett, 1932). This conclusion would only be partly correct. Despite systematic biases in memory, people at the same time often show considerable accuracy in their recall. For example, Levine (1997) found that people were better able than chance to recall their past emotions about a political event, and that correlations between the actual intensity of past emotions and recalled intensity were substantial. In other words, respondents who recalled experiencing emotions of greater intensity were most likely to have actually experienced more intense emotions. Accuracy may reflect in part that we actually retrieved the correct fragments from our histories. It probably also reflects the fact that the beliefs and goals that we use to aid our reconstruction are often effective tools. A palaeontologist will likely arrive at a better representation of a dinosaur armed with a theory of how it should be constructed than if she began with no present knowledge to aid her reconstruction. We too, may benefit from the reconstruction strategies available to us, even if they may sometimes lead us astray.

SUMMARY

- Theorists and researchers suggest that memory is largely reconstructed on the basis of current knowledge, beliefs, and goals.
- The illusion of stability occurs when the consistency between past and present states is exaggerated.
- The illusion of change occurs when the discrepancy between past and present states is inflated.
- People's implicit theories about change and stability over time help to determine their reconstructions of the past.
- People's motivations may also influence the type of revisions they make to past selves and events.
- Despite robust systematic biases in people's memories, recall for the personal past can still be relatively accurate in many instances.

FURTHER READING

An excellent early discussion and demonstration of reconstructive memory can be found in Bartlett's (1932) classic book, *Remembering*. In addition, Ross (1989) published a thorough overview of research and theory related to implicit theories contributing to memory illusions. More recently, Wilson and Ross (2001) presented empirical demonstrations of the illusions of change and stability, highlighting the motivational determinants and the moderating influence of perceived temporal distance.

REFERENCES

Albert, S. (1977). Temporal comparison theory. *Psychological Review, 84*, 485–503.

Bartlett, F. C. (1932). *Remembering*. Oxford: Oxford University Press.

Bork, R. (1996). *Slouching toward Gomorrah: Modern liberalism and American decline*. New York: Regan Books/Harper Collins.

Conway, M., & Ross, M. (1984). Getting what you want by revising what you had. *Journal of Personality and Social Psychology, 47*, 738–748.

Eibach, R. P., Libby, L. K., & Gilovich, T. (2003). When change in the self is mistaken for change in the world. *Journal of Personality and Social Psychology, 84*, 917–931.

Festinger, L. (1957). *A theory of cognitive dissonance*. Stanford, CA: Stanford University Press.

Fleeson, W., & Baltes, P. B. (1998). Beyond present-day personality assessment: An encouraging exploration of the measurement properties and predictive power of subjective lifetime personality. *Journal of Research in Personality, 32*, 411–430.

Goethals, G. B., & Reckman, R. F. (1973). The perception of consistency in attitudes. *Journal of Experimental Social Psychology, 9*, 419–423.

Greenwald, A. G. (1980). The totalitarian ego: Fabrication and revision of personal history. *American Psychologist, 35*, 603–618.

Karney, B. R., & Frye, N. E. (2002). "But we've been getting better lately": Comparing prospective and retrospective views of relationship development. *Journal of Personality and Social Psychology, 82*, 222–238.

Keyes, C. L. M., & Ryff, C. D. (2000). Subjective change and mental health: A self-concept theory. *Social Psychology Quarterly, 63*, 264–279.

Levine, L. J. (1997). Reconstructing memory for emotions. *Journal of Experimental Psychology: General, 126*, 165–177.

McFarland, C., & Alvaro, C. (2000). The impact of motivation on temporal comparisons: Coping with traumatic events by perceiving personal growth. *Journal of Personality and Social Psychology, 79*, 327–343.

McFarland, C., & Ross, M. (1987). The relation between current impressions and memories of self and dating partners. *Personality and Social Psychology Bulletin, 13*, 228–238.

Neisser, U. (1967). *Cognitive psychology.* East Norwalk, CT: Appleton Century Crofts.

Polivy, J., & Herman, P. (2002). If at first you don't succeed: False hopes of self-change. *American Psychologist, 57*, 677–689.

Ross, M. (1989). The relation of implicit theories to the construction of personal histories. *Psychological Review, 96*, 341–357.

Ross, M., & Wilson, A. E. (2000). Constructing and appraising past selves. In D. L. Schacter & E. Scarry (Eds.), *Memory, brain, and belief* (pp. 231–258). Cambridge, MA: Harvard University Press.

Ross, M., & Wilson, A. E. (2002). It feels like yesterday: Self-esteem, valence of personal past experiences, and judgments of subjective distance. *Journal of Personality and Social Psychology, 82*, 792–803.

Safer, M. A., & Keuler, D. J. (2002). Individual differences in misremembering pre-psychotherapy distress: Personality and memory distortion. *Emotion, 2*, 162–178.

Sanitoso, R., Kunda, Z., & Fong, G. T. (1990). Motivated recruitment of autobiographical memories. *Journal of Personality and Social Psychology, 59*, 229–241.

Wilson, A. E., & Ross, M. (2001). From chump to champ: People's appraisals of their earlier and current selves. *Journal of Personality and Social Psychology, 80*, 572–584.

Woodruff, D. S., & Birren, J. E. (1972). Age changes and cohort difference in personality. *Developmental Psychology, 6*, 252–259.

APPENDIX

Your current and past attributes

Please rate yourself on the following attributes, *as you are now, at this point in time in your life.* Rather than rating yourself *in general* (e.g., how you have been across several years), please think about what you are like *now and very recently* (within the past *two weeks*). Please answer the following questions about yourself at your current age, *by comparing yourself to other people in the same age group as yourself in the present.* For each question, choose the number from the scale below that best represents your response, and write that number in the space next to that question.

```
 0    1    2    3    4    5    6    7    8    9    10
```
Much *less*   *Same* as   Much *more*
than most   most   than most

Myself within the past two weeks, relative to other people of my current age . . .

1. How socially skilled are you now?   _____
2. How self-confident are you now?   _____
3. How narrow-minded are you now?   _____
4. How well do you adapt to new situations now?   _____
5. How independent/self-reliant are you now?   _____
6. How immature are you now?   _____
7. How naïve (inexperienced) are you now?   _____

(A) DISTANT CONDITION:	*(B) RECENT CONDITION:*
Now, take a moment to think back to another point in time. *Think all the way back to the beginning of the term.* What were you like way back then?	Now, take a moment to think of a point in time *in the recent past, the beginning of this term.* What were you like then?
Please rate yourself on the following attributes, *as you were way back then, at the beginning of the term.* Rate yourself specifically as you were at the beginning of the term (within the *first two weeks*). Please answer the following questions about yourself at the beginning of the term, *by comparing yourself to other people in the same age group as yourself at the beginning of the term.*	Please rate yourself on the following attributes, *as you were at the beginning of this term.* Rate yourself specifically as you were at the beginning of the term (within the *first two weeks*). Please answer the following questions about yourself at the beginning of the term, *by comparing yourself to other people in the same age group as yourself at the beginning of the term.*

```
 0    1    2    3    4    5    6    7    8    9    10
```
Much *less*   *Same* as   Much *more*
than most   most   than most

(A) DISTANT	*(B) RECENT*
Myself in the past, all the way back at the beginning of the term, relative to other people at the beginning of the term . . .	*Myself in the recent past, at the beginning of this term, relative to other people at the beginning of the term* . . .

1. How socially skilled were you then?   _____
2. How self-confident were you then?   _____

3. How narrow-minded were you then? ____
4. How well did you adapt to new situations then? ____
5. How independent/self-reliant were you then? ____
6. How immature were you then? ____
7. How naïve (inexperienced) were you then? ____

Perspectives

22 Suggestion and illusion

*Vladimir A. Gheorghiu,
Günter Molz, and Rüdiger F. Pohl*

illudere (Latin) = to play one's game, to pass, to ridicule, to misguide

Research on cognitive illusions has developed a tradition of its own. This book documents the state of the art for an impressive list of cognitive illusions, thus supplying profound insight into the relevant factors causing or modifying these illusions. Looking back at the history of the respective research shows that most of these illusions have been studied in complete isolation without any reference to the other ones, and moreover without any reference to the large body of research on suggestions. As a matter of fact, the editor of this book noted that the first versions of the chapters' manuscripts contained almost no explicit links to any of the other chapters. Experimental methods as well as theoretical explanations of cognitive illusions thus resembled an archipelago spread out in a vast ocean without any sailor having visited more than one (or at the most two) of these small islands yet. In trying to further explore this largely unknown territory, we believe that cognitive illusions are more connected than previously acknowledged, that they show parallels to suggestions so that both research domains should benefit from each other methodologically as well as theoretically, and that both should be placed within the broader context of general cognitive processes.

We start this chapter by summarizing some common issues of research linking suggestions and illusions. Next, we discuss a conceptual framework for these two domains, before turning to the main part of the chapter: Borrowing from the research on suggestion and suggestibility, we introduce the domain of "illusionality" as a theoretical framework encompassing different illusive situations as well as general and individual characteristics of someone's "illusionability".

In this paper, we pursue several goals:

(1) It is time to move from explanations of single illusions to more general characteristics: What are the basic cognitive mechanisms and conditions leading to illusions? As a cornerstone of our considerations, we would

like to emphasize that we see cognitive illusions as resulting from regular elements of our cognitive equipment.
(2) We also want to discuss illusions within the broader context of evolutionary adapted capacities, thereby stressing the role of motivational functions: Where and how could illusions be helpful (e.g., in coping with onerous situations)? In pursuing such questions, we want to replace an overly pessimistic view of human cognitive abilities with a more optimistic one.
(3) As a consequence, we want to look at the illusions' importance in applied settings, thereby also referring to individual differences: How do illusions arise in everyday life?

The result of this endeavour could be to have a somewhat more reasonable map of the archipelago, showing that – underneath the ocean – all belong to the same continental shelf. Of course, in the long run one must not forget that there are other continental shelves representing other disciplines relevant for cognitive psychology, like the neurosciences or linguistics. At least we are aware of the fact that ignoring these shelves is not a protection for the own discipline against thorough earthquake-like turbulences.

COMMON ISSUES OF RESEARCH ON COGNITIVE ILLUSIONS AND ON SUGGESTIONS

Unfortunately, research on cognitive illusions and on suggestions has proceeded mainly in parallel without too many references from one to the other. However, there are a number of common issues and relations, which we will point out in this section. For example, suggestion research has incorporated cognitive-illusion methods to induce and measure suggestions, while on the other hand, some cognitive-illusion phenomena were explicitly explained by assuming suggestive processes. This section highlights the points of contact between the two research traditions and presents some recent empirical studies. The goal of this enterprise is to unveil the common mechanisms underlying both suggestion and illusion, thus allowing deduction from the study of some curious phenomena to "normal" processes of cognitive functioning. Knowing these basic processes might then lead to a more general theory encompassing both illusion and suggestion.

Points of contact

In its beginnings, suggestion research addressed primarily hypnotic contexts in which a certain behaviour was forced to occur by means of *direct* and authoritative methods. In order to be able to work with more representative and more ecologically valid suggestions in non-hypnotic contexts, *indirect* methods were developed. These were based on illusions: Stimulus presentations were simulated (Seashore, 1895), or memories were biased by means of suggestive interrogations (Binet, 1900). The common feature of these procedures was to hide the researchers' aim to measure individual influenceability. For example, Binet (1900) had developed the indirect suggestibility test of progressive lines (or weights). He demonstrated that suggestible persons who had to judge the lengths of successively presented lines (which originally became progressively longer) continued to "see" longer lines even if their length remained constant. This reminds one of cognitive illusions in thinking where experience with previous problem-solving tasks allows one to deduct a complicated, but successful rule that is then unquestioningly applied to future tasks that, however, could have been solved much more easily.

In the subsequent period of suggestion research, the early techniques were further developed and applied in research on suggestibility and persuadability (e.g., Eysenck & Furneaux, 1945) and in classical experiments in social psychology (e.g., Asch, 1956). Most of these, as well as the contemporary illusion techniques, addressed the manipulation of perception and sensory judgements (see examples of recent studies below).

Until today, the connection between suggestion research and work on cognitive illusions remained rather vague. But this integration is desirable because suggestion research will surely benefit from cognitive psychology's results concerning, for example, knowledge representation and inferential processes. On the other hand, suggestion research may also be helpful for understanding cognitive illusions, as is demonstrated by the following examples, though not all of the authors use explicitly the term *suggestion*:

(1) Gudjonsson and colleagues investigated the psychology of interrogations and confessions. In a recent publication, Gudjonsson (2003) demonstrated the decisive role of suggestions in this context; for example, that a false belief could even lead to a false confession to murder.
(2) Studies by Loftus and others on the misinformation effect (see Chapter 19) have convincingly shown that suggestions can distort memory, here in the case of eyewitness testimony. In this research paradigm, the misleading information suggests that one adapt one's memory accordingly. This in turn leads to having a poorer memory for the original information than in the control group, which did not receive misleading information.
(3) Research on hindsight bias (see Chapter 20) focused on the recall of earlier judgements, which were evaluated to be wrong and dysfunctional because of their non-congruency with later provided information. Recall of the earlier judgements is typically biased towards the new information. Some researchers interpreted this bias to be adaptive and to support ecologically valid behaviour (e.g., Pohl, Bender, &

Lachmann, 2002). It allows people to cope better with undesirable situations. In order to prevent getting compromised a second time (which may have happened for the first time while producing the earlier erroneous judgement), the new information may act as a directive and suggestive cue bringing memory more in line with the present knowledge, which then leads to hindsight bias. Similarly, Conway and Ross (1984) claimed that biasing one's memories may lead to being more satisfied in the actual situation (see Chapter 21).

(4) In a similar paradigm, namely anchoring (see Chapter 10), participants tend to base their numerical judgements on a previously presented "anchor" (a numerical value) that could even be a random number, that is, completely meaningless. But still it exerts its influence on judgement, just as would be expected from a suggestion.

(5) In research on labelling effects (see Chapter 18), a word that is used to label an ambiguous figure was found to bias later reconstruction of that figure in the direction of the given label.

(6) Another example is given by the work of Roediger, McDermott, and others on the associative memory illusion (see Chapter 17). A list of words is presented that contains words which are all highly associated to a target word, but the target word itself is not on the list. Later, people reliably tend to recall the target word as having been on the list. The converging associations in this case provided a suggestive direction in which to integrate the given list of words.

In order to understand the close links between suggestions and cognitive illusions, it may be helpful to look at everyday situations. As an example for the whole class of illusions, we pick just one, namely illusory correlations (see Chapter 5). The tendency to attribute a connection between two simultaneously, but in reality independently, occurring events or to ascribe causality to two contiguous, but again independent, events (*post hoc, ergo propter hoc*), appears to be a general human characteristic. These illusory correlations and causalities could lead to rigid or even superstitious behaviour (e.g., meaningless rituals). Persons in these cases tend to confirm their subjective beliefs through auto-suggestive techniques, thereby increasing the subjective sense of stability in a changing environment.

Some recent studies

Besides gaining more knowledge on single illusions, research should also always strive for a more integrative point of view. This seems to be especially important if one thinks of professionals in different applied fields who might be affected: philosophers, anthropologists, sociologists, psychologists, therapists and many others. They could all benefit from more integrative research, overcoming today's tendency to have several research traditions on similar topics, but independent from one another. Examples for such a more integrative approach, in addition to those studies reported below, can be found in several books on suggestional phenomena (DePascalis, Gheorghiu, Sheehan, & Kirsch, 2000; Gheorghiu, Netter, Eysenck, & Rosenthal, 1989; Schumaker, 1991).

A recent study by Gheorghiu, Koch, Fialkovski, Pieper, and Molz (2001) demonstrated the close link between the classical suggestion research and cognitive factors in an experiment on the influence of suggestional processes on *warmth sensations*. In addition to the type of alleged source of warmth (lamp or hand) and affected skin area (finger tips, palm, wrist, bend of elbow), the authors manipulated a third variable, the so-called "set factor". Half of the participants were allegedly made familiar with the sensation of feeling the warmth prior to the main experiment, for example by putting one's palm on a piece of styrofoam (made of polystyrene which has no objective source of warmth) and feeling a subjective increase of warmth. These participants then showed much stronger effects on the dependent variables measuring sensation of warmth (percentage of persons feeling warmth, reaction times, and intensity of sensation) than control participants without such prior "experience". Thus, this study demonstrated the influence of a cognitive set on the success of suggestive influences: Participants in the experimental group who had a high expectancy to be able to feel warmth reported significantly more often and more intensively feeling warmth, although according to objective stimuli this group should not differ from the control group.

In a series of experiments, Gheorghiu, Koch, and Götz (2000) showed that motions can be induced, modified, or blocked by *pseudo-rational* explanations. For example, participants in the experimental condition were told that they might fall backwards if they relaxed their bodies and pressed their hands continuously against their chests while standing upright. This explanation is pseudo-rational, because even strong pressure is not sufficient to make the body fall. The control-group participants were only instructed to press their hands continuously against their chests. The results showed that more persons in the pseudo-rational group tended to fall backwards than persons in the control group, thus demonstrating again the influence of cognitive factors. Tasks like this one can easily be used as a classroom demonstration (see Text box 22.1 for all necessary information and also a more detailed discussion of the influence of pseudo-rational explanations).

In order to assess the correlation between more cognitive and more suggestional variables, Molz (2000) conducted an exploratory study using the Ellsberg (1961) task. In that task, two urns are given: urn A with a 50/50 distribution (called "unambiguous") and urn B with an unknown distribution (called "ambiguous") of red and white balls. The participant will win whenever he or she draws a red ball. The task is simply to select from which urn to draw. Typically, people prefer the unambiguous urn A to urn B (by about 80 to 20%). Before running this task, Molz administered a motor test

Text box 22.1 Classroom demonstration

This demonstration of suggestive effects is based on the possible consequences of *leading ideas* (Binet, 1900). in the context of tension-and-relaxation exercises. The procedure allows making some personal experiences, but does not include all controls that would be necessary for a more sophisticated experiment.

Method

Participants

The experimenter should ask one person who does not know about the expected results to serve as the naïve instructor. Both the experimenter and the instructor are present throughout the whole study. We recommend asking at least 20 students to participate: 50% should be assigned to the experimental group, the others to the control group.

Material

The material consists of four tension-and-relaxation exercises that the participants are asked to carry out. These tasks are described in written instructions that are read to the participants by the instructor. The four tasks and their descriptions for the experimental group are as follows (for the control group, the sentences in italics are simply omitted):

Exercise 1: Relaxation of upper torso while sitting upright
Please sit up straight on the chair as far to the front edge as possible. Put your right hand on your breastbone. Now conduct a relaxation exercise of your upper torso. First, tense the muscles of your upper torso and then relax these muscles. Try to keep your upper torso relaxed without leaning back on your chair. Repeat this relaxation exercise twice, keeping your right hand on your breastbone. Please exert a continuous pressure on your breastbone in each phase counting slowly from one to five. *If the relaxation is successful, pressure against the breastbone might cause you to fall backwards.* Please notice whether you fell backwards.

Exercise 2: Convergence of eyeballs with closed eyes
Your task now is to close your eyes and to move your eyeballs towards each other, that is, towards your nose, as if focusing on some close object. Keep them in this position for about 10 seconds. This requires a tensing of all eye-muscles. *If the relaxation is successful, you might not be able to open your eyes. Instead of opening your eyes, you tend to raise your eyebrows upwards.* Now please try to open your eyes. Please notice whether you did not open your eyes. After completing this exercise move your eyeballs into their normal position by opening and closing your eyes for a few times.

Exercise 3: Strong tension of arm muscles
Please stand up. Let your arms hang down beside your body. Now make a fist with your right hand. Tense your right arm and hand so hard that you can distinctly feel your fingernails on the inside of your hand. Now try to raise your straight right arm in front of you upwards to the level of your head. *Due to the strong muscle tension, it could happen that your arm cannot be lifted to that height. It might stop moving below shoulder height.* Please notice whether you interrupted your arm movement before you reached the level of your head.

Exercise 4: Relaxation of arms and hands
Please sit down comfortably. Hold both bent arms in front of you at chest level so that the insides of your hands touch each other with the finger tips pointing away from you. Continue by tensing the muscles of both arms and pressing your hands firmly together for a few seconds. Keeping the tension, move both bent arms and hands slowly apart until they reach shoulder width. Now relax your hands and arms. *If this relaxation is successful, it might happen that both hands move back towards each other in an involuntary movement.* Please notice whether you moved your hands back together.

Procedure

Depending on the time frame, the study could either be run as a group experiment (with either all experimental participants or all control participants together) or in single sessions. If it is carried out as a group experiment, participants should be asked to close their eyes, in order to not imitate the behaviours of others.

The instructor reads all four instructions in the given order one at a time to the participant. The experimenter is present, but only records the dependent measures (see Design). The instructor makes it clear to the participant that it is absolutely necessary to follow the instructions as *closely* as possible and to *fully* concentrate on the tasks presented.

Each of the four exercises proceeds as follows. First, the instructor reads the instruction to the participant and demonstrates the intended postures, while the participant only listens and observes. (The experimenter should carefully tell the instructor in advance *not* to show the suggested movements.) Then the instructor reads the instruction again, now with the participant doing the exercise at the same time. After each exercise, the instructor asks the participant to shake out the tensed muscles and to relax.

Design

The experimental design consists of one between-subjects factor with two conditions (experimental vs control group). The dependent variables are the number of participants

- who fell backwards with their upper torso (Exercise 1);
- who did not open their eyes (Exercise 2);
- who failed to raise their arm up to the level of their head (Exercise 3);
- who moved their hands back together (Exercise 4).

Analysis

On a descriptive level, the number of participants who showed the suggested reaction are compared between experimental and control group. For each single exercise, a 2 (Group: experimental vs control) × 2 (Reaction: shown vs not shown) chi-square test of independence can be run.

Results and discussion

Typical results are as follows: In the experimental condition, about 75% of the participants behave according to the pseudo-arguments, whereas in the control condition, only about 25% are likely to show the suggested reactions.

In discussing these results it is essential to note that the four exercises used in this classroom demonstration are not based on reflex-like mechanisms. The critical arguments presented in the experimental conditions are pseudo-rational in nature. In Exercise 1, pressure against the breastbone alone cannot cause the upper body to fall backwards. Also, convergence of the eyeballs cannot prevent the eyes opening (Exercise 2). Strongly tensing the arm muscles may perhaps make arm movements difficult, but will not cause a block (Exercise 3). The termination of muscle tension does not automatically cause both hands to move back together (Exercise 4). In all these experimental conditions, a pseudo-rational explanation is provided which can be accepted by the participant without being questioned, that is, as if no other reaction were possible. Note that the instructions for the control group do not include "explanations" for these potential reactions. Any difference in the reaction frequency between experimental and control group is therefore based on the pseudo-rational explanations given to the experimental group only.

The effectiveness of the described and similar methods have been tested under various experimental conditions (Gheorghiu, 1991; Gheorghiu et al., 2000). One of the results indicated that the readiness to react as suggested is significantly higher if the participant is given pseudo-arguments (as was done here). However, in the control condition a few participants typically also show the suggested reactions. This might be due to an *implicit*, suggestive directedness in the instructions (e.g., in the third exercise, the task of tensing one's arm might convey the idea that this tensing does not allow simultaneous lifting of the arm). In contrast, the pseudo-rational explanations in the experimental condition reflect an *explicit*, suggestive directedness.

In the latter cases, a "logic of the matter" seems to arise, triggering hypothesis-guided behaviour in the participant. In suggestibility research, this basic form of a "top-down" effect was first described in Binet's (1900) concept of "leading ideas", according to which apparently valid observations and conclusions could produce changes in attitude and behaviour. Presumably, we are prone to the influence of such "guiding ideas" every single day.

scale (from suggestion research) and also recorded ratings of subjective feelings. Then his participants expressed how confident they were to choose either urn A or B. He found a strong correlation (of $r = .50$) between amount of positive feelings during the motor test and subsequent preference for the unambiguous urn A. Although these results are only preliminary, research of this type helps to illuminate the relationships between cognitive illusions and suggestions and will thus be continued by our research group in the near future.

A CONCEPTUAL FRAMEWORK LINKING SUGGESTIONS AND ILLUSIONS

General reaction patterns and strategies

In order to fulfil demands of everyday life, people have general reaction patterns that could be categorized into three groups. These patterns could be labelled as *immediate*, *mediate*, and a *combination* of both.

(1) *Immediate* patterns consist of unconditioned as well as conditioned reflexes and reactions, which are evoked automatically or forced to be performed. Behaviour based on these reactions is deterministic, because there are no other options for reacting. These reflex and reflex-like reactions therefore appear as exclusive.

(2) With respect to the *mediate* reaction patterns, there are always at least two options available, one of which must be selected. In order to decide which option to use, thereby rejecting the other ones, people may use one or more of several complementary mechanisms of disambiguation, namely rational, suggestive, intuitive, or aleatoric strategies (Gheorghiu, 1992):

- In *rational* strategies, the underlying decisional process is based primarily on a reflected comparative assessment of all available options. The outcome thus gains the character of a consciously induced solution.
- In *suggestive* strategies, one-sided explicit or implicit cues lead to a differential evaluation of the available options. Individuals who follow this strategy behave as if the implemented options were the only ones, without any alternatives.
- *Intuitive* strategies are similar to suggestive ones. However, evaluation and decision here involve emotional aspects. Bowers (1984) characterized intuitivity as "sensitivity and responsiveness to information that is not consciously represented, but which nevertheless guides inquiry towards productive and sometimes profound insights" (p. 256). These aspects then guide the selection of the

preferred option, accompanied by certainty of having decided correctly (which is not always true as we all know).
- And finally, selecting an option by chance is an *aleatoric* strategy. These random decisions can easily be overlooked in everyday life. But there are certainly many situations in which none of the other strategies could be applied, because the information appears too fragmentary for a rational decision and it does not show any obvious (suggestive or intuitive) clues as to which alternative to prefer.

In everyday life, these different mediate reaction patterns are often used in complex combinations with one another, possibly with a certain individual prevalence for one or the other of these strategies for judgement, evaluation, and decision. (Neglecting this intricate interplay would amount to a cognitive illusion itself that could result from the exaggerated desire to more clearly disentangle the possible strategies.)

(3) There are tasks in which a *combination* of both immediate and mediate patterns of reaction are involved and needed. A situation may automatically activate immediate reaction patterns, but will still leave some degrees of freedom for the individual. An example from social psychology is that evoked attitudes, prejudices, or convictions would generally suffice to "choose" an option to act, but we might also feel free to overcome this impulse and to act otherwise. Similarly, developmental findings on imitative behaviour provide evidence for these complex reaction patterns: While infants simply cannot avoid imitating, older children and adults mostly have other options available and thus may or may not imitate the given behaviour.

Coming back to cognitive illusions, heuristics such as general search and judgement mechanisms as well as coping strategies represent such mixtures as well. They are partly deliberate in the sense of a rational calculus, but also partly reflex-like in the sense of affective reactions. Both involve rational and intuitive strategies, and both can be prone to suggestive influences. For example, Bayesian reasoning might be facilitated by the suggestion to use frequencies instead of probabilities (see Chapter 3). On the other hand, a suggestive process can be supported by providing rational explanations.

Suggestive strategies and cognitive illusions

We assume that many errors and biases (typically labelled as cognitive illusions) represent the outcomes of suggestive strategies employed in everyday life. This is made clearer by discussing suggestive and intuitive strategies in relation to the reflex and reflex-like (immediate) strategies on one side and rational (mediate) strategies on the other.

In general, reflex-like mechanisms are too rigid for the many complex demands to dissolve ambiguity. The challenge of overcoming these narrow patterns also results from the necessity to gain more room for interpersonal influence. To maintain subtle interactions between the individual and his or her social environment, fixed and routinely performed actions will certainly not suffice. Rational strategies surely play an important role to dissolve social and other types of ambiguity, but may be too complicated and too time-consuming in a rapidly changing environment. In addition, rational strategies may also block themselves by running into a deadlock if no decision can be reached.

As a solution to this state of affairs, suggestive and intuitive strategies (as well as heuristics) may show an efficient way out. On one hand, they allow for more complexity than immediate reactions (thus overcoming too rigid behaviour) and, on the other hand, they are also fast and smooth (thus avoiding strategies that are too complicated and time-consuming). This might explain why suggestive strategies play such an important role in our lives (see Gheorghiu, 1993; Gheorghiu & Kruse, 1991).

In general, a suggestive situation can be characterized as given in Text box 22.2. These characteristics might also apply to cognitive illusions. Someone who falls prey to a cognitive illusion has opted for a certain outcome, ignoring the other potentially available ones. The illusioned person reacts as if his or her behaviour were the only applicable one in this situation. This process is based neither on reflex-like nor on deliberate processes alone. In addition, the behaviour is not only biased or wrong with respect to some normative standard, but the direction in which it will be biased can also be predicted (just as with suggestions). Hell (1993) even used predictability as a defining characteristic of cognitive illusions. So the main question – both for suggestions and illusions – is: Which conditions allow a prediction about which of all

---

Text box 22.2 Description of a suggestive situation

1. In a given context, a person (suggestee) is guided to react in a certain way by simple or complex, explicit or implicit, coarse or subtle cues.
2. The suggestee may choose among two or more options how to react. He or she might follow the given cues or might react in another way. Opting for the suggested option is not a matter of reflex or deliberate mechanisms.
3. Readiness for reacting in the suggested way can be impaired or supported by many biological, psychological, and sociological factors and may depend on the single individual. Taking these variables into account allows improvement of prediction of whether the suggestion will succeed or not.
4. The effects of suggestions result in *initiation* or *blocking, accentuation* or *diminution, conservation* or *transformation* of thoughts, judgements, memories, attitudes, sensations, feelings, and behaviour.

potential reactions and responses can be suggested and thus implemented into a person's behaviour?

THE HEURISTIC CHALLENGE OF SUGGESTION: THE DOMAIN OF ILLUSIONALITY

The close connections between cognitive illusions and suggestions as outlined above can be viewed as a heuristic challenge to develop theoretical frameworks that encompass both. In order to overcome conceptual problems and to allow a reasonable classification of different aspects of suggestions, Gheorghiu (2000) proposed a "domain of suggestionality", which was thought of as being analogous to the terms "rationality" or "emotionality" referring to the whole areas of rational or emotional processes, respectively. Likewise, suggestionality was supposed to represent the general frame for classifying and understanding specific elements of suggestions. These elements were ordered under four headings: (a) suggestive situations and phenomena, (b) suggestibility (encompassing general as well as individual characteristics), (c) techniques of suggestions, and (d) theory of suggestionality.

In analogy to this framework, we here describe a "domain of illusionality" consisting of the same categories. We will present these in the following subsections, with the exception of the techniques of cognitive illusions, which have been omitted here (due to space constraints and because they have been dealt with more thoroughly in the preceding chapters of this book).

The illusive situation

We propose to differentiate between three types of illusive situations: Perceiving illusion as reality, reality as illusion, and reality as non-reality.

Perceiving illusion as reality

This tendency is the most prominent illusion in research on suggestions. In fact, most of the biases described in this book belong to this category. Examples for these distortions can be described in terms of "as-if" relations (see Table 22.1). Thinking, judgement, comprehension, and memory processes may be affected.

In sum, confusions of this type can be characterized by three main aspects: First, things are summed despite having different qualities (*pars-pro-toto* principle), for example, in perceiving independent events as dependent or random events as deterministic. Second, equivalent things are interpreted to be different, for example, in attributing different trait values to the same person depending only on the clothes that the person is wearing. And third,

Table 22.1 Examples for perceiving illusion as reality in different cognitive domains

Domain	Illusions
Thinking and judgement	People react . . . • as if effects of an event were its causes, • as if random effects had specific meaning, • as if an example or authority could replace the necessary line of argumentation (*ignoratio elenchi*), • as if judgements on persons or situations were independent from previous prepossessions.
Comprehension	People react . . . • as if the conception of a fact were the fact itself, • as if everything based on common sense were unconditionally correct, • as if complex argumentation necessarily implied plausibility, • as if a single aspect were congruent with the entire situation.
Memory and perception	People react . . . • as if remembered events had taken place in exactly the same way they are recalled, • as if something they perceive themselves were more true than the same event perceived by others, • as if perceived sensations were obligatorily based on equivalent real world stimuli.

quantitative differences are taken to be valid indicators of different qualities. This would be the case, for example, if a scientist who has published a lot is believed to do good research.

Perceiving reality as illusion

This tendency is also widespread, but it has not been investigated so much. It has mainly been analyzed in therapeutic settings dealing with neglect and repression within the context of reframing strategies. The applied importance of this tendency makes us focus on a central cognitive feature, namely the impressive cognitive flexibility to even turn reality into fiction.

An early empirical demonstration of this effect was provided in the classical experiment of Perky (1910). She made her participants imagine a banana on a dark and allegedly blank surface. But in fact, participants were actually presented with an unobtrusive picture of a banana on that surface. When the participants were asked to describe the banana, they thought they were describing a fictitious object solely generated by their own imagination, rather than by the actually presented picture. Another more recent and more dramatic example is the World Trade Center-disaster on 9/11, which many people who were watching the scene on TV first interpreted as part of a Hollywood action movie. They just could not believe this to be truly happening, even though it was bitter and tragic reality. (This is just the opposite of what Orson Wells had elicited when his production of *The war of the worlds* was broadcast on radio and taken as a true report by many listeners.)

Generally, any fallacies and biases where reality is exchanged for fiction might be placed into this category. For example, Conway and Ross (1984) favoured such an explanation for subjective theories of change or stability (see Chapter 21). Similarly, Davidsson and Wahlund (1992) suggested that the confirmation bias (see Chapter 4) might be due to an avoidance strategy of not testing relevant information, which could possibly disconfirm one's assumptions (cf. the data of Molz, 1997, supporting this explanation).

Perceiving reality as non-reality

This tendency is similar to the second one. However, it differs in one crucial point. Whereas perceiving reality as an illusion is a matter of reinterpretation, this third tendency is a matter of leaving out substantial aspects of the given setting. People tend to focus on central aspects, thereby neglecting any important interactions. The segregated parts then appear to be non-existent.

Such observations have been analyzed, for example, in research on mindlessness (Langer 1989). Probably the best example of a corresponding cognitive illusion is the optimism bias, also known as unrealistic optimism (Weinstein, 1980), often resulting in an illusion of control (see Chapter 6): People retain an optimistic attitude even in the face of evidence completely contrary to their expectations (see also Chapter 14 on the Pollyanna principle).

The intention of listing these three types of illusions is to demonstrate that there are interdisciplinary aspects that generate useful links between cognitive illusions in research, in applied settings, and in everyday life. The theoretical challenge now is to relate these types to the cognitive illusions described in this book. We gave some examples for each type, but are still far from having a complete categorization available (and perhaps we never will).

Finally, it should be mentioned that the three tendencies described above share one feature, which was first identified by research on suggestions: Illusioned people in these situations possess in theory different alternative ways to react, but in the end they choose the suggested option. Why they do so is a matter of illusionability, which will be described next.

Illusionability

This section focuses on illusionability as the main reason for not realizing alternative possible ways to react. We define illusionability as readiness to be illusioned. However – and this is different from the research on suggestibility where mainly individual factors were investigated – illusionability research so far puts more emphasis on general cognitive and other psychological factors.

General psychological features of illusionability

In light of the variety and the often remarkable robustness of cognitive illusions, we assume that cognitive illusions should be explicable from a more general psychological perspective. This includes assuming the influence of specific but regular properties that foster the occurrence of illusions. We view these as the "hotbed" of cognitive illusions. In addition, basic cognitive processes have evolved to deal with the permanent and manifold uncertainties of the world. We discuss these two areas – the "hotbed" and the basic processes – in turn.

As one of the main factors for building a "hotbed" of cognitive illusions, there are certain *restrictions* that impair strictly rational information processing and thus favour the influence of illusionability. These restrictions could result from permanent ambiguity, limitations of control and rationality, segregation tendencies, and other cognitive and affective factors.

Ambiguity appears to be a permanent companion of human life. The relevant information to allow valid conclusions is often missing, because the situation is poorly structured or probabilistic, involves a lack of transparency or accessibility, or is simply difficult to predict. Limitations of control and rationality may result from our incapacity to process all relevant information. Interdependencies and correlations in the real world are usually complex and non-deterministic. In order to get orientated and to make predictions, reductions and simplifications are therefore inevitable (Simon, 1955). In addition, the tendency to segregate certain aspects (by means of non-pathological dissociation procedures) appears quite natural in everyday life. For example, emotions may get separated from rational thought. In extreme cases, these tendencies might even result in experiences of alienation. And finally, emotional factors usually exert their influence on cognitive processing, often in a more subtle way, but sometimes also in more drastic or even traumatic ways.

The second area of general psychological factors that determine illusionability consists of basic cognitive propensities that are connected to possible illusions. We consider these as built-in aspects of our information-processing system that resemble "normal" functioning. In this sense, illusions are nothing special. They are simply bound to occur. Due to the restrictions discussed above, several cognitive mechanisms (which are useful for thinking and judging in everyday life) could be made responsible. These include striving for economy (involving reduction and simplification strategies), ascribing meaning (i.e., searching for connections and associations, comparing, and categorizing), acting in anticipation of expected results, relying on one's own imaginary capacities (including wishes, dreams, and fantasies), pretending (i.e., simulating and dissimulating), and last but not least, acting self-centred. Generally, all these tendencies suggest that the individual chooses one or only a few out of many options, thus leading to the elimination of those options that are no longer pursued. As a consequence, all these mechanisms are inherently related to the occurrence of cognitive illusions. However, these illusions need not be detrimental, but could rather be adaptive as well.

Let us look at one of these mechanisms more closely, namely the propensity for *economic* processing. In this case, alternative options are ignored a priori, thus leading to a premature cognitive commitment (Langer, 1989). This includes the application of *pars-pro-toto* strategies. In addition, people are typically only interested in the results of their cognitive processes, but not in the processes themselves (which, however, could provide valuable information). Everyday experiences provide many examples of such economic processing. To name just one, we refrain from being overly redundant in communication because we typically (but sometimes erroneously) assume that our communication partner has already understood what we had in mind.

With respect to suggestion research (Gheorghiu, 1996), this propensity for economic processing appears similar to the editing mechanism assumed in prospect theory, the most important theory in behavioural decision making (Kahneman & Tversky, 1979). Furthermore, research on fast and frugal heuristics has also shown the relevance and importance of such mechanisms, for example, in one-reason decision making (Gigerenzer, Todd, & ABC Research Group, 1999). Another economic mechanism focuses on facilitating information search. This has, for example, been described in the availability and representativeness heuristics (see Chapters 8 and 9, respectively).

Individual differences

In addition to the general psychological factors discussed above, individuals differ in their degree of illusionability. Several authors have recently examined the relationships between individual differences and cognitive illusions (e.g., Pohl, 2000; Read & Winograd, 1998; Stanovich, 1999). However, they did not address the problem of how to measure the illusionability of an individual person. Therefore, this section is devoted to appropriate proposals from suggestibility research that might be used as starting points for developing similar instruments to assess illusionability.

As mentioned above, individual differences (in addition to other variables) determine the probability with which an individual will follow a suggested direction. Gudjonsson and others (e.g., Gudjonsson, Sigurdsson, Brynjolfsdottir, & Hreinsdottir, 2002) made several notable contributions with respect to such individual differences as acquiescence, intelligence, and memory capacity. Gudjonsson (1997) also published probably the most well-known suggestibility scale (GSS, Gudjonsson Suggestibility Scales).

Gheorghiu and co-authors introduced several suggestibility scales for sensory judgements and motor reactions. In traditional research, suggestibility is assessed by pretending that test persons are presented with real stimuli, but in fact these are faked. This implies the possibility that results are strongly influenced by participants' compliance. Avoidance of compliance was the main motive for constructing the Sensory Suggestibility Test (SST; Gheorghiu, Netter, & Tichi, 1989). This was achieved by warning the participants: They were told that stimuli might or might not occur and that they should only react to actually presented stimuli. In fact, a real stimulus was never presented in experimental trials (only in control trials). Given these objectives, a scale of sensory suggestibility was developed for the tactile, auditory, and visual senses.

Gheorghiu and Hübner (1992) addressed an additional problem related to the theme of this book. Their Sensory Suggestibility Scale (SSK) can be applied in two variants differing only in their instruction. One instruction pretends that the purpose of the test is to assess one's sensory thresholds (as in the SST), whereas according to the other instruction the purpose of the test is to measure the individual deception. The idea of this latter test instruction is to avoid persons trying to behave according to the assumed test's intention. Accordingly, test scores were lower in the second condition ("deception") than in the first one ("threshold"). This can be taken as evidence for the impact of cognitive factors while being tested for sensory suggestibility. Apart from that, both versions have similar satisfactory psychometric qualities, and variants of them have been successfully applied for assessing the placebo effect (DePascalis, Chiaradia, & Carotenuto, 2002).

Having discussed two of the four cornerstones of the domain of illusionality (i.e., illusive situations and illusionability) and having omitted the third one (illusive techniques), we now turn to the one of the most theoretical importance: What are the functions of cognitive illusions with respect to human thinking, judgement, and memory?

THE THEORETICAL CHALLENGE OF ILLUSIONALITY: WHAT ARE THE FUNCTIONS OF COGNITIVE ILLUSIONS?

Preliminary considerations

In early research on cognitive illusions, any biases in thinking, judgement, or memory were judged to be malfunctions of the cognitive system (e.g., Tversky & Kahneman, 1974). Later, the focus shifted towards a viewpoint incorporating the possibly adaptive advantages of these biases (e.g., Gigerenzer, 1991), for example, to allow for coping in stressful situations. From the perspective of research on suggestion, this change is completely justified and also desired.

During our entire lifetime, human beings are influenced by suggestions and illusions in a great variety of situations. It seems unlikely that all these cases reflect nothing but a malfunction of nature. Due to the frequent occurrence of illusions, there is no need to answer the question *whether* we are illusioned. More important is to find the reasons *why* we are influenced by illusions, or as Alan Baddeley (debating the role of autobiographical memory) once exclaimed: "But what the hell is it for?" (Baddeley, 1988).

In animal behaviour, illusions are also of adaptive relevance. Consequently, the phylogenetic perspective as suggested by Cosmides and Tooby (1992) should be considered here as well. This change of perspective appears suitable and long overdue for the development of integrative research on common aspects of different illusions, ranging from manipulative techniques to complex judgement, thinking, and memory illusions. One area in which such illusions could possibly be helpful, and which will be discussed next, is in coping mechanisms.

Coping functions

The crucial functions of adaptive coping mechanisms are *orientation*, *support*, and *protection*. These mechanisms are related to suggestive and illusive processes and, typically, they do not work independently but are complementary to each other.

Orientation

Orientation is in many situations the prerequisite for fast and efficient acting (Gigerenzer et al., 1999). But it can be severely hampered by ambiguity or uncertainty, which is all too common. These shortcomings can in principle be reduced or even resolved by means of suggestive directions for one's behaviour. Orientation in this sense can be achieved by pseudo-rules, normative rules, rituals, conventions, leading ideas, or self-fulfilling prophecies. The underlying suggestions are supported by pseudo-rationalizations and pseudo-attributions, or by elaboration of subjective criteria for the truth of personal constructs (Gheorghiu & Kruse, 1991).

Support

Coping functions leading to support ensure that biological, psychological, and social necessities are met. Different illusive techniques may serve the satisfaction of needs concerning food, sexuality, and social relations. This can be achieved in different ways, for example, by encouragement to carry on (by suggesting advantages or by stimulating curiosity), or by activation of potential capabilities (by influence of feedback or evaluative judgements), or by reduction or elimination of negative implications (by reframing the problem or by increased positivity). These illusions are also used in order to reach personal advantages and social power (Cialdini, 2000).

Protection

Conservation and defence of the self are enhanced by protective coping functions. To this end, complex self-illusion techniques may be employed. *Defensive* strategies, for example, protect or enhance self-esteem and reduce dissonance. A number of cognitive illusions belong to this kind of coping functions, even though the self-esteem-protection hypothesis does not represent the only explanation for these illusions. Conway and Ross (1984), for example, discussed the protective function in relation to hindsight bias (see Chapter 20). *Compensational* strategies offer substitute "solutions" within an illusionary environment including religion, esotericism, and magic. In scientific contexts, these coping functions have been discussed in relation to the placebo effect (e.g., Kirsch, 1999). *Ludic* or *playful* strategies are also important and common to all age groups. Both words, "ludic" and "illusion", derive from the same Latin word *ludere*, which means "to play". Human readiness to playfully share and take part in different roles may ease identification, regression, and dissociative procedures. These are relevant in applied contexts like self-healing and psychotherapy, but also in everyday settings, for example, to reduce boredom.

These are some examples of coping functions. The adaptive functions of suggestions and illusions in this context can also become effective in combination with other cognitive strategies (like rational or intuitive ones). The individual not only welcomes and accepts the possibility of an illusion, but also sometimes even reacts with frustration (or disappointment), if the illusion is involuntarily uncovered, forcing him or her to face the naked truth. To prevent this, people often seek refuge in the belief that they have a personal guardian angel and that some dangers (like getting killed in a car accident) are in fact much smaller for themselves than for others. In this way, people may build their own private and secure world. These observations underline the importance of illusions in coping with stressful situations.

Three general qualities of human judgement, thinking, and memory are crucial in this context. These are the directionality of behaviour, the capacity to interpret and evaluate, and the capacity to reach decisions. Humans act directedly because of their own or others' goals, motives, values, hypotheses, expectancies, etc. These are likely to become autonomous and to influence cognition. Interpretation and evaluation of experiences allow the (re-)construction of reality and are essential for the orientation function mentioned above. Meaning is attributed to events based on internal or external information. What is most important is the personal relevance that is ascribed to the current situation or aspects thereof (cf. Gheorghiu & Wallbott, 1994). In many situations there are no unambiguous decision criteria – therefore, besides rational strategies, people often use pseudo-rational, suggestional, or intuitive decision rules simply because they are forced to choose one option.

CONCLUDING REMARKS

One important parallel between research on suggestional processes and research on cognitive illusions (cf. Molz, 2000) is that systematic deviations from normatively correct behaviour were in both domains typically judged to be malfunctions of the human cognitive system. Jungermann (1986) characterized this point of view as *pessimistic*, which was the predominant perspective until the 1980s. Tversky and Kahneman's (1974) work on heuristics and biases can be interpreted as such a perspective searching for systematic errors in human judgements. Beach, Christensen-Szalanski, and Barnes (1987) promoted an orientation towards an epistemic instead of an aleatoric logic, which we have already mentioned above: Logics of random variables and axioms of probability are not necessarily the appropriate yardsticks for evaluating human performance. This – in Jungermann's terms *optimistic* – perspective is shared by Gheorghiu (1996, Gheorghiu & Kruse, 1991) and the other authors of this chapter, not only for cognitive illusions but also for suggestional processes. According to that argumentation, suggestions very often have a positive effect on everyday life and thus should be considered to be basically adaptive. In future research, a double-tracked approach seems wise – that is, to further investigate the decisive conditions leading to single cognitive illusions, but at the same time to pursue the goal of developing a more integrative account of illusionality, uncovering the regular set of basic cognitive processes that are responsible for illusions.

In this chapter we set out to sail across a wide and mainly unknown ocean to visit a multitude of small islands called "cognitive illusions". The idea was that despite their apparent isolation, all of these islands might be connected to each other, thus forming a network of relations that are waiting (and need) to be discovered. Inspired by the domain of suggestionality, we sketched a first result of our journey: a map called "the domain of illusionality", which captures the main aspects of the archipelago of cognitive illusions. Whether that map will prove helpful to other sailors (as we sincerely hope) remains to be seen. At least we can already feel the fair wind that will take us beyond the known territory.

REFERENCES

Asch, S. E. (1956). Studies of independence and conformity: A minority of one against a unanimous majority. *Psychological Monographs*, 70, 17–190.
Baddeley, A. (1988). But what the hell is it for? In M. M. Gruneberg & R. N. Sykes (Eds.), *Practical aspects of memory* (Vol. 1, pp. 3–18). Wiley: New York.

Beach, L. R., Christensen-Szalanski, J. J. J., & Barnes, V. E. (1987). Assessing human judgment: Has it been done, can it be done, should it be done? In G. Wright & P. Ayton (Eds.), *Judgmental forecasting* (pp. 49–62). Chichester, UK: Wiley.

Binet, A. (1900). *La suggestibilité* [Suggestibility]. Paris: Schleicher Frères.

Bowers, K. S. (1984). On being unconsciously influenced and informed. In K. S. Bowers & D. Meichenbaum (Eds.), *The unconscious recondidererd* (pp. 227–272). New York: Wiley.

Cialdini, R. B. (2000). *Influence: Science and practice.* Boston: Allyn & Bacon.

Conway, M., & Ross, M. (1984). Getting what you want by revising what you had. *Journal of Personality and Social Psychology, 47,* 738–748.

Cosmides, L., & Tooby, J. (1992). Cognitive adaptations for social exchange. In J. H. Barkow, H. Jerome, & L. Cosmides (Eds.), *The adapted mind: Evolutionary psychology and the generation of culture* (pp. 163–228). London: Oxford University Press.

Davidsson, P., & Wahlund, R. (1992). A note on the failure to use negative information. *Journal of Economic Psychology, 13,* 343–353.

DePascalis, V., Chiaradia, C., & Carotenuto, E. (2002). The contribution of expectation to placebo analgesia phenomenon in an experimental setting. *Pain, 96,* 393–402.

DePascalis, V., Gheorghiu, V. A., Sheehan, P. W., & Kirsch, I. (Eds.), (2000). *Suggestion and suggestibility. Theory and research. Hypnosis International Monographs* (Vol. 4). München: M.E.G.-Stiftung.

Ellsberg, D. (1961). Risk, ambiguity, and the Savage axioms. *Quarterly Journal of Economics, 75,* 643–669.

Eysenck, H. J., & Furneaux, W. D. (1945). Primary and secondary suggestibility: An experimental and statistical study. *Journal of Experimental Psychology, 35,* 485–503.

Gheorghiu, V. A. (1991). Untersuchungen über die Beeinflussung motorischer Abläufe unabhängig vom hypnotischen Kontext: Das Problem der Plausibilität der Testsituation [Investigations on the influenceability of motor processes independent from a hypnotic context: The problem of plausibility of the test situation]. In E. Bagdy & M. Szönyi (Eds.), *Proceedings of the 1st Congress of Psychotherapeutical Relaxation, Budapest* (pp. 24–31). Budapest: Agroinform.

Gheorghiu, V. A. (1992). Suggestion vs. Rationalität: Eine Wasser–Feuer-Beziehung? [Suggestion vs. rationality: A water–fire-relationship?]. In B. Peter & G. Schmidt (Eds.), *Erickson in Europa. Europäische Ansätze der Ericksonschen Hypnose und Psychotherapie* (pp. 304–327). Heidelberg: Carl-Auer-Verlag.

Gheorghiu, V. A. (1993). Die Psychologie der Suggestion: Eine kognitivistische Perspektive [The psychology of suggestion: A cognitivistic perspective]. *Hypnose und Kognition, 10,* 3–26.

Gheorghiu, V. A. (1996). Die adaptive Funktion suggestionaler Prozesse. Zum Stellenwert suggestionsbedingter Einflüsse [The adaptive function of suggestional processes. Status of influences caused by suggestions]. *Hypnose und Kognition, 13,* 125–146.

Gheorghiu, V. A. (2000). The domain of suggestionality: Attempt to conceptualize suggestional phenomena. 1. Particularities of suggestion. In V. DePascalis, V. A. Gheorghiu, P. W. Sheehan, & I. Kirsch (Eds.), *Suggestion and suggestibility. Theory and research. Hypnosis International Monographs* (Vol. 4, pp. 1–28). München: M.E.G.-Stiftung.

Gheorghiu, V. A., & Hübner, M. (1992). Die Sensorische Suggestibilitätsskala (SSK) als Erhebungsverfahren für Täuschbarkeit [The Scale of Sensory Suggestibility as assessment of deception]. *Experimentelle und Klinische Hypnose, 8*, 117–129.

Gheorghiu, V. A., Koch, E., Fialkovski, H., Pieper, W., & Molz, G. (2001). Factors influencing the illusion of warmth. *Contemporary Hypnosis, 18*, 2–31.

Gheorghiu, V. A., Koch, E., & Götz, C. (2000). Initiation, modification, and inhibition of motor reactions through indirect suggestion approaches. In V. DePascalis, V. A. Gheorghiu, P. W. Sheehan, & I. Kirsch (Eds.), *Suggestion and suggestibility. Theory and research. Hypnosis International Monographs* (Vol. 4, pp. 177–197). München: M.E.G.-Stiftung.

Gheorghiu, V. A., & Kruse, P. (1991). The psychology of suggestion: An integrative perspective. In J. Schumaker (Ed.), *Human suggestibility: Advances in theory, research, and application* (pp. 59–75). New York: Routledge.

Gheorghiu, V. A., Netter, P., Eysenck, H. J., & Rosenthal, R. (Eds.). (1989). *Suggestion and suggestibility: Theory and research*. Berlin: Springer.

Gheorghiu, V. A., Netter, P., & Tichi, H. J. (1989). A test of sensory suggestibility. In A. F. Bennet & K. M. McConkey (Eds.), *Cognition in individual and social contexts* (pp. 507–517). Amsterdam: Elsevier.

Gheorghiu, V. A., & Wallbott, H. G. (1994). Suggestion and attribution of meaning: A cognitive and social psychological perspective. *Communicazioni Scientifiche di Psicologia Generale/Scientific Contributions to General Psychology, 12*, 117–139.

Gigerenzer, G. (1991). How to make cognitive illusions disappear: Beyond "heuristics and biases". *European Review of Social Psychology, 2*, 8–115.

Gigerenzer, G., Todd, P. M., & The ABC Research Group (Eds.). (1999). *Simple heuristics that make us smart*. New York: Oxford University Press.

Gudjonsson, G. H. (1997). *The Gudjonsson Suggestibility Scales Manual*. London: Psychology Press.

Gudjonsson, G. H. (2003). *The psychology of interrogations and confessions: A handbook*. New York: Wiley.

Gudjonsson, G. H., Sigurdsson, J. F., Brynjolfsdottir, B., & Hreinsdottir, H. (2002). The relationship of compliance with anxiety, self-esteem, paranoid thinking and anger. *Psychology, Crime and Law, 8*, 145–153.

Hell, W. (1993). Gedächtnistäuschungen [Memory illusions]. In W. Hell, K. Fiedler, & G. Gigerenzer (Eds.), *Kognitive Täuschungen. Fehl-Leistungen und Mechanismen des Urteilens, Denkens und Erinnerns* [Cognitive illusions. Fallacies and mechanisms of judgment, thinking, and memory] (pp. 13–38). Heidelberg: Spektrum.

Jungermann, H. (1986). The two camps on rationality. In H. R. Arkes & K. R. Hammond (Eds.), *Judgement and decision making: An interdisciplinary reader* (pp. 627–641). Cambridge, MA: Cambridge University Press.

Kahneman, D., & Tversky, A. (1979). Prospect theory: An analysis of decision under risk. *Econometrica, 47*, 263–291.

Kirsch, I. (Ed). (1999). *How expectancies shape experience*. Washington: American Psychiatric Association.

Langer, E. J. (1989). *Mindfulness*. Reading, MA: Addison Wesley.

Molz, G. (1997). *The confirmation bias: Does it result from mental accounting? An exploratory analysis*. Giessen: Giessener Electronic Library (http://bibd.uni-giessen.de/ghtm/uni/p010006.htm)

Molz, G. (2000). Behavioural decision making and suggestional processes: Some considerations for integration. *Hypnose und Kognition, 17*(Supplement), 91–92.

Perky, C. W. (1910). An experimental study of imagination. *American Journal of Psychology, 21,* 422–452.

Pohl, R. F. (2000). Suggestibility and anchoring. In V. DePascalis, V. A. Gheorghiu, P. W. Sheehan, & I. Kirsch (Eds.), *Suggestion and suggestibility: Theory and research. Hypnosis International Monographs* (Vol. 4, pp. 137–151). München: M.E.G.-Stiftung.

Pohl, R. F., Bender, M., & Lachmann, G. (2002). Hindsight bias around the world. *Experimental Psychology, 49,* 270–282.

Read, J. D., & Winograd, E. (Eds.). (1998). Individual differences and memory distortions. *Applied Cognitive Psychology, 12*(SI).

Schumaker, J. (Ed.). (1991). *Human suggestibility: Advances in theory, research, and application.* New York: Routledge.

Seashore, C. E. (1895). Measurements of illusions and hallucinations in normal life. *Studies from the Yale Psychophysiological Laboratory, 2,* 1–67.

Simon, H. A. (1955). A behavioral model of rational choice. *Quarterly Journal of Economics, 69,* 99–119.

Stanovich, K. E. (1999). *Who is rational? Studies of individual differences in reasoning.* Mahwah, NJ: Lawrence Erlbaum Associates Inc.

Tversky, A., & Kahneman, D. (1974). Judgment under uncertainty: Heuristics and biases. *Science, 185,* 1124–1131.

Weinstein, N. D. (1980). Unrealistic optimism about future life events. *Journal of Personality and Social Psychology, 39,* 806–820.

Author index

Abelson, R. P. 120
Abramson, L. Y. 97, 116, 119, 120, 121, 123
Adams, J. K. 236
Adams, P. A. 236
Agnoli, F. 23, 35
Aikins, S. 297, 298, 301
Akamatsu, S. 296
Akers, K. 335
Alba, J. W. 9, 239, 242
Albert, S. 390
Allison, K. 222, 229
Alloy, L. B. 26, 97, 116, 119, 120, 121, 123
Allwood, C. M. 243
Alvaro, C. 391
Amir, Y. 218
Anderson, A. K. 302
Anderson, C. 1, 37
Anderson, J. R. 285, 310
Anderson, N. H. 46
Andrus, D. E. 189
Anes, M. D. 322
Angle, S. T. 120
Angstadt, P. 289
Aristotle 166, 309
Arkes, H. R. 201, 202, 203, 205, 206, 207, 210
Armor, D. A. 268
Armour, V. 201, 207
Armstrong, W. 119, 124
Arndt, J. 318
Arterberry, M. E. 222
Asch, S. E. 401
Ashby, F. G. 268
Attanasio, J. S. 176
Ayeroff, F. 120
Ayers, M. S. 277, 286, 287, 288, 289, 351

Ayton, P. 171

Bacon, F. 89
Bacon, F. T. 201, 205
Baddeley, A. 416
Bakan, P. 301, 305
Balota, D. A. 318
Baltes, P. B. 391
Bandy, D. 14
Barber, B. C. 121
Bar-Hillel, M. 63, 67, 166
Barnes, V. E. 418
Barnsley, R. H. 335
Barron, F. 223
Barston, J. L. 137, 138, 139
Bar-Tal, D. 223, 227, 230
Bartlett, F. C. 9, 13, 346, 380, 392
Bassok, M. 83, 84
Bayes, Rev. Thomas 43, 61
Bazerman, M. H. 187
Beach, L. R. 62, 418
Beck, J. R. 24, 29, 36
Begg, I. 201, 205, 207
Belli, R. F. 334, 335
Bender, M. 3, 14, 364, 374, 375, 401
Benjamin, A. S. 321
Berg, C. A. 230
Berlyne, D. E. 220, 227, 228
Berscheid, E. 84, 86
Betsch, T. 67, 70, 88, 156
Betz, A. L. 261
Billings, F. J. 353
Binder, N. 215, 217, 227
Biner, P. M. 120
Binet, A. 401, 404, 406
Birnbaum, M. H. 1, 37, 45, 46, 47, 48, 49, 53, 54, 55, 56, 57, 62
Birrell, P. 152
Birren, J. E. 382, 384

Biswas, A. 187
Bjorklund, D. F. 250
Björkman, M. 248
Black, P. M. 322
Blackmore, S. 124
Bless, H. 157, 158, 160, 161
Blitz-Miller, T. 124
Bodenhausen, G. V. 193
Boehm, L. 201, 202, 203, 205, 206, 207, 210
Bolger, F. 242, 245, 246
Boneau, A. C. 209
Bördlein, C. 81
Borgida, E. 27, 38
Bork, R. 389
Bornstein, B. H. 185
Bornstein, M. H. 327, 333, 334
Bornstein, R. F. 215, 216, 217, 218, 219, 220, 221, 222, 223, 224, 225, 227, 228, 229, 230
Boucher, J. 255, 260
Bouts, P. 121
Bower, G. H. 154
Bowers, K. S. 407
Brainerd, C. J. 318
Brandimonte, M. A. 338, 339
Brase, G. 71
Braun, K. 334, 355
Bredart, S. 278, 286–7
Bregman, N. J. 335
Breiter, H. C. 302
Brekke, N. 186, 188, 190, 195
Brenner, L. A. 249
Brewer, W. F. 9
Brier, G. W. 236
Brigham, J. C. 338, 339
Brinkmann, B. 67, 70
Brody, N. 221, 228
Brooks, C. I. 336, 340
Brown, A. L. 204
Brown, J. D. 123
Brown, N. R. 160
Bruce, A. C. 244
Brun, W. 29
Brunswik, E. 248
Brynjolfsdottir, B. 414
Budescu, D. V. 244, 247, 248
Budson, A. E. 322
Buehler, R. 17, 235
Burns, H. J. 347, 348, 349, 350
Burton, S. 187
Burton, A. M. 296
Byrne, R. M. J. 127, 129, 135, 139, 142

Cabral, K. 340
Cacciapaglia, H. 340
Calderwood, K. 124
Calkins, M. 310
Campbell, J. D. 374, 375
Carlson, B. W. 24, 27, 28, 34
Carmichael, L. 327, 328, 329, 330, 331, 332
Carotenuto, E. 415
Castellan, W. 336, 340
Caverni, J.-P. 2, 8, 13, 14, 32, 35, 71
Ceci, S. J. 352
Cervone, D. 185
Chapman, G. B. 185, 186, 191, 192, 193
Chapman, J. P. 97
Chapman, L. J. 97
Chase, V. M. 31, 36, 37
Chater, N. 131
Chiaradia, C. 415
Chiesi, H. L. 207
Chokron, S. 305
Christensen, I. P. 31
Christensen-Szalanski, J. J. J. 62, 363, 366, 371, 374, 375, 418
Chromiak, W. 204
Cialdini, R. B. 417
Clemens, S. L. 262
Clements, C. M. 123
Clode, D. 297, 300, 303
Cohen, J. 23
Cohen, M. S. 302
Collins, H. R. 354
Combs, B. 153
Conway, M. 382, 384, 402, 412, 417
Copeland, D. E. 296
Corkill, A. J. 14
Cornell, K. R. 217, 220, 223, 224, 225, 227, 228
Cosmides, L. 63, 70, 71, 81, 416
Cox, J. R. 132
Coyle, J. T. 9
Craver-Lemley, C. 222, 228, 229
Crawley, S. E. 16
Crocker, J. 88, 97
Csikszentmihalyi, M. 268
Curran, T. 14
Czerlinsky, J. 10, 12

Daffner, K. Y. 322
D'Agostino, P. R. 221, 222, 228, 230
Daneman, M. 283, 286
Daniel, T. C. 329, 333
Dardis, G. J. 266
Davey, S. J. 9

Davidoff, J. 303–4
Davidsson, P. 412
Dawes, R. 251
De Agostini, M. 305
de Mul, S. 278, 279, 283
Dearnaley, E. J. 23
DeCapito, A. 333
Deese, J. 312, 317
Demarest, I. H. 328, 329, 330, 332, 333
Dempster, F. N. 14
DePascalis, V. 403, 415
Devine, P. G. 83, 84, 86
DiGirolamo, G. J. 302
Doherty, M. E. 87, 168
Donovan, S. 23, 33, 34
Donovan, W. L. 123
Dorner, W. W. 102
Dougherty, M. R. P. 248
Downs, J. H. 302
Dragonetti, R. 124
Drivdahl, S. B. 354
Duensing, S. 352
Dunn, D. S. 120
Dunning, D. 265
Dywan, J. 320, 356

Ebbinghaus, H. 310
Ebert, A. 72
Eddy, D. M. 62
Edwards, W. 8, 45, 46, 52, 55, 62
Eibach, R. P. 389
Eisenhauer, M. 15, 364, 366, 367, 368, 369, 370, 371, 372, 375
Ellsberg, D. 403
Englich, B. 183, 185, 186
Engstler-Schooler, T. Y. 337, 338, 339
Epley, N. 188, 189
Epstein, S. 23, 33, 34, 38
Erev, I. 244, 247, 248
Erickson, T. A. 275, 279, 282, 283
Ericsson, K. A. 318, 339, 340
Etling, K. M. 186, 188, 190, 195
Evans, J. St. B. T. 8, 29, 34, 38, 127–8, 129, 130–2, 134, 135, 137, 138, 139, 140, 141, 142
Eysenck, H. J. 3, 401, 403

Fabiani, M. 358
Fabre, J. M. 2, 8, 13, 14, 32
Fanselow, C. 372, 373, 374, 375
Ferrell, W. R. 243, 246
Festinger, L. 195, 390
Fialkovsky, H. 403
Fiedberg, E. L. 1

Fiedler, K. 7, 23, 26, 28, 61, 67, 70, 88, 97, 102, 103, 104, 105, 108, 109
Finger, K. 355
Finkel, S. E. 189
Fiore, S. M. 338, 339
Fischbach, G. D. 9
Fischhoff, B. 45, 48, 153, 186, 237, 238, 239, 242, 243, 244, 245, 363, 371, 373, 374
Fisher, A. V. 340
Fisk, J. E. 24, 25, 26, 28, 30, 31, 32, 33, 34, 36, 37, 38
Fiske, S. T. 174
Fleeson, W. 391
Fodor, J. 39
Fong, G. T. 89, 92, 390
Forys, K. 222, 228, 229
Fox, P. T. 302
Frederick, S. 179, 180
Freeman, H. R. 220
Freund, T. 223, 227, 230
Frey, D. 88
Freytag, P. 102
Friedland, N. 121
Friedrich, J. 91
Frisch, D. 178
Frydenlund, R. 29
Frye, N. E. 383, 384, 391
Fulero, S. 152
Furneaux, W. D. 401

Gabriel, S. 193
Gadenne, V. 89
Gagné, F. M. 88
Galinsky, A. D. 185, 187
Galley, D. J. 218, 221
Gallo, D. A. 315, 317, 318, 320, 321
Garb, H. N. 174
Gardiner, J. M. 313
Garry, M. 353, 354, 355
Garza, A. A. 229, 230
Gatto, J. T. 211
Gauggel, S. 367, 368, 369, 371
Gavanski, I. 24, 175
Gawlik, B. 334
Gehrke, E. M. 83, 84, 86
Gheorghiu, V. A. 3, 341, 403, 406, 407, 409, 410, 414, 415, 416, 417, 418
Gibson, J. 330
Gifford, R. K. 98, 99
Gigerenzer, G. 2, 3, 4, 7, 10, 11, 12, 14, 32, 49, 62, 63, 64, 65, 66, 67, 68, 69, 70, 71, 72, 81, 134, 150, 177, 178, 201, 239, 241, 246, 247, 252, 367,

368, 369, 371, 372, 373, 375, 414, 415, 416
Giladi, E. E. 267
Gilbert, C. 301, 305
Gilinsky, A. S. 140
Gilovich, T. 8, 10, 12, 186, 188, 189, 389
Girotto, V. 35, 69, 70, 71
Glass, T. 302
Glöckner, A. 88
Goethals, G. B. 381, 382, 384
Goethe, J. W. von 379
Goldsmith, R. W. 37
Goldstein, D. 201, 204
Goldstein, D. G. 32, 252
Gonzales, M. 2, 8, 13, 14, 69, 70, 71
Goodwin, K. A. 318, 319
Götz, C. 403, 406
Graesser, A. C. 88
Graham, S. A. 340
Gramm, K. 103
Green, J. D. 261, 262
Greenwald, A. G. 382
Gregory, R. L. 223, 226
Grice, H. P. 184, 190, 278
Griffin, D. 8, 10, 12, 17, 235, 243
Griggs, R. A. 132
Gude, C. 201, 204
Gudjonsson, G. H. 401, 414

Ha, Y. 81, 82, 86, 93, 103, 132, 192
Haar, T. 88
Haberstroh, S. 88
Hackett, C. 201, 202, 203, 205, 206, 207, 210
Haddock, G. 158
Halpern, A. R. 222
Hamid, P. N. 221
Hamilton, D. L. 98, 99, 103
Hamm, R. M. 72
Hammerton, M. A. 46, 48
Hanawalt, N. G. 328, 329, 330, 332, 333
Handley, S. J. 29, 127–8, 135
Hannon, B. 283, 286
Hansel, C. E. M. 23
Hardin, D. P. 266
Hardt, O. 15, 364, 366, 367, 368, 369, 370, 371, 372, 375
Harper, C. 135
Harris, G. 205
Harrison, A. A. 210, 216
Harrison, D. A. 267
Hartley, D. 309

Hasher, L. 9, 161, 201, 204
Hashtroudi, S. 317
Hassett 358
Hastie, R. 363, 366, 371, 374, 375
Hawkins, S. A. 363, 366, 371, 374, 375
Heaps, C. M. 357, 358
Hearst, E. 102
Heine, S. J. 266
Hell, W. 2, 3, 7, 9, 13, 14, 363, 367, 368, 369, 371, 409
Helson, H. 195
Helweg-Larsen, M. 266, 267
Henkel, L. A. 320
Herbst, K. C. 266
Herman, P. 382
Hertwig, R. 3, 11, 14, 31, 36, 37, 64, 69, 72, 150, 178, 371, 372, 373, 374, 375
Herz, R. S. 327, 337
Hicks, J. L. 320
Higgins, E. T. 148, 192, 340
Hiraki, K. 289
Hirsch, T. B. 302
Hirshman, E. 318
Hirt, E. R. 83, 84, 86
Hobbes, T. 309
Hockney, D. 297
Hodge, D. 355
Hodgins, H. S. 83, 84, 86
Hodgson, R. 9
Hoffrage, U. 3, 11, 14, 49, 62, 63, 64, 65, 66, 67, 68, 69, 70, 71, 72, 239, 241, 246, 247, 252, 363, 371, 372, 373, 374, 375
Hogan, H. P. 327, 328, 329, 330, 331, 332
Holstein, C. 34, 38
Holzworth, R. J. 168
Horchler, S. 222, 229
Houston, C. 186, 188, 190, 195
Howard, J. 152
Hreinsdottir, H. 414
Hübner, M. 415
Hug, K. 81, 134
Huh, E. 34, 38
Humphrey, N. K. 297
Husband, T. H. 353
Hutchinson, J. W. 239, 242
Hyman, I. E. 352, 353, 356
Hynan, L. G. 1, 37

Isen, A. M. 268
Israel, L. 321

Jacoby, L. L. 320, 352, 356

Jacowitz, K. E. 190
James, W. 345
Jamis, M. 351
Janiszewski, C. 218
Jeannerod, M. 302
Jensen, C. 152
Johnson, E. J. 185, 186, 191, 192, 193
Johnson, J. E. V. 244
Johnson, M. K. 14, 317, 320
Johnson-Laird, P. N. 35, 71, 127, 129, 130, 132, 135
Jones, C. R. 192, 340
Jones, G. V. 293, 295, 296, 298, 299, 300, 302, 303, 305
Jones, K. T. 178
Jones, S. K. 178
Joram, E. 178
Judd, B. B. 140
Jungermann, H. 7, 12, 27, 31, 32, 418
Juslin, P. 240, 242, 245, 246, 248, 249

Kahn, A. S. 265
Kahneman, D. 1, 4, 6, 8, 10, 11, 12, 24, 27, 31, 32, 45, 46, 47, 48, 51, 55, 62, 147, 148, 149, 150, 152, 156, 157, 160, 165, 167, 169, 170, 172, 173, 174, 176, 179, 180, 183, 184, 186, 187, 188, 189, 190, 195, 245, 305, 371, 414, 415, 418
Kail, R. V. 220
Kale, A. R. 217, 220, 223, 224, 225, 227, 228
Kamas, E. N. 277, 285, 286, 287, 288, 289
Kao, S. -F. 98, 102
Kareev, Y. 112
Kariyazono, A. 31
Karmiloff-Smith, A. 39
Karney, B. R. 383, 384, 391
Karoni, P. 14
Kassin, S. 358
Kato, T. 296
Katz, R. C. 340
Kauff, D. M. 221, 228
Keinan, G. 121
Kelley, C. M. 289, 320, 352, 356
Kelly, S. W. 296
Kennedy, C. A. 256
Kent, D. R. 124
Keren, G. 65, 68, 69, 71, 237, 242
Kerr, T. 201, 207
Keuler, D. J. 382, 384
Keyes, C. L. M. 390

Kingsolver, B. 345
Kirkpatrick, E. A. 310, 311
Kirsch, I. 355, 403, 417
Kitayama, S. 266
Klar, Y. 267
Klauer, K. C. 103
Klayman, J. 81, 82, 86, 89, 93, 103, 130, 132, 192
Kleinbölting, H. 72, 239, 241, 246, 247
Kleiter, G. D. 70
Klumpp, G. 157, 158, 161
Knee, C. R. 83, 84, 86
Koch, E. 403, 406
Koehler, J. J. 45, 62, 72
Kok, I. 282, 283
Kontis, T. C. 295
Kosslyn, S. M. 302
Kounios, J. 14
Krantz, D. H. 23, 35
Krauss, S. 61, 65, 70, 71, 72
Krist, H. 1
Kronzon, S. 46, 48, 53, 55
Kruger, J. 257, 265, 266, 267
Kruglanski, A. W. 90, 223, 227, 230
Krugman, H. E. 208
Krull, D. S. 260
Kruse, P. 409, 416, 418
Kunda, Z. 81, 89, 92, 390
Kunst-Wilson, W. R. 221
Kurzenhäuser, S. 72
Kusbit, G. W. 276, 277, 278, 279, 280, 283
Kutas, M. 304
Kwong, J. Y. Y. 190
Kyle, D. 119, 120, 121, 122

Lachmann, G. 3, 14, 364, 374, 375, 402
Lake, C. 222, 228, 229
Lampinen, J. M. 315
Langer, E. J. 115, 118–19, 120, 121, 122, 123, 124, 412, 414
Laplace, P. S. 166
Larkin, J. H. 39
Lather, P. 255, 256
Lawrence, C. P. 189
Layman, E. 175
Layman, M. 153
Leavitt, L. A. 123
Lebiere, C. 285
Legrenzi, M. S. 35
Legrenzi, P. 35, 71
Lehman, D. R. 266, 357, 358
Lemos, K. 267
Leone, D. R. 218, 221

Lepper, M. R. 80, 89
Levidow, B. 352
Levine, L. J. 381, 384, 392
Levy, J. 301
Lewis, C. 65, 68, 69, 71
Libby, L. K. 389
Liben, L. S. 1
Liberman, A. 90, 91, 92, 93
Lichtenstein, S. 45, 48, 153, 187, 237, 238, 239, 242, 243, 244, 245
Lindsay, D. S. 289, 317, 354
Lindsey, S. 64, 69, 72
Lineberger, M. 193
Link, B. G. 327, 340
Lipscomb, T. J. 335
Lipson, A. 34, 38
Lo, Y. F. 340
Locke, J. 309
Loftus, E. F. 327, 334, 335, 347, 348, 349, 350, 352, 353, 355, 356, 358, 401
Lombardi, L. 289
Lopez, S. J. 268
Lord, C. G. 80, 89
Luh, K. E. 301
Luo, C. R. 318
Lupfer, M. B. 175
Lydon, J. E. 88
Lynch, J. S. 130, 131
Lynn, S. 353.
Lyon, D. 45

Maass, A. 371, 372, 373, 374
Macchi, L. 67, 68, 71, 72
MacCoun, R. 11
MacKay, D. G. 283, 284
Mall, M. 367, 368, 369, 371
Malmi, R. A. 97
Mandel, D. R. 170, 178
Mandler, G. 218, 222, 228, 229
Manktelow, K. I. 133, 134, 139
Manning, C. G. 353, 355
Markowitsch, H. J. 14
Markus, H. R. 266
Marsh, R. L. 320
Martignon, L. 10, 12, 65, 70, 71, 72, 252
Martin, C. C. 302
Martin, M. 293, 295, 296, 298, 299, 300, 302, 303, 305
Mather, M. 14, 320
Matlin, M. W. 255, 259, 263, 264, 265
Mattson, M. E. 275, 279, 282, 283
May, R. S. 243

Mayer, E. 322
Mayseless, O. 90
Mazzoni, G. A. L. 353, 355
McAllister, H. A. 335
McClelland, A. G. R. 242, 245, 246
McClelland, J. 310
McCloskey, M. 348, 351
McClure, M. 119, 120, 121, 122
McDermott, J. 39
McDermott, K. B. 3, 9, 10, 13, 14, 309, 312, 314, 315, 317, 318, 320, 321, 356, 358, 402
McDonald, J. 87
McFarland, C. 380, 384, 391
McGoey, P. J. 243, 246
McGraw, P. 68, 69, 72
McKelvie, S. J. 297, 298, 301
McKenna, F. P. 116, 117, 118, 123
McKenna, P. A. 215, 217, 227
McKenzie, C. R. M. 111
McManus, C. 298, 301
McManus, I. C. 297
McMillan, D. 88, 102
Medvec, V. H. 186
Meiser, T. 103
Meissner, C. A. 318, 339
Melcher, J. M. 336
Mellers, B. A. 45, 46, 47, 48, 49, 54, 55, 56, 57, 62, 68, 69, 72
Mellinger, A. E. 120
Memon, A. 339
Mesulam, M. M. 9
Meyers, J. 208
Mill, J. S. 175
Miller, D. G. 347, 348, 349, 350
Miller, D. T. 195
Miller, E. 14
Miller, M. B. 315
Mitra, N. 222, 229
Mitterer, J. 205
Miyake, K. 83, 84, 86
Modolo, K. 278, 286–7
Mojardin, A. H. 318
Molz, G. 403, 412, 418
Monahan, J. L. 215, 229
Montgomery, H. 243
Morrier, D. M. 27, 38
Morris, M. W. 175
Morris, W. N. 263
Mosconi, G. 71
Müller, M. 367, 368, 369, 371
Murphy, A. H. 237, 243
Murphy, S. T. 215, 219, 221, 229
Murray, L. A. 26

Musch, J. 374
Mussweiler, T. 183, 184, 185, 186, 187, 189, 190, 191, 192, 193, 194, 195, 196
Myers, D. G. 265
Mynatt, C. R. 87

Nakamura, G. V. 9
Nakamura, Y. 218, 222, 228, 229
Nash, M. 357, 358
Neale, M. A. 185, 186, 187, 188, 190
Neely, J. H. 192
Neill, C. M. 265
Neisser, U. 88, 380
Netter, P. 3, 403, 415
Neuschatz, J. S. 315, 319
Newman, J. 102
Newstead, S. E. 129, 135, 139, 142
Nhouyvanisvong, A. 281, 287, 289
Nicholls, M. E. R. 297, 300, 303
Nickel, S. 103, 104, 105, 108, 109
Nisbett, R. E. 154, 155
Nolde, S. F. 14
Northcraft, G. B. 185, 186, 188, 190
Novemsky, N. 46, 48, 53, 55

Oaksford, M. 131
O'Connor, M. G. 222, 242
Oishi, S. 265
Olsson, H. 242, 243, 245, 246, 248, 249
Onslow, M. 176
Osgood, A. 119, 120, 121, 122
Osgood, C. E. 255, 260
Oswald, M. 89, 93
Over, D. E. 29, 34, 38, 70, 71, 133, 139, 140, 141

Packman, A. 176
Palmer, J. C. 327, 335, 347
Park, J. H. 120
Parsons, L. M. 302
Pavlov, I. 310
Payne, D. G. 315
Peake, P. K. 185
Pentland, J. 352, 356
Percer, J. M. 320, 321
Perham, N. 29
Perky, C. W. 411
Persson, M. 249
Pezdek, K. 355
Pezzo, M. V. 364, 373
Pfeiffer, P. E. 185, 247
Phan, L. B. 268
Phelan, J. C. 327, 340

Phillips, D. J. 119, 120, 121, 122
Phillips, L. D. 237, 238, 239, 242, 243, 245
Piatelli-Palmarini, M. 8, 11, 13
Pickrell, J. E. 353, 356, 358
Pidgeon, N. 24, 25, 26, 28, 31, 32, 33, 34, 38
Pieper, W. 403
Pitz, G. 45
Plessner, H. 102
Plous, S. 185
Pohl, D. 156
Pohl, R. F. 3, 14, 15, 327, 334, 336, 340, 363, 364, 365, 366, 367, 368, 369, 370, 371, 372, 373, 374, 375, 401, 414
Poletiek, F. H. 87
Polivy, J. 382
Pollard, P. 137, 138, 139
Popper, K. R. 79, 81
Porter, E. H. 255
Porter, S. 357, 358
Potter, M. C. 289
Prentice, W. C. H. 332, 333, 335
Price, J. R. 222, 227, 230
Pring, L. 16
Pushkar, D. 264

Quattrone, G. A. 186, 189
Quirouette, C. C. 264
Quist, R. M. 119, 120, 121, 122

Racine, C. 321, 322
Radvansky, G. A. 296
Raiijmakers, J. 310
Read, D. 178
Read, J. D. 14, 335, 354, 414
Reber, R. 158, 161
Reckman, R. F. 381, 382, 384
Reder, L. M. 276, 277, 278, 279, 280, 281, 282, 283, 285, 286, 287, 288, 289, 351
Redl, J. 301
Reeves, A. 222
Regev, Y. 121
Regier, T. 12
Reiman, E. 14
Renner, C. H. 208, 211
Renner, M. J. 208, 211
Reyes, R. M. 154
Reyna, V. F. 318
Rholes, W. S. 192, 340
Richards, D. R. 281, 287
Richardson, J. T. E. 296

Richardson-Klavehn, A. 313
Rittenauer-Schatka, H. 157, 158, 161
Ritter, F. 281
Rivkin, I. D. 268
Robinson, K. J. 309, 316, 318
Rodin, J. 115
Roediger, H. L. III 2, 3, 9, 10, 13, 14, 309, 312, 314, 315, 316, 317, 318, 320, 321, 356, 358, 402
Rose, R. L. 98
Rosenthal, R. 3, 403
Roskos-Ewoldsen, D. R. 24
Ross, D. F. 352
Ross, L. 80, 89, 154, 155
Ross, M. 17, 147, 155, 235, 267, 380, 381, 382, 383, 384, 385, 388, 390, 391, 402, 412, 417
Roth, J. 120
Rothbart, M. 152
Rothman, A. J. 158, 159
Rubin, D. C. 295
Rumelhart, D. 310
Russer, S. 103
Ryff, C. D. 390

Safer, M. A. 382, 384
Samuels, M. C. 87
Sanders, J. D. 229, 230
Sanitioso, R. 89, 92, 390
Sassler, M. A. 260
Savitsky, K. 186
Schacter, D. L. 9, 14, 321, 322
Schiavo, M. D. 87
Schneider, S. 243
Schooler, J. W. 336, 337, 338, 339
Schum, D. A. 48
Schumaker, J. 403
Schunn, C. D. 281, 285, 287, 289
Schwartz, M. 201
Schwarz, N. 156, 157, 158, 159, 160, 161, 190
Schwarz, S. 327, 336, 364, 371, 372, 373
Scott-Kakures, D. 90
Sczesny, S. 327, 336
Seamon, J. G. 215, 217, 221, 227, 228, 318
Seashore, C. E. 401
Sedikides, C. 261, 262, 266
Sedlmeier, P. 3, 11, 14, 72, 150
Seitz, A. 353
Seligman, M. E. P. 265, 268
Shackle, G. L. S. 30–1, 32
Shaffer, M. A. 267

Shaffer, V. A. 208, 211
Shafto, M. 283, 284
Shannon, L. 261
Shanon, B. 302
Shanteau, J. 45, 46, 54
Sheehan, P. W. 403
Shefrin, H. 174
Shepperd, J. A. 266, 267
Sherman, S. J. 89, 103, 353, 355
Shiffrin, R. 310
Sicoly, F. 147, 155
Sieck, W. R. 249
Sigurdsson, J. F. 414
Silvera, D. H. 260
Sim, D. L. H. 175
Simon, D. P. 39
Simon, H. A. 39, 413
Simons, A. 157, 158, 161
Skov, R. B. 89
Skowronski, J. J. 261
Sloman, S. A. 12, 70, 71
Sloutsky, V. M. 340
Slovak, L. 70, 71
Slovic, P. 1, 8, 10, 45, 48, 153, 187, 244
Slowiaczek, L. M. 89
Smith, H. D. 167–8
Smith, S. L. 72
Sneed, J. R. 265
Snodgrass, J. G. 304
Snyder, C. R. 268
Snyder, M. 83, 84, 86
Soll, J. B. 248
Solomons, W. 336
Sonino-Legrenzi, M. 71
Souza-Silva, K. 189
Spacapan, S. 115
Spilich, G. J. 207
Srull, T. K. 193
Stadler, M. A. 312, 358
Stahlberg, D. 327, 336, 364, 371, 372, 373, 374
Stang, D. J. 219, 220, 221, 228, 255, 259, 264, 265
Stangor, C. 88, 102
Stanovich, K. E. 14, 35, 38, 139, 140, 177, 414
Stegner, S. E. 46, 47, 54, 55, 56, 57
Sternberg, R. J. 230
Stewart, H. L. 267
Stibel, J. M. 70, 71
Story, A. L. 264
Strack, F. 157, 158, 161, 184, 185, 186, 187, 189, 190, 191, 192, 193, 194, 196

Stroffolino, P. J. 281, 287
Suantak, L. 246
Sullivan, A. L. 322
Sullivan, L. E. 9
Sully, J. 8
Suls, J. 267
Swann, W. B. Jr 83

Tanke, E. 84, 86
Tassoni, C. J. 174
Taylor, H. A. 24, 29, 36
Taylor, S. E. 88, 123, 174, 263, 268
Teigen, K. H. 29, 175, 179
Tesser, A. 210, 374, 375
Tetlock, P. E. 91
Thaler, R. 11, 13
Thomas, C. 119, 124
Thomas, D. R. 333
Thomas, N. 222, 228, 229
Thompson, C. P. 261, 262, 263
Thompson, D. M. 346
Thompson, S. C. 115, 119, 120, 121, 122, 124
Thompson, V. A. 29
Thompson, W. C. 154
Thompson, W. L. 302
Thorndike, E. 310
Thüring, M. 27, 31
Tichi, H. J. 415
Titchener, E. B. 215
Todd, P. M. 4, 10, 11, 12, 177, 414, 416
Toglia, M. P. 315, 319, 352
Toneatto, T. 124
Tooby, J. 63, 70, 71, 416
Toppino, T. 201, 204
Trope, Y. 83, 84, 90, 91, 92, 93
Troscianko, T. 124
Troutman, C. M. 46, 54
Tsanos, A. 124
Tulving, E. 148, 313, 346, 363
Turken, A. U. 268
Tversky, A. 1, 4, 6, 8, 10, 12, 24, 27, 31, 32, 45, 46, 47, 48, 51, 55, 62, 147, 148, 149, 150, 152, 156, 157, 160, 165, 167, 169, 170, 172, 173, 174, 176, 180, 183, 184, 186, 187, 188, 189, 190, 195, 243, 245, 371, 414, 415, 418
Tweney, R. D. 87

Underwood, B. J. 311, 317
Upfold, D. 205

Van Avermaet, E. 121

Van der Lely, H. K. J. 39
van Oostendorp, H. 278, 279, 282, 283
Van Zandt, B. J. 218, 222, 228, 229
Vanderwart, M. 304
Vannucci, M. 304
Vasta, R. 1
Verfaellie, M. 322
Viggiano, M. P. 304
Villejoubert, G. 170, 178
Viscusi, D. 121
Vogl, R. J. 262, 263
von Clef, J. 327, 337
von Restorff, H. 103
von Winterfeldt, D. 8
Voss, J. F. 207
Vrungos, S. 124

Wade, K. A. 354
Wahlund, R. 412
Walker, W. R. 262, 263
Wallbott, H. G. 340, 417
Wallsten, T. 45, 46, 53, 56, 244, 247, 248
Walsh, R. O. 123
Walters, A. A. 327, 328, 329, 330, 331, 332
Walther, E. 103, 104, 105, 108, 109
Wänke, M. 160, 161
Wardle, J. 336
Warren, D. L. 189
Warrington, E. K. 303–4
Wason, P. C. 79, 80, 81, 82, 84, 86, 129, 130, 132
Wasserman, E. A. 98, 102
Watson, J. M. 317, 318, 320, 321
Weinstein, N. D. 155, 412
Welder, A. N. 340
Wells, G. L. 24, 28, 175
Welsh, G. S. 223
Wennerholm, P. 245, 248
Wessels, P. M. 358
West, R. F. 35, 38, 177
Whishaw, I. Q. 335
Whitbourne, S. K. 265
White, R. W. 115
Whitehouse, W. G. 26
Whittlesea, B. W. A. 222, 227, 230
Wild, B. 67, 70
Wilkening, F. 1
Willham, C. F. 363, 366, 371, 374, 375
Wilson, A. E. 267, 382, 383, 384, 385, 388, 390, 391
Wilson, T. 340
Wilson, T. D. 120, 186, 188, 190, 195

Winkielman, P. 159
Winkler, R. L. 243
Winman, A. 243, 245, 246, 248
Winograd, E. 14, 414
Wolff, W. T. 102
Wolford, G. 24, 29, 36, 315
Woll, S. B. 88
Wong, K. F. E. 190
Wong, L. 46, 55
Wong, R. 46, 55
Wood, A. G. 297, 300, 303
Wood, S. J. 297, 300, 303
Woodruff, D. A. 382, 384
Woolfolk, A. 340
Woolfolk, M. E. 336, 340
Woolfolk, R. 340
Wright, G. 171
Wright, R. 318

Wundt, W. 330
Wyer, R. S. 37, 193

Xu, G. 206, 207

Yates, J. F. 24, 27, 28, 34, 242, 249
Yuille, J. C. 357, 358
Yun, L. S. 14

Zacks, R. T. 161
Zajonc, R. B. 210, 215, 219, 221, 227, 229, 230
Zaragoza, M. 348, 351, 354
Zarate, M. A. 229, 230
Zechmeister, E. B. 201, 204
Zuckermann, M. 83, 84, 86
Zupanek, N. 161

Subject index

absolute judgement 184, 187
accessibility, selective 191–2
acquiescence tendency 86
activation 322
adaptive learning 375
affective primacy model 229
aggregation rule 56
aggression type 104
aleatoric reaction strategies 408
ambiguity 403, 413
anchoring effect 4, 6, 148, 183–97, 246, 336
   vs hypothetical design 364
   as knowledge accessibility effect 192–3
   paradigms 187–8
   pervasiveness and robustness 185–6
   relevance 186–7
   as two-stage process 195–6
anchors 8, 184–5, 371, 392, 402
applicability 192
applications 14
appraisal value 188
Ark question 279, 283
Armstrong illusion 283–4
arousal model (Berlyne) 227
artificiality 11
assimilation 373
assimilative perception 330
association 309
association-based theories of DRM 316–18
associative activation 318, 320, 321
associative learning 140
associative memory illusion 6, 309–23, 402
asymmetry 296–7
attitude polarization 206, 210, 212
attribution processes 320

autobiographical memory 16, 89, 293, 300, 355, 357, 416
automatic process 204–5
availability 4, 6, 147–61
   amount of recall 149–50, 156–60, 161
   applications 151–6
   biased encoding and retrieval of information 152–4
   direct access to information 158
   ease of recall 156–60, 161
   famous-names experiment 149–50
   letter-frequency experiment 150–1
   naive theories 159–60
   processing motivation 158–9
   vividness of information 154
averaging 27, 36–8, 40
averaging model of source credibility 46–7, 53

backward associative strength (BAS) 317, 321
base rate 61, 63, 66
   in Bayesian inference 43–58
base-rate effect 243, 251
base-rate fallacy 48, 49, 55, 57
base-rate neglect 5, 62, 166, 172, 178, 180
Bayes' rule 61, 66, 67, 71, 72
Bayes' theorem 4, 5, 30, 44–7, 51, 170
Bayesian inference 11
   base rates in 43–58
   statistical formats in 61–77
Bayesian reasoning 62, 63
behavioural measures 218
belief bias 135, 136–9
Belief Index 138
believability 39
bias(es) 2, 4, 10–12, 13, 57

434 Subject index

belief 135, 136–9
  confirmation 5, 79–94, 130–2
  in deductive reasoning 6, 127–43
  heuristics 245–6
biased recall 260–1
biased-reconstruction theory 372–3
biased sampling 373
Brier score 236–8
Brunswikian error 248

cab problem 47–9, 49–55
calibration 237
causality 175–6
ceiling rule 36, 37, 40
CHARM theory 351
chimeric perception 301–2
classroom experiment 16
  anchoring 184–5
  associative memory 311–12
  availability 150, 151
  base rates in Bayesian inference 50
  belief bias 136–8
  confirmation bias in interrogation 85–6
  conjunction fallacy 24–6
  hindsight bias 367–8
  illusions of control 117–19
  illusions of stability and change 385–8
  illusory correlation 104–10
  labelling 327, 328–9
  memory for spatial orientation 294–5
  mere exposure effect 225–7
  misinformation effect 349–50
  Moses illusion 276–7
  overconfidence 239–41
  Pollyanna Principle 257–9, 271–2
  Representatives 167–70
  statistical formats in Bayesian inference 67–70
  suggestion 404–6
  validity effect 201–3
cognitive experiential self theory (CEST) 27, 33–5
cognitive illusions
  defining features 2–3
  categories 3–5
  selection of 5–7
  status 12–13
colour, memory for 333–5
commission 9
commission errors 3
comparative judgement 184, 193
comparison 195
compensational strategies 417

computational model 372–3
conditional events 30
conditional probability 33, 37, 66
confidence 173
  in knowledge 209–10
confidence-frequency effect 243, 251
confirmation bias 5, 79–94, 130–2
congruency effect 88, 89, 93
conjunction fallacy 5, 9, 11, 23–41, 72, 172, 178, 180
conjunction rule 23, 24, 29–30
conservatism 62
contingent phenomenon 38
contralaterality 299–300
control heuristic 122
conversational inference 190
conversational postulate 278
cooperative principle 278
coping function 416–18
covert aggression 114
criterion shift 315
cues 32, 36
cultural differences 265

debiasing 132–4, 136
decision routine 88
deductive reasoning, biases in 127–43
Deese-Roediger-McDermott (DRM) paradigm 312–16, 320, 322
defensive strategies 417
delusion 14
depression 123
diagnosis 170–2, 174
diagnostic strategy 83
dissonance theory 88
distinctiveness 103
distorted term 279, 280, 282, 283, 287, 288–9
distortions 3
domain-sensitive reasoning 134
drinking-age problem 132
dual code theory 338
dual-process thinking 180
dual processes 139–40
dual processing 139, 143
dust-bowl empiricism 245, 250

ecological models 246–7, 251
ecological validity 32, 208–10
error models 247–8, 251
  combined 248–9
error of commission 91
error of omission 91

Subject index 435

expectancy-based illusory correlation 98, 101–2, 107
expertise 207
expertise effect 243, 251
experts 174
exposure effect 220
external-validity problem 142

failure emphasis 120
fallacy, conjunction 5, 9, 11, 23–41, 72, 172, 178, 180
false-alarm rate 63
false memory 345–6, 353, 354, 356–9
false recall 312–22
false recognition 312–22
falsification 4, 79, 82
familiarity 206
familiarity effect 230
fast and frugal heuristics 4, 10, 12, 27, 36
feature level 287–9
feature-positive effect 102
figure assimilation 330
flashbulb memories 353
fluency-based attributions 320–1
fluency illusions 9
focus of attention 286–7
focus of hypothesis 104
forced-choice preference judgements 218
format dependence 244–5
format effect 251
forward telescoping effect 16
Free Recall by Associative Nets (FRAN) 310
free recall task 236
frequencies 28–9, 160–1
frequency judgements 178
frequency of three 208
frequency-validity effect 6
frequentist interpretations 27, 28–9
fundamental attribution error 155
fuzzy trace theory 318, 321

gambler's fallacy 168, 172, 178, 180
gambling 124, 244
game show paradigm 281
general intelligence 140
geometric averaging model 37
gist condition 278, 280, 318
Gudjonsson Suggestibility Scales (GSS) 414

handedness 293, 297–300
handwriting 305

hard—easy effect 242, 251
hemispheric differences 301–2
heuristic 4, 10–12, 245–6
heuristic/analytic system 34–5
hindsight bias 7, 265, 336–7, 363–75, 392, 401–2
  cognitive processes 371–2
  definition 365
  z index 365, 366
  designs 363–4
  experiment 367–71
  individual differences 374
  measures 364–5
  metacognitions 373–4
  relevance 366
Human Associative Memory (HAM) 310
hypothesis-consistent testing 191
hypothesis testing 4, 81
hypothetical design 363–4

illusion 399–418
  of change 379–93
  of control 5, 115–25
  as reality 410–11
  of stability 379–93
  of validity 173, 180
illusionability 399, 413–15
illusionality 7, 399
illusory control 120, 121–2, 124
illusory correlation 5, 97–112
illusory recollection 321
imagination inflation 353
imperfect encoding 279–80
imperfect memory retrieval 278, 280–1
implicit associative response (IAR) 317
implicit theories 389–90
inadequate retrieval hypothesis 280–1
incongruency effect 88, 89, 93
individual differences 13, 14, 140, 222–3
  in hindsight bias 374–5
inference 44
information retrieval, biased encoding and 152–4
innate cognitive modules 134
insufficient adjustment 189
intensity principle 261
Interaction Index 138
interference 9, 339, 345
interpretation problem 141
interquartile index 238–9
intrusion of reality 121

436 Subject index

intuitive reaction strategies 407–8
inverse fallacy 170, 178

judgement 2, 3–4, 5, 6, 8
  absolute 184, 187
  comparative 184, 193
  forced-choice preference 218
  frequency 178
  of odour 336–7
  Pollyanna principles in 264–8
  probability 174, 179
  of taste 336–7
judgemental anchoring 197

knew-it-along effect *see* hindsight bias

label 335
labelling 7, 327–42, 402
Lake Wobegon effect 257–9, 265–6, 267
language 260
laterality 297–300
Law of Prägnanz 330
leading ideas 404
lexical decision 194
Likert ratings 217
limited cognitive capacity 286
Linda scenario 5, 24–6, 34, 36
linguistic misunderstanding 27
local mental model 246
logic 4, 128, 129, 143
Logic Index 138
ludic strategies 417

matching bias 130–2, 140, 142
memory 2, 3, 4, 5, 6–7, 8–10, 260–4, 345, 388
  encoding, storage, and retrieval 346–7
Memory Assessment Procedure (MAP) 357
memory bias 392
Memory Characteristics Questionnaire (MCQ) 320, 321
memory design 363
memory distortion 9, 345, 352–3, 355–6
memory illusions 293–306, 309–12
memory impairment 348, 351, 372
mental models 27, 35
mere exposure 210–11
mere exposure effect (MEE) 6, 215–34
  experimental designs 217
  moderating variables 219–27
  naturalistic designs 216–17
  relevance 218–19
metacognitions 373–4

Michigan Omnibus Personality Inventory (MOPI) 261, 262
MINERVA-DM model (MDM) 248–9
misaggregation 55
misattribution
  of causality 1
  recall and 157–8, 160–1
misconceptions of physics 1
misinformation 327, 334–5
misinformation effect 7, 345–59, 401
mismatch 282
misperception 55, 56
mobilization-minimization approach 263
model theory of probabilistic reasoning 71
modularity 39
monitoring, reality 317, 321
Monte Carlo simulations 111
mood-congruent memory 260, 263–4
mood, illusions of control and 121
Moses illusion 4, 6, 275–90
motivationally supported hypotheses 90–2
motive for control 120–1
motor imagery 302–5
Mueller-Lyer illusion 57

natural frequencies 63–7, 70–3
need for control 120–1
negative test strategy 82, 83, 93
neglect of base rate 47, 48
negotiation 185
neuropsychology 13, 14
nonregressive predictions 173
nonspecific activation model 228
norm 16
normalized frequencies 64, 70
normative goodness 236
normative models 4
normative system problem 141
numeric priming 190–1
numerosity 104

odour, judgements of 336–7
omission 9
omission errors 3
one-reason algorithm 32, 40
optical illusions 2, 3, 13
optimistic bias 255
orientation bias 9
orientation illusions in memory 293–306

Subject index

overconfidence 6, 11, 17, 235–51, 265
  confidence intervals 238–9
  probability estimates 236–8
  tasks and measures 235–41
  theoretical accounts 245–9
  typical findings 242–5
overconfidence bias 72
overgeneralization 293–7
overshadowing 339
overt aggression 114

paired-associated learning techniques 310
paradox of rationality 141
pars-pro-toto principle 410, 414
partial match 281–2, 283–6
partitiveness 71
perceived control 115
perception [see above]
perceptions of control 124
perceptual fluency/attributional model 228–9
permanence theory, memory 347
permission rules 133
perspective 151
  of others, adopting 155–6
planning fallacy 17, 235
plausibility strategy 282
playful strategies 417
point of subjective equality (PSE) 333–4
Pollyanna hypothesis 255
Pollyanna Principle 4, 5, 6, 17, 255–69
portrait asymmetry 296–7
positive psychology 268
positive testing 103–4
positive test strategy 81–4, 86–7, 93, 94, 103
positivity 6
positivity bias 132
post-decisional regret 88
posterior probability 61, 62
potential surprise 30
pragmatic reasoning schemas 134
pragmatic relevance 134
preciseness paradox 175
prediction 57, 170–2
preference analysis (Langer) 124
priming, numeric 190–1
prior probability estimate 61
probabilistic mental models (PMMs) 239–41, 246–7, 251–2
probabilistic reasoning, model theory of 71
probability judgements 174, 179

probability theory 4
PROBEX 249
pseudo-rational explanations 403
psychography 9
Psychology Information Test (PIT) 209

qualitative likelihood ratio 28
quasi-modularity 39

randomness 167–9, 171
rational reaction strategies 407
rational thinking 128
rationality 14, 16, 129, 140–2
reaction patterns 407–8
reality
  as illusion 9, 411–12
  monitoring 317, 321
  as non-reality 412
recoding interference 338, 339
reconstruction 340, 371, 379–80, 389–90
referential validity 204
regression 173
regression analysis 37
regression effects 2
relatedness effects 9
relative frequencies 64, 70
repetition 201, 206, 212
representation of information 72, 73
representative heuristic 166, 244
representativeness 4, 6, 8, 27, 28, 31, 32, 148, 165–81
response bias 287
response distortion 55, 56
retrieval cue 372
reverse probabilities 36, 38
revision of opinion 45

sample size 169–70, 172
samples-size effect 103, 107
sampling 242–3, 251
SARA (Selective Activation and Reconstructive Anchoring) 372–3
Scale-Adjustment Averaging Model of source credibility 46
schema 88, 295, 346–7
schema pointer plus tag model 88
Search of Associative Memory (SAM) 310
selection task (Wason) 129–34, 140, 142
selective accessibility 191–2
selective activation 373
Selective Activation and Reconstructive Anchoring (SARA) 372–3

438 *Subject index*

selective attention and encoding 98, 103–4
selective remembering 84, 88
self 383, 390–1
self appraisal theory 390
self-esteem 260
self fulfilling prophecy 86
self-help programmes 382, 384, 390
self-presentation motive 374
semantic cohesion 283
semantic memory 6
semantic priming 191
semantic relatedness 282–3
sensory sampling model 249
Sensory Suggestibility Scale (SSK) 415
Sensory Suggestibility Test (SST) 415
serial anticipation learning 310
signal-detection approach 246
signal-detection theory 48
signed summation 27, 28, 40
similarity-based illusory correlation 102
similarity-based theories of DRM 318–20
simultaneous conservatism 244
single-event probabilities 64
skill-related factors 119–20
source bias 56
source credibility 46, 56
source dissociation 206
source expertise 57
source monitoring 9
Source of Activation Confusions (SAC) 281, 351
speed, memory for 335–6
spiritualism 9
spreading activation 285–6
spurious confirmation 90
standard for comparison of performance 2
standard information menu 62
statistical format 73
stereotypes 152–3
subjective probability 43
subliminal MEEs 229, 230
subset principle 71
substantive goodness 236
success emphasis 120
suggestibility 355, 399, 401, 410

suggestion 2–3, 340, 399–418
suggestionality 7, 418
suggestive reaction strategies 407
sum of squared deviations (SSD) 54–5
suppositional reasoning 128
surprise 373
surprise index 238–9
surprise theory 27, 30–3, 37, 40
syllogism 134–6
syllogistic reasoning 3, 134–6, 140
System 1/System 2 processes 12, 35

Take The Best 252
taste, judgements of 336–7
temporal self-appraisal theory 390–1
thinking 3–4, 5–6, 8
Thurstonian error 248
transfer inappropriate retrieval 339
true confirmation bias 86–90
two-alternative forced-choice tasks (2AFC) 236, 237
two-factor model of MEE 228
two systems models of judgement under uncertainty 12

uncertainty 43
underconfidence 244, 245
unequal weighting 98, 102
unrealistic optimism 155

validity effect 201–12
   as an automatic process 204–5
   expertise in 207
   source of information in 206–7
   types of information producing 205–6
verbal overshadowing 9, 329, 337–9, 342
visual forms, memory for 329–33
vividness of information 154

warnings 186, 315, 415
Wason selection task 129–34, 140, 142
well-being 265–6
witness credibility 50–4
writing system 305

yield sign 351–2

Printed in Poland
by Amazon Fulfillment
Poland Sp. z o.o., Wrocław